Dictionary of Banking Terms

Dictionary of Banking Terms

Sixth Edition

by

Thomas P. Fitch

Consulting Editors

Dr. Irwin L. Kellner
Chief Economist, CBS MarketWatch

Donald G. Simonson
Anderson Schools of Management
University of New Mexico

BARRON'S

Barron's books are available at special quantity discounts to use as premiums and sales promotions, or for use in corporate training programs. For more information, please write to the Special Sales Manager, Barron's Educational Series, Inc., at the mailing address indicated below.

All inquiries should be addressed to:
Barron's Educational Series, Inc.
250 Wireless Boulevard
Hauppauge, NY 11788
www.barronseduc.com

Library of Congress Catalog Card No. 2011043738

ISBN: 978-0-7641-4756-2

Library of Congress Cataloging-in-Publication Data
Fitch, Thomas P.
Dictionary of banking terms / by Thomas P. Fitch ; consulting editors, Irwin L. Kellner, Donald G. Simonson.—6th ed.
p. cm.
Includes bibliographical references and index.
ISBN 978-0-7641-4756-2 (alk. paper)
1. Banks and banking—Dictionaries. I. Title.

HG151.F57 2012
332.103—dc23 2011043738

PRINTED IN CHINA

9 8 7 6 5 4 3 2 1

CONTENTS

PREFACE TO THE SIXTH EDITION

It has been more than 20 years since the *Dictionary of Banking Terms* was initially published. As we prepare to go to press with the 6th—and by far most extensive—edition, a quick review of the events reshaping the world of banking and finance is very timely. Obviously, the financial world is a different place than it was back in 1990.

In the preface to the 1st edition, we commented on the gradual breaking down of the traditional barriers separating companies. Commercial banks won the right to underwrite and deal in limited amounts of corporate debt and equity securities. Thrift institutions (savings and loan associations, savings banks, and credit unions) were able to offer many of the same services as commercial banks thanks to deregulation legislation enacted in the 1980s. Interest rate ceilings limiting what banks and thrifts could pay depositors—restrictions dating back to the 1930s—were eased, allowing banks to compete more openly for consumer deposits with nonbank financial companies. While all this was happening, legislative barriers limiting banks to doing business in a single state or within a geographic region were gradually phased out. Nationwide banking was just a few years away. "The banking system has been made over, and the transition is not yet complete," we observed.

Another revolution in financial services was well underway in the mid 1990s as more consumers began doing their banking at automated teller machines in banking offices and in retail locations or at home from their personal computers. "Self-service banking reached maturity in the last decade," we noted in the preface to the 3rd edition. In the 4th edition, published in 2000, we noted how the landmark Gramm-Leach-Bliley Act of 1999 finally removed the 1933 Glass-Steagall Act barriers separating banking and commerce. A new type of banking structure, the financial holding company, came into existence. While structural barriers were crashing to the ground, another revolution in financial services was quietly going on. More consumers—and businesses—began paying their bills and buying goods or services with debit cards and various types of electronic payments. A little-known federal law, the Check 21 law, was more than a contributing factor in the switch to less costly and more efficient payments. Check 21, which became law in 2004, allowed banks to "truncate" or stop the flow of paper checks after initial deposit at a consumer's bank, eliminating further handling of billions of checks written every year. In 2004, noncash electronic payments in the United States surpassed check writing for the first time.

By 2005, when the 5th edition went to press, the mortgage finance boom, aided by record low interest rates and rising house prices, was gathering steam. Much of this loan production was eventually repackaged as investment securities, mortgage-backed securities, and collateralized debt obligations (CDOs), and resold to investors in the U.S. and around the world. The new powers granted federally insured banks back in 1999—the ability to compete on an equal footing with investment banking giants—would be tested within a few short years. As we noted back in 2005, "Deregulation in the financial services industry has been a work in progress since the 1980s, with a few bumps in the road along the way."

The big story since 2008 is the Great Recession, a financial downturn triggered by the financial crisis of that year, a series of events that shook the worldwide banking system to its core. The bumps in the road became apparent in the fall of that year when investment banking giant Lehman Brothers collapsed in a matter of weeks. More than a liquidity crisis, the financial crisis of 2008 was a crisis of confidence. Major players worried that their counterparties on the other side of a trade would somehow become insolvent, resulting in a wider panic. In quick succession, several major firms—American International Group, Fannie Mae, and Freddie Mac—were put on government support in the form of capital infusions. Merrill Lynch was acquired by Bank of America. The financial crisis also led to enactment of a new federal law, the Dodd-Frank Wall Street Reform and Consumer Protection Act of 2010. This law was most sweeping rewrite of the federal regulatory system since the Great Depression.

The unfolding events since 2008 have served up a rich stew of new terms and phrases enriching the banking vocabulary. Many of these are included in this updated edition: QUANTITATIVE EASING, SHADOW BANK STRESS TEST, TOO BIG TO FAIL, and TOXIC ASSET. Newer terms used in everyday banking, MOBILE BANKING, PAPERLESS STATEMENT, and TEMPORARY ACCOUNT NUMBER, to name a few, are also defined. In general, the 6th edition takes a fresh look at the world of banking and finance in the 21st century and supplants previous editions of the *Dictionary of Banking Terms*.

Many individuals and organizations contributed to the banking dictionary since its inception. For this edition, the author wishes to thank Amherst Group, American Bankruptcy Institute, Bettinger & Leech, Conference of State Bank Supervisors, Davis Polk, Equifax, The European Commission, Fair Isaac Corporation, Federal Deposit Insurance Corporation, Federal Reserve Bank of New York, Federal Reserve Board of Governors, Internal Revenue Service, MasterCard Worldwide, Mayer Brown, Milken Institute, Morrison Foerster, Mortgage Bankers Association, Office of the Comptroller of the Currency, Skadden Arps, Standard & Poor's, Sullivan & Cromwell, TRW, TransUnion, and Visa Inc.

Thomas P. Fitch

HOW TO USE THIS BOOK EFFECTIVELY

Alphabetization: All entries are alphabetized by letter rather than word, so that multiple-word terms are treated as single words. For example, **ASSET MANAGEMENT ACCOUNT** follows **ASSET LIABILITY COMMITTEE (ALCO), DUN & BRADSTREET** follows **DUE TO ACCOUNT, GOODWILL** follows **GOOD MONEY**, and **SELLING GROUP** follows **SELLER-SERVICER**.

Many terms commonly used in banking have distinctly different meanings depending on the context in which they are used. Readers must determine the context relevant to their purpose. When a term has several entries, subentries are presented in alphabetical sequence. In some entries the various meanings are presented as simple numerical headings.

Abbreviations and Acronyms: A separate list of abbreviations and acronyms follows the dictionary. It contains a shortened version of terms defined in the book, plus related business terms.

Cross-References: To add to your understanding of a term, related, or contrasting terms are sometimes cross-referenced. The cross-referenced terms will appear in SMALL CAPITALS either in the body of the entry (or subentry) or at the end of the definition. These terms will be printed in SMALL CAPITALS only the first time they appear in the entry. When a term is fully defined by another term, a reference rather than an entry is provided; for example, **COMMUNITY BANK** *see* INDEPENDENT BANK.

Italics: Italic type is used to indicate that another term has a meaning identical or very closely related to that of the entry. Italic type is also used to highlight words or phrases that have a special meaning to the trade. Italics are also used for the titles of publications.

Parentheses: Parentheses are used in entry titles for two reasons. The first is to indicate that a word or phrase has a meaning so closely related to the term defined that only one entry is necessary; for example **CAPITAL GAIN (OR LOSS)**. The second is to indicate that an abbreviation is used with about the same frequency as the term itself. For example: **CERTIFICATE OF DEPOSIT (CD)**, or **FEDERAL DEPOSIT INSURANCE CORPORATION (FDIC)**.

Examples, Illustrations, and Tables: The examples in the dictionary are designed to help readers gain understanding and to help them relate abstract concepts to the real world of banking. Line drawings are presented in some entries, in addition to text to clarify concepts best understood visually.

A

AAA highest rated corporate or municipal bond, with full payment of principal and interest expected at maturity. Bonds rated AAA, AA, A, and BBB by Standard & Poor's, and Baa or better by Moody's Investors Service, are considered investment grade bonds, eligible for purchase by banks and savings institutions as INVESTMENT SECURITIES. *See also* BOND RATING.

ABANDONMENT voluntary surrender of rights, title, or claim to property, and forfeiture of any legal rights of ownership. A savings account or brokerage account will be considered abandoned property if it is unused for a certain number of years and the owner cannot be found; the account legally becomes property of the state under the laws of ESCHEAT.

ABA TRANSIT NUMBER numeric coding facilitating check clearing. The ABA numbering system, managed by the American Bankers Association, assigns a unique identifier to each U.S. financial institution. The ABA number is the numerator (upper portion) of a fraction in the upper right corner on checks; the denominator is the bank's CHECK ROUTING SYMBOL, which identifies the Federal Reserve Bank servicing that financial institution. *See also* MAGNETIC INK CHARACTER RECOGNITION.

ABILITY TO PAY capacity to meet future obligations from earnings or income.

1. **Banking.** A borrower's capacity to make principal and interest payments from disposable income. Lenders look closely at a credit applicant's current salary and expected future earnings, and at an organization's CASH FLOW from conversion of assets into cash. *See also* BALANCE SHEET RATIOS; FIVE C'S OF CREDIT; QUALIFYING RATIO.
2. **Securities, municipal bonds.** The issuer's capacity to generate sufficient income from taxes or other sources to meet contractual obligations.
3. **Finance.** The ability to meet DEBT SERVICE payments on bonds and other long-term obligations.

ABOVE PAR *see* PAR VALUE.

ABSOLUTE PRIORITY RULE *see* BANKRUPTCY.

ABSOLUTE TITLE clean title, free of liens or attachments, replacing all previous titles. Accepted as the sole document of title, it is defensible against claims by third parties.

ABSTRACT OF TITLE summary of title to real property, listing current owners, liens, judicial proceedings, satisfaction of claims, and other information affecting title. A title abstract is a necessary step in obtaining TITLE INSURANCE.

ABSTRACTION OF BANK FUNDS *see* DEFALCATION or EMBEZZLEMENT.

ACCELERATED DEPRECIATION accounting method of reducing the book value of an asset at a higher rate than comparable methods in the early years of ownership. Since 1981, the most common form of accelerated depreciation is the *accelerated cost recovery system* (ACRS), which later was modified by the TAX REFORM ACT of 1986. Previous methods of accelerated depreciation included the *declining balance method* and the *sum-of-the-years digits* method.

ACCELERATION CLAUSE clause in a mortgage bond or promissory note stating that the unpaid balance is payable if specified conditions of default, defined in a loan COVENANT or bond INDENTURE, should occur. Acceleration, exercisable at the option of the lender, calls for immediate payment of the remaining balance, plus interest due. *See also* CREDIT EVENT.

ACCEPTANCE promise to pay created when the drawee of a TIME DRAFT stamps or writes the word "accepted" above his signature and a designated payment date. Once accepted, the draft is the equivalent of a promissory note; the drawee becomes the ACCEPTOR, and is obligated to pay the amount shown at maturity. Acceptances are NEGOTIABLE INSTRUMENTS, which means they can be sold to another holder before maturity.

1. **Banking.** A time draft honored by a bank, known as a BANKER'S ACCEPTANCE. It is used primarily in financing international trade, for example, an overseas manufacturer selling goods to an importer. *See also* DOCUMENTARY CREDIT; THIRD COUNTRY ACCEPTANCE.
2. **Finance.** Trade acceptance that is issued by a finance company affiliated with a manufacturer or by an importer acting as agent for a manufacturer. It is often backed by a bank LETTER OF CREDIT.

ACCEPTOR person or party, normally the DRAWEE, who accepts a bill of exchange or TIME DRAFT and becomes responsible for payment at maturity to the party named in the draft.

ACCESS right to use banking services. Specifically, it means the right to make deposits to or withdrawals from a bank account, verify an account balance, use a safe deposit box, or make electronic transfers using a bank card or other ACCESS DEVICE.

ACCESS DEVICE bank card or personal security code giving consumers the means to make deposits, withdraw funds, transfer funds, or pay bills electronically. Financial institutions may issue an access device only at the consumer's request. *See also* SMART CARD.

ACCOMMODATION ENDORSER person who endorses a PROMISSORY NOTE as a favor to the borrower, without compensation or benefit. The endorser is a GUARANTOR or surety, and remains secondarily liable in event of default. *See also* COMAKER.

ACCOMMODATION PAPER PROMISSORY NOTE or NEGOTIABLE INSTRUMENT signed by a third party, who acts as accommodation maker, endorser, or party. *See also* ACCOMMODATION ENDORSER.

ACCORD AND SATISFACTION legal term for *payment in full* toward discharge of an obligation; the satisfactory completion of an agreement and acceptance of payment. When a new contract is accepted in place of an expiring one, it is a NOVATION.

ACCOUNT contractual relationship between two parties involving an exchange of funds, as between buyer and seller, or an agreement by one party to hold funds in trust for the other. Examples include a charge account, checking account, or trust account.

1. **Accounting.** A bookkeeping entry in a ledger. Examples are accounts receivable, accrued interest, allowance for bad debt.
2. **Banking.** (1) A record of funds on deposit under a particular name or ACCOUNT NUMBER, such as a checking account, also called a DEMAND DEPOSIT account, which allows the account holder to withdraw funds by writing checks; a NEGOTIABLE ORDER OF WITHDRAWAL (NOW) account, a check-like account that pays interest; a PASSBOOK account, a savings account with no specified maturity; and a TIME DEPOSIT account, which pays interest on funds deposited for specified periods (7 days up to 7 years or more), and may be subject to an EARLY WITHDRAWAL PENALTY if funds are taken out before the maturity date. *See also* ALL SAVERS CERTIFICATE; AUTOMATIC TRANSFER SERVICE (ATS); DRAFT; MONEY MARKET DEPOSIT ACCOUNT; SMALL SAVER CERTIFICATE; STATEMENT SAVINGS ACCOUNT; SUPER NOW ACCOUNT; TRUST ACCOUNT; (2) A transaction record of a CREDIT CARD or home equity credit line, or a commercial ACCOUNTS RECEIVABLE FINANCING.
3. **Securities.** A contractual arrangement under which securities, mutual fund shares, futures and options, and so on are bought and sold; a brokerage account.

ACCOUNT ACTIVITY deposits, withdrawals, earnings credits for deposit balances, and service charges on a checking or savings account during a particular time period. These are summarized in an ACCOUNT STATEMENT.

ACCOUNT ANALYSIS summary of banking services provided for a business. Account analysis statements are issued periodically, usually monthly. Relevant information reported in the account analysis statement includes: the company's AVERAGE DAILY BALANCE, AVERAGE DAILY FLOAT on uncollected checks, EARNINGS CREDIT RATE on collected balances, account activity charges, and account balances needed to pay for bank services (COMPENSATING BALANCES). An analytical tool mostly used in pricing corporate CASH MANAGEMENT services, account analysis is also used by banks to evaluate profitability of CORRESPONDENT banking services, such as check clearing, performed for other financial institutions.

ACCOUNTANT'S OPINION statement describing results of an examination of a firm's books and records, following generally accepted auditing and accounting standards. The opinion may be qualified or unqualified, depending on the scope of the examination and the accountant's confidence in the information reviewed. A qualified opinion, although not necessarily negative, indicates information that the accountant was not able to directly confirm, normally because of limitations in the scope of the audit. *See also* GENERALLY ACCEPTED ACCOUNTING PRINCIPLES.

ACCOUNT BALANCE *see* BALANCE.

ACCOUNT HISTORY

1. summary of a deposit account's activity, including interest earned, during a particular period.
2. summary of transaction activity by a credit card or other OPEN-END CREDIT account, including late payments, overlimit activity, average daily balance, and so on. *See also* ACCOUNT STATEMENT; CREDIT FILE; CREDIT REPORT.

ACCOUNT HOLD

1. CHECK HOLD, or the number of days that a bank can legally hold uncollected balances before giving customers use of those funds. *See also* AVAILABILITY SCHEDULE.
2. notation limiting an account owner's access to his or her funds, as when a savings account is used as collateral for a loan.

ACCOUNT INQUIRY request for a copy of an individual's ACCOUNT HISTORY, usually in connection with a credit approval or renewal of an existing line of credit. *See also* CREDIT REPORT.

ACCOUNT IN TRUST account managed by one party for use by another, who is named the BENEFICIARY. A parent or guardian opening a child's savings account under the UNIFORM GIFTS TO MINORS ACT approves any withdrawals until the child reaches legal age.

ACCOUNT NUMBER numeric code identifying the holder of an account. Account numbers have a standardized number of characters, and may contain coded information for internal security purposes. *See also* ABA TRANSIT NUMBER; CHECK DIGIT.

ACCOUNT RECONCILEMENT cash management service for business customers. Typically, the customer receives a listing of checks paid, checks still outstanding, and account balances by date. This service reduces clerical costs, and functions as an outside audit control over funds collection and disbursement.

ACCOUNTS RECEIVABLE FINANCING form of secured lending giving businesses short-term financing by selling their trade receivables or pledging receivables as collateral for a loan. Direct sale of accounts receivable is a nonrecourse type of financing called FACTORING. An accounts receivable loan from a bank is a DISCOUNT: the borrower draws against a line of credit that is less than the full dollar value of his trade credits. Accounts receivable financing is a rather flexible way of obtaining credit, since borrowers' financing costs are directly related to their business cycle. Receivables financing is often priced at spreads above the bank PRIME RATE and is relatively expensive compared to other forms of credit. *See also* BORROWING BASE; INVENTORY FINANCING; PURCHASE ORDER FINANCING.

ACCOUNTS RECEIVABLE TURNOVER ratio of total credit sales to average accounts receivable during an accounting period, a measure of an organization's ability to convert inventory into cash, and thus, financial efficiency. Close attention should be paid to credit terms, billing procedures, and company and industry trends. *See also* BALANCE SHEET RATIOS; RATIO ANALYSIS.

ACCOUNT STATEMENT any summary of transaction activity occurring during an accounting period, usually monthly, but sometimes quarterly, or annually.

1. **Banking.** A listing of deposits, withdrawals, checks paid, interest earned, and service charges against an account. It is issued monthly, as required by Federal Reserve regulations, to give customers an opportunity to review their financial records and correct any error. Customer account statements may be delivered by mail, or if the customer chooses, by electronic mail (e-mail) message. *See also* ACCOUNT ANALYSIS; COMBINED STATEMENT; CONSOLIDATED FINANCIAL STATEMENT; PERIODIC STATEMENT; PAPERLESS STATEMENT.
2. **Securities.** A record of transactions showing status of an account maintained at a broker-dealer firm, net market value of securities owned, cash and securities positions, and so on. Brokerage statements are issued monthly or quarterly.

ACCOUNTS RECEIVABLE CONVERSION *see* CHECK CONVERSION.

ACCOUNTS UNCOLLECTIBLE loans in DEFAULT that have been charged off, or are likely to be charged off, as losses. Lenders report the condition of loans with principal and interest in arrears in quarterly CALL REPORTS to bank regulatory agencies. *See also* ADVERSELY CLASSIFIED ASSETS; CHARGE-OFF; LOAN LOSS RESERVES.

ACCRETION OF DISCOUNT accounting process for adjusting the book value of a bond purchased at a discount (the ORIGINAL ISSUE DISCOUNT) to the PAR VALUE at maturity. Accretion is, in effect, a noncash payment of interest, reflecting interest earned while a bond is owned.

ACCRUAL BASIS accounting system in which revenues and expenses are recognized in the period in which they arise, regardless of when the cash for the revenue or the expenditure actually occurs. Accrual accounting is the only basis of accounting approved under GENERALLY ACCEPTED ACCOUNTING PRINCIPLES, and is used by public companies and most privately owned companies. *See also* CASH BASIS.

ACCRUAL BOND long-term, deferred interest COLLATERIZED MORTGAGE OBLIGATION (CMO) bond, also called a Z-Bond, that pays no interest until all prior bonds have been retired. An accrual bond is similar to a ZERO-COUPON BOND, except that it has an explicit coupon rate and pays both principal and coupon interest. *See also* STRIP; STRIPPED MORTGAGE-BACKED SECURITIES.

ACCRUAL RATE stated annual rate at which interest is calculated. On an ADJUSTABLE RATE MORTGAGE, the accrual rate is determined from an independent market INDEX, plus a MARGIN, which is fixed at loan origination. The accrual rate is also called the *note rate, coupon rate,* or *contract rate.*

ACCRUED INTEREST interest earned, though not credited or otherwise paid. Interest earned by a deposit account may be added to the account balance or paid by check. Bonds pay interest every six months, but interest is earned (accrued) every month. An investor buying a bond midway between interest payment dates must pay the seller any interest accrued from the last payment date up to, but not including, the settlement date. *See also* UNEARNED DISCOUNT; UNEARNED INTEREST.

ACID TEST RATIO *see* BALANCE SHEET RATIOS.

ACKNOWLEDGMENT admission of the truth of a statement or validity of a document. *See also* ATTEST.

1. **Banking.** A notification by a paying bank that an item presented for payment has been paid, or that it cannot be honored. *See also* WIRE FATE ITEM.
2. **Securities.** A verification, that a customer's signature is genuine, required when transferring accounts to another broker or fiduciary. *See also* MEDALLION SIGNATURE GUARANTEE.

ACQUIRER

1. in bank cards, a bank that purchases merchant sales drafts, also called the MERCHANT BANK. Merchants receive credit for the dollar value of credit card receipts, less a processing fee (the MERCHANT DISCOUNT RATE).
2. in AUTOMATED TELLER MACHINE networks, the financial institution that dispenses the cash, collecting a transaction fee from the card issuing bank.
3. bank gaining control over another financial institution, either through an exchange of stock, payment in cash, or a combination.

ACQUISITION purchase of an asset, such as real estate, chattels, or securities, with title and rights of ownership passing to the new owner.
Banking:
1. addition of new accounts through marketing, resulting in deposit growth or new money. Deposit growth is accomplished by direct mail promotion, advertising, in-branch promotions, and so on.
2. takeover of one company by another through a PURCHASE ACQUISITION, a mostly cash transaction, or a POOLING OF INTERESTS in which two entities agree to swap common stock. *See also* BAILOUT.

ACQUITTANCE document or receipt evidencing full payment of an obligation, releasing the lender's SECURITY INTEREST. When a borrower completes the last payment on a mortgage, the lender issues a SATISFACTION OF MORTGAGE document, indicating the debt is fully repaid. *See also* TERMINATION STATEMENT.

ACTIVE ACCOUNT
1. checking or savings account with deposits or withdrawals listed in account statements for a specified period. Bank service charges are often determined on the basis of account activity.
2. credit card account showing new charges or an outstanding balance in the most recent billing period.

Contrast with INACTIVE ACCOUNT.

ACTIVITY CHARGE fee charged to cover servicing costs. Some activity fees are triggered when the account balance falls below a certain level. Others are transaction fees based on account usage, such as checks written or a service charge for automated teller machine withdrawals. *See also* ACCOUNT ANALYSIS; BREAK-EVEN YIELD; MINIMUM BALANCE; TARGET BALANCE.

ACT OF BANKRUPTCY behavior deemed an admission of bankruptcy—generally the failure to pay obligations when due. The Bankruptcy Reform Act of 1978 simplified the filing of involuntary petitions by eliminating specific tests of bankruptcy, such as transferring assets to defraud creditors. Since then, inability to pay bills on time is sufficient grounds for filing a creditor's petition. *See also* CREDITORS' COMMITTEE.

ACTUALS any physical commodity or financial instrument (Treasury bills, bonds, currencies) sold at the SPOT rate at the expiration of a contract. In a FINANCIAL FUTURE, it is the commodity underlying the futures contract as distinguished from the futures contract itself. In the futures market, delivery of the physical commodity or financial instrument rarely occurs, as most traders close out their forward positions before a contract expires.

ADDITIONAL COLLATERAL *see* SIDE COLLATERAL.

ADD-ON INTEREST finance charges computed by adding the interest payable to the full amount of loan principal. The add-on interest is added to the original principal amount, and becomes a part of the face amount of the promissory note.

Computing interest due under the add-on interest method is fairly simple. The loan PRINCIPAL is divided into a number of fixed payments, and each payment is multiplied by the finance charge, to calculate the interest cost to the borrower: Add-On Interest = Principal × Rate × Number of Months in the loan/12. *See also* AMORTIZATION; DISCOUNT, RULE OF THE 78'S; SIMPLE INTEREST.

ADEQUATE NOTICE printed notice clearly stating terms and conditions of a consumer loan or extension of credit. Lenders are required by the TRUTH IN LENDING ACT to disclose key credit terms, such as the ANNUAL PERCENTAGE RATE, annual fee, GRACE PERIOD, and other pertinent information when a new account is opened, and notify customers of any subsequent changes in credit terms.

ADJUDICATION settlement of opposing arguments by notice and trial in a court of law; also a court's ruling, such as adjudication of bankruptcy. Contrast with ARBITRATION.

ADJUSTABLE-RATE MORTGAGE (ARM) residential mortgage in which the interest rate floats up or down according to changes in an index rate. Adjustable-rate mortgages usually have lower initial interest rates than fixed-rate mortgages, so there is an opportunity for substantial interest savings over the life of the loan if rates remain steady or decline. Adjustable-rate mortgages first appeared in the 1960s but did not gain wide popularity until the 1980s, when lenders began promoting ARM loans as a low-cost alternative to thirty-year, fixed-rate mortgage loans. ARMs are structured with built-in limits, called interest-rate caps, to cushion the impact of interest-rate fluctuations on loan payments in any year or over the life of the loan. An adjustable-rate mortgage with an initial rate of 4½%, an annual cap of 1%, and a lifetime cap of 4% will have an interest rate no higher than 9½%. ARM rates are usually adjusted every six months or once a year, depending on the type of loan. Loan payment caps do not limit the amount of interest the lender is earning, which means an ATM loan may cause NEGATIVE AMORTIZATION if the accrued loan interest exceeds the interest actually paid.

When computing the loan interest rate, the lender adds a margin to an index rate selected as the benchmark, or base rate. The most common indexes are the CONSTANT MATURITY TREASURY (CMT) INDEX of Treasury issues with the same final maturity; the Treasury Bill index, based on the current auction yield of 3-month, 6-month or 1-year Treasury bills; the 12-month Moving Treasury Average, computed from the Treasury CMT index for the previous 12 months; the 11th District Cost of Funds Index, the weighted average cost of savings accounts, Federal Home Loan Bank advances, and other sources of funds paid by savings institutions in the 11th Federal Home Loan Bank district; the LONDON INTERBANK OFFERED RATE (LIBOR), the rate major London banks charge each other for borrowings; the certificate of deposit (CD) index, the average rate earned by nationally traded certificates of deposit; and the bank PRIME RATE, the rate banks charge their prime business borrowers. The most popular are the Treasury indexes, the 11th District Cost of Funds Index, and the LIBOR index. A popular variation of the adjustable-rate mortgage is the HYBRID ARM, in which the loan has a fixed interest rate for 3 to 10 years and thereafter adjusts according to market conditions. *See also* ALTERNATIVE MORTGAGE INSTRUMENT.

ADJUSTABLE RATE PREFERRED STOCK cumulative preferred stock with dividends paid and adjusted quarterly. Adjustable rate issues have no maturity date, but may be called at the option of the issuer. Shareholder dividends are nonaccruing, and are paid on scheduled DIVIDEND dates.

ADJUSTED CAPITAL RATIO ratio of adjusted CAPITAL to total assets, used in computing CAPITAL ADEQUACY. A bank's adjusted capital includes LOAN LOSS RESERVES for bad debt and securities gains or losses that are charged to earnings, less loans classified as DOUBTFUL LOANS or LOSS. The risk-adjusted capital guidelines, adopted by banking regulators in 1988, are aimed at developing uniform bank capital guidelines. *See also* CAPITAL ADEQUACY; RISK-BASED CAPITAL.

ADJUSTED GROSS INCOME individual's income from all sources, as reported on the IRS 1040 tax return, after certain allowable deductions such as IRA contributions, moving expenses, and alimony.

ADJUSTMENT accounting entry for ledger entries not previously posted and transferred to subsidiary accounts, or to correct bookkeeping errors. *See also* ADJUSTED CAPITAL RATIO; ADVERSELY CLASSIFIED ASSETS; RISK-BASED CAPITAL.

ADJUSTMENT CREDIT short-term ADVANCE by a Federal Reserve Bank, secured by a bank's own promissory note—the most common form of borrowing from a Federal Reserve Bank to meet RESERVE REQUIREMENTS and support short-term lending.

ADJUSTMENT INTERVAL time interval between changes in interest rates or monthly payment on an ADJUSTABLE RATE MORTGAGE. Mortgage rates are adjusted at preset intervals ranging from six months to five years, depending on the mortgage index.

ADMINISTRATOR

1. bank or party appointed by a probate court to distribute an estate of a person who dies INTESTATE, that is, without leaving a WILL, fails to name an EXECUTOR or when the executor refuses to serve. The administrator has legal authority to pay claims against the estate and distribute assets to heirs.
2. person who manages any business.

AD VALOREM valuation based on the monetary worth of an asset, from the Latin phrase *ad valorem* meaning "to the value." It is a widely accepted basis for such tax assessments (ad valorem taxes) as sales taxes, property taxes, and import tariffs.

ADVANCE

1. PRINCIPAL amount available when a borrower draws from a line of credit, takes a CASH ADVANCE against a bank credit card, or disburses a loan at specific periodic stages. Advances may be secured or unsecured. *See also* OVERDRAFT.
2. to draw against a preapproved line of credit.
3. disbursement of funds to finance payment of collections or refinance a maturing loan, as in a BRIDGE LOAN.
4. DISCOUNT WINDOW loan from a FEDERAL RESERVE BANK to a commercial bank maintaining a RESERVE ACCOUNT at one of the 12 district Fed banks. These loans are backed by U.S. Treasury securities or acceptable collateral.

   Most Federal Reserve credit is by advances, as this form of credit is easier to execute than rediscounting (selling) loans, and also because banks are reluctant to let their customers know they occasionally have to borrow. Contrast with REDISCOUNT. *See also* ADJUSTMENT CREDIT; EMERGENCY CREDIT; EXTENDED CREDIT; SEASONAL CREDIT.

ADVANCE COMMITMENT written promise or agreement to take some future action. The most common example is a contractual commitment a financial institution makes to lend funds to a borrower at a future date on terms agreed upon in advance, for example, a REVOLVING CREDIT agreement. The lender ordinarily charges a COMMITMENT FEE and may require the borrower to keep part of the loan as a COMPENSATING BALANCE in a checking account at the lending institution. A FIRM COMMITMENT is absolutely binding on the lender, whereas a CONDITIONAL COMMITMENT is binding only if certain terms are met in the future, such as meeting certain tests of creditworthiness. In mortgage banking, an advance commitment is called a STANDBY COMMITMENT.

ADVANCE REFUNDING *see* DEFEASANCE.

ADVERSE ACTION in consumer credit, denial of an applicant's credit application. If turned down because of DEROGATORY INFORMATION in a CREDIT REPORT, the applicant is entitled to examine, without cost, his or her credit report and request corrections of any inaccurate negative information reported by a lender. *See also* EFFECTS TEST; REGULATION B.

ADVERSELY CLASSIFIED ASSETS loans and other assets that are at risk to some degree, in the opinion of bank examiners. Such assets fail to meet acceptable credit standards, and totals of classified loans are reported separately in bank CALL REPORTS. State and national banking examiners have adopted uniform guidelines (the National Bank Examiners risk classification system) listing poorly performing loans as follows, from worst to least serious: LOSS, or complete write-off; DOUBTFUL LOAN, where repayment in full is questionable; SUBSTANDARD, where some loss is probable unless corrective actions are taken; and SPECIAL MENTION, indicating such potential problems as missing documentation or insufficient collateral.

Supervisory agencies require that lenders write down loans classified as doubtful to 50% of the original book value and loans classified as loss by 100% in calculating their net capital (adjusted capital plus reserves for possible loan losses) available for making new loans. *See also* NONACCRUAL LOAN; NONPERFORMING ASSET.

ADVICE written confirmation of payment received, funds transferred, service performed, or payment made. Examples in banking include a credit advice, indicating a debit advice, a withdrawal or transfer, and an account service charge.

AFFIDAVIT Latin for "has pledged his faith," a sworn statement in writing witnessed by a notary public or other public official. Federal agencies, such as the Federal Housing Administration, or the Veterans Department sometimes require affidavits from borrowers to show eligibility for a mortgage loan. Depository institutions may require affidavits before distributing trust assets to beneficiaries. *See also* ATTEST.

AFFILIATE any firm closely related to another through ownership by a parent company. If only two companies are involved and one owns more than 50% of the stock in the second, the preferred term is SUBSIDIARY.

Banking:

1. organization owned or controlled by a bank through stock ownership, or whose officers are directors of a BANK HOLDING COMPANY or FINANCIAL HOLDING COMPANY.
2. company owned by a federally insured bank or bank holding company that performs services such as credit card processing or data processing for financial institutions. Except for deposit taking, bank-owned service corporations engage in a wide range of bank-related functions, that are approved by the Federal Reserve Board as permissible activities for bank holding companies. *See also* REGULATION Y.
3. financial institution that issues MasterCard or Visa debit cards and credit cards. Also called AGENT BANK.

Finance:

1. any company directly or indirectly owning 5% or more of the voting stock in another company, as defined by the Investment Company Act.
2. company whose actions are controlled by another company through a joint agreement, or a company that, with others, controls the accounting company.

AFFINITY CARD credit card promoted under a sponsoring agreement between an organization and a card issuing bank. The issuer may waive annual fees for affinity cardholders, or even offer the card at a lower rate than ordinary bank cards. *See also* CO-BRANDED CARD.

AFFIRMATIVE COVENANT *see* COVENANT.

AFGHANI monetary unit of Afghanistan.

AFRICAN DEVELOPMENT BANK regional financial institution created by agreement among independent African countries in 1964. Membership, originally restricted to African countries, became open to nonregional countries in 1981. The bank provides long-term development loans, primarily for agriculture and capital improvement projects.

AFTER ACQUIRED CLAUSE

1. clause stating that any property acquired by the borrower after the mortgage is signed will be included as collateral in the mortgage lien. Such clauses provide additional protection for lenders and may also help borrowers obtain financing at a better rate, although they limit the ability to raise capital through new borrowings.
2. in ASSET-BASED LENDING, lien extending the lender's security interest to any additional inventory or receivables acquired by the borrower. Sometimes called a FLOATING LIEN, this gives the lender adequate protection against loss when the loan collateral is constantly changing.

AGENCY relationship between a principal and another party, named as agent, who is authorized to carry out the principal's instructions in transactions with a third party. For example, giving another person POWER OF ATTORNEY to negotiate a contract.

1. **Finance.** Account managed by one party for another, as by a bank trust department for an institutional client. A bank, acting as agent, can purchase or sell securities for individuals.
2. **Securities.** Federal agency securities other than those issued by the U.S. Treasury Department, such as obligations of the Government National Mortgage Association (Ginnie Mae), the Federal Intermediate Credit Banks, the Export-Import Bank. Some agency securities are backed by the full faith and credit of the U.S. government.

AGENCY FOR INTERNATIONAL DEVELOPMENT (AID) federal agency created in 1961 to administer assistance programs to less developed countries (LDCs) by making loans on more favorable terms than private banks. AID loans arranged through letters of credit drawn on commercial banks, are fully backed by the U.S. government.

AGENT BANK

1. bank named by members of a multibank lending syndicate to protect the interests of the participating banks in administering a loan to a foreign or domestic borrower. Its role is similar to a bond trustee. The agent bank is responsible for notifying other banks of

advances or drawdowns by the borrower and changes in interest rate. Often synonymous with LEAD BANK or lead manager.

2. bank that participates in the credit card program of another bank, by issuing credit cards and acting as a merchant depository, but does not finance the card receivables. Most financial institutions participating in bank card programs are agents rather than principal issuers.

3. foreign bank doing business in the United States on behalf of its parent. Such banks negotiate terms for international letters of credit and act as collection agents for the parent bank, but do not accept deposits or make loans in their own name. Also called *agency bank.*

AGGREGATE DEMAND (AGGREGATE SUPPLY) consumer spending plus government spending and investment spending by producers, considered a measure of total demand for goods and services in the economy. Both MONETARY POLICY and FISCAL POLICY attempt to influence aggregate demand to meet desired objectives of economic growth and employment. Aggregate supply is the economy's overall production of goods and services to meet anticipated demand.

AGING SCHEDULE classification of accounts receivable, inventory, or loans by the time intervals they are held. In a loan portfolio, aging shows the distribution of accounts from the date they are acquired, and is an indication of overall ASSET QUALITY or probability of repayment. Aging of accounts also reveals delinquency patterns, for example, any loans past-due 30 days, 60 days, 90 days or more—a useful guide in planning collection efforts. Loans 90-days delinquent are listed as NONACCRUAL LOANS, which means the bank is no longer posting interest due on the income statement. If this situation persists these loans may have to be charged off as BAD DEBT.

In ASSET-BASED LENDING, aging of accounts is a listing of accounts receivable by invoice date, and is used in determining the BORROWING BASE of eligible receivables against which funds are advanced. *See also* ADVERSELY CLASSIFIED ASSETS; LOAN GRADING.

AGREEMENT language defining the terms and conditions of a legally binding contract between two parties, such as an extension of CREDIT, or a LOAN secured by COLLATERAL. Examples include a deposit agreement as specified by an account SIGNATURE CARD, lease agreement, loan agreement, and credit card agreement.

AGREEMENT AMONG UNDERWRITERS contract between members of an UNDERWRITING GROUP offering a new issue of securities by which rights and responsibilities are assigned. A SYNDICATE is a group of bankers who underwrite and distribute an offering of securities. The agreement designates the MANAGING UNDERWRITER and additional participating underwriters; the ALLOTMENT or portion of the offering to be assigned each member; the life of the syndicate; and the method for offering the securities, that is, whether the underwriters agree to purchase the securities from the issuer or try to place them on a BEST EFFORT basis. Ordinarily, the offering syndicate dissolves after the securities have been placed, usually within 60 days, or sometimes earlier if by mutual consent.

AGREEMENT CORPORATION state chartered corporation engaged in international banking. These banking offices agree to limit their activities, under Federal Reserve Board regulations, to those permitted EDGE ACT CORPORATIONS, but have more liberal capital guidelines. Agreement corporations are chartered to conduct international operations through domestic offices, thereby allowing local firms access to international markets through local banks.

AGRICULTURAL CREDIT loans, notes, bills of exchange, and bankers' acceptances financing agricultural transactions. Banks lend to farmers for a variety of purposes, including (1) short-term credit to cover operating expenses; (2) intermediate credit for investment in farm equipment and real estate improvements; (3) long-term credit for acquisition of farm real estate and construction financing; and (4) debt repayment and refinancing. Commercial banks are the largest source of agricultural credit, followed by the Farm Credit Banks. *See also* FARM CREDIT SYSTEM; FARMER MAC; FARMERS HOME ADMINISTRATION.

ALGORITHM set of rules for solving a problem using a mathematical formula. In banking, algorithms are used in loan pricing, financial modeling and asset-liability management, transfer pricing, and data security. *See also* DATA ENCRYPTION STANDARD.

ALIENATION CLAUSE type of acceleration clause allowing the lender to demand full payment when mortgaged property is conveyed to another owner. An example is a DUE-ON-SALE clause in a mortgage deed. *See also* ASSUMABLE MORTGAGE.

ALIEN CORPORATION company incorporated in a foreign country. It is sometimes used interchangeably with FOREIGN CORPORATION, although there is a technical distinction between the two. In state laws throughout the United States, the term foreign corporation refers to a corporation chartered in another state. In general business usage and in federal tax laws, the term foreign corporation indicates a company incorporated in a country other than the United States.

ALL-IN COST total cost, whether explicit or implied. The all-in cost of a certificate of deposit is the rate of interest paid the depositor, the deposit insurance premium, and the opportunity cost of maintaining a RESERVE REQUIREMENT balance at a Federal Reserve Bank. In bank lending, the term refers to borrower's total cost of credit, including net interest charged, origination fees, service fees, utilization fees, and so on. *See also* COST OF FUNDS; MARGIN; SPREAD.

ALLOCATED TRANSFER RISK RESERVE (ATRR) special portion of a bank's LOAN LOSS RESERVE covering so-called COUNTRY RISK, for example, a private borrower's inability to raise the necessary foreign exchange to pay external debt. *See also* COUNTRY RISK; SOVEREIGN RISK.

ALLONGE paper attached to a NEGOTIABLE INSTRUMENT (check or promissory note, for example) for additional endorsements when there isn't enough space on the instruments themselves.

ALLOTMENT allocation, or share, usually of securities in an underwriting of new issues. It is also a method of filling bids in U.S. Treasury security auctions. In corporate securities, the most common usage occurs in *syndicated underwriting* where members of the SYNDICATE subscribe to underwrite and distribute a certain number of shares. In a *ratable allotment* if 20 million syndicate subscriptions are received for a new issue of only 10 million shares, a participant who subscribed to 5 million shares would receive an allotment of 2.5 million shares to offer for sale.

ALLOWANCE

1. **Accounting.** An account for adjusting the value of an asset through charges to current income; a reserve for depreciation.
2. **Banking.** LOAN LOSS RESERVE for anticipated CHARGE-OFF of bad debt.
3. **Trusts.** A probate court's award to a fiduciary, for example, a WIDOW'S ALLOWANCE.

ALLOWANCE FOR BAD DEBT *see* LOAN LOSS RESERVES.

ALL SAVERS CERTIFICATE one-year federally tax-exempt certificate account, authorized by the Economic Recovery Tax Act of 1981 to attract funds to mortgage lenders. None have been issued after December 1982.

ALPHA

1. expected price performance of a stock attributable to earnings, management, or other factors, as opposed to general market conditions. A stock with an alpha of 1.10 can be expected to outperform the market regardless of what happens to the market as a whole.
2. *risk-adjusted rate of return* of a mutual fund. Alpha measures the portfolio manager's contribution to investment return. A mutual fund with an alpha of 2.0% would have performed 2.0% better than expected for funds in its category. *See also* BETA.

ALTERED CHECK check or other NEGOTIABLE INSTRUMENT with the date, dollar amount, or payee's name changed or erased, usually for fraudulent purposes. Banks may refuse to honor checks if tampering is suspected.

ALTERNATIVE MORTGAGE INSTRUMENT (AMI) residential mortgage loan that differs from a fixed-rate, fully amortizing mortgage in the interest rate, the monthly or periodic payments, or the terms of repayment. These loans first became popular in the early 1980s, when high interest rates put buying a home beyond the reach of many first-time homeowners. Banks and savings institutions quickly introduced a variety of alternative mortgages, all designed to reduce the home buyer's mortgage payment or allow the buyer to finance a larger home. Included are the ADJUSTABLE-RATE MORTGAGE, which has an interest rate tied to an index; the HYBRID ARM, an adjustable-rate mortgage that has a fixed rate of interest in the first 3 to 10 years of the loan; and the INTEREST-ONLY LOAN, in which the borrower makes only interest payments for the first several years. Alternative mortgages have their advantages and disadvantages; critics say their primary benefit, a more affordable housing market for middle-class home buyers, may be offset by rising home finance costs if borrower incomes do not grow at the same pace as mortgage payments. *See also* BALLOON MORTGAGE; BIWEEKLY MORTGAGE; 15-YEAR MORTGAGE; GROWING EQUITY MORTGAGE; HYBRID ARM; OPTION ARM; PRICE LEVEL ADJUSTED MORTGAGE; PIGGYBACK MORTGAGE; REVERSE MORTGAGE; SHARED APPRECIATION MORTGAGE; TWO-STEP MORTGAGE.

AMENDMENT addition, deletion, or change to a legal document. All parties to the agreement must formally consent to an amendment by signing it. Afterward, the amendment becomes an integral part of the document, binding on all parties to the original agreement.

AMERICAN BANKERS ASSOCIATION (ABA) *see* TRADE ASSOCIATION.

AMERICAN DEPOSITARY RECEIPT (ADR) negotiable certificate issued by a U.S. bank for shares of stock issued by a foreign corporation. The securities are held in a custodial account, either at the issuing bank or an agent. ADRs are registered with the Securities and Exchange Commission, and give the holder the same benefits of ownership as shareholders. Two common types are sponsored ADRs, which are approved and promoted by the issuing corporation; and unsponsored ADRs, which are not backed by the issuer. ADRs are priced in dollars, and traded on stock exchanges and over-the-counter in the same fashion as U.S.-issued securities. *See also* INTERNATIONAL DEPOSITARY RECEIPT.

AMERICAN INSTITUTE OF BANKING (AIB) educational division of the AMERICAN BANKERS ASSOCIATION. AIB promotes professional advancement in banking through classroom instruction, seminars, study groups, and correspondence courses, and is supported by participating financial institutions through local chapters.

AMERICAN NATIONAL STANDARDS INSTITUTE (ANSI) nonprofit organization that sponsors industry standards for information management and data communication. The AMERICAN BANKERS ASSOCI-

ATION oversees the ANSI financial industry standards committee (ANSI X9). *See also* INTERNATIONAL ORGANIZATION FOR STANDARDIZATION.

AMERICAN RULE *see* PRUDENT MAN RULE.

AMERICAN STOCK EXCHANGE (AMEX) U.S. stock exchange with the third largest trading volume, located at 86 Trinity Place, New York City. Its market derivatives include DIAMONDS, which track the Dow Jones Industrial Average, and Standard & Poor's Depositary Receipts (SPIDERS), which track the Standard & Poor's 500 Index. The American Stock Exchange was acquired in 2009 by NYSE Euronext, the holding company that owns the New York Stock Exchange.

AMORTIZATION reduction in the value of an asset over the period owned; also the liquidation of debt through payments to a creditor or to a SINKING FUND.

1. **Banking.** The payment of a loan by periodic payments of principal and interest, resulting in a declining principal balance and eventual repayment in full. This form of debt repayment is LEVEL PAYMENT AMORTIZATION. Other methods have repayment schedules in which the early loan payments don't fully cover the interest due (NEGATIVE AMORTIZATION).

   Even though level payment amortization calls for the same payment in every installment, the loan payments are divided unequally between principal balance and interest owed. In the early years of a 30-year mortgage, a higher portion of early loan payments goes toward payment of interest than reducing the principal; as the loan is gradually paid down, an increasing portion of each payment is allocated to the PRINCIPAL until a zero-balance is eventually reached. *See also* ADD-ON INTEREST; AMORTIZATION SCHEDULE; BALLOON MORTGAGE; REBATE; RULE OF THE 78'S; SIMPLE INTEREST.
2. **Securities.** An accounting process for adjusting the book value of bonds purchased above PAR VALUE to the face value. Compare to ACCRETION OF DISCOUNT.
3. **Accounting.** A gradual reduction in book value of patents and other intangible assets. The preferred term for writing off fixed assets such as equipment is DEPRECIATION.

AMORTIZATION SCHEDULE table commonly used in mortgages and installment loans, showing the number of payments due, the amount due in each installment, the declining principal balance, and the number of years needed to fully extinguish the debt. *See chart on next page.*

AMOUNT FINANCED credit or advance actually made available to a borrower, repayable according to terms of the loan. It is equal to the loan PRINCIPAL less any prepaid finance charges, and does not include upfront payments such as prepaid DISCOUNT POINTS. *See also* ADD-ON INTEREST; AMORTIZATION.

AMORTIZATION OF ONE-YEAR $1,000 LOAN AT 10%, SIMPLE INTEREST

Monthly Payment (P&I): 87.92

To Principal	To Interest	Balance
79.59	8.33	920.41
80.25	7.67	840.16
80.92	7.00	759.24
81.59	6.33	677.65
82.27	5.65	595.38
82.96	4.96	512.42
83.65	4.27	428.77
84.35	3.57	344.42
85.05	2.87	259.37
85.76	2.16	173.61
86.47	1.45	87.14
87.19	.73	–.05

ANALYST *see* CREDIT ANALYST.

ANNOUNCEMENT EFFECT market reaction to reports from regulatory agencies, such as borrowing by the Treasury Department or changes in key interest rates, as when the Federal Reserve Board raises or lowers the FEDERAL FUNDS RATE, potentially a warning of changes in credit conditions and interest rates. Also known as *signal effect.*

ANNUAL CAP clause in an ADJUSTABLE RATE MORTGAGE limiting any increase in the interest rate during a calendar year to a preset amount or ceiling, giving the borrower a cushion against a sudden increase in mortgage payments and PAYMENT SHOCK when the loan rate is adjusted, particularly in periods of rising interest rates. A 10% mortgage with a 2% annual cap will increase only to 12% even if the mortgage INDEX rate goes up by 3%. *See also* LIFE OF LOAN CAP; PAYMENT CAP.

ANNUAL CLEAN UP *see* CLEAN-UP REQUIREMENT.

ANNUAL PERCENTAGE RATE (APR) effective cost of credit in consumer loans and real estate loans expressed as a percentage rate. The annual percentage rate is the finance charge the borrower actually pays, including loan INTEREST, points, and origination fees.

The Federal TRUTH IN LENDING ACT of 1968 requires lenders to calculate the cost of credit as an annual percentage and disclose the APR in large bold type in loan application documents. APR rates and the dollar amount (principal and interest) for various fixed-rate amortizing loans can be found in APR tables available from the Federal Reserve Board. *See also* ADD-ON INTEREST; EFFECTIVE RATE; NOMINAL INTEREST RATE; SIMPLE INTEREST.

ANNUAL PERCENTAGE YIELD (APY) amount of interest expressed as a percentage rate, a deposit account (or a share draft account) would earn in a year at a stated interest rate. The APY disclosure, showing the effect of interest compounding, assumes that funds remain on deposit for a full 365-day year at the advertised rate, and no additional deposits or withdrawals are made. *See also* TRUTH IN SAVINGS.

ANNUAL REPORT audited annual disclosure of performance to shareholders of a public corporation, as required by the Securities and Exchange Commission. It contains management's review of financial performance, the corporate income statement, balance sheet, as well as other schedules, such as flow of funds and changes in capital accounts. Also in the annual report is the auditor's letter, a statement containing the ACCOUNTANT'S OPINION. *See also* FORM 10K.

ANNUITY investment contract purchased from a life insurance company that makes guaranteed payments at some future date, usually after retirement. A *fixed annuity* pays a fixed-dollar income for a predetermined number of years, or for the remaining life of the annuitant. A *variable annuity* pays an investment return tied to the market value of securities owned (stocks, bonds, or money market securities), and is designed to preserve purchasing power. There is usually no annual limit on annuity contributions, and distributions are generally not required at age 70½. Capital invested in annuities grows tax-free and at withdrawal is taxed at ordinary income tax rates. Financial soundness of the insurance company, past investment performance, and broker sale commissions are important considerations in buying an annuity. Unlike bank deposit accounts, annuities are not protected by deposit insurance. *See also* BANK INVESTMENT CONTRACT.

ANTEDATE *see* BACK DATING.

ANTICIPATED BALANCE estimated balance of a SAVINGS ACCOUNT or TIME DEPOSIT account at maturity or other future date, including compounded interest, assuming no additional deposits or withdrawals occur.

ANTICIPATED INTEREST estimated interest a savings account will earn as of a future date, assuming that there is normal compounding of interest and no additional deposits or withdrawals occurring during the interest period.

ANTICIPATION any advance payment of an obligation prior to the date payment is due, usually to save interest costs.

1. **Accounting.** Charges to income or future earnings before these earnings are realized.
2. **Banking.** Borrower's legal right, if allowed by a mortgage instrument, to repay the outstanding principal and interest on a loan, as when refinancing the loan at a lower rate. Also, deposit of funds for payment of an ACCEPTANCE prior to the maturity date, reducing the customer's liability.

ANTITRUST LAWS legislation designed to prevent monopolies or business practices limiting free market competition. Although some 40 states have adopted such legislation, the more important acts are these federal laws: (1) the Sherman Antitrust Act of 1890, which outlawed monopolies, restraints of trade, and business combinations (called trusts) created for the sole purpose of restricting competition, though it did not define these terms; (2) the Federal Trade Commission Act of 1914, creating the Federal Trade Commission, a federal agency with power to regulate interstate commerce, investigate business activities (except those by banks) and issue enforcement orders; (3) the Clayton Antitrust Act of 1914 and amendments, which banned tie-in contracts, interlocking directorates, and certain types of holding company acquisitions.

The U.S. Department of Justice and bank supervisory agencies look closely at deposit account CONCENTRATION or the market share an acquirer would gain from a merger. Local deposit share, in an era of nationwide banking and convenient access to non-local banks, is one of several factors the banking regulators examine when approving a merger application. The bank agencies also review mergers for their impact on financial stability and ability to deliver banking services to local communities.

APPORTIONMENT proportional division of rights, ownership, or expenses, as between buyer and seller in a real estate conveyance. In trusts and estates, it applies to the division of income and administration expenses between two or more accounts, for example, principal and interest income, or the division of estate taxes among heirs of an estate. Compare with *allocation,* which assigns income earned or expenses paid to a single account for accounting purposes.

APPRAISAL written estimate of market value by a qualified appraiser. Appraised value is one of the key factors determining loan size in loans secured by real estate. The estimated value of real property is based on replacement cost, sales of comparable property, or expected future income from income producing property. *See also* AUTOMATED VALUATION MODEL (AVM).

APPRECIATION

1. increase in the value of an asset through a rise in market price, appraised value, or income earned, as compared to an earlier period. The opposite is DEPRECIATION.
2. increase in the value of one currency vis-à-vis another, without any change in official value occurring. It results from growth in market demand under floating exchange rates rather than official action such as a currency revaluation.

APPROVED LIST

1. **Banking.** Bonds or other securities that a bank may hold as investments, usually based on RATINGS from bond rating firms such as Standard & Poor's, Moody's Investors Service, Fitch Ratings, and

others. Federal Reserve regulations limit investments by national banks to investment grade securities as determined by a ratings service. State chartered banks are subject to the same investment requirements as national banks by the Federal Reserve Act.

2. **Investments.** A list of investments authorized for a fiduciary, by state statute, or by directors of a mutual fund.

ARBITRAGE profit making by buying a security, currency, or commodity at a low price in one market and simultaneously selling in another market at a higher price. Alternately, an arbitrageur borrows in one market and lends in another. The effect is to diminish price differences between markets.

There are several forms of arbitrage transactions.

Securities traders engage in *risk arbitrage* when their profit from a transaction is dependent on completion of a corporate merger, takeover, or recapitalization.

In the futures market, arbitrage is sometimes called maturity arbitrage, for example, buying three-month delivery contracts and selling six-month contracts in a particular currency (also known as FORWARD FORWARD).

Arbitrage also relates to SWAP transactions where similar issues of fixed-income securities are exchanged and later resold. *See also* CARRY TRADE; COVERED INTEREST ARBITRAGE; CURRENCY SWAP; HEDGE/HEDGING; INTEREST RATE SWAP.

ARBITRATION

1. settlement of a dispute after a hearing of opposing arguments, by an arbitrator, rather than a court of law. If binding arbitration is accepted, the parties involved agree to follow the arbitrator's decision, which is binding only on the parties to the dispute, and is not a legal precedent, as is a judicial ruling.
2. in the securities industry, a method for settling disputes between member firms, or between banker-dealers and their customers. Arbitration of disputes involving broker-dealers and their customers is often part of a brokerage agreement, but can limit a brokerage client's right to sue a broker-dealer.

ARIARY monetary unit of Madagascar.

ARM'S LENGTH TRANSACTION transaction carried out by unrelated or unaffiliated parties, as by a willing buyer and a willing seller, each acting in his own self-interest. Pricing based on such transactions is the basis of fair market valuations.

ARREARS

1. debt, installation loan payment, or bond interest due but unpaid. Loans unpaid after an allowed GRACE PERIOD are considered delinquent. The term also applies to unpaid preferred stock dividends.
2. mortgage or installment loan interest payable at specific dates for the use of borrowed money in the previous period.

ARTICLE 9 section of the UNIFORM COMMERCIAL CODE dealing with loans secured by collateral. Amendments to Article 9 in 2001 add new types of collateral (for example, deposit accounts as collateral for commercial loans) and new types of transactions (sales of promissory notes) that can be pledged as loan collateral, supplementing other assets (such as accounts receivable, business inventory, real property, and securities) that have for many years been used as loan collateral. *See also* PERFECTED LIEN; SECURED LOAN.

ARTICLES OF INCORPORATION document stating the purpose of a private corporation, filed by founders at a designated state office, e.g., with the Secretary of State. When approved, it becomes the firm's *certificate of incorporation,* giving the corporation its legal existence, subject to the laws of the state where incorporated. After the charter is granted, corporate directors adopt bylaws stating, among other things, the operating rules of the corporation.

ARTICLES OF PARTNERSHIP written agreement by persons establishing a partnership, stating among other things, the nature of the business being formed, the capital contribution of each partner as well as their duties and responsibilities, and the share in net profits of the organization.

Owners share equally in the profits of the business unless stated otherwise and pay taxes as individuals. *See also* GENERAL PARTNER; LIMITED PARTNERSHIP.

ARTICLE XII COMPANY investment company chartered under New York state law to finance international banking transactions. An Article XII company can hold credit balances and offer other banking services but cannot accept deposits. These companies, usually owned by foreign banks, are exempt from RESERVE REQUIREMENTS of the Federal Reserve System.

ASIAN CURRENCY UNIT (ACU) unit of account for dollar denominated deposits held in separate accounts in banks in Singapore, Hong Kong, and other Asian financial centers. The term refers to nonresident dollar deposits. Contrast with EURODOLLAR.

ASIAN DEVELOPMENT BANK *see* MULTILATERAL DEVELOPMENT BANK.

ASKED PRICE lowest price at which a seller is willing to offer securities or financial futures, also called OFFERING PRICE. It is then compared against the BID price, the highest price offered by a potential buyer.

ASSAY test of a precious metal or oil commodity to determine if it meets quality standards for trading on commodities exchanges. An assay test also determines the cost of materials (*assay value*) in coins.

ASSESSED VALUATION appraisal of real and personal property by taxing authorities for computation of AD VALOREM taxes. This is used to determine debt limits for municipal governments, as set by charter or by statutory limit. Local property taxes are computed from an assessment ratio that sets taxes payable against a percentage of fair market value.

ASSESSMENT

1. tax on real property, whether an annual property tax based on current fair market value, or special assessments for sewers or public improvements.
2. amount sometimes levied by banks, corporations, and insurance companies on stockholders to cover an impaired capital position or unanticipated losses.
3. in bankruptcy, special charge to the holders of stock not fully subscribed, payable to the bankruptcy trustee for benefit of creditors.

ASSET anything owned by a person or organization having monetary value, usually its cost or fair market value. An asset may be a specific property, such as title to real estate or other tangible property, or enforceable claims against others.

1. **Banking.** Loans, discounts, investment securities (government bonds, municipal bonds), and claims against other banks. Loans account for the largest portion of interest earning assets held by banks and savings (thrift) institutions. Also included are FEDERAL FUNDS sold to other banks; checks in the process of collection. *See also* REAL ESTATE OWNED; TRADING ACCOUNT ASSETS.
2. **Finance.** There are several major asset categories: (1) current assets—cash and short-term items convertible into cash within one year; (2) FIXED ASSETS—furniture, plant, and equipment owned by a firm, which are depreciated over their useful life; (3) INTANGIBLE ASSETS—patents, trademarks, or goodwill, which have a value and carry a cost; and (4) pledged assets—collateral for a bank loan or purchase of securities on margin.

ASSET ALLOCATION distributing assets among stocks, bonds, and other investment classes to achieve goals, such as income or capital appreciation. Asset allocation, a service available from financial planners and investment advisers, is a central concept in personal financial planning and portfolio management.

ASSET-BACKED SECURITIES bonds or debt securities collateralized by the cash flow from a pool of auto loans, credit card receivables, vehicle and equipment leases, consumer loans, insurance policies, and other obligations. The bonds give the holder an UNDIVIDED INTEREST in the securitized assets, and are funded by the cash flows received by the issuer from regular payments of principal and interest from borrowers.

The process of converting loans into marketable securities is known as SECURITIZATION. When mortgage loans, consumer loans, commercial loans, and leases are securitized, the pools of assets backing a particular issue are transferred to a GRANTOR TRUST, a passive entity that issues the securities that are purchased by investors. Virtually any debt obligation with regularly scheduled principal and interest payments can be securitized: auto loans, credit card receivables, home improvement loans, leases, residential mortgages, and second mortgages. Examples are MORTGAGE-BACKED SECURITIES, such as COLLATERALIZED MORTGAGE OBLIGATIONS (CMOS), and REAL ESTATE MORTGAGE INVESTMENT CONDUITS (REMICS). Debt securitizing also gives lenders another source of funds for making new loans, and is a technique actively used in ASSET-LIABILITY MANAGEMENT. *See also* ASSET SALES; SECONDARY MORTGAGE MARKET.

ASSET-BASED LENDING financing secured by a firm's balance sheet assets, such as inventory, receivables, or collateral other than real estate. The most common forms are ACCOUNTS RECEIVABLE FINANCING, in which the lender advances funds against trade receivables, inventory lending, and equipment leasing. Asset-based lending covers a broad range of secured lending activities, and is used to support the credit needs of firms that cannot obtain bank financing on a fully unsecured basis. Also called *"asset financing"* or *"asset-based financing." See also* FACTORING; PURCHASE ORDER FINANCING; WAREHOUSE RECEIPT.

ASSET COVERAGE measure of an organization's SOLVENCY or its ability to pay back bank debt and other credit obligations from earnings. The result can be expressed as a ratio, a percentage, or in dollar terms. *See also* DEBT SERVICE COVERAGE RATIO (DSCR).

ASSET LEDGER subsidiary ledger of asset accounts in which journal entries of transactions are summarized and classified into debits and credits. Depending on the size of an organization and the complexity of its accounting system, it may have many different ledgers for different types of assets, for example, fixed assets.

ASSET-LIABILITY COMMITTEE (ALCO) senior management committee in a bank or thrift institution, responsible for coordinating borrowing and lending strategy, and funds acquisition to meet profitability objectives as interest rates change. This committee also monitors actions by the Federal Reserve that may affect interest rates, such as a change in the Federal Reserve FEDERAL FUNDS RATE.

ASSET-LIABILITY MANAGEMENT active management of a bank's BALANCE SHEET to maintain a mix of loans and deposits consistent with its goals for long-term growth and risk management. Banks, in the normal course of business, assume financial risk by making loans at interest rates that differ from rates paid on deposits. Deposits often have shorter maturities than loans and adjust to current market rates faster than loans. The result is a balance sheet mismatch between assets (loans) and liabilities (deposits).

The function of asset-liability management is to measure and control three levels of financial risk: INTEREST RATE RISK (the pricing difference between loans and deposits), CREDIT RISK (the probability of default), and LIQUIDITY RISK (occurring when loans and deposits have different maturities).

A primary objective in asset-liability management is managing NET INTEREST MARGIN, that is, the net difference between interest earning assets (loans) and interest paying liabilities (deposits) to produce consistent growth in the loan portfolio and shareholder earnings, regardless of short-term movement in interest rates. The dollar difference between assets (loans) maturing or repricing and liabilities (deposits) is known as the rate sensitivity GAP (or *maturity gap*). Banks attempt to manage this asset-liability gap by pricing some of their loans at variable interest rates.

A more precise measure of interest rate risk is DURATION, which measures the impact of changes in interest rates on the expected maturities of both assets and liabilities. In essence, duration takes the gap report data and converts that information into present-value worth of deposits and loans, which is more meaningful in estimating maturities and the probability that either assets or liabilities will reprice during the period under review. Besides financial institutions, nonfinancial companies also employ asset-liability management, mainly through the use of derivative contracts to minimize their exposures on the liability side of the balance sheet. *See also* DYNAMIC GAP; GAPPING; LIQUIDITY; MATCHED MATURITIES; MISMATCH; NEGATIVE GAP; POSITIVE GAP; REFINANCE RISK; REINVESTMENT RISK; REPRICING OPPORTUNITIES; STATIC GAP; ZERO GAP.

ASSET MANAGEMENT ACCOUNT money-management account combining an array of investment services with convenient access by check writing, credit or debit card, and a combined statement of financial position. Bank sponsored accounts are usually built around a checking or NOW account, and allow securities buying. *See also* WRAP ACCOUNT.

ASSET QUALITY estimation of the quality of bank assets (principally loans and leases) as measured by a lender's credit standards, and the liquidity of securities held in the investment portfolio. If assets are packaged for resale to investors in the secondary market, the criterion for determining quality of assets is, "What can I expect to get in the market if I sell my loans?" In this context, asset quality has less to do with CHARGE-OFF analysis than the marketability of the credit portfolio.

ASSET SALES nonrecourse sale of bank receivables to a third party, either through the sale of WHOLE LOANS or WHOLE POOLS of loans, or SECURITIZATION, that is, issuing securities collateralized by the receivables of bank credits (residential mortgages, auto loans, leases, credit card receivables). Accounting treatment of asset sales is complicated, and determines whether a transaction is a sale of assets. In general terms, the test of an asset sale is whether the seller gives the buyer control over the assets transferred, and also any residual interest, without recourse to the seller. Transfers with recourse—allowing the buyer to resell a portion of the assets back to the seller—are treated by Financial Accounting Standards Board Rule 77 as a financing rather than a sale of assets.

If the agreement requires the seller to take back any bad loans, it is not considered for accounting purposes a true sale of assets and the seller cannot deduct the value of loans sold from its loan portfolio. *See also* ASSET-BACKED SECURITIES; PRIVATE PLACEMENT; REAL ESTATE MORTGAGE INVESTMENT CONDUIT (REMIC); SECURITIZATION.

ASSET SWAP exchange of one asset for another, often done to improve the quality of a bank's loan portfolio by, for example, converting a fixed rate asset into an asset with a floating rate. There are numerous examples: converting a EUROBOND into a synthetic floating rate note through an exchange of interest payments; an exchange of one commodity for another, as in a commodity swap; or a DEBT FOR EQUITY SWAP.

ASSIGNMENT

1. signing over title, rights, or other interests to another person.
2. in a LETTER OF CREDIT, transfer by a BENEFICIARY of all or part of the credit facility to another party, which must be confirmed by the advising bank.
3. writing on the back of a stock certificate transferring ownership to another holder.
4. transfer of debtor's property to creditors, called an assignment for the benefit of creditors. Transfers in the 90 days prior to a bankruptcy petition may, however, be set aside by a bankruptcy trustee. *See also* VOIDABLE PREFERENCE.
5. option writer's notice to the Options Clearing Corp. of intent to fulfill an offsetting buy, resulting in assignment in favor of the seller.

ASSOCIATE BANK bank that is a member of a corporation or joint venture providing common benefits. Examples include banks that are members in a clearing house association and those affiliated with a bank card system such as Visa or MasterCard. Typically, associations have different classes of membership, depending on equity ownership, and other factors.

ASSUMABLE MORTGAGE MORTGAGE giving the borrower the right to assign the unpaid balance of his obligation, without prepayment penalty, to another person upon sale of the mortgaged property. The buyer assumes payment of the loan at the same rate and terms for the remainder of the mortgage, and the seller remains secondarily liable for the obligation. Department of Veterans Affairs mortgages and mortgages insured by the FEDERAL HOUSING ADMINISTRATION are generally assumable by the buyer. Contrast with PORTABLE MORTGAGE. *See also* ASSUMPTION; DUE-ON-SALE CLAUSE.

ASSUMPTION mortgage clause stating the terms under which an existing mortgage or deed of trust may be conveyed to another party. Generally, a mortgage cannot be transferred at the same rate and terms without written consent of the lender. *See also* ASSUMABLE MORTGAGE.

AT PAR *see* PAR VALUE.

AT SIGHT denotes a negotiable instrument, such as a check, bill of exchange, or draft payable when presented to the drawee.

ATTACHMENT

1. writ authorizing seizure of property after a court approved judgment in favor of a creditor. The creditor must obtain a property execution authorizing garnishment of wages or seizure of personal assets, such as bank accounts.
2. creditor's lien, which is said to attach to the borrower's assets in exchange for a loan or advance against a line of credit. *See also* SECURITY INTEREST.

ATTEST sworn statement of fact or condition, duties or responsibilities. In the case of a will, the person signs in the presence of two or more witnesses, or before a notary public.

AT THE MARKET *see* MARKET ORDER.

AT THE MONEY refers to the STRIKE PRICE of an option contract when the option is about equal in price to the current market price of the underlying security or futures contract. *See also* IN THE MONEY; OUT OF THE MONEY.

ATTORNEY AT LAW person licensed by a state to practice law, give legal advice, and represent clients in legal proceedings before a court or administrative agency. Generally, a lawyer.

ATTORNEY IN FACT person named by another to act as an agent in his behalf. Assignment is in writing, and is commonly referred to as a POWER OF ATTORNEY assignment, and may be general or limited to specific acts.

AUCTION MARKET system by which securities are bought and sold at the best possible price through competitive bidding. Prices are established by brokers acting as agents of buyers and sellers, as well as principal dealers acting for their own accounts. In the securities market, the best example is the New York Stock Exchange, where buyers and sellers make competitive bids for exchange listed securities by submitting order tickets to the exchange. The commodity futures market where interest rate fixtures are traded, is in contrast, an open outcry market, where market prices are set by direct interaction of exchange members, standing in a pit on the trading floor.

The U.S. Treasury Department sells new issues of Treasury bills on a DISCOUNT YIELD basis through competitive auction bidding in which the price of bills offered for sale is gradually lowered, starting with the lowest yield (and highest price) until the entire amount being offered is sold. *See also* COMPETITIVE BID; DUTCH AUCTION.

AUDIT examination and verification of a company's books and records by a qualified accountant. An auditor's letter of opinion, which may be qualified or unqualified, is included in the company's annual report. Audits are also required by the SECURITIES AND EXCHANGE COMMISSION for companies with registered securities.

AUDIT DEPARTMENT internal management control group responsible for maintaining accuracy of financial data through periodic inspections of branch offices and bank departments. The internal audit department also insures adherence to law, regulation, and policy.

AUDITOR'S OPINION *see* ACCOUNTANT'S OPINION.

AUDIT TRAIL chronological record of a transaction, loan, or investment, including credit memos and related documents. Such a record reveals the step-by-step history of a transaction as it flows through the organization, enabling an after-the-fact review to determine the time and place where errors occurred. *See also* CREDIT REVIEW.

AUTHENTICATION legal verification of the genuineness of a bond, document, or signature. In electronic funds transfers, authentication is a method of verifying that a payment instruction has in fact originated at the sending bank, and has not been tampered with by an unauthorized party. *See also* ATTEST; MESSAGE AUTHENTICATION CODE.

AUTHORITY TO PURCHASE advice used in Far East trade, authorizing a correspondent bank to purchase drafts on an importer rather than the importer's bank. Many banks add their own guarantee, giving the advice the same authority as a LETTER OF CREDIT.

AUTHORIZATION issuance of approval to complete a transaction or pay funds, for example a bank card authorization or payment authorization. In bank cards, the card issuing bank notifies the merchant processing bank (the merchant bank) that a cardholder has available credit and issues an AUTHORIZATION CODE for the transaction.

AUTHORIZATION CODE in bank cards, a message from a merchant processing bank to a card accepting merchant approving transactions against the card presented by the cardholder. *See also* NEGATIVE AUTHORIZATION; POSITIVE AUTHORIZATION; ZERO-FLOOR LIMIT.

AUTHORIZED INVESTMENT investment by a fiduciary or trustee, following written instructions in a trust instrument. Contrast with legal investment conforming with regulations by state banking authorities or state law concerning permissible investments by fiduciaries and mutual savings banks.

AUTHORIZED SETTLEMENT AGENT bank that is authorized to submit checks or CASH ITEMS to a Federal Reserve Bank for collection.

In bank cards, a bank authorized to honor clearing drafts for the settlement of interchange.

AUTHORIZED STOCK (SHARES) maximum number of shares in each class of capital stock that a corporation can legally issue. (It may not actually issue all of the shares authorized.) The total shares per class of stock, for example common stock, or preferred stock, is specified in the corporate charter or ARTICLES OF INCORPORATION. The number of authorized shares can be increased by amending the articles of incorporation or charter, which is usually accomplished by shareholder vote.

AUTOMATED CLEARING HOUSE (ACH) computer-based clearing and settlement facility for interchange of electronic debits and credits among financial institutions. ACH entries can be substituted for checks in recurring payments such as mortgages, or in DIRECT DEPOSIT distribution of federal and corporate benefits payments, including Social Security payments. Since the mid-1970s, the ACH has functioned as a unified payment clearing system consisting of regional clearing house associations owned by U.S. financial institutions. The ACH system is being used increasingly as a payments processor for business-to-business trade payments and household bill payments. *See also* CASH CONCENTRATION & DISBURSEMENT; CORPORATE TRADE EXCHANGE; CORPORATE TRADE PAYMENT; ELECTRONIC DATA INTERCHANGE; NET SETTLEMENT.

AUTOMATED TELLER MACHINE (ATM) computer terminal allowing consumers to make deposits, obtain cash from checking or savings accounts, pay bills, transfer money between accounts, and do other routine transactions as they would at a bank teller window. Today bank ATMs do much more than dispense cash in preset increments. Some ATM machines cash checks to the penny, accept envelope-free deposits, and print monthly statements for mortgage, brokerage, or regular banking accounts. Some U.S. banks have programmed their machines to offer ATM customers access to all of the banking services available on the bank's Internet Web site, effectively duplicating the bank's Web site on the ATM display screen.

AUTOMATED UNDERWRITING mortgage lender's analysis of a new loan application using a computer program to collect all the information necessary to approve the loan application. In the United States, automated underwriting systems such as Fannie Mae's Desktop Underwriter® and Freddie Mac's Loan Prospector® review the loan applicant's credit history, and ability to repay the loan and determine if the price the applicant is offering to pay is supported by the property value. The main advantage these systems offer is their speed in approving loans scheduled to be sold to investors in the secondary mortgage market.

AUTOMATED VALUATION MODEL (AVM) computer generated estimate of residential property value, accepted by most lenders as a substitute for a full property APPRAISAL for second mortgage loans and home equity lines of credit. Valuations are calculated using computer software models and recent sales of similar homes.

AUTOMATIC DEPOSIT *see* DIRECT DEPOSIT.

AUTOMATIC TRANSFER SERVICE (ATS) prearranged transfer of funds from a savings account to checking, allowing the depositor to earn interest until funds are needed to cover checks written or to maintain a minimum balance. Also called *automatic savings transfer*.

AVAILABILITY time period, expressed in days, from the day of deposit until funds are credited to an account's COLLECTED BALANCE, are available for spending or investment. Funds availability is determined by average clearing time, allowing for MAIL FLOAT and FEDERAL RESERVE FLOAT. *See also* AVAILABILITY SCHEDULE; CHECK HOLD; DEFERRED AVAILABILITY.

AVAILABILITY SCHEDULE table showing the number of days needed to clear a deposited check. Under the EXPEDITED FUNDS AVAILABILITY ACT, financial institutions must give their customers access to deposited funds within a fixed number of days, depending on whether a check is drawn on a local or nonlocal bank. Local checks (checks deposited at a bank in the same Federal Reserve REGIONAL CHECK PROCESSING CENTER as the paying bank) must be available for use within two business days after the day of deposit.

AVAILABLE BALANCE checking account balance a customer actually has use of: the current balance, less deposits not yet posted to the account. A bank may include the checking account CASH RESERVE credit line in computing available balance. *See also* COLLECTED BALANCE.

AVAILABLE CREDIT credit ready for use in new purchases, sometimes called open to buy. In bank cards, it is the difference between the AVERAGE OUTSTANDING BALANCE and the cardholder's preapproved credit limit. Also, the unused portion of a bank LINE OF CREDIT.

AVAILABLE FUNDS

1. funds that a bank can put to use in meeting loan demand or hold in its investment portfolio, depending on market competition, demand for credit, interest rates, and other factors. The total is equal to cash on hand (VAULT CASH) and checks payable by other banks (cash due from banks on the balance sheet) plus aggregate loans and investments.
2. AVAILABLE BALANCE in a depositor's account, which is the amount that can be invested readily, disbursed to pay creditors, or transferred to another account.

AVAILABLE RESERVE net difference between EXCESS RESERVES balances maintained in a RESERVE ACCOUNT at a Federal Reserve Bank or branch office, and funds borrowed at the DISCOUNT WINDOW.

AVAILABILITY OF FUNDS

Type of Deposit	When Funds Are Available for Use
—First $100 of any deposit of checks —Government checks, cashier's checks, certified checks, teller's checks —Checks written on another account at the same institution —Direct deposit and other electronic credits	Next business day after the day of deposit
—Checks written on local institutions*	Second business day
—Checks written on nonlocal institutions —Deposits made at an automated teller machine owned by another institution	Fifth business day

*Under the Expedited Funds Availability Act, a check is a local check if deposited in the same Federal Reserve check processing region as the paying bank.

AVAL European term for a bank guarantee ensuring payment of a note, bond, promissory note, or draft. *See also* MEDALLION SIGNATURE GUARANTEE.

AVERAGE ANNUAL YIELD average return per year for the entire term of a multiyear CERTIFICATE OF DEPOSIT (CD), assuming that compound interest earned remains the same. The average annual yield of a CD will be higher than the EFFECTIVE ANNUAL YIELD because it includes interest earned over a longer period of time.

AVERAGE BALANCE *see* AVERAGE DAILY BALANCE.

AVERAGE COLLECTED BALANCE average dollar amount on deposit in a checking account during an accounting period, equal to daily ledger balances less uncollected checks, divided by the number of days in a reporting period, usually a month. *See also* AVAILABLE BALANCE; UNCOLLECTED FUNDS.

AVERAGE DAILY BALANCE

1. average amount in a deposit account, equal to the sum of daily deposit balances during an accounting period, usually a month, divided by the number of days.

2. method of computing CREDIT CARD finance charges, computed by taking the daily beginning balance, adding new charges for that day, and subtracting any payments applied to purchases. The resulting total, divided by the number of days in the billing period, is multiplied by the finance charge.

AVERAGE DAILY FLOAT average dollar amount of checks or drafts in the process of collection, and not credited to the account as collected funds or available funds. Also referred to as *items in collection.*

AVERAGE LIFE number of years until the date when one-half of each dollar of principal value in a security will be paid. Average life is a shorthand method of computing a bond's retirement date, which determines its YIELD TO MATURITY. This calculation is only an approximation, as it depends on borrower prepayments and other factors. For example, some 30-year conventional mortgages will prepay much faster than others. Half lives of corporate and municipal bonds frequently are determined by prepayments into a SINKING FUND. Also called WEIGHTED AVERAGE LIFE in mortgage-backed securities or *average maturity* in corporate and municipal bonds. *See also* CASH FLOW YIELD; DURATION; HALF LIFE.

AVERAGE OUTSTANDING BALANCE average unpaid balance in a credit card portfolio, including interest-paying balances carried over from previous billing periods. The average outstanding balance, a measure of profitability and account usage, is equal to the total number of accounts divided by the number of accounts with balances.

AVERAGE TICKET average merchant transaction in a bank card program. It is computed by dividing total dollars charged in a time period by the number of sales drafts and is indicative of account activity and indirectly a measure of bank card INTERCHANGE income collected from other banks.

AWARD

1. decision by a board of arbitration, after hearing arguments presented by the parties to a dispute, in favor of either of the parties.
2. acceptance of a competitive bid in AUCTION MARKET sale for U.S. Treasury securities or municipal bonds.

B

BACK DATING writing a check or draft with a date earlier than today's date. This does not affect its negotiability, as long as the check is cashed or deposited within six months of the date written. The opposite is a POST-DATED check.

BACK-END LOAD mutual fund that charges a sales commission, or load, if the investor disposes or sells shares in the fund. Also called *trail commissions*. Compare with FRONT-END LOAD.

BACK OFFICE area in a bank where checks are paid, deposits and withdrawals are posted to accounts, and interest earned on deposits is credited to the account holders. *See also* AUTOMATED CLEARING HOUSE; CUSTOMER INFORMATION FILE; PROOF AND TRANSIT; PROOF OF DEPOSIT; WIRE TRANSFER.

BACK-TO-BACK COMMITMENT two-part commitment by a lender. The first part is an advance on a construction loan; the second is a long-term commitment, also called the TAKE-OUT COMMITMENT, by the same bank lender for permanent mortgage financing.

BACK-TO-BACK LETTERS OF CREDIT two letters of credit, one in favor of the buyer's agent and one financing the seller. A back-to-back credit is created when an exporter holding an irrevocable LETTER OF CREDIT persuades the buyer's bank (the advising bank) to open a second credit in favor of the merchandise supplier. The two credits are identical in all respects, except that the supplier becomes the BENEFICIARY of the back-to-back credit, and the amount of the second credit is less than the original export credit. The difference is the import agent's commission.

BACK-TO-BACK LOAN two-party loan between a parent company in one country and subsidiaries in another. Similar to a PARALLEL LOAN, with the important difference that a back-to-back loan gives the lender the right to OFFSET claims against pledged collateral if the borrower defaults, while the parallel loan does not. The two-party, or parallel loan, is less risky for the lender because the parent company is obligated to step in if a foreign subsidiary fails to pay the note.

BACKUP LINE bank line of credit serving as an alternate source of liquidity for an issuer of commercial paper, and a source of credit for the buyer, or purchaser in the event the issuer is unable to rollover the paper at maturity. The amount of backup varies from as little as 50% for some AAA rated issuers to 100% for lower quality paper. Ordinarily, the line is a CONFIRMED LETTER OF CREDIT or a contractual facility (revolving credit agreement or revolving underwriting facility) in place at issue time. Or, it may be cash set aside by the issuer. A bank line typically is a SWING LINE. Bank credit lines are paid for by compensating balances or by straight fee.

BACKUP WITHHOLDING IRS rule requiring banks to withhold a percentage of interest or dividends (up to 20%) payable to taxpayers who did not pay taxes on interest or stock dividends in a prior tax year, or who did not disclose their Social Security number to their financial institutions.

BAD BANK specially chartered bank, acting as a self-liquidating trust, chartered by a bank holding company to hold nonperforming assets owned by a federally insured bank. Transfer of bad loans improves the ASSET QUALITY of the seller. Also known as a *collection bank.*

BAD CHECK any check dishonored, for wrong endorsement, lack of endorsement, insufficient funds, account closed, and so on. State laws vary on penalties for bad checks. *See also* CHECK KITING.

BAD DEBT loans classified as a probable LOSS and having no economic values. These loans, past due as to payment of interest and principal, are removed from the loan portfolio and their book value loss is charged to a reserve account (LOAN LOSS RESERVES). *See also* BAD DEBT RECOVERY; LOAN LOSS PROVISION.

BAD DEBT RECOVERY collection of loans written off as uncollectible and charged to the lender's LOAN LOSS RESERVES account. Recoveries may come from several sources: the borrower's voluntary payment of some or all of the principal or interest payments due; FORECLOSURE and sale of the borrower's assets pledged as loan COLLATERAL; or GARNISHMENT of the borrower's wages, salary, or bank assets. *See also* REAL ESTATE OWNED; WORKOUT AGREEMENT.

BAHT monetary unit of Thailand.

BAILMENT delivery of personal property for safekeeping with control and possession passing from the *bailor* (the owner) to the *bailee*. An example is personal items or stock certificates, held in trust in a bank SAFE DEPOSIT BOX. The bailee has no knowledge of the items delivered and no fiduciary relationship is created, as in a TRUST agreement.

BAILOUT financial assistance given to a financial institution or savings institution suffering a loss of earnings resulting from loan losses, deteriorating market conditions, or a sudden outflow of deposits in a depositor RUN. When the infusion of funds is from a federal agency such as the DEPOSIT INSURANCE FUND, which insures bank deposits, it is the depositors who are bailed out. The insurance agency may arrange open bank assistance to a troubled bank, or arrange an acquisition by a healthy financial institution. In either case, the deposit insurance fund gives enough assistance, usually in the form of promissory notes, to cover the difference between the estimated market value of the bank's assets and its liabilities (the bank's negative net worth), thereby recapitalizing the institution. *See also* BRIDGE BANK; INSURED DEPOSIT; MODIFIED PAYOFF; PURCHASE AND ASSUMPTION.

BALANCE

1. amount available in an account after payment of service charges, less withdrawals or debits and deposits not credited. In a checking account, the most important figure is the account's COLLECTED BALANCE representing the total of deposits cleared, less checks paid and bank service charges.
2. to reconcile a checking account by comparing bank statement with check book register.
3. amount payable in a mortgage or installment loan payment. Also called the BALANCE DUE.

BALANCE DUE amount payable at regular intervals in a mortgage, installment loan, or open-end credit account. With credit cards, a nominal payment called the MINIMUM PAYMENT is due, although the cardholder may pay any amount, up to the full amount advanced against the account.

BALANCE OF PAYMENTS accounting of a country's economic transactions with foreign countries in a stated period of time, normally one year. The balance of payments for any country is divided into two broad categories: the CURRENT ACCOUNT, representing import and export trade, plus income from tourism, profits earned overseas, and interest payments; and the capital account, representing the sum of bank deposits, investments by private investors, and debt securities sold by a central bank or official government agencies.

In economic terms, a balance of payments surplus means a nation has more funds from trade and investments coming in than it pays out to other countries, resulting in an APPRECIATION in the value of its national currency versus currencies of other nations. A deficit in the balance of payments has the opposite effect: an excess of imports over exports, a dependence on foreign investors, and an overvalued currency. Countries experiencing a payments deficit must make up the difference by exporting gold or HARD CURRENCY reserves, such as the U.S. dollar, that are accepted currencies for settlement of international debts. *See also* INTERNATIONAL RESERVES; SPECIAL DRAWING RIGHTS.

BALANCE REPORTING reporting of an organization's collected balances, by telephone or computer connection with a reporting bank's BACK OFFICE, usually on a daily basis. Daily reporting of account balances in one or more banks, normally done early in the business day, is a major component of CONTROLLED DISBURSEMENT services for corporate cash management customers.

BALANCE SHEET

1. statement of a bank's financial position listing assets owned, liabilities owed, and owner's equity as of a specific date. Banks accept deposits (counted as bank liabilities) and make loans (counted as assets). This explains the importance of ASSET-LIABILITY MANAGEMENT in managing bank profitability and stability in earnings.

Bank ledger accounts are balanced daily, resulting in a daily statement of condition, providing verification that a bank's books are in balance that day. This balance sheet information is reported quarterly to stockholders and the public, and to banking regulatory agencies in a bank's CALL REPORT or report of condition. Contrast with INCOME STATEMENT.

2. financial picture indicating assets owned and liabilities owed. The difference is referred to as *net worth.*

BALANCE SHEET RATIOS

1. ratios used in examining the financial condition, and changes in financial position, of any company, based on data reported in the BALANCE SHEET. Certain ratios are particularly applicable to banks. The most important are the CAPITAL RATIOS (measuring the ratio of equity capital to total assets) and LIQUIDITY RATIOS (measuring a bank's ability to cover deposit withdrawals and pay out funds to meet the credit needs of its borrowers). Other useful ratios are the loan-to-deposit ratio (total loans divided by total deposits) the CHARGE-OFF ratio (net charge-offs as a percentage of total loans), the loan loss reserve ratio (LOAN LOSS RESERVES for potential bad loans as a percentage of total loans), and the ratio of nonperforming loans to total loans. *See also* EFFICIENCY RATIO; NET INTEREST MARGIN; RETURN ON ASSETS; RETURN ON EQUITY.

2. accounting ratios used by bank credit officers in evaluating creditworthiness of borrowers. The most widely used are: the *acid-test ratio* or *quick ratio* (short-term assets divided by current liabilities); the *current ratio* (current assets divided by current liabilities); and the *debt coverage ratio* (working capital divided by long-term debt). Financial ratios can be measured against ratios in prior years, or industry averages, for quick, easy comparison. Key performance ratios, such as the *leverage ratio* (long-term debt as a percentage of shareholder net worth), are frequently used in pricing commercial loans. A loan might have an interest spread over a BASE RATE, for example, the bank PRIME RATE plus 25 basis points if financial leverage is kept at, or below, a certain level. *See also* RATIO ANALYSIS.

BALANCE TRANSFER CARD credit card allowing the transfer of outstanding balances from a high-interest rate card to a card with a lower interest rate. Such cards are ideal for debt consolidation.

BALBOA monetary unit of Panama.

BALLOON MATURITY bank loan, usually a mortgage, requiring a large, lump-sum payment at maturity. The balloon extinguishes the debt. Also, a bond issue requiring larger payments at the later maturity dates. *See also* BALLOON MORTGAGE; BALLOON PAYMENT.

BALLOON MORTGAGE mortgage that does not fully repay principal and interest by the maturity date. A balloon mortgage, also known as a *nonamortizing mortgage*, has a lower debt repayment than a conventional fixed rate mortgage loan, and thus is attractive to new home buyers whose incomes may be expected to increase, or to people who expect to sell their property and pay off the loan in a much shorter period than if they had borrowed with a conventional, fully-amortized mortgage. The two types of balloon mortgages are the INTEREST-ONLY LOAN—a mortgage with payments that cover only the interest owed and the partially amortizing mortgage, also known as a ROLLOVER mortgage—a short-term mortgage that must be refinanced at the end of a stated term, usually three to five years. *See also* ALTERNATIVE MORTGAGE INSTRUMENTS; NEGATIVE AMORTIZATION.

BALLOON PAYMENT final lump-sum payment of unpaid principal remaining at the end of a BALLOON MORTGAGE and in certain types of leases. The extra payment extinguishes the debt.

B AND C LOAN *see* SUBPRIME LOAN.

BANK organization, usually a corporation, that accepts deposits, makes loans, pays checks, and performs related services for the public. The Bank Holding Company Act of 1956 defines a bank as any depository financial institution that accepts checking accounts (checks) or makes commercial loans, and its deposits are insured by a federal deposit insurance agency. A bank acts as a middleman between suppliers of funds and users of funds, substituting its own credit judgment for that of the ultimate suppliers of funds, collecting those funds from three sources: checking accounts, savings, and time deposits; short-term borrowings from other banks; and equity capital. A bank earns money by reinvesting these funds in longer-term assets. A COMMERCIAL BANK invests funds gathered from depositors and other sources principally in loans. An investment bank manages securities for clients and for its own trading account. In making loans, a bank assumes both interest rate risk and credit risk; market rates may rise above the NET INTEREST MARGIN a bank earns on its loan portfolio and investments, and borrowers may default.

In addition to their role as credit intermediaries, banks act as agents for customers in a number of bank-related functions: initiating payment orders to third parties, either by check or electronic funds transfer; purchasing or selling securities, as for a trust account customer; and operating cash management for corporate customers. These NON-CREDIT SERVICES are an important, and growing, source of fee income. Banks also offer safe deposit boxes; manage trust accounts for individuals and endowment funds; clear checks and drafts for other financial institutions; underwrite securities through SECURITIES AFFILIATES; and, in general, perform other bank related services as permitted by federal and state banking regulations. Advances in the financial services industry occurring since the mid-1970s allow consumers to get banking services from many different financial institutions, such as SAVINGS BANKS, FEDERAL SAVINGS BANKS, SAVINGS AND LOAN ASSOCIATIONS and CREDIT UNIONS, in addition to commercial banks. Savings banks, S&Ls, and credit unions (known collectively as THRIFT INSTITUTIONS) make auto loans, consumer loans, and residential mortgages, and offer checking accounts and NEGOTIABLE ORDER OF WITHDRAWAL (NOW) ACCOUNTS, competing openly with commercial banks. Financial modernization has also removed many of the key functional distinctions between commercial banks and investment banking companies. Commercial banks are permitted by the GRAMM-LEACH-BLILEY ACT to deal in securities, offer investment advisory services, and perform other functions related to banking through subsidiary companies.

See also AFFILIATE; AGENT BANK; AGREEMENT CORPORATION; ASSOCIATE BANK; BAD BANK; BANK EXAMINATION; BANK HOLDING COMPANY; BANKERS' BANK; BANKING POWER; BRIDGE BANK; CENTRAL BANK; COMPTROLLER OF THE CURRENCY; COOPERATIVE BANK; CORRESPONDENT; COUNTRY BANK; DE NOVO; DEPOSITORY INSTITUTION; DUAL BANKING; FEDERAL RESERVE BANK; FEDERAL RESERVE SYSTEM; FEDERAL HOME LOAN BANK SYSTEM; FULL-SERVICE BANK; GARN-ST GERMAIN ACT; GLASS-STEAGALL ACT; INDEPENDENT BANK; INDUSTRIAL BANK; INSURED BANK; INTERSTATE BANKING; MCFADDEN ACT; MEMBER BANK; MONEY CENTER BANK; MUTUAL SAVINGS BANK; NATIONAL BANK; NONBANK BANK; NON-MEMBER BANK; RETAIL BANKING; REGULATION A; REGULATION D; RELATIONSHIP BANKING; RESERVE CITY BANK; SHADOW BANK; STATE BANK; SUPER-REGIONAL BANK; UNIT BANKING; UNIVERSAL BANKING; WHOLESALE BANKING; ZOMBIE BANK.

BANK ADMINISTRATION INSTITUTE nonprofit organization, based in Chicago, Illinois, that promotes banking industry standards in bank operations and auditing through professional schools, technical conferences, and a research affiliate, the Foundation for Financial Institutions Research. The Bank Administration Institute, founded in 1924, is the oldest and largest technical organization serving the U.S. banking industry.

BANK CALL *see* CALL REPORT.

BANK CAPITAL *see* CAPITAL.

BANK CARD transaction card giving bank customers the ability to pay for goods and services at retail merchants, and get cash at bank teller windows or at automated teller machines. A bank card may be a CREDIT CARD, tied to a pre-approved line of credit, or a DEBIT CARD, drawing funds from the holder's checking or savings account. A bank card is also a useful form of identification when cashing a check.

BANK CARD ASSOCIATION organization, owned by financial institutions, that licenses a bank card program or performs transaction processing for its owners. The present-day national card associations, MASTERCARD and VISA, perform four key functions: licensing bank cards and service marks to card issuing banks; authorizing transactions by cardholders; settling interchange transactions when the transaction processing bank (called the MERCHANT BANK) is different from the card issuer; and setting the INTERCHANGE rate, or the transaction processing fee paid by association members. Mailing of new cards and billing to cardholders is done by the banks themselves.

BANK CHECK *see* CASHIER'S CHECK.

BANK CREDIT

1. sum of bank LOANS and DISCOUNTS (loans with the interest deducted when the loan is made) extended by COMMERCIAL BANKS and savings institutions, and a major source of EARNING ASSETS in banks. Bank lending is influenced mostly through OPEN MARKET OPERATIONS of the Federal Reserve System, and to a much lesser extent through DISCOUNT WINDOW lending by Federal Reserve Banks directly to banks and savings institutions. When the Fed purchases securities from dealers in the open market, bank credit is expanded; credit is drained from the banking system when the Fed sells securities.
2. FEDERAL RESERVE CREDIT, a credit the Federal Reserve Banks contribute to depository financial institutions, either directly, from Reserve Banks loans through the DISCOUNT WINDOW facility, or indirectly, from securities owned by Reserve Banks through open market operations, plus FEDERAL RESERVE FLOAT.

BANK DEBITS checks paid, drafts honored, and other instruments drawn against deposited funds of individuals, partnerships, corporations, and other legal entities, during a given period of time—usually daily. Economists track bank debits to forecast national trends.

BANK DISCOUNT RATE

1. rate quoted by dealers for short-term noninterest bearing money market instruments, such as commercial paper and Treasury bills. When a bank accepts or agrees to pay a time draft, thus creating a BANKER'S ACCEPTANCE, the difference between what the bank pays and the face value of the instrument is the bank's charge (called a DISCOUNT) for honoring the draft. The rate is the bank discount rate.
2. rate that banks charge on discount loans (loans with the interest deducted when the loan is made). The borrower receives the face value of the note, less the discount. A borrower taking out a $1,000 one-year loan pays the lender $50 in interest and receives $950 for use over the year. The rate of interest is 5.263%. ($50 ÷ $950) in this example.

BANK DRAFT check, drawn by a bank against its own funds deposited in another bank. In international banking, a SIGHT DRAFT or DEMAND DRAFT drawn on a foreign bank allows payment in a local currency at the SPOT exchange rate, minimizing foreign exchange risk in import/export trade financing. Contrast with CASHIER'S CHECK.

BANK ENDORSEMENT bank's endorsement of checks paid and presented to the check writer's bank for collection. This identifies the bank to other financial institutions and indicates the words "pay any bank" and the date the check is paid.

BANKER'S ACCEPTANCE negotiable time draft financing international trade. The draft is guaranteed by the accepting bank. By accepting the draft, the bank agrees to pay the face value of the obligation if the issuer (the DRAWER of the draft) fails to pay, hence the name TWO-NAME PAPER. By lending its name to the transaction, the accepting bank makes it easier for an importer or exporter to obtain trade financing. A bank, once it has accepted a draft, can hold the paper until maturity or sell it in the money market. The accepting bank assumes some risk, although in most cases the credit risk is minimal as banks generally deal only with very credit worthy companies. Maturities on accepted drafts generally range from 30 to 180 days; payment is due at maturity, which usually coincides with delivery of goods to the buyer.

Bankers' acceptances are most widely used in international trade, although domestic acceptances are not uncommon. Acceptances used in trade finance are eligible for REDISCOUNT at a Federal Reserve Bank, and are not subject to RESERVE REQUIREMENTS. Bankers' acceptances are more marketable than trade drafts issued by finance companies, and there is an active secondary market for bank accepted paper. Some banks even purchase acceptances nearing maturity to increase their liquidity. *See also* DOLLAR EXCHANGE ACCEPTANCE; FINANCE BILL; RISK PARTICIPATION; THIRD-COUNTRY ACCEPTANCE.

BANKERS' BANK depository institution, usually a commercial bank, organized and chartered to do business with other banks and owned by the banks it services. These banks do not take deposits or make loans to the public. They may be chartered as NATIONAL BANKS, invest in an EXPORT TRADING COMPANY, and may be exempted from RESERVE REQUIREMENTS.

BANKER'S BLANKET BOND fidelity bond purchased from an insurance broker that protects a bank against losses from a variety of criminal acts: employee fraud, robbery, burglary, and forgery. Some states require blanket bond coverage as a condition of operating a bank.

BANK EXAMINATION periodic review of a bank's balance sheet assets and liabilities by chartering agency or bank supervisory agency. Bank examiners focus their attention on three main areas: the competence of bank management; the quality of bank assets, principally loans; and compliance with state or federal banking regulations. Today, examiners also look closely at OFF-BALANCE SHEET ITEMS such as loan commitments or guarantees, which are contingent claims on the bank's assets.

Supervisory examinations are carried out by federal, state, and independent agencies. National banks are examined by the Comptroller of the Currency, state chartered banks by the Federal Deposit Insurance Corporation or the state banking department, and bank holding companies by the Federal Reserve Board. Savings and loan associations are examined by the Comptroller of the Currency, savings banks and credit unions by state banking departments. *See also* COMPLIANCE EXAMINATION.

BANK FAILURE closing of an insolvent bank by the chartering agency. The bank is placed in receivership with the FEDERAL DEPOSIT INSURANCE CORPORATION, which then settles any claims against the bank by its creditors, including the claims of insured depositors up to $250,000 per account. The FDIC has the authority to liquidate, if necessary, the bank's assets to meet these claims, and by law is obligated to dispose any creditor claims by selecting the failure-resolution method bearing the lowest cost to the DEPOSIT INSURANCE FUND, managed by the FDIC.

The least disruptive way of disposing of a failed bank is a PURCHASE AND ASSUMPTION, a transaction in which another bank steps forward and purchases some or all of the failed bank's assets and assumes its deposit liabilities. In drastic situations where a failed bank has almost no salvageable value, and thus no interested bidders willing to acquire it, the insurance fund pays the insured depositors of the liquidated bank the value of their claim, up to the FDIC insurance limit. This is known as a MODIFIED PAYOFF; the insurance payout to depositors is modified in the sense that an UNINSURED DEPOSITOR, someone who has deposits in the failed bank greater than the insurance limit, may suffer some loss of principal or interest. The major difference between the two methods is, in a purchase transaction, the acquiring bank assumes all deposit liabilities, so the claims of both insured and uninsured depositors are fully covered.

Since federal deposit insurance began in the 1930s, no major bank in the United States has been allowed to fail by banking regulatory agencies, mainly out of fear that a failure would be too disruptive to financial markets. The "too big to fail" argument has been tested on several occasions, most recently in the 2008 financial crisis. *See also* BAILOUT; BRIDGE BANK; TOO BIG TO FAIL.

BANK FOR INTERNATIONAL SETTLEMENTS (BIS) international organization, based in Basel, Switzerland, that acts as a bank for central banks of major industrial countries. Chartered in 1930 by a group of European central banks, the BIS has evolved since the 1960s into an influential monetary institution, assisting central bankers in investing monetary assets. The RISK-BASED CAPITAL standard, adopted by banks in the GROUP OF 10 countries by 1988, in which loans and other bank assets are classified by risk, was formulated by central bankers.The Federal Reserve Board of Governors regularly takes part in BIS meetings, and the bank is a member of the Federal Reserve's SWAP NETWORK with other central banks. *See also* BASEL COMMITTEE; BASEL I, BASEL II, BASEL III.

BANK GIRO *see* GIRO.

BANK HOLDING COMPANY entity controlling one or more commercial banks. Bank holding companies are closely supervised by the Federal Reserve Board. Companies owning 25% or more of the voting stock in a bank, or controlling a majority of its directors, are required to file periodic financial statements with the Federal Reserve Board of Governors. U.S. branch offices of foreign banks also are supervised by the Federal Reserve Board. The Bank Holding Company Act sets standards for acquisitions and permits interstate acquisitions and nationwide branch banking. The GRAMM-LEACH-BLILEY ACT OF 1999 significantly widened the scope of authorized activities, allowing any well-capitalized bank holding company to become a FINANCIAL HOLDING COMPANY, providing a wide range of banking, investment advisory, and insurance-related services. Bank holding companies are often identifiable by the words *banc* or *bancshares* in the corporate name. *See also* ONE BANK HOLDING COMPANY; PERMISSIBLE NONBANK ACTIVITIES; REGULATION Y.

BANK HOLIDAY

1. uniform schedule of national holidays honored by financial institutions. Under the Uniform Commercial Code, interbank payments delayed by a holiday are payable the next business day.
2. temporary closing of a bank by government officials. The most famous "bank holiday" is the one-week nationwide closing in 1933, ordered by President Franklin D. Roosevelt to control a wave of bank failures and restore confidence in the banking system.

BANK IDENTIFICATION NUMBER (BIN)

1. ABA TRANSIT NUMBER.
2. numeric code identifying bank card issuing financial institutions affiliated with Visa or MasterCard. The BIN number is the first six digits of the ACCOUNT NUMBER. Banks use BIN tables in routing transactions to the appropriate bank for credit approval and final settlement.

BANKING ACT OF 1933 major banking reform legislation enacted by Congress as a remedy to the financial instability in the banking system during the Great Depression, creating the FEDERAL OPEN MARKET COMMITTEE, and the FEDERAL DEPOSIT INSURANCE CORPORATION. The act gave effective control of MONETARY POLICY to the Federal Reserve Board of Governors. Sections 16, 20, 21, and 32 of the act, separating commercial banking from investment banking, are more commonly known as the GLASS-STEAGALL ACT. The Glass-Steagall Act enforced a legal separation of commercial and investment banking activities until these restrictions were removed by the GRAMM-LEACH-BLILEY ACT OF 1999.

BANKING AND SECURITIES INDUSTRY COMMITTEE (BASIC) committee organized in 1970 to promote uniform bank office standards in securities trading and settlement. Its members are drawn from the major stock exchanges, the National Association of Securities Dealers, and the New York Clearing House banks.

BANKING DEPARTMENT *see* STATE BANKING DEPARTMENT.

BANKING POWER

1. ability of a bank to lend, specifically its power to "create money" by depositing a portion of a new loan in a bank account. The borrower doesn't take out the loan in cash; instead, the loan proceeds are deposited in a new or existing checking account. The lender agrees to honor checks drawn against the account, and can use part of that balance to make new loans.

   Unlike most other corporations, which are free to engage in almost anything not prohibited by law, U.S. banks may undertake only those activities specifically approved by law or regulation. Banking powers generally fall into two categories: express powers, including the ability to lend money granted by state legislatures or Congress; and implied powers given by the courts through judicial rulings. *See also* MONEY MULTIPLIER.
2. financial services regarded as closely related to banking and approved by Congress or banking supervisory agencies as PERMISSIBLE NONBANK ACTIVITIES. In the 1990s, many barriers limiting bank activities in securities dealing, insurance, mutual funds, and investment advisory services were lifted, allowing banks to compete more freely with non-bank financial institutions. *See also* FINANCIAL HOLDING COMPANY; GRAMM-LEACH-BLILEY ACT, SECURITIES SUBSIDIARY.

BANKING SYNDICATE *see* SYNDICATE; TENDER PANEL.

BANK INSURANCE FUND (BIF) *see* DEPOSIT INSURANCE FUND.

BANK INVESTMENT CONTRACT (BIC) contract issued by a bank, guaranteeing a fixed rate of return on invested capital over the life of the contract. A bank investment contract is similar to a guaranteed investment contract (GIC) sold by insurance companies, has a maturity of one to ten years, and the added protection of federal deposit insurance.

BANK LINE bank's moral commitment to lend, as distinct from its contractual, legal, commitment; alternate name for a LINE OF CREDIT. A bank line is an indication of a bank's willingness to lend to a particular borrower up to a predetermined amount, usually for working capital purposes, and for a one-to-three-year period. The line is renewable at the option of the lender, so long as the borrower meets certain conditions, for example, agreeing to keep a portion of the line in a COMPENSATING BALANCE with the lender to maintain the business in sound financial condition. In some cases, the borrower may be asked to demonstrate his ability to operate without bank financing by periodically reducing the borrowed amount to zero (called a CLEAN-UP REQUIREMENT).

Ordinarily, no commitment fee is charged, although the lender may assess a usage fee on funds actually advanced. An *advised line* is disclosed to the borrower, whereas a *guidance line* is used for internal credit monitoring by the lender and is not disclosed. *See also* EVERGREEN LOAN; REVOLVING CREDIT.

BANK-LOAN FUND mutual fund-holding adjustable-rate bank loans, typically used to finance leveraged buyouts. Such funds are attractive in periods of rising interest rates. Also called *floating rate loan fund.*

BANK MERGER *see* MERGER.

BANK NOTE

1. non-interest bearing promissory note, issued by an authorized bank for payment of debts. The FEDERAL RESERVE NOTE is the only officially authorized circulating note. Synonymous with currency and LEGAL TENDER.
2. unsecured interest-bearing notes sold to institutional investors. These notes are similar to CERTIFICATES OF DEPOSIT, except that these obligations are not protected by deposit insurance. Bank notes resemble bonds more than deposits, paying semiannual interest, and are liabilities of issuing banks rather than bank holding companies. *See also* DEPOSIT NOTE.

BANK OF FIRST DEPOSIT bank where a check in the process of collection is initially deposited. If the check is drawn on another bank, the collecting bank presents the check directly to the paying bank, or to a Federal Reserve Bank, for settlement against the paying bank's RESERVE ACCOUNT. *See also* CASH ITEMS; COLLECTION ITEMS; DIRECT SEND.

BANK QUALITY bonds given one of the top four ratings by bond rating firms, for example, a STANDARD & POOR'S rating of BBB or better. Commercial banks are permitted to purchase these securities, also known as INVESTMENT GRADE bonds, for their own account. These bonds also are considered acceptable investments for fiduciaries, such as trust departments and pension funds. Bonds with a lower rating are known collectively as JUNK BONDS, and are considered speculative investments.

BANK RATE MONITOR INDEX index of money market rates on consumer deposit accounts paid at 100 banks around the country, compiled weekly and reported in daily newspapers. The Bank Rate Monitor Index is compiled weekly by Bank Rate Monitor Inc., Pompano Beach, Florida, and lists the average rate paid on a variety of consumer savings deposits and time deposit accounts. Web site: www.banknote.com.

BANK RATING *see* RATING.

BANK RESERVES bank funds allocated for a specific purpose. LEGAL RESERVES are funds that banks maintain in a noninterest earning account at a Federal Reserve Bank or at a correspondent bank, plus vault cash, to meet their RESERVE REQUIREMENTS. Legal reserves protect depositors' assets, and also permit the Federal Reserve System to more easily regulate bank credit, the funds that banks have available for lending, by controlling the total supply of reserves in the banking system through Federal Reserve MONETARY POLICY.

LOAN LOSS RESERVES, a percentage of outstanding loans, are kept in a separate account to cover anticipated loan losses. When interest payments on a loan have not been made for a reasonable period, usually 90 days, the loan is no longer considered an earning asset and a reserve is set aside to cover the expected loss. If this loan is later written off as a worthless asset, a charge is made against the reserve for loan losses.

PRIMARY RESERVES are checking account balances in a Federal Reserve Bank, vault cash, plus checks in the process of collection; SECONDARY RESERVES are mostly marketable short-term securities, such as U.S. Treasury bills, that are easily convertible to cash. *See also* EARMARKED RESERVES.

BANK RUN series of unexpected cash withdrawals, caused by a sudden decline of depositor confidence or fear that a bank will be closed by the chartering agency. Today, the silent run is much more prevalent than bank runs in the past, when customers lined up in front of tellers' windows and demanded their savings in cash. Depositors simply transfer their interest-sensitive funds—called HOT MONEY deposits—to other institutions. Also called a *run on a bank.*

BANKRUPTCY the state of insolvency or inability to pay debts.

Bankruptcy courts deal with two broad types of cases: VOLUNTARY BANKRUPTCY by debtors seeking a fresh start, and INVOLUNTARY BANKRUPTCY filed by a sufficient number of creditors, who believe the debtor has committed an ACT OF BANKRUPTCY by concealing assets or favoring one creditor over another. In both cases, the objective is a fair and equitable settlement of claims and distribution of assets. Filing a petition initiates an automatic stay against further debt collection until a debt is discharged, the petition is dismissed, or a repayment plan is accepted by creditors. Once a petition is filed, the bankruptcy remains on a debtor's credit bureau report for up to 10 years.

The Bankruptcy Reform Act of 1978, the first major revision in the bankruptcy code in four decades, brought about several important changes: the new code simplified the procedures for filing petitions, modified the *absolute priority rule* giving secured creditors seniority over other creditors, limited creditor rights to set-off claims against a debtor's assets, and expanded the powers of federal bankruptcy judges to decide cases. Amendments to the code in 1984 gave bankruptcy courts the power to dismiss so-called abusive petitions by debtors concealing assets. Amendments enacted in 2005 (the Bankruptcy Abuse Prevention and Consumer Protection Act) further modified the code. Individuals who have sufficient income to repay some of their debts (as determined by a "means test") must instead file a Chapter 13 bankruptcy petition.

The important chapters in the revised code are the following:

Chapter 7: called a LIQUIDATION, allows a court-appointed trustee with broad discretionary powers to distribute assets among creditors and arrange interim financing. In general, the trustee represents the interests of the unsecured creditors, or general creditors. If, however, there are no assets, the debt is discharged, and the creditors receive nothing.

Chapter 9: a rarely used section of the code, designed for adjustment of debts of a municipality. Also called a *municipal reorganization.*

Chapter 11: a REORGANIZATION, normally by a business, allowing the debtor (called a DEBTOR-IN-POSSESSION if no trustee is named) to maintain operating control, while restructuring debts and working out a repayment schedule acceptable to creditors. Creditor loans to Chapter 11 debtors are permitted under certain conditions.

Chapter 12: a provision dealing with agricultural bankruptcies, allows small family-owned farms with debts under $1.5 million to repay obligations based on fair market value of the loan collateral.

Chapter 13: a debt repayment plan, called a WAGE EARNER PLAN, filed by individuals earning regular income. The debtor files a budget with the court, and agrees to make partial payment (less than 100%) of obligations owed to creditors over a three- to five-year period, normally within three years. *See also* COMPOSITION; CRAMDOWN; DISCHARGE OF BANKRUPTCY; PREFERENCE; PRIORITY OF LIEN; REAFFIRMATION; REDEMPTION; VOIDABLE PREFERENCE.

BANKRUPTCY MEANS TEST 2005 amendment to the U.S. Bankruptcy Code limiting discharge of debts when debtors have an ability to repay at least some of their obligations. Debtors who fail the means test may convert their case to another chapter of bankruptcy.

BANKRUPTCY TRUSTEE person named by a bankruptcy judge, with the consent of creditors, to manage the affairs of a debtor in bankruptcy. The trustee has legal authority to file claims on behalf of the debtor, set aside a PREFERENCE to one or more creditors, and also represent the interests of unsecured creditors or general creditors. Most bankruptcy courts have a U.S. Trustee, a permanent trustee who handles all cases filed in that jurisdiction.

BANK SECRECY ACT federal law enacted in 1970, intended to discourage the use of currency in illegal transactions, requiring banks to report all cash deposits, withdrawals, or transfers of $10,000 to the Internal Revenue Service. International transactions are reportable to the U.S. Customs Department. Banks are required to fill out a CURRENCY TRANSACTION REPORT within 15 days of the transaction date to avoid having to pay stiff penalties. Amendments to the Bank Secrecy Act (the USA PATRIOT Act of 2001) require individuals opening a deposit or loan account to provide some proof of identity, such as a driver's license or passport. The new procedures are designed to deter money laundering or misuse of personal financial information through identity theft or account fraud. *See also* MONEY LAUNDERING.

BANKS FOR COOPERATIVES *see* FARM CREDIT SYSTEM.

BANK STATEMENT

1. REPORT OF CONDITION, financial statement disclosing a bank's income and condition of its balance sheet, filed quarterly with its primary regulator. These statements are also available on request for public inspection.
2. customer's ACCOUNT STATEMENT of deposits, withdrawals, transaction activity, and bank service charges, usually mailed monthly.
3. bank's statement of deposit accounts subject to RESERVE REQUIREMENTS, filed every other week with a Federal Reserve Bank.

BANK WIRE electronic payment service for transfer of high-value payments between banks when prompt communication and immediate transfer of funds are important. A bank wire payment, also called a WIRE TRANSFER, moves through the Federal Reserve's FEDERAL WIRE (FED WIRE) network.

See also AUTOMATED CLEARING HOUSE; CLEARING HOUSE INTERBANK PAYMENTS SYSTEM.

BANQUE D'AFFAIRES *see* MERCHANT BANKING.

BANXQUOTE MONEY MARKETS INDEX index of rates paid by investors on negotiable certificates of deposit and high yield savings accounts, compiled weekly by Banx Corp. The index offers a side-by-side comparison of rates paid by selected national, regional, and local banks and savings institutions. Web site: www.Banx.com.

BARBELL PORTFOLIO portfolio of INVESTMENT SECURITIES concentrating the bulk of assets in bonds or other securities with very long or very short-term maturities. This is a more sophisticated form of investing than *laddering* (the practice of buying bonds in each maturity range, producing a higher return), but it may create liquidity risk if a bank wants to restructure its portfolio. More frequent adjustments are necessary to maintain the desired asset mix, especially when rates change.

Barbelling an investment portfolio through the heavy use of short-term and long-term issues, with few securities of intermediate maturity, is designed to maximize liquidity, with minimal market impact from the short-term issues, while the long-term debt brings the highest yield and the highest return. This strategy, of course, does not make much sense when the yield curve is flat, that is, when short-term rates are roughly the same as long-term rates, or when the yield curve is inverted, and short-term rates are higher than those at the long end. *See also* LADDERED PORTFOLIO.

BARREN MONEY cash or money earning no interest, such as cash in a safe deposit box or reserve account balances in a Federal Reserve Bank. Also called *idle funds.*

BARTER trade of goods or services without the exchange of cash, checks, or another form of monetary payment. A barter system functions as a *local currency* system for exchanging products of comparable value. Barter trading facilitates import-export commerce by less-developed countries lacking HARD CURRENCY reserves through a form of barter known as *counter-trade.*

BASEL COMMITTEE joint committee of banking supervisory agencies in the 12 major industrial countries organized in 1975. The Basel Committee (also spelled *Basle Committee*) promotes uniform policies for bank capital and supervision of financial institutions. The United States is represented on the Basel Committee by the Federal Reserve Board. *See also* BANK FOR INTERNATIONAL SETTLEMENTS.

BASEL I, BASEL II, BASEL III informal name for a series of agreements defining bank capital adequacy. Recommendations are issued by the Basel Committee on Banking Supervision at its headquarters in Basel, Switzerland, and enforced through national laws and regulations. National banking supervisors participating in Basel 1, issued in 1988, agreed on an international framework for capital adequacy guidelines for the first time. Basel I set a minimum capital-to-assets ratio of 8%. This means that a bank with $100 million in loans and other assets would have to maintain at least $8 million in equity capital as a buffer against financial losses. Bank assets were given a risk weighting to determine capital requirements. Risk-free assets (cash and equivalents) required no capital reserves. Riskier assets (residential mortgages, commercial loans, and so on) would need a capital reserve of 50% to 100% of risk-weighted assets.

Basel II modified the original agreement, allowing bank supervisory agencies to increase the 8% capital-to-assets ratio for riskier banks. Basel II has three supporting principles (called "pillars"): minimum capital requirements, supervisory review by supervisory agencies, and market discipline.

Basel III strengthens the previous accords by improving the banking sector's ability to absorb shocks from financial or economic stress and also adds new risk management and disclosure rules. Under Basel III, large bank-holding companies are subject to stricter rules than smaller banks. Basel III also adds a "capital conservation buffer" (exclusively common stock) and raises the required ratio of equity capital (common stock and retained earnings) to 6% of bank assets. These revised capital adequacy guidelines under Basel III are to be phased in by 2018. *See also* RISK-BASED CAPITAL; TIER 1; TIER 2.

BASE I data processing network operated by VISA USA for authorization of bank card transactions by banks affiliated with the Visa card system. *See also* BASE II.

BASE II data processing network operated by VISA USA for clearing and settlement of bank card transactions between card honoring merchant banks and card issuers for net daily account settlement among Visa member institutions. *See also* BASE I.

BASE RATE interest rate used as an index for pricing a bank loan or line of credit, for example, the BANKER'S ACCEPTANCE rate, CERTIFICATE OF DEPOSIT rate, LONDON INTERBANK OFFERED RATE (LIBOR), or the PRIME RATE. A MARGIN is added to, or subtracted from, the base rate. *See also* COST OF FUNDS INDEX (COFI).

BASE YEAR ANALYSIS examination of an organization's financial statements by a bank credit department, by which financial data reported in a prior year are compared to data reported in the period under review. The prior year is called the base year. *See also* BALANCE SHEET RATIOS; TREND ANALYSIS.

BASIC BANKING *see* LIFELINE BANKING.

BASIS

1. original cost of an asset plus capital improvements, from which any taxable gains (or losses) are determined, after deducting depreciation expenses. In investments, the purchase price, plus out-of-pocket costs such as brokers' commissions, is used in computing short-term or long-term capital gains reportable to the Internal Revenue Service.
2. in the futures market, the difference between the SPOT price, or cash market price, of a security (or commodity) and its price in the futures market. As the delivery date of a FUTURES CONTRACT approaches, this difference gradually disappears, and at maturity the cash market and futures market prices should be the same. Most investors use financial futures only as a hedging tool to limit possible losses as interest rates change.
3. number of days used in calculating the interest earned in an investment or interest payable on a bank loan. Also called the *accrual base.*

   There are different interest calculation methods:

   365-day year base—savings and time deposit accounts paying interest from date of deposit to date of withdrawal, U.S. Treasury bills, and bank loans (interest computed using actual days in the loan). Also called *money market basis.*

   360-day year base—federal agency securities, municipal bonds, corporate bonds, and LONDON INTERBANK OFFERED RATE (LIBOR) based instruments. Also called *corporate bond equivalent basis.*

   The difference in interest earned, comparing a 360-day year and 365-day year can be substantial with a large principal invested. For example, $100 invested at 8%, using a 360-day year earns $8.00 at 360 days, whereas $100 invested at 8% using a 365-day year earns $7.89 at 360 days. Comparing interest yield on an investment with a 365-day yield basis to one with a 360-day year is easy; to convert from 365- to 360-day interest, simply multiply the 365-day interest by 1.0139; to convert from 360- to 365-day interest, multiply the 365-day interest by .98630.
4. in FOREIGN EXCHANGE, adjustment in the forward market price of different currencies for variance in interest rates. For example: if interest rates are 5% above U.S. rates, British pound sterling is

priced at a 5% discount vis-à-vis the U.S. dollar, allowing different currencies to be traded on a comparable basis. *See also* PURCHASING POWER PARITY.

BASIS POINT smallest measure in quoting yields on bonds, mortgages, and notes, equal to one one-hundredth of one percentage point, or .01%. A bond whose yield to maturity changes from 8.50% to 9.25% is said to move 75 basis points in yield.

BASIS PRICE price of a bond expressed as an annual percentage rate; the YIELD TO MATURITY expected by the purchaser. Contrast with dollar price, the price actually paid by the investor.

BASIS RISK in ASSET-LIABILITY MANAGEMENT, the risk that changes in interest rates will cause interest-bearing deposit liabilities to reprice at a different rate than interest-bearing assets, creating an asset liability MISMATCH. For example, a 1% rise in 30-day money market rates may produce a 0.5% increase in the yield on bank loans and a full 1% rise in rates paid on corresponding deposit accounts. Basis risk also means the risk that prices on financial instruments in the cash market will react differently to changes in rates than prices on futures market contracts.

BASIS SWAP swap agreement involving exchange of two floating rate financial instruments denominated in the same currency, one pegged to one reference rate and the other tied to a second reference rate. Contrast with CURRENCY SWAP and INTEREST RATE SWAP.

BASIS SWAP

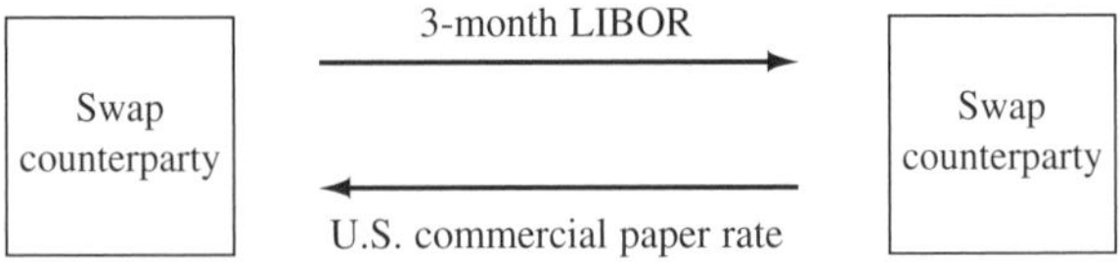

Notional amount: $5 million.
Maturity: 3 years.
Payment schedule: every three months.

Source: Recent Innovations in International Banking (Bank for International Settlements, 1986).

BATCH group of checks, drafts, or items handled as a unit for BACK OFFICE processing later during the day. Also called *block.* Contrast with ON-LINE processing.

BATCH HEADER RECORD

1. 94 character format, the bank address for sending AUTOMATED CLEARING HOUSE (ACH) payments. This may not be the same as the ABA TRANSIT NUMBER if payments ordinarily are processed through a correspondent bank.
2. identifier for any group of accounts processed as a unit.

BEAR BOND bond considered likely to increase in value in a bear market, i.e., when interest rates are rising. The typical bond pays the investor a stream of cash fixed in terms of the dollar amount and the dates paid, and will decline in price when rates increase. Certain bonds, for example, an INTEREST-ONLY (IO) STRIP, or a mortgage-backed security paying interest only, are likely to rise in value in a bear market because prepayments on the underlying mortgages slow down. This slowing in loan prepayments increases the total amount of cash the investor can expect to receive over the life of the investment.

BEARER BOND bond payable to holder rather than an owner registered on the books of the issuer's bank or agent. These bonds are negotiable instruments with no record of ownership. Title is held by anyone who possesses the security and holds it in good faith. Bond interest is paid semiannually when detachable coupons are clipped and presented to a bank for collection, just like a check. Contrast with REGISTERED BOND.

BEAR SPREAD trading strategy in which a trader sells contracts (goes short) in nearby months and buys contracts (goes long) in months further out, acting on the belief that short-term interest rates are rising faster than long-term rates and market prices of currencies, financial instruments, and so on, are falling. This is *selling the spread* in futures trading. In options trading, a combination of puts and calls intended to take advantage of falling prices. The opposite is a BULL SPREAD.

BEAR SQUEEZE official INTERVENTION by central banks in the foreign exchange markets to force speculators short selling a currency to cover their positions, preventing the speculators from making quick profits. This generally is done by bidding to purchase more of a local currency than is available in the markets, usually causing large losses to currency speculators.

BEIGE BOOK Federal Reserve survey of regional business conditions. The Beige Book is published eight times a year and released to the public about two weeks before meetings of the FEDERAL OPEN MARKET COMMITTEE, which sets monetary policy for the Federal Reserve System.

BELLY UP slang expression for a borrower, corporation, or development project that has failed, and is unable to pay obligations to creditors. An insolvent bank or savings institution, in particular a financial institution closed down by its financial regulator, is also said to go "belly up."

BELOW MARKET RATE rate below conventional rates in a given market. The term also describes a low introductory rate in an ADJUSTABLE RATE MORTGAGE, known as a TEASER RATE.

BELT AND SUSPENDERS slang expression for an overly cautious lender, who takes an assignment of collateral plus personal guarantees from a borrower. It also characterizes a lender who follows loan policies to the letter, saying, "When in doubt, file," meaning a new lien is filed at nearly every opportunity.

BENEFICIARY

1. person named to receive income from a trust, insurance policy, or endowment.
2. in trade finance, the person or company in whose favor a LETTER OF CREDIT is opened or a DRAFT is drawn.
3. the last-named party receiving payment in a transaction. Also called *ultimate beneficiary.*
4. person to whom an estate passes, as provided by a WILL.

BEQUEST gift of personal property according to a WILL, synonymous with legacy. A gift of real property is a DEVISE.

BEST EFFORT

1. securities team for underwriting a new offering of securities. The distributor of the securities offered for sale pledges to sell as much as can be sold, but makes no guarantee to purchase the entire offering from the issuer. Best effort underwriting is seen most often in the over-the-counter market for initial public offerings by DE NOVO companies and financial institutions, as opposed to established companies.
2. in banking, a loan to a corporate borrower in which the participating banks (the SYNDICATE group) agree to underwrite only a portion of the financing. Compare with FIRM COMMITMENT.

BETA measure of price volatility of mutual funds and financial instruments. Beta is usually expressed as a covariance; in mutual funds, it measures how responsive a fund is to the market as a whole. A fund with a 1.10 beta is expected to perform 10% better than the Standard & Poor's 500 Index in rising markets and 10% worse in falling markets.

BIAS Federal Reserve's view concerning interest rates. A bias toward higher rates means the FEDERAL OPEN MARKET COMMITTEE, the Fed's rate-setting committee, may raise the federal funds target rate at its next meeting.

BID

1. price at which market participants are willing to buy securities, futures contracts, or foreign currencies. The bid price, in other words, is the highest price a prospective buyer is willing to pay at a particular time. The difference between the bid price and the OFFER price (the lowest price a seller will accept) is known as the SPREAD, which is a dealer's commission in buying and selling securities. *See also* COMPETITIVE BID; NONCOMPETITIVE BID; QUOTATION.
2. offer to acquire a failed bank at a liquidator's auction.

BID AND ASKED range of price quotes in the OVER-THE-COUNTER market, the bid price being the highest price a buyer is willing to pay; the asked price being the owner's selling price. When combined, the two prices are a broker's QUOTATION.

BID WANTED indicates the owner of a security or financial instrument is seeking bids by interested buyers, generally when prices are rising. A bid wanted quote is signified by the notation BW in published market sheets.

BIG BANG sudden deregulation of financial markets. The best such example is the London "Big Bang" of 1986, acclaimed as a major step toward a single world financial market. It eliminated fixed-rate brokerage commissions and ownership limits on non-British firms.

BILATERAL CREDIT LIMIT agreement by member banks in the CLEARING HOUSE INTERBANK PAYMENTS SYSTEM (CHIPS) in New York to limit the payments they are willing to accept from each other to an agreed-upon level. This limits their intraday credit risk when they authorize payments to other CHIPS members, but have not yet collected funds from other banks to back up those transfers. *See also* DAYLIGHT OVERDRAFT; SENDER NET DEBIT CAP; SYSTEMIC RISK.

BILATERAL NETTING *see* NETTING.

BILL

1. bill of exchange, a payment order written by one person (the drawer) to another, directing the latter (the drawee) to pay a certain amount of money at a future date to a third party. An important document in international trade, a bill of exchange is a bank draft when drawn on a bank or, a trade draft when drawn on another party. It is sometimes used interchangeably with DRAFT (although drafts are negotiable instruments transferable by endorsement) whereas bills of exchange are not always negotiable. *See also* BANKERS ACCEPTANCE.
2. bill of lading, a receipt issued by a common carrier for transporting trade goods from one point to another. When presented to a collecting bank along with an accepted bank draft, the bank releases the goods after it has been paid by the paying bank. A bill of lading is a title document and a receipt for goods transported. *See also* DOCUMENTARY DRAFT.
3. TREASURY BILL, a security with a maximum maturity of one year, issued by the U.S. Treasury Department. Three-month and six-month bills are auctioned weekly by the Treasury; one-year bills are auctioned monthly. In all cases, bills are sold at a discount from principal amount and redeemed at face value.
4. due bill, a statement of money owed, as when a bank sells a security and receives payment but has not delivered the security or equivalent asset. Outstanding due bills are considered borrowed funds by a bank issuing a bill, and a loan by the holder of the obligation. In the securities industry, a due bill indicates the amount owed by a buying broker to a selling broker. It can also be an IOU for interest or dividend payments to the owner of record, if such payments are owned by the buyer.

BILL DISCOUNTED *see* BANK DISCOUNT RATE; DISCOUNT.

BILLING CYCLE interval between periodic payment-due dates on a consumer installment loan or credit card account, usually every 25 or 30 days. Billing periods are considered roughly equal if they vary by no more than four days from the regular statement date.

BILLING ERROR charge to a customer's ACCOUNT STATEMENT disputed by the account holder, resulting from unauthorized use, incorrect billing date, payments to a credit card account not credited, or errors in computation, such as transposition of numbers or late mailing of the periodic billing statement. These are corrected through ERROR RESOLUTION procedures in the FAIR CREDIT BILLING ACT and the ELECTRONIC FUNDS TRANSFER ACT.

BILL PAYMENT *see* HOME BANKING; TELEPHONE BILL PAYMENT.

BILLS PAYABLE

1. trade obligations of a firm, such as a trade acceptance or BANKER'S ACCEPTANCE, payable at maturity.
2. a bank's indebtedness to other banks, principally an ADVANCE from a Federal Reserve Bank, backed by the bank's own promissory note and a pledge of government securities as collateral. *See also* BORROWED FUNDS.

BILL PRESENTMENT *see* ELECTRONIC BILL PAYMENT & PRESENTMENT.

BIRR monetary unit of Ethiopia.

BIWEEKLY MORTGAGE fixed-rate mortgage with loan payments every two weeks, rather than monthly as with most residential mortgages. The loan payment is one-half that of a regular 30-year mortgage, but the accelerated repayment allows the borrower to pay off the mortgage much faster than the mortgage with monthly amortization. The borrower makes 26 half-payments a year or one extra full-month payment. The result is accelerated buildup of equity and lower interest expense over the loan term. *See also* ALTERNATIVE MORTGAGE INSTRUMENTS.

BLACK SCHOLES MODEL mathematical formula widely used in pricing option contracts. The model attempts to gauge whether option contracts are fairly priced, by comparing the price of this instrument and the STRIKE PRICE (or exercise price) of the option, the volatility of the instrument, the time remaining until the expiration of the option contract, and current interest rates. The Black Scholes model has also been adapted to bank asset-liability management, pricing of interest rate CAPS and COLLARS, and is widely used in the currency markets.

BLANK ENDORSEMENT endorser's writing on a check, promissory note, or bill of exchange without indicating the party to whom it is payable. The endorser merely signs his name, making the instrument "payable to bearer" and negotiable by delivery alone. Also called *endorsement in blank.*

BLANKET LIEN term describing a floating lien, covering all personal property owned by a borrower, as opposed to real property. As used by some lenders, it is meant as a catchall security interest covering every imaginable type of collateral owned by the borrower. Compare to CROSS-COLLATERAL.

BLANKET MORTGAGE mortgage secured by two or more parcels of property, frequently used by developers who acquire a single large tract of land for subdivision and resale to individual homeowners. Also called a *blanket trust deed.*

BLENDED RATE

1. rate in an assumable mortgage (also a WRAPAROUND MORTGAGE combining a first and second mortgage), combining the old, below market rate and the new higher rate.
2. in commercial loan refinancings, a formula rate used to adjust for the current rate; a fair and equitable composite rate. For example, if the borrower's old rate is 7%, and the current market rate is 12%, the lender may agree to make the loan at 9%, provided the borrower maintains a compensating balance and/or brings in additional collateral.
3. in cost of funds accounting, a POOLED COST OF FUNDS, for example, a blend of the Federal Funds rate and the bank certificate of deposit rate.

BLIND BROKERING form of securities trading that promises anonymity to either side to a transaction, common in the primary dealer market for U.S. government securities. The broker, who acts as agent for an unnamed third party, assumes the responsibilities of a PRINCIPAL to a trade.

BLIND TRUST trust created to avoid appearance of conflict of interest by an individual whose job involves a conflict with investing. The party named as trustee can be a bank trust department or any third party, other than a relative, employee, or business partner.

BLOCK

1. **Banking.** A group of checks, or checks and cash, collected during business hours and submitted, along with relevant deposit slips, for sorting into the check collection system, and also for proving (reconciling) deposits with deposit slips. For example, a teller's block. Checks are routinely processed as single units. *See also* BATCH.
2. **Securities.** The shares of a security bought or sold in a single transaction, the most common unit being 10,000 shares.

BLOCKED ACCOUNT

1. bank account in a currency subject to EXCHANGE CONTROLS by monetary authorities. Some countries restrict or prohibit out-of-country

transfers from domestic bank accounts in the local currency. The result is an overvalued currency, in relation to free-market currencies that are not inhibited by currency controls.

2. any bank account frozen for political reasons, usually during wartime or national emergency. In the United States, funds in these blocked accounts owned by foreign governments or private individuals may not be touched, unless released by the U.S. Treasury. *See also* FROZEN ACCOUNT; WARNING BULLETIN.

BROKER PRICE OPINION (BPO) estimate of probable selling price of a residential property based on selling prices of comparable properties in the area or a drive-by inspection, often used by a mortgage servicer as an alternative to a full property APPRAISAL. Also called *comparative market analysis*.

BLUE LIST trade publication, "The Blue List of Current Municipal Offerings," listing par value, coupon rate, and yield to maturity of municipal bonds and notes, compiled daily by a STANDARD & POOR'S affiliate since 1935. Dealers pay a fee for each daily listing.

BLUE SKY LAWS popular name for state securities laws designed to safeguard investors from buying worthless securities. Many states have patterned their securities laws after federal legislation.

BOARD

1. official governing body of an organization; the BOARD OF DIRECTORS of a bank or corporation, the BOARD OF TRUSTEES of a mutual savings bank or savings and loan association.
2. shorthand reference for the BOARD OF GOVERNORS of the Federal Reserve System.
3. popular name for a stock exchange, in particular the New York Stock Exchange or the Big Board.

BOARD OF DIRECTORS governing body of a corporation, elected by shareholders to represent their interests in managing the firm. Directors adopt the bylaws and operating rules of a corporation, appoint its operating officers, and set the stock dividend rate paid to shareholders. Directors of national banks are required to own shares of stock in the bank and are elected by shareholders at an organizational meeting before the bank opens for business, and at regular annual meetings afterwards. Most large corporations have a certain number of INSIDE DIRECTORS who are also officers of the firm, and outside directors who are elected from the community at large. Each FEDERAL RESERVE BANK is governed by a nine-member board elected by MEMBER BANKS that own stock in the Reserve Bank in that region of the country. These boards have three separate classes of directors, who are named to serve three-year terms: Class A Directors, representing the member banks, and are usually bankers; and Class B Directors and Class C Directors, representing the interests of business, labor, and consumers. Class A and Class B directors are elected by member banks in a Federal Reserve district; Class C directors are named by the BOARD OF GOVERNORS of the Federal Reserve System. Directors appoint each Reserve Bank's president, and first vice president, who serve for five-year terms, and name the district's representatives to the FEDERAL ADVISORY COUNCIL, which advises the Board of Governors on policy issues relating to bank supervision and regulation.

BOARD OF GOVERNORS seven-member board, appointed by the President of the United States and confirmed by the Senate, governing the Federal Reserve System. Federal Reserve governors, who serve for 14-year terms, set RESERVE REQUIREMENTS for depository financial institutions; approve the DISCOUNT RATE for short-term Reserve Bank loans to financial institutions, as proposed by each of the 12 Federal Reserve Banks; regulate state chartered MEMBER BANKS and bank holding companies; and cast a majority of the votes on the influential FEDERAL OPEN MARKET COMMITTEE, through which the Federal Reserve directs MONETARY POLICY. The chairman of the Board of Governors, serving a four-year term, is the senior policy maker in the Federal Reserve System, and represents the Federal Reserve before Congress and federal agencies.

BOARD OF TRUSTEES group of individuals named to manage a nonstock corporation, for example a mutual savings bank, mutual fund, foundation, or university. The trustees of a mutual savings bank are elected by depositors to establish operating rules, set lending policies, appoint its executive officers, and have a fiduciary duty to protect assets of depositors.

BOILER PLATE slang term for standard clauses in loan agreements, insurance policies, wills, and other official documents. Some states have adopted so-called plain English laws, requiring lenders to write consumer credit agreements in everyday language so consumers have a clear understanding of their rights and responsibilities.

BOLIVAR monetary unit of Venezuela.

BOLIVIANO monetary unit of Bolivia.

BONA FIDE ERROR *see* BILLING ERROR.

BOND interest-bearing or discounted certificate of indebtedness, paying a fixed rate of interest over the life of the obligation, hence the name *fixed income security*. The issuer is obligated by a written agreement (the bond INDENTURE) to pay the holder a specific sum of money, usually semiannually but sometimes at maturity, as is the case with a ZERO-COUPON SECURITY, and the face value, or PAR VALUE, of the certificate at maturity. Bonds are long-term obligations, meaning they have maturities of five years, and frequently, ten years or longer.

Bondholders have different rights than stockholders; the holder of a bond has a claim against the issuer as provided in the indenture, but has no ownership rights, as stockholders have. A CONVERTIBLE bond, however, may be swapped for common stock. Most convertibles are DEBENTURES, or unsecured promises to pay.

Bonds, even though they pay only a fixed rate of interest, and thus are vulnerable to a decline in price when interest rates are rising, are popular with financial institutions for a number of reasons. They allow the issuer to raise additional capital without selling stock, through the financial technique known as LEVERAGE; issuers, by selling bonds secured by loans, are able to liquify the balance sheet, by converting balance sheet assets (residential mortgages, leases, credit card receivables) into marketable securities. Banks, individual investors, and insurance companies are major buyers of bonds.

Typically, bonds are classified by several different categories:

Collateral Backing—fully unsecured promise to pay a DEBENTURE or bonds secured by mortgages or claims to specific assets, for example, ASSET-BACKED SECURITIES.

Maturity—single maturity term bond or SERIAL BOND having several maturities.

Method of transfer—book entry registered on the books of a central depository; BEARER BOND payable to the holder; or REGISTERED BOND.

Price—Discount bond, sold at an ORIGINAL ISSUE DISCOUNT from face value or premium bond, sold ABOVE PAR.

See also ACCRUAL BOND; BOND EQUIVALENT YIELD; BOND RATING; BOOK-ENTRY SECURITY; CONTROLLED AMORTIZATION BOND; EUROBOND; INDUSTRIAL DEVELOPMENT BOND; I-BONDS; INFLATION-INDEXED SECURITIES; JUNK BOND; MORTGAGE-BACKED BOND; PRIVATE PURPOSE BOND; PUBLIC PURPOSE BOND; SAVINGS BOND; STATE AND LOCAL BONDS; SURETY BOND; TREASURY BOND; YANKEE BOND; YEN BOND.

BOND ANTICIPATION NOTE (BAN) short-term debt instrument with a maturity under a year, issued by a municipality or local government, usually for capital improvement projects, that is paid off when long-term bonds are issued.

BOND BUYER INDEX index published by *The Bond Buyer*, a daily newspaper covering the municipal bond market. Actually, there are several Bond Buyer indices:

—the Bond Buyer average of 40 long-term bonds, compiled daily from quotations by five municipal bond brokers, is used by the Chicago Board of Trade as the basis for long-term municipal bond contracts. The index is adjusted to an 8% average yield.

—the Bond Buyer 20 bond index, estimating the composite yield of 20 general obligation bonds rated A or better.

—the Bond Buyer 11 bond index of select AA rated bonds, several of which are included in the 20 bond index.

BOND CIRCULAR *see* PROSPECTUS; REGISTRATION STATEMENT.

BOND EQUIVALENT YIELD investment yield of a bond purchased at discount from face value, such as a U.S. Treasury bill or municipal bond, expressed as a percent. These securities do not pay monthly, quarterly, or semi-annual interest, as interest-bearing securities do. For Treasury bills with maturities of three or six months, the formula for converting discount yield basis to the bond equivalent is as follows:

Yield equals face value minus the purchase price, divided by the purchase price; multiplied by the number of days in the year following the issue date/the number of days to maturity.

Also called *coupon equivalent yield* or *equivalent bond yield.*

BOND POWER a type of assignment by the registered owner of securities, allowing transfer to another holder. Bond assignments often are executed in blank, when the bond owner cannot sign the certificates in person. When securities are pledged as loan collateral, a bond power assignment allows the lender to sell the securities if the borrower defaults.

BOND RATING evaluation by rating company of the probability that a particular bond issue will default. Bonds are rated by STANDARD & POOR'S, Moody's Investors Service, and Fitch Ratings and are given bond ratings from AAA (least likely to default) to D (default). Bonds rated BBB by Standard & Poor's (Baa by Moody's) or better are rated BANK QUALITY bonds or investment grade bonds suitable for purchase by commercial banks, fiduciaries, mutual savings banks, trust companies, and insurance companies. Bonds given lower ratings are considered speculative investments.

BOND RATING—CORPORATE AND MUNICIPAL BONDS

	Bond Rating Service	
Explanation of Rating	Moody's Investors Service	Standard & Poor's
Highest quality	Aaa	AAA
High quality	Aa	AA
Upper medium grade	A	A
Medium grade	Baa	BBB
Predominantly speculative	Ba	BB
Speculative, low grade	B	B
Poor quality	Caa	CCC
Highest speculation	Ca	CC
Lowest quality, no interest paid	C	C
In default		DDD
In arrears		DD
Questionable value		D

BOND SWAP selling a bond prior to its maturity and purchasing another. Bond swapping is a popular portfolio management technique. There are several types of swaps: A maturity swap exchanges bonds of different maturities; a quality swap upgrades safety by purchasing high-grade bonds; a yield swap aims to maximize return on invested capital by, say, purchasing deep discount bonds when rates are falling; and a tax swap creates a tax loss offsetting capital gains earned by a substitute bond while preserving the original investment. *See also* ASSET SWAP; CURRENCY SWAP; INTEREST RATE SWAP; WASH SALE.

BOND TRUSTEE financial institution with trust powers, such as a commercial bank trust department or trust company, given fiduciary powers by a bond issuer to enforce the terms of the bond INDENTURE. The trustee sees that bond interest payments are made as scheduled, and protects the interests of the bondholders if the issuer defaults.

BOOK

1. trader's log of purchases and sales creating a market position; also called a *position sheet.* A trader's book may be LONG (an excess of assets or forward market purchases over liabilities in the same asset), SHORT (an excess of liabilities or forward sales contracts over assets), or matched in which assets are roughly equivalent to liabilities of the same maturities. A trader who has more liabilities than assets, or vice versa, is said to be running an open book or UNMATCHED BOOK.

   In the securities industry, specialists on the New York Stock Exchange maintain a book of orders to buy and sell stocks in which they are authorized to make markets.
2. to put a loan or LOAN PARTICIPATION on the balance sheet as an earning asset.
3. shorthand expression for BOOK VALUE of a bank's common stock in relation to market value, as in "ABC Bank is selling at twice book."

BOOK BALANCE funds on deposit prior to any adjustment for check clearing FLOAT, uncollected funds, or RESERVE REQUIREMENTS. Also called *gross balance.*

BOOK ENTRY SECURITY security represented by an account entry on the records of a private depository or, in the case of U.S. government securities, a Federal Reserve Bank.

BOOK PROFIT (OR LOSS) *see* UNREALIZED PROFIT (OR LOSS).

BOOK TRANSFER transfer of funds from one deposit account into another at the same financial institution. Book transfers are an efficient method of consolidating funds because they eliminate check clearing FLOAT.

BOOK VALUE

1. current value of an asset as it appears on the balance sheet. It can be the same as market value, or it can represent the difference

between the purchase price and market price, less accumulated depreciation.

2. NET WORTH of a corporation, sometimes expressed in terms of value dollars per share of common stock, after deducting the outstanding preferred stock.
3. original purchase price of an asset.

BORROWED FUNDS generic term for funds loaned to a bank, generally on a short-term basis, by another bank. It covers the following: BILLS PAYABLE; EURODOLLARS purchased and FEDERAL FUNDS purchased; REDISCOUNTS of promissory notes and business paper at a Federal Reserve Bank; and REPURCHASE AGREEMENTS with other financial institutions and securities dealers. Also called *borrowings. See also* BORROWED RESERVES; MANAGED LIABILITIES.

BORROWED RESERVES Federal Reserve loan to a bank or a savings institution with insufficient reserves on hand to meet its legal RESERVE REQUIREMENTS. An increase in borrowed reserves signals tighter Federal Reserve credit policy and potentially higher interest rates for bank borrowers. When the Federal Reserve provides less credit to the banking system, banks must borrow to maintain the required reserves. These loans, in the form of an ADVANCE or DISCOUNT by a Federal Reserve Bank, are normally collateralized by Treasury securities. *See also* DISCOUNT WINDOW; REDISCOUNT.

BORROWER person or organization obtaining funds from another, called a *lender,* normally repayable with INTEREST at a future date. An extension of credit by a financial institution, for example a bank LOAN, is evidenced by a PROMISSORY NOTE, a legally enforceable agreement to repay. *See also* MORTGAGOR.

BORROWING BASE amount a lender is willing to advance against the value of pledged collateral. The borrowing base is determined by multiplying the value of the assigned collateral (receivables, inventory, equipment) by a discount factor, a process known as *margining.* In accounts receivable financing, the lender may agree to advance funds against 80% of current receivables. For example, the borrowing base of a customer pledging receivables of $200,000 is $160,000. As a rule, receivables qualify for a higher borrowing base (and a smaller margin) than inventory because receivables are one step closer to being converted into cash. *See also* FLOATING LIEN.

BOUNCED CHECK *see* RUBBER CHECK.

BOURSE French for stock exchange; a generic term for European exchanges trading listed securities, and in some countries, foreign exchange. It is used most often in France and Belgium. Called *borsa* in Italy and *borse* in Germany.

BOUTIQUE popular name for a bank-owned company or holding company affiliate that acts as an INVESTMENT ADVISOR for institutional investors or a particular segment of the industry, e.g., mergers and acquisitions, money management for institutional clients, and so on.

BOW-TIE LOAN short-term variable rate loan that defers any unpaid interest charges above a pre-determined interest rate. A bow-tie loan rolls any interest due into the loan principal in a long-term loan from a bank lender or investor.

B-PIECE BUYER investor buying the lowest-rated securities in a new issue of mortgage-backed or asset-backed securities. Such bonds are usually classified as JUNK BONDS in credit quality; the B-Piece Buyer could lose all or part of the invested principal if the issuer gets into financial trouble.

BRADY BOND dollar-denominated bond converting international bank loans to long-term bonds, named after Nicholas Brady, U.S. Treasury secretary in the 1980s. Brady bonds are collateralized by 30-year zero-coupon Treasury bonds for bond principal value and an INTERNATIONAL MONETARY FUND reserve fund for interest earned.

BRANCH AUTOMATION *see* PLATFORM AUTOMATION.

BRANCH BANKING multi-office banking, generally defined as accepting deposits or making loans at facilities away from a bank's home office. Branch banking has gone through significant changes since the 1980s as banks responded to a more competitive nationwide financial services market.

In the 1990s, regulatory limitations on bank branching, such as the 1920s era MCFADDEN ACT that restricted branching to a bank's home state, were finally lifted. The Riegle-Neal Interstate Banking & Branching Efficiency Act of 1994 authorized well-capitalized banks to acquire branch offices, or open new ones, anywhere in the United States outside their home state after June 1, 1997. Most states passed laws enabling interstate branching prior to that date. Branch banking networks are gradually evolving into multi-state financial services networks where depositors can access their accounts from any banking office. Financial innovation such as INTERNET BANKING will also influence the future of "bricks and mortar" banking by potentially reducing the need to maintain extensive branch networks to service consumers. *See also* AGENCY BANK; CHAIN BANKING; GROUP BANKING; INTERSTATE BANKING; REGIONAL INTERSTATE BANKING; UNIT BANKING.

BREAK-EVEN YIELD yield required to cover the cost of bringing to market a new product or banking service. In COST ACCOUNTING, it is the point at which a sale covers the cost of a product or service. Each additional sale brings profit to the bottom line, considering the cost of offering the service, normally the fully loaded cost that includes fixed costs, such as building rent, and equipment costs, and variable costs such as the cost of funds.

BREAKPOINT

1. deposit account balance below which zero reserves are required. The current value is published in the Federal Reserve Bulletin.
2. account balance where the interest rate earned (or paid) is raised or lowered.
3. in mutual funds, the point at which the sales commission charged is lowered, because of the size of the transaction. Most funds have several breakpoints.

BRETTON WOODS SYSTEM international monetary system created in 1944 at an international conference of 44 nations in Bretton Woods, New Hampshire. A direct result of this conference was the creation of the INTERNATIONAL MONETARY FUND (IMF), the INTERNATIONAL BANK FOR RECONSTRUCTION AND DEVELOPMENT (known informally as the World Bank), and the FIXED EXCHANGE RATES that existed until the 1970s. The original agreement, which became law in the United States in 1945, was modified in 1971 when the par value exchange system was replaced by a system of FLOATING EXCHANGE RATES.

BRICKS AND MORTAR popular name for the fixed assets owned by a bank, either owned or leased, including branch offices, and the BACK OFFICE. Generally it refers to retail offices or branch offices in conventional multibranch banking. Branch banking has a high number of distribution points for retail customers, at a high fixed cost. Contrast with AUTOMATED TELLER MACHINE; HOME BANKING.

BRIDGE BANK bank organized to assume the deposits and secured liabilities of an insolvent bank. The FEDERAL DEPOSIT INSURANCE CORPORATION was given authority to charter these temporary banks by the Competitive Equality Banking Act of 1987. The FDIC has the authority, using a bridge bank, to operate a failed bank for up to three years until a buyer can be found.

BRIDGE LOAN

1. short-term loan to cover a home buyer's financing costs when selling one house and purchasing another. The loan provides funds to buy a new house before proceeds are available from sale of the old house.
2. in corporate finance, interim financing covering the time lag between redemption of a bond or commercial paper issue, and replacement by a new one. Bridge loans, commonly replacing short-term debt with longer term financing, are an integral part of corporate restructurings, mergers, and leveraged buy-outs. Banks and insurance companies supply funds to pay off old debts before proceeds are raised from new debt or issuance of stock. Also known as *gap financing* or *swing loan.*
3. short-term multinational credit extended to a LESS DEVELOPED COUNTRY, arranged through the International Monetary Fund and the World Bank, in anticipation of longer-term financing by private banks.

BROKEN DATE term used in FOREIGN EXCHANGE trading and the Euromarket for a forward exchange contract or money market contract with delivery of currency, CDs, and so on, to take place on a nonstandard date; for example 28 days instead of 30 days. Also called *cock date.*

BROKER

1. **Securities:** Person acting as an AGENT, or intermediary between buyer and seller, usually charging a fee, or commission, for performing that service. Banks acting as brokers on behalf of their customers must register with the Securities and Exchange Commission and with state regulatory agencies. *See also* INTER-DEALER BROKER.
2. **Mortgages:** State-licensed person who, for a fee or commission, represents property owners in real-estate transactions. Some brokers act on behalf of borrowers in arranging mortgage financing and negotiating terms of sale.

BROKERED DEPOSIT high-value bank deposit, usually a CERTIFICATE OF DEPOSIT, purchased from a broker acting as an agent for the depositor. The broker negotiates a higher interest rate with the participating banks and sells off smaller pieces to the account owners, usually in blocks close to the FDIC insurance limit of $250,000 per account. These accounts are reported on a bank's records in the name of the broker rather than that of the account owner. For this reason, federal law bars undercapitalized banks and thrift institutions from accepting brokered deposits.

BROKER'S CALL LOAN short-term demand loan to a broker secured by pledged securities. Brokers use the loans to finance underwriting or to secure advances to customers who maintain margin accounts. Broker loans are usually callable on 24-hour notice, hence the term *call loan rate.*

BUILDING AND LOAN ASSOCIATION *see* SAVINGS AND LOAN ASSOCIATION.

BULK FILING check processing operation involving the high-speed sorting of checks and storage of cancelled checks by statement cycle rather than by ACCOUNT NUMBER.

BULL BOND bond considered likely to increase in value in a bull market, that is, when interest rates are falling. Whereas most bonds will increase in value in a declining rate market, bonds that perform especially well in a bull market are PRINCIPAL-ONLY (PO) STRIP mortgage-backed securities. POs, which consist entirely of mortgage principal payments, do well in a falling rate market because mortgagors refinance their loans at lower interest rates. Investors are repaid their original investment more quickly, increasing the CASH FLOW YIELD of the security.

BULLET LOAN loan that has a one-time payment of principal and interest at its termination. A bullet loan is similar to a BALLOON MATURITY loan, with the important difference that a bullet loan, unlike a balloon loan, has no obvious source of repayment. To pay off the bullet loan the borrower may have to refinance at the current rate, liquidate assets, or sell collateral.

BULLION gold or other precious metals in bar or coin form. The major gold trading centers are London and Zurich, with gold futures trading based in New York. Monetary reserves of central banks are kept mostly in gold bullion. *See also* EARMARKED RESERVES; GOLD FIX.

BULL SPREAD trading strategy in which a trader buys contracts in nearby months (goes long), and sells contracts in future months (goes short), expecting to realize a profit if prices rise. Also called *buy a spread.* The opposite is BEAR SPREAD.

BUMP-UP CD savings certificate giving the account owner the option to request a one-time increase (or bump-up) in interest earned. These CDs normally pay a lower yield than ordinary CDs but have advantages when prevailing market interest rates are rising. The rate increase does not change the CD's original date of maturity.

BUNDLING packaging several related banking services as a single account, for which the customer pays an annual fee or monthly fee, plus applicable service charges.

BUSINESS COMBINATION *see* MERGER.

BUSINESS CREDIT loans made to corporations and partnerships, as distinct from consumer loans or personal loans. A TERM LOAN provides financing for short-term working capital or long-term capital improvements, and is repaid in a lump sum. A LINE OF CREDIT allows businesses to borrow repeatedly up to a certain amount. Most lenders ask for business financial statements, and many want personal guarantees, even when making loans to established small businesses. *See also* CORPORATE RESOLUTION; DEMAND LOAN; FINANCING STATEMENT; TIME LOAN.

BUSINESS DAY

1. day on which a bank is open for business, ordinarily most calendar days other than Sundays and legal public holidays.
2. day that two related markets, for example, futures exchanges or stock exchanges in different cities, are open for business.

BUSINESS PLAN document required of new businesses or corporations in REORGANIZATION, where the business is planning a major change in operations. This plan may be a chronological explanation of how the firm will use the bank loan, plus management goals and earnings objectives over the next three to five years. This statement usually is accompanied by a PRO FORMA STATEMENT of anticipated earnings and expenses over the same period. The two statements should complement each other.

BUTTERFLY SPREAD options strategy designed to profit from stable or decreasing volatility. The spread involves trades in four call options, all with the same expiration date: an option with a low exercise price; the sale of two call options with an intermediate exercise price; and the purchase of a call option with a high exercise price.

BUY A SPREAD *see* BULL SPREAD.

BUYBACK

1. in a foreign debt restructuring, an agreement by a debtor nation to buy outstanding loans from creditor banks at fair market value. Funds to purchase unpaid loans, normally at a deep discount from face value or book value, come from a variety of sources: export earnings, tourism, and direct loans or grants from the INTERNATIONAL MONETARY FUND and other international credit agencies.
2. offer by a corporation to repurchase its own stock from shareholders, done to raise the price of its stock or fend off a hostile takeover.
3. REPURCHASE AGREEMENT.

BUY CONTRACT contract to purchase Treasury bills, money market instruments, or other assets in the future.

BUYDOWN money advanced, usually by a builder, to reduce the borrower's monthly payment in the early years of a mortgage, below the level required for normal amortization. Buydowns are most prevalent in periods of high interest rates, when prospective home buyers might otherwise not qualify for a mortgage loan. Contrast with *buy-up*, which reduces points paid on a loan in exchange for a higher interest and higher monthly payments.

BUY IN

1. **Futures.** Covering a futures market short position by purchasing an offsetting long position, or taking delivery of securities or commodities.
2. **Securities.** The process whereby a broker or dealer bank, after purchasing securities that a selling broker cannot deliver, completes the transaction with another source at current market prices and charges the original selling broker the difference in cost.

BUYING FORWARD buying money market instruments or currencies in anticipation of a price rise or future demand. The opposite side is a sell contract by a counter-party.

BUY ON MARGIN buying an asset by making an initial payment—called the MARGIN—and borrowing the balance needed to cover the purchase price from a bank or broker. The margin represents a down payment. There are numerous examples: buying a house by making a down payment and financing the rest through a mortgage, buying securities through a broker, and so on. In securities purchasing, the amount of margin needed is regulated by the Federal Reserve Board.

BUY-SELL AGREEMENT

1. agreement between a bank or MORTGAGE BANKER making a construction loan for a project and the permanent lender assigning to the latter the long-term mortgage on the completed project. Many lenders providing interim financing during the construction phase will not advance funds without a permanent TAKE-OUT lender, who in effect buys out the original lender's interest in the project.
2. agreement in a closely held corporation or partnership, whereby, in the event of death of one of the partners or other triggering event, the survivor offers to buy the interest of the other owners of the firm.

C

CABLE
1. international bank draft transmitted by cable transfer between correspondent banks, as opposed to payment through the mail.
2. trader's shorthand for the U.S. dollar–pound sterling exchange rate.

CALAMITY CALL clause in a COLLATERALIZED MORTGAGE OBLIGATION (CMO) requiring the issuer to retire a portion of the CMO issue on a monthly basis if prepayments reach a level high enough to cause an insufficient cash flow to meet scheduled payments of principal and interest. A calamity call reduces the issuer's REINVESTMENT RISK, although that risk can also be covered by a prepayment reserve fund. *See also* CLEAN UP REQUIREMENT.

CALENDAR schedule of upcoming securities that will be brought to market. For example, the weekly auctions of U.S. Treasury securities, municipal bonds offered for sale, and also ASSET-BACKED SECURITIES offered for sale by banks and investment banks.

CALL
1. lender's demand for early payment of a loan, because the borrower has failed to meet contractual commitments such as maintaining adequate insurance or making timely payments; or, in a DEMAND LOAN, the lender's exercise of his right to ask for repayment in full at any time.
2. comptroller's call issued to NATIONAL BANK by the COMPTROLLER OF THE CURRENCY, to file a CALL REPORT or Report of Condition.
3. regulatory agency's order to a distressed bank to raise more capital, sometimes referred to as a capital call.
4. broker's demand for additional MARGIN or collateral when the value of customer's pledged collateral falls below a stated value, known as a *margin call.*
5. REDEMPTION privilege exercised by a bond issuer, as permitted in the INDENTURE agreement. It permits the issuer to retire the bonds if only a small portion of the issue is outstanding, in order to keep servicing costs from becoming unreasonable. Also called *nuisance call.*

CALLABLE *see* CALL OPTION.

CALLABLE CERTIFICATE OF DEPOSIT CERTIFICATE OF DEPOSIT that includes a CALL feature by the issuing bank. The bank may call the CD if interest rates decline prior to maturity. Callable CDs pay a higher rate than noncallable CDs due to this investment risk. Callable CDs are issued in a variety of options to meet investor needs: the fixed-interest rate CD, step-up CD and multi-step CD (giving the holder the right to adjust the yield upward once in the life of the CD or at predetermined intervals); and the step-down CD (the yield is adjusted downward if market rates fall). Most callable CDs credit interest to the holder's account semi-annually, but monthly payment and ZERO-COUPON CDs are also issued. Most callable CDs offer a put option exercisable at the death of the account holder, allowing beneficiaries to sell the CD back to the issuing bank.

CALL DATE *see* FIRST CALL DATE.

CALL LOAN *see* BROKER'S CALL LOAN; DEMAND LOAN.

CALL OPTION

1. bond issuer's right to redeem a bond at current value before its maturity date. Also called *call provision*.
2. contract giving the buyer of an option the right to purchase currencies, financial futures, or securities at a stated price, called the STRIKE PRICE.

CALL PROTECTION

1. provisions in a bond INDENTURE limiting redemption of callable bonds for a specified period, usually ten years for municipal and corporate bonds.
2. feature in MORTGAGE-BACKED SECURITIES designed to minimize prepayment risk during a so-called LOCK-IN PERIOD. If loans are prepaid during this period, funds are not passed through immediately to the investor. Buyers of mortgage-backed securities like this feature because it provides a more consistent cash flow. *See also* CALAMITY CALL.

CALL REPORT

1. quarterly report of income and condition required by a financial institution's primary supervisory agency: the Comptroller of the Currency for national banks; Federal Reserve Banks for state member banks; the Federal Deposit Insurance Corp. for insured nonmember banks; or state banking agencies for state chartered banks and trust companies. Call reports are published by the FDIC on the FDIC's Web site (www.fdic.gov) approximately one month after the quarterly filing date.
2. lender's written report of new business development.

CAMELS RATING measure of the relative soundness of a bank. CAMELS ratings—the term stands for CAPITAL, ASSETS, *management*, *earnings*, LIQUIDITY and *sensitivity* to market risk—are calculated on a 1–5 scale, and are used by bank supervisory agencies to evaluate bank condition. A rating of 1 is given to banks with the strongest performance ratings; banks given a CAMELS rating of 4 or 5 are placed on the watch list of banks in need of supervisory attention. Individual CAMELS ratings are disclosed to bank management, though not to the general public. *See also* CAPITAL ADEQUACY.

CANADIAN ROLLOVER MORTGAGE *see* ROLLOVER MORTGAGE.

CANCEL to endorse or mark a check (or negotiable instrument) in such a way that it is no longer negotiable.

CANCELLED CHECK check voided by endorsement, indicating it has been paid by the drawee bank and cannot be renegotiated.

CAP

1. INTEREST RATE CAP in a commercial loan negotiated at loan origination. The lender agrees to set the maximum interest rate on a floating rate loan, for which the borrower pays a fee.
2. clause in a residential mortgage loan agreement limiting any interest rate or payment increases to a specified amount until the loan is fully paid. An ANNUAL CAP limits yearly increases; a LIFE OF LOAN CAP remains in force throughout the term of the loan; a PAYMENT CAP limits month-to-month increases in loan payments.
3. upper end of a COLLAR, a two-way credit agreement protecting both borrower and lender against fluctuating interest rates; the lower end is a FLOOR.
4. in a wire transfer payment system, the originating bank's net debit cap, placing a limit on its aggregate DAYLIGHT OVERDRAFT exposure in its RESERVE ACCOUNT it is willing to accept during a single business day.

CAPACITY one of the FIVE C'S OF CREDIT—the borrower's ability to pay an obligation when due, normally determined by verifying salary given on a credit application with an employer and considering probability of continued employment.

CAPITAL

1. **Banking.** Measure of financial strength; funds invested in a bank, including COMMON STOCK and qualifying PREFERRED STOCK, MANDATORY CONVERTIBLE securities, such as CAPITAL NOTES, plus retained earnings. Equity capital is the initial funding (called contributed capital or PAID IN CAPITAL) needed to charter a bank, a cushion against operating losses, such as BAD DEBT, and a source of protection for depositors' money.

   In 1989, banking regulatory agencies revised the capital standards for banking institutions after the FINANCIAL INSTITUTIONS, REFORM, RECOVERY & ENFORCEMENT ACT required savings and loan associations to meet the same standards for CAPITAL ADEQUACY as national banks. Under the Risk-Based Capital guidelines, bank assets are classified by risk (because they represent loans and investment of funds), and capital requirements are determined from the risks assigned to each asset category. Thus, an asset defined as needing 100% of capital would require 100% of the prevailing 8% risk-based capital requirement. In other words, for every $100 in loans and investments, a bank would need, on average, $8 in capital coverage. *See also* BASEL I, BASEL II, BASEL III; CAPITAL RATIO; TOTAL CAPITAL.

2. **Finance.** Owner's share in a business plus operating profit or surplus, financing its long-term growth. Also called *contributed capital* or *owner's equity. See also* NET WORTH; PAID-IN CAPITAL.

CAPITAL ADEQUACY amount of capital relative to a financial institution's loans and other assets. Almost all banking regulators require that banks hold a certain minimum of equity capital against their risk-weighted assets. The Basel Committee on Bank Supervision, a coordinating body within the Bank for International Settlements, supervises the administration of capital reserves for central bankers around the world. *See also* BASEL I, BASEL II, BASEL III; RISK-BASED CAPITAL.

CAPITAL ASSET PRICING MODEL mathematical formula comparing expected RISK to expected reward. Investors expect higher risk asset classes to pay higher returns. For example, investors expect common stocks to pay a higher investment return (the risk premium) than the three-month Treasury bill, a risk-free security. The theory assumes that stock market investors are rewarded for market-related risk, which is known as BETA risk.

CAPITAL GAIN (OR LOSS) difference between selling price of an asset and cost when purchased. If the difference is positive, a gain is realized; if negative, a loss results.

CAPITALIZED COST base dollar cost of a leased asset, excluding finance charges, that is amortized over the life of the lease. The figure may include taxes, insurance, service agreements, and outstanding balances from previous leases. Disclosure of capitalized cost is required in consumer leases. Also called *capitalization cost.*

CAPITAL LEASE *see* FINANCE LEASE.

CAPITAL MARKET financial market where corporations and government agencies raise funds by selling stocks, bonds, and marketable securities with maturities greater than one year. Securities are distributed through public exchanges or through private placement sales to investors. Compare with MONEY MARKET.

CAPITAL NOTE any NOTE or DEBENTURE issued by a bank or bank holding company that qualifies as bank capital. Capital notes are unsecured liabilities that are considered supplementary capital or Tier 2 capital in meeting a bank's required capital-to-asset ratio. Under regulatory capital guidelines, notes qualify as capital if they have original maturities of at least seven years, are noncallable before the maturity date, and have a mandatory conversion clause requiring the issuer to exchange the notes for common stock at a future date at a preset price.

CAPITAL RATIO key financial ratio measuring a bank's CAPITAL ADEQUACY or financial stability. As a general rule, the higher the ratio the more sound the bank. A bank with a high capital-to-asset ratio is protected against operating losses more than a bank with a lower ratio, although this depends on the relative risk of loss at each bank.

There are several standard measures of capital adequacy:

—Risk-adjusted capital ratio: TIER 1 capital (common stock and qualifying preferred stock) divided by risk-adjusted assets.

—TOTAL CAPITAL to total assets ratio: tier 1 capital plus TIER 2 capital (preferred stock, subordinated debt, and loan loss reserves) divided by total average assets.

—LEVERAGE ratio: tier 1 capital divided by total average assets, excluding goodwill.

—total risk-adjusted capital ratio: total RISK-BASED CAPITAL for certain loans and investments divided by risk-adjusted assets.

CAPITAL STRUCTURE the mix of long-term debt, common and preferred stock, and owner's equity financing a business enterprise. Analysts look at the proportion of long-term debt versus short-term debt and the amount of debt issued when analyzing capital structure. Companies more heavily financed by debt are said to be more risky when applying for bank loans.

CARD ACT federal law requiring credit card issuers to give advance notice of changes in interest rate, annual fees, late payment fees, and overlimit fees and to disclose financing costs to cardholders making minimum payments. Applicants under age 21 must show proof of sufficient income or have a cosigner. Full name: Credit Card Accountability, Responsibility, and Disclosure Act of 2009.

CARDHOLDER AGREEMENT written statement of terms and conditions relating to a bank card, as required by Federal Reserve regulations. In credit cards, the agreement states the ANNUAL PERCENTAGE RATE, the monthly minimum payment, annual card fee if any, and the cardholder's rights in billing disputes.

CARD RECOVERY BULLETIN *see* WARNING BULLETIN.

CARRY FORWARD/CARRY BACK

1. excess bank reserves (up to 2%) that may be carried over from one week to the next RESERVE maintenance period to help meet that period's reserve requirements. Deficiencies in reserves are also carried forward to the next accounting period.
2. TAX LOSS CARRY FORWARD, a tax benefit allowing corporations and individuals to carry forward losses to reduce their tax liability.

CARRYING CHARGES

1. portion of the FINANCE CHARGE in bank loans covering the lender's costs in booking the loan and collecting payments plus a portion of bad debt expense.
2. broker's charge to customers for a MARGIN account financing securities purchased on credit.

3. dealer's out-of-pocket expenses, usually bank loans, for holding a cash security or commodity until sold or delivered. Carrying charges can also refer to storage, insurance, and other costs.

CARRY TRADE borrowing short-term funds and simultaneously buying longer-maturity, higher-return investments. Banks use the carry trade to manage their loan funding costs, which can translate into lower mortgage rates and credit card rates for consumers. The trade can be very profitable for institutional investors when the difference between short-term and long-term rates is greatest.

CASH

1. currency (including bills and coin) in circulation, including checking account balances. Cash held by a bank, for example VAULT CASH, requires no capital backing under RISK-BASED CAPITAL rules adopted by bank regulatory agencies.
2. to convert a check to cash by endorsing and presenting to a bank. Also called *negotiating a check.*

See also CURRENCY IN CIRCULATION.

CASH ADVANCE cash loan against a personal line of credit, obtained by presentment of a CREDIT CARD at a bank teller window, at an automated teller machine, or by mail. Finance charges are paid from the transaction date.

CASH BASIS accounting system in which revenues are recognized when cash is received and when expenses are paid. This form of accounting is easier for smaller firms to adopt than the ACCRUAL BASIS, in which income and expenses are recognized in the period in which they arise.

CASH BASIS LOAN loan on which interest payments are recorded when collected. These are loans in which the borrower has fallen behind in interest payments, and are classified as NONACCRUAL LOANS. In extreme situations where the lender reasonably expects that only a portion of the principal and interest owed ultimately will be collected, payments are credited directly to the outstanding principal. *See also* NONPERFORMING ASSET.

CASH CARD plastic card encoded with a preset value. Cash cards are like cash; there is no built-in security and if lost or stolen can be used by anyone. Card-accepting retailers deduct the value of each purchase until the card value is used up. Contrast with CHECK CARD.

CASH COLLATERAL negotiable instruments, documents of title, securities, bank deposits, and other short-term assets that readily are convertible into cash.

CASH CONCENTRATION & DISBURSEMENT (CCD) corporate electronic payment used in business to business and intracompany transfers of funds. Vendors, including numerous federal agencies, have used the CCD payment format, an electronic payment record developed by the National Automated Clearing House Association, to make single invoice payments to suppliers. Funds are cleared on an overnight basis through the nationwide AUTOMATED CLEARING HOUSE network. *See also* CONCENTRATION ACCOUNT; CORPORATE TRADE EXCHANGE; CORPORATE TRADE PAYMENT.

CASH DELIVERY *see* SAME DAY FUNDS.

CASH DISCOUNT *see* DISCOUNT.

CASH DISPENSER card activated banking terminal similar to an AUTOMATED TELLER MACHINE that dispenses currency in various denominations, but does not accept deposits. The earliest ATMs were cash dispensers only.

CASH EQUIVALENTS investments or securities of such high liquidity and safety that they are regarded as good as cash, generally those with maturities under three months. Examples are short-term certificates of deposit, money market funds, and Treasury bills.

CASH FLOW

Banking:

1. cash available to an organization from its business operations and investments. A positive cash flow indicates net operating income is sufficient to cover expenses, while a negative cash flow means expenses are growing faster than revenues. Lenders, when making loans to a business, often look first at cash flow from operations, before COLLATERAL pledged by the borrower, as the primary source of loan repayment.
2. flow of funds through a bank, an important measure of its overall LIQUIDITY, or ability to meet customer demand for funds. It is usually summarized in a cash flow report indicating a bank's sources of funds (mostly deposits) and uses of funds (mostly loans). *See also* CASH POSITION.
3. the flow of principal and interest payments as borrowers pay down consumer and mortgage loans to investors holding MORTGAGE-BACKED BONDS and ASSET-BACKED SECURITIES.
4. an estimate of property income from leases in commercial mortgage securitizations. It is calculated by deducting leasing commissions, improvements, and other capital expenses from net operating income.

CASH FLOW LOAN short-term loan that is normally unsecured by pledge of assets or collateral, and is repayable from cash generated from business operations. *See also* COLLATERAL LOAN.

CASH FLOW YIELD monthly rate of return of a mortgage-backed security, based on principal and interest mortgage payments and an estimated rate of loan prepayment. Cash flow yield is the monthly INTERNAL RATE OF RETURN of a mortgage-backed security, producing the rate of return that approximates the actual return to the holder. Because some mortgage pools are paid off faster than others, cash flow yield offers a more realistic way to price mortgage-backed securities than the 12-year prepayment assumptions prevalent in the 1970s.

CASHIER bank officer responsible for custody of the bank's earning assets, and whose signature is required on official bank checks, called CASHIER'S CHECKS and all official correspondence.

CASHIER'S CHECK bank-issued check, also called *official check* or *treasurer's check*, signed by a bank officer and drawn against funds of the bank itself. A cashier's check is generally regarded as good as cash. Contrast with CERTIFIED CHECK.

CASH ITEMS any check given immediate credit to a customer's account, before a bank has received payment from the paying bank. Examples are a DEPOSITORY TRANSFER CHECK and a pre-authorized check. *See also* COLLECTION ITEMS.

CASH JOURNAL book of original accounting entries, where transactions are recorded in chronological order. Entries from the cash journal are later entered in the balance sheet ledger. A cash journal is a basic service to bank MASTER TRUST customers.

CASH LETTER group of checks sent to a clearing house or the Federal Reserve check collection system, accompanied by letter that lists the amounts and instructions for payment to other banks. Also called a *transit letter.*

CASH MANAGEMENT

1. financial management technique used by corporate treasurers to accelerate the collection of receivables, control payments to trade creditors, and efficiently manage cash. Large corporations collect funds from many different accounts into a single CONCENTRATION ACCOUNT, and invest excess funds in the MONEY MARKET. The local accounts are frequently drawn down to zero-funds every day. In disbursing payments to trade creditors, treasurers attempt to control the outflow of funds by timing payments with the receipt of invoices from trade creditors. A frequently used tool in cash management is CONTROLLED DISBURSEMENT of corporate payments to match the collection of accounts receivables against disbursements to trading partners. *See also* BALANCE REPORTING; DELAYED DISBURSEMENT; ELECTRONIC DATA INTERCHANGE; LOCK BOX; TREASURY WORKSTATION; ZERO-BALANCE ACCOUNT.
2. personal financial management account at a bank or brokerage firm, combining a money market fund and a brokerage or investment account with check writing and debit card access.

CASH MANAGEMENT BILL short-term debt instrument normally issued with maturity up to 50 days by the U.S. Treasury as an alternative to Treasury notes or Treasury bills. Cash management bills are sold to institutional investors. These bills are issued to cover temporary cash shortages, for example, just before a major tax collection date, such as April 15 or June 15.

CASH MARKET market where securities, financial instruments, or currencies are transferred from buyer to seller, and paid for at the current market price. Cash market transactions are for immediate, on the spot delivery, as opposed to financial futures, forward market contracts, options, and swaps, which call for delivery at some future date. Also called *spot market.*

CASHOUT REFINANCE refinanced mortgage on a property resulting in a new mortgage with a larger principal balance. The cash taken out reduces the owner's equity but can be applied to pay down other debts and finance home improvements or be used for other purposes.

CASH POSITION

1. cash assets in a bank, synonymous with LIQUIDITY. Specifically, cash position is a measure of cash on hand, including vault cash and teller cash, and cash that can be raised from the sale of short-term assets, such as certificates of deposit, government securities, repurchase agreements, and so on. Also included are excess RESERVE ACCOUNT balances with a Federal Reserve Bank or correspondent, deposits with other banks, and checks in the process of collection.
2. funds in a bank's reserve account at a Federal Reserve Bank or a correspondent bank.

CASH RATIO ratio of total cash plus short-term investment securities to total bank assets; a LIQUIDITY ratio.

CASH RESERVE

1. bank's vault cash (including currency and coin), that may be used to satisfy RESERVE REQUIREMENTS.
2. revolving LINE OF CREDIT attached to a checking account allowing a consumer to write checks for amounts greater than the account balance without paying overdraft charges. Also called *cash reserve checking.*

CASH SETTLEMENT

1. settlement provision in some options and futures contracts that do not require delivery of the underlying instrument. For options, the difference between the settlement price on the underlying instrument or security and the option's exercise price is paid to the option holder at the exercise date. For futures contracts, the exchange establishes a settlement price on the final day of trading and all remaining open positions are marked to market at that price.
2. in securities trading the optional delivery of stocks purchased on the trade date, rather than the settlement date. *See also* DELIVERY VERSUS PAYMENT.

CASH SURRENDER VALUE accumulated paid-in value of a life insurance policy that qualifies as collateral on a bank loan. Banks usually will advance amounts up to the cash surrender value of a life insurance policy, less the interest charged on the loan. Besides taking an ASSIGNMENT of the insurance policy, which transfers title to the policy to the lender, the lender usually will ask the borrower to sign a separate contract stating the lender's rights. The lender usually advances up to 90% of paid-up cash value, as of the most recent payment date. The paid-up value may be used as collateral for a bank loan, although bank rates are often higher than rates insurance companies charge for policy loans.

CAVEAT VENDITOR Latin for "let the seller beware." Financial institutions selling loans in the SECONDARY MARKET are bound by written agreement to see that loans delivered to a buyer are documented properly and meet contract specifications. The opposite of caveat emptor (let the buyer beware).

CEASE AND DESIST ORDER order issued by a bank regulatory agency, after notice and opportunity for hearing, requiring a depository institution or a bank officer to suspend any unlawful, unsafe, or unsound practices, such as excessive lending to an insider. These orders are issued by the appropriate regulatory agencies under the FINANCIAL INSTITUTIONS REGULATORY ACT of 1978 and are enforceable in the courts.

CEDI, NEW CEDI monetary unit of Ghana.

CEILING

1. maximum INTEREST RATE on interest-bearing deposit accounts. Interest rates were deregulated starting in the 1980s, allowing banks and savings institutions to pay market rates for savings accounts and certificates of deposit. *See also* DEPOSITORY INSTITUTIONS DEREGULATION & MONETARY CONTROL ACT; MARKET RATE OF INTEREST.
2. USURY ceiling, the highest rate of interest permitted by state law on consumer installment loans and other extensions of credit.
3. in FOREIGN EXCHANGE, the price level of a particular currency that triggers INTERVENTION by central banks in the exchange markets.

CENTRAL BANK government agency that performs a number of key functions: (1) issues the nation's currency; (2) regulates the supply of credit in the economy; (3) manages the external value of its currency in the foreign exchange markets; (4) holds deposits representing reserves of other banks and other central banks; (5) acts as FISCAL AGENT for the central government, when the government sells new issues of securities to finance its operations; and (6) attempts to maintain an orderly market in these securities by actively participating in the government securities market.

The FEDERAL RESERVE SYSTEM, the central bank in the United States. It typically regulates BANK CREDIT by buying and selling government securities. This process, known as OPEN MARKET OPERATIONS, aims to promote stable economic growth while controlling the rate of inflation. Other major central banks are the Bank of England, the European Central Bank, and the Bank of Japan. *See also* BANK FOR INTERNATIONAL SETTLEMENTS; BASEL COMMITTEE; INTERVENTION; LENDER OF LAST RESORT; MONETARY POLICY; SWAP NETWORK.

CENTRAL INFORMATION FILE *see* CUSTOMER INFORMATION FILE.

CENTRAL LIABILITY list combining all of a borrower's liabilities, including direct and indirect loans, letters of credit, guarantees, and other accommodations. Grouping all related credit with a borrower gives the lender a history of the borrower, and is useful in controlling credit overextensions.

CENTRAL LIQUIDITY FACILITY (CLF) government corporation within the NATIONAL CREDIT UNION ADMINISTRATION that lends funds to member credit unions. Membership is voluntary. The CLF, which began operating in 1979, is capitalized by credit union contributions of capital stock and is authorized to make short-term and long-term loans to credit unions needing temporary financial assistance.

CERTIFICATE paper establishing an ownership claim; also, an assertion of facts.

1. bank CHARTER or certificate of authority issued by a chartering agency, authorizing a newly organized bank to open for business.
2. CERTIFICATE OF DEPOSIT, a receipt for a time deposit.
3. certificate of accounts, an auditor's opinion, filed by a certified public accountant after examination of an organization's books and records.
4. CERTIFICATE OF TITLE evidencing ownership of real estate or personal property.
5. certificate of claim, a borrower's written promise to reimburse specified expenses, for example, debt collection costs.
6. SAFEKEEPING CERTIFICATE issued by custodian for a certificate of deposit, stock certificate, or other security assigned to a new nominee.
7. PROTEST certificate issued by a bank refusing to honor a check.
8. CERTIFICATE OF INDEBTEDNESS.

CERTIFICATE ACCOUNT *see* SAVINGS CERTIFICATE.

CERTIFICATE AUTHORITY electronic affidavit validating an individual or business as authorized to conduct electronic commerce transactions over the Internet. Certificates are issued by a commercial bank or an independent, third-party organization acting as the middleman in an electronic commerce transaction. The issuer validates digital certificates identifying a consumer, merchant, or financial institution. *See also* DIGITAL SIGNATURE.

CERTIFICATE OF DEPOSIT (CD) receipt for a TIME DEPOSIT issued for a stated time period and normally paying a fixed rate of interest.

Bank CDs, are issued in negotiable and non-negotiable form, have maturities as short as seven days to seven years or longer, and pay a market rate of interest. The interest earned on consumer CDs, which are non-negotiable debt instruments protected by federal deposit insurance, is stated as an annual rate and an EFFECTIVE RATE that shows the effect of interest compounding. Since 1983, when time deposit rates were deregulated, CDs have been enormously popular investment accounts with consumers. Banks and savings institutions also have issued zero-coupon CDs, which pay no interest until the maturity date, much like ZERO-COUPON BONDS.

A NEGOTIABLE CERTIFICATE OF DEPOSIT has a principal of $100,000 (frequently $1 million or more), and can be sold to a new owner before maturity. Negotiable CDs are generally purchased by institutional investors, rather than individuals, and are actively traded in the secondary market,

Cashing in a bank CD before the maturity date can trigger an EARLY WITHDRAWAL PENALTY, usually a partial loss of interest. *See also* AVERAGE ANNUAL YIELD; BUMP-UP CD; BROKERED DEPOSIT; EURODOLLAR CERTIFICATE OF DEPOSIT; JUMBO CERTIFICATE OF DEPOSIT; MONEY MARKET CERTIFICATE; VARIABLE RATE CERTIFICATE; YANKEE CERTIFICATE OF DEPOSIT.

CERTIFICATE OF DEPOSIT ACCOUNT REGISTRY SERVICE (CDARS) type of certificate of deposit account that enables users to place a large deposit in federally insured accounts. CDARS (pronounced "cedars") transfers account balances above the Federal Deposit Insurance Corporation's maximum insurable amount to another financial institution in a network of banks managed by Promontory Interfinancial Network LLC, Arlington, Virginia. Web site: *www.CDARS.com.*

CERTIFICATE OF INDEBTEDNESS

1. short-term IOU issued by the U.S. Treasury Department until 1981. These special certificates have since been replaced by six-month and one-year Treasury bills; none are currently outstanding.
2. unsecured promissory note issued by a corporation, giving the holder a claim to the unpledged assets of the issuer.

CERTIFICATE OF TITLE opinion by an attorney or title searcher, after an inspection of public tax and land records, of the condition of the title to a specific piece of property. It does not provide warranties as to the authenticity of a title; that is done by a title insurance company.

CERTIFIED CHECK business or personal check stamped with the paying bank's certification that: (1) the maker's signature is genuine; and (2) there are sufficient funds in the account to cover the check. Once certified, a check becomes an obligation of a bank, and is paid out of bank funds. Banks charge a fee for certifying customer checks. Contrast with CASHIER'S CHECK.

CFA FRANC monetary unit of Cameroon, Central African Republic, Chad, Congo, Equitorial Guinea, and Gabon.

CHAIN BANKING control of three or more independently chartered banks by a few individuals, usually through stock ownership or interlocking directorates. Chain banking differs from BRANCH BANKING, or multioffice banking within a single institution and GROUP BANKING by affiliate banks within a BANK HOLDING COMPANY. Its importance in the banking system has declined since the late 1980s with the rapid growth of INTERSTATE BANKING and, in several states, more liberalized branching laws.

CHARACTER one of the five elements (the FIVE C'S OF CREDIT) in credit analysis. A loan backed by only a borrower's reputation in the community is called a *character loan* or GOOD FAITH loan.

CHARGEBACK paying bank's refusal to honor a check or draft, causing the check to be returned to the presenting bank.

CHARGE-OFF

1. loan written off as uncollectible bad debt. When full repayment is considered unlikely, loans are removed from the lender's balance sheet and charged against the LOAN LOSS RESERVES account for bad debt. Loans removed from the lender's books may be partially or fully recovered by the lender's collection department or an outside debt collection agency if the loan is secured by collateral or the borrower has additional assets. Also called *write-off. See also* BAD DEBT; PROBLEM LOAN; WORKOUT AGREEMENT.
2. process of removing uncollected loans or closed accounts from a bank's balance sheet.

CHARITABLE TRUST trust created for educational, scientific, or other purposes, organized as a legal charity. There are two types: a *charitable lead trust* pays income to a charity for a period of time, say 20 years, after which the property is distributed to noncharitable beneficiaries; a *charitable remainder trust* pays its income to taxable beneficiaries and the principal to charity when the trust ends.

CHARTER legal authorization to conduct business as a bank or thrift institution, granted by the COMPTROLLER OF THE CURRENCY for national banks, and state banking departments for state-chartered banks. Among requirements for charter approval are competent management, a commitment to the local community, and ability to obtain deposit insurance. *See also* ARTICLES OF INCORPORATION.

CHARTER CONVERSION *see* CONVERSION.

CHARTING *see* TECHNICAL ANALYSIS.

CHATTEL MORTGAGE lien giving a lender a security interest in personal property, as opposed to real estate (land, buildings) pledged as collateral for repayment of a loan. Chattels can be any kind of movable property, such as automobiles, jewelry, and so on. *See also* CONDITIONAL SALES CONTRACT.

CHEAP MONEY said of credit available when interest rates are low and banks are willing to lend their EXCESS RESERVES, presumably with minimal repayment risk, to a creditworthy borrower.

CHECK demand draft drawn on a bank, payable to the writer or to a third party; also called a DEMAND DEPOSIT. Checks are NEGOTIABLE INSTRUMENTS, transferable to another person. A check signed by the DRAWER, or MAKER, can be voided only by a STOP PAYMENT order. The ability to offer checking accounts is one of the criteria determining whether a financial institution is, in fact, a bank, as defined by the Bank Holding Company Act. *See also* CASHIER'S CHECK; CERTIFIED CHECK; DRAFT; NEGOTIABLE ORDER OF WITHDRAWAL (NOW) ACCOUNT; PAYMENT ORDER; SUPER NOW ACCOUNT; THIRD PARTY CHECK.

CHECKABLE DEPOSITS deposit accounts that may be drawn against by writing CHECKS or DRAFTS. The term includes, in addition to DEMAND DEPOSIT accounts, any negotiable payment order, such as a NOW account—Negotiable Order of Withdrawal—or a SUPER NOW ACCOUNT. The Monetary Control Act of 1980 placed all check-like bank deposits under the same category for the purpose of calculating Reserve Requirements. The Dodd-Frank Act of 2010 gave approval to payment of interest on corporate checking accounts, reversing a long-standing ban dating to the 1930s.

CHECK CARD Visa or MasterCard debit card that deducts funds from a cardholder's checking account. Check cards are frequently accepted by restaurants and other merchants that also accept Visa or MasterCard credit cards as a replacement for personal checks.

CHECK CLEARING movement of a check from the bank or depository institution where it was deposited back to the bank on which it was written (the DRAWEE bank or paying bank). The term also covers the movement of funds from paying bank to receiving bank, the corresponding credit and debit to the accounts involved, and the return of checks (for insufficient funds in the check writer's account, for example) back to the paying bank. The Federal Reserve Banks operate a nationwide check clearing system. *See also* REGIONAL CHECK PROCESSING CENTER.

CHECK CONVERSION bank merchant service that reformats payments, for example, a check written to pay a utility bill, into an ELECTRONIC CHECK, which is then forwarded to the paying bank through the U.S. banking system's AUTOMATED CLEARING HOUSE. Merchants receiving electronic check payments get access to their funds more quickly, as electronic checks are paid before paper checks. Also called *accounts receivable conversion*.

CHECK CREDIT unsecured revolving line of credit, often used as a substitute for bank credit cards. Check credit functions as a cash advance against a bank card line of credit, but the drafts are processed as checks. Check credit may be a CASH RESERVE line of credit, or a special set of drafts that access a credit line. *See also* OVERDRAFT.

CHECK DIGIT final character in the nine-digit bank transit/routing number (ABA TRANSIT NUMBER plus CHECK ROUTING SYMBOL), validating a bank's transit and routing numbers in check processing. Some banks also use check digits to verify the accuracy of ACCOUNT NUMBERS.

CHECK GUARANTEE merchant service that, for a fee, guarantees that a customer's check will be paid. Check guarantee services compare checking account numbers against a file of known bad check writers.

CHECK HOLD number of days a bank can legally hold uncollected funds before crediting deposited funds to a customer's account. The Expedited Funds Availability Act of 1987 limits check holds to two business days for LOCAL CHECKS and five days for nonlocal checks. The first $100 of any check must be available for use the next business day. *See also* AVAILABILITY SCHEDULE; REGULATION CC.

CHECK KITING drawing against balances credited to uncollected checks. For example: a person deposits a $1,000 check in bank ABC, drawn on funds in bank XYZ. Before the first check clears he deposits a $1,000 check in bank XYZ, drawn on the first bank, and a $2,000 check drawn on bank XYZ in bank ABC. By carefully timing the checks, he has accumulated $3,000 in fictitious balances. Check kiting schemes can be very elaborate, and have been known to cause bank failures. Kiting is best controlled by monitoring unpaid checks in the process of collection.

CHECKLESS SOCIETY notion that ELECTRONIC FUNDS TRANSFER (EFT) would someday replace check writing as the accepted way of transferring economic value. Innovations in financial services develop slowly, often taking 20 years or longer to become mature systems with broad consumer acceptance. However, financial innovation alone cannot completely reduce check writing. While newer services such as AUTOMATED TELLER MACHINES and INTERNET BANKING appeal to many consumers, banks also continue to offer popular low-cost checking accounts and personal service.

CHECK ROUTING SYMBOL denominator (lower number) of a fraction appearing in the upper right corner of checks paid through the Federal Reserve System. The ABA TRANSIT NUMBER is the upper number. The routing symbol is a three- to four-digit number identifying the Federal Reserve district of the drawee (paying) bank, the Federal Reserve facility through which the check is collected, and the funds availability assigned by the Fed. Checks given IMMEDIATE CREDIT, indicated by a 0 as the final digit in the routing symbol, are payable the same day as presented to a Federal Reserve Bank for collection. A

DEFERRED AVAILABILITY check (identifiable by the numbers 1 through 9 in the final digit) is paid by a Federal Reserve Bank in two business days. For example: 50-226/ 213

CHECK 21 federal law enacted in 2003 allowing the recipient of a check to create a digital version of the original check (a SUBSTITUTE CHECK), thereby eliminating the need for further handling of the physical document. The Check 21 law became effective one year later, in 2004. Full name: Check Clearing for the 21st Century Act. *See also* TRUNCATION.

CHECK, STOP PAYMENT *see* STOP PAYMENT.

CHICAGO BOARD OF TRADE *see* FUTURES EXCHANGES.

CHINESE WALL popular name for the legal separation between a commercial bank and its trust department, designed to prevent conflicts of interest that may influence the trust department's role as a FIDUCIARY and investment advisor for trust accounts. *See also* VOLCKER RULE.

CHIP CARD *see* SMART CARD.

CHRISTMAS CLUB *see* CLUB ACCOUNT.

CHURNING

Banking:

1. lending and refinancing, replacing old debt with new debt to collect commitment fees and other fees.
2. in collection of past-due loans, extracting token payments from delinquent borrowers, without curing the delinquency (restoring the debt to current paid status).
3. in a loan portfolio, replacing expired accounts with new accounts, without increasing the number of accounts. This happens most often in a highly competitive market, as in bank credit cards.

Securities: excessive trading in a customer's account designed solely to increase broker's commissions—an illegal practice under SEC rules.

CITY BANK *see* RESERVE CITY BANK.

CLAIM

1. rights to assets held by another, for example, a depositor's claim to assets of a bank or a creditor's claim represented by a LIEN.
2. rights to an estate, for example, a life interest in the property of a deceased spouse.
3. owner's right of possession, represented by a CERTIFICATE OF TITLE.

CLASS

1. securities issued as part of a group, or having similar characteristics, such as bonds issued under the same INDENTURE. Synonymous with TRANCHE.

2. one of several types of stock issued by a corporation, for example, Class A or Class B. Usually only one class has voting rights.
3. group of creditors in a bankruptcy case, ranked by seniority of claim. For example, secured creditors holding liens or mortgages.

CLASSIFIED LOAN *see* ADVERSELY CLASSIFIED ASSETS; NONACCRUAL ASSET.

CLEAN

1. **Accounting.** Auditor's certificate in which no irregularities are disclosed. Also called an *unqualified opinion.*
2. **Banking.** To be free of debt, as during a borrower's annual clean-up period when bank lines of credit are paid down to a zero balance owed. *See also* CLEAN-UP REQUIREMENT.
3. **International Trade.** A bill of exchange, draft, or LETTER OF CREDIT without shipping documents attached, usually issued to organizations with good credit.

CLEAN FLOAT market condition in which the value of a nation's currency in relation to other currencies is determined purely by free market forces. There are almost no cleanly floating Western currencies, i.e., currencies that are not supported one way or another through INTERVENTION by central banks. *See also* DIRTY FLOAT.

CLEAN TITLE TITLE to real property, free of liens or judgments giving the named title holder legal rights of ownership. A clean title is normally required to get a MORTGAGE from a bank. Contrast with CLOUD ON TITLE.

CLEAN-UP REQUIREMENT contractual requirement that a borrower pay off any outstanding balance on a one-year renewable LINE-OF-CREDIT and reduce usage of the line to zero for a specified period. Once required as a proof that the borrower is not dependent on the lender for permanent financing, these provisions are becoming less common in banking. Also called *annual clean-up.*

CLEAR

1. COLLECTION of checks deposited in a bank, with payment to the depositor. *See also* CLEARINGS.
2. matching of trades between buyers and sellers of securities, financial futures contracts, and so on, by an exchange or clearing house.
3. clear TITLE, or marketable title, without liens or encumbrances.

CLEARING CORPORATION organization affiliated with a financial exchange through which brokers, financial institutions, and other parties settle trades efficiently and with minimum paperwork. Clearing corporations handle the validation, delivery, and settlement of securities transactions. Examples are the Depository Trust and Clearing Corporation (DTCC; formerly Depository Trust Company), National Securities Clearing Corporation (a DTCC subsidiary).

CLEARINGHOUSE

1. **Banking.** Association of banks organized to exchange checks, drafts, or other payments types, including electronic transfers. A clearinghouse maintains a daily log of transactions it accepts. At the close of business the clearinghouse arranges the SETTLEMENT of obligations and transfer of funds from members who owe money to members who have money due. In its capacity as a central facility, the clearinghouse acts as buyer to all sellers and seller to all buyers. *See also* AUTOMATED CLEARINGHOUSE; CLEARING CORPORATION; CLEARING HOUSE FUNDS; NETTING; NET SETTLEMENT.
2. **Futures.** An agency affiliated with a commodities exchange through which transactions are settled, through delivery of the commodity or purchase of offsetting futures positions.

CLEARING HOUSE AUTOMATED PAYMENTS SYSTEM (CHAPS) private telecommunication and payment system for interbank clearing of British POUND STERLING payments, operated since 1984 by the Bankers Clearing House of London.

CLEARINGHOUSE FUNDS funds passed through the check clearing system prior to approval or credit. Personal or business checks are available in one to three business days, if drawn on a local bank, or five days if payable by a nonlocal financial institution. Contrast with FEDERAL FUNDS, which are available the same day.

CLEARING HOUSE INTERBANK PAYMENTS SYSTEM (CHIPS) privately owned funds transfer system that handles time-sensitive, high-value payments between the world's major banks. This clearing house processes about 95% of the dollar-denominated payments moving between countries around the world, including trade-related payments and foreign exchange trades. CHIPS, which is operated by the Clearing House Payments Co. LLC in New York City, has operated since 2001 as a real-time clearing and settlement system. *See also* FEDERAL WIRE; SOCIETY FOR WORLDWIDE INTERBANK FINANCIAL TELECOMMUNICATION.

CLEARINGS *see* CHECK CLEARING.

CLOSE to consummate an agreement, sale, or transfer of assets.

1. **Accounting.** The transfer of final entries from subsidiary ledgers to a balance sheet ledger, a process known as closing the books.
2. **Real Estate.** The rights of ownership are transferred in exchange for monetary and other considerations. At a loan closing, promissory notes are signed and checks exchanged.
3. **Securities.** End-of-day trading, referring to trades occurring within half an hour of the closing bell. Also, the final price of a security traded on a public exchange.
4. **Underwriting.** Exchange of checks and securities after an offering of securities has been placed with investors.

CLOSED ACCOUNT account with a zero-balance, debits equaling credits.

CLOSED-END CREDIT loan or extension of credit in which the loan principal cannot be increased after funds are disbursed and the loan is partially repaid. The loan may require periodic payment of principal and interest, as in an installment loan, or repayment of the entire loan principal at maturity. Contrast with OPEN-END CREDIT, such as a bank credit card or a home equity line of credit.

CLOSED-END FUND investment trust that pools the assets of investors and issues a fixed number of shares. In contrast, an open-end fund or a MUTUAL FUND that continuously offers new shares to the public or offers to repurchase shares at NET ASSET VALUE. Shares of closed-end funds are traded over-the-counter or on stock exchanges and may trade at a premium or discount from the net asset value per share.

CLOSED-END LEASE consumer lease that does not give the lessee the option of buying the leased property when the lease expires. The lessee makes a fixed monthly payment for a specified number of months, and has no further obligation afterward. This type of lease is most common in automobile leasing. Contrast with OPEN-END LEASE, which may have a BALLOON PAYMENT at the end of the lease.

CLOSED-END MORTGAGE bond secured by a mortgage on real estate prohibiting the borrower from using the mortgaged property as collateral for any other debts or repaying the debt early except with consent of the bondholders.

CLOSING COSTS borrower's out-of-pocket expenses in closing a mortgage loan as listed in the HUD-1 SETTLEMENT STATEMENT. These costs include origination fees and closing points, title insurance, attorney fees, land survey, and such prepaid items as taxes and insurance escrow payments.

CLOSING DATE date on which ASSET-BACKED SECURITIES are first authenticated and delivered by the issuer. The bond indenture or indenture supplement is finalized, collateral is delivered to the trustee, legal documents are executed, and cash is received by the issuer on this date.

CLOSING POINTS sum paid by a home buyer to the mortgage lender at loan closing to increase the loan's effective yield. One point is equal to 1% of the loan amount. Also called a *discount point.*

CLOSING STATEMENT *see* HUD-1 SETTLEMENT STATEMENT.

CLOUD ON TITLE TITLE that is encumbered by prior liens, attachments, or court judgments, impairing the owner's ability to transfer title to someone else. Distinguish from CLEAN TITLE.

CLUB ACCOUNT
1. deposit accounts of unincorporated voluntary associations.
2. special purpose savings account, often issued with a coupon book. These accounts normally pay interest and have a maximum one-year maturity. Examples are Christmas club, Chanukah club, holiday club, and vacation club.

CO-BRANDED CARD Visa or MasterCard credit card jointly sponsored by a bank and retail merchant. Co-branded cards can be issued at less cost than conventional retail private label cards, and give issuing banks access to new customers. Cardholders may be given incentives, such as discounts on merchandise, rebates, or discounts off purchases. A co-branded card has a tie-in with a specific merchant rather than an association or professional group. It also can be used at other merchants. Contrast with AFFINITY CARD.

CODE OF ETHICS rules and procedures of professional conduct, for example, the Risk Management Associates Code of Ethics.

COLLAR two-sided interest rate guaranty protecting both the borrower and lender. It consists of a FLOOR and an INTEREST RATE CAP. The lower end, the floor, assures the lender the rate will not fall below a fixed amount; the upper end, the cap, assures the borrower that the cost of credit will not rise above a stated level. The cap protects the borrower from interest rate risk if rates rise quickly. Often, the lender is willing to reduce the cost of an interest rate cap if the borrower accepts an interest rate floor as well.

COLLATERAL asset pledged as security to ensure payment or performance of an obligation. In bank lending, it is generally something of value owned by the borrower. If the borrower defaults, the asset pledged may be taken and sold by the lender to fulfill completion of the original contract. Four types of collateral, as recognized by the Uniform Commercial Code, are commonly used in secured lending: (1) trade goods, (2) paper (negotiable instruments and title documents), (3) intangibles, and (4) business proceeds (cash). Collateral assigned to the lender can even be the asset being financed, as in ASSET-BASED LENDING, where a loan might be secured by business inventory or accounts receivable. In a home mortgage loan, the borrower gives the lender a MORTGAGE on the house being purchased.

When bank assets are securitized, or converted into marketable securities in the SECONDARY MARKET, the PRINCIPAL and INTEREST payments serve as collateral for the securities offered for sale to investors.

See also ASSET-BACKED SECURITIES; COLLATERAL LOAN; SECURITY AGREEMENT; SECURITY INTEREST; SIDE COLLATERAL.

COLLATERALIZE to secure a debt in part or in full by pledge of COLLATERAL. *See also* ASSIGNMENT; HYPOTHECATION.

COLLATERALIZED BOND OBLIGATION (CBO) multiclass security backed by a pool of corporate bonds. CBO securities are similar to collateralized mortgage obligations but are divided into various classes, called bond tranches, according to credit quality. There is at least one class of investment-grade bonds that provides liquidity to a bond portfolio holding mostly noninvestment grade or high-yield junk bonds.

COLLATERALIZED DEBT OBLIGATION (CDO) diversified, multiclass security similar to a COLLATERALIZED MORTGAGE OBLIGATION and backed by pools of bonds, bank loans, or other assets. A CDO may own corporate bonds, commercial loans, asset-backed securities, residential mortgage-backed securities, commercial mortgage-backed securities, and emerging market debt. These securities are typically divided into several classes, or bond tranches, that have differing levels of credit tolerances and typically contain at least one class of investment-grade bonds. Most CDO issues are structured in a way that enables the senior bond classes and mezzanine classes to receive investment-grade credit ratings; credit risk is shifted to the most junior class of securities. If any defaults occur in the assets backing a CDO, the senior bond classes are first in line to receive principal and interest payments, followed by the mezzanine classes and finally by the lowest rated (or nonrated) class, which is known as the equity tranche. The term CDO may also refer to the investment vehicle—known formally as a SPECIAL-PURPOSE VEHICLE—created to hold assets backing a CDO investment portfolio.

COLLATERALIZED LOAN OBLIGATION (CLO) multiclass security similar to a COLLATERALIZED DEBT OBLIGATION except that the assets securing the obligation are commercial bank loans. By issuing collateralized loan obligations, banks can reduce their regulatory capital requirements and reduce the risk associated with commercial lending.

COLLATERALIZED MORTGAGE OBLIGATION (CMO) mortgage-backed bond secured by the cash flow of a pool of mortgages. In a CMO, the regular principal and interest payments made by borrowers are separated into different payment streams, creating several bonds that repay invested capital at different rates.

A given pool generally secures several different classes of CMO bonds. A CMO pays the bondholder on a schedule that differs from the mortgage pool as a whole, and includes fast pay, medium pay, and slow pay bonds to suit the needs of different investors. The common arrangements include: a fast-pay bond with a maturity much shorter than the total pool; a bond paying interest only for a period that may be fixed on contingent on how prior CMOs perform, before payment of principal begins; and a bond paying variable interest based on an index, typically the LONDON INTERBANK OFFERED RATE (LIBOR), even though the mortgages themselves may be fixed rate loans.

Fast paying bonds appeal mostly to financial institutions seeking short-term liquidity investments, whereas longer-term CMOs appeal to the investment needs of pension funds and institutional investors. The first CMOs were issued by the Federal Home Loan Mortgage Corp. (Freddie Mac) in 1983. CMOs manage the prepayment risk associated with mortgage-related securities by splitting the pools of mortgage loans into different categories. CMOs pay principal and interest semiannually.

A CMO can be a nonrecourse sale of assets by the issuer, or a liability of the issuer, depending on how a transaction is arranged. The accounting rules in issuing these securities are complex.

See also ACCRUAL BOND; PASS-THROUGH SECURITY; PAY-THROUGH SECURITY, REAL ESTATE MORTGAGE INVESTMENT CONDUIT.

COLLATERAL LOAN loan secured by a pledge of assets. Loans secured by collateral are primarily commercial loans where the ultimate source of repayment is the borrower's assets, rather than the borrower's character or reputation in the community. The lender's FINANCING STATEMENT lists the collateral securing the loan, and the location and condition of the collateral. When filed with a public records office, a LIEN is created, giving the lender priority over other creditors. *See also* ASSET-BASED LENDING; CASH FLOW LOAN; MORTGAGE; PERFECTED LIEN; SECURITY AGREEMENT; SECURITY INTEREST; UNIFORM COMMERCIAL CODE.

COLLATERAL TRUST NOTE

1. short-term COMMERCIAL PAPER issued by a mortgage banker to finance its inventory of loans. These notes are issued under a trust indenture, and are collateralized by a pool of mortgages. Holders of the notes have equal claim with lenders originating the mortgages.
2. short-term notes secured by pledged bonds or other securities, most often issued by railroads, holding companies, and investment trusts.

COLLATERAL VALUE estimate of value of borrower's pledged collateral as determined by APPRAISAL. *See also* LOAN-TO-VALUE RATIO.

COLLATERAL VALUE INSURANCE business insurance that guarantees the value of appraised collateral and establishes a minimum liquidation value. Generally, the machinery, inventory, or equipment offered for collateral is appraised, and a certificate of guarantee is then issued. This form of lender protection is available from insurers and is used mostly in ASSET-BASED LENDING.

COLLECTED BALANCE checking account cash balance after deducting checks drawn on other banks. Generally defined as account ledger balances, less unpaid checks in the process of collection. A bank may count a deposited check as funds available for use by its customer in two business days, but usually will not include it in the depositor's collected balance for five or six days. This allows time for the drawer bank to return the check because of insufficient funds in the check maker's account or for other reasons. Contrast with AVAILABLE BALANCE.

COLLECTION

1. PRESENTMENT of checks, drafts, and other negotiable instruments to the point of origin, and receiving payment from the paying bank. The term covers CASH ITEMS such as checks and drafts, and also *noncash items,* including acceptances, bonds, and notes, which are referred to as COLLECTION ITEMS. Cash items receive immediate credit, but collection items are credited only when paid.
2. handling of past-due accounts by specialists, who attempt to get a promise to pay from the delinquent borrower and ultimately recover all or part of the debt. *See also* SKIP ACCOUNT.

COLLECTION ITEM

1. banking term for checks, drafts, or negotiable instruments that are credited to the customer's account after final payment is received. Also called *noncash item. See also* WIRE FATE ITEM.
2. delinquent or past due obligation turned over to a debt collection agency.

COLLECTION PERIOD period of time required to convert deposited checks into collected balances. The Expedited Funds Availability Act of 1987 requires banks to credit funds to a customer's account within two days from the date of deposit for local checks, and within five days for nonlocal checks. *See also* AVAILABILITY SCHEDULE.

COLLECTIVE INVESTMENT FUND pooled fund operated by a bank or trust company for investment of the assets of separate trust accounts; also known as MASTER TRUST accounting. Pooling helps the investors obtain diversification of investments, improved earnings, and economies of scale. National banks and many state chartered banks are authorized to manage master trust accounts.

COLON monetary unit of Costa Rica and El Salvador.

COMAKER person who signs a borrower's PROMISSORY NOTE to give a loan additional security or to enhance the quality of a loan. A comaker has a liability similar to an *endorser* or *guarantor,* although in a strict legal sense a guarantor or endorser cannot be compelled to honor the note until certain conditions are met.

COMBINED LOAN-TO-VALUE RATIO (CLTV) sum of the face value of all mortgages on a property divided by the market value of that property. The CLTV ratio is a measure of credit risk in the second lien and high loan-to-value sectors of the home equity market.

COMBINED STATEMENT ACCOUNT STATEMENT listing account activity in demand deposit, including statement savings; time deposit account and balances owed on revolving credit lines, telephone banking transactions, and so on. Combined statements save postage and the costs of printing and mailing separate statements; *See also* DESCRIPTIVE STATEMENT; PAPERLESS STATEMENT.

COMFORT LETTER

1. in UNDERWRITING, a letter from an independent auditor reporting the procedures followed in reviewing unaudited financial statements and other data in preparing the registration statement and prospectus. Sometimes called *cold comfort letter.*
2. letter indicating that a bank holding company will honor its end-of-day net settlement position in an electronic payment system. Comfort letters are commonly used in the Clearing House Interbank Payments System network in New York to reduce the possibility that a CHIPS member will fail to meet its payment obligations to other banks.

COMMERCIAL AND INDUSTRIAL (C&I) LOAN LOAN to a corporation, commercial enterprise, or joint venture, as opposed to a loan to a consumer. C&I loans can be a source of working capital, or finance the purchase of manufacturing plants and equipment. These loans are generally short-term, are secured by COLLATERAL pledged by the borrower or are fully unsecured, and usually are made at flexible rates. Generally, the rate is pegged to the bank PRIME RATE: or a money market rate, such as the LONDON INTERBANK OFFERED RATE (LIBOR). Many lenders also require borrowers to file periodic financial statements, usually annually, and meet other conditions, such as maintaining proper insurance on the loan collateral. *See also* CONTINUATION STATEMENT; CORPORATE RESOLUTION; COVENANT; DEMAND LOAN; FINANCING STATEMENT; SECURITY AGREEMENT; SECURITY INTEREST; TERM LOAN; TIME LOAN.

COMMERCIAL ACCOUNT bank account maintained by a business, generally a checking account. Business checking accounts generally have higher monthly activity fees and service charges than accounts owned by individuals but receive an EARNINGS CREDIT RATE (ECR) based on average collected balances. *See also* ACCOUNT ANALYSIS; BUSINESS CREDIT; NONPERSONAL TIME DEPOSIT.

COMMERCIAL BANK state bank or NATIONAL BANK, owned by stockholders, that accepts demand deposits, makes commercial and industrial loans, and performs other banking services for the public. The term commercial bank is synonymous with FULL SERVICE BANK, because many commercial banks supply trust services, foreign exchange, trade financing, and international banking. Most state chartered trust companies are also commercial banks. Commercial bank deposits are insured by the DEPOSIT INSURANCE FUND, a federal insurance fund managed by the Federal Deposit Insurance Corporation. *See also* INDEPENDENT BANK; NONBANK BANK; SECURITIES SUBSIDIARY.

COMMERCIAL LETTER OF CREDIT *see* LETTER OF CREDIT.

COMMERCIAL LOAN *see* COMMERCIAL & INDUSTRIAL LOAN.

COMMERCIAL MORTGAGE loan secured by commercial real estate, usually with a 20- to 40-year term. Commercial mortgages differ in many ways from residential mortgage loans. These are highly customized financings and are usually pegged to a BASE RATE such as the bank PRIME RATE, and are sometimes made at fixed rates. Rates and payment terms are negotiated in each loan by the borrower and the lender. Commercial mortgages have commitment fees and can be quite profitable for mortgage lenders, although there is some default risk. Commercial mortgage financing is frequently arranged through multilender SYNDICATES or LOAN PARTICIPATIONS arranged by a lead bank. *See also* INTEREST ONLY LOAN; ZERO-COUPON MORTGAGE.

COMMERCIAL MORTGAGE-BACKED SECURITIES (CMBS) securities backed by mortgages on commercial properties such as multifamily apartment buildings, office towers, industrial buildings, hotels, and retail shopping malls. Commercial mortgage securities are usually collateralized by fixed-rate mortgages that are locked out from prepaying for 5 to 10 years but may also have floating-rate bonds collateralized by shorter-term prepayable mortgages. The pool of securities has a multiclass structure starting with investment—grade bonds that are rated triple-A extending all the way down to unrated junior class bonds. If any mortgage loan defaults, losses are allocated to the lowest rated bonds and recoveries are credited to the senior-level investment-grade bonds. This allocation of loss enables the entire collateral loan pool to be sold to a variety of investors. Investor analysis usually focuses on the pools' default and liquidation potential to prepay higher-rated classes or create losses for the lower rated credit classes.

COMMERCIAL PAPER short-term promissory note, or unsecured money market obligation, issued by prime rated commercial firms and financial companies, with maturities from 2 days up to 270 days. The most active market is in issues under 30 days.

Commercial paper is, in effect, a promissory note of the issuer used to finance current obligations, and is a NEGOTIABLE INSTRUMENT as defined by the UNIFORM COMMERCIAL CODE. Interest rates on commercial paper are often lower than bank loan rates, which makes the commercial paper market an attractive alternative to issuers, particularly in periods of TIGHT MONEY and high interest rates.

Most commercial paper rates are quoted on a discount basis, although some paper is interest-bearing. Issuers market their paper through dealers, or alternatively through direct placement with an investor. Commercial paper is rated by debt rating agencies and generally is backed by a bank LINE OF CREDIT. Secondary market sales are limited, as issuers are able to closely match the maturity needs of investors.

COMMINGLED FUNDS

1. **Asset-Based Lending.** A borrower's cash collateral account mixed with other accounts kept by the lender.
2. **Trusts.** A COMMON TRUST FUND managed by a bank trust department for employee benefit plans, retirement plans of self-employed workers. These funds give the participants greater investment diversifi-

cation and safety of principal, at lower operating cost for the bank. The Federal Reserve Board has permitted bank trust departments to offer commingled accounts, much like MUTUAL FUNDS, to customers with INDIVIDUAL RETIREMENT ACCOUNTS. *See also* MASTER TRUST.

COMMISSION

1. broker's charge for executing a trade.
2. fee, a percentage of the selling price of property, paid to a real estate broker.
3. fee paid to a bank's TRUST DEPARTMENT, normally a percentage of the income from a trust account.

COMMISSION HOUSE *see* FUTURES COMMISSION MERCHANT.

COMMISSIONER OF BANKING *see* STATE BANKING DEPARTMENT.

COMMITMENT

1. lender's agreement to make a loan at a quoted rate during a specific future period. Usually, a COMMITMENT FEE is charged for this service. *See also* LOCK-IN PERIOD.
2. mortgage originating bank's contractual agreement to deliver a specified number of mortgage loans to a secondary market CONDUIT. *See also* STANDBY COMMITMENT.

COMMITMENT FEE lender's charge for holding credit available. The fee may be waived for some borrowers. In business credit, commitment fees often are charged for an unused portion of a LINE OF CREDIT.

COMMITMENT LETTER form letter from a lender stating willingness to advance funds to a named borrower, repayable at a specified rate and time period. This is a common notice in loans that are real estate secured, such as home equity lines of credit and second mortgages, subject to an escape clause allowing the lender to rescind the agreement in event of materially adverse changes in the borrower's financial condition.

COMMITTEE ON UNIFORM SECURITIES IDENTIFICATION PROCEDURES (CUSIP) *see* CUSIP NUMBER.

COMMODITIES FUTURES TRADING COMMISSION (CFTC) independent federal agency created by Congress in 1974 to regulate the commodity futures market. Traders engaged in the commodities markets are required to register with the CFTC. The CFTC has authority to set margin requirements, regulate options contracts in commodities, and supervise registered FUTURES COMMISSION MERCHANTS.

COMMODITY CREDIT CORPORATION government corporation under the U.S. Department of Agriculture that finances public price supports for farm commodities. The agency gives its financial backing to bank letters of credit supporting commodity exports.

COMMODITY PAPER note, bill of exchange, or trade acceptance secured by shipping documents or a warehouse terminal receipt, which is payable on demand. Bank endorsed commodity paper is eligible for REDISCOUNT under Federal Reserve REGULATION A.

COMMON LAW body of law based on judicial decisions and precedent that has become the basis of the legal system in Great Britain and the United States (except in Louisiana, where *civil law* is the legal foundation). Many of the legal concepts in use today, including the law of contracts, are derived from common law.

COMMON STOCK security representing equity ownership in a corporation. Holders of common stock have the right to elect directors and collect dividends. Common stock claims are subordinate to bondholder claims, preferred stockholders, and general creditors.

COMMON TRUST FUND collective investment fund managed by a bank trust department. A common trust fund is similar to an open-end investment company or MUTUAL FUND, but participation is limited to those with trust accounts. Federal law permitted the tax-free conversion of common trust fund assets into mutual funds after December 31, 1995.

COMMUNITY BANK *see* INDEPENDENT BANK.

COMMUNITY DEVELOPMENT BANK bank-sponsored financial institution, also called a *community development corporation,* making business loans and mortgages in economically distressed communities. Community development banks are backed by federal deposit insurance and may receive startup capital from federal grants or from banks and savings associations.

COMMUNITY PROPERTY property shared by husband and wife, each having a half-interest in the earnings of the other; the form of joint property ownership in several states. Most states adhere to common law rules of property ownership where each spouse owns what he or she earns.

COMMUNITY REINVESTMENT ACT (CRA) federal law requiring banks to meet the credit needs of their entire community where they accept deposits, including low- and moderate-income neighborhoods. Financial supervisory agencies use a four-tier rating system in assessing compliance with the CRA, and make available for public inspection the CRA rating assigned to a lender. CRA compliance ratings *(outstanding, satisfactory, needs to improve,* and *substantial noncompliance)* are available from the FEDERAL DEPOSIT INSURANCE CORPORATION and bank regulatory agencies. *See also* REDLINING; REGULATION C.

COMORTGAGOR *see* COMAKER.

COMPENSATING BALANCE checking account balance used to pay for bank services. The balance offsets bank expenses in servicing a loan or line of credit. A loan contract, for example, may call for 10 and 5 compensating balances—10% of the credit line at commitment time and an additional 5% when the borrower draws against the credit.

COMPETITIVE BID public auction bid containing prices and terms offered by an underwriter for a new issue of securities. Issuers select the underwriter bidding the best (highest) price and lowest interest cost. The highest price must be combined with the interest coupon to arrive at NET INTEREST COST or NIC.

Underwriting proposals for most municipal general obligation bonds, railroad bonds, and public utility bonds are submitted in this bid form. U.S. Treasury securities also are marketed through competitive bidding by dealer banks bidding the highest price (and lowest yield) for new Treasury bills, notes, and bonds. Contrast with NEGOTIATED UNDERWRITING. *See also* NONCOMPETITIVE BID.

COMPETITIVE BID OPTION commercial loan SYNDICATE where banks submit auction bids for a loan, and have the option of selling loan participations to other banks or investors. The lead bank in the syndicate generally retains only a small portion of the financing in its own portfolio. Competitive bidding by U.S. banks for commercial and industrial (C&I) loans is similar to TENDER PANEL bidding in the Eurocredit market where a group of banks make bids to purchase short-term corporate notes through a REVOLVING UNDERWRITING FACILITY.

COMPLIANCE EXAMINATION periodic bank examination by a federal regulatory agency to ensure compliance with consumer protection regulations, such as the COMMUNITY REINVESTMENT ACT, the EQUAL CREDIT OPPORTUNITY ACT, or the TRUTH IN LENDING ACT. Compliance exams are intended to uncover any violations of consumer protection regulations so that remedial action can be taken.

COMPOSITION agreement between an insolvent debtor and his creditors, whereby the creditors accept less than the full value of their claims. Considered an expedient alternative to bankruptcy, composition plans are most often agreed to in small, unincorporated businesses rather than larger firms. Creditors are inclined to accept partial repayment in the belief that an operating business is better than one that liquidates to pay off its creditors. Compare WAGE-EARNER PLAN.

COMPOUND INTEREST interest added to interest previously earned on a principal balance. Compounding increases the depositor's rate of return on bank balances and the lender's effective yield on the unpaid principal of outstanding loans. For example: take a $1,000 savings account paying 5% interest, compounded monthly; the EFFECTIVE RATE earned is 5.116%, assuming the $1,000 remains on deposit for a full year and no additional deposits are made. The more frequently interest is compounded, the higher the effective rate earned. Contrast with SIMPLE INTEREST, where interest is computed only on the original principal. *See also* DAILY INTEREST; RULE OF 72.

COMPOUND RATE OF RETURN *see* INTERNAL RATE OF RETURN.

COMPOUND INTEREST

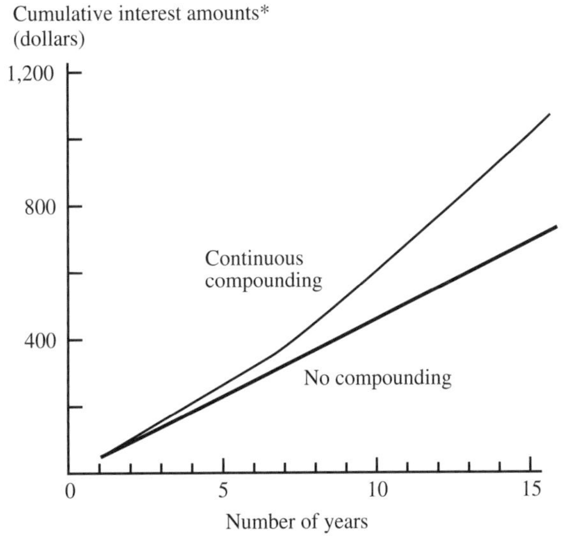

*Amount paid on $1,000 at 5% annual interest rate.

Source: John R. Brick, ed., *Bank Management* (Richmond, Virginia: Robert F. Dame, Inc., 1980), p. 475.

COMPTROLLER OF THE CURRENCY chief regulator of national banks, appointed by the President for a five-year term, with Senate confirmation. The Office of the Comptroller of the Currency, the supervisory agency for nationally chartered banks, is the oldest federal regulator of financial institutions. The Comptroller of the Currency also serves as one of the three directors of the Federal Deposit Insurance Corp. The GRAMM-LEACH-BLILEY ACT OF 1999 authorized the Office of the Comptroller of the Currency, a U.S. Treasury Department agency, to approve non-banking activities of national banks that are determined by the Treasury Department to be "financial in nature," and thus permissible activities for national banks. The Dodd-Frank Act gave the Comptroller's Office authority to supervise federally chartered thrifts and also gave the Comptroller authority to write regulations implementing banking legislation (rule-making authority) for thrifts of all sizes. *See also* FEDERAL FINANCIAL INSTITUTIONS EXAMINATION COUNCIL.

COMPUTERIZED LOAN ORIGINATION (CLO) online network that lists residential mortgage loans, including rates and fees, offered by different mortgage lenders, accessible through mortgage brokers and real estate agents. Many CLO networks also support online mortgage applications. CLO networks give home buyers the convenience of comparison shopping mortgage loans from competing lenders directly from the broker's office. A downside risk is the list of participating lenders may not be very extensive. Mortgage originators use CLO networks to offer home buyers rapid approval of mortgage applications, and also to pool mortgages for resale in the SECONDARY MORTGAGE MARKET.

CONCENTRATION

1. condition of a bank's loan portfolio measured by the number of loans extended to a particular industry. Excessive lending to a single industry (agriculture, oil and gas exploration, real estate) indicates a lack of DIVERSIFICATION in the loan portfolio, and potential credit risk. In general, most banks report loan concentrations above 50% of equity. The Securities and Exchange Commission requires banks to disclose in financial reports any concentration exceeding 10% of loans. *See also* ASSET QUALITY; LIQUIDITY.
2. share of deposits owned by a bank in a given market. The U.S. Department of Justice uses a statistical yardstick, the Herfindahl Index, in gauging the anticompetitive effects of bank mergers. The index is calculated by adding the market shares of a product, such as deposits, owned by banks in a market and squaring the results. The index indicates both the number of firms in a market and their relative size. For example, a market with five firms, each having individual market shares of 30, 20, 20, 20, and 10 percent would have an index of 2200. Generally, the Justice Department will not challenge a merger unless the post-merger index is at least 1800 and the merger causes an increase of at least 200 on the scale.

CONCENTRATION ACCOUNT deposit account into which funds are periodically transferred from various local banks, via wire transfer or automated clearing house debit, from other accounts in the same bank, or in different banks. *See also* LOCK BOX; ZERO-BALANCE ACCOUNT.

CONCENTRATION BANK bank that maintains a CONCENTRATION ACCOUNT for a corporate customer. Usually this bank is also the corporation's LEAD BANK, having the firm's primary deposit account, and may offer investment advice, funds transfer, and other NONCREDIT SERVICES. *See also* TREASURY WORKSTATION.

CONDITIONAL COMMITMENT

1. lender's agreement to provide financing to a qualified borrower, provided the borrower obtains insurance or satisfies other requirements.
2. notice from a federal loan guaranty agency, such as the Federal Home Administration, that it has agreed to insure a mortgage loan, subject to the limitations in the guarantee.

CONDITIONAL PREPAYMENT RATE (CPR) mortgage prepayment model in which the average monthly prepayment rate is annualized by multiplying by 12. CPR expresses prepayment as ratio of prepayments to outstandings, usually a percentage of the mortgage balance outstanding at the beginning of the year that will be prepaid that year. CPR is a predictor of CASH FLOW YIELDS from Collateralized Mortgage Obligation issues.

CONDITIONAL SALES CONTRACT agreement commonly used in real estate finance and commercial finance, whereby the seller retains title through a purchase money security interest. Ownership passes to the purchaser when installments are fully paid. *See also* FINANCE LEASE.

CONDOMINIUM single housing unit in a multiple-unit building. The owner holds legal title to the unit and pays property taxes plus a share of the building's common charges for maintenance and upkeep. The owner may sell, rent, or mortgage the unit just as if it were a single-family house. Compare to COOPERATIVE.

CONDUIT government or private organization that assembles mortgage and other loans into a large pool, and issues pass-through or pay-through securities in its own name to investors. The first mortgage conduits were established by the Government National Mortgage Association and the Federal Home Loan Mortgage Corp. Private sector conduits have since been organized by mortgage insurance companies and financial institutions to issue securities backed by mortgages, credit card receivables, boat loans, and other loans, without federal agency guarantee. Mortgage conduits make it easier for a large number of banks and thrifts to sell their loans to secondary market investors, as smaller lenders are not limited by pool size or eligibility restrictions. *See also* ASSET-BACKED SECURITIES; COLLATERALIZED MORTGAGE OBLIGATION; PASS-THROUGH SECURITY; PAY-THROUGH SECURITY.

CONFERENCE OF STATE BANK SUPERVISORS (CSBS) *see* TRADE ASSOCIATION.

CONFESSION OF JUDGMENT loan clause by which the borrower waives his claim to mortgaged property without hearing or notice if the lender obtains a DEFICIENCY JUDGMENT in event of default. This credit practice was prohibited by regulation in 1985.

CONFIRMATION

1. written communication to the counterparty reciting all the relevant details of a transaction.
2. audit function whereby a bank requests customers to verify account balances; a means of detecting deposit fraud. *Positive confirmation* requests that every balance be checked; *negative confirmation* requests a reply only if errors or account differences are found. *See also* POSITIVE PAY.
3. in bankruptcy, acceptance of a debt repayment plan by creditors.

CONFIRMED LETTER OF CREDIT LETTER OF CREDIT in international trade guaranteed by a second bank, in addition to the bank originally issuing the credit. The confirming bank agrees to pay or accept drafts against the credit even if the issuer refuses. A confirmed letter of credit also protects against unfavorable exchange regulations and shortages of foreign currency in the importing country.

CONFORMING LOAN residential mortgage loan that meets Fannie Mae or Freddie Mac underwriting guidelines. Conforming loans may be retained by the originator or sold in the secondary mortgage market to Fannie Mae or Freddie Mac. The loan limit for single-family homes is revised annually according to year-to-year changes in average purchase prices.

CONSERVATOR

1. court appointed person to manage and protect the interests of an estate or the affairs of a person judged incompetent.
2. official appointed by a banking regulator to protect the assets of a troubled bank or savings institution while a permanent solution to its financial problems is worked out. A bank declared to be insolvent is placed under control of a RECEIVER, and assets sold to pay its creditors.

CONSIDERATION something of value voluntarily exchanged by parties to an agreement, making the agreement a legally binding CONTRACT on all of the parties involved. In banking, it is the lending of money in exchange for a borrower's promise to repay the loan, put up collateral, or both.

CONSOLIDATED FINANCIAL STATEMENT

1. accounting statement combining the assets and liabilities of a bank, its domestic branches, and major subsidiaries in a single statement. Major commercial banks report changes in their financial position weekly to the Federal Reserve Board of Governors. *See also* REPORT OF CONDITION.
2. FINANCIAL STATEMENT combining assets, liabilities, and shareholder's equity of affiliated companies for reporting or disclosure purposes.

CONSOLIDATION LOAN installment loan that enables a borrower to combine several outstanding loans under one loan, rather than several smaller ones, often with a lower monthly payment.

CONSORTIUM BANK European MERCHANT BANK owned by banks from different countries, and engaged primarily in international banking. Consortium banks, originating in the 1960s and 1970s, are less active in Euromarket lending than they once were.

CONSTANT MATURITY TREASURY (CMT) INDEX weekly average of bond dealer quotes on Treasury securities with the same remaining time to maturity. The one-year CMT yield, calculated from Treasury issues maturing in one year, is a widely used index for adjustable-rate mortgages. Other Treasury indexes used in mortgage lending are the three-year and five-year CMT.

CONSTANT PAYMENT periodic payment of a fixed amount that includes interest and principal. As the loan is paid off, a greater portion of each payment is allocated to reducing the principal. For example, a fixed-rate home mortgage loan.

CONSTANT PERCENT PREPAYMENT annualized estimate of mortgage loan prepayments, computed by multiplying the average monthly prepayment rate by 12. *See also* CONDITIONAL PREPAYMENT RATE.

CONSTRUCTION LOAN *see* CONSTRUCTION MORTGAGE.

CONSTRUCTION MORTGAGE interim loan covering construction and development costs, secured by a MORTGAGE on the property financed, also called a *construction loan.* Funds are advanced at specific stages of construction, in so-called *progress payments*, with a portion held back until completion of the project, a certain percentage of the building has been leased, or other criteria have been met. Construction financing is paid off from the proceeds of a permanent mortgage by an INSTITUTIONAL LENDER, for example a life insurance company, pension fund or bank. However, some lenders have made construction loans on speculation, without a FIRM COMMITMENT by a take-out lender.

CONSTRUCTIVE NOTICE notice in a newspaper or public record presumed to be legally sufficient notice of actions taken, for example, the recording of liens, escheats of abandoned property to the state, and so on. Constructive notice is enforceable under the law if given in a legally prescribed manner. Distinguish from *actual notice*, in which a person is notified of a pending action by letter or in person.

CONSULAR INVOICE certification by a consul or government official covering an international shipment of goods. A consular invoice, obtained from the consul of the importing country at the point of shipment, insures that the exporter's trade papers are in order and the goods being shipped do not violate any laws or trade restrictions. AD VALOREM taxes or specific import duties are determined from a consular invoice.

CONSUMER ADVISORY COUNCIL group established by Congress in 1976 to advise the Federal Reserve Board on its responsibilities under the Consumer Credit Protection Act and other credit related issues. The council, drawn from a diverse group of consumers and lenders, meets three times a year, but has no real power.

CONSUMER BANKERS ASSOCIATION *see* TRADE ASSOCIATION.

CONSUMER CREDIT credit extended to individuals for personal or household use, rather than businesses. Broadly defined, consumer credit includes all forms of INSTALLMENT CREDIT other than loans secured by real estate (home mortgages, for instance) plus OPEN-END CREDIT such as credit cards. New forms of credit, however, have blurred these distinctions; a HOME EQUITY CREDIT line is a revolving line of credit secured by real estate—a lien on the borrower's home.

Many traditional forms of consumer credit, such as auto loans, have standard monthly payments—fixed repayment schedules of one to five years or more—and are made at either fixed interest rates or variable rates that are based on an INDEX. Consumer loans fill a variety of needs: financing the purchase of an automobile or household appliance, home improvement, debt consolidation, and so on. These loans may be unsecured or secured by an assignment of title, as in an auto loan, or money in a bank account. Consumer debt is monitored by the Federal Reserve Board, and is one of the leading indicators of growth in the economy. *See also* AMORTIZATION SCHEDULE; CLOSED-END CREDIT; HOME EQUITY CREDIT; RULE OF THE 78'S; REGULATION B; REGULATION Z; SIMPLE INTEREST.

CONSUMER CREDIT PROTECTION ACT *see* TRUTH IN LENDING ACT; REGULATION Z.

CONSUMER FINANCIAL PROTECTION BUREAU (CFPB) agency created by the Dodd-Frank Act of 2010 to enforce consumer protection regulations across all federal agencies. An independent agency within the Federal Reserve, the CFPB can write rules for banks, payday lenders, debt collectors, mortgage brokers, and credit unions; examine banks and credit unions with assets of $10 billion or more, mortgage-related businesses, and some nonbank financial firms; impose fines or ask courts to order relief to curb abusive practices; monitor markets for potential consumer risks; require banks and financial companies to disclose costs and risks of financial products; and also review and comment on consumer complaints. Web site: *www.consumerfinance.gov.*

CONSUMER INTEREST finance charge on bank card and retail credit card purchases, cash advances, educational loans, and other types of consumer credit. Since 1991, consumer interest is no longer deductible for tax purposes. Contrast with mortgage-related interest and business interest, which remain tax deductible. *See also* TAX-DEDUCTIBLE INTEREST.

CONSUMER LEASE contract for a lease of personal property, such as an automobile, boat, or household appliance with a total obligation under $25,000. Lease financing has a fixed schedule of monthly payments, usually over a three- to five-year period, and may include an option to purchase the leased property at maturity. Bank lessors are required by Federal Reserve REGULATION M to disclose the actual cost to the consumer. This includes security deposits, monthly payments, taxes, and registration costs, and in an OPEN-END LEASE, whether a BALLOON PAYMENT is due at maturity.

CONSUMER REPORTING AGENCY *see* CREDIT BUREAU.

CONSUMMATION actual time when a credit agreement becomes a legally binding contract between a financial institution and a borrower. Depending on state laws, this may occur when the loan documents are signed, as in a mortgage closing, when the lender accepts a credit application, or when the lender makes a firm commitment to extend credit.

CONTACTLESS CARD bank card enabling users to make purchases by waving or tapping the card at a retail merchant's checkout. Contactless cards, currently tested by a small number of banks, also have applications as mass transit fare cards and personal identification cards.

CONTEMPORANEOUS RESERVES method of calculating bank RESERVE REQUIREMENTS for deposit accounts and VAULT CASH based on currently outstanding balances. Bank assets and liabilities used in calculating reserve requirements maintained at a Federal Reserve Bank are added up on Monday and reported on the Wednesday of that same week. *See also* LAGGED RESERVES.

CONTINGENT INTEREST *see* FUTURE INTEREST.

CONTINGENT LIABILITY

1. obligation of a person who signs a promissory note as an ACCOMMODATION ENDORSER, COMAKER, or GUARANTOR, becoming liable for payment in the event the original borrower defaults.
2. financial obligation of a bank that is dependent on future events or actions of another party, such as a standing agreement to lend money if a borrower cannot obtain alternate financing. Included are standby letters of credit, commitments to make or purchase loans, and participations in acceptances, financial futures, and forward contracts. These are ordinarily reported as OFF-BALANCE SHEET ITEMS in a bank's CALL REPORT.

CONTINGENT RESERVE funds set aside from net earnings to cover unexpected needs, such as unanticipated loan losses, future taxes, and interest expense. *See also* LOAN LOSS RESERVES.

CONTINUATION STATEMENT amendment to a borrower's financing statement extending a lender's lien. A lender's FINANCING STATEMENT granting a security interest in pledged collateral ordinarily expires after five years under the UNIFORM COMMERCIAL CODE. It may be extended beyond that period by filing a continuation statement with the secretary of state and other public officials, as specified in the laws in the jurisdiction where the property is located. *See also* PERFECTED LIEN.

CONTRA ACCOUNT accounting entry offsetting another account; its balance is subtracted. For example, the LOAN LOSS RESERVES account offsets a bank's LOAN account, an earning asset on the BALANCE SHEET.

CONTRACT

1. **General.** An agreement backed by lawful consideration to carry out actions, exchange assets, or refrain from doing things. A legally

valid contract is reached through mutual agreement by persons with the capacity to negotiate, in which each gives up something of value. It must be for a lawful purpose.

2. **Futures.** (1) A trading unit in a financial future; (2) An agreement between buyer and seller of a futures contract as defined by a commodities exchange or exchange clearinghouse.
3. **Foreign Exchange.** An agreement by two parties to exchange one currency for another at a specified future date.

CONTRACT MONTH month in which contracts to deliver commodities or financial instruments in a futures exchange are satisfied by making or taking delivery. In reality, most commodity and interest rate futures contracts are closed out or liquidated before the contract delivery date by reversing the original transaction. Also called *delivery month.*

CONTRACT OF SALE agreement to transfer title to real property or tangible assets at a given price. Actual delivery is effected by delivery of a signed, sealed, and acknowledged deed. This may happen days or months later, normally when the buyer has fulfilled certain conditions, such as making a certain number of payments. *See also* CONDITIONAL SALES CONTRACT.

CONTRACTUAL CLEARING BALANCE amount a bank maintains at a Federal Reserve Bank in addition to any funds deposited to meet its RESERVE REQUIREMENTS. The arrangement gives the bank flexibility to pay its daily transaction obligations without overdrawing its reserve account. The additional funds deposited in a reserve account can also be used to pay for services provided by Federal Reserve Banks.

CONTROLLED AMORTIZATION BOND (CAB) *see* PLANNED AMORTIZATION CLASS.

CONTRIBUTION

1. amount invested annually in a retirement savings plan or salary reduction plan.
2. donation or gift to a charitable organization.

CONTROLLED DISBURSEMENT in corporate CASH MANAGEMENT, a funds management technique designed to maximize the funds available for investment or for payment to trade creditors. Excess funds can be invested in the money market. Contrast with DELAYED DISBURSEMENT, which emphasizes clearing of checks through remote locations to extend check clearing time and FEDERAL RESERVE FLOAT on uncollected checks. *See also* FEDERAL RESERVE FLOAT.

CONVENTIONAL MORTGAGE residential MORTGAGE not backed by federal insurance or guarantee. In the secondary mortgage market, Fannie Mae and Freddie Mac are the major purchasers of conventional loans.

CONVERSION

1. exchange of banking charter by a bank or thrift institution, for example, a state chartered bank applying for a national charter from the Comptroller of the Currency, or vice versa. Charter conversions allow a bank to take advantage of differences in banking regulation, such as more liberal LEGAL LENDING LIMITS for state chartered banks in some states.
2. switching from mutual ownership to stock ownership through a common stock RIGHTS OFFERING, done by a savings bank or savings and loan association to raise equity capital.
3. switching an ADJUSTABLE RATE MORTGAGE to a fixed rate loan, often at no additional charge to the borrower if done within a specified period.
4. exchange of a convertible security, such as a CAPITAL NOTE or a DEBENTURE for a specified number of common stock shares.
5. exchange of mutual fund shares for shares in another fund, often at no charge if the transfer is within a family of funds.
6. in tort law, the wrongful taking of property that belongs to someone else, as when a TRUSTEE uses assets in a trust fund for personal benefit.

CONVERSION PRIVILEGE feature in some ADJUSTABLE RATE MORTGAGES allowing the borrower to switch to a fixed rate loan usually at the end of the first rate adjustment period.

CONVERTIBLE

1. ADJUSTABLE RATE MORTGAGE that can be exchanged, at the borrower's option, for a fixed rate mortgage, usually in the first one to five years. The cost of switching to a fixed rate loan is generally less than the cost of refinancing.
2. DEBENTURE or PREFERRED STOCK that can be exchanged at a set price for a predetermined number of common stock shares.
3. currency easily exchanged for another currency or an equivalent amount of gold.
4. revolving line of credit exchanged for a fixed-maturity term loan.

CONVEXITY in bonds and other fixed-income securities, a measure of the rate of change in DURATION, the actual maturity of a fixed-income security. It is called convexity because the shape of the typical yield curve measuring price versus maturity of a security, for example, a ten-year Treasury bond, is somewhat rounded or convex in shape. The ten-year Treasury bond is said to have *positive convexity*.

In contrast, mortgage-backed securities and pools of mortgage loans have *negative convexity* because when current interest rates drop to a certain point below the rate at which the loans were made, borrowers tend to refinance their loans, paying off their old mortgages and taking out new loans. Mortgage prepayments shorten the duration of mortgage-backed securities, causing a drop in price. Thus, convexity tries to explain the difference between estimated prices of a security and market prices that are influenced by changes in interest rates.

CONVEXITY

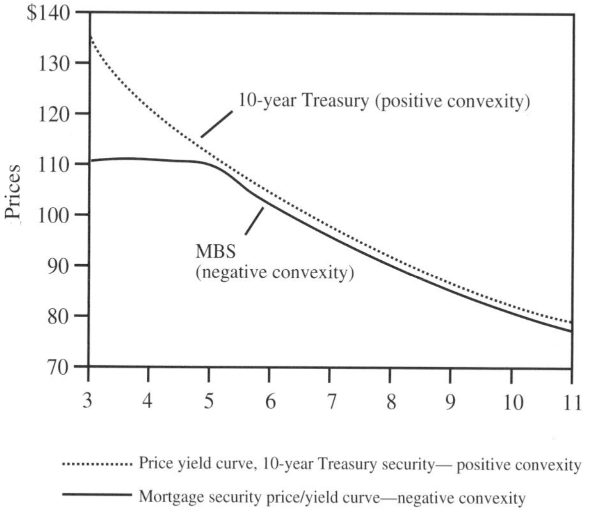

Source: William W. Barlett, *Mortgage-Backed Securities* (New York: Institute of Finance, 1989), p. 203.

CONVEYANCE transfer of TITLE to real property from buyer to seller by MORTGAGE or deed of trust. Also the document effecting a legal transfer.

COOPERATIVE form of multiple ownership real estate in which property units are owned by a nonprofit corporation or business trust, which grants occupancy rights to individual tenants; also called a co-op. Property owners buy shares in the corporation representing their ownership of an apartment or office, and pay the corporation a share of real estate taxes, building maintenance, and other overhead expenses. Loan interest and property taxes paid by the corporation are tax deductible by individual tenants.

COOPERATIVE BANK member-owned organization, similar to a mutual SAVINGS AND LOAN ASSOCIATION, that makes loans and pays interest on pooled deposits. Cooperatives in the United States are CREDIT UNIONS, Federal Intermediate Credit Banks, and Banks for Cooperatives in the FARM CREDIT SYSTEM, and state chartered savings associations in several New England states.

CORDOBA (GOLD CORDOBA) monetary unit of Nicaragua.

CORE CAPITAL common stock, preferred stock, paid-in capital, and retained earnings included in the calculation of a financial institution's required minimum capital. In financial reports filed with banking regulatory agencies, core capital is generally referred to as TIER 1 capital.

CORE DEPOSITS deposits acquired in a bank's natural market area, counted as a stable source of funds for lending. These deposits have a predictable cost, imply a degree of customer loyalty, and are less interest rate sensitive than short-term CERTIFICATES OF DEPOSIT and BROKERED DEPOSIT accounts. Included are small denomination TIME DEPOSITS and checking accounts.

CORPORATE AGENT banking services performed on an agency basis for corporations and government entities. Among these are check clearing, dividend and interest payment, stock registration and redemption, and tax collection for government agencies. These generate fee income for the providing bank. *See also* NONCREDIT SERVICES.

CORPORATE RESOLUTION legal document adopted by a corporation's board of directors and signed by the corporate secretary, specifying who may sign checks, borrow money, and otherwise do business with a bank. Many banks have adopted standard corporate resolution forms to facilitate the loan documentation in commercial credit. The corporate resolution, and often a copy of a corporation's charter and bylaws, are kept in the loan files at the various lending institutions where it does business. Also called *corporate borrowing resolution.*

CORPORATE TRADE EXCHANGE (CTX) electronic funds transfer used by corporations and government agencies to pay trading partners through the AUTOMATED CLEARING HOUSE (ACH) system. The CTX payment format combines payment information and a variable length record (called an addendum record) with related information, such as invoice numbers, allowing multiple payments to trade creditors in a single transfer of funds. *See also* CASH CONCENTRATION & DISBURSEMENT; CORPORATE TRADE PAYMENT; ELECTRONIC DATA INTERCHANGE.

CORPORATE TRADE PAYMENT (CTP) electronic funds transfer used by corporations and government agencies to pay trade creditors through the AUTOMATED CLEARING HOUSE (ACH). The CTP is less flexible than the CORPORATE TRADE EXCHANGE, and was phased out in 1996. *See also* CASH CONCENTRATION & DISBURSEMENT; ELECTRONIC DATA INTERCHANGE.

CORPORATION business organization treated as an entity—an artificial person distinct from its owners—in the eyes of the law. Ownership is represented by shares of stock. A corporation has three distinguishing characteristics: (1) separation of ownership from management and limited liability, i.e., its liability to creditors is limited to its resources, unlike partnerships or sole proprietor businesses that have unlimited personal liability; (2) the ability to negotiate contracts and own property; and (3) transferable ownership, assuring its existence beyond the lives of its stockholders. Stockholders elect corporate directors, who in turn decide its policies. *See also* ARTICLES OF INCORPORATION; CORPORATE RESOLUTION; LIMITED LIABILITY COMPANY; SUB-CHAPTER S.

CORPUS

1. PRINCIPAL of a trust, as distinct from interest income, which may consist of stocks, bonds, bank accounts, real estate, or other property contributed by the donor.
2. principal amount of an investment note or bond. Compare to COUPON.
3. principal in a zero-coupon debt issue, which pays no interest to the holder until final maturity.

CORRESPONDENT

1. bank that holds deposits for other banks and performs services, such as check clearing. The deposit balance is a form of payment for services. Many community banks clear checks drawn on out-of-town banks through RESERVE ACCOUNTS at a larger bank. Correspondent banks also buy participations in loans exceeding the LEGAL LENDING LIMIT of a smaller bank, called the RESPONDENT, and give these banks access to financial markets, such as the foreign exchange market or financial futures market, that are ordinarily beyond the reach of smaller financial institutions.
2. mortgage banker or broker who services mortgage loans for a fee, collecting principal and interest payments plus real estate taxes.

COSIGNER *see* ACCOMMODATION ENDORSER; COMAKER.

COST ACCOUNTING accounting system allocating direct and indirect costs of bank services to various departmental units. Internal cost accounting considers various factors in pricing bank services, and typically includes the following: overhead, including building rent, utilities, administrative support, and executive salaries; selling costs, which include advertising, promotional expenses, and salaries of account executives and branch employees; and interest cost, or the cost of acquiring funds for lending or investing. Some bank expenses have fixed costs that remain more or less constant, such as employee salaries and rent; others have variable costs and are volume sensitive.

The MARGINAL COST OF FUNDS measures the cost of expanding deposits at the margin, that is the cost of one additional dollar unit of deposit or loan volume. Fully absorbed costing takes into consideration both interest expense and noninterest expenses, such as rent, insurance, and taxes, and frequently it is the basis of pricing banking services. A bank carries out a cost analysis of the product or service being considered and determines the yield required to meet its required return. Fully absorbed costing, also called *cost plus pricing,* often disadvantageously ignores customer demands and competitive pricing by other financial institutions.

See also BREAK-EVEN YIELD; COST OF FUNDS; RELATIONSHIP BANKING; TRANSFER PRICING.

COST OF FUNDS dollar cost of interest paid or accrued on funds acquired from various sources within a bank, and BORROWED FUNDS acquired from other banks, including time deposits, advances at the Federal Reserve DISCOUNT WINDOW, Federal Funds purchased, and Eurodollar deposits. A bank may use its internal cost of funds in pricing the loans it makes. *See also* COST OF FUNDS INDEX.

COST OF FUNDS INDEX (COFI) measure of interest paid on funds borrowed from depositors, or from other banks. The index is expressed as a percentage, such as the Federal Home Loan Bank index in mortgage lending, or the 11th district Federal Home Loan Bank index. A cost of funds index published by the Office of Thrift Supervision is often used by mortgage lenders as the base rate for adjusting rates on ADJUSTABLE RATE MORTGAGES.

COUNTERFEIT security, currency, or bank card made to appear genuine, with the intention of defrauding an unsuspecting person. Counterfeiting U.S. currency and bank cards is a felony under federal law, punishable by fines and prison terms. The U.S. Secret Service, a bureau of the Treasury Department, has responsibility for detecting and arresting counterfeiters.

COUNTER-PARTY

1. person at the opposite side of a repurchase agreement or swap agreement. The person who agrees to sell back securities sold in a repurchase agreement, or exchange at a later date currency values or interest rates in a swap agreement with another party.
2. bank that either purchases or sells back overnight Federal Reserve Funds (Fed Funds).

COUNTERSIGN signature vouching the authenticity of another's handwriting; a form of dual control when corporate checks are signed by more than one MAKER. A company's authorized check writers are listed in its CORPORATE RESOLUTION.

COUNTER-TRADE *see* BARTER.

COUNTRY BANK bank whose main office is outside a city with a Federal Reserve Bank or branch. Country banks generally have lower RESERVE REQUIREMENTS than RESERVE CITY BANKS, which are located in major cities having a Federal Reserve Bank. The term *country collections* is often used in reference to all banks outside the region where the sending bank is located.

COUNTRY CLUB BILLING credit card billing system in which copies of the original sales drafts are included with the monthly statement. Bank card issuers abandoned country club billing in the 1970s in favor of less costly DESCRIPTIVE STATEMENT billing—an itemized listing of account charges.

COUNTRY EXPOSURE LENDING SURVEY survey released by the Interagency Country Exposure Review Committee disclosing information on foreign lending of U.S. banks on a consolidated basis. Borrowers are ranked by loan type (public or private, maturity, cross-border, and nonlocal currency loans). The report, detailing loans to more than 190 countries, is issued quarterly.

COUNTRY LIMIT limit on the amount of money a bank is willing to lend to all borrowers, both public and private, in one country.

COUNTRY RISK risk that economic or political changes in a foreign country, for example, lack of currency reserves (FOREIGN EXCHANGE), will cause delays in loan payments to creditor banks or even repudiation of debt. Country risk is broader in scope than SOVEREIGN RISK as it takes into account the probability of debt repayment by private borrowers as well as central governments. Banks set aside funds in a reserve account, called the ALLOCATED TRANSFER RISK RESERVE, as a cushion against possible bad debt losses from foreign loans. The Asian financial crisis of 1997—which began with a currency devaluation in Thailand led to serious balance of payment problems in Asia, Russia, and Latin America—underscored this broad definition of country risk. Following the Asian crisis, international lenders came to view country risk as any event causing non-payment by private borrowers due to macroeconomic developments beyond their control. *See also* COUNTRY EXPOSURE LENDING SURVEY; COUNTRY LIMIT.

COUPON detachable certificates showing the dollar amount of interest payable to a bond holder at regular intervals, ordinarily semiannually. Coupons on a BEARER BOND are negotiable instruments and are processed just like checks. Bond interest on BOOK-ENTRY securities is credited to the owner's account.

COUPON RATE

1. nominal annual rate of interest the issuer of a note or bond promises to pay the holder during the period the securities are outstanding. In mortgage banking, it refers to the contract rate of interest on MORTGAGE-BACKED SECURITIES.
2. the annual rate of interest shown on the face of a loan agreement or mortgage.

COUPON STRIPPING process of separating the interest on a bond from the underlying principal. Coupon stripping is used most often to create U.S. Treasury zero-coupon securities known as STRIPS (Separate Trading of Registered Interest and Principal Securities) and similar zero-coupon investments. *See also* STRIPPED MORTGAGE-BACKED SECURITIES.

COUPON SWAP *see* INTEREST RATE SWAP.

COVENANT

1. language in a loan agreement by which the borrower pledges to do certain things and refrain from others. An *affirmative covenant* may require the borrower to maintain adequate property insurance, make timely loan payments, and provide audited financial statements. A *negative covenant* (also called a *restrictive covenant)* prohibits the borrower from selling or transferring assets, defaulting, or taking specific actions that would diminish the value of the collateral or impair the value of the lender's ability to collect the loan. Failure to perform as agreed might cause the lender to accelerate the loan, or call (demand full payment of) the loan.
2. enforceable clause in a bond contract protecting the interests of bondholders. There are various kinds of bond covenants: an agreement to charge sufficient fees, common in municipal bonds, to produce the required revenue (a *rate covenant*); an agreement not to sell or encumber the project (a *negative covenant*); an agreement to maintain adequate insurance and debt service (a *protective covenant*).

COVER

1. taking assignment of collateral as protection against borrower default. Synonymous with security. Also, allocating a part of net income against possible BAD DEBT losses.
2. to offset an account withdrawal by making a DEPOSIT.
3. purchase of currency or financial futures to offset or close a previously taken position. A short cover involves buying against contracts expiring in the same delivery month.
4. buying back securities previously sold in a SHORT SALE.
5. in corporate finance, ability of a corporation to service its debt obligations out of earnings.
6. in UNDERWRITING, the second highest bid in competitive bidding for a bond issue, called the *covering bid.*

COVERAGE RATIO financial ratio measuring a bank's ability to absorb potential losses from nonperforming loans. The ratio is calculated by dividing the ending balance of the LOAN LOSS RESERVES balance by total nonperforming loans.

COVERDELL EDUCATION SAVINGS ACCOUNT *see* EDUCATION SAVINGS ACCOUNT.

COVERED BOND debt securities backed by a pool of high-quality mortgages or public sector loans (the cover pool). Covered bonds are similar to ASSET-BACKED SECURITIES but legally are balance sheet obligations of the issuing bank. These bonds offer some investor protections, specifically the issuer's pledge to maintain credit quality. If default occurs, investors have recourse to both the pool and the issuing bank. Widely used in the Eurobond market, this type of financing entered the U.S. market in 2006 with a covered bond issue by Washington Mutual Savings.

COVERED INTEREST ARBITRAGE currency arbitrage carried out by purchasing financial instruments in different currencies and using a FORWARD EXCHANGE CONTRACT to lock in a yield. An investor buying a two-year bond dominated in German deutschemarks, yielding 5%, might exchange D-marks for dollars in the forward market to buy a U.S. dollar denominated security of comparable maturity yielding 9%.

COVERED OPTION call option backed by the security underlying the option contract. The writer, or seller, of the option collects a premium for writing the option, and has the securities to deliver if the option is exercised. Contrast with NAKED OPTION.

CRAMDOWN (1) debt repayment plan paying creditors less than the full amount owed. The confirmation is approved by the bankruptcy court as long as at least one class of adversely affected creditors agrees, and the debtor's repayment plan does not discriminate.

CRAMDOWN (2) loss of principal or interest caused by a bankruptcy court allowing a change in the original terms of a loan or mortgage.

CREATIVE FINANCING

1. **In general.** Any funds acquisition, bank lending, or capital raising technique that differs from standard industry practices. Borrowers often resort to innovative financing when financing from conventional sources is unavailable or can be arranged at more favorable terms using nonstandard financing techniques. Such techniques have become more common in the fixed income and equity markets in recent years.
2. **Commercial lending.** A customized loan in which the rate paid and credit terms are negotiated by borrower and lender. The lender may agree to arrange financing at an attractive rate and terms if a borrower assumes part of the credit risk in funding a loan. So-called *performance based loan pricing* also allows a lender to tailor a line of credit or revolving credit so that pricing is set according to the borrower's usage of the credit.
3. **Mortgages.** Any mortgage that differs from a 30-year CONVENTIONAL MORTGAGE in rate, credit terms, or other factors. Creative financing allows a lender to tailor mortgage financing to suit a borrower's income and financial situation, making home ownership more affordable by a wider group of borrowers. Reduced interest rate loans, seller buydowns, or jumbo loans are examples. Creative financing also can involve taking out a SECOND MORTGAGE at loan origination to lower the required down payment. Most creative mortgages are ineligible for purchase by federal agencies in the SECONDARY MORTGAGE MARKET. *See also* ALTERNATIVE MORTGAGE INSTRUMENT; SALE AND LEASEBACK.

CREDIT faith, from the Latin *credito.* An agreement by which something of value—goods, services, or money—is given in exchange for a promise to pay at a later date.

Banking:

1. lender's agreement to advance funds, based on an estimation that the debt will eventually be repaid, or to refrain from collecting a previously existing debt, as in a refinancing.

   Bank credit is classified by: type of borrower, for example, loans to consumers (mortgages, auto loans, credit cards) as opposed to loans to businesses (commercial lines of credit, working capital loans); type of collateral pledged, if any; and terms of repayment. Some bank loans are repaid according to a fixed schedule, for example, a 30-year mortgage; others such as a DEMAND LOAN to a business that may be called at any time by the lender.
2. used by bank credit analysts and lenders instead of BORROWER or LOAN. A lender might say, "I'll approve the credit if it's a four-year loan," or "I think the credit is good."
3. bookkeeping entry representing a deposit of funds into an account. In accounting, a credit entry notes an increase in liabilities, owner's equity, and revenues, and a decrease in assets and expenses. Contrast with DEBT. *See also* ABILITY TO PAY; CLOSED-END CREDIT; CREDIT ENHANCEMENT; CREDIT LINE; CREDIT RATING; CREDIT REPORT; CREDIT RISK; EQUAL CREDIT OPPORTUNITY ACT; EXTENSION AGREEMENT; FAIR CREDIT BILLING ACT; FAIR CREDIT REPORTING ACT; FORBEARANCE; INSTALLMENT CREDIT; LINE OF CREDIT; OPEN-END CREDIT; REGULATION B; REGULATION G; REGULATION T; REGULATION Z; REVOLVING CREDIT; SECURED LOAN; USURY.

CREDIT ANALYST

1. person who evaluates the financial history and financial statements of credit applicants, with an eye toward assessing creditworthiness. An analyst is trained to evaluate: 1) the applicant's financial strength; 2) the probability of full repayment; and 3) whether collateral or a cosigner is needed to adequately secure the loan.
2. person who evaluates the earnings and financial performance of corporations. The preferred term is financial analyst or securities analyst.

CREDIT APPLICATION oral or written request for an extension of credit, following the lender's procedures for the credit requested. Information regarding the cost of credit must be disclosed, such as the ANNUAL PERCENTAGE RATE, under Federal Reserve REGULATION Z, when a consumer formally applies for credit. A completed application means the lender has received all the information ordinarily received in evaluations for the amount and type of credit requested, including credit reports from a credit bureau, government guarantees, or approvals to insure or provide security for the credit. An application fee may be charged to cover loan processing and property appraisal costs, as in a mortgage. Advances under an existing credit arrangement, or rate shopping generally are not considered applications for credit, and do not require TRUTH IN LENDING disclosures by the lender.

CREDIT BALANCE account with payments exceeding the principal balance owed, as when a customer pays down a loan by making extra payments. In FACTORING, it is the amount owed to a customer when accounts receivable are purchased by a factor.

CREDIT BUREAU agency gathering data for banks, savings institutions, and other credit grantors on consumers' experience—their credit history—meeting obligations, based on information reported by credit grantors. This information is distributed for a fee to other credit grantors, who use it in deciding whether to approve or decline credit applications, and how much credit to offer any particular borrower. For example, credit card issuers offering preapproved credit cards routinely determine who gets an offer by screening credit bureau reports; accepting a card on the terms offered will open an account.

Amendments to the EQUAL CREDIT OPPORTUNITY ACT in 1996 broadened the rights of consumers (who are allowed to review their credit reports annually and dispute inaccurate information) by requiring credit bureaus to maintain a toll-free consumer service telephone number and to disclose the names of organizations requesting a consumer's credit report. Credit information is gathered by about 500 regional credit bureaus that report to three nationwide automated systems: Equifax, Inc., 1550 Peachtree Street NE, Atlanta, Georgia; Experian, 475 Anton Boulevard, Costa Mesa, California; and TransUnion LLC, 555 West Adams Street, Chicago, Illinois. *See also* CREDIT REPORT.

CREDIT CARD plastic card authorizing the account holder to charge purchases against a preapproved credit line. Credit cards are issued by banks, thrift institutions, retailers, gasoline companies, and other credit grantors. Card issuers may charge an ANNUAL FEE to cover account servicing costs.

Credit card purchases normally become payable after a GRACE PERIOD (up to 30 days) during which no finance charge is imposed. Afterward, the balance due may be paid in full or paid down in monthly installments of principal plus interest. Some issuers charge credit card interest from the purchase date if the cardholder's account has an outstanding balance. Credit card interest rates, annual fees, and repayment terms may vary considerably.

See also BALANCE TRANSFER CARD; CO-BRANDED CARD; DEBIT CARD; GOLD CARD; TRAVEL & ENTERTAINMENT CARD.

CREDIT CONTROL infrequently used powers of the Federal Reserve Board in carrying out MONETARY POLICY. The Federal Reserve's authority to assess SURCHARGES on bank reserves and impose reserve requirements on nonbank financial companies expired in 1982.

CREDIT COUNSELING credit advisory service offered to persons with excessive debts as an alternative to bankruptcy. Debt counselors affiliated with the National Foundation for Consumer Credit charge only a nominal monthly fee for helping consumers work their way out of debt. Consumers are budgeted a portion of take-home income to pay off current obligations and voluntarily curb their use of credit until debts are repaid.

CREDIT CRITERIA factors employed to determine a borrower's CREDITWORTHINESS, or ability to repay debt. Factors include the following: income, amount of personal debt carried, number of accounts from other credit sources, and credit history. A lender is free to use any credit-related factor in approving or denying a credit application so long as they do not violate the equal credit protections of Federal Reserve REGULATION B prohibiting credit discrimination on the basis of race, sex, or other factors.

CREDIT DEFAULT SWAP swap agreement enabling the transfer of third-party credit risk in exchange for a stream of regular payments (essentially a form of credit insurance) for a set time period. Commercial banks use credit default swaps to manage the credit risk associated with making large loans to their corporate customers. If a borrower defaults on a loan or another predefined CREDIT EVENT occurs, the counterparty providing the insurance purchases the defaulted asset.

Credit default swaps are a very common form of CREDIT DERIVATIVE. The objective in many credit derivatives, including default swaps, is to split market risk from credit risk; doing so effectively reduces a bank's exposure and its risk of loss.

CREDIT DENIAL turndown of an application for credit; also called a credit decline or rejection. The EQUAL CREDIT OPPORTUNITY ACT requires lenders who deny consumer credit applications to state in writing the reasons why the applicant was rejected. Reasons for denial can vary from insufficient information in the credit application or lack of previous borrowing experience to a poor credit history. If turned down on the basis of information supplied by other creditors, applicants have the opportunity, under REGULATION B, to review a copy of their credit report. *See also* ADVERSE ACTION; CREDIT SCORING; EFFECTS TEST.

CREDIT DEPARTMENT department in a bank that evaluates the financial condition of credit applicants and maintains a log of loan payments on currently outstanding loans. Credit information is gathered on a confidential basis and stored for future reference. The credit department also responds to requests by other lenders for credit information on a particular borrower. *See also* CREDIT REVIEW.

CREDIT DERIVATIVE derivative contract whose redemption value is linked to specified credit-related events, such as bankruptcy, credit downgrade, nonpayment, or default. These agreements gained popularity in the 1990s and have assumed numerous forms: credit default swaps, credit-linked notes, and total return swaps. Banks use credit derivatives to actively manage their credit risk to selected customers or counter-parties.

CREDIT ENHANCEMENT techniques used to improve the credit rating of an asset-backed security or a municipal bond, generally to get an investment grade rating from a bond rating agency and to improve the marketability of the securities to investors. There are two general classifications of credit enhancements: third-party enhancement, in which an insurance company or another third party pledges its own creditworthiness and guarantees repayment in exchange for a fee; and self-enhancement, which is generally done by the issuer through OVERCOLLATERALIZATION, i.e., pledging loans with a book value greater than the face value of the bonds offered for sale.

Third party enhancements take the form of a STANDBY LETTER OF CREDIT or COMMERCIAL LETTER OF CREDIT issued by a bank, a surety bond from an insurance company, or a special reserve fund managed by a FINANCIAL GUARANTEE firm. The type of enhancement used and the amount of credit protection purchased varies according to the characteristics of the portfolio. Holders of the securities issued have recourse against the guarantor to the extent of the guarantee. Lines of credit are sometimes referred to as *soft capital* because they would not ordinarily be called upon. *See also* BACKUP LINE.

CREDIT EVENT sudden change in a borrower's credit standing, such as bankruptcy or violation of a bond indenture or loan agreement, that raises doubts about the borrower's ability to repay future obligations. Credit events can trigger a payoff in a CREDIT DEFAULT SWAP, a common form of credit derivative, and are clearly defined in the swap agreement between the two counterparties. The defined events refer to changes in the underlying asset, not events affecting either of the contract counterparties.

CREDIT FILE record containing historical data on open or fully paid credit accounts. Credit files may contain personal financial statements, credit applications, and comments by credit analysts, as well as the current status of the account, payment history, current balance, credit limit, and so on.

CREDIT FREEZE account owner's instructions to a credit reporting agency barring sale or release of his or her financial information until the owner gives permission. Credit freezes are permitted by state law in most states. A credit freeze is different from credit monitoring, which notifies the account owner of suspicious activity reported to a credit bureau. Also called *security freeze*.

CREDIT HISTORY *see* CREDIT FILE.

CREDIT INSURANCE various types of insurance purchased by the borrower, and in some instances by the lender. If purchased by the bank, insurance is a hedge against abnormal credit losses. In consumer credit, credit life insurance or disability insurance purchased by the borrower pays the creditor in the event the borrower suffers an accident or dies before the debt is repaid. *See also* CREDIT ENHANCEMENT; PRIVATE MORTGAGE INSURANCE (PMI); SINGLE INTEREST INSURANCE.

CREDIT INVESTIGATION appraisal of a prospective borrower's ability and willingness to repay a loan, carried out by a CREDIT ANALYST. Before approving a loan, a lender may ask for credit references and personal or corporate financial statements, obtain a copy of the applicant's CREDIT REPORT, and also verify the applicant's salary with his or her employer.

CREDIT LIMIT credit card term, referring to the maximum balance allowed for a credit card customer, often set by a CREDIT SCORING model.

CREDIT LINE

1. maximum amount of credit available in an open-end credit arrangement such as a bank credit card, which the lender may change at any time. The line is disclosed in the credit card agreement.
2. funds available to a borrower for a specified period, subject to review before renewal, for example, a revolving LINE OF CREDIT.

CREDIT MONEY money backed by the full faith and credit of the issuing country as opposed to hard currency or gold. Most currencies in circulation today are credit money. Also called *fiat money.*

CREDITOR any lendor who, in the course of business, regularly extends credit, repayable by agreement, by a second party, the debtor. The loan may be repayable in several equal installments over a specified period, or in certain business loans, repayable in full at the option of either the borrower or the lender. A lender who takes an assignment of collateral has a claim on the borrower's assets, whereas a lender who lends on the strength of a borrower's character can look only to the borrower's future income.

CREDITORS' COMMITTEE group representing a class of creditors holding secured claims against a company in REORGANIZATION under Chapter 11 of the Bankruptcy Code. Large companies in bankruptcy, for example, a New York Stock Exchange listed company, may have several committees of creditors. The debtor company must offer an acceptable repayment plan to its creditors before a reorganization can be approved. *See also* CRAMDOWN; INVOLUNTARY BANKRUPTCY.

CREDIT QUALITY *see* ASSET QUALITY.

CREDIT RATING

1. lender's estimate of an individual's creditworthiness, based on past history of borrowing and repaying, employment, and information supplied by the prospective borrower in a credit application, as well as the applicant's CREDIT REPORT. Lenders often ask businesses to furnish tax returns and financial statements.

2. evaluation of creditworthiness of individuals and businesses by a CREDIT BUREAU. Many organizations are active in assigning credit ratings, including consumer credit bureaus, such as TransUnion LLC, and mercantile agencies, such as DUN & BRADSTREET.
3. BOND RATING.

CREDIT REFERENCE previous borrowing history offered as demonstration of creditworthiness in a CREDIT APPLICATION. Credit references are a source of supporting documentation in applying for bank credit.

CREDIT REPAIR consumer's right under the FAIR CREDIT REPORTING ACT to dispute credit history items disclosed in a CREDIT REPORT. CREDIT BUREAUS will investigate, and remove verifiable errors at the consumer's request. But accurate, though derogatory, information cannot be removed; legal judgments against the borrower remain in a credit report for seven years, and bankruptcies for ten years.

CREDIT REPORT

1. **Asset-Based Lending.** Periodic report listing merchandise returns, credit allowances, and so on, allowing the lender to monitor collateral backing the loan.
2. **Banking.** A report furnished by a CREDIT BUREAU when requested by a lender or the individual named in a report. A credit report lists available credit and a borrower's payment history including on-time payments, late payments, and the number of times a loan payment was missed. It also may include judgment liens to collect a debt, bankruptcy petitions, and tax liens. Credit reports retain adverse credit information for seven years, and bankruptcy petitions for a ten-year period. Federal law requires credit bureaus to give consumers the right to inspect their credit report and write comments if they disagree with it. Amendments to the Fair Credit Reporting Act enacted in 2003 allow consumers to get a free copy of their credit report annually from a Web-based clearinghouse, *www.annualcreditreport.com.*

CREDIT REPORTING AGENCY *see* CREDIT BUREAU.

CREDIT REVIEW follow-up monitoring of a loan or extension of credit by a senior loan committee, bank auditor, or regulatory agency. Credit review is intended to determine whether the loan was made in accordance with the lender's written credit standards and in compliance with banking regulations. Missing documentation or signatures on loan documents, if detected by the credit review process, can then be corrected by the lending officer, thus preventing a deterioration in credit quality and possible loss. Also called *loan review.*

CREDIT RISK risk that a borrower will not pay a loan as called for in the original loan agreement, and may eventually DEFAULT on the obligation. Credit risk is one of the primary risks in bank lending, in addition to INTEREST RATE RISK.

CREDIT SCORE numeric index estimating an individual's creditworthiness and ability to repay financial obligations, taking into account promptness in paying bills, length of credit history, available credit actually used, bankruptcy, and other negative events, and other factors. Consumer credit scoring models were originally developed in the 1950s by Fair Isaac Corporation and have since been widely used by banks, retail merchants, and others to evaluate credit risk and consumer probability of repayment.

FICO scores range from about 300 to a high of 850, with a score above 720 generally considered a "good credit" and a score below 600 a higher risk. Variations in credit scores can occur because credit reporting agencies process information in a borrower's credit report in different ways.

The three U.S. credit reporting companies, Equifax, Experian, and TransUnion, have a competing credit scoring model called VANTAGESCORE that evaluates creditworthiness in a slightly different way but uses many of the same credit variables—including payment history, credit balances, and length of credit history.

CREDIT SCORING methodology used by banks and other lenders, usually through computation of a numeric CREDIT SCORE, to determine how much credit, if any, to extend to an individual borrower. Banks use scoring to determine credit limits and interest rates. Scoring models have many applications besides risk scoring of credit applications, including estimating probability of default or bankruptcy and evaluating loan portfolio profitability and success probability in credit marketing. Credit reporting agencies have developed scoring systems that insurance companies can use in rating the quality of potential customers. *See also* CUT-OFF SCORE; DECISION TREE; EFFECTS TEST; JUDGMENTAL CREDIT ANALYSIS.

CREDIT SPREAD

1. yield difference between Treasury securities and comparable non-Treasury securities, such as mortgage-backed bonds, expressed in basis points. Credit spreads widen in recessions and grow tighter in economic expansions.
2. difference in value of two options on the same underlying security when the value of the option written (or sold) exceeds the value of the one bought.

CREDIT SWEEP business SWEEP ACCOUNT linked to a bank line of credit. Excess balances are automatically transferred from a checking account to pay down existing lines of credit; any remaining balances are invested in a money market fund or short-term investment. Also called *loan sweep*.

CREDIT TICKET bookkeeping memo for a credit transaction. For example, a deposit to a checking account or savings account. *See also* DEBIT TICKET.

CREDIT TRANCHE *see* TRANCHE.

CREDIT UNION not-for-profit financial cooperative that makes personal loans and offers other consumer banking services to persons sharing a common bond, typically employment at the same firm. Deregulation in the banking industry since the late 1970s has allowed credit unions to offer many of the same banking services as commercial banks, savings banks, and savings and loan associations. Federally chartered credit unions can write residential mortgages and issue credit cards. Many credit unions also offer interest-bearing transaction accounts (called a SHARE DRAFT ACCOUNT). Credit unions can charge below-market rates on loans while paying higher rates to savers, as they are exempt from federal and state taxes. The Credit Union Membership Access Act of 1998 permits credit unions to expand their membership to individuals residing in their local area (a community credit union). Credit unions get their operating funds from shares purchased by individual owners, who are called members, and pay dividends (representing the payment of interest) out of earnings.

The NATIONAL CREDIT UNION ADMINISTRATION, an independent federal agency chartered in 1970, is the primary regulator of national (federally chartered) credit unions. It also operates the National Credit Union Share Insurance Fund, which offers share deposit insurance up to $100,000 per account for qualifying federal and state credit unions, and the CENTRAL LIQUIDITY FACILITY, a lender-of-last resort for credit unions. *See also* SHARE ACCOUNT; SHARE DRAFT ACCOUNT.

CREDIT UNION NATIONAL ASSOCIATION *see* TRADE ASSOCIATION.

CREDITWORTHINESS general qualification for borrowing, based largely on a borrower's credit history, in the opinion of a lender or as determined by a CREDIT SCORING system if credit scoring is used.

CROSS-BORDER OUTSTANDINGS aggregate total of dollar-denominated loans and contingent obligations to foreign borrowers, including loans, bankers' acceptances, and standby letters of credit, plus deposits with foreign banks. Excluded are local currency transactions in foreign countries and deposits with branches of U.S. banks.

CROSS-COLLATERAL collateral covering several loans under a single security agreement, also called a *dragnet clause*. In essence, collateral for each loan backs the entire package of loans.

Language in a second mortgage loan stating the loan is in default if the borrower defaults on other loans secured by the same property is another type of cross-collateral.

CROSS-CURRENCY SWAP *see* CURRENCY SWAP.

CROSS-HEDGE hedge against INTEREST RATE RISK by purchase of a financial future in a different, but related, asset. A cross-hedge is used when there is no futures market for the asset owned or when it is more profitable not to use the same market. It assumes that similar financial instruments show correlation in their price movements. For example, hedging corporate bonds with Treasury bond futures.

CROSS-RATE currency EXCHANGE RATE computed by pricing two currencies against a third, usually the U.S. dollar. Foreign exchange dealers use currency cross-rate tables to look for arbitrage opportunities. Each major currency, such as the U.S. dollar or the British pound, has its own cross-rate.

CROSS-RATE TABLE

	U.S. Dollar	Euro	Yen	Canadian Dollar	Pound Sterling
Pound Sterling	0.6158	0.6384	0.5874	0.4207	—
Canadian Dollar	1.5679	1.5174	1.3962	—	2.3770
Yen	104.83	108.69	—	71.63	170.26
Euro	0.9646	—	0.9201	0.6590	1.5665
U.S. Dollar	—	1.0368	0.6429	0.6832	1.6241

CROSS-SELL selling more than one banking product at the customer service desk, for example, check OVERDRAFT protection to a customer opening a checking account. Cross-marketing is perfectly legal as long as there are no tie-in arrangements, i.e., making the sale conditional on acceptance of the add-on product.

CROWDING OUT heavy government borrowing when private sector organizations also want to borrow. Government agencies can theoretically pay almost any interest rate, but individuals and business borrowers may be unwilling to borrow at high interest rates. Crowding out rarely happens except in periods of sharply rising interest rates, and very tight money.

CRUMMEY TRUST trust allowing tax-free gifts to minors and limited withdrawals of interest or principal by the BENEFICIARY during a specified period, say 30 days a year, while the trust is in effect. A Crummey trust, unlike a *minor's trust,* does not require distribution of trust assets by age 21.

CURING OF DELINQUENCY *see* REINSTATEMENT.

CURRENCY

1. circulating money accepted as a medium of exchange for payment of debts; also called LEGAL TENDER. Generally, the term applies only to paper money—FEDERAL RESERVE NOTES in the United States—not coins. *See also* CURRENCY IN CIRCULATION.

2. NATIONAL CURRENCY, such as the U.S. dollar and the British pound sterling.

CURRENCY BAND range of upper and lower prices within which currencies are allowed to move against a reference currency or currencies of major trading partners. *See also* EUROPEAN MONETARY SYSTEM.

CURRENCY BASKET artificial currency used as reference notes in international monetary transactions. Nominal values of currency baskets vary as the prices of constituent currencies fluctuate. Examples are the ASIAN CURRENCY UNIT (ACU), the EUROPEAN CURRENCY UNIT (ECU), and International Monetary Fund SPECIAL DRAWING RIGHTS (SDRS).

CURRENCY FUTURES contract in the futures markets for exchange of currencies at a specific exchange rate. A futures contract is a standard contract, hedging against currency risk, for purchase of standard amounts of a specific currency (normally major currencies, such as the U.S. or Canadian dollar, British pound sterling, Japanese yen, German mark, or Chinese yuan). Contrast with FORWARD EXCHANGE CONTRACT.

CURRENCY IN CIRCULATION paper money and coins in the hands of consumers and businesses, as opposed to cash (VAULT CASH) held by financial institutions, or currency reserves of Federal Reserve Banks and the U.S. Treasury. Circulating currency is only a small fraction of the cash available for spending and it understates the MONEY SUPPLY, which is largely demand deposits or checking accounts in banks and savings institutions.

Currency held by the public is one of the key factors affecting BANK RESERVES. It is one of the statistical measures watched by the FEDERAL OPEN MARKET COMMITTEE trading desk at the Federal Reserve Bank of New York when the Fed decides to add or drain reserves from the banking system to stay within monetary policy targets.

CURRENCY OPTIONS contract giving the right, not the obligation, to buy or sell a specific quantity of one foreign currency in exchange for another at a fixed price; called the exercise price or STRIKE PRICE. The buyer of a currency option pays a premium to the seller. American-style options are exercisable on any date up to the contract expiration date; in contrast, European style options only can be exercised at specific future dates.

Foreign currency options for U.S. dollar, deutschmark, Canadian dollar, pound sterling, Swiss franc, and Japanese yen are traded OVER-THE-COUNTER by banks in major financial centers around the world. Exchange-traded currency options (British pound sterling, Canadian dollar, deutschmark, French franc and Swiss franc, and Japanese yen) are traded in the United States on the Philadelphia Stock Exchange. OTC trading in some markets coincides with the quarterly expiration cycles—March, June, September, and December—of exchange traded currency options.

CURRENCY SWAP agreement to exchange one currency for another at an agreed upon exchange rate. In a currency swap, the holder of an unwanted currency exchanges that currency for an equivalent amount of another currency to improve the market liquidity of a currency owned or to obtain bank financing at a lower rate. For example, company ABC obtains five-year below market financing from a German bank, and swaps deutschmarks for dollars with company ZYX, which has more U.S. dollars than it needs. At maturity, the swap is reversed. A *cross-currency swap* involves the exchange of a fixed rate obligation in one currency for a floating rate obligation in another. Swaps are technically borrowings, but unlike bank loans they are not ordinarily disclosed on the balance sheet. *See also* INTEREST RATE SWAP.

CROSS-CURRENCY INTEREST RATE SWAP

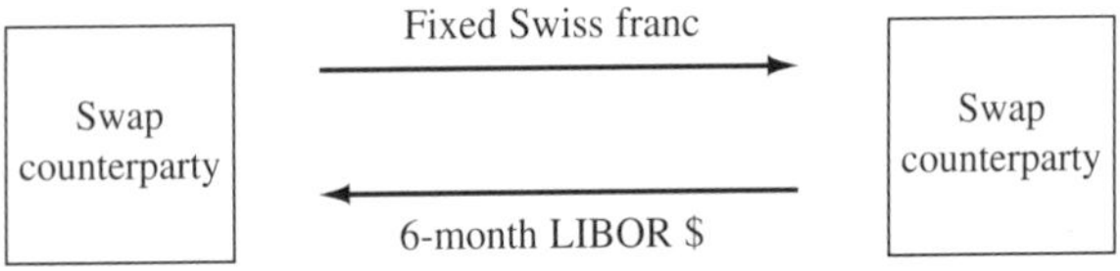

CURRENCY TRANSLATION process of restating balance sheet amounts denominated in one currency in terms of a second currency at current exchange rates. No actual exchange of funds takes place. Multinational corporations restate assets and liabilities, plus earnings of foreign subsidiaries in terms of a national reference currency. The resulting foreign currency translation exposure is recorded as an equity account on the balance sheet. At large banks, adjusted foreign currency translation is included as part of equity capital.

CURRENCY TRANSACTION REPORT (CTR) Internal Revenue Service (IRS) report that banks and thrift institutions are required by the Bank Secrecy Act to fill out detailing currency transactions of $10,000 or more.

CURRENCY WARRANTS detachable options in securities issues giving the holder the right to purchase additional securities denominated in a currency different from that of the original issue. The coupon and the price of the securities covered by the warrant are fixed at the time of the sale of the original issue.

CURRENT ACCOUNT portion of the BALANCE OF PAYMENTS consisting of exports and imports of goods and services, as well as transfer payments such as foreign aid grants. A current account surplus (or deficit) is the amount by which exports of goods and services plus inward transfers exceeds, or falls short of, imports of goods and services. It is the most widely accepted definition of international payment flows between countries.

CURRENT COUPON bond interest rate comparable to that earned by newly issued bonds with a similar COUPON RATE and maturity, and is the rate closest to prevailing market rates of interest. In other words, the bond is selling at a price close to its PAR VALUE. Its YIELD TO MATURITY is the same or nearly the same as its interest rate, or, in the case of floating rate bonds, the interest payable in the current period.

CURRENT MATURITY time interval from the present date to the maturity of a bond issue. Contrast with the ORIGINAL MATURITY, which is the time difference from the issue date to the scheduled maturity date.

CURRENT POOL FACTOR ratio of the outstanding principal of pass-through securities or COLLATERALIZED MORTGAGE OBLIGATIONS in relation to the original principal amount issued, expressed as a percent. The ratio indicates the prepayment experience of different classes (called TRANCHES) of asset-backed securities issued under the same indenture, or comparable issues.

CURRENT YIELD annual rate of interest paid by a bond, computed by dividing the coupon interest by original purchase price. The current yield of an 8% bond selling at $800 is 10%. Current yield is different from YIELD TO MATURITY, which includes the annual accretion of interest as the price rises from $800 to $1,000 at maturity. Current yield is useful in comparing year-to-year changes in bond yield.

CURTESY legal interest, referred to as a LIFE ESTATE, of a husband in the property of his wife after her death. The legal interest held by a widow is a DOWER.

CUSHION

1. interval between the issue date of a security and the earliest CALL DATE. This is referred to as CALL PROTECTION; also, the degree of protection given investors holding discount pool mortgage-backed securities, which are essentially mortgage bonds backed by low-rate mortgages.
2. *cushion bond*—a bond with a high coupon selling at a price below what might be considered a market price. This occurs when a bond is trading at a high premium but is callable at a lower price. The call option holds down the market price, creating a cushion between the market price and what could justifiably be a higher price.
3. function served by a reserve account, such as a bank's LOAN LOSS RESERVES for possible bad debt.

CUSIP NUMBER nine digit identifier—seven numbers and two letters—identifying U.S. securities issued in book-entry or certificate form since 1970. The CUSIP numbering system (short for Committee on Uniform Securities Identification Procedures) was expanded in 1989 with the addition of foreign registered securities, identified by a nine-digit CUSIP International Numbering System (CINS).

CUSTODIAN CORPORATE AGENT, usually a commercial bank, that holds securities under a written agreement for a corporate client and buys or sells securities when instructed. Custody services include securities safekeeping, and collection of dividends and interest. Custodian banks, and their agents in various countries called subcustody banks, also buy, sell, and deliver securities when instructed by a bank's corporate clients. The bank acts only as transfer agent and makes no buy-sell recommendations.

CUSTODY ACCOUNT

1. account held in trust by a parent for a minor under the UNIFORM GIFT TO MINORS ACT. Minors cannot transfer assets without approval of the account trustee.
2. account held by a CUSTODIAN for an institution such as a mutual fund, pension fund, or a corporate customer. The bank holds the customer's property in safekeeping, as provided by a written agreement, collects dividends and interest payments, and sells or delivers securities when instructed by the principal. *See also* MASTER TRUST.

CUSTOMER ACTIVATED TERMINAL (CAT) any card activated terminal that gives customers access to balance accounts information; also any video interactive terminal that gives rate and current balance information, and so on.

CUSTOMER INFORMATION FILE (CIF) computerized accounting system that maintains a record of a bank's customers including such information as deposit accounts owned, credit relationships, trust accounts, joint ownership of accounts, and so on. The CIF is a bank's customer control file, allowing the bank to look at its customers by total relationship, rather than single accounts (checking, savings). It is updated periodically, frequently daily, to reflect changes as new accounts are opened, checks written, and loan payments made. When used in product marketing, a CIF can help identify CROSS-SELL opportunities at the new accounts desk, produce customer lists for direct mail marketing, and analyze the profitability of customer relationships. *See also* RELATIONSHIP BANKING.

CUSTOMER INITIATED ENTRY (CIE) banking transaction from a self-service banking terminal, for example, an automated teller machine, personal computer, or smartphone. Customer-initiated entries substitute customer labor for bank labor, and in theory are less costly to process as transaction volume increases.

CUSTOMER SERVICE REPRESENTATIVE (CSR) bank employee who opens new accounts, accepts loan applications, and assists customers with service related questions. In recent years, some banks have upgraded the customer service representative to PERSONAL BANKER.

CUT-OFF DATE predetermined date in a billing or processing cycle when account activity for the previous reporting period is summarized (when checks written against an account are collected and summarized in a monthly statement). Checks paid or deposits received after the cut-off date are included in the next month's statement.

CUT-OFF SCORE minimum number of points needed in a CREDIT SCORING system to qualify as creditworthy. Applicants scoring below the cut-off score are denied credit, unless the credit grantor decides to approve the credit request anyway and OVER-RIDE the score. Those whose scores exceed the cut-off generally are approved.

CUT-OFF TIME

1. point in the business day before which electronic payments, such as Federal Reserve Fed Wire transfers or AUTOMATED CLEARING HOUSE (ACH) payments, must be submitted to a processing bank for entry into the interbank clearing system.
2. transaction processing time, measured in seconds, at which an electronic banking terminal automatically disconnects from a host computer if unable to process a transaction. Also called *time-out.*
3. latest time of day a bank will credit deposits made to a customer's account. Also called *ledger credit cut-off.*

CYCLE

1. grouping of accounts in batches, which are processed as a single unit, to distribute the work load and make identification of accounts easier. Checking account statements are processed in batch cycles, as are credit cards and installment loans.
2. business cycle—the periodic expansion and contraction of the economy, as measured by growth in the U.S. Gross Domestic Product (GDP). According to the U.S. Bureau of Economic Research, which tracks economic trends, business cycles, on average, last about 52 months or 2½ years. Among the factors affecting the rate of economic expansion (as the economy moves from recession to growth and stable employment) are expansion and contraction in bank credit, which is influenced by Federal Reserve MONETARY POLICY. *See also* LAGGING INDICATORS; LEADING INDICATORS.

CY PRES DOCTRINE rule applied to trust agreements, for example a TESTAMENTARY TRUST created by a will, which says that in the event the agreement cannot be carried out as intended, it should be followed as closely as possible—literally *near to it.*

D

DAILY INTEREST deposit account interest compounded daily and credited to the depositor's account monthly, quarterly, or at other intervals. For example, $100 deposited for a year (365 days) earns $.84 in daily compound interest at 30 days, $2.53 at 90 days, $5.13 at 180 days, and $10.67 after a full year. *See also* COMPOUND INTEREST.

DALASI monetary unit of Gambia.

DATA CAPTURE electronic collection of merchant bank card sales draft receipts directly from the merchant's point-of-sale terminal or electronic cash register. Bank card data capture, also called *draft capture,* accelerates collection of funds for retail merchant accounts by eliminating mail float in bank card processing.

DATA ENCRYPTION STANDARD (DES) financial industry protocol for protection of sensitive transaction information, including account balances, bank identification codes (called issuer keys), and consumer account access codes. The DES standard, published by the National Institute of Standards and Technology, is also known as the Data Encryption Algorithm (DEA). *See also* ALGORITHM; KEY MANAGEMENT; PERSONAL IDENTIFICATION NUMBER.

DATED DATE date from which a newly issued bond begins to accrue interest, ordinarily one month after the closing date of a mortgage-backed bond or municipal bond. The securities actually may be delivered after the closing date.

DATE OF RECORD *see* RECORD DATE.

DATING

1. **Banking.** The period of time from issuance of a TIME LOAN or DISCOUNT and maturity of the note.
2. **Factoring.** An extension of the payment period in which payment is expected.
3. **Value Dating.** An electronic transfer to assure money will be available when needed.

DAY CYCLE daytime processing cycle for transmitting AUTOMATED CLEARING HOUSE debits or credits between regional clearing house associations, ordinarily from 8 A.M. to 1 P.M. Eastern time. Also called *daytime window*. Compare with NIGHT CYCLE.

DAYLIGHT OVERDRAFT intraday loan that occurs when a bank transfers funds in excess of its RESERVE ACCOUNT. Daylight overdrafts are caused when banks transfer funds in excess of reserve account balances at a Federal Reserve Bank. Since 1994 Federal Reserve Banks have charged banks a processing fee for daylight overdrafts. *See also* BILATERAL CREDIT LIMIT; NET SETTLEMENT; SENDER NET DEBIT CAP.

DAY LOAN bank loan to a broker for purchase of securities, usually arranged in the morning, hence the name *morning loan*. Securities delivered to the broker later that day become the collateral for a regular BROKER'S CALL LOAN.

DAY ORDER order to purchase securities or financial futures good for one day only. If the order cannot be filled that day it is automatically cancelled.

DAYS OF GRACE *see* GRACE PERIOD.

DEALER person or firm that acts as a PRINCIPAL, buying (or selling) from their own account for position and risk, as opposed to a BROKER, who acts as an agent for customers and is paid a commission. Dealers expect to make a profit by selling at a higher price or by correctly guessing future interest rate movements.

The GRAMM-LEACH-BLILEY ACT OF 1999 removed many Depression-era restrictions on dealer activities of commercial banks. Banks are permitted to register their investment securities subsidiaries with the Securities and Exchange Commission, which supervises the securities underwriting of bank-owned securities firms. The Gramm-Leach-Bliley Act excludes bank underwriting of permissible securities (such as municipal revenue bonds), bank activities as TRUSTEE or FIDUCIARY, and the sale of asset-backed securities originated by the issuing bank from SEC registration. *See also* DEALER BANK; PRIMARY DEALER; SECURITIES SUBSIDIARY.

In the securities industry, investment banking firms often act as both broker or dealer, depending on the transaction, and the term *broker-dealer* is commonly used when referring to a dealer firm. *See also* DEALER BANK; PRIMARY DEALER; SECURITIES SUBSIDIARY.

DEALER BANK commercial bank that underwrites and makes markets in securities of the U.S. government and federal agencies, municipal general obligation bonds, and other debt securities. Banks that deal in municipal securities are registered dealers with the Municipal Securities Rulemaking Board.

DEALER FINANCING financing arrangement where a bank purchases, at a discount, loans originated by a car dealer or other retailer. In dealer financing, the dealer's customer becomes a customer of the bank. *See also* INDIRECT LOAN.

DEATH TAXES generic name for state estate taxes assessed on property transferred at the death of an owner, including estate and inheritance taxes.

DEBENTURE unsecured promise to pay, backed only by the general credit of the issuer. Debentures, like corporate bonds, are issued under a deed of trust or INDENTURE. Some debentures can be exchanged for common stock at a specific price and are called CONVERTIBLE debentures. Contrast with BOND.

DEBIT bookkeeping entry on the left-hand side of a balance sheet. A debit transaction increases an asset account or an expense, and decreases a liability, equity account, or revenue account.

DEBIT BALANCE

1. **Banking.** The amount owed by a bank customer who writes checks greater than the balance in his checking account, creating an OVERDRAFT.
2. **Securities.** The balance owed by a broker's customer with insufficient margin in a trading account. *See also* CREDIT BALANCE.

DEBIT CARD plastic card giving consumers access to their funds electronically. Debit cards act like checks when paying for goods and services or withdrawing cash at automated teller machines. Debit cards with MasterCard or Visa logos are more readily accepted than checks in many retail establishments. Consumer purchases with a debit card, unlike a credit card, do not offer the convenience of paying over time, because funds are withdrawn immediately (date of purchase with ON-LINE transactions, or in the next two to three days with *off-line* transactions). Debit card purchases are free of finance charges, making them advantageous for low-dollar purchases.

DEBIT TICKET bookkeeping memo for a debit transaction. When a bank processes a check as a cash item, it credits the customer's account and writes a debit ticket, charged to the general ledger account for "cash items in the process of collection." When it receives payment from the paying bank, a corresponding credit entry cancels the debit entry.

DEBT CANCELLATION CONTRACT bank's contractual agreement to cancel all or part of a customer's agreement to repay a loan, contingent on a triggering event such as death, disability, or loss of job. The borrower pays a bank fee instead of credit insurance premiums.

DEBT FORGIVENESS reduction in loan value when a loan is discounted from its original principal or charged off as a bad debt. As an example, a $100,000 loan, if discounted to $90,000, yields a debt forgiveness amount of $10,000. Under IRS rules that $10,000 is reportable as taxable income to the borrower.

DEBT INSTRUMENT written promise to repay a debt, evidenced by an acceptance, promissory note, or bill of exchange. The term also applies to formal debt securities, such as bonds and debentures.

DEBT LIMIT maximum borrowing power of a government entity, as set by the state constitution or legislative authority. The federal debt ceiling is adjusted by joint congressional resolution, whereas debt limits of most state governments are established by state constitution, and borrowing limits of municipal governments are imposed by state legislatures. In municipal securities, an issuer's debt limit is normally stated as a percentage of ASSESSED VALUATION.

DEBT LOADING adding up personal debts in anticipation of BANKRUPTCY. Personal debts, if acquired within 90 days of a bankruptcy filing, may be excluded from bankruptcy protection by a bankruptcy court. *See also* INSOLVENCY.

DEBTOR IN POSSESSION legal name for a firm or business concern filing for protection from creditors under Chapter 11 of the Bankruptcy code, acting as its own BANKRUPTCY TRUSTEE.

Financing arrangements given to an insolvent borrower under court supervision may have some attractions to lenders because these are supervised closely by the bankruptcy court.

DEBTOR NATION nation that is in arrears in interest or principal payments on debts to bank lenders or international development agencies, such as the World Bank. Debtor nations have an unfavorable balance of trade, meaning an excess of imports over exports, or have a net inflow of capital from foreign investors.

DEBT REPAYMENT SCHEDULE

1. consumer loan AMORTIZATION SCHEDULE showing the number of payments needed to pay off a loan.
2. WAGE EARNER PLAN in a Chapter 13 bankruptcy calling for the debtor to pay a certain amount every month to the court for distribution to creditors over a three-year period in partial repayment of debts owed.

DEBT RESCHEDULING *see* RESCHEDULING.

DEBT SERVICE

1. cash outlay needed to meet principal and interest payments on a mortgage or other note, usually expressed as a monthly or annual payment. Fixed rate consumer loans, including mortgages, are often referred to as CONSTANT PAYMENT obligations, as the regular payments needed to fully amortize the debt remain the same through the life of the loan.
2. amount needed in a calendar year or fiscal year to meet bond interest payments, retire the principal on maturing bonds, or make payments to a sinking fund.

DEBT SERVICE COVERAGE RATIO (DSCR) measure of a mortgaged property's ability to cover monthly debt service payments, defined as the ratio of net operating income (or net operating cash flow) to debt service payments. A coverage ratio of less than 1.0 means the property is generating insufficient cash flow to cover the debt service payments.

DEBT SUSPENSION AGREEMENT contractual agreement by which a bank agrees to suspend all or part of a borrower's obligation to repay a loan owing to job loss, hospitalization, military service, or other predefined triggering event. Repayment of the existing debt is temporarily deferred. *See also* DEBT CANCELLATION CONTRACT.

DEBT-TO-EQUITY RATIO

1. a company's balance sheet debt divided by shareholder's equity, a measure of financial leverage, or the use of borrowed money to boost financial performance.
2. total long-term debt, including interest-bearing debt, divided by shareholder's equity, a measure of a company's ability to pay off creditors' claims in event of liquidation.

DEBT-TO-INCOME RATIO ratio of monthly debt payments, including mortgage debt, to monthly gross income. Lenders use the debt-to-income ratio to determine whether a borrower qualifies for home mortgage. Mortgage lenders often set this ratio of total debt at a maximum 33–36% of household income, but may go higher if the borrower has other assets available to pay down the loan or has substantial equity in the mortgaged property.

DECEASED ACCOUNT deposit account whose owner is deceased. Once notified of the death, a bank places a hold on the account until authorized by court to make payment to the legal heirs.

DECEDENT person who has died. The term is used in connection with wills, estates, and inheritances. A person leaving a valid will is a TESTATOR; if there is no will, the decedent is said to have died INTESTATE.

DECISION TREE

1. diagram in financial analysis showing the interaction of financial ratios, and how one ratio affects another ratio, allowing a financial analyst or bank examiner to see the cause and effect relationship in different ratios.
2. CREDIT SCORING model that examines the interaction between different factors of credit, for example, a borrower's age, income, type of residence, by means of a tree-like chart. It differs from the more widely accepted point scoring analysis, which assigns points to each credit factor considered in approving or rejecting a credit application.

See illustration on next page.

DECLINING YIELD CURVE *see* INVERTED YIELD CURVE.

DEED *see* QUITCLAIM DEED; WARRANTY DEED.

DEED OF TRUST legal document used in some states in lieu of a MORTGAGE. Title to the property passes from seller to a trustee, who holds the mortgaged property until the mortgage has been fully paid. The trustee is authorized to sell the property if the borrower defaults, paying the lender the amount of the mortgage loan and any remaining balance to the former owner.

DEEP DISCOUNT bond trading at a price below 80% of its PAR VALUE. This normally occurs when the coupon interest is far below the current market rate, or the credit quality is poor. Commercial loans or mortgages sold to investors at prices well below their acquisition cost or book value are also said to be trading at deep discounts.

DECISION TREE

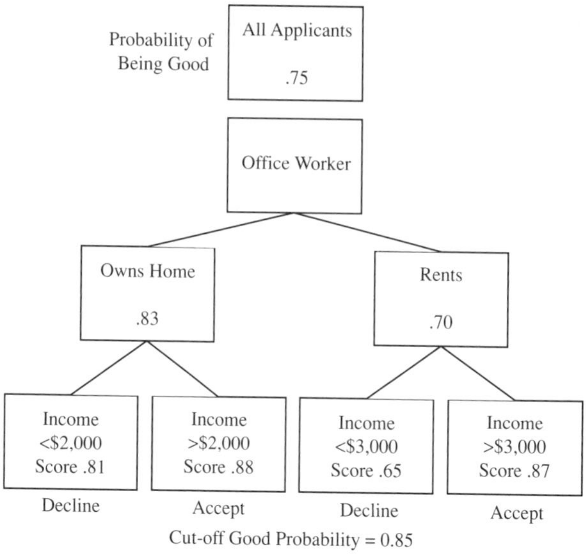

DEFALCATION wrongful diversion of funds held in trust by a FIDUCIARY. Usually said of public officials or officers of corporations. *See also* EMBEZZLEMENT.

DEFAULT failure to meet a contractual obligation, such as repayment of a loan by a borrower or payment of interest to bond holders. Default gives the note holder, or the holder of a mortgage bond, rights and recourse under the mortgage indenture to institute foreclosure proceedings or to accelerate the maturity date.

DEFEASANCE

1. **Banking.** A clause in a loan agreement, such as a MORTGAGE, giving the borrower the right to redeem the title to property securing the debt when the loan is fully paid.
2. **Finance.** A refinancing technique in which a bond issuer, instead of redeeming the bonds at the call date, continues to make coupon interest payments from an IRREVOCABLE TRUST. The cash flow from trust assets, ordinarily U.S. Treasury securities or zero-coupon securities, must be sufficient to service the bonds until the expected maturity. Defeasance effectively removes the bonds from the issuer's balance sheets, even though the issuer continues to meet bond interest payments.

In mortgage banking defeasance allows a bond trustee to protect mortgage-backed bonds from early redemption, if the issuer fails to keep sufficient collateral or defaults.

DEFERRED AVAILABILITY temporary delay in funds availability on checks drawn on out-of-town banks. Checks with 1-day or 2-day availability—the average time it takes to clear checks drawn on distant banks—are credited to the depositing bank's Federal Reserve account. Even so, a bank may get credit for checks deposited before funds are collected from the paying bank, which in turn creates FEDERAL RESERVE FLOAT.

DEFERRED CREDIT *see* DEFERRED AVAILABILITY; UNEARNED DISCOUNT.

DEFERRED INTEREST

1. bond paying interest at a later date, at maturity in the case of a ZERO-COUPON SECURITY. Interest payments accumulate during the holding period but no interest is actually paid until the redemption date. *See also* ACCRETION OF DISCOUNT.
2. unpaid interest in an ADJUSTABLE RATE MORTGAGE. If monthly payments do not cover the loan interest cost, the unpaid interest is added to the loan principal. Deferred interest may occur when the mortgage is originated at a below-market rate, and the borrower agrees to pay the difference (the deferred interest) in later years of the loan.

DEFERRED PAYMENTS

1. deferral of principal and interest payments in a GRADUATED PAYMENT MORTGAGE.
2. skip payment privilege sometimes offered credit card or installment loan customers, a consumer convenience though less common today than in the years before credit cards became popular.

DEFICIENCY JUDGMENT court order authorizing a lender to collect part of an outstanding debt from foreclosure and sale of the borrower's mortgaged property or repossession of property securing a debt, after a finding that the property is worth less than the book value of the outstanding debt.

DEFINED BENEFIT PLAN retirement income plan set up by a corporation to pay a specified sum to qualified employees, based on the number of years in service. Corporate contributions are placed in a separate trust account. These plans pay no taxes on their investments, and are managed according to federally mandated standards under the EMPLOYEE RETIREMENT INCOME SECURITY ACT.

DEFINED CONTRIBUTION PLAN any of a number of savings plans allowing employers, and also employees, to make contributions from earned income on a tax-deferred basis, for retirement income. Included are profit sharing plans and 401(K) PLANS. Many plans allow matched funding by employers, sometimes on a dollar-for-dollar basis with employee contributions. *See also* DEFINED BENEFIT PLAN.

DEFINITIVE SECURITIES securities issued in certificate form, as distinguished from BOOK-ENTRY SECURITY, where ownership is indicated by entries in a computer. *See also* BEARER BOND; REGISTERED BOND.

DEFLATION decrease in the general level of prices, usually the result of an economic downturn. Deflation may result from (1) tight money monetary policies causing a rise in interest rates and shrinkage in the money supply; or (2) falling demand for goods and services, resulting in excess supply and falling prices. Deflation is not the same as DISINFLATION, which is characterized by a lower growth in prices.

DELAY *see* PAYMENT DELAY.

DELAYED DISBURSEMENT practice in cash management whereby firms pay vendors and other corporations by disbursing the payments from a bank in a remote city. Delayed disbursement, also called *remote disbursement,* maximizes clearing FLOAT, and differs from CONTROLLED DISBURSEMENT.

DELINQUENCY failure to pay an obligation when due. A delinquent loan is subject to a LATE CHARGE penalty and can be noted on the borrower's credit report as a past due payment. Loans with more than two missing payments (60 to 90 days past due) are regarded as seriously delinquent and debt collection efforts are initiated to recover the amount due.

DELIVERY

Banking:

1. PRESENTMENT of a check or negotiable instrument, endorsed by the payee, to the paying bank.
2. in the secondary market, forwarding of loan documents by a selling bank to the purchaser, under the terms of a FORWARD COMMITMENT or STANDBY COMMITMENT.

Futures: taking possession of the financial instrument, security, or commodity underlying a futures market contract at specified times, normally at the beginning of a contract delivery month.

DELIVERY DATE

1. day in the month when financial instruments or commodities are deliverable under a financial futures contract. This may occur any day during the contract month at the seller's option, so long as proper notice is given. Actual delivery normally takes place two days after the seller's DELIVERY NOTICE. *See also* FIRST DAY NOTICE.
2. day that a purchaser of securities takes possession. Delivery may take place under five-day regular way delivery, cash basis delivery, or seller's option delivery at a later date. *See also* SETTLEMENT.
3. maturity date of a FORWARD EXCHANGE CONTRACT in foreign exchange, at which time the exchange of currencies takes place.

DELIVERY NOTICE in financial futures, a written notice given by a seller to a clearinghouse stating the date when a commodity or financial instrument will be delivered. The futures clearing house assigns the contract to the longest-standing buyer on record. Also called *notice of intention to deliver.*

DELIVERY VERSUS PAYMENT securities industry term indicating payment is due when the buyer has securities in hand or a book entry receipt. It is also called *delivery against cash, cash on delivery,* or from the sell side, *receive versus payment.* Commonly used by institutional accounts, payment can be made to the seller, or a bank acting as the seller's agent, by check, wire transfer, or cash.

DELTA TECHNICAL ANALYSIS term used in measuring the interaction between the price of an option premium and the price of the underlying security or futures contract. The delta rises toward 1.0 for IN THE MONEY options and approaches zero for options that are OUT OF THE MONEY. Compare with *gamma,* which is the sensitivity of an option's delta to small changes in the price of the underlying instrument.

DEMAND DEPOSIT account paying funds on demand without notice of intended withdrawal; also called a *checking account.* Federal and state banking laws define a demand deposit as any bank deposit payable within 30 days. Bank demand deposit drafts, or checks, are NEGOTIABLE INSTRUMENTS, as defined by Article 3 of the UNIFORM COMMERCIAL CODE. *See also* CHECK; NEGOTIABLE ORDER OF WITHDRAWAL (NOW) ACCOUNT; SUPER NOW ACCOUNT.

DEMAND DRAFT written order directing that payment be made, on sight, to a third party. The person writing the draft is called the *drawee*; the bank making the payment is the *drawer*, or the payor bank. The beneficiary of a demand draft, the person receiving the payment, is the *payee.* Drafts may be payable at some future date (time drafts) or on sight (demand drafts). Demand drafts drawn on banks are known as CHECKS.

DEMAND LOAN loan with no specific maturity date, but payable at any time. Only interest is paid until the principal is paid off, or until the lender demands repayment of principal. The borrower may, however, pay off the loan early, without incurring a prepayment penalty. If the funds are advanced to a broker, it is referred to as a call loan. *See also* TERM LOAN; TIME LOAN.

DENAR monetary unit of Macedonia.

DENOMINATION face value of coins, currency, or securities. FEDERAL RESERVE NOTES, the legal currency in the United States, are issued with values of $1 to $100. Bonds typically are $1,000 or $5,000.

DE NOVO newly chartered bank, as opposed to a bank acquired through a purchase ACQUISITION or a newly opened branch banking office. Banking expansion usually occurs through chartering of new banks and approval of new branch offices by state banking departments, or through the acquisition of existing banks (and banking offices).

DEPOSIT

1. funds placed with a bank in a savings account, or in a demand account subject to withdrawal by check. A deposit balance in a deposit accepting bank—a depository financial institution—is merely a credit, representing the depositor's right to an equivalent amount of money from the bank. The opposite is a WITHDRAWAL, removing funds from an account.
2. crediting of cash, checks, or drafts to a customer's account at a depository financial institution.
3. EARNEST MONEY given as intention of fulfilling a contract, for example, a DOWN PAYMENT towards purchase of a house.

DEPOSITARY an agent authorized to place funds or securities in safekeeping in a DEPOSITORY institution.

DEPOSITARY RECEIPT *see* AMERICAN DEPOSITARY RECEIPT; INTERNATIONAL DEPOSITARY RECEIPT.

DEPOSIT INSURANCE *see* DEPOSIT INSURANCE FUND; FEDERAL DEPOSIT INSURANCE CORPORATION; GUARANTY FUND; INSURED DEPOSIT; UNINSURED DEPOSITOR.

DEPOSIT INSURANCE FUND (DIF) fund administered by the Federal Deposit Insurance Corporation (FDIC) that insures deposits of banks and thrift institutions from losses in event of bank failure. Insured deposits are covered up to $250,000 per account. The DIF is funded by insurance premiums (assessments) paid by member institutions. The fund was created in 2006 with the merger of the Bank Insurance Fund (BIF), which insured deposits in commercial banks, and the Savings Association Insurance Fund (SAIF), which insured deposits in thrift institutions (savings banks, federal savings banks, and savings and loan associations). Although the FDIC is not a government agency backed by the full faith and credit of the U.S. Treasury, depositors and financial markets treat the DIF as if it had an implicit guarantee.

DEPOSIT INTEREST RATE interest rate paid on deposit accounts by commercial banks and other depository financial institutions. Interest-bearing deposit accounts have been completely deregulated since March 31, 1986, when the old interest rate ceilings under Regulation Q were abolished.

DEPOSIT NOTE debt security issued by a bank, backed by federal deposit insurance and carrying an original maturity of two to five years. Deposit notes, which pay a fixed rate of interest, can be issued in book entry or certificate form.

Deposit notes are marketed through brokers, have an active secondary market, and hold some appeal with investors unwilling to buy bank holding company debt. Compare to BANK NOTE.

DEPOSITORY

1. bank holding funds or marketable securities, usually under a specific agreement. Distinguish from DEPOSITARY.
2. bank authorized to accept public deposits for state and local governments, or federal tax payments in a TREASURY TAX AND LOAN ACCOUNT.
3. CORRESPONDENT bank holding deposits for other banks, used for check clearing or meeting RESERVE REQUIREMENTS.

DEPOSITORY INSTITUTIONS ACT OF 1982 *see* GARN-ST GERMAIN DEPOSITORY INSTITUTIONS ACT.

DEPOSITORY INSTITUTIONS DEREGULATION AND MONETARY CONTROL ACT federal law, enacted in 1980, deregulating deposit interest rates and expanding access to the Federal Reserve DISCOUNT WINDOW in the first major reform of the U.S. banking system since the 1930s. The act has two main sections: Title 1, the Monetary Control Act, which extends RESERVE REQUIREMENTS to all U.S. banking institutions and also deals with the banking services furnished by the Federal Reserve System; and Title 2, the Depository Institutions Deregulation Act of 1980, phasing out Federal Reserve REGULATION Q deposit interest rate ceilings.

The following are highlights of the act:

(1) Mandatory reserves for all depository institutions were phased in over an eight-year period ending in 1988.

(2) Federal Reserve Banks were required to begin charging banks for clearing checks through the Federal Reserve System, and pricing reserve bank services at levels competitive with private sector pricing.

(3) a five-member committee, the DEPOSITORY INSTITUTIONS DEREGULATION COMMITTEE, was created to phase out federal interest rate ceilings on interest-earning deposit accounts over a six-year period ending in 1986.

(4) nationwide NEGOTIABLE ORDER OF WITHDRAWAL (NOW) accounts were authorized.

(5) federal deposit insurance coverage was raised from $40,000 to $100,000 per insured account.

(6) all depository institutions, including savings and loans and other thrift institutions, were given access to the Federal Reserve DISCOUNT WINDOW for credit advances.

(7) savings and loan associations were authorized to make consumer loans, including auto loans and credit card loans, up to 20% of total assets.

(8) savings and loans were authorized to offer TRUST accounts.

(9) state USURY laws limiting rates lenders could charge on residential mortgage loans were pre-empted.

(10) state chartered, federally insured banks were allowed to charge the same interest rates on bank loans as national banks.

(11) Federal Reserve REGULATION Z, implementing the consumer credit protections in the Truth in Lending Act, was simplified.

(12) authorized federal credit unions to originate residential mortgages. *See also* GARN-ST GERMAIN DEPOSITORY INSTITUTIONS ACT; MONEY MARKET DEPOSIT ACCOUNT; PRIVATE SECTOR ADJUSTMENT FACTOR; SUPER NOW ACCOUNT.

DEPOSITORY INSTITUTIONS DEREGULATION COMMITTEE (DIDC) five-member committee established by the Banking Act of 1980 (the DEPOSITORY INSTITUTIONS DEREGULATION AND MONETARY CONTROL ACT) to gradually phase out interest rate ceilings on deposit accounts. The DIDC's authority expired March 31, 1986 when Federal Reserve REGULATION Q abolished interest rate ceilings on passbook savings accounts.

DEPOSITORY TRANSFER CHECK (DTC) preprinted DEMAND DRAFT used by corporations to make transfers of cash from a checking account at one bank to a CONCENTRATION ACCOUNT at another bank. This nonnegotiable instrument requires no signature. Also called a *depository transfer draft.*

DEPOSITORY TRUST COMPANY (DTC) *see* CLEARING CORPORATION.

DEPOSIT SLIP two-part form listing checks deposited into a customer's account. One copy is the customer's transaction receipt, the other serves as an audit trail and is a record of original entry legally admissible in a court of law.

DEPRECIATION

1. **Accounting.** The amortization of fixed assets, such as furniture and fixtures, allocating the purchase cost of the asset over its useful economic life. ACCELERATED DEPRECIATION allows faster write-off than would ordinarily occur under straight-line depreciation.
2. **Foreign Exchange.** A decline in price of one currency relative to another without market INTERVENTION by central banks. Contrast with APPRECIATION.

DEPRESSION economic downturn characterized by falling prices, high unemployment, and a reduction in purchasing power. Economic depressions were regular occurrences in the United States in the 19th century. A depression cannot be fixed by MONETARY POLICY, but may be overcome by government spending or FISCAL POLICY. Contrast with RECESSION.

DEPTH OF THE MARKET amount of a currency, commodity, or security that can be traded at any given time without causing a price distortion. Thin markets usually are characterized by wide bid-asked spreads and substantial price fluctuations during a short period of time. Strong markets are characterized by relatively narrow spreads or stable prices.

DEREGULATION business environment in which market competitors are controlled more by market forces rather than by government regulation. The aim is to create a more efficient marketplace by substituting MARKET DISCIPLINE for the hand of government. The regulatory framework in the financial services industry, created by the BANKING ACT OF 1933, was modified substantially in the 1980s and 1990s. Financial institutions were permitted to offer a wider range of new services, allowing commercial banks and thrift institutions to pay market rates for deposits and compete more effectively with nonbank financial companies. *See also* DEPOSITORY INSTITUTIONS DEREGULATION AND MONETARY CONTROL ACT; GARN-ST GERMAIN DEPOSITORY INSTITUTIONS ACT.

DERIVATIVE financial contract whose value is linked to another asset. Derivatives—literally, *derivative contracts,* are often used to protect assets against changes in value.

Derivatives cover a wide assortment of financial contracts, including forwards contracts, futures, options, and swaps. *Exchange-traded derivatives* are traded on the floor of an organized exchange and usually require a good faith deposit, or MARGIN, when buying or selling a contract. Examples are interest rate futures and options on futures contracts.

Over the counter derivatives, such as currency swaps and interest rate swaps, are privately negotiated bilateral agreements, and are often traded off the organized exchanges. In the currency markets, forward delivery contracts allow traders to lock in current prices when buying or selling baskets of currencies for future delivery.

Derivative securities are bond-like securities created when pools of loans and mortgages are packaged and sold to investors and are another type of derivative widely used.

In the hands of knowledgeable users, derivative contracts have many applications in today's floating interest environment: managing currency and interest rate risk, or locking in financing costs by swapping floating rate debt for fixed-rate. Derivatives gained public notoriety in the 1990s when some corporations and municipalities used derivatives for speculative purposes (known as *taking a view* on the market), and suffered large losses when interest rates moved against them.

See also ASSET-BACKED SECURITIES; COLLATERALIZED MORTGAGE OBLIGATION; CURRENCY SWAP; DERIVATIVE MORTGAGE-BACKED SECURITIES; INTEREST RATE SWAP; MORTGAGE-BACKED SECURITIES; SWAP.

DERIVATIVE MORTGAGE-BACKED SECURITIES mortgage-backed securities formed by dividing the cash flows from a pool of mortgages into obligations with payment characteristics substantially different from the underlying mortgages. Innovation in the mortgage market has led to numerous derivative mortgage instruments: the COLLATERALIZED MORTGAGE OBLIGATION, consisting of a series of bonds with different maturity classes; the INTEREST ONLY (IO) STRIP, receiving only interest payments; the PRINCIPAL-ONLY (PO) STRIP, a security receiving only loan principal payments; and mortgage RESIDUALS, which are the excess cash flow after debt service payments. Derivative securities often are used as hedging devices to immunize a loan portfolio against interest rate risk. *See also* ACCRUAL BOND; CONTROLLED AMORTIZATION BOND; INVERSE FLOATER; STRIPPED MORTGAGE-BACKED SECURITIES.

DEROGATORY INFORMATION information in a borrower's credit history (credit report) that lenders may legally use to turn down a loan request or application for credit. Included are such things as bankruptcies, late payments, and previously charged off loans.

DESCRIPTIVE BILLING credit card billing in which monthly statements list the merchant name and location, transaction amount, and date of purchase. Bank credit card systems also include a merchant reference number to identify and investigate charges disputed by a cardholder. Contrast with COUNTRY CLUB BILLING. *See also* COMBINED STATEMENT.

DESCRIPTIVE STATEMENT ACCOUNT STATEMENT listing deposits, withdrawals, and account service charges in chronological order, or as they are posted to the customer's account. If the transaction was initiated by an ELECTRONIC FUNDS TRANSFER, Federal Reserve regulations require financial institutions to disclose the transaction date, location of the terminal, and amount of the transaction. This rule also covers preauthorized payments, direct payroll deposits, and automated teller machine transactions.

DESK

1. money desk at the Federal Reserve Bank of New York, where Federal Open Market Committee buy-sell orders are executed, increasing or reducing the supply of available bank reserves.
2. any trading desk where orders are executed for bank customers, correspondent banks, or a bank's own account. For example, a foreign exchange desk, Federal Funds (Fed Funds) desk, loan sales desk, and so on.

DEVALUATION downward adjustment by monetary authorities in the official exchange rate of a nation's currency in relation to a KEY CURRENCY, such as the U.S. dollar or an established monetary standard such as gold. Devaluation occurs when a government increases the amount of its currency it is willing to exchange with other currencies at current exchange rates. Contrast with DEPRECIATION. *See also* REVALUATION.

DEVISE gift of real property or real estate provided by will. Distinguish from BEQUEST, a gift of personal property to a beneficiary.

DIAMONDS exchange traded security issued by the American Stock Exchange that replicates price movements in the Dow Jones Industrial Average.

DIFFERENTIAL

1. **Banking.** Refers to the ¼ of 1% difference between deposit interest rates paid by commercial banks and rates paid by savings and loans. The rate differential on time deposit accounts, created in the 1960s to give thrift institutions a stable funding source for mortgage lending, was phased out in January 1984.
2. **Finance.** A broker's commission for handling small, odd-lot orders, which normally is higher than with regular orders.

DIGITAL SIGNATURE digital code attached to an electronically transmitted message that guarantees the sender is who he or she claims to be and that the message has not been tampered with by third parties. The Electronic Signatures in Global and National Commerce Act of 2000 (commonly called the E-SIGN law) gives digital signatures the same legal status as handwritten signatures. Experts say routine use of digital signatures will occur when businesses grow more comfortable with e-commerce security and verification systems. *See also* AUTHENTICATION.

DINAR monetary unit of Algeria, Bahrain, Kuwait, Libya, Serbia, and Tunisia.

DIRECT BANKING *see* HOME BANKING; INTERNET BANKING; MOBILE BANKING.

DIRECT DEBIT method of collecting loan or mortgage payments by deducting the amounts owed from the borrower's checking account on the date payment is due.

DIRECT DEPOSIT automatic deposit of wages or benefits (such as Social Security payments) into a consumer's bank account. Direct deposit payments are processed through the Federal Reserve's AUTOMATED CLEARING HOUSE. Since January 1, 1999, all federal payments, including Social Security payments to newly enrolled beneficiaries, are made by electronic direct deposit to the recipient's bank account, as required by the Debt Collection Improvement Act of 1996. Direct deposit payment remains optional for previously enrolled beneficiaries.

DIRECT INVESTMENT real estate investments by state chartered banks and thrift institutions. State chartered banks are permitted by state regulations in about 20 states to take equity positions in real estate development. Direct investments by savings and loan associations in speculative real estate projects contributed to heavy losses in savings and loan associations in the late 1980s and a federal bailout of the S&L deposit insurance fund in 1989. National banks are prohibited by law from making such investments. The FINANCIAL INSTITUTIONS REFORM, RECOVERY AND ENFORCEMENT ACT of 1989 restricts direct real estate investments by savings institutions to separately capitalized subsidiaries.

DIRECT LOAN loan by a bank to its own customer without the use of third parties, such as dealers. Direct lending gives the lender more opportunities to screen credit applicants than indirect lending, and to monitor the loan through the CREDIT DEPARTMENT once a loan is approved and funds are disbursed. Compare with INDIRECT LOAN.

DIRECTOR person elected by shareholders of a corporation at the annual meeting to represent their interests, select the firm's officers, and carry out company policy. Directors name operating officers, such as president, and decide when dividends are paid. *See also* INSIDE DIRECTOR.

DIRECTORS & OFFICERS' (D&O) INSURANCE liability insurance protecting a bank director or officer against lawsuits by third parties, for example, shareholders, loan customers, or banking regulatory agencies seeking damages for losses caused by errors in loan administration or negligent acts. Directors and officers of failed banks and savings institutions have been sued by the federal insurance funds to recover costs absorbed by the insurance fund in liquidating the failing institution or arranging a friendly takeover by another bank. Some banks have funded their own coverage through SELF-INSURANCE.

DIRECT PLACEMENT sale of securities to a long-term institutional investor, such as a life insurance company or pension fund, without the use of underwriters, also known as a sale of loans, such as mortgages directly to an investor. The term also refers to PRIVATE PLACEMENT.

DIRECT SEND private agreement among banks to exchange checks drawn on accounts at each other's bank, bypassing local clearinghouses or the Federal Reserve.

Direct presentment increases funds availability. Contrast with TRANSIT LETTER.

DIRECT VERIFICATION *see* CONFIRMATION.

DIRHAM monetary unit of Morocco and the United Arab Emirates.

DIRTY FLOAT foreign exchange rate that is influenced to one degree or another by market INTERVENTION by the issuing country's monetary authority. Most western currencies, including the French franc, Italian lira and, to a lesser extent, U.S. dollar and Japanese yen, fall into this category. The opposite is CLEAN FLOAT.

DISBURSEMENT

1. payment of funds that partially or fully settles a debt. Also, an outflow of cash that reduces a liability.
2. periodic release of construction loan in installments, called *progress payments*, at specific phases of construction. A portion of the loan is normally held back until completion of the project. *See also* CONTROLLED DISBURSEMENT; DELAYED DISBURSEMENT.

DISCHARGE OF BANKRUPTCY bankruptcy court's order releasing a debtor from his obligations, except for obligations the debtor voluntarily agreed to assume. Although the debtor is no longer liable for discharged obligations, the bankruptcy will remain on his CREDIT REPORT up to 10 years. A discharge of obligations is available only to individual debtors, but not to corporations.

DISCHARGE OF LIEN notification to a borrower of a lender's release of a lien on property securing performance of a loan after payment of the debt, for example, a SATISFACTION OF MORTGAGE document. The discharge is also noted in public land records.

DISCLOSURE

1. **Banking.** Information on credit terms required by federal or state laws to give their customers. Disclosure is normally required in all

consumer loans and residential mortgages. Items subject to disclosure are the finance charge expressed as the ANNUAL PERCENTAGE RATE, method of interest rate computation, minimum monthly payment, and also procedures for error resolution in billing disputes. Banks also must disclose the reason for a turndown when rejecting a consumer loan application.

2. **Securities.** The release of relevant information to a buyer of securities. The Securities Act of 1933 and other regulations require issuers to give buyers sufficient information to make an informed decision. It is up to the customer to evaluate the information and make a purchase decision. The SEC and securities exchanges do not care what is sold, only that all the relevant information is presented to the buyer.
3. **Accounting.** A fact or condition stated on the balance sheet or in footnotes. *See also* MARKET DISCIPLINE.

DISCOUNT

1. bank loan with interest deducted from the face amount of the note when the credit is extended. The borrower repays the full amount indicated on the note.
2. price difference between a bond's current market price and its stated PAR VALUE, when the market price is lower.
3. BANK DISCOUNT RATE, or a bank's quoted price when it accepts payment liability for a bill of exchange, which then becomes a BANKER'S ACCEPTANCE.
4. Treasury Department's method of issuing U.S. Treasury bills at less than face value, with redemption at par at maturity. The discount on the bill represents interest.
5. price difference between two currencies, when one is trading at less than par value in relation to another currency.
6. fee charged by a bank for processing and crediting credit card receivables to a merchant's bank account.
7. cash discount offered by merchants for payment in cash. *See also* DEEP DISCOUNT; MERCHANT DISCOUNT RATE.

DISCOUNT BROKERAGE cut-rate brokerage service, involving execution of securities buy or sell orders, without offering research or investment advice. Discount brokerage through affiliated companies has been an approved banking activity for bank holding companies since 1983, by an amendment to Federal Reserve REGULATION Y.

DISCOUNTED CASH FLOW accounting technique for estimating the present value (market value) of anticipated future income and expenditures, such as earnings from loan principal and interest payments, and income from investment securities. It is calculated as either net present value, which expresses future cash flows in terms of current money by applying a discount rate to future receipts, or INTERNAL RATE OF RETURN, which figures the average annual yield or return on capital of an investment or a bank loan over its expected lifetime.

DISCOUNT HOUSE organization that purchases bankers' acceptances and trade acceptances, bills of exchange, and commercial paper. Acceptances are money market instruments. They are counted as loans when held by the reporting bank. Discount houses are financial intermediaries in Great Britain and several European countries, but not in the United States.

DISCOUNT INTEREST loan interest deducted when a loan is made. A borrower taking out a $1,000 loan at 10% receives $900 from the lender. The difference ($100) is discount interest.

DISCOUNT POINT upfront payment by a home buyer to the lender at the outset of a mortgage, typically at loan closing, to increase the loan's effective yield. One point equals 1% of the principal; on a $100,000 mortgage loan, one discount point is $1,000.

DISCOUNT POOL pool of loans originated below the current market interest rate; these pools tend to have slower prepayment characteristics, because the borrower is unlikely to refinance unless rates drop dramatically. As such, these are a CUSHION for long-term investors, such as pension funds. The lower rate is a kind of built-in CALL PROTECTION.

DISCOUNT RATE

1. rate charged by Federal Reserve Banks for loans at the Federal Reserve DISCOUNT WINDOW. The discount rate is set by each Federal Reserve Bank and approved by the Federal Reserve Board of Governors in Washington. Each Reserve Bank submits its own rate to the board, which then either approves the rate or denies it. The discount rate is not necessarily the same across all 12 Federal Reserve Banks. Occasionally, one or more of the district Fed banks has insisted on a different rate than other Fed banks. This situation could persist for several weeks, although in recent years the Reserve Banks have tended to fall into line with a uniform discount rate, reflecting the emergence of a national market for bank credit. The discount rate is one of the policy tools the Federal Reserve Board employs to carry out monitory objectives; the others are OPEN MARKET OPERATIONS and RESERVE REQUIREMENTS. As of March 31, 1980, when the MONETARY CONTROL ACT OF 1980 became law, all depository financial institutions holding transaction accounts were able to borrow at the discount window.
2. BANK DISCOUNT RATE, quoted by banks when they accept acceptances and bills of exchange. The best names, those holding prime paper, qualify for the lowest rates.

DISCOUNT WINDOW Federal Reserve facility for direct loans to a financial institution with a deficiency in its RESERVE ACCOUNT. The term originated with the practice of sending a bank representative to a reserve bank teller window when a bank needed to borrow money.

The discount window provides credit through discounts (actually, rediscounts) of notes and acceptances already accepted, and discounted by a bank, and advances that are collaterized by a bank's holdings of Treasury securities. Today, most Federal Reserve credit is in the form of advances, which are a more convenient way of borrowing. In 2003 the Federal Reserve relaxed its rules on direct loans to financial institutions. Financially sound banks can borrow directly from Federal Reserve Banks even if they have not exhausted other sources of funds. *See also* ADJUSTMENT CREDIT; EXTENDED CREDIT; SEASONAL CREDIT.

DISCOUNT YIELD yield computation based on face amount of a security rather than the purchase price. Treasury bill yields are calculated this way, and also yields on most commercial paper and some municipal notes. Discount yield is calculated by:

discount / face amount × 360 / days to maturity.

DISCRETIONARY ACCOUNT account managed by a bank acting as an ATTORNEY IN FACT or FIDUCIARY, usually through its TRUST DEPARTMENT. The bank has the right to buy or sell assets, usually securities, without prior consent.

DISCRETIONARY MONETARY POLICY authority of the Federal Reserve Board to influence market interest rates, such as the FEDERAL FUNDS (FED FUNDS) RATE or the DISCOUNT RATE. When the Fed decides to lower the Fed Funds target rate, it instructs the Open Market Desk at the Federal Reserve Bank of New York to buy Treasury bills, notes, and bonds in the financial markets.

This puts money in the banking system because it increases the supply of bank RESERVES, thereby pushing Fed Funds rates lower so commercial banks can charge each other a lower rate on overnight loans of Fed Funds. The Fed lowers the Funds Rate when it wants to stimulate the economy, usually when consumer spending is weak and economic output is declining. When the Fed wants to raise the Fed Funds target rate, it sells securities to dealers, which drains reserves from the banking system. *See also* MATCHED-SALE PURCHASE AGREEMENT; OPEN MARKET OPERATIONS; QUANTITATIVE EASING; TERM AUCTION FACILITY; TERM DEPOSIT FACILITY; TERM SECURITIES LENDING FACILITY.

DISCRETIONARY TRUST trust that gives the trustee a degree of latitude in paying income from the trust to a beneficiary, usually to keep the beneficiary from wasting the trust's assets.

DISCRIMINATION denial of credit to an applicant, based on factors prohibited by federal credit laws. The EQUAL CREDIT OPPORTUNITY ACT allows credit denials based on the applicant's credit history, such as late payments, as long as credit denial is not based on race, color, age, religion, national origin, or other factors specified by law.

DISHONOR

1. refusal by a drawee bank to accept a promissory note, or to pay a check or draft, as might happen if the check writer's account has insufficient funds. To collect payment, the holder of the instrument must look to the endorsers or guarantors through a legal process known as PROTEST. But, unless the drawee bank gives prompt notice, by returning the check the same day, the endorser's liability is voided.
2. refusal by a check writer or maker to pay a check or other negotiable instrument. *See also* NOTICE OF DISHONOR; WRONGFUL DISHONOR.

DISINFLATION slowing of the rate of increase in consumer and wholesale prices. Federal Reserve monetary policy is designed to contain the rate of inflation by controlling the supply of credit available for borrowing and keeping the inflation rate at a manageable level.

DISINTERMEDIATION withdrawal of funds from interest-bearing deposit accounts when rates on competing financial instruments, such as money market mutual funds, stocks, bonds, and so on, offer the investor a better return. The double-digit inflation of the late 1970s, which caused many consumers to put their liquid assets in short-term money funds, led to federal legislation in 1980 deregulating deposit interest rates, allowing banks and thrifts to compete more effectively with nonbank financial intermediaries.

DISPOSABLE INCOME net income remaining after state, federal, and local taxes are paid, and available for consumption or saving. Distinguish from discretionary income, which is income remaining after meeting essential household expenses, such as food and housing costs.

DIVERSIFICATION

1. **Lending.** The allocation of a bank's assets over a wide group of borrowers to keep ASSET QUALITY of the loan portfolio at an acceptable level and maintain consistent earnings, while minimizing CREDIT RISK, or potential losses from borrower defaults. The LEGAL LENDING LIMIT prevents a bank from making excessive loans to a single borrower, but a lender can still "put too many eggs in one basket" by lending to many borrowers in a particular industry.
2. **Investments.** The distribution of assets in a portfolio among different types of securities, such as bonds, stocks, commercial paper, and so on, and also by buying securities of the same type with different maturities. *See also* BARBELL PORTFOLIO; IMMUNIZATION; LADDERED PORTFOLIO.

DIVESTITURE sale of an asset to achieve a desired objective. A bank may sell branch offices, or even an entire operating division, to cut operating expenses or carry out its business plan for long-term growth. Assets sold without recourse are taken off the selling bank's balance sheet and transferred to the purchaser. In accounting terms, the sale is treated as a nonrecurring gain (or loss). *See also* ANTITRUST LAWS; ASSET SALES.

DIVIDEND

1. quarterly payment to stockholders of record, as a return on investment. Dividends may be in cash, stock, or property, and are declared from operating surplus. If there is no surplus, the payment is considered a return on capital. Dividend payments are, in effect, taxed twice—once when corporate profits are taxed and again when the dividend is received by a taxpaying stockholder.
2. money paid to the holder of a SHARE ACCOUNT in a credit union; the payment is the equivalent of INTEREST.

DIVIDEND PAYING AGENT corporate agent, often a commercial bank, assigned the responsibility for paying quarterly dividends to stockholders of record. This agent may or may not be the same as the TRANSFER AGENT, the firm that keeps track of securities redemptions and new issues.

DOBRA monetary unit of São Tomé and Principe.

DOCUMENTARY COMMERCIAL BILL draft accepted by a bank with bills of lading and other documents attached. The attached documents are delivered to the drawee when it accepts or pays the draft, and ordinarily controls title to the merchandise.

DOCUMENTARY CREDIT commercial letter of credit provided for payment by a bank to the named beneficiary, usually the seller of merchandise, against delivery of documents specified in the credit.

DOCUMENTS AGAINST ACCEPTANCE instructions given by an exporter to a bank that the documents attached to the draft for collection are deliverable to the importer only when the importer accepts the draft by signing it.

DOCUMENTS AGAINST PAYMENT instructions by an exporter to a bank that the documents attached to the draft for collection are deliverable only after payment of the draft.

DODD-FRANK ACT financial reform legislation following the near collapse of the U.S. banking system in the 2008 financial crisis. This federal law (full name: Dodd-Frank Wall Street Reform and Consumer Protection Act of 2010) added an interagency committee to the federal regulatory system, created a new agency to enforce consumer financial laws, and required trading of many types of over-the-counter derivative contracts through an exchange or clearinghouse. The Dodd-Frank Act:

1. created a new agency, the FINANCIAL STABILITY OVERSIGHT COUNCIL, chaired by the U.S. Treasury Secretary, to identify potential risks to the U.S. financial system.
2. authorized the Federal Reserve Board to supervise investment banks and selected nonfinancial companies.
3. established a new resolution procedure for liquidating troubled large financial companies and authorized the Treasury Secretary

to designate the Federal Deposit Insurance Corporation as receiver for distressed financial companies.

4. imposed tougher capital requirements on large banks designated *systemically important financial institutions.*
5. created an Office of Financial Research within the Treasury to support the Oversight Council.
6. created an independent CONSUMER FINANCIAL PROTECTION BUREAU to enforce compliance with federal consumer protection laws.
7. created the Federal Insurance Office, a Treasury Department agency, to advise Congress and federal agencies on insurance issues.
8. revised the formula for calculating federal deposit insurance assessments; insurance assessments must be based on an insured bank's total deposit base, including deposits held in non-U.S. banking offices.
9. created the Office of Credit Rating Agencies within the Securities and Exchange Commission to oversee credit rating agencies.
10. prohibited many types of proprietary trading by depository financial institutions—the so-called VOLCKER RULE.
11. required large, complex banks and financial companies to write a LIVING WILL document in the event insolvency by a major bank threatened stability of the U.S. financial system.
12. required hedge funds managing more than $100 million to register with the Securities and Exchange Commission and appoint a chief compliance officer.
13. transferred supervision of thrift-holding companies from the Office of Thrift Supervision to the Federal Reserve.
14. transferred supervision and examination functions of the Office of Thrift Supervision (OTS) to the Comptroller of the Currency and the Federal Deposit Insurance Corporation; closed down the OTS as a financial regulator.
15. required trading of many types of swap contracts on a regulated exchange or a SWAP EXECUTION FACILITY.
16. made significant changes in corporate governance and executive compensation.
17. allowed banks to pay interest on corporate checking accounts effective July 2011.

DOLLAR monetary unit of the United States and 14 other countries. Since 1971, when the U.S. officially abandoned the gold exchange standard and convertibility of the dollar into gold, the value of the U.S. dollar has been allowed to float freely against other currencies in foreign exchange markets.

DOLLAR BOND

1. popular name for a municipal revenue bond quoted and traded in dollar price, rather than YIELD TO MATURITY. Dollar bonds are usually municipal bonds with a single large amount due at one time, usually

the TERM BOND portion of a financing, as opposed to SERIAL BONDS, which consist of numerous maturities of smaller amounts. Dollar bonds come in the same $5,000 principal amounts as other bonds.
2. EUROBOND denominated in U.S. dollars and issued in a financial center outside the United States. *See also* DUAL CURRENCY BOND.

DOLLAR-DAY collected balance of one dollar, held for one day. The term is often used as a measure for quantifying the comparative benefits of alternative CASH MANAGEMENT systems.

DOLLAR EXCHANGE ACCEPTANCE time draft drawn by central banks in different countries and accepted by banks for the purpose of furnishing foreign exchange.

DOLLAR ROLL sale of a MORTGAGE-BACKED SECURITY to a dealer, with an agreement to repurchase a substantially identical security at a future date and at a specified price. This normally is done as a short-term financing technique or to generate income from ARBITRAGE.

DOMESTIC EXCHANGE checks, drafts, and acceptances drawn in one city and payable in another in the United States. Checks cleared through the Federal Reserve System are exchanged at par, or face value, i.e., without discount. Before the Federal Reserve check collection system was established in 1916, many banks imposed an exchange charge, or a fee deducted from the face amount of checks drawn on other banks. This practice, known as nonpar banking, has since disappeared. Contrast with FOREIGN EXCHANGE.

DONG monetary unit of Vietnam.

DONOR person making a gift; a voluntary transfer of property to another, who accepts the gift without CONSIDERATION. A GIFT INTER VIVOS is an irrevocable transfer occurring during the donor's lifetime.

DON'T KNOW securities term for a questioned trade, indicating refusal to complete a transaction due to a disagreement on the trade details or because errors are discovered in the comparison sheets exchanged by broker-dealers.

DORMANT ACCOUNT account showing no activity, other than posting of interest for a specified period. These are generally low balance accounts. If unclaimed for a certain number of years, ownership reverts to the state under ESCHEAT laws.

DOUBLE LEVERAGE use of holding company debt to finance bank equity. Double leveraging occurs when a bank holding company borrows in the debt market, and transfers the proceeds to a subsidiary bank. The practice is discouraged by bank regulators if an excessive proportion of net income is used to retire holding company debt.

DOUBTFUL LOAN loan in which full repayment is considered uncertain. Some losses are expected. A loan classified as doubtful has all the characteristics of a SUBSTANDARD loan (well-defined credit weaknesses), with the added characteristic that credit weaknesses make full collection or liquidation in full highly questionable and improbable. *See also* ADVERSELY CLASSIFIED ASSETS.

DOUGLAS AMENDMENT amendment to the BANK HOLDING COMPANY ACT of 1956 prohibiting interstate bank acquisitions unless expressly authorized by state statute. Reciprocal agreements by states' legislatures in the mid-1980s authorized cross-border mergers in neighboring states, and the Riegle-Neal Banking Act of 1994 eliminated all legislative barriers to interstate bank mergers, including the Douglas Amendment.

DOWER right of a widow to some or all of the property of her deceased husband. Years ago some states recognized a common law dower, giving a widow a fixed portion of the estate; today this right has generally been abolished.

DOW JONES INDUSTRIAL AVERAGE price-weighted average of 30 leading industrial stocks traded on the New York Stock Exchange, compiled by Dow Jones & Co. and published daily in the *Wall Street Journal.* The industrial average is one of four securities averages computed by Dow Jones; the others are a 20-stock transportation average, an average of 15 utility stocks, and a composite averaging all of these securities. The industrial average is the most popular, and is widely quoted as an indicator of stock prices and investor confidence in the securities market.

DOWN PAYMENT initial good faith deposit made by a home buyer, indicating intention to purchase real estate offered for sale and obtain financing from a bank or mortgage company. Also called a GOOD FAITH deposit.

DOWNSTREAM

1. RESPONDENT bank, generally a community bank serviced by a larger CORRESPONDENT bank.
2. funds borrowed by a bank holding company for use as a subsidiary, generally to obtain a more favorable rate; a downstream loan. Contrast with UPSTREAM.

DRACHMA monetary unit of Greece.

DRAFT payment order directing a second party, the DRAWEE, to pay a specified sum to a third party (the payee). A draft is actually a bill of exchange, although the term *draft* is ordinarily used if drawn on a bank. A CHECK is a bank draft payable when presented (a SIGHT DRAFT). Drafts may also be payable at a future date (a TIME DRAFT). *See also* DOCUMENTARY DRAFT; FOREIGN DRAFT; PAYABLE THROUGH DRAFT.

DRAGNET CLAUSE *see* CROSS-COLLATERAL.

DRAINING RESERVES *see* TIGHT MONEY.

DRAW DOWN

1. to activate or borrow against a LINE OF CREDIT.
2. bank customer's instructions to transfer funds to another bank, as when a corporation transfers temporarily idle funds into a CONCENTRATION ACCOUNT for reinvestment at market interest rates.
3. periodic advance of funds to a developer, as authorized by the terms of a construction loan.

DRAWEE person (or bank) who is expected to pay a check or draft when the instrument is presented for payment.

DRAWER party instructing the drawee to pay someone else, by writing, or drawing a check or draft. The drawer is also known as the *maker* or *writer*.

DUAL BANKING banking system in the United States, consisting of STATE BANKS, chartered and supervised by state banking departments, and NATIONAL BANKS, chartered and regulated by the Office of the Comptroller of the Currency. The side-by-side existence of state banks and national banks accounts for wide variations in credit regulation, LEGAL LENDING LIMITS, and permissable activities from one state to another, and even within a state.

DUAL CONTROL actions requiring approval by two persons, each being held accountable. When a teller cashes a check for a noncustomer, a bank officer's signature is often required. If authorization by two individuals is required, it is a joint custody arrangement. Access to a safe deposit box requires approval by banker and customer, each possessing a key to the box.

DUAL CURRENCY BOND bond paying interest in one currency, but convertible into another at redemption. A dual currency bond might be issued by a German bank, paying interest in deutschmarks, but is repaid in dollars at redemption.

DUALITY membership in both of the two national bank card organizations. Prior to 1976, credit card issuing banks belonged to either Visa (then National BankAmericard Inc.) or MasterCard (Interbank Card Association).

DUE BILL *see* BILL.

DUE DILIGENCE

1. **Banking.** The responsibility of bank directors and officers to act in a prudent manner in evaluating credit applications; in essence, using the same degree of care that an ordinary person would use in making the same analysis.
2. **Securities.** The responsibility of securities underwriters to explain relevant details of a new issue of securities to interested purchasers. Called a due diligence meeting.

3. **General Business.** In a corporate MERGER or ACQUISITION, close examination of the books to examine the quality of both assets and liabilities of a target company.

DUE FROM ACCOUNT general ledger asset account representing funds on deposit at another bank. In international banking, the term Nostro *(due from* in Latin) is often used.

DUE-ON-SALE CLAUSE provision in a mortgage requiring payment of the unpaid loan balance if the property is sold. The mortgage cannot be transferred to another borrower (permitted in an ASSUMABLE MORTGAGE) without approval by the lender, and normally only at current market interest rates. The due-on-sale clause provides mortgage secondary market investors with a continuous supply of residential mortgages originated at market interest rates.

DUE TO ACCOUNT general ledger liability account representing funds payable to other banks. In international banking, the term Vostro *(due to* in Latin) is often used.

DUN & BRADSTREET (D&B) company that supplies corporate credit reports and ratings, based on industry reported information and its own analytical data. D&B reports (compiled by Dun & Bradstreet Credibility Corporation) on estimated financial strength, promptness of trade payments, and capital adequacy, plus statistical data, such as financial performance ratios of rated companies. Dun & Bradstreet clients receive extracts of balance sheet and income statement data, as reported by D&B listed companies. Credit information on some three million U.S. and Canadian companies is listed in a ratings directory, *The Reference Book.* The absence of a D&B rating for a particular company means that Dun & Bradstreet did not have sufficient information available to classify a company.

Credit analysts, when evaluating publicly traded companies, supplement D&B reports with audited financial statements.

DURATION expected life of a fixed-income security, taking into account its coupon yield, interest payments, maturity, and call features. Duration attempts to measure actual maturity, as opposed to final maturity, by measuring the average time required to collect all payments of principal and interest. The duration of a callable bond, also called its *effective duration,* may be considerably shorter than its stated maturity in a period of rising interest rates. Thus, as market interest rates rise, the duration of a financial instrument decreases. For example, a 30-year conventional mortgage may have an effective duration of only 11 to 12 years, which means the loan will probably be paid off in about one-third of the time it is supposedly carried by the originating lender as an earning asset. Duration differs from other measurements such as AVERAGE LIFE and HALF LIFE. Duration measures the time required to recover a dollar of price in present value terms (including principal and interest), whereas average life computes the average time needed to collect one dollar of principal. *See also* DYNAMIC GAP; GAPPING; IMMUNIZATION; STATIC GAP.

DURBIN AMENDMENT amendment to the Dodd-Frank Act of 2010 capping the debit card interchange fee (SWIPE FEE) that banks charge for processing debit card transactions. Debit card processing fees are capped at a fixed amount per transaction. The amendment, named after Senator Richard Durbin, also gave the Federal Reserve Board power to regulate debit card interchange fees.

DUTCH AUCTION auction system, also called a *single price* auction, in securities underwriting where the issuer gradually lowers the price until a responsive bid is met. Buyers can bid any price they want, and securities are sold at a single price to all buyers whose bid price is at or higher than the auction-set price. The U.S. Treasury Department sometimes employs the dutch auction technique in auctions of Treasury notes and inflation-indexed securities.

DYNAMIC GAP asset-liability gap model that takes into account projected future balances or the difference between INTEREST SENSITIVE ASSETS and INTEREST SENSITIVE LIABILITIES at specific future time periods, as opposed to STATIC GAP.

E

EARLY AMORTIZATION accelerated payment of bond principal in an asset-backed security, usually triggered when there is a sudden increase in delinquencies in the underlying loans or when EXCESS SPREAD, the issuer's net profit after deducting servicing fees, charge-offs, and other costs, falls below an acceptable level. Early amortization protects investors from prolonged exposure to a pool of receivables whose credit performance has deteriorated.

EARLY WITHDRAWAL PENALTY forfeiture of interest or service fee charged depositors for withdrawing money from a savings or time deposit prior to maturity. Banks may require 30 days' notice before withdrawing funds, but penalties for early withdrawals have been sharply reduced from levels prior to interest rate deregulation.

EARMARKED RESERVES funds set aside for a specific purpose. For example, a bank's LOAN LOSS RESERVES for possible bad debt. The Federal Reserve Bank of New York holds gold bullion in trust for foreign central banks and various international organizations. Earmarked gold is used to back up monetary agreements, such as currency swaps to stabilize exchange rates. *See also* EXCHANGE STABILIZATION FUND; GOLD STOCK.

EARNEST MONEY good faith sum of money given to bind a contract, for example an agreement to purchase real property, or a commitment fee to assure an advance of funds by a lender. In a real estate transaction, the money is applied to the purchase price and is forfeited if the purchaser fails to carry out the terms of the agreement.

EARNING ASSETS any asset generating INTEREST or yielding FEE income—the major source of a bank's net income. Included are loans and leases, but not UNEARNED INTEREST income; U.S. government, corporate, and municipal securities held as INVESTMENT SECURITIES; securities purchased under agreements to resell (REPURCHASE AGREEMENTS); TIME DEPOSIT accounts in other banks; FEDERAL FUNDS sold to other banks; and TRADING ACCOUNT ASSETS.

EARNING POWER demonstrated ability of a business to earn a profit on invested capital after paying owners and employees, servicing obligations, and fully recognizing its costs while following good accounting practices. A bank loan officer looks at a company's ability to generate earnings as an important test of business risk when approving a loan application.

EARNINGS ALLOWANCE *see* EARNINGS CREDIT.

EARNINGS CREDIT RATE (ECR) adjustment factor that reduces bank service charges on business checking accounts. Large banks often peg their earnings credit rate to the U.S. Treasury bill rate.

EARNINGS PER SHARE (EPS) portion of a company's profit allocated to each outstanding share of common stock. Companies usually report the weighted average of the number of shares outstanding over the reporting period. Earnings per share, a widely used measure of profitability, is usually reported in two ways: basic earnings per share and diluted earnings per share, which includes any convertibles and warrants outstanding.

EARNING THE POINTS in foreign exchange, market condition that exists when the buying price of a currency in the forward market is cheaper than the SPOT MARKET price. A trader selling at the spot rate and buying at a cheaper one-month forward rate is earning the points. The opposite is LOSING THE POINTS.

EASY MONEY said of credit available to the public through the banking system when the Federal Reserve allows bank credit to expand. When the Federal Reserve allows reserves to accumulate, interest rates are stable, if not declining. Easy money policies could encourage economic growth and, eventually, inflation, if carried out for a sustained period. Contrast with TIGHT MONEY.

E BOND *see* SAVINGS BOND.

ECONOMETRICS economic modeling technique that seeks to explain in mathematical terms the relationships between key economic variables such as capital spending, wages, bank interest rates, population trends, and also government fiscal and monetary policies. An econometric model helps business planners test different hypotheses explaining why the economy acts as it does, for example, the relationship between bank RESERVE REQUIREMENTS and interest rate volatility. This helps organizations explore various options available in forecasting business growth. *See also* REGRESSION ANALYSIS; TECHNICAL ANALYSIS.

ECONOMIC RECOVERY TAX ACT federal law enacted in 1981 that cut taxes across-the-board, modified the depreciation tables used by businesses in writing off capital equipment, and indexed tax brackets to the inflation rate. The act reduced the individual tax rate by 23%, cut the corporate capital gains tax to a maximum of 20%, and introduced the accelerated cost recovery system used by businesses in calculating ACCELERATED DEPRECIATION.

To encourage individual savings, the act made INDIVIDUAL RETIREMENT ACCOUNTS (IRAS) available to anyone earning regular income, and introduced the ALL SAVERS CERTIFICATE, a one-year savings certificate free of federal taxes.

The act also reduced the federal tax on estate and gift taxes, making the first $600,000 tax free after 1987, and allowed an unlimited MARITAL DEDUCTION on property transfers as provided by a will.

EDGE ACT CORPORATION banking corporation financing international commerce, chartered by the Federal Reserve Board under a 1919 amendment to the Federal Reserve Act. Edge Act corporations have reserve accounts in a Federal Reserve bank, accept deposits outside the United States, and invest in non-U.S. firms. A bank-owned Edge Act corporation buys and sells notes, drafts, and bills of exchange, and complements the international banking activities of its parent bank. The International Banking Act of 1978 approved ownership of Edge corporations by foreign banks. *See also* AGREEMENT CORPORATION; EXPORT TRADING COMPANY.

EDUCATION LOAN loan made for college or vocational training expenses, often at a BELOW MARKET RATE. Loans backed by the STUDENT LOAN MARKETING ASSOCIATION (Sallie Mae) are 90% guaranteed for repayment of principal and interest. A guaranteed student loan (called a Stafford Student Loan, after Sen. Robert T. Stafford of Vermont) is insured by a state guarantee agency and reinsured by Sallie Mae. Repayment of a Stafford Student Loan is deferred until after college graduation.

EDUCATION SAVINGS ACCOUNT (ESA) savings plan for education expenses authorized by the Economic Growth and Tax Relief Act of 2001, which greatly expanded both contributions and income eligibility. Annual contribution limits in these accounts (formerly Education IRAs) were raised from $500 to $2,000 per year per child from birth to age eighteen, and the adjusted gross income limitation was increased to $95,000 for singles and $190,000 for married couples. The 2001 legislation renamed the tax-favored savings plan (created by the 1997 tax law) the Coverdell Education Savings Account, in recognition of its primary backer, the late Senator Paul Coverdell of Georgia.

Coverdell Education Savings Account earnings and withdrawals are tax-free, although annual contributions cannot be deducted from personal income taxes. Contributions can be made at any time up to the April 15 filing deadline for the applicable tax year (instead of December 31 under the previous law). Distributions may be used for a much wider range of education expenses, including books; elementary, secondary, and postsecondary school tuition and fees; personal computers; room and board; tutoring; and extended day-care expenses. Taxpayers taking a distribution from an education savings account may also claim a so-called hope credit for postsecondary education expenses or a lifetime learning credit to improve job skills for the same year they took a Coverdell ESA distribution as long as the ESA distribution is not used for the same expenses. Contributions to a Coverdell savings account and a qualified state tuition 529 plan in the same year are allowed without penalty.

EE BOND *see* SAVINGS BOND.

EFFECTIVE ANNUAL YIELD depositor's yield earned on a savings account or time deposit, including compounded interest, assuming the funds remain in the account for a full calendar year. The effective yield of a six-month certificate of deposit, for instance, is the rate earned by the CD over the course of the year, including interest compounding. Effective yield may overstate the yield earned on a six-month CD because the calculation assumes the funds will automatically be reinvested (rolled over) at the original rate.

EFFECTIVE DATE date on which a transaction is posted, or an agreement becomes effective.

1. **Banking.** The time when an expiring CERTIFICATE OF DEPOSIT is renewed at the current rate, and interest paid is adjusted accordingly. Also, the date on which a bank card becomes valid.
2. **Securities.** The date on which a registered offering of securities may be sold, ordinarily 20 days after filing of the issuer's registration statement with the Securities and Exchange Commission. *See also* SHELF REGISTRATION.

EFFECTIVE NET WORTH stockholder's equity in a corporation, plus subordinated debt, such as debentures or loans to the firm by an owner. Credit analysts sometimes count loans by a principal toward a company's worth, provided the principal owners sign a SUBORDINATION AGREEMENT assuring that bank loans are paid first. This is especially true of closely held corporations where officers and owners are often the same.

EFFECTIVE RATE

1. rate of interest paid on a loan, or earned on an interest-bearing deposit, as distinguished from the NOMINAL RATE. In a bank loan, it is the ANNUAL PERCENTAGE RATE. *See also* ADD-ON INTEREST; ANNUAL PERCENTAGE YIELD; SIMPLE INTEREST.
2. investor's yield realized on a bond or security, which is different from the COUPON RATE. The effective rate takes into account the price paid, the time to maturity, and the amortization of premium or accretion of a discount. Also called *effective yield.*
3. weighted average cost of Federal Funds purchased in the inter-bank market, calculated by the Federal Reserve Bank of New York. Banks that have a deficiency in their RESERVE ACCOUNTS are charged at a rate equal to the effective rate of the Federal Funds.

EFFECTS TEST method of assessing the discriminatory impact of supposedly neutral credit policies. In general, the effects test works this way: a person who alleges illegal discrimination need only establish that the action in question has a disproportionately discriminant effect on a member of a protected class, and therefore is discriminatory in effect. The statutory basis of the effects test is the EQUAL CREDIT OPPORTUNITY ACT, which prohibits credit denials on the basis of marital status, national origin, age, or whether applicants are receiving public assistance, and also the Fair Housing Act. The effects test is most frequently applied in evaluating the fairness of statistically based CREDIT SCORING systems and alternative mortgages, such as graduated payment mortgages, where future income is considered.

EFFICIENCY RATIO ratio of bank expenses to revenue. The efficiency ratio can be calculated in any of four ways: noninterest expense divided by total revenue, less interest expense; noninterest expense divided by net interest income before deducting the LOAN LOSS PROVISION for possible bad loans; noninterest expense divided by revenue; or operating income divided by fee income plus tax equivalent net interest income. A lower efficiency ratio generally means a bank is managing growth in operating expenses; a higher number means operating costs are increasing. Also called *overhead burden* or *overhead efficiency ratio.*

EFFICIENT MARKET theory that financial markets fully reflect all publicly available information. Good news expected next week will affect stock prices today, so someone who waits a week to buy or sell may be too late to cash in. This widely contested theory maintains that all investors have access to essentially the same information, and for this reason small investors can do as well as professional investment managers.

ELECTRONIC BANKING form of banking where funds are transferred through an exchange of electronic signals between financial institutions, rather than an exchange of cash, checks, or other negotiable instruments. The ownership of funds and transfers of funds between financial institutions are recorded on computer systems connected by telephone lines. Customer identification is by access code, such as a password or PERSONAL IDENTIFICATION NUMBER, instead of a signature on a check or other physical document. Electronic banking systems can be low-dollar retail payment systems, such as AUTOMATED TELLER MACHINE networks and POINT-OF-SALE systems; and large-dollar interbank payment systems, such as the Federal Reserve Fed Wire or the CLEARING HOUSE INTERBANK PAYMENTS SYSTEM operated by the New York Clearing House Association. *See also* AUTOMATED CLEARING HOUSE; BOOK ENTRY SECURITY; ELECTRONIC FUNDS TRANSFER; WIRE TRANSFER.

ELECTRONIC BENEFITS TRANSFER distribution of government benefits, such as food coupons or public assistance, to qualified recipients with the use of automated teller machines (ATMs) and retail point-of-sale terminals to effect transfer of payment. *See also* ELECTRONIC TRANSFER ACCOUNT (ETA).

ELECTRONIC BILL PAYMENT & PRESENTMENT Internet-based billing service allowing consumers to pay credit card and other retail bills from a personal computer. Funds are deducted electronically from the consumer's checking account and cleared through the Federal Reserve's AUTOMATED CLEARING HOUSE network.

ELECTRONIC CHECK electronic version of a paper check, including date, payee name, payment amount, and signature. Electronic checks (e-checks), are meant for paying bills, transferring funds, or any purpose where a paper check is used today. Such checks have a DIGITAL SIGNATURE security code proving payment was authorized by the account holder.

ELECTRONIC CHECK PRESENTMENT (ECP) in check clearing, electronic transmission of the check writer's account number and other payment data directly to the paying bank. Electronic check presentment does not eliminate use of paper checks, but it does allow for a more efficient and less costly method for clearing checks. The Check Clearing for the 21st Century (or Check 21) Act permits banks to send a digital image of a paper check instead of the actual check and thus eliminates much of the labor-intensive costs associated with clearing the billions of checks Americans write every year. *See also* RE-PRESENTED CHECK; SUBSTITUTE CHECK.

ELECTRONIC DATA INTERCHANGE (EDI) transfering data between companies using computer networks such as the Internet. With EDI, electronically transmitted data replaces paper documents in the business accounts receivable cycle. Electronic messages are sent through public data transmission networks or the banking system. When payments also are made through EDI, the payment instructions flow through the banking system. *See also* CORPORATE TRADE EXCHANGE; CORPORATE TRADE PAYMENT; ELECTRONIC FUNDS TRANSFER; X12.

ELECTRONIC FUNDS TRANSFER (EFT) transfer of funds between accounts by electronic means rather than conventional paper-based payment methods, such as CHECK writing. As defined by the ELECTRONIC FUND TRANSFER ACT of 1978, an electronic funds transfer is any financial transaction originating from a telephone, electronic terminal, computer, or magnetic tape.

There are two categories of EFT systems:

1. large dollar WIRE TRANSFER systems such as Fed Wire, the Federal Reserve communication system linking Federal Reserve Banks, member banks, and the Treasury; and the Clearing House Interbank Payment System (CHIPS), a private wire network that handles most of the U.S. dollar volume in foreign trade.
2. consumer electronic payment systems, including AUTOMATED TELLER MACHINE networks, retail merchant POINT-OF-SALE (POS) debit card systems, and telephone bill payment systems. *See also* ELECTRONIC DATA INTERCHANGE; INTERNET BANKING.

ELECTRONIC FUND TRANSFER ACT federal law enacted in 1978 providing the legal framework for ELECTRONIC FUNDS TRANSFER into, or out of, a consumer's bank account. These payments are not regulated by the UNIFORM COMMERCIAL CODE, which limits its coverage of consumer payments to negotiable instruments, such as checks or drafts. The act specifies protections available to consumers sending or receiving funds electronically, and limits consumer liability for UNAUTHORIZED TRANSFER to $50, provided the bank is notified promptly. The act requires financial institutions to inform consumers of their financial rights under the act, provide written receipts of all electronic transfers, list transfers on an ACCOUNT STATEMENT, and develop procedures for error resolution. These guidelines are implemented in Federal Reserve REGULATION B. *See also* PERSONAL IDENTIFICATION NUMBER; PROVISIONAL CREDIT.

ELECTRONIC TRANSFER ACCOUNT (ETA) bank account for electronic DIRECT DEPOSIT of Social Security and other federal payments to individuals. Intended for consumers without regular checking or savings accounts, electronic transfer accounts were authorized by the Debt Collection Improvement Act of 1996. Accounts became available to the public in 1999. Account holders can draw against deposited funds at automated teller machines or electronic point-of-sale terminals. *See also* ELECTRONIC BENEFITS TRANSFER

ELIGIBLE PAPER notes, drafts, bankers' acceptances, and negotiable instruments that are acceptable collateral for DISCOUNT WINDOW loans at a Federal Reserve Bank or sale to investors. To be acceptable for rediscount, paper must arise from a commercial transaction, have a maturity not exceeding 90 days, and bear the member bank's endorsement. The Monetary Control Act of 1980 extended discount window access to all financial institutions holding transaction accounts or business time deposits.

ELIGIBLE SECURITIES

1. debt securities banks may buy from issuers and trade in the dealer market—principally Treasury obligations and general obligation municipal bonds. Trading in "ineligible" securities such as corporate bonds is restricted to a bank's SECURITIES SUBSIDIARY.
2. securities regarded as acceptable bank investments: Treasury and agency securities, and municipal bonds in the four top rating categories.

EMBEDDED OPTION option that is part of the structure of a bank loan, bond, or financial instrument. Common examples are prepayment options in mortgages, early withdrawal options in certificates of deposit, annual caps in adjustable-rate mortgages, and call (early redemption) provisions in corporate bonds. Embedded options are very interest rate sensitive and add uncertainty in the calculation of projected returns and interest risk because the probability they will be exercised is always present. Also called *hidden option*.

EMBEZZLEMENT unlawful conversion of assets held in trust, as when a bank teller diverts money in a cash drawer to personal use. Misappropriation of bank funds can take many forms, which makes detection difficult.

EMERGENCY CREDIT extended term loan, usually more than 30 days, from a Federal Reserve Bank to nonbank financial institutions when assistance is not available from other sources. Reserve Banks are also authorized by the Federal Reserve Act and the Dodd-Frank

Act enacted after the 2008 financial crisis to extend credit to corporations other than banks. *See also* EXTENDED CREDIT.

EMPLOYEE RETIREMENT INCOME SECURITY ACT (ERISA) federal law enacted in 1974 that set investment guidelines for management of private pension plans and profit sharing plans, including employee vesting and conduct of plan administrators. The act also established a pension insurance fund, the Pension Benefit Guaranty Corp.

EMPLOYEE SAVINGS PLAN group savings plan, involving tax-deferred employee contributions to a pooled investment account. Contributions are often matched, up to a certain dollar amount, by employers. Other examples are 401(K) PLANS and profit sharing plans.

EMPLOYEE STOCK OWNERSHIP PLAN (ESOP) stock ownership plan whereby employees purchase shares in their company's stock. Shares can be sold directly through a STOCK PURCHASE OPTION, or through a company sponsored 401(K) PLAN. A leveraged ESOP allows a company to raise its capital-to-asset ratio by issuing new shares of stock to an employee trust, which finances the transaction with a loan from a bank. The ESOP loan is repaid in pretax corporate dollars, and dividend payments to employees and the dividends reducing the bank loan are tax deductible expenses. An ESOP is often used as a retirement benefit to current employees. Employees receive shares of stock and future dividends that can be reinvested in new stock. These plans often are started by companies seeking to avoid hostile takeover by keeping company stock in friendly hands.

EMPLOYEE TRUST pension or profit-sharing plan set up by an employer, usually a corporation, to provide retirement income for its employees. Known as an employee benefit trust, or DEFINED BENEFIT PLAN, the plan is managed by a trustee, often a bank, which pays out funds at retirement or as instructed by the plan's corporate sponsor.

ENCODING imprinting of the dollar amount in machine readable characters—MAGNETIC INK CHARACTER RECOGNITION (MICR), on checks sent through the banking system for collection, as well as checks deposited at the same bank from which the items are drawn. All preprinted checks have standard MICR line coding on the bottom edge, and for a good reason; the Federal Reserve refuses to handle unencoded checks as CASH ITEMS, which means delayed funds availability for the depositor.

ENCRYPTION scrambling of sensitive information, such as account numbers or access codes, to prevent unauthorized use. The DATA ENCRYPTION STANDARD (DES), the encryption format adopted by the financial industry, requires that information scrambling take place in a computer or terminal before transmission. *See also* MESSAGE AUTHENTICATION CODE.

ENCUMBRANCE right or claim to real property that passes with title, for example, easements, judgment liens, and mortgages. An encumbrance does not hinder transfer of ownership, though it may reduce the market value of the property.

ENDORSEMENT signature on the back of a negotiable instrument, such as a CHECK. Endorsement legally transfers ownership to another party. The UNIFORM COMMERCIAL CODE recognizes five kinds of endorsement: (1) BLANK ENDORSEMENT or unqualified endorsement; (2) special endorsement; for example, "Pay to the order of ABC Company"; (3) restrictive endorsement, writing limiting further negotiation, such as "for deposit only"; (4) qualified endorsement, "Pay to ABC Bank, without recourse"; and (5) conditional endorsement, "Pay XYZ Company upon completion of contract." (Rarely used.)

The Expedited Funds Availability Act of 1987 imposes certain restrictions on check endorsements, requiring endorsers to write their names in the top 1½ inches on the back of a check, leaving space for bank endorsements.

ENDORSER person who, by signing a check or negotiable instrument, transfers his ownership interest to another party. The endorser promises to make good on the check if it is dishonored for any reason.

END-TO-END foreign exchange term for the end-of-month working date against another end-of-month working date, regardless of the actual number of days in between. The term also can apply to the forward maturities in a CURRENCY SWAP. For example, an end-to-end January-February forward contract would go from January 31 to February 28, not 30 days from January 31. Also called *fixed dates.*

EQUAL CREDIT OPPORTUNITY ACT (ECOA) federal law enacted in 1974 requiring lenders to give businesses and consumers equal access to credit. The act specifically prohibits credit discrimination on the basis of race, marital status, national origin, age, or dependence on public assistance. Borrowers who exercise their consumer rights under the Consumer Credit Protection Act are also protected from credit discrimination. Lenders are required to respond to credit applications within 30 days, and if the application is rejected, to offer reasons for denying credit. The act is implemented by Federal Reserve REGULATION B. *See also* EFFECTS TEST; PROHIBITED BASIS.

EQUITY

1. value of stockholders' ownership interest in a corporation after all claims have been paid, and thus a claim on its assets in proportion to the number, and class, of shares owned. Equity, also called net value or net worth, is total assets less total liabilities. Common stock equity of a bank is counted as part of its RISK-BASED CAPITAL.
2. fairness in settling legal disputes, as opposed to a strict interpretation of common law rules.
3. residual value of a brokerage or futures margin account, assuming its liquidation at the current market prices.
4. credit union member's ownership interest, represented by a SHARE ACCOUNT.
5. market value of real property, less any outstanding mortgages.

EQUITY KICKER *see* KICKER.

EQUITY OF REDEMPTION mortgagor's right to redeem property after DEFAULT, and avoid a FORECLOSURE sale, by paying the outstanding principal, plus interest and other costs, to the mortgagee. Some states permit redemptions even after a foreclosure auction.

EQUIVALENT BOND YIELD *see* BOND EQUIVALENT YIELD.

EQUIVALENT TAXABLE YIELD *see* TAXABLE EQUIVALENT YIELD.

ERROR RESOLUTION procedures for correcting disputed transactions to a consumer's bank account, under Federal Reserve REGULATION E. A consumer claiming that funds were taken from an account by another person's UNAUTHORIZED TRANSFER without prior consent, or a transaction was posted improperly due to a bank bookkeeping error, can have the error corrected by notifying the financial institution holding the account. Once notice is given, the financial institution has from 10 to 45 days to investigate the complaint and recredit funds debited in error. The consumer's account liability is limited by regulation to $50 if the bank is notified of the error, but otherwise can be as high as $500. *See also* PROVISIONAL CREDIT.

ERRORS AND OMISSION INSURANCE liability insurance protecting a lender against losses due to negligence, improper documentation, and other errors, but not gross negligence or fraud. An example is TITLE INSURANCE. Errors and Omission coverage is required of financial institutions originating mortgage loans for resale in the secondary mortgage market.

ESCHEAT reversion of property to the state under certain prescribed conditions when the owner dies without heirs or if a depositor's account remains inactive for a specified number of years and the owner cannot be located. Property may be redeemed if the owner reappears.

ESCROW written agreement authorizing the holding of funds by a third party (the escrow agent). Banks typically hold escrow accounts for real estate taxes and property insurance due on mortgaged property.

ESSENTIAL PURPOSE BOND *see* PUBLIC PURPOSE BOND.

ESTATE

1. ownership rights or claims to property, both real estate and personal property, at the time of death. The total of a person's assets passes to his heirs, according to the terms of a will, or is disposed of at the discretion of a probate court if no will is left. Individuals plan for the orderly distribution of an estate through *estate planning,* which involves the drawing of wills and creation of trusts, to achieve maximum benefit for heirs or trust beneficiaries in event of death.
2. assets owned by a debtor entering bankruptcy; also any assets acquired within 180 days of filing petition. Some assets are

excluded from the debtor's estate, such as 401(k) savings plans and education savings accounts.

ESTOPPEL CERTIFICATE contract clause in which one party asserts that mortgage debt, collateral pledged, and so on, is correct on the date the agreement was made. This prevents the borrower from claiming differently at a later date. Also called an *estoppel clause.*

EURO monetary unit of 17 member countries in the European Union. Several additional countries, not EU members, also use the Euro as their official currency. These included (as of 2011) Andorra, Kosovo, Montenegro, Monaco, San Marino, and Vatican City. The Euro was officially adopted on January 1, 1999 by 11 European nations—Austria, Belgium, Finland, France, Germany, Ireland, Italy, Luxembourg, the Netherlands, Portugal and Spain, followed by Greece in 2001. On its debut as the common currency in the European Monetary Union (EMU) group of nations, the Euro replaced the EUROPEAN CURRENCY UNIT (ECU) and the initial value of the Euro was fixed at a one-to-one equivalence with the ECU. Euro-denominated currency and coins went into circulation on January 1, 2002, replacing all national currencies.

The common currency was adopted by the Maastricht Treaty on European Union, signed in Maastricht, the Netherlands, in 1992 and ratified in 1993 by the parliaments of the member nations. Public referendums approved the treaty in some countries. The economic rationale behind the Euro was that a single currency would promote cross-border trade within Europe and international trade with the rest of the world. Converting to a single currency also helps companies cut costs and promotes a more efficient banking system because businesses would no longer have to conduct business in several different currencies.

The European countries converting to the Euro qualified by meeting a series of economic conditions, known as the convergence criteria as certified by the European Commission in 1998.

—inflation cannot exceed more than 1.5% of the inflation rate of the three best performing countries.

—budget deficit targets must fall within 3% of gross domestic product (GDP) and government debt below a reference value of 60% debt-to-GDP ratio.

—currency exchange rates are to stay within the normal fluctuation margin (currency bands) of the EUROPEAN MONETARY SYSTEM (EMS) for at least two years.

EUROBOND corporate or government bond denominated in a currency other than the national currency of the issuer. These bonds are ordinarily issued in bearer form by international syndicates of commercial banks and investment banks that bid on securities offered for sale through a TENDER PANEL. *See also* SAMURAI BOND; YANKEE BOND; YEN BOND.

EUROCOMMERCIAL PAPER short-term unsecured promissory note issued in London and other European financial centers for same-day settlement in U.S. dollars in New York. Paper is issued in either discount or interest-bearing form and distributed through dealers on a best-effort basis, in contrast to EURONOTE facilities, which are issued through a TENDER PANEL. Eurocommercial paper gives issuers quicker access to funds than Euronotes, sometimes same-day funds.

EUROCREDIT *see* FLOATING RATE NOTE; REVOLVING UNDERWRITING FACILITY.

EUROCURRENCY deposit in any bank outside the country of origin. Eurocurrency deposits are time deposits that can be loaned from one owner to another, ordinarily on a short-term basis.

EURODOLLAR dollar denominated deposit in a bank or bank branch outside the United States. The majority of Eurodollar deposits are found outside the United States, primarily in London based banks, where there is an active secondary market for large Eurodollar deposits. Banks holding Eurodollar deposits use them to make loans, denominated in dollars, to corporations, foreign governments and government agencies, domestic U.S. banks, and others.

EURODOLLAR CERTIFICATE OF DEPOSIT certificate of deposit issued by a U.S. bank branch located outside the United States. Virtually all Euro CDs are issued in London at rates pegged to the LONDON INTERBANK OFFERED RATE.

EURO FEDS overnight advances of Eurodollars between U.S. based banks, transmitted by FEDERAL WIRE. U.S. banks with excess reserves may find a Euro placement (a deposit of dollars in the Euromarket) more attractive than selling Fed funds. Consequently, the rate on overnight Euros closely tracks the Fed funds rate.

EURO INTERBANK OFFERED RATE (EURIBOR) benchmark interest rate for Euro-denominated loans and debt instruments. Euribor rates are compiled by the Euopean Banking Federation and released each business day at 11 A.M. Brussels time. Rates are quoted for one week and monthly maturities out to a year.

EURONOTE

1. Short-term unsecured promissory notes issued in the Euro Zone by a high credit quality corporate, financial, or sovereign institution.
2. Euro Zone legal tender, issued in 5, 10, 15, 20, 50, 100, 200, and 500 euro denominations by the European Central Bank.

EURO OVERNIGHT INDEX AVERAGE (EONIA) benchmark interest rate in the Euro Zone for overnight bank loans. Eonia is a weighted average of the rates charged by major European banks (the panel banks) for unsecured overnight loans to other banks in the interbank market. The Eonia rate is the underlying rate for interest rate swaps and other financial derivatives.

EUROPEAN BANK FOR RECONSTRUCTION AND DEVELOPMENT development bank created in 1990 by the twelve member nations of the European Community to recapitalize the former Soviet bloc countries in Eastern and Central Europe. Nations contributing funding also include the United States and Japan. Also known as *European Development Bank.*

EUROPEAN CENTRAL BANK (ECB) bank founded to oversee monetary policy in the European Community countries adopting the EURO common currency. The European Central Bank coordinates policy with the central banks of the participating countries. Collectively, the ECB and the central banks of the European countries make up the European System of Central Banks (ESCB). The ECB itself is run by a Governing Council, whose members are drawn from the bank's executive board and governors of the national central banks. The ECB executive board, consisting of the bank's president, vice president, and four appointed members, serve non-renewable terms of up to eight years.

The European Central Bank was created by the Maastricht Treaty on European Union ratified in 1993, which established the European Monetary Union (EMU) and the EURO, the common currency of European countries. The ESCB's tasks are defining and implementing the monetary policy of the European Community, conducting foreign exchange operations to achieve price stability, holding and managing the foreign currency reserves of members states, and promoting stability in the overall financial system.

The ESCB is governed by the decision-making bodies of the ECB: 1) the Executive Board; 2) the Governing Council, whose members are governors of the national central banks of European Union nations participating in the Euro and the ECB Executive Board; 3) the General Council, made up of the ECB president and vice president, and the governors of all national central banks.

The ECB, working jointly with the national central banks, operates the TARGET (Trans European Automated Real-Time Gross Settlement Express Transfer) funds transfer system for large-value Euro payments. The TARGET cross-border payment system is similar to the FEDERAL RESERVE FEDERAL WIRE (FEDWIRE), and provides immediately available transfers of funds.

EUROPEAN COMMUNITY economic alliance formed in 1957 by Belgium, France, Italy, Germany, Luxembourg, and the Netherlands to promote trade and cooperation among its members.

With ratification of the Maastricht Treaty on European Union in 1993, the European Community dropped its previous name, the European Economic Community (EEC). The European Community is closely identified with the EUROPEAN UNION, an economic and social policy group of which it is a part.

EUROPEAN CURRENCY UNIT (ECU) monetary unit of the EUROPEAN COMMUNITY from 1979 until the introduction of the EURO in January

1999. The ECU, a basket currency, was made up from predetermined amounts of all the EC countries except the Spanish peseta and the Portuguese escudo. Its principal application was ECU-denominated securities. When the Euro became Europe's common currency, the ECU ceased to exist as a monetary unit; the initial value of the Euro was set to ensure one-to-one equivalence between the ECU and the Euro.

EUROPEAN MONETARY SYSTEM (EMS) 1979 agreement by European nations to link their currencies with the objective of limiting currency variations to a narrow range and keeping inflation in check. A forerunner of today's EUROPEAN UNION, the EMS eventually became strained by the differing economic policies of its members and in the early 1990s by the permanent withdrawal of Britain. These differences led to formation of the European Monetary Institute in 1994, an interim step toward a common economic policy, and in 1998 the EUROPEAN CENTRAL BANK.

EUROPEAN UNION group of countries taking part in the economic unification of Europe. (There were 27 countries in the European Union in 2011. Only 17 of the 27 members of the European Union (EU) are part of the Euro Zone, the name for the collection of EU countries that utilize the euro.) The term also refers to the pan-European governmental and social agencies involved in inter-governmental cooperation: the European Commission (based in Brussels, Belgium), which oversees Europe's economic and monetary unification; the European Parliament, directly elected by citizens of member countries; the Council of Ministers, consisting of the foreign ministers of EU member governments; the European Court of Justice, the court of last resort for interpreting EU treaties; and the Court of Auditors, which monitors government budgets of EU countries. The 1993 Maastricht treaty gave the European Parliament equal decision-making powers with the Council and Commission.

EVERGREEN LOAN revolving line of credit with no CLEAN-UP REQUIREMENT requiring the borrower to pay off the outstanding balance periodically. Evergreen loans are generally made for specific terms, for example three years, and may be renewed or cancelled at the end of that period. This is also a de facto condition of short-term loans that are constantly renewed without a reduction in loan principal. *See also* BULLET LOAN; REVOLVING CREDIT.

EXACT INTEREST interest calculated on a 365-day year, as opposed to a 360-day year, which is known as ORDINARY INTEREST. Banks use the 365-day basis in paying DAILY INTEREST on certificates of deposit and other time deposits.

EXCEPTION ITEM check that cannot be paid for one reason or another, such as a customer's STOP PAYMENT order, closed account, missing endorsement, and so on. Also, any item requiring special handling by the paying bank.

EXCESS CASH FLOW payments from loans or mortgages underlying mortgage-backed bonds or other asset-backed bonds in excess of the amount needed to retire the bonds. This additional cash flow, from overcollateralization, mismatched coupons, prepayments, or reinvestment income, may be used toward bond redemption or passed to investors who purchased a residual interest in the securities.

EXCESSIVE PURCHASES credit card charges deviating from normal usage. Frequent use of a credit card in a 24-hour period is an alert to the possibility that a card has been stolen or is being used fraudulently.

EXCESS LOANS loans exceeding the LEGAL LENDING LIMIT for loans to a single borrower. State banks are limited to making loans to a single borrower equal to 10% of their available capital, and national banks are limited to a 15% maximum. Bank directors may be held personally accountable for losses resulting from excessive loans. *See also* INSIDER LENDING.

EXCESS RESERVES surplus balances above what banks are legally required to hold to meet RESERVE REQUIREMENTS. The Federal Reserve began paying interest on excess reserve balances in 2008; this was authorized by Congress in 2006 after decades of discussion. The program gives smaller banks the option to earn interest on excess balances held at a Federal Reserve bank.

EXCESS SPREAD an ASSET-BACKED SECURITIES term for yield remaining after payments to bondholders are made, expenses paid, and losses covered. Excess spread is the issuer's profit and the first layer of protection for bondholders.

EXCHANGE CONTROLS restrictions on currency flows between countries, imposed by central banks or monetary authorities. A country may: (1) prohibit residents from owning a bank account denominated in another currency or an account in a foreign bank; (2) prohibit exporters from drawing against a bank account except for internal transfers; and (3) limit bank trading in a domestic currency to discourage currency speculation. Exchange controls are common in some European countries and in most developing countries; a bank account in one of these currencies is known as a BLOCKED ACCOUNT. These currencies frequently are overvalued in relation to unimpeded currencies, and may not be CONVERTIBLE easily into other currencies or a monetary standard, such as gold. *See also* DIRTY FLOAT; RESTRICTED MARKET.

EXCHANGE RATE conversion price for exchanging one currency for another. Exchange rates are influenced by a number of factors, including domestic interest rates and inflation rates, and whether central banks are attempting to influence the market price through INTERVENTION in the exchange markets.

EXCHANGE STABILIZATION FUND U.S. currency reserve fund employed to stabilize rates in the foreign exchange market. The fund is managed by the Federal Reserve Bank of New York, acting in its role as fiscal agent for the Treasury Department. The exchange stabilization fund is also a clearing house for CURRENCY SWAPS by the world's central banks and SPECIAL DRAWING RIGHTS allocated to various countries by the INTERNATIONAL MONETARY FUND.

EXCHANGE-TRADED FUND (ETF) security representing a market index and traded on a stock exchange. Exchange-traded funds are similar to index mutual funds but can be bought or sold any time during the day and have lower expense ratios. Two popular ETFs are Standard & Poor's Depositary Receipt (SPIDERS), which started in 1993, and the NASDAQ-100 Tracking Stock Index first offered in 1999.

EX-COUPON *see* COUPON STRIPPING.

EXECUTOR person or institution, often a trust company, named in a WILL to distribute the assets of a decedent. The executor assumes control of the assets of an estate, pays estate taxes, debts, and expenses.

EXEMPT SECURITIES securities exempt from registration and reporting rules of the Securities and Exchange Commission and Federal Reserve margin requirements. U.S. Treasury securities, as well as federal agency issues, municipal bonds, commercial paper and private placements are exempt from these rules. Direct obligations of a bank or savings institution and Ginnie Mae pass-through certificates are exempt from SEC registration.

EXERCISE PRICE *see* STRIKE PRICE.

EX-LEGAL denotes the absence of a legal opinion. Municipal bonds are sometimes issued without the customary legal opinion of a bond counsel printed on the certificates, which may hinder the marketability of the bonds when they are traded.

EXOTIC CURRENCY currency that is not traded easily; there is no depth to the market. Exotic currencies have wide BID AND ASKED spreads in the over-the-counter foreign exchange market. *See also* WEAK CURRENCY.

EXPECTATIONS THEORY interest rate theory that says the anticipated YIELD on successive maturities of the same security is determined by investor expectations of future interest rates. The expectations theory tries to explain the term structure of interest rates by saying that any combination of maturities produces roughly the same average yield. Investors anticipating rising short-term interest rates will buy more short maturity securities, which influences the slope of the YIELD CURVE. Contrast with the MARKET SEGMENTATION THEORY. *See also* INVERTED YIELD CURVE; LIQUIDITY PREFERENCE THEORY.

EXPEDITED FUNDS AVAILABILITY ACT federal law enacted by Congress in 1987 limiting CHECK HOLDS on checks deposited into a bank account, and requiring banks and other depository financial institutions to follow a uniform funds availability schedule in processing checks or drafts deposited into an account. Under the Expedited Funds Availability Act, the first $100 of a check is to be available for use at the opening of business the day after a deposit is made, remaining funds on the second day after the deposit if payable by a local bank, and within five days if drawn on more distant banks, after September 1, 1990. Cash deposits, U.S. Treasury checks, official bank checks (cashier's checks, certified checks, and teller's checks), and checks paid by government agencies are also included in checks subject to next day availability. The Expedited Funds Availability Act is implemented by Federal Reserve Regulation CC.

EXPIRATION DATE

1. last date a bank CREDIT CARD can be used. The date is embossed on the card.
2. in options trading, the last date an options contract can be exercised. In American style options, options can be exercised any time during the option cycle; in European style options, they can be exercised only on the maturity date.

EXPORT-IMPORT BANK independent federal agency set up by Congress in 1934 to finance exports of U.S. products by making intermediate and long-term nonrecourse loans when financing is unavailable from private lenders. The Eximbank borrows from the Treasury Department to make direct credits and discount loans to foreign borrowers, and also provides credit guarantees and insurance against political risk. The bank competes with similar financing agencies in other industrialized nations. *See also* FOREIGN CREDIT INSURANCE ASSOCIATION.

EXPORT TRADING COMPANY (ETC) trading organization supplying support services required for export trade. An ETC may warehouse, ship, and insure goods, as well as supply clients with market information. U.S. commercial banks are permitted to own and operate export trading companies under the Bank Export Services Act of 1982.

EXPOSURE

1. total amount of credit committed to a single borrower, or to a single country if EXTERNAL DEBT is considered.
2. in foreign exchange and futures market trading, the potential for suffering a gain or loss from fluctuations in market prices.
3. bank's risk of suffering a loss when it credits a customer's account before funds are collected from the payer. This is called a DAYLIGHT OVERDRAFT in wire transfer systems. *See also* MISMATCH; POSITION.

EXPRESS TRUST trust created by explicit instructions, given either orally or in writing, as opposed to a *constructive trust* created by a court of equity.

EXTENDED CREDIT advance from a Federal Reserve Bank for a longer period than the customary ADJUSTMENT CREDIT arranged at a discount window. Extended credit is often for periods longer than 30 days, priced at a surcharge above the Fed's discount rate, and it fills the needs of seasonal credit by small banks lacking direct access to money markets and credit to meet the liquidity needs of banks holding long-term fixed rate assets. *See also* EMERGENCY CREDIT; SEASONAL CREDIT.

EXTENSION AGREEMENT agreement by a lender to roll back the due date on a loan. Lenders are sometimes willing to do this when they believe a borrower's financial condition will eventually improve, and that extending the maturity is preferable to calling the loan. *See also* STANDSTILL AGREEMENT.

EXTENSION RISK risk that rising interest rates will slow bond repayments beyond the scheduled maturity date, causing investors owning low-yielding mortgage-backed or asset-backed securities to find their principal committed for longer time periods than expected. Investors risk losing the opportunity to buy new issue bonds paying a higher rate of interest.

EXTERNAL DEBT

1. funds obtained from outside an organization, including bank loans and subordinated debt—a measure of financial leverage. In general, external debt is anything that is not equity capital such as common stock or preferred stock.
2. total amount of bank debt owed by debtor nations to foreign lenders and creditor banks.

F

FACE VALUE principal of a security, insurance policy, or unit of currency. In securities, the face value (or the PAR VALUE) and market value are usually different until maturity. That price difference is the PREMIUM or DISCOUNT.

FACILITY FEE lender's charge for making a line of credit or other credit facility available to a borrower, for example, a COMMITMENT FEE.

FACSIMILE DRAFT computer generated copy of an original sales draft. In a disputed credit card transaction, for example, a facsimile draft shows enough information—account number, signature, transaction amount—to validate a transaction.

FACTORING short-term financing from the nonrecourse sale of accounts receivable to a third party, known as a *factor.* The factor assumes the full risk of collection, including credit losses. Factoring is most common in the garment industry, but has been used in other industries as well. There are two basic types of factoring: (1) discount factoring, in which the factor pays a discounted price for the receivables prior to the maturity date; and (2) maturity factoring, where the factor pays the client the purchase price of the factored accounts at maturity.

Factoring can be on a notification, or a non-notification basis. The typical method in accounts receivable factoring is non-notification financing, in which the client's debtors are not notified and the client remits payments to the factor as they are received. Factoring is normally done WITHOUT RECOURSE, meaning that the factor assumes the risk of nonpayment. Financing carried out on a RECOURSE basis is called ACCOUNTS RECEIVABLE FINANCING. *See also* ASSET-BASED LENDING; PURCHASE ORDER FINANCING.

FAIL

1. **Banking.** The inability of a bank to meet its credit obligations to other banks, possibly causing settlement failures at other banks. This is known as SYSTEMIC RISK. *See also* TOO BIG TO FAIL.
2. **Securities.** A trade in which delivery does not take place on the settlement date. If it is the fault of the seller, that is, the seller fails to deliver the securities, the trade is noted as a fail to deliver. If buyer fails to pay because securities have not been delivered by the seller's broker, it is a fail to receive. Fails normally occur when the buyer and seller disagree on whether the securities delivered meet the specifications of the purchase order.

FAIR CREDIT BILLING ACT federal act specifying procedures for resolution of billing disputes in consumer credit. Enacted by Congress in 1974, the Fair Credit Billing Act amends the TRUTH IN LENDING ACT by: (1) requiring lenders to correct billing errors within

90 days of receiving a consumer complaint; (2) prohibiting credit card issuers from offsetting an unpaid bill against a deposit account without obtaining a court order; and (3) limiting a credit cardholder's liability to a maximum of $50. Consumers must be given a statement of their credit rights. *See also* PROVISIONAL CREDIT; REGULATION Z.

FAIR CREDIT REPORTING ACT federal law enacted in 1970 to ensure confidentiality of consumer credit information held by lenders and credit reporting agencies. The act prohibits disclosure of credit files, other than for specific purposes, such as employment, insurance, and bona fide credit applications; requires credit bureaus to give consumers a copy of their credit report when requested; and specifies procedures whereby consumers can dispute any DEROGATORY INFORMATION in a credit report.

FAIR MARKET VALUE price at which an asset passes from a willing seller to a willing buyer, each having access to all the relevant facts and acting freely—frequently the basis for tax assessments and judicial awards.

FANNIE MAE federally chartered corporation that purchases qualifying mortgages from lenders and sells securities backed by mortgage loans to investors. Fannie Mae, the largest source of home mortgage funding in the United States, purchases mortgages and mortgage-backed securities from financial institutions and guarantees timely payment of principal and interest to buyers of Fannie Mae–issued mortgage securities. When a bank lender delivers a pool of mortgage loans to Fannie Mae, Fannie Mae creates a MORTGAGE-BACKED SECURITY in exchange for the loans. The lender can hold the mortgage security in its own portfolio or sell it to investors.

Fannie Mae buys federally insured or guaranteed mortgages and conforming mortgage loans (loans with an original principal amount under a CONFORMING LOAN limit). This figure is adjusted annually. Fannie Mae raises its operating capital from issuance of common stock, from the sale of notes and debentures, and from the guaranty fees it charges mortgage lenders. Created in 1938 as the Federal National Mortgage Association, Fannie Mae became an investor-owned corporation in 1968. In 1986 Fannie Mae made an important advance in mortgage securitization, issuing the first stripped mortgage-backed security—a mortgage security with an unequal distribution of principal and interest in a single mortgage pool.

As a buyer of mortgages in the secondary market, Fannie Mae functions in much the same way as its major competitor, FREDDIE MAC. While similar, their historical origins are quite different: Fannie Mae was organized to purchase loans from mortgage bankers and thereby encourages bankers to originate new loans. Freddie Mac was created in 1970 to help savings and loan associations (or thrift institutions, as they were known) distribute their loans in the secondary market. Both are government-sponsored enterprises, meaning the companies have a government-defined mission and charter, but they obtain operating funds from the capital markets. In 2008, Fannie Mae was placed under government control (supervised by the Federal Housing Finance Administration) after suffering large losses in its mortgage securities portfolio. The U.S. Treasury Department pledged to provide capital as needed to ensure Fannie Mae's support of the housing and mortgage markets.

FARM CREDIT SYSTEM (FCS) nationwide cooperative system of banks and associations providing credit to farmers, agricultural concerns, and related businesses. The system is comprised of the Banks for Cooperatives, which makes loans to farmer-owned marketing, supply, and service cooperatives, and rural utilities; the Farm Credit Banks, which make short and intermediate term farm loans secured by real estate; and the Federal Farm Credit Banks Funding Corp., which acts as a conduit through which the FCS issues debt in the credit markets. The Farm Credit Banks were created by merger of the old Federal Intermediate Credit Banks, making intermediate term farm loans, and the Federal Land Banks. A new agency, the Federal Agricultural Mortgage Corporation (FARMER MAC) was established by the Agricultural Credit Act of 1987 to create a secondary market for farm credit. Bonds, notes, and other obligations issued by Farm System institutions, other than the FAC, are insured by the Farm Credit System Insurance Corporation. Another federal agency, the Farm Credit Financial Assistance Corporation, provides capital assistance by issuing government guaranteed bonds. The Farm Credit System, originally capitalized by the federal government, is now self-funding and owned by its member-borrowers.

FARMER MAC nickname for the Federal Agricultural Mortgage Corporation, a stockholder-owned company created by the Agricultural Credit Act of 1987 to improve the availability of long-term credit for America's farmers. Farmer Mac provides secondary market liquidity and lending support by purchasing newly originated and existing agricultural loans directly from farm lenders; exchanging Farmer Mac guaranteed securities for eligible farm loans; issuing long-term standby purchase commitments for eligible loans; and by purchasing and guaranteeing securities backed by eligible agricultural loans, which are known in the market as AgVantage® bonds.

FARMERS HOME ADMINISTRATION (FmHA) agency of the U.S. Department of Agriculture supplying loans, including operating loans, water conservation loans, and residential mortgages to farmers in rural areas. Farmers Home Administration loans are funded by annual appropriations by Congress, and by private lenders, whose loans are guaranteed up to 90% of principal and interest by the Farmers Home Administration.

FASIT a rarely used structure (short for Financial Asset Securitization Investment Trust) for the pooling of credit card receivables, home equity loans and auto loans, and sale of multi-class securities to investors. FASITs were phased out by the American Jobs Creation Act of 2004.

FEDERAL ADVISORY COUNCIL advisory group consisting of one member from each Federal Reserve District, usually a banker, selected annually by the board of directors in each of the 12 Federal districts. Members meet with the Federal Reserve Board at least four times a year to make recommendations on business and financial issues relating to banking, but have no real power.

FEDERAL AGENCIES interest-bearing debt securities of U.S. departments and agencies. Among these are the 12 Federal Home Loan Banks, the Export-Import Bank, the Government National Mortgage Association, and the Federal Housing Administration.

Federal agencies lend directly to qualified borrowers or guarantee loans made by private lenders. Some agency securities are backed by the FULL FAITH AND CREDIT of the U.S. government, for example, Ginnie Mae pass-through securities and participation certificates, whereas Fannie Mae debentures are backed only by the issuer.

FEDERAL CREDIT UNION (FCU) federally chartered non-profit consumer cooperative. Federal credit unions, which hold the majority of credit union assets in the United States, originate a wide variety of consumer credit, from auto loans to residential mortgages at competitive rates.

FEDERAL DEPOSIT INSURANCE CORPORATION (FDIC) federal agency managing the DEPOSIT INSURANCE FUND (DIF), insuring depositor accounts in banks and thrift institutions up to $250,000 in principal and interest. The FDIC maintains the DIF by assessing depository institutions an insurance premium, which is based on the insured deposits in each financial institution as well as each bank's degree of risk to the insurance fund. FDIC insurance coverage is mandatory for Federal Reserve member banks and banks supervised by the Comptroller of the Currency.

Insured banks and thrift institutions must maintain certain liquidity and reserve requirements to receive deposit insurance coverage. They are classified into five groups based on their RISK-BASED CAPITAL ratio: from well capitalized (capital ratio of 10% or higher) to critically undercapitalized (risk-based capital ratio under 2%). The FDIC has authority to force undercapitalized banks to take corrective action and declare critically undercapitalized banks insolvent. Changes to the FDIC's formula for assessing deposit insurance premiums, authorized by the Dodd-Frank Act of 2010, take into account an insured bank's total deposit base (including overseas deposits) when computing deposit insurance assessments for individual financial institutions.

FEDERAL DEPOSIT INSURANCE CORPORATION IMPROVEMENT ACT (FDICIA) federal law enacted in 1991 to address the thrift industry crisis. FDICIA recapitalized the BANK INSURANCE FUND of the Federal Deposit Insurance Corporation (FDIC), expanded the authority of banking regulators to seize undercapitalized banks, and expanded consumer protections available to banking customers.

Among its major provisions:

(1) raised the FDIC's authority to borrow from the Treasury Department from $5 million to $30 million.

(2) revised deposit insurance coverage, linking the premiums banks pay for FDIC insurance to their financial strength.

(3) required banking regulators to intervene in restructuring banks and thrifts that fail to meet minimum capital requirements.

(4) required the FDIC to use the method least costly to the insurance fund when merging insolvent banks into healthy ones.

(5) required annual on-site examinations of banks and thrifts.

(6) required banks and thrifts to disclose fair market value of their assets.

(7) required audited financial statements in annual reports of banks and thrifts with assets of $150 million or more.

(8) introduced a new formula for computing capital adequacy.

(9) imposed new limits on executive compensation and lending to senior officers and bank directors.

(10) extended U.S. banking regulations and on-site examinations to branches of foreign banks.

(11) required disclosure of more information (TRUTH IN SAVINGS) on interest rates paid to depositors.

See also REGULATION F; RISK-BASED DEPOSIT INSURANCE; UNINSURED DEPOSITOR.

FEDERAL FINANCIAL INSTITUTIONS EXAMINATION COUNCIL (FFIEC) coordinating group of federal and state banking regulators. The FFIEC was created to promote uniform supervision of U.S. financial institutions. Current members include the Board of Governors of the Federal Reserve System, the Federal Deposit Insurance Corporation, the National Credit Union Administration, and the Office of the Comptroller of the Currency. The State Liaison Committee (representing the Conference of State Bank Supervisors, the American Council of State Banking Supervisors, and the National Association of State Credit Union Supervisors) became a voting member of the FFIEC in 2006. The CONSUMER FINANCIAL PROTECTION BUREAU was added in 2011. *See also* UNIFORM BANK PERFORMANCE REPORT.

FEDERAL FINANCING BANK (FFB) agency in the U.S. Treasury established by Congress in 1973 to centralize borrowing by federal agencies. The FFB makes loans at favorable rates to agencies that do not have ready access to the credit markets; its debt is a direct obligation of the U.S. Treasury.

FEDERAL FUNDS unsecured loans of immediately available funds from excess balances in RESERVE ACCOUNTS held at Federal Reserve

Banks. Technically, Fed Funds are not borrowings, but purchases of bank reserves. A bank advancing Fed Funds sells excess reserves; a bank receiving Fed Funds buys reserves from the selling bank. Although most Fed Funds sales are made on an overnight basis, some are negotiated for much longer periods as Term Fed Funds. The term *federal funds* also refers to money made available from one party to another for immediate use. Some deals are described as "payable in federal funds." Contrast with CLEARINGHOUSE FUNDS. *See also* FEDERAL FUNDS RATE.

FEDERAL FUNDS RATE rate charged in the interbank market for purchases of EXCESS RESERVE balances. The rate of interest paid on overnight Fed Funds, the Fed Funds rate, is a key money market interest rate, and is the benchmark interest rate for other short-term credit arrangements. Because the Fed Funds rate reprices with each transaction, unlike the Federal Reserve DISCOUNT RATE, it is the most sensitive of the money market rates and is watched carefully by the Federal Reserve Board.

FEDERAL HOME LOAN BANK SYSTEM largest collective source of mortgage financing in the U.S. Its functions are similar to what the Federal Reserve System does for commercial banks. The Federal Home Loan Bank System consists of twelve regional federal home loan banks that make low-rate advances to savings and loan associations, cooperative banks, and commercial banks. It raises money by selling notes and bonds in the financial markets. The system was created in 1932 following a wave of bank failures to help restore confidence in the nation's financial system and improve the supply of funds available for home loans. In 1989 the Federal Home Loan Bank System's public policy mission was expanded to include affordable housing and community development lending. Since 1997 the regional home loan banks have purchased pools of conforming mortgage loans under a cooperative risk-sharing arrangement (called Mortgage Partnership Finance or Mortgage Purchase, depending on the district bank involved) with the originating financial institutions. The Financial Services Modernization Act of 1999 (the GRAMM-LEACH-BLILEY ACT) expanded the types of collateral for credit advances to include small business loans and farm and agribusiness loans and permitted commercial banks to become member institutions if they originated a certain percentage of their loans as residential mortgages. *See also* QUALIFIED THRIFT LENDER.

FEDERAL HOME LOAN MORTGAGE CORPORATION (FHLMC) *see* FREDDIE MAC.

FEDERAL HOUSING ADMINISTRATION (FHA) federal agency that insures residential mortgages. Created by the National Housing Act of 1934, the FHA is now a part of the Department of Housing and Urban Development. Both the FHA and the Department of Veterans Affairs have single family mortgage programs to assist home buyers that are unable to obtain financing from conventional mortgage lenders (banks, savings and loans, and other financial institutions). Private lenders are the sources of funds for FHA loans, but the FHA loans often have a rate ceiling below prevailing market rates. There are also limits on the loan amount the FHA will insure for a single borrower.

FEDERAL INTERMEDIATE CREDIT BANK *see* FARM CREDIT SYSTEM.

FEDERAL LAND BANK *see* FARM CREDIT SYSTEM.

FEDERAL NATIONAL MORTGAGE ASSOCIATION (FNMA) *see* FREDDIE MAC.

FEDERAL OPEN MARKET COMMITTEE (FOMC) policy committee in the Federal Reserve System that sets short-term MONETARY POLICY objectives for the Fed. The committee is made up of the seven governors of the Federal Reserve Board, plus five of the 12 presidents of Federal Reserve Banks. The president of the Federal Reserve Bank of New York is a permanent FOMC member. The other four slots are filled on a rotating basis by presidents of the other 11 Federal Reserve Banks. The committee carries out monetary objectives by instructing the Open Market Desk at the Federal Reserve Bank of New York to buy or sell government securities from a special account, called the OPEN MARKET ACCOUNT, at the New York Fed. When the FOMC purchases securities, it adds reserves to the banking system, expanding the supply of credit and allowing banks to make more loans; when it sells securities, it drains reserves and tightens credit.

The Federal Open Market Committee generally buys and sells securities, normally U.S. Treasury bills, for longer-term impact. For short-term adjustment of bank reserves, it will sell securities to a securities dealer with an agreement to repurchase (a MATCHED SALE—PURCHASE AGREEMENT), or buy securities from a dealer, followed by a subsequent resale back to the dealer (a REPURCHASE AGREEMENT). Open market operations are one of several monetary policy tools of the Federal Reserve; the others are the discount rate and reserve requirements on transaction and time deposit accounts. *See also* DISCOUNT WINDOW; OPEN MARKET OPERATIONS; REPURCHASE AGREEMENT; RESERVE REQUIREMENTS.

FEDERAL RESERVE BANK one of 12 regional banks in the FEDERAL RESERVE SYSTEM. These banks are located in Boston, New York, Philadelphia, Cleveland, Richmond, Atlanta, Chicago, St. Louis, Minneapolis, Kansas City, Dallas, and San Francisco. The role of each bank, and its branches, is to provide central bank services, such as check collection, access to the Federal Reserve Wire Network (FEDERAL WIRE or Fed Wire) and credit advances at the Fed DISCOUNT WINDOW. In addition, Federal Reserve Banks establish monetary policy along with the Federal Reserve Board of Governors, and monitor commercial and savings banks to ensure that financial institutions follow Federal Reserve regulations. Reserve banks act as depositories for member banks in their regions. Each Federal Reserve Bank is owned by commercial banks in its Federal Reserve district that hold stock in the Fed district bank. These commercial banks are MEMBER BANKS in the Federal Reserve System. *See also* FEDERAL RESERVE BOARD; REGIONAL CHECK PROCESSING CENTER.

FEDERAL RESERVE BOARD (FRB) seven-member board governing the FEDERAL RESERVE SYSTEM. Its members are appointed by the president, subject to Senate confirmation, and serve 14-year terms. The board supervises the banking system by issuing regulations controlling the activities of bank holding companies, and also issues regulations implementing federal laws regulating banking; holds a voting majority at meetings of the influential FEDERAL OPEN MARKET COMMITTEE, which exercises control over the supply of credit in the banking system; and sets RESERVE REQUIREMENTS for NATIONAL BANKS and state chartered banks that own stock in Federal Reserve Banks. The financial modernization act of 1999 (the Gramm-Leach-Bliley Act) expanded the Federal Reserve Board's authority to supervise financial holding companies, a new type of BANK HOLDING COMPANY. It also established a supervisory process in which the Federal Reserve would consult with the U.S. Treasury Department to determine activities that are both closely related to banking and financial in nature, and thus acceptable activities for financial holding companies. The Dodd-Frank Act of 2008 expanded the board's authority, giving the Fed the power to supervise thrift-holding companies, subsidiaries of thrift-holding companies, investment banks, and selected nonfinancial companies. *See also* FEDERAL RESERVE BANK; FUNCTIONAL REGULATION.

FEDERAL RESERVE CREDIT credit contributed to the banking system by Federal Reserve Banks. This is derived from a variety of sources (1) Reserve Bank discounts and advances at the DISCOUNT WINDOW, secured by bank endorsed business paper (discounts) or credit advances secured by government securities put up as collateral (advances); (2) Treasury and federal agency securities owned by reserve banks through OPEN MARKET OPERATIONS of the Federal Reserve System; and (3) additional sources of credit, including longer-term EXTENDED CREDIT to financial institutions having liquidity problems, and FEDERAL RESERVE FLOAT on checks presented to Reserve Banks for collection.

Reserve Banks exert more influence over lending by financial institutions through the actions of the FEDERAL OPEN MARKET COMMITTEE than the Fed DISCOUNT WINDOW loans. *See also* MONETARY BASE.

FEDERAL RESERVE FLOAT temporary credit to a bank's reserve account caused by the time lag in the collection of checks. Float is checkbook money on the books of both the paying bank and the depositing bank, in effect fictitious reserves created when a Federal Reserve Bank credits a DEFERRED AVAILABILITY check to a bank's

Reserve Account at the Fed but before it has collected payment on the check from the paying bank.

Checks drawn on banks in cities with a Federal Reserve Bank or branch office are treated as IMMEDIATE CREDIT checks and no Fed float is created. Processing and transportation delays are the major causes of Fed float, the largest source of collection float in the U.S. banking system.

FEDERAL RESERVE NOTE circulating currency issued by Federal Reserve Banks to meet the public's seasonal needs for money. Federal Reserve notes are non-interest bearing promissory notes issued in denominations of $1 to $100, and are official LEGAL TENDER for payment of debts. The notes bear the name of the issuing Federal Reserve Bank.

FEDERAL RESERVE REGULATIONS *see* REGULATION A through REGULATION EE.

FEDERAL RESERVE SYSTEM central banking system in the United States, the "Fed," established by the Federal Reserve Act of 1913 and comprising the 12 district Federal Reserve Banks and their 24 branch offices, the Federal Reserve Board of Governors in Washington, D.C., the Federal Open Market Committee, the Federal Advisory Council, and member banks owning stock in one of the 12 Federal Reserve Banks. National banks are required by law to own stock in the Federal Reserve Bank in their region. State chartered banks have the option of becoming member banks.

As its name implies, the Federal Reserve System is a federal central bank, with operational responsibilities shared by the Board of Governors and the 12 regional banks. The Federal Reserve System regulates the cost and availability of bank credit through MONETARY POLICY decisions of the Federal Open Market Committee; sets the DISCOUNT RATE banks pay when borrowing from a Federal Reserve Bank; approves interstate banking mergers; supervises bank holding companies, and oversees international banking operations through agreements with other central banks. *See also* FEDERAL RESERVE BANK; FEDERAL RESERVE BOARD; FEDERAL WIRE.

FEDERAL SAVINGS AND LOAN (S & L) ASSOCIATION federally chartered savings and loan association supervised by the Comptroller of the Currency. Federal savings and loans (S&Ls) derive their funds mostly from consumer deposits and invest primarily in long-term residential mortgages. Congress authorized federally chartered savings institutions to serve the needs of home buyers under the Home Owners' Loan Act of 1933. Since the early 1980s, deregulation in the banking industry gave federal savings institutions the right to offer checking accounts and Negotiable Order of Withdrawal (NOW) accounts. The Garn-St Germain Act of 1982 allowed federal savings institutions to make consumer loans, offer discount brokerage accounts, and invest up to 5% of assets in commercial loans. Even with these expanded powers, federal S&Ls are required to keep at least 70% of assets in residential mortgages or mortgage securities. *See also* FEDERAL SAVINGS BANK; QUALIFIED THRIFT LENDER; THRIFT INSTITUTION.

FEDERAL SAVINGS AND LOAN INSURANCE CORPORATION (FSLIC) federal agency established by Congress in 1934 to insure deposits in savings and loan associations and savings banks. During the 1980s, heavy losses by savings institutions depleted the reserves of the FSLIC, causing it to become insolvent. Assets and liabilities of the FSLIC were transferred to a new agency, the Savings Association Insurance Fund in 1989. In 2006, deposit insurance funds for banks and thrift institutions were merged into a single entity, the DEPOSIT INSURANCE FUND.

FEDERAL SAVINGS BANK (FSB) savings bank, chartered and supervised by the Office of Thrift Supervision. Federal savings banks, designated by the letters FSB or FA in an institution's name, were authorized by a 1978 amendment to the Home Owners' Loan Act of 1933. Federal savings banks can put up to 10% of assets in commercial, business, or agricultural loans, and can be chartered as mutual or stockholder-owned institutions.

FEDERAL WIRE (FED WIRE) high-speed electronic communications network linking the Federal Reserve Board of Governors, the 12 Federal Reserve Banks and 24 branches, the U.S. Treasury Department, and other federal agencies. The Federal Reserve Wire Network, more commonly known as *Fed Wire*, is used by the Reserve Banks and the Treasury for high-value time-sensitive payments, such as funds transfers between reserve banks, purchases or sales of FED FUNDS transfers between correspondent banks, and sales of book entry U.S. government securities.

Federal Reserve MEMBER BANKS and other depository financial institutions also have access to the Fed Wire network to their own account and in transferring funds on behalf of a customer, when timeliness and certainty of payment are important. The Treasury Department and federal agencies make extensive use of the Fed Wire in collection of funds from Treasury TAX AND LOAN ACCOUNTS in commercial banks, and in disbursement of funds.

Fed Wire transfers are immediate transfers of funds, and are effective usually within minutes of the time a payment is initiated. They are guaranteed as final payments when the receiving financial institution is notified of the credit to its reserve account. *See also* AUTOMATED CLEARING HOUSE; CLEARING HOUSE INTERBANK PAYMENTS SYSTEM; SOCIETY FOR WORLDWIDE INTERBANK FINANCIAL TELECOMMUNICATIONS.

FED FUNDS *see* FEDERAL FUNDS.

FED WIRE *see* FEDERAL WIRE.

FEE a charge for services performed.

1. **Banking.** A lender's charge for making credit available, for example, a COMMITMENT FEE or credit card annual fee. Also, charges for

noncredit services, such as a trust department's allowance or commission.

2. **Estates.** An inheritable estate in land, usually referred to as a fee simple estate or freehold estate. A *fee simple absolute* is an estate to which the holder has unquestioned ownership, whereas a fee tail is inheritable only by a limited group of heirs.

FIAT MONEY paper money that is backed only by the issuing government's decree that it is acceptable as LEGAL TENDER currency. Its value stems from public confidence, rather than convertible into gold or other hard currency.

FIDELITY BOND *see* BANKER'S BLANKET BOND.

FIDUCIARY person or legal entity that administers investments for the benefit of others. A fiduciary is legally obligated to safeguard assets in trust in the best interests of those for whom it acts. State law, the Uniform Fiduciaries Act, controls what fiduciaries can or cannot do with entrusted assets. *See also* PRUDENT MAN RULE.

FIELD WAREHOUSE *see* WAREHOUSE.

15-YEAR MORTGAGE popular variation of the fixed-rate mortgage that pays off a home mortgage over a 15-year period. The monthly payments are slightly higher than those in a regular 30-year mortgage, but a greater portion of each loan payment is applied to the principal, so the interest actually paid is significantly less than with a regular 30-year loan at the same interest rate and amount borrowed. A disadvantage for borrowers with growing incomes is the 15-year mortgage lowers the amount of tax-deductible interest paid over the life of the loan.

FINALITY OF PAYMENT guaranty of payment to the party receiving an electronic funds transfer. Interbank payments over the Federal Reserve Wire Network (FEDERAL WIRE) are final and irrevocable when transmitted, and are credited to the receiving bank's reserve account at the time of the transaction. *See also* NET SETTLEMENT; SAME DAY FUNDS.

FINANCE BILL bill of exchange that, when accepted by a bank, becomes a source of short-term credit for working capital rather than import or export finance. Finance bills, which usually have maturities longer than 60 days, are sometimes issued in tight money periods. They are subject to reserve requirements, unlike ordinary bankers' acceptances, and cannot be rediscounted at the Federal Reserve window. Also called a *bankers' bill* or *working capital acceptance.*

FINANCE CHARGE borrower's total cost of credit, including loan interest, commitment fees, and prepaid interest, in a consumer loan. Under the Truth in Lending Act, the finance charge must be disclosed as the total dollar cost of credit. Contrast with ANNUAL PERCENTAGE RATE, which states the cost of credit as an annualized rate.

The finance charge does not include late payment fees, annual charges, such as a credit card annual fee, and credit insurance, except in situations where the lender requires insurance before a loan is made.

FINANCE COMPANY financial intermediary, often affiliated with a holding company or a manufacturer, that makes loans to individuals or businesses. As a group, finance companies service several distinct segments of the financial services market. Captive finance companies owned by manufacturers finance their dealers' inventory and provide direct financing, sometimes at below-market rates, to consumers buying the manufacturer's goods. Sales finance companies purchase, at a discount, the installment sales contracts of retail merchants. Commercial finance companies, also known as commercial credit companies, make loans to wholesalers and manufacturers, secured by the assets of the business (ASSET-BASED LENDING), and engage in lease financing. Credit receivables of finance companies are the basis of many ASSET-BACKED SECURITIES that are traded in the capital markets as ordinary bonds and notes. Some diversified finance companies, such as General Electric Capital (G.E. Capital), are among the largest financial intermediaries and are involved in all phases of credit, from consumer and equipment financing to aircraft leasing.

Finance companies raise most of the funds needed for lending from sale of commercial paper and short-term debt in the capital markets. *See also* FINANCIAL INSTITUTION; FINANCIAL SUPERMARKET.

FINANCE LEASE fixed-term lease, usually noncancellable, used by businesses in financing capital equipment. The lessor's service is limited to financing the asset, whereas the lessee pays all other costs, including maintenance and taxes, and has the option of purchasing the asset at the end of the lease for a nominal price. It is also called *a full-payout lease* because the lease is fully paid out (amortized) over its lifetime. Contrast with OPERATING LEASE.

FINANCIAL ACCOUNTING STANDARDS BOARD (FASB) seven member self-regulatory board, based in Norwalk, Connecticut, that sets accounting rules for certified public accountants. Organized in 1973, its Statements of Financial Accounting Standards are the basis for GENERALLY ACCEPTED ACCOUNTING PRINCIPLES.

FINANCIAL COUNSELING *see* CREDIT COUNSELING; FINANCIAL PLANNING.

FINANCIAL FUTURE FUTURES CONTRACT on a financial instrument. The value of the contract rises or falls in accordance with the movement of interest rates. Contracts gain in value as rates fall, and lose value when interest rates rise. Traders use financial futures to speculate on the future directions in interest rates, while financial institutions (such as banks, mortgage bankers, and savings institutions) use futures contracts to hedge against falling prices and protect the value of their portfolios' assets. Trading in financial futures is supervised by the Commodity Futures Trading Commission, a federal self-regulatory organization. Financial futures traded on commodities exchanges include contracts in Treasury bill and bond futures, certificates of deposit, commercial paper, Government National Mortgage Association (Ginnie Mae) pass-through securities, foreign currencies, and stock market indexes. *See also* CURRENCY FUTURES; INTEREST RATE FUTURES.

FINANCIAL GUARANTEE noncancellable indemnity bond guaranteeing the timely payment of principal and interest due on securities by the maturity date. If the issuer defaults, the insurer will pay a fixed sum of money to holders of the securities. Financial guarantees are similar to a STANDBY LETTER OF CREDIT, but are issued by an insurance company. *See also* CREDIT ENHANCEMENT; MUNICIPAL BOND INSURANCE.

FINANCIAL HOLDING COMPANY (FHC) financial entity engaged in a broad range of banking-related activities, created by the GRAMM-LEACH-BLILEY ACT OF 1999. These activities include: insurance underwriting, securities dealing and underwriting, financial and investment advisory services, merchant banking, issuing or selling securitized interests in bank-eligible assets, and generally engaging in any non-banking activity authorized by the Bank Holding Company Act. Financial holding companies are authorized to engage in activities that are "financial" in nature and "incidental" to financial activities. The Federal Reserve Board is responsible for supervising the financial condition and activities of financial holding companies.

Similarly, any non-bank commercial company that is "predominantly" engaged in financial activities, earning 85% or more of its gross revenues from financial services, may choose to become a financial holding company.

FINANCIAL INNOVATION payment system advances altering or modifying the role of banks, and financial institutions in general, as intermediaries between suppliers and users of funds. Technological innovations, such as ELECTRONIC FUNDS TRANSFER payments, replace checks with electronic debits and credits. Risk transferring innovations, such as ADJUSTABLE RATE MORTGAGES, transfer credit risk from one party to another. Credit generating innovations, for example, HOME EQUITY CREDIT lines, give borrowers new ways to use financial assets, increasing the supply of available credit. Equity generating innovations, such as TRUST PREFERRED STOCK, give banks a less costly way to raise equity capital than issuing new shares of common stock.

FINANCIAL INSTITUTION government agency or privately owned entity that collects funds from the public, and from other institutions, and invests those funds in financial assets, such as loans, securities, bank deposits, and income generating property. Broadly defined, financial institutions act as intermediaries between savers and borrowers and are differentiated by the way they obtain and invest their funds. Depository financial institutions—a group that includes commercial banks, savings and loan associations, mutual savings banks, and credit unions—conduct business by accepting public deposits, which are insured by the federal government against loss, and channeling their depositors' money into lending activities. Nondepository financial institutions, such as brokerage firms, life insurance companies, pension funds, and investment companies, fund their investment activities directly from the financial markets by selling securities to the public or by selling insurance policies, in the case of insurance companies. Increasingly, the boundaries between depository and nondepository institutions have become less distinct. Brokerage firms can invest their customers' money in bank CDs, whereas banks and savings institutions offer securities brokerage and mutual funds.

FINANCIAL INSTITUTIONS REFORM, RECOVERY AND ENFORCEMENT ACT (FIRREA) federal legislation of 1989 providing government funds to insolvent savings and loan associations, and mandating sweeping changes in the examination and supervision of savings and loans. The act required savings and loans to adopt new capital standards, transferred the regulatory powers of the Federal Home Loan Bank Board to the OFFICE OF THRIFT SUPERVISION, a bureau within the U.S. Treasury Department; and placed the 12 district Federal Home Loan Banks under control of an oversight board, the Federal Housing Finance Board. The act also abolished the defunct Federal Savings and Loan Insurance Corporation (FSLIC).

Among its major provisions:

(1) established two federal deposit insurance funds, the BANK INSURANCE FUND, insuring deposits in commercial banks, and the SAVINGS ASSOCIATION INSURANCE FUND, insuring deposits in savings institutions. Both funds are to be managed by the Federal Deposit Insurance Corporation.

(2) authorized a new federal agency, the RESOLUTION FUNDING CORPORATION, to finance the liquidation of insolvent savings associations.

(3) established a federal agency, the RESOLUTION TRUST CORPORATION (RTC), to dispose of assets of failed savings associations.

(4) expanded the board of directors of the Federal Deposit Insurance Corporation from three to five members, including the director of the Office of Thrift Supervision, and two others appointed by the President and confirmed by the Senate.

(5) required savings and loans to meet minimum capital standards: tangible capital of 1.5% of total assets, "core capital," which is tangible capital plus goodwill equal to 3% of total assets that may have been acquired in a merger; and RISK-BASED CAPITAL equal to 6.4% of risk-weighted assets (rising to 8% after January 1, 1993). GOODWILL was excluded from inclusion in core capital after 1994.

(6) authorized a new insurance logo for savings and loans including the words "backed by the full faith and credit of the United States Government."

(7) required savings and loans to meet a new "qualified thrift lender" test of 70% of portfolio assets in residential mortgages or mortgage related securities.

(8) raised deposit insurance premiums paid by commercial banks and savings and loans to recapitalize the federal deposit insurance funds.

(9) permitted commercial banks and savings and loans to acquire financially sound savings associations in other states.

(10) permitted banking regulators to seize assets of healthy banks when an affiliated bank becomes insolvent.

(11) banned, with certain exceptions, savings and loans from converting from the Savings Association Insurance Fund to the Bank Insurance Fund for a five-year period ending in 1994.

(12) required savings associations to adhere to the same risk-based capital standards as national banks.

(13) required savings associations to adhere to the same lending limit in loans to a single borrower as national banks: a legal loan limit equal to 15% of capital in unsecured loans and 25% of capital in secured loans.

(14) required savings associations to divest their holdings in junk bonds by July 1, 1994, and generally follow the same investment guidelines as commercial banks. Junk bonds and direct investments of savings and loans must be held in separately capitalized subsidiaries.

(15) permitted the district Federal Home Loan Banks to accept commercial banks as member institutions and make credit advances to commercial banks with at least 10% of assets in residential mortgages.

(16) banned the use of brokered deposits by savings associations failing to meet minimum capital requirements.

(17) required the district Home Loan Banks to establish an Affordable Housing Program, and pledge a percentage of their retained earnings to mortgages to low income borrowers.

(18) banned tax breaks to acquirers of insolvent savings associations.

(19) directed the Treasury Department and the General Accounting Office to conduct studies of risk-based deposit insurance, market valuation accounting, and other matters.

(20) allowed commercial banks to market bank services directly to nonbank affiliates and bank-owned affiliates.

(21) restructured the Federal Home Loan Mortgage Corporation as a stockholder owned corporation with an 18-member board of directors. Holders of Freddie Mac preferred stock were authorized to exchange shares of preferred stock for voting common stock.

(22) amended the Home Mortgage Disclosure Act to require mortgage lenders to collect and report to their primary regulator data on mortgage activities by census tract.

(23) amended the Community Reinvestment Act to require federal banking regulators to disclose lender compliance annually on an A-B-C-D scale.

(24) directed that real estate appraisals comply with state certification and licensing standards.

(25) expanded the enforcement powers of banking regulators, authorizing banking agencies to assess civil money penalties up to $1 million a day and criminal penalties up to $5 million a day, and added bank fraud to crimes covered under the Racketeer Influenced and Corrupt Organizations Act (RICO).

FINANCIAL INSTITUTIONS REGULATORY ACT federal law enacted in 1978 that (1) created the FEDERAL FINANCIAL INSTITUTIONS EXAMINATION COUNCIL to coordinate the activities of federal supervisory agencies; (2) authorized banking regulators to issue CEASE AND DESIST orders against officers and directors of financial institutions; (3) required banks to make loans to directors, officers, and major stockholders on the same terms as other borrowers; (4) created a credit union CENTRAL LIQUIDITY FACILITY to meet short-term liquidity needs of insured credit unions; and (5) placed ELECTRONIC FUNDS TRANSFERS between financial institutions and consumers under federal regulation. *See also* ELECTRONIC FUND TRANSFER ACT.

FINANCIAL INSTITUTIONS REGULATORY AUTHORITY (FINRA) self-regulatory organization created by the merger of the National Association of Securities Dealers (NASD) and the New York Stock Exchange's regulation committee. The Financial Industry Regulatory Authority oversees business among brokerage firms, registered securities representatives, and the investing public. The FINRA Investor Education Foundation, created in 2003, is the largest U.S. foundation dedicated to investor education.

FINANCIAL INTERMEDIARY financial institution, such as a commercial bank or savings and loan association, that accepts deposits from the public and makes loans to those needing credit. By acting as a middleman between cash surplus units in the economy (savers) and deficit spending units (borrowers), a financial intermediary makes it possible for borrowers to tap into the vast pool of wealth in federally insured deposits in banks and other depository financial institutions. The movement of capital from surplus units through financial institutions to deficit units seeking bank credit is an indirect form of financing known as *intermediation*—consumers are net suppliers of funds, whereas business and government are net borrowers. A bank gives its depositors a claim against itself, meaning that the depositor has recourse against the bank (and, if the bank fails, the deposit insurance fund protecting insured deposits), but has no claim against the borrower who takes out a bank loan. *See also* DISINTERMEDIATION.

FINANCIAL LEVERAGE *see* LEVERAGE.

FINANCIAL PLANNING

1. **Banking.** Capital budgeting and profit planning carried out by a bank's senior management committee, with the aim of managing

asset growth, net income, and expenses to meet specific objectives in future time periods. Financial planning is broader in scope than ASSET-LIABILITY MANAGEMENT, which is largely concerned with pricing interest sensitive deposits and bank loans and managing interest rate risk and liquidity risk. In a larger sense, bank financial planning is synonymous with strategic planning and market planning, both of which are concerned with setting specific targets for deposit growth, net income, and expected payback or return from new branch offices, automated teller machines, and other facilities. Through financial planning, a bank's senior management committee formulates plans for meeting competition from other financial services companies and sets objectives for profitability, growth in market share, types of customers to be served, and so on, all of which determine the future direction of the bank.

2. **Investments.** Financial counseling designed to help individuals make the best use of their financial assets and achieve specific economic objectives, such as adequate funding of a child's college education expenses, or post-retirement needs. Financial planning entails writing objectives, setting up budgets, and periodically reviewing a plan. Many banks and bank trust departments offer financial planning services to help private banking or retail customers select customized financial services suiting their individual needs, charging an hourly rate or a flat fee for writing a financial plan. Professional financial planners are certified by the College for Financial Planning.

FINANCIAL PRIVACY consumer protection expressed in the Right to Financial Privacy Act of 1978 and expanded by subsequent laws. Depository institutions may give federal agencies access to financial account information in connection with a law enforcement action if the request is: (1) authorized by a consumer, or (2) obtained by formal written request, subpoena or search warrant. The financial modernization act of 1999 establishes a national standard for financial privacy, and gives consumers the option to disallow disclosure of their financial data (such as account numbers) to unaffiliated companies. This right of refusal (called an *opt-out right*) is to be given to consumers together with a copy of their financial institution's privacy policy.

FINANCIAL SERVICES MODERNIZATION ACT *see* GRAMM-LEACH-BLILEY ACT OF 1999.

FINANCIAL STABILITY BOARD international committee of central bankers, finance ministers, and multinational financial organizations created in 2009 to coordinate bank supervision in the major world economies. The Board is based in Basel, Switzerland. Web site: *www.financialstabilityboard.org.*

FINANCIAL STABILITY OVERSIGHT COUNCIL interagency group chaired by the U.S. Treasury Secretary to monitor the U.S. financial system and identify potential threats to the country's financial stability. The council has 10 voting and five nonvoting members. The voting members include Treasury officials, Federal Reserve Board members, and insurance experts.

FINANCIAL STATEMENT report summarizing the financial condition of an individual, partnership, or business organization. Statements that bank lenders use most often in making loans are the BALANCE SHEET (assets, liabilities, and net worth as of a certain date); the INCOME STATEMENT summarizing income and expenses; and the statement of cash flows summarizing the sources and uses of funds in a given year.

FINANCIAL SUPERMARKET popular name for a company offering a market basket of financial services. The financial supermarket became part of the banking industry's vocabulary in the 1980s, when nonbanking financial companies, unrestricted by banking regulations, began offering financial services in competition with banks and thrifts.

The GRAMM-LEACH-BLILEY ACT OF 1999, authorizing banks and nonbank financial services companies to enter each other's businesses, signals the beginning of a new era in marketing financial services. With the Gramm-Leach-Bliley Act, banks have the authority to market mutual funds, annuities and life insurance, in addition to federally insured deposit accounts. The biggest drawback to *one-stop shopping* at a bank or brokerage company is consumer unwillingness to put all of their eggs, financially speaking, in one basket.

FINANCING STATEMENT document filed with a lender detailing personal property taken as collateral from a borrower. The financing statement, a standard document under the UNIFORM COMMERCIAL CODE, is filed with the secretary of state or designated public official. The document is time stamped, the filing date is noted, and a file number is assigned, securing the lender's claim to the assigned collateral. *See also* CONTINUATION STATEMENT; PRIORITY OF LIEN.

FINDER'S FEE

1. fee paid by a lender to a broker, or sometimes by a borrower to a broker, for obtaining a loan, usually a mortgage, or for referring business to a lender.
2. fee paid by a lender to a third party and sometimes to a bank's own customers, for referring new business.
3. in real estate, a commission paid to a broker for locating a property.
4. in securities, a fee paid by an investment banker to someone who brings in a deal.

FIREWALLS

1. regulations meant to segregate a bank's securities underwriting from its deposit gathering and lending activities. The intended purpose of Federal Reserve Board regulations dealing with securities

underwriting is maintaining the functional separation of banking and commerce. *See also* VOLCKER RULE

2. combination of hardware and software separating a computer network from external networks, mainly the Internet.

FIRM COMMITMENT

Banking:

1. lender's agreement to fund a commercial loan, installment loan, or mortgage loan at a quoted rate for a specific period of time. Called a LOCK-IN PERIOD in mortgage lending. A COMMITMENT FEE is often required; is usually forfeited if the borrower does not take the loan.
2. in the secondary mortgage market, a lender's agreement to sell loans to a buyer in a specific future time period. Secondary market buyers, such as Fannie Mae or Freddie Mac, buy loans with a 60- to 120-day forward delivery. *See also* GOING LONG; GOING SHORT.

Securities: securities offering in which the underwriters assume all the risk, as opposed to a BEST EFFORT deal in which the underwriter acts as agent for the issuer.

FIRST CALL DATE earliest date a bond issuer may redeem all or part of the issue at a price specified in the indenture. The first exercisable call date is noted in the bond offering sheets. Mortgage-backed bonds may become callable if original principal falls to a certain level, even if no call date is given. *See also* YIELD TO CALL; YIELD TO MATURITY.

FIRST DAY NOTICE first date on which a seller in the futures market notifies a clearing house of his intention to deliver a financial instrument, in fulfillment of a futures contract. Also, the date on which a clearinghouse notifies a buyer.

FIRST MORTGAGE mortgage creating a primary lien against real property, and having priority over subsequent mortgages, which are known as junior mortgages. It is the first to be paid when the property is sold. *See also* HOME EQUITY CREDIT; SECOND MORTGAGE.

FIRST TO FILE RULE *see* PRIORITY OF LIEN.

FISCAL AGENT

1. organization, usually a bank or trust company, that disburses funds for dividend payments, redeems bonds and coupons, and performs other services for a bond issuer.
2. agent for a municipal, state, or national government. The Federal Reserve is fiscal agent for the Treasury Department in dealings with other central banks and international monetary organizations. *See also* EXCHANGE STABILIZATION FUND.

FISCAL POLICY taxation and spending policies of the federal government. Fiscal policy is carried out by adjusting budgetary deficits (or surpluses) to achieve desired economic goals. When federal expenditures grow at a faster rate than tax revenues, the U.S. Treasury raises additional funds by borrowing in the capital markets. When tax revenues exceed federal spending, surplus funds can be used to reduce the national debt. In practice, Congress has found it difficult to adjust the federal budget to balance revenues and expenditures.

Fiscal policy is administered independently of the Federal Reserve System's MONETARY POLICY, although the two have similar goals—balanced economic growth and stable employment at low rates of inflation—and together exert considerable influence over the demand for bank credit and pricing of bank loans. Deficit spending by the federal government must be financed through periodic borrowings in the public debt market by the Treasury Department. These auctions of new Treasury debt are closely watched by the Federal Reserve, and by the financial markets in general. *See also* CROWDING OUT; KEYNESIAN ECONOMICS; MONETARY ACCORD OF 1951; SUPPLY SIDE ECONOMICS.

FISCAL YEAR any 12-month period or period of 52 weeks, designated by a corporation, government agency, or any other organization as the time period for filing financial reports, balance sheets, and income statements. This period may differ from the calendar year.

FIVE C'S OF CREDIT judgmental method of evaluating a potential borrower's creditworthiness, based on five criteria: *character, capacity, capital, collateral,* and *conditions.* The first four deal with a borrower's ABILITY TO PAY, whereas the last point refers to general business conditions in the borrower's industry.

FIXED ASSET tangible property used in the operation of a business. Fixed assets are stated on the balance sheet by their net depreciated value. Plant, machinery and equipment, furniture and fixtures, and leasehold improvements are the fixed assets of most companies.

FIXED EXCHANGE RATES FOREIGN EXCHANGE rate system that existed under the BRETTON WOODS SYSTEM, in which the value of national currencies is set vis-à-vis the value of other currencies. Each country is required to maintain its currency at or near this fixed rate. Fixed exchange rates were used until the early 1970s, when the United States abandoned the gold standard and a system of FLOATING EXCHANGE RATE was adopted. *See also* CLEAN FLOAT; SMITHSONIAN AGREEMENT.

FIXED RATE LOAN loan with an interest rate that does not vary over the term of the loan, as opposed to a variable rate loan or ADJUSTABLE RATE MORTGAGE. Fixed rate loans generally are constant payment, fully-amortizing loans, for example, a 30-year fixed rate mortgage. Many consumer installment loans, such as auto loans, boat loans, and home improvement loans, are made at fixed rates. Fixed rate loans often have a higher initial cost than adjustable rate loans because the lender isn't protected against increases in money costs—the lender's cost of funds—but the borrower has the comfort of knowing the rate and payment will not vary over the life of the loan.

FLAT

1. bond traded without accrued interest. This happens if the transaction settlement date is the same as the semiannual interest payment date. Income bonds issued by companies in reorganization—interest is paid only if earned—and bonds in default usually are traded flat.
2. market maker's position that is neither short nor long at the end of a trading session. The net exposure is zero.
3. underwriter's position if all securities are sold from inventory.
4. in the foreign exchange market, broker's position in which commitments to buy a particular currency are identical to commitments to sell that currency. Also called a SQUARE POSITION.

FLAT BED IMPRINTER manual device that copies the embossed characters of a bank card or charge card on all copies of a sales draft. Flat bed imprinters have been largely replaced by electronic cash registers. Card owners' account numbers are captured by swiping credit or debit cards through a card reading device. *See also* POINT-OF-SALE TERMINAL.

FLEXIBLE RATE MORTGAGE *see* ADJUSTABLE RATE MORTGAGE.

FLEXIBLE SPENDING ACCOUNT tax-advantaged account allowing individuals to set aside a portion of their earnings through payroll deduction for medical expenses, dependent care, or other expenses. Employee deductions are not subject to payroll taxes, resulting in substantial tax savings. The most common type is a HEALTH SAVINGS ACCOUNT, which provides funding for current and future medical expenses. Funds deducted from an employee's pay into an FSA are not subject to federal payroll taxes, resulting in substantial payroll tax savings. Paper checks or debit cards may be used to access account funds. Also called *flexible spending arrangement.*

FLOAT dollar value of cash balances created by the time lag in processing unpaid checks. Collection float is interest that may be lost to the depositor; payment float is interest that may be gained by the payer. The largest component of float is FEDERAL RESERVE FLOAT, created when a Federal Reserve Bank credits the reserve account of a collecting bank before it has collected from the paying bank. Other kinds of float are MAIL FLOAT, caused by delays in mail handling between cities; holiday float created when a bank is not open for business due to a state or national holiday; and return item float, created when checks are returned for insufficient funds or other reasons. A bank customer's AVERAGE DAILY FLOAT is often calculated for purposes of ACCOUNT ANALYSIS. *See also* AVAILABLE BALANCE; REGULATION CC.

FLOATER debt instrument with a variable coupon, paying a rate indexed to a money market rate.

FLOATING DEBT one-year to five-year municipal notes issued to meet short-term financing needs, for example, Revenue Anticipation Notes and Tax Anticipation Notes. Municipal obligations that have been rolled into longer-term bonds are known as *funded debt*.

FLOATING EXCHANGE RATE EXCHANGE RATE system in which rates of each national currency are determined by interaction of market supply and demand. Factors affecting demand and supply of each currency include a country's CURRENT ACCOUNT balance, the general strength of its economy, its rate of INFLATION, and interest rates as compared against other nations.

In the years since 1971 when the United States finally abandoned the fixed exchange rate system and convertibility of the dollar into gold, most world currencies have traded at floating, or flexible, exchange rates. A downside to the floating exchange rate system is that central banks have to intervene in the markets from time to time, by buying or selling currencies to keep exchange rates from getting too high or too low. CLEAN FLOAT currency has a minimum of official intervention, except to maintain market stability, and its exchange rate is mostly determined by market demand. DIRTY FLOAT, on the other hand, denotes a varying amount of official INTERVENTION to keep a nation's currency within a desired range of currency prices in relation to other currencies. *See also* CONVERTIBILITY; EXCHANGE CONTROLS; FIXED EXCHANGE RATES.

FLOATING INTEREST RATE loan interest rate that changes whenever an index rate, or BASE RATE, such as the bank PRIME RATE, the LONDON INTERBANK OFFERED RATE (LIBOR). There are numerous examples: (1) consumer loan rate, for example, the rate charged on adjustable rate mortgages or variable rate auto loans, that is indexed to another rate, such as the commercial bank prime rate, a COST OF FUNDS INDEX, or a lender's internal cost of funds; (2) key lending rate, such as the PRIME RATE that moves upward or downward, depending on market demand for funds, available reserves in the banking system, and other factors. Contrast with FIXED RATE LOAN.

FLOATING LIEN loan or credit facility secured by inventory or receivables. This type of security agreement gives the lender an interest in assets acquired by the borrower after the agreement, as well as those owned when the agreement was made. When the agreement covers proceeds from sales, the lender also has recourse against receivables. *See also* BORROWING BASE; INVENTORY FINANCING.

FLOATING RATE CERTIFICATE OF DEPOSIT large dollar certificate of deposit (CD) paying a rate tied to a money market rate. Commonly used in the Euromarket to finance interbank lending, floating rate CDs or floaters are usually denominated in units of $250,000 with a coupon rate tied to the six-month London Interbank Offered Rate (LIBOR). *See also* BROKERED DEPOSIT.

FLOATING RATE LOAN *see* VARIABLE RATE LOAN.

FLOATING RATE NOTE (FRN) variable rate bonds with an interest rate that is periodically reset, usually every three to six months, and that carry a fixed spread, usually over the six-month London Interbank Offered Rate (LIBOR). Floating rate notes, also called FLOATERS, have been an important source of medium-term international credit for commercial banks active in Euromarket lending. Competition in the Euromarket has led to a wide variety of notes: a perpetual floating rate note is a variable rate note with no stated maturity; a capped floating rate note sets an upper limit on the borrower's interest rate; and a mini-max FRN carries a rate that can fluctuate only within a preset range. Floating rate notes are usually subordinated to the claims of the depositors, and usually count toward a bank's capital base.

FLOOD INSURANCE federally subsidized hazard insurance protecting home owners against property damage from flooding. Coverage is mandatory when lenders make federally insured or guaranteed mortgages to home buyers purchasing property in designated flood hazard areas. Flood insurance coverage, obtained from private insurers, is available only to residents of communities participating in the National Flood Insurance Program, administered by the Federal Insurance and Mitigation Administration.

FLOOR minimum rate that a bank can impose on a floating rate or variable rate loan. A floor rate is often negotiated together with a rate ceiling, called an INTEREST RATE CAP; the two financial guarantees are collectively referred to as an interest rate COLLAR. The floor protects the lender from a sharp drop-off in rates; the cap assures the borrower that financing costs will not rise excessively.

FLOOR LIMIT largest credit card a retail merchant may accept without obtaining authorization by the card issuer. Contrast with ZERO-FLOOR LIMIT.

FLOOR LOAN initial funding of a CONSTRUCTION MORTGAGE that a lender agrees to advance without regard for tenant leasing, or requiring the builder to substantially complete the project and have a certificate of occupancy. The lender may fund 80% of the total cost of a project, with the remainder, called a HOLDBACK, held aside until the builder has leased the majority of units or has the building ready for occupancy. A *floor to ceiling loan*, in contrast, has two separate fundings: one at satisfactory completion of the project, and a second funding when the building is fully occupied or meets cash flow requirements set by the lender.

FLOOR PLANNING bank loan made to finance a dealer's inventory. The dealer issues a TRUST RECEIPT to the bank, and the bank is repaid when the inventory is sold. Floor planning has a lower profit margin and is less desirable than other forms of commercial lending. In addition to bearing the financing risk, the bank stands to lose money if the dealer makes a sale without notifying the lender, known as *selling out of trust.* Dealer financing is usually done only on goods for which broad consumer demand exists.

FLORIN monetary unit of Aruba.

FLOW OF FUNDS

1. quarterly Federal Reserve survey showing the movement of funds between different sectors of the economy—households, businesses, governments, and financial institutions. The survey, the "Flow of Funds Accounts," is reported monthly in the *Federal Reserve Bulletin* and is a useful indicator of buying preferences of institutional investors.
2. statement in the bond resolution of a municipal bond issuer stating how municipal revenues are to be applied, generally giving priority to maintenance and operations, and bond debt service. *See also* CASH FLOW.

FOOTINGS expression for the bottom line figure on a bank's balance sheet: the sum of assets or liabilities, plus equity capital.

FORBEARANCE

1. lender's decision not to exercise a legally enforceable right against a borrower in default, in exchange for a promise to make regular payments in the future. For example, a mortgage lender will agree not to initiate foreclosure proceedings against a mortgagor whose loan is in arrears. *See also* MORTGAGE MODIFICATION.
2. temporary relief granted a bank by a regulatory agency from compliance with minimum capital requirements or other banking regulations, extended to financial institutions in economically depressed areas. Banks given capital forbearance must file a plan to restore their capital base within a specified period.

FORECASTING

1. in bank ASSET-LIABILITY MANAGEMENT, an estimate of future expectations based on historical information, current and projected market conditions, and management assumptions about interest rates and market demand for credit. As used in an asset-liability model, forecasting is a planning tool that estimates interest earning assets and interest sensitive liabilities to determine whether the balance sheet will be asset sensitive or liability sensitive during specific time periods in the future. The forecast is normally revised periodically as market conditions or management assumptions change. *See also* DYNAMIC GAP.
2. in corporate CASH MANAGEMENT, an estimate of future cash receipts from conversion of assets into cash. Forecasting tries to anticipate changes in cash flow for purposes of funds management and debt management.
3. projecting corporate earnings, financial institutions, sales, and so on in future time periods. *See also* ECONOMETRICS.

FORECLOSURE legal proceeding initiated by a creditor to take possession of collateral securing a defaulted loan. Some states allow lenders to reclaim property by simply declaring the borrower has defaulted, a process known as *strict foreclosure.* Most states, though, require lenders to file a foreclosure suit and obtain a judgment before seizing and auctioning off a borrower's property. Proceeds from a foreclosure sale are applied first to pay off the mortgage debt and foreclosure expenses, with the remainder, if any, going to the borrower. A borrower in default has the legal right, in most states, to redeem his property, called the RIGHT OF REDEMPTION, by paying the lender the balance of the outstanding debt, plus out-of-pocket expenses.

FOREIGN BRANCHES branches of U.S. banks in foreign countries or branches of foreign banks in the United States. By reciprocal agreement among central banks, foreign branches are subject to the banking laws and regulations in their host country. The International Banking Act of 1978, for example, requires U.S. offices of foreign banks to maintain reserve accounts with a Federal Reserve Bank, choose a home state as their U.S. base of operations, and meet federal regulations covering bank holding companies.

FOREIGN CORPORATION legal term for a corporation chartered in a state other than the one where it does business. A bank chartered in New York, but owning a loan production office in California, is a foreign corporation in California. The less confusing designation, *out-of-state corporation,* is preferred in general usage. Contrast with ALIEN CORPORATION.

FOREIGN CREDIT INSURANCE ASSOCIATION (FCIA) voluntary association of some 50 U.S. insurance companies formed in 1961 under the sponsorship of the EXPORT-IMPORT BANK. Acting as agent for the EximBank and its member companies, it provides insurance coverage for credits extended by U.S. exporters to foreign purchasers. FCIA provides some degree of insurance for commercial risk, whereas EximBank assumes coverage for political risk.

FOREIGN CURRENCY FUTURES *see* CURRENCY FUTURES.

FOREIGN CURRENCY OPTIONS *see* CURRENCY OPTIONS.

FOREIGN CURRENCY TRANSLATION *see* CURRENCY TRANSLATION.

FOREIGN DEPOSITS deposits at branch offices of domestic banks outside the United States or its overseas territories. Such deposits are not subject to deposit insurance premiums or reserve requirements, and are not included in computing the net demand deposits of domestic banks. This freedom from bank regulation was one reason the INTERNATIONAL BANKING FACILITY was authorized by state governments—mostly in New York and California—to create a domestic environment competitive with the relatively unrestricted Bahama and Cayman Islands Offshore Banking Centers.

FOREIGN DRAFT check denominated in a specific foreign currency, usually drawn to the seller on a bank account in the country of the currency's origin.

FOREIGN EXCHANGE currency—literally foreign money—used in settlement of international trade between countries. Trading in foreign exchange is the means by which values are established for commodities and manufactured goods imported or exported between countries. Creditors and borrowers settle the resulting international trade obligations, such as bank drafts, bills of exchange, bankers' acceptances, and letters of credit, by exchanging different currencies at agreed upon rates.

The result of all this international trade is that financial institutions accumulate surpluses of different currencies from loan repayments by foreign borrowers, and also from import-export trade financing on behalf of bank customers.

The interbank foreign exchange market is an over-the-counter market, a network of commercial banks, central banks, brokers, and customers who communicate with each other throughout the world's major financial centers. Foreign exchange traders also make markets (or speculate) in different currencies, usually anticipating future appreciation of stronger currencies against weaker ones, through the foreign exchange FORWARD MARKET and the CURRENCY FUTURES market.

See also FORWARD EXCHANGE CONTRACT; FORWARD FORWARD; VALUE DATE.

FOREIGN EXCHANGE VALUE DATES

TODAY (Transaction Date)	TOMORROW	NEXT DAY	BEYOND TWO DAYS
Cash delivery date (U.S. dollar, Canadian dollar, Mexican peso)	Spot date for Canadian dollar tomorrow / next	Spot delivery date Tomorrow / next delivery date	Forward delivery date

FOREIGN ITEMS check drawn on any bank other than the bank where it is presented for payment. Also called TRANSIT ITEMS.

FORGERY alteration of a document or negotiable instrument with intent to defraud; signing another's signature to a document with intent to defraud. *See also* ALTERED CHECK; RAISED CHECK.

FORINT monetary unit of Hungary.

FORM 8K report disclosing significant events potentially affecting a corporation's financial condition or the market value of its shares, required by the Securities and Exchange Commission. The report is filed within 30 days after the event (a pending merger, an amendment to the corporate charter, a charge to earnings for loan losses) took place, and summarizes information that any reasonable investor would want to know before buying or selling securities.

FORM 10K annual financial report filed with the Securities and Exchange Commission. Issuers of registered securities are required to file a 10K, as well as corporations with 500 or more shareholders, assets of $2 million, and exchange listed corporations. The report, which becomes public information once filed with the SEC, summarizes key financial information, including sources and uses of funds by type of business, net pre-tax operating income, provision for income taxes and loan losses, plus comparative financial statements for the last two fiscal years. A summary of the 10K report is included in the annual report to stockholders.

FORM 1099 official disclosure of calendar year payments, such as bank interest earned on deposit and escrow accounts, stock dividends, bond interest, pension payments, and royalties required for income tax reporting. Banks and other organizations reporting interest or dividend payments mail a 1099 notice to their customers early in a new year.

FORM 10Q quarterly financial report filed by companies with listed securities and corporations required to file an annual 10K report with the Securities and Exchange Commission. The 10Q report, which does not have to be audited, summarizes key financial data on earnings and expenses, and compares current financial information to data reported in the same quarter in the previous year.

FORWARD BOOK total of a foreign exchange dealer's forward contracts in various maturities for a given currency or for all currencies.

FORWARD COMMITMENT agreement by a lender to make a loan at a quoted rate, purchase a loan from another lender, or sell a loan to a secondary market CONDUIT in the future. The commitment, spelled out in a binding contract, may expire if unexercised by a certain date. *See also* LOCK-IN PERIOD.

FORWARD DELIVERY

1. agreement between two parties whereby currency or other financial instruments are exchanged at a specified future date beyond the SPOT settlement date.
2. agreement by a mortgage originating bank to deliver mortgages at a specific future date, for example, 30, 60, or 120 days, to a secondary market purchaser. Also called *deferred delivery.*

FORWARD DISCOUNT price for future delivery of a currency that is lower than the SPOT price for immediate delivery. For example, if a dealer is quoting $1.7510 and $1.7520 (BID AND ASKED) for current delivery of British pound sterling, and the discounts for six months' forward delivery are .0040 and .0030, the forward quotes would be adjusted to $1.7470 and $1.7490. The forward discount normally adjusts for the difference in interest rates between two countries, but also can indicate market expectation of a lower price.

FORWARD EXCHANGE CONTRACT agreement between two parties to exchange one currency for another at a forward or future date. Forward contracts call for delivery on a date beyond the SPOT contract settlement, which ordinarily takes place within ten days of the transaction date. Unlike a futures contract, forward contracts do not take place on regulated exchanges and do not involve delivery of standard currency amounts. They are cancelable only with consent of the other party to a trade. A forward contract allows a bank, or a bank's customer, to arrange for delivery (or sale) of a specific amount of currency on a specified future date, at the current market price. This protects the buyer against the risk of fluctuating rates when acquiring foreign exchange needed to meet future obligations.

FORWARD EXCHANGE RATE price quoted for delivery of a currency beyond the SPOT delivery date, or delivery in two business days. The forward rate may be quoted with a discount (FORWARD DISCOUNT) or with a premium (FORWARD PREMIUM), depending on interest rates, market demand, and so on, or as an OUTRIGHT FORWARD transaction without an offsetting purchase or sale in the SPOT MARKET.

FORWARD FORWARD forward market contract where the dealer takes two different forward positions at opposite sides of the market. For example, a purchase of three-month dollars and simultaneous sale of six-month dollars in the foreign exchange market.

FORWARD MARGIN *see* FORWARD DISCOUNT; FORWARD PREMIUM.

FORWARD MARKET market where dealers agree to deliver currency, commodities, or financial instruments at a fixed price at a specified future date. Most forward contracts are made for delivery at specific future dates, for example, one week from the transaction date, one month, and so on. Longer term contracts are more speculative in nature, and are substantially more risky. *See also* ROLLOVER; SPOT NEXT; TOMORROW NEXT.

FORWARD PREMIUM price for future delivery of a currency or a financial instrument that is higher than the immediate delivery price, or SPOT market price. A dealer quoting $1.7110 and $1.7120 (bid and asked) for British pound sterling and the premiums for six months forward delivery are .0025 and .0030, respectively, the bid and asked prices would be adjusted to $1.7135 and $1.7140. *See also* FORWARD DISCOUNT.

FORWARD RATE AGREEMENT (FRA) contract by which two parties agree on the interest rate to be paid at a future settlement date. The contract period is quoted as, for example, six against nine months, the interest rate for a three-month period commencing in six-months time. The principal amounts are agreed, but never exchanged, and the contracts are settled in cash; exposure is limited to the difference in interest rates between the agreed and actual rates at settlement.

FORWARD SPREAD price difference between SPOT price and one-month FORWARD RATE. Say the spot rate is $1 = 1.6510 euro, and the one-month forward rate is $1 = 1.6460. The difference, or .0050, is the forward spread.

401(k) PLAN employer-sponsored salary deferral plan allowing individuals to contribute a portion of gross salary to a savings plan or company profit-sharing plan. Contributions and income earned are tax-deferred until withdrawn at age 59½, or when the employee retires or leaves the company. Plan participants can make pretax contributions to a 401(k) plan up to a certain amount. These contribution limits have increased dramatically since 2004. In 2012, the maximum contribution to a 401(k) plan was $16,500 plus an annual inflation adjustment ($500 a year). Plan participants who reach age 50 before the calendar year is over can put aside an additional catch-up contribution of $5,500 adjusted upward for inflation ($500 a year). Employees classified as highly compensated (2011 salaries above $110,000) may be subject to participation limits determined by the Internal Revenue Service; a portion of their 401(k) contribution may become reportable as taxable income.

A new Roth-style plan, the ROTH 401(K) PLAN, allows after-tax contributions to an employer-sponsored employee savings plan in exchange for the right to withdraw both contributions and earnings tax-free in some future year.

Early withdrawals from a 401(k) plan are subject to a 10% penalty tax except for certain conditions, such as disability or a qualifying hardship. *See also* ROTH 401(K) PLAN.

403(b) PLAN tax-deferred savings plan similar to a 401(K) PLAN but created for employees in public schools, colleges, universities, public hospitals, churches, and 501(c)(3) nonprofit organizations. As with the 401(k) plan, participating employees defer a portion of their pretax salary into a tax-deferred retirement account. A 403(b) savings plan can be funded in any of three ways: elective deferrals or funds transferred from salary, nonelective deferrals (employer contributions), and after-tax contributions if permitted by the plan sponsor. Funds contributed to a 403(b) account are not taxed until withdrawn. Participants may contribute payroll-deducted funds up to a maximum amount ($16,500 in annual salary deferrals). Starting in 2012, this annual funding limit is adjusted upward in $500 increments based on a measure of inflation. Plan participants who reach age 50 are allowed to make the same catch-up contributions as 401(k) plan participants—an additional $5,500 a year plus a $500 inflation adjustment.

FRACTIONAL RESERVES proportion of bank deposits that must be kept as LEGAL RESERVES. Bank reserves are a tool of central bank monetary policy; an increase in the ratio of required reserves to deposits indicates a tightening in credit policy by the Federal Reserve. Large banks are required to keep up to 12% of checking account deposits in a noninterest earning account at the Fed. Smaller banks have lower reserve requirements. The *multiplier effect* of money allows a bank to re-lend most (88¢ of $1 in deposits, at a 12% reserve requirement) of the funds in new deposits, in effect, creating new deposits. Because only a portion of deposits are backed by reserves, banks can suffer losses, or even fail, due to a sudden runoff of deposits, as in a BANK RUN. This risk is known as LIQUIDITY RISK. *See also* BANK RESERVES; MONEY MULTIPLIER.

FRANC monetary unit of Burundi, Comoros, Djibouti, Guinea, Rwanda, and Switzerland.

FRAUD intentional deception resulting in injury to another, as when a person makes false statements, conceals or omits material facts. A false statement is fraudulent if it is made knowingly, without believing it to be true, or is carelessly stated, without regard for the truth. Persons suffering a loss from a fraudulent transaction have legal recourse under the UNIFORM COMMERCIAL CODE if the contract is a written agreement, is valued at $500 or more, and is signed by the person owing the money or his agent. Legal protections against consumer credit fraud, for example, credit card fraud, are enforceable under federal and state laws. *See also* STATUTE OF FRAUDS.

FREDDIE MAC investor-owned corporation chartered by Congress in 1970 to create a secondary market for conventional mortgage loans—loans not backed or guaranteed by a government agency—and promote affordable home ownership. Freddie Mac purchases single-family and multifamily mortgage loans (called conforming loans) that have an original principal amount not greater than the conforming loan ceiling. An early pioneer in mortgage securitization, Freddie Mac issued the first conventional mortgage pass-through certificate (a type of mortgage security that pays monthly principal and interest payments from the underlying mortgage loan pool) in 1971 and the first COLLATERALIZED MORTGAGE OBLIGATION in 1983.

Freddie Mac provides funding to mortgage lenders in two ways: it borrows money by selling debt securities, and it purchases mortgages and mortgage-backed securities; second, it guarantees investors against credit losses on securities backed by pools of conforming mortgages. These guaranteed mortgage-backed securities can be held as investments by financial institutions selling loans to Freddie Mac or sold to mortgage investors, including Freddie Mac itself. In return for guaranteeing the timely payment of principal and interest to investors owning mortgage-backed securities, Freddie Mac collects fees from mortgage-originating financial institutions.

Originally owned by the nation's savings and loan associations (then part of the Federal Home Loan Bank System), Freddie Mac became a public corporation in 1989, the year the savings and loan industry restructured under the Financial Institutions Recovery and Enforcement Act. The company's legal name is still the Federal Home Loan Mortgage Corporation, but it conducts business as Freddie Mac.

In 2008, Freddie Mac was placed under government control (supervised by the Federal Housing Finance Administration) after suffering large losses in its mortgage securities portfolio. The U.S. Treasury Department pledged to provide capital as needed to ensure its support for the U.S. housing and mortgage finance markets.

FREE BALANCE *see* MINIMUM BALANCE.

FREEHOLD legal estate in land, giving the owner the right to hold the property for life, passing it down to his or her legal heirs. There are three types of freehold estates: LIFE ESTATE, an estate limited to the life of the holder; *fee simple*, an estate without any restrictions; and *fee tail*, an estate inherited by the donor's direct descendants. Contrast with LEASEHOLD.

FREE PERIOD in credit cards, the time interval in which interest is charged for current purchases. This period usually runs anywhere from 10 to 25 days after the billing date. Also called GRACE PERIOD or *days of grace.*

FREE RESERVES funds available to banks for lending or investment, widely regarded as an indicator of available BANK CREDIT. The total of free reserves is computed by subtracting from a bank's EXCESS RESERVES (or reserve account balances above its RESERVE REQUIREMENTS) any borrowings from the Federal Reserve.

FRONT-END LOAD

1. sales charge when mutual fund shares are purchased, payable to the broker handling the sale. The sales load is added to the NET ASSET VALUE per share when computing the offering price. Annuities, life insurance policies, and limited partnerships also may have a front-end sales charge. Contrast with BACK-END LOAD; NO-LOAD FUND; 12B-1 MUTUAL FUND.
2. loan disbursement schedule that is higher in early years of a loan and lower in subsequent years. This is a fairly common arrangement in construction lending.
3. loan structured with above normal usage fees in the early years of a loan.

FRONT MONEY *see* SEED MONEY.

FROZEN ACCOUNT account barred by a judicial ruling or legal process from further withdrawals. An account owned by a deceased person is frozen until the lawful heirs of the person's estate can be found. An account that is subject to a legal dispute is frozen until the legal ownership has been determined by a court of law. In the securities industry, the term refers to a customer's account blocked from further trading because of trading violations. *See also* BLOCKED ACCOUNT.

FULL COUPON BOND *see* CURRENT COUPON.

FULL FAITH AND CREDIT expression for the commitment by a state, local, or national government to pledge its taxing authority, plus nontax revenues, in payment of principal and interest on outstanding debt securities. For example, a GENERAL OBLIGATION BOND is backed by the issuing municipality's AD VALOREM taxing power. U.S. Treasury obligations and some federal agency securities also are backed by this pledge.

FULL RECOURSE type of indirect lending in which a merchant or dealer sells loan contracts to a bank or finance company with an unconditional guarantee. The dealer assumes full responsibility for repayment and agrees to indemnify the bank if the borrower defaults.

FULL SERVICE BANK bank offering the public most, if not all, of the services traditionally expected of banking institutions. Services typically found in full service banks include consumer credit, mortgage financing, commercial lending, trust services, and corporate agency services, such as funds transfer and cash management. *See also* FINANCIAL SUPERMARKET.

FULL SERVICE BROKER bank or brokerage firm offering investors a full line of brokerage, asset management services, and investment advice. Full-service firms generally have a research department that furnishes reports to institutional clients and retail clients, and a buy or recommended list for all clients. DISCOUNT BROKERAGE firms, in contrast, only execute orders to buy or sell securities.

FULLY AMORTIZING LOAN loan in which regular payments of principal are sufficient to fully pay off the loan by the maturity date, without additional payments. A typical example is a 30-year fixed rate or adjustable rate conventional mortgage loan.

FUNCTIONAL COST ANALYSIS voluntaary survey by the Federal Reserve Board of the costs of banking services. The functional cost analysis, comparing various asset, income, and cost ratios, is the only widely available measurement of the cost of providing banking products, such as deposits, withdrawals, and transit items. Functional costing measures the cost of providing each item, and can be readily compared to prior years. Although useful, functional cost analysis has a number of flaws. The number of participants is generally small and costs are based on ledger balances, which ignore balance sheet entries such as cash items (checks) in the process of collection.

FUNCTIONAL REGULATION notion that bank supervision should be divided by business activity. Thus, banks involved in selling or underwriting securities would have these activities reviewed by the Securities and Exchange Commission, and not by the Federal Reserve or other banking supervisor. The SEC is involved as a banking regulator by reviewing financial reporting and investments of many companies, including bank holding companies.

Enactment of the GRAMM-LEACH-BLILEY ACT OF 1999 signaled a significant shift in the supervision of bank holding companies, financial holding companies, and their subsidiaries and affiliates. The act provides that, where, specialized functional regulators already oversee permissible activities, these same regulatory agencies will continue to have primary supervisory responsibility. Thus, the Securities and Exchange Commission will review a BROKER-DEALER operating subsidiary, and state insurance commissioners will bear responsibility for supervising insurance marketing activities.

FUNDAMENTAL ANALYSIS study of interest rate trends, unemployment, gross domestic product and other factors to predict growth patterns for the economy as a whole. In securities analysis, fundamental analysis is the study of stocks and bonds through examination of historical ratios and trends and comparisons with other companies. Contrast with TECHNICAL ANALYSIS.

FUNDS

1. cash or its equivalents, drafts and money orders. The term generally applies to short-term money market instruments and securities that are readily convertible into cash.
2. trader's jargon for Canadian dollar, abbreviated Can$ or $C.

FUNDS AVAILABILITY *see* AVAILABLE BALANCE.

FUNDS MANAGEMENT management of net funds available for investment and external funds purchased from other banks. Funds management attempts to match the cash flow needs of a bank against maturity schedules of its deposits as loan demand increases or decreases. Funds management is more of a Treasury function than ASSET-LIABILITY MANAGEMENT, which deals mainly with control of *interest rate risk* and *liquidity risk,* and the pricing of loans in specific time periods.

Funds management examines the mix of funds raised by a bank, including large dollar deposits, nondeposit borrowings, and credit advances from a Federal Reserve Bank or Federal Home Loan Bank. Its aim is supplying funds sufficient to meet the bank's asset growth objectives at the lowest funding cost, and at acceptable levels of risk (credit risk, liquidity risk, and interest rate risk).

On the asset side of the balance sheet, funds management deals with the control of discretionary portfolios by the corporate treasurer, including the investment securities portfolio and trading account assets. On the liability side, it focuses on wholesale sources of funds and hedging techniques, such as interest rate futures and interest rate swaps to control these balance sheet exposures. Also called *balance sheet management. See also* LIABILITY MANAGEMENT.

FUNDS TRANSFER

1. moving funds between accounts or to a third party account at the same financial institution, also called a *book transfer.*
2. external transfers between an originating financial institution and receiving financial institution. The term covers all types of interbank ELECTRONIC FUNDS TRANSFER, including the Federal Reserve's FED WIRE (FEDERAL WIRE); the interbank AUTOMATED CLEARING HOUSE (ACH) system, and the CLEARING HOUSE INTERBANK PAYMENTS SYSTEM (CHIPS) in New York City, through which the majority of international trade payments involving U.S. financial institutions and overseas banks are channeled. The Fed Wire and the CHIPS networks account for more than 90% of transfers of funds on an annual basis. All other forms of payment, including checks, cash, and credit cards, collectively account for less than 10% of total dollar value, but about 99% of the transactions in the U.S. economy.

FUNGIBLE financial instrument equivalent in value to another, and easily exchanged or substituted. A dollar bill loaned has the same value as a dollar paid back. Bearer securities and stocks issued in the same class have this quality, as well as exchange traded options and mortgages in a pool of loans supporting a mortgage-backed security.

FURTHEST MONTH in futures trading, the farthest month from the contract delivery date. It is the most distant of the contract delivery months in financial instruments or commodities approved for trading by a futures exchange. A contract calling for delivery in 18 months is the furthest month, while a three-month contract is a nearby contract or NEAREST MONTH.

FUTURE ADVANCE mortgage clause allowing the lender to advance funds after the initial loan closing and disbursement of funds, without executing a new mortgage deed or taking additional collateral. An example is a CONSTRUCTION MORTGAGE secured by the building financed. Construction advances are made at specific stages of completion according to a preset schedule, and ordinarily take precedence over liens recorded after the loan closing date, but before the additional funds are disbursed. *See also* OPEN-END MORTGAGE.

FUTURE DATING *see* VALUE DATING.

FUTURE ESTATE *see* FUTURE INTEREST.

FUTURE INTEREST interest in land or personal property giving the holder the right of possession, though not ownership. A vested interest conveys the right to claim, as of a specific date, assets held in trust, for example, an employee's interest in a corporate pension plan, payable upon retirement; a contingent interest transfers ownership only when specific events occur, for example, the death of the grantor or creator of a trust. *See also* REMAINDERMAN.

FUTURES COMMISSION MERCHANT (FCM) firm or person engaged in soliciting or accepting orders for the purchase or sale of futures contracts. A futures commission merchant accepts cash or securities for margin trading, subject to the rules of a futures exchange, and is licensed by the Commodities Futures Trading Commission.

FUTURES CONTRACT negotiable contract to make or take DELIVERY at an agreed price of a standardized amount of a commodity or financial instrument during a specific month, under terms and conditions established by a federally regulated futures exchange market where trading takes place. Futures contracts are often used as a HEDGING device against interest rate or price risk. Mortgage lenders who believe that mortgage rates are falling might sell 90-day forward contracts in Government National Mortgage Association (Ginnie Mae) pass-through securities; if they think rates are rising, they can buy futures contracts. At contract delivery time, the price of the futures contract and the cash price of the mortgages should cancel each other out. Normally, in futures trading the seller of a contract (known as a *short)* will notify the exchange of his intention to deliver contracts to a buyer (called the *long)* as the contract delivery month draws near. Of course, buyers and sellers of futures contracts have the option of exchanging an expiring contract for a new one, which is what most participants in the futures market actually do, rather than take delivery. *See also* FUTURES EXCHANGES; OPTION.

FUTURES EXCHANGES commodities market where futures contracts in financial instruments or real commodities (wheat, soybeans) are traded. Stock and bond indexes and options also are traded on these exchanges.

Major financial futures exchanges around the world are the following: CBOE Futures Exchange; Chicago Mercantile Exchange; New York Mercantile Exchange; NYSE Liffe U.S., New York; Sydney Futures Exchange, Sydney, Australia; Montreal Exchange, Montreal, Quebec; Toronto Stock Exchange Futures Market; Winnipeg Commodity Exchange; London International Futures Exchange; London Metal Exchange; Singapore Commodity Exchange; and the Tokyo Financial Exchange.

G

GAP amount by which INTEREST SENSITIVE ASSETS differ from INTEREST SENSITIVE LIABILITIES for a designated time period, for example, the net difference between loans and deposits maturing in one year or less. An excess of liabilities over assets means there are more liabilities than interest earning assets, resulting in a NEGATIVE GAP. The opposite, an excess of interest earning assets compared to deposits, is a POSITIVE GAP. *See also* GAPPING; REPRICING OPPORTUNITIES.

GAP FINANCING *see* BRIDGE LOAN.

GAPPING acquiring assets with anticipated maturities, or durations, longer or shorter than the liabilities used to fund those assets. This is the conventional circumstances of bank lending, in other words, borrowing short and lending long, creating interest rate risk that is managed through ASSET LIABILITY MANAGEMENT.

GARNISHMENT process granted by a court order by which a lender obtains, directly from a third party such as an employer, part of an employee's salary in satisfaction of an unpaid debt.

Part of the employee's salary will be taken out in each pay period until the debt is fully paid. *See also* ATTACHMENT; WAGE ASSIGNMENT.

GARN-ST GERMAIN DEPOSITORY INSTITUTIONS ACT federal law enacted by Congress in 1982 authorizing banks and savings institutions to offer a new account, the MONEY MARKET DEPOSIT ACCOUNT—a transaction account with no interest rate ceiling to compete with money market mutual funds; gave savings and loan associations the authority to make commercial loans; and gave federal regulatory agencies the authority to approve, for the first time, interstate acquisitions of failed banks and savings institutions.

The following are highlights of the numerous provisions of the act:

(1) savings and loan associations were authorized to make commercial, corporate, business, or agricultural loans up to 10% of assets after January 1, 1984.

(2) the deposit interest rate differential, allowing savings and loans and savings banks to offer rates on interest-bearing deposit accounts ¼ of 1% higher than commercial banks was lifted, as of January 1984.

(3) the act authorized a new capital assistance program, the Net Worth Certificate Program, under which the Federal Savings and Loan Insurance Corp. and the Federal Deposit Insurance Corp. would purchase capital instruments called Net Worth Certificates from savings institutions with net worth to assets ratios under 3%, and would later redeem the certificates as they regained financial health.

(4) the act permitted savings associations to offer checking accounts (demand deposit accounts) to individuals and business checking accounts to customers who had other accounts.

(5) savings and loans were authorized to increase their consumer lending, from 20% to 30% of assets, and to expand their dealer lending and floor-plan loan financing.

(6) the act raised the ceiling on direct investments by savings institutions in nonresidential real estate from 20% to 40% of assets, and also allowed investment of 10% of assets in education loans for any educational purpose, and up to 100% of assets in state and municipal bonds.

(7) the act preempted state restrictions on enforcement by lenders of due-on-sale clauses in most mortgages for a three year period ending October 15, 1985, and authorized state chartered lenders to offer the same kinds of alternative mortgages permitted nationally chartered financial institutions.

(8) authorized the Comptroller of the Currency to charter Bankers' Banks, or depository institutions owned by other banks.

(9) made state chartered industrial banks eligible for federal depository insurance.

(10) raised the legal lending limit for national banks from 10% to 15% of capital and surplus.

GATEWAY means by which users of one computer system can gain access to another without making a separate connection. Gateway access is commonly used in AUTOMATED TELLER MACHINE (ATM) systems, and electronic POINT OF SALE systems through a single gateway. *See also* INTERNET BANKING; SWITCH.

GENERAL ACCOUNT

1. general ledger account for assets or liabilities other than accounts of bank customers, such as loans and deposits.
2. Federal Reserve term for brokerage accounts subject to REGULATION T margin requirements, which regulates broker loans for purchase or short sale of securities. The Fed requires that broker loans secured by marginable stock be made from this account. *See also* TREASURY GENERAL ACCOUNT.

GENERAL AGREEMENTS TO BORROW (GAB) arrangements, whereby members of the GROUP OF TEN countries make loans to the INTERNATIONAL MONETARY FUND (IMF) in their own currencies to finance drawings by a member of the G-10 group. Switzerland has also joined in the accord. The G-10 countries, and Switzerland, have since decided to make the GAB funding commitment available to all members of the IMF.

GENERAL ENDORSEMENT *see* BLANK ENDORSEMENT.

GENERAL EXAMINATION detailed examination of a bank by its primary financial regulator. National banks are examined approximately every two years by the Comptroller of the Currency, state banks by state banking departments. The Federal Reserve Board examines state banks that are MEMBER BANKS in the Federal Reserve System and inspects financial records of bank holding companies (and financial holding companies).

GENERAL LEDGER central accounting record of an organization, summarizing changes in financial position as transactions are posted during an accounting period. Accounts owned by a bank's customers are kept separately in the bank's bookkeeping department on subsidiary accounts, or control accounts, which are used to update the general ledger. Control accounts may list customer accounts by type, maturity, collateral, and so on, although most banks follow the accounting format required by the Comptroller of the Currency and other regulatory agencies in listing accounts for the Reports of Condition and Income (call reports). The general ledger is also the basis for financial disclosures in the CALL REPORT filed with banking regulatory agencies, stockholders, and other outside organizations.

GENERAL LIEN lien against a borrower's personal assets, as opposed to a claim against real property. The lender may use the lien to seize property in satisfaction of a debt, including assets not specifically covered by the obligation.

GENERALLY ACCEPTED ACCOUNTING PRINCIPLES (GAAP) accounting rules and conventions defining acceptable practices in preparing financial statements. The FINANCIAL ACCOUNTING STANDARDS BOARD (FASB), an independent self-regulatory organization, is the primary source of accounting rules followed by auditors and certified public accountants. The aim of GAAP accounting principles is uniformity in financial statements.

GENERAL MORTGAGE BOND bond secured by a BLANKET MORTGAGE on all mortgageable property of the issuing corporation. Commonly used by railroads, a general mortgage may not necessarily have priority of claim over other liens on specific assets or parcels of land.

GENERAL OBLIGATION BOND state or municipal bond (a G-O bond) backed by the issuer's full faith credit and taxing authority. General obligation bonds are normally issued to finance nonrevenue producing public works projects, such as schools, roads, and public buildings, although some G-O projects do generate revenue, for example, a bond financing a water or sewage treatment plant. A bond having no restrictions as to dollar amount of taxes or tax rate that can be assessed to make debt service payments to bondholders is known as an *unlimited tax bond.* Often, however, local governments are restricted by local or state regulations limiting property taxes that can be raised to make bond principal and interest payments; such a bond is called a LIMITED TAX BOND. *See also* PRIVATE PURPOSE BOND; PUBLIC PURPOSE BOND; REVENUE BOND.

GENERAL PARTNER co-owner of an unincorporated business, who holds a share of the firm's profits or losses, and is fully liable for its debts; the managing partner in a venture capital limited partnership. A general partner has unlimited personal liability for the debts of the partnership. *See also* LIMITED PARTNERSHIP.

GENERIC SECURITIES securities backed by newly issued mortgages or other loans. They are less valuable to investors than SEASONED SECURITIES.

GEN-SAKI short-term money market in Japan, used as a secondary market for repurchase and resale of medium-term and long-term corporate and government bonds. The gen-saki market is open to corporations as well as financial institutions.

GIFT CARD prepaid Visa card, MasterCard, or American Express card that enables the user to purchase goods or services up to the value of the card. Bank-issued gift cards work much like retail merchant gift cards, serving as redeemable gift certificates. Card-issuing financial institutions profit from the float or interest earned from the date of purchase to the transaction date. Banks may treat gift cards like credit card cash advances by charging users transaction fees.

GIFT CAUSA MORTIS gift of personal property by a person anticipating death. The gift, which is legally effective only after the donor's death, can reduce inheritance taxes that would otherwise be payable. Contrast with GIFT INTER VIVOS.

GIFT INTER VIVOS gift of property between living persons, made during the donor's lifetime, as opposed to a GIFT CAUSA MORTIS. The gift is irrevocable, provided the donor relinquishes ownership and makes the gift without reference to his death. *See also* INTER VIVOS TRUST.

GIFT TAX graduated federal tax, also imposed by some states, on property transfers by gift during the donor's lifetime. Gifts subject to the tax include irrevocable living trusts. The tax, paid by the donor, is based on fair market value.

GI LOAN popular name for a Department of Veterans Affairs guaranteed mortgage, authorized under the Serviceman's Readjustment Act of 1944. GI loans, guaranteed up to a certain amount, are all used for residential purposes such as buying a home or a condominium unit, refinancing, or making home improvements. Unlike most conventional mortgage loans, these loans are ASSUMABLE MORTGAGES—transferable to a new mortgagor when a house is sold. The Department of Veterans Affairs, a cabinet-level agency succeeding the Veterans Administration, also makes direct loans to qualified veterans.

GILT-EDGED British pound sterling bonds (gilts), issued by the Bank of England, and known as gilts in the market, as these securities have little risk of default. It also refers to AAA-rated U.S. corporate bonds.

GINNIE MAE informal name for the Government National Mortgage Association, a federal agency under the Department of Housing and Urban Development (HUD). Ginnie Mae guarantees the timely payment of monthly principal and interest, with the full faith and credit support of the U.S. government, on mortgage pass-through securities backed by federally insured or guaranteed mortgage loans. It does not issues mortgage-backed securities in its own name. Ginnie Mae works with approved lenders, adding its guarantee to residential mortgages insured by the Federal Housing Administration (FHA) or guaranteed by the Department of Veterans Affairs (VA) or to loans originated under the Department of Agriculture's Rural Housing Service and the Department of Housing and Urban Development's Office of Public and Indian Housing. Ginnie Mae was created in 1968, when the Federal National Mortgage Association (FANNIE MAE) was spun off from HUD and became a stand-alone corporation. In 1970 Ginnie Mae guaranteed the first publicly traded mortgage pass-through securities representing an undivided interest in FHA loans and VA loans. *See also* FREDDIE MAC; GINNIE MAE PASS-THROUGH.

GINNIE MAE PASS-THROUGH mortgage-backed security giving the holder a proportional interest in a pool of residential mortgages, guaranteed by the GOVERNMENT NATIONAL MORTGAGE ASSOCIATION. Ginnie Mae securities are called passthroughs because the originating banks, mortgage bankers, and savings institutions pass all principal and interest, plus repayments, directly to the investor. There is no reinvestment of principal, as there is in mortgage-backed bonds.

Ginnie Mae securities are collateralized by Department of Veterans Affairs guaranteed and Federal Housing Administration insured mortgages. There are two different types of Ginnie Mae securities available to investors. GNMA I certificates remit payments directly from the issuer to the investor on the 15th of each month. The holder gets a separate payment of principal and interest for each certificate issued. Payments on GNMA IIs are made on the 20th of each month. These securities, unlike GNMA I's, are backed by guaranteed loans from geographically dispersed multiple loan pools, and pay a coupon interest rate that can vary up to 1%. Originating financial institutions deduct a servicing fee of ½ of 1% before remitting mortgage payments to Ginnie Mae. (The servicing fee on GNMA II pass-throughs can vary from ½ of 1% to 1.5%.) Ginnie Mae securities are called *modified passthrough* securities because the COUPON RATE (also called the *production rate)* of the securities is reduced by the issuer's servicing fee. Because Ginnie Mae securities are backed by the FULL FAITH AND CREDIT of the U.S. government, these issues have a wide SECONDARY MARKET. Futures contracts in Ginnie Maes have been traded on the Chicago Mercantile Exchange since 1972. *See also* PARTICIPATION CERTIFICATE; SECONDARY MARKET.

GIRO electronic payment system widely used in Europe and Japan for consumer bill payments. Unlike the CHECK system in the United States, which is a debit-based system, giros are credit transfers. In giro systems, a payment order automatically transfers funds from the consumer's account to the creditor's account and notifies creditors when the transfer is made. Multiple payments from a single giro are also possible.

GLASS-STEAGALL ACT federal law enacted by Congress in 1933 forcing a separation between commercial banking and investment banking. This act, which required commercial banks to dispose of their securities affiliates, bears the same name as the BANKING ACT OF 1933, and is part of the landmark 1933 act. Since then, the name Glass-Steagall has been more commonly used when referring to the four sections of the banking act (Sections 16, 20, 21, and 32) pertaining to underwriting and sale of securities.

The late 1980s saw legislative barriers between banking and investment banking significantly eroded, as banks were granted more powers by banking regulators to deal in securities as both principal and agent for bank customers. Commercial banks own securities, broker-dealer and investment management firms, and mutual fund companies, and they act as investment advisors for municipal governments and corporations. Banks won Federal Reserve Board approval to underwrite commercial paper in 1987, and corporate equity securities and bonds in 1990 (through subsidiaries of bank holding companies). The GRAMM-LEACH-BLILEY ACT repealed the affiliation (Section 20) and management interlock (section 32) prohibitions of Glass-Steagall.

Other key provisions of the Glass-Steagall Act still remaining in effect are Section 16, prohibiting Federal Reserve MEMBER BANKS from directly underwriting securities, except for those of the U.S. Treasury and federal agencies, and the general obligations of state and municipal governments; and Section 21, prohibiting securities underwriters from accepting federally insured deposits. *See also* PERMISSIBLE NONBANK ACTIVITIES; SECURITIES SUBSIDIARY.

GLOBALIZATION interdependence of buyers and sellers of financial instruments in financial centers around the world. This phenomenon is due mainly to several factors: (1) the maturation of the EUROPEAN UNION countries markets since the 1960s; (2) introduction of the Internet, providing market makers and consumers with near instantaneous access to current market data on financial products; (3) a desire by financial institutions to expand lending and other activities beyond geographic boundaries; and (4) a desire to control balance sheet risk through INTEREST RATE SWAPS and other financial swap agreements.

For example, the growing use in international financial markets of marketable debt instruments, principally in the EUROBOND market, as opposed to traditional bank lending, as a financing vehicle for major corporate borrowers, and also sovereign governments. The shift away from bank credit instruments, such as Note Issuance Facilities, toward Floating Rate Notes and Eurocommercial paper began in the early 1980s, and was aided by the strong secondary market in Eurobond financings. Both commercial banks and investment banks participate in this market. Outside the United States, U.S. commercial banks are not confined by Glass-Steagall Act limitations on securities underwriting, and are active participants in the Eurobond market.

Advances in INFORMATION TECHNOLOGY allowed traders in foreign exchange and other money market instruments to manage positions on a 24-hour basis, by moving their trading book to a different financial center at the close of trading. This practice, known as *passing the book,* permits financial institutions that make markets in New York, London, or Tokyo, for instance, to maintain a single trading book listing positions, limits, and exposures for the entire firm, rather than keeping separate books in each trading center.

GNOMES popular name for 15-year fixed rate Participation Certificates sold by the Federal Home Loan Mortgage Corporation (Freddie Mac). Gnomes are PASS-THROUGH SECURITIES collateralized by mortgage payments from 15-year mortgages.

GO-AROUND process of soliciting competitive quotes from dealers when the Federal Open Market Committee buys (or sells) securities in the open market, in carrying out the Fed's monetary policy. The go-around, a telephone survey by the Open Market Desk at the Federal Reserve Bank of New York, signals the Fed's intention to do business with primary government securities dealers. Buying securities increases bank reserves, or funds available for bank lending; selling securities has the opposite effect.

GOING LONG originating mortgage loans without a firm commitment from a SECONDARY MARKET investor. If interest rates are stable, a lender may hold these loans in his own portfolio or try to place them with a buyer at a later date. In the securities industry, buying securities for investment or speculation, with no immediate plans of reselling.

GOING SHORT hedging strategy whereby a bank obtains either a FORWARD COMMITMENT or a STANDBY COMMITMENT from a SECONDARY MARKET buyer to purchase loans before the loans actually are booked. By getting a commitment first, the lender is able to lock in a mortgage rate if interest rates are expected to rise or fall.

In the securities industry, selling a security not actually owned by the investor—a SHORT SALE—anticipating that the open position created by the sale can be closed when the security is purchased later at a lower price.

GOLD CARD Credit card offering extra advantages or services, such as a higher spending limit. These cards have a higher annual fee than standard bank credit cards, and are marketed to consumers with above average incomes. Sometimes called a *prestige card* or *premium card.*

GOLD CERTIFICATE certificate issued by the U.S. Treasury Department to Federal Reserve Banks, certifying ownership of official U.S. gold reserves. Except for certificates kept for educational displays, no paper certificates actually are issued; these are bookkeeping credits. When the Treasury purchases gold and wants to replenish its dollar balances, it issues gold certificates to the Federal Reserve

Board, which are kept in a separate gold certificate account. Federal Reserve Banks use gold certificates to settle payments between reserve banks, carried in the books of the INTERDISTRICT SETTLEMENT account.

GOLD EXCHANGE STANDARD international monetary exchange system, a variation of the GOLD STANDARD in which central bank reserves are held in gold BULLION and in reserve currencies that are convertible into gold. Some economists believe the gold standard acts as a brake on inflation, because commodity prices are linked to gold. From the 1930s until 1971, the U.S. dollar was convertible into gold at $35 an ounce, and foreign exchange rates were fixed, or pegged, to the dollar. In 1971 the United States finally abolished the convertibility of the U.S. dollar into gold, ushering in the floating exchange rates that are the basis of the international monetary system as it exists today. *See also* INTERVENTION.

GOLD FIXING process by which the daily price is set for gold traded on the spot market. It occurs in London, Paris, and Zurich at 10:30 A.M. and 3:30 P.M. London time of every business day. This price is the average price at which all major bid orders are filled, and is set by gold trading specialists at gold trading financial institutions operating in these cities.

GOLD OPTION right to buy or sell any amount of gold bullion in the future if a specific price is reached. These options are quoted on the Commodity Exchange Inc. New York; the Mid-America Commodity Exchange; and the Philadelphia Stock Exchange.

GOLD STANDARD monetary system that pegs or fixes the value of a nation's currency unit to a fixed amount of gold bullion. Paper currency in such systems is convertible freely into gold. The gold standard was introduced in Great Britain in 1821 and was the basis for the U.S. monetary system from the 1870s to 1971, when the U.S. Treasury Department announced it would no longer back the U.S. dollar, for foreign exchange purposes, with its gold reserves. (The Gold Act of 1934 abolished the right of U.S. citizens to exchange paper currency for gold.) The gold standard insures a fixed rate of exchange in international trade, while limiting the amount of paper currency a central government can issue for domestic spending. Its main drawback is that it hinders the ability of a government to control the supply of money and it makes it very difficult for a country to isolate itself from depressions or inflation in the economies of its major trading partners. A country experiencing a large BALANCE OF PAYMENTS deficit may thus find it impossible to properly address the situation without coming off the gold standard. *See also* GOLD EXCHANGE STANDARD.

GOLD STOCK monetary gold reserves maintained by the U.S. Treasury. It consists of (1) monetized gold, or the total of GOLD CER-

TIFICATE credits issued by the Treasury to Federal Reserve Banks; and (2) nonmonetized gold, or gold bullion against which no certificates have been issued. The value of the Treasury's gold supply is carried on the books at $42.22 a troy ounce, the official U.S. government price set in 1973. The Treasury's gold stock does not include gold reserves held by the EXCHANGE STABILIZATION FUND, U.S. gold subscriptions to the INTERNATIONAL MONETARY FUND, and gold held as EARMARKED RESERVES at the Federal Reserve Bank of New York for foreign and international accounts.

GOOD DELIVERY securities industry term for a certificate bearing the proper endorsement and signature guarantee, and meeting other requirements of National Association of Securities Dealer's Uniform Practice Code, making it transferable by delivery to the buyer, who is obligated to accept it.

GOOD FAITH

1. UNSECURED LOAN made on the basis of the borrower's reputation in the community, called a *character loan.*
2. in BAD DEBT collection, an agreement by the lender to modify efforts to recover the amount owed if the borrower makes certain payments or delivers collateral.
3. legal requirement that a lender extend credit in the belief that the borrower will repay the debt according to the terms of the loan agreement.
4. a lender's reasonable estimate of mortgage closing costs, which must be listed in a good faith statement, formally known as a HUD-1 SETTLEMENT STATEMENT, as required by banking regulation.
5. token sum of money given to indicate interest in fulfillment of a contract, called good faith money. In a real estate transaction, it is known as EARNEST MONEY.

GOOD FAITH ESTIMATE (GFE) *see* HUD-1 SETTLEMENT STATEMENT.

GOOD MONEY immediately available funds, or FEDERAL FUNDS. The term is applied to interbank funds transfers over the Federal Reserve's Fed Wire, available for withdrawal the same day, as opposed to CLEARINGHOUSE FUNDS, which take a minimum of 1–2 days to clear.

GOODWILL

1. intangible asset representing the difference between the purchase price of an asset and its fair market value. Goodwill is created when a bank pays a premium to acquire the assets of another bank in a take-over transaction. For example, bank ABC pays the shareholders of bank XYZ $100 per share for XYZ's outstanding common stock, which has a book value per share of only $50. Bank ABC reports the difference ($50) as goodwill. Goodwill is also created when a bank pays a premium above estimated market value to acquire loans, credit card accounts, and so on.

Goodwill is a non-tax-deductible asset. It has no independent market or liquidation value, and accepted accounting principles require that it be written off (amortized) over the time period in use. Goodwill and other intangibles do not qualify as Tier 1 bank CAPITAL after December 31, 1992, under RISK-BASED capital guidelines.

2. informally, an expression for good customer relations, employee morale, and a well-respected business name.

GOURDE monetary unit of Haiti.

GOVERNMENT BOND long-term debt securities of the United States government, given the highest rating available. The term refers to Treasury bonds, which have original maturities of 10 to 30 years, and Series EE and Series HH Savings Bonds.

GOVERNMENT DEPOSITORY bank eligible to accept government deposits. Banks so designated are Federal Reserve Banks, national banks, and state chartered member banks in the Federal Reserve System. Commercial banks act as agents of the U.S. Treasury by holding tax receipts in a TREASURY TAX AND LOAN ACCOUNT, which allows the Treasury to leave funds on deposit locally until needed. See also PLEDGING REQUIREMENTS.

GOVERNMENT NATIONAL MORTGAGE ASSOCIATION (GNMA) *see* GINNIE MAE.

GOVERNMENTS negotiable securities issued by the U.S. Treasury Department, including Treasury bills, notes, and bonds. Also, federal agency securities, many of which are backed by the FULL FAITH AND CREDIT of the U.S. government. Others are only MORAL OBLIGATION BONDS.

GRACE PERIOD

1. time period allowed for making payments on a loan. Payments made after the due date, but within this 10–15 day period are considered timely payments, and not subject to late charges or other penalties.

2. in credit cards, the time period, ranging anywhere from 10 to 25 days, in which interest is not charged on current purchases. This is also called *free period.* Some credit card issuers, though, allow a grace period only on paid-up accounts with no balances carried over from the previous month.

3. in international banking, the length of time during which the borrower is excused from making loan principal payments. For example, multilateral soft loans to developing countries are long-term loans arranged through the World Bank, with lenient credit terms and grace periods that are measured in years.

GRADUATED PAYMENT MORTGAGE (GPM) fixed rate mortgage with low payments in the early years, and higher payments later on, designed to meet the financing needs of young home owners with growing incomes. This is also known in the trade as a "Jeep" mortgage. The most popular versions of the GPM are 30-year mortgages with payments that rise by a fixed amount each year for the first five to ten years and then level off. Lenders usually charge a slightly higher rate on a GPM than a CONVENTIONAL MORTGAGE, because part of the interest due is deferred until the later years. Even though borrowers ultimately pay more for a GPM, the lower initial payments make this kind of mortgage more affordable to home buyers whose incomes could not support a conventional mortgage loan. A variation is the adjustable rate graduated payment mortgage, which has an interest rate that is adjusted every three to five years. *See also* ADJUSTABLE RATE MORTGAGE; ALTERNATIVE MORTGAGE INSTRUMENT.

GRAMM-LEACH-BLILEY ACT OF 1999 federal legislation that removed Depression-era Glass prohibitions of the GLASS-STEAGALL ACT barring cross-ownership of banks, securities firms, and insurance companies. Commercial banks are now permitted to own insurance companies and engage in securities underwriting through federally regulated subsidiaries. A complex piece of legislation, the act marks the culmination of efforts dating to the early 1980s to modernize the U.S. financial services industry.

Important provisions include:

(1) repealed the sections of the 1933 Glass-Steagall Act mandating the legal separation of commercial banking and investment banking.

(2) eliminated the Bank Holding Company Act of 1956's prohibition on bank underwriting of insurance.

(3) established the Federal Reserve Board as the primary regulator of financial holding companies.

(4) provided for functional regulation of financial activities by state regulatory agencies and other federal agencies.

(5) permitted financial holding companies to conduct activities that are "complementary" to banking.

(6) grandfathered for 10 years the nonfinancial activities of firms engaged in financial business.

(7) allowed bank-owned subsidiaries to underwrite corporate securities, but limited the size of bank-owned securities firms to 45% of total assets or $50 billion, whichever is lower.

(8) prohibited banks from insurance sales or real estate development.

(9) gave the Treasury Department and the Federal Reserve the right to veto each other's decisions on new financial powers.

(10) permitted national banks to directly underwrite municipal revenue bonds.

(11) barred bank holding company mergers with securities firms or insurance companies if any subsidiary bank has a less than *satisfactory* COMMUNITY REINVESTMENT ACT (CRA) rating.

(12) required banks and community groups to disclose the terms of certain CRA-related agreements.

(13) extended the time period between CRA examinations to five years for banks and thrift institutions with assets under $250 million that have *outstanding* CRA ratings.

(14) prohibited sharing of customer account numbers with third-party marketing firms and required financial institutions to establish privacy policies and disclose these policies to customers once a year.

(15) prohibited approval of UNITARY THRIFT holding company applications received after May 4, 1999, and barred commercial companies from buying existing unitary thrifts.

(16) prohibited states from interfering with insurance sales by national banks.

(17) stripped the Comptroller of the Currency of legal advantage in court disputes with state insurance regulators over state laws enacted after September 3, 1998.

(18) allowed FEDERAL HOME LOAN BANK members to use small business loans and farm loans as collateral for advances from a regional Federal Home Loan Bank.

(19) requires operators of automated teller machines to post notices of fees at ATMs.

GRANDFATHERED ACTIVITIES nonbanking activities prohibited by law, regulation or agreement, but approved for organizations that were already engaged in those activities as of a specific date. Entry by other firms is, however, disallowed.

In banking, the term is used widely in reference to activities of certain bank holding companies, allowed to continue by the Bank Holding Company Act of 1956 and its 1970 amendment, or by subsequent legislation. For example, the GRAMM-LEACH-BLILEY ACT closed a loophole in the law by banning new charters of UNITARY THRIFT companies, a type of savings and loan holding company, after May 4, 1999, but allowed existing unified thrifts to stay in business.

GRANTOR

1. person who executes a deed conveying property to another, or who creates a trust instrument. Also called *settlor.*
2. writer or seller of an option contract, either a call option or a put option. A call option conveys the right to buy the underlying securities; a put option gives the right to sell.

GRANTOR TRUST any trust other than one created by a WILL. In the SECONDARY MORTGAGE MARKET and securitized asset sales market, a grantor trust is a legal, passive entity through which pass-through securities are sold to investors. Grantor trusts are not subject to taxation.

GREEN BOOK

1. U.S. Treasury Department publication listing procedures to be followed in handling DIRECT DEPOSIT payments of government benefits and other payments through the AUTOMATED CLEARING HOUSE (ACH) system.

2. economic forecast outlining different economic scenarios, prepared by the Federal Reserve Board staff for members of the FEDERAL OPEN MARKET COMMITTEE at a regular meeting of the FOMC. *See also* BEIGE BOOK.

GRIDLOCK *see* SYSTEMIC RISK.

GROSS COUPON the interest rate earned on mortgages underlying a mortgage-backed security, for example, the rate earned by mortgages underlying a PASS-THROUGH SECURITY as opposed to the COUPON RATE on the bonds.

GROSS ESTATE property in a decedent's estate before payment of debts, estate taxes, and other expenses. After these expenses and funeral costs are deducted, beneficiaries are paid from the amount remaining, which is the net estate.

GROSS MARGIN

1. **Banking.** Synonymous with SPREAD or yield. The difference between the lender's cost of funds, and the rate paid by the borrower, including upfront fees, usage fees, and cancellation fees.
2. **Finance.** A disclosure on the Profit and Loss (P&L) statement of the borrower; the difference between sales and gross earnings.

GROSS SETTLEMENT funds transfer system providing immediately available transfers of funds. Examples are the Federal Reserve's FEDERAL WIRE (FEDWIRE) in the United States, and TARGET (Trans European Real-Time Gross Settlement Express Transfer) in the European Union countries. Also called *real-time gross settlement.* Compare with NET SETTLEMENT.

GROSS SPREAD underwriter's margin in issuing new securities, or the difference between the price at which securities are sold to the public and the price paid by the underwriter to the issuer. The difference, the selling cost, includes the manager's fee and selling concession (the discount offered) to members of the underwriting syndicate.

GROUP BANKING form of HOLDING COMPANY in which a management group has control of several existing banks. Each bank in the group has its own board of directors, but the holding company coordinates the activities of all banks in the group, and owns a majority of capital stock in member banks. *See also* BANKERS' BANK; CHAIN BANKING; INTERLOCKING DIRECTORATE.

GROUP OF 7 international group comprised of finance ministers of the seven leading industrial democracies who meet to coordinate economic and monetary policy. The group, also known as the G-7, includes Japan, West Germany, France, Britain, Italy, Canada and the United States. Organized in 1986.

GROUP OF 10 organization of central banks of the major industrial countries. Member banks coordinate banking industry supervision through the BANK FOR INTERNATIONAL SETTLEMENTS and monetary policy through the INTERNATIONAL MONETARY FUND (IMF). Founding members are central banks from Belgium, Canada, France, Germany, Italy, Japan, the Netherlands, Sweden, the United Kingdom, and the United States. Switzerland has also joined as a full-fledged member.

GROUP OF 24 *see* ORGANIZATION FOR ECONOMIC COOPERATION AND DEVELOPMENT.

GROUP OF 30 international organization of major banks and investment firms whose mission is improving back-office procedures and book-entry processing of securities.

GROWING EQUITY MORTGAGE (GEM) mortgage with a fixed interest rate but varying monthly payments. Monthly payments of principal and interest rise monthly, semi-annually, or yearly according to an agreed upon schedule, with extra payments used to reduce the loan principal and shorten the loan term. Also called a rapid payoff mortgage. *See also* ALTERNATIVE MORTGAGE INSTRUMENT.

GUARANI monetary unit of Paraguay.

GUARANTEED LOAN loan guaranteed as to repayment of principal and interest by a federal agency, such as the Department of Veterans Affairs or the Small Business Administration. Also, a student loan guaranteed by the Student Loan Marketing Association.

GUARANTEED MORTGAGE CERTIFICATE (GMC) mortgage backed bond, backed by a pool of mortgages, issued by the Federal Home Loan Mortgage Corporation (Freddie Mac) since 1975. The bonds, representing an undivided interest in a pool of residential mortgages, have a guaranteed average life, and pay principal and interest semiannually. The investor receives full payment of principal if the underlying mortgages prepay at a rate faster than the guaranteed minimum rate.

GUARANTEED STUDENT LOAN *see* EDUCATION LOAN; STUDENT LOAN MARKETING ASSOCIATION.

GUARANTOR

1. person or corporation who guarantees payment by another. Also known as a SURETY. A guarantor becomes a co-endorser and assumes liability in event of default.
2. corporation that provides assurances, either through a LETTER OF CREDIT or the strength of its own balance sheet, to step in and pay the outstanding obligation of, for example, a municipal bond issuer. *See also* FINANCIAL GUARANTEE.
3. Federal Home Loan Mortgage Corp. MORTGAGE SWAP in which mortgage lenders exchange loans for Freddie Mac PARTICIPATION CERTIFICATES.

GUARANTY three-party agreement, involving a promise by one party (the guarantor) to fulfill the obligation of a person owing a debt if that person fails to perform. The guaranty (also spelled guarantee) is a CONTINGENT LIABILITY of the guarantor. *See also* FINANCIAL GUARANTEE.

GUARANTY FUND

1. mutual savings bank reserve fund required by some states as cushion against short-term losses. The fund is set aside from current earnings. Also called a *surplus account.*
2. privately sponsored deposit insurance fund, the predecessor of federal deposit insurance. Even after federal deposit insurance was enacted in 1933, private guaranty funds co-existed with federal insurance programs for many years until the mid-1980s when a series of savings and loan failures in Ohio and Maryland forced private insurers in those states to liquidate.

GUARDIAN person who has legal responsibility for care of a minor, or a person incapable of managing his affairs. This right may be conveyed by a court, or it may be a natural guardianship, for example, a parent providing for a child under legal age.

GULF RIYAL monetary unit of Dubai and Qatar.

H

HAIRCUT

1. valuation formula used by broker-dealers in computing net capital positions. A dealer's haircut is an estimate of potential losses, taking into account credit risk, market risk, time to maturity, and other factors. Haircuts vary according to class of security: ranging from a nearly 0% haircut for short-term U.S. Treasury securities to 100% for issues in default, where total loss is probable. Haircuts in government securities trading are based on weekly yield volatility, as tabulated by the Federal Reserve Bank of New York. Dealer capital requirements are governed by the Securities and Exchange Commission's Rule l5c3-1. The lowest haircuts are given to securities considered least likely to default, for example, Treasury bills.
2. in lending, difference between the amount advanced by a lender and the market value of collateral securing the loan. For example, if a lender makes a loan equal to 90% of the dollar value of marketable securities, the difference (10%) is the haircut. Also called *haircut financing.*
3. spread in a repurchase agreement, or the difference between the market value and the value actually used.
4. in a bank failure, a depositor's potential loss as an UNINSURED DEPOSITOR when deposits exceed the $250,000 coverage limit.

HALF LIFE number of years needed for half of the loan principal in a mortgage-backed security to be repaid. Half lives are determined by interest rate volatility, borrower prepayments, and to some extent by geographic region. In general, when interest rates fall, borrowers refinance at substantial savings in interest costs, causing half lives to drop.

Rising rates have the opposite effect. Borrowers hold on to their loans for a longer period and half lives lengthen. *See also* AVERAGE LIFE; DURATION.

HANDLE trader's shorthand where the whole number is eliminated from a trade quote and understood by the parties to the trade. Quotes are in fractions: 1/16 bid, 3/16 offered.

HANDLING CHARGE see INTERCHANGE RATE.

HARD CURRENCY

1. currency expected to remain stable, if not appreciate in value, in relation to other currencies; also a currency that is readily CONVERTIBLE, or exchanged for the currency of another country. A sizable portion of international trade and bank lending is denominated in hard currencies; central banks keep a portion of their reserves in these currencies. Also called STRONG CURRENCY.

2. gold bullion of gold coins, as opposed to paper money, which is not convertible into an equivalent amount of gold or other precious metal.

HARD MONEY LOAN loan secured by real estate at an interest rate above prevailing market rates, often granted to a borrower in financial distress such as bankruptcy or foreclosure. Hard money loans are typically extended by private investors rather than commercial banks.

HAZARD INSURANCE property insurance carrying protection against losses from fire, certain natural causes, vandalism, and malicious mischief. Home owners generally maintain hazard insurance coverage through regular mortgage payments, a portion of which goes into an ESCROW account for insurance and property taxes. Mortgage lenders require hazard insurance coverage before a loan is made.

H BOND *see* SAVINGS BOND.

HH BOND *see* SAVINGS BOND.

HEAD TELLER bank teller whose duties include supervising other tellers, controlling cash in tellers' drawers, preparing a daily cash report for the general ledger, and helping other tellers find a difference if end-of-day debits and credits are out of balance. Actual duties vary by financial institution.

HEALTH SAVINGS ACCOUNT tax-advantaged savings plan that covers current and future medical expenses. A health savings account (HSA; formerly medical savings accounts) has two main components: 1) a high-deductible health insurance plan purchased from an insurance company; 2) a savings account at a commercial bank or savings institution similar to an individual retirement account. Self-employed individuals and individuals who are not covered by another qualified health insurance plan (or who have not yet enrolled in the federal Medicare health insurance program) can make tax deductible contributions up to $2,650 ($5,250 for families) annually.

Health savings account earnings accumulate tax-free, and withdrawals for qualified medical expenses are also tax-free. Individuals age fifty-five or older can increase their annual HSA contributions. Contributions for any year may be made any time up to the April 15 tax filing deadline. Health savings accounts, authorized by federal legislation enacted in 2003, are designed to pay for medical expenses covered by the insurance policy until the insurance deductible are met. Once the deductible limit has been reached, the insurance policy pays for medical expenses exceeding the policy deductible.

HEDGE/HEDGING financial technique to offset the risk of loss from price fluctuations in the market. Hedgers employ a variety of techniques, including futures contracts, options on futures, and interest rate swaps. An investor wanting protection against a fall in price can sell forward contracts (a LONG HEDGE); in the futures market, to protect against a rise in price, the investor buys forward contracts (a SHORT HEDGE). For example, a borrower in the money market can use INTEREST RATE FUTURES as protection against increases in short-term rates with a short or sell hedge, by selling an interest rate contract for future delivery. If rates happen to rise between the contract sale date and the delivery date, the value of the futures contract will drop and the hedger can make a gain by buying back, at a lower price, the contract sold earlier.

Other forms of hedging involve purchase of interest rate and currency options, INTEREST-ONLY (IO) STRIP and PRINCIPAL ONLY (PO) STRIPS, and RESIDUAL tranches of a COLLATERALIZED MORTGAGE OBLIGATION. *See also* ARBITRAGE; COVERED INTEREST ARBITRAGE; CROSS-HEDGE; DERIVATIVE MORTGAGE-BACKED SECURITIES; SHORT SALE; TRANCHE.

HERFINDAHL INDEX *see* CONCENTRATION.

HIGH-GRADE BOND bond rated triple-A or double-A by Standard & Poor's or Moody's rating services. It may be supported by a CREDIT ENHANCEMENT, such as a letter of credit to obtain a high debt rating. *See also* INVESTMENT GRADE.

HIGHLY LEVERAGED TRANSACTION bank loan financing a corporate acquisition, recapitalization, or LEVERAGED BUYOUT, usually at high interest rates. The financing often results in a doubling of the borrower's liabilities and debt-to-assets ratio above 50%, or when the borrower has total liabilities (including preferred stock) exceeding 75% of its total assets. Also, a loan designated as highly leveraged by a banking regulator or a syndicating agent.

HIGH LOAN-TO-VALUE MORTGAGE second mortgage loan that, when combined with a related first-lien mortgage, substantially exceeds the value of the mortgaged property. High loan-to-value mortgages are used most often in consolidating consumer obligations, such as credit card debt, in one second mortgage. This loan is sometimes called a *125 percent mortgage loan* because the combined loan-to-value ratio of the two loans may be as high as 125% of the property value.

HIGH RATIO LOAN mortgage loan in which the amount advanced by the lender is close to the appraised value of the property. Generally, any mortgage with a loan-to-value ratio higher than 80% is considered a high ratio loan. Lenders often require the borrower to obtain MORTGAGE INSURANCE to guard against default risk.

HIT THE BID expression for a seller's willingness to accept the bid price offered by a buyer. The opposite is TAKE THE OFFER.

HOLDBACK portion of a construction loan that is not funded until the project is nearing completion, or the borrower has satisfied certain performance requirements, such as leasing a majority of the units in the building. The amount kept back often is equal to the construction firm's expected profit when the building is completed.

HOLDER IN DUE COURSE party who becomes the good faith owner of a NEGOTIABLE INSTRUMENT (such as a check, note, or draft), for value received, without knowledge of any claims against it, or that the instrument was dishonored when presented for payment, or in any way defective. Under the UNIFORM COMMERCIAL CODE, the body of law governing legal contracts, the person holding a check endorsed by another is the presumed legal owner, and can sue in his or her own name. A person accepting a THIRD PARTY CHECK is a holder in due course, and holds legal title to the instrument, regardless of any prior claims. By contrast, a good faith buyer of an asset does not necessarily acquire title; an innocent buyer of a stolen car never gains title to the car.

A bank acquiring installment loan contracts, as a holder in due course, from a retailer or other lender, can be held liable in some cases for any claims by the original borrower against the seller of the note. This is the Federal Trade Commission's *holder in due course* rule, intended to prevent abusive credit practices. The rule, issued in 1976, says the holder of a note must honor warranties of the original seller. This means a consumer cannot be required to make payments when the seller of the note refused to honor a manufacturer's guarantee on merchandise that turned out to be defective, or the seller refused to perform work, such as home improvements, financed by a bank loan.

HOLD HARMLESS CLAUSE clause in a construction mortgage or loan contract relieving the borrower from liability in unforeseen events, such as labor strikes or natural disaster, that limit or inhibit the borrower in meeting contractual obligations.

HOLDING COMPANY *see* BANK HOLDING COMPANY; FINANCIAL HOLDING COMPANY; ONE-BANK HOLDING COMPANY; UNITARY THRIFT.

HOLDOVERS transit checks in collection that, for one reason or another, are delayed until the next processing cycle, which is usually the next business day, for bundling in cash letters and presentment to a clearing house or directly to the paying bank for collection. Most holdovers are found in large clearing banks.

HOLIDAY FLOAT *see* FLOAT.

HOME BANKING self-service banking for consumers and small business owners, enabling users to perform many routine functions at home by telephone, or cable modem connection. Home banking, also called *on-line banking* or *PC banking,* gives consumers an array of convenient services: they can move money between accounts, pay bills, check balances, and buy and sell mutual funds and securities. They can also look up loan rates and see if they qualify for a credit card or mortgage.

Home banking services date to the early 1980s, and since then have grown enormously as home computers become more affordable and easier to use. The ability to transact banking accurately and in the privacy of the home any time of the day has made home banking an attractive alternative to visiting local financial institutions. In the 1990s, financial institutions broadened their home banking services by giving consumers direct access to banking information via the INTERNET, enabling many to do their banking from anywhere in the United States or around the world.

See also INTERNET BANKING; MOBILE BANKING.

HOME EQUITY CONVERSION MORTGAGE *see* REVERSE MORTGAGE.

HOME EQUITY CREDIT loan secured by equity value in a borrower's home. A home equity loan allows the home owner to tap into the accumulated equity in his home—the difference between the current fair market value and the amount secured by a first mortgage—by writing checks that are drawn against a line of credit. Most home equity loans require an initial sign-up fee and an APPRAISAL of the property to determine the LOAN-TO-VALUE RATIO. Equity credit policies vary regionally, but a common practice is to set the upper limit on equity lines at an amount equal to 80% of the current market value of a home, less the outstanding mortgage balance. Also called *home equity line of credit. See also* SECOND MORTGAGE.

HOME IMPROVEMENT LOAN consumer loan, usually secured by collateral or a mortgage, taken out to finance alterations, remodeling, or structural renovations to an existing dwelling. These loans are generally short-term, but may be for longer periods. *See also* HOME EQUITY CREDIT; SECOND MORTGAGE.

HOME MORTGAGE DISCLOSURE ACT *see* REGULATION C.

HOMESTEAD EXEMPTION state laws allowing debtors to exclude equity in a home from seizure by creditors in a BANKRUPTCY filing or other legal proceeding. Some states give debtors the option of choosing a federal exemption, which is usually lower than state allowances.

HONOR

1. payment of a check when presented or agreement to pay a time draft at a future date. *See also* ACCEPTANCE.
2. acceptance of a bank card or travel & entertainment (T&E) card offered as payment for goods or services.

HOT CARD bank card that cannot be honored for payment, most often because the card has been reported lost or stolen, or has been cancelled by the issuer. Hot cards are listed in the combined Visa and MasterCard WARNING BULLETIN.

HOT MONEY

1. interest-sensitive deposits in domestic accounts, such as short-term bank CDs, that are subject to withdrawal at maturity if another bank offers a higher rate. Much of the interest-sensitive money

flowing in and out of banks is owned by corporate or institutitional investors who seek out the currency and country offering the best return. When rates fall, funds are often withdrawn on short notice.

2. surplus funds that banks purchase or sell to each other in the money market, normally on an overnight or short-term basis, such as FEDERAL FUNDS or overnight repurchase agreements. See also MANAGED LIABILITIES.
3. uninsured deposits, for example certificates of deposit, in amounts above the $250,000 FDIC limit. Depositors who seek the highest return look for banks and savings institutions paying the highest nationally advertised rate on short-term CDs. *See also* BROKERED DEPOSIT.
4. bank teller's bait money: specially marked bills in a teller's drawer, meant to help identify cash taken in robberies.

HOUSING AND URBAN DEVELOPMENT, DEPARTMENT OF (HUD) cabinet-level federal agency, founded in 1965, that promotes housing development in the United States through direct loans, mortgage insurance and guarantees. The FEDERAL HOUSING ADMINISTRATION, which insures mortgage loans originated by private lenders, and GINNIE MAE (Government National Mortgage Association), which guarantees residential mortgages pooled for resale in the secondary mortgage market, are within HUD. Ginnie Mae was separated from the Federal National Mortgage Association (FANNIE MAE) and established as a wholly owned federal agency under HUD by the Housing Act of 1968. Other HUD-assisted programs finance the construction of subsidized public housing, and rehabilitation of single family and multifamily housing. *See also* MUTUAL MORTGAGE INSURANCE FUND.

HOUSING AUTHORITY BOND short-term note or long-term bond issued by a public housing authority and guaranteed as to repayment of principal and interest by the U.S. Department of Housing and Urban Development. The bonds finance construction of low- and moderate-income housing, paying competitive rates.

HOUSING STARTS award of a building permit for construction of new residential multifamily and single family housing. The volume of housing starts, gauging consumer demand for residential mortgages, is one of the 12 leading economic indicators compiled by the U.S. Department of Commerce.

HRYVNIA monetary unit of Ukraine.

HUD-1 SETTLEMENT STATEMENT a document that provides an itemized listing of the funds that were paid at closing. Items that appear on the statement include real estate commissions, loan fees, points, and initial escrow (impound) amounts. Each type of expense goes on a specific numbered line on the sheet. The totals at the bottom of the HUD-1 statement define the seller's net proceeds and the buyer's net payment at closing. It is called a HUD-1 statement because the form is printed by the Department of Housing and Urban Development (HUD). The HUD-1 statement is also known as the *closing statement* or *settlement sheet*.

HUMPED YIELD CURVE unusual situation where medium-term rates are higher than rates on short-term and long-term instruments. Also called a *bell-shaped yield curve*.

HUMPED YIELD CURVE

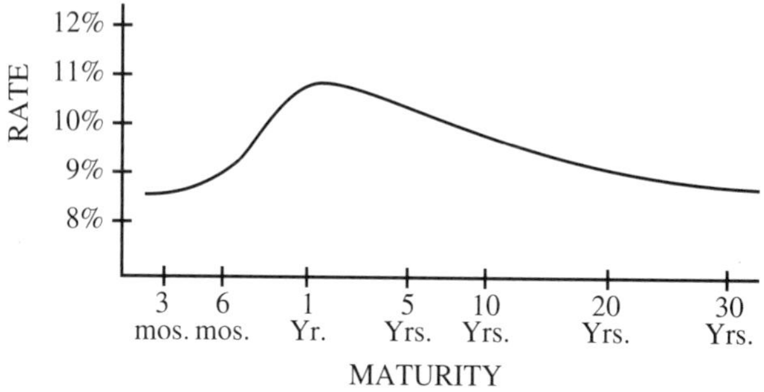

HURDLE RATE

1. capital budgeting term referring to a bank's minimal rate of return in extending a loan or making an investment. Loans are funded if the bank's expected return exceeds the hurdle rate. Also called the MARGINAL COST OF FUNDS.
2. BREAK-EVEN YIELD; the point at which sales equals cost.

HYBRID ARM variation of an ADJUSTABLE-RATE MORTGAGE (ARM) loan that has a fixed rate of interest in the early years of the loan. The initial fixed-rate period in a hybrid ARM can be set for 3 years, 5 years, 7 years or 10 years, after which the loan converts to an adjustable-rate mortgage and the interest rate is adjusted once a year according to changes in market conditions for the remaining term of the loan. Hybrid ARMs are ideal for borrowers who plan to live in their homes for a relatively short period, want a lower monthly payment, or would like to qualify for a larger mortgage. The 5/1 hybrid ARM, a popular choice, has a fixed rate of interest for the first five years; in subsequent years the rate is adjusted annually.

HYPERINFLATION economic condition characterized by rapidly rising prices of freely traded goods, and declining purchasing power, threatening economic stability and ability to repay EXTERNAL DEBT. The term usually is applied when consumer prices are rising at rates in excess of 50% per month, particularly in developing countries. Also called *runaway inflation*.

HYPOTHECATION

1. **Banking.** Offer of stocks, bonds, or other assets owned by a party other than the borrower as COLLATERAL for a loan, without transferring title. If the borrower turns over the property to the lender, who holds it in safekeeping, the action is referred to as a *pledge;* if the borrower retains possession, but gives the lender the right to sell the property in event of default, it is a *true hypothecation.*
2. **Securities.** The pledging of negotiable securities to collateralize a broker's MARGIN loan. If the broker pledges the same securities to a bank as collateral for a broker's loan, the process is referred to as *rehypothecation.*

I

I-BONDS inflation-adjusted SAVINGS BONDS issued by the U.S. Treasury. I-Bonds are available in eight denominations from $50 to $10,000 and earn interest up to 30 years. The interest payout on these bonds is determined by a composite of two rates: a fixed rate of return (ranging from 3% to 3.5%) set by the Treasury Department, and a semi-annual inflation rate determined by the Bureau of Labor Statistics from a version of the consumer price index. I-Bonds, like other savings bonds, offer investors special tax benefits. Investors may defer paying federal taxes on their earnings, which are automatically reinvested, as long as they own the bonds. I-Bonds are also exempt from state and local income taxes. If used for college tuition and other college fees, investors may exclude all or part of I-Bond earnings in calculating federal taxes. *See also* INFLATION-INDEXED SECURITIES.

IDENTIFICATION any means of verifying a bank's customer, for example, the drawer (maker) of a negotiable instrument or the person initiating an electronic funds transfer. Also, any industry assigned number identifying a paying bank (the ABA TRANSIT NUMBER or CHECK ROUTING SYMBOL), or the owner of marketable securities.

1. bank customer's signature on a check, either as drawer or endorser. Banks have an obligation to examine paid checks for proper endorsement, but this is now done on an exception basis.
2. in electronic transfers of funds, a sending bank's password, called an issuer KEY, used in place of a bank officer's signature. *See also* MESSAGE AUTHENTICATION CODE.
3. PERSONAL IDENTIFICATION NUMBER (PIN) assigned to a bank account.
4. biometric identification, a means of identifying bank customers by unique physical characteristics, such as voice, fingerprint, or handwriting. The most promising of these new technologies is signature dynamics, which identifies handwriting.
5. personal information known by the account holder, such as mother's maiden name, recorded on a SIGNATURE CARD when a new account is opened.
6. Social Security Number of an individual or federal TAXPAYER IDENTIFICATION NUMBER of an organization.
7. BANK IDENTIFICATION NUMBER (BIN).
8. machine readable characters such as the MAGNETIC INK CHARACTER RECOGNITION (MICR) line on the bottom edge of checks.
9. CUSIP NUMBER.

IDENTITY THEFT misappropriation of an individual's identifying information with the intent to commit fraud. An individual who knowingly uses another person's Social Security number or driver's license or other personal identifying data to open fraudulent bank accounts or apply for fraudulent loans is committing identity theft. In a common version, called account takeover theft, the thief uses the information to access existing accounts. Computerized records and the ability to transact business anonymously over the Internet have contributed greatly to the rise of identity theft crimes since the late 1990s.

ILLIQUID asset not easily sold for cash, for example, a loan with a limited secondary market. Such loans can, however, be sold through private placement with an investor, sometimes at a discount from face value.

Also, assets that are not counted toward a bank's core capital, such as real estate owned through foreclosure and nonmarketable securities.

IMMEDIATE BENEFICIARY beneficiary of a trust who is entitled to receive immediate benefits, which may be unrestricted or limited to trust income. Contrast with *ultimate beneficiary*, the person named to receive the final distribution from the trust.

IMMEDIATE CREDIT check given SAME-DAY FUNDS availability when presented to a Federal Reserve Bank for collection. Only banks in a city where the Fed has a Reserve Bank or branch, called a RESERVE CITY BANK, are given immediate availability on checks cleared by the Fed, as opposed to the normal two-day DEFERRED AVAILABILITY on most checks. Also, banks usually give same-day credit to on-us checks, or checks drawn against accounts in the same bank where they are deposited.

IMMUNIZATION actions taken to safeguard against market risk. A bond portfolio is said to be *immunized* when it is structured to produce a target rate of return, regardless of any changes in bond prices or market interest rates. Banks can immunize the balance sheet by holding approximately equal amounts of assets and liabilities for a defined period of time. More generally, immunization can refer to investment strategies, such as interest rate and currency swaps to minimize investment risk. *See also* DURATION; GAPPING; REINVESTMENT RISK.

IMPAIRED CAPITAL condition where a bank's total paid-in capital is less than the stated value, through excessive loan losses or other unsound practices. If the impairment is severe, a bank may be called upon by a regulatory agency's capital call to make up the deficiency by raising new capital or go into liquidation.

IMPAIRED CREDIT bank loan where full repayment is considered uncertain. An impaired credit is classified as a DOUBTFUL LOAN, SUBSTANDARD, or LOSS, depending on the severity of the impairment.

IMPLIED VOLATILITY degree of volatility implied by the market price of an option. Some options traders deal in volatility, buying options when their implied volatility is low and selling options when their implied volatility is high. By using the BLACK SCHOLES MODEL, an investor who knows the option price, the strike price and other factors, can determine the price volatility.

IMPOUND ACCOUNT account established by a mortgage lender to pay a borrower's property tax and insurance costs. Mortgage payments are increased to include these costs, and the funds collected are disbursed when the payments are due. Lenders prefer this arrangement, as it minimizes the possibility of a lapse in tax or insurance payments, which could potentially reduce the value of the mortgaged property.

IMPUTED INTEREST interest that legally may be considered part of the principal of a debt, if the interest paid is less than the amount estimated for tax purposes by the Internal Revenue Service.

INACTIVE ACCOUNT account with infrequent deposits or withdrawals. If no activity is recorded for a specified period, other than crediting of interest, it is considered a DORMANT ACCOUNT and removed from the file of active accounts.

INADVERTENT ERROR clerical or billing error that, although a technical violation of consumer protection laws, does not give cause to a civil liability complaint if a bank can assert the error was unintentional, was made in good faith despite safeguards to prevent such mistakes, and then corrects the error. For example, a lender may assess a LATE CHARGE on a mortgage payment even though the payment was received during the allowed grace period.

INAS network for exchange of bank card authorizations among financial institutions affiliated with MASTERCARD INTERNATIONAL. Full name: Interbank National Authorization System. *See also* INET.

INCENTIVE PRICING transaction pricing intended to encourage consumers to use banking services. *See also* TEASER RATE.

INCOME LIMITS maximum amounts that moderate income or low income families may earn to qualify for subsidized rental housing or a low-interest mortgage. Limits are based on family size and geographic location.

INCOME PROPERTY MORTGAGE *see* COMMERCIAL MORTGAGE.

INCOME STATEMENT profit and loss statement detailing a firm's financial operations for a specific period, including net profit or loss for the period in question. It usually is accompanied by a BALANCE SHEET for the end of that period. Income statements are included in quarterly 10Q reports and annual 10K reports filed with the Securities and Exchange Commission.

INCONVERTIBLE currency or security that cannot be freely exchanged for another, or sold for cash. An inconvertible currency is less desirable to investors than a freely CONVERTIBLE currency.

INCORPORATED TRUSTEE trust company or bank trust department authorized to act as a FIDUCIARY for a trust account, as opposed to an individual who is appointed TRUSTEE.

INCREMENTAL COST OF FUNDS *see* MARGINAL COST OF FUNDS.

INDENTURE

1. written agreement specifying the terms and conditions for issuing bonds, stating the form of the bond being offered for sale, interest to be paid, the maturity date, call provisions and protective covenants, if any, collateral pledged, the repayment schedule, and other terms. It describes the legal obligations of a bond issuer and the powers of the bond TRUSTEE, who has the responsibility, under the TRUST INDENTURE ACT of 1939, for ensuring that interest payments are made to registered bondholders.
2. mortgage or deed of trust securing a lien against real property, specifying covenants and conditions, as agreed by the seller (the grantor) and the buyer.

INDEPENDENT BANK locally owned and operated commercial bank. It derives its sources of funds from, and it lends money to, the community where it operates, and is not affiliated with a multibank holding company. Also called *community bank.*

INDEPENDENT COMMUNITY BANKERS OF AMERICA *see* TRADE ASSOCIATION.

INDEX

1. **In general.** A numerical figure adjusted periodically to reflect changes in the quantity of goods produced, prices paid, loan interest rates, by comparing current activity to a base year, previous month, or previous year. The Consumer Price Index, measuring changes in prices paid for consumer goods, is a widely used example.
2. **Banking.** The interest rate used as the base rate in pricing variable rate loans, often called a COST OF FUNDS INDEX. In an ADJUSTABLE RATE MORTGAGE, the borrower's loan rate is reset periodically at a MARGIN above the index rate. Numerous index rates are used in bank lending, for example, the Federal Home Loan Bank Board's cost of funds index or the National Average Mortgage Contract Rate Index.
3. **Economics.** A statistical measure of the rate of change in the economy, for example, the index of leading economic indicators, which tends to anticipate changes in the business cycle.
4. **Securities.** An indicator of financial market performance, for example, the Standard & Poor's 500 Index of industrial stocks, or the Dow Jones Industrial Average.

INDEXED INVESTMENT *see* INFLATION-INDEXED SECURITIES; MARKET INDEX CD.

INDICATION

1. **Banking.** A notation next to a money market dealer's price quote signifying that the quotation is for information only and the dealer is unwilling to do business (make a market) at that price.

2. **Securities.** A willingness to buy securities in registration from an underwriter—an expression of interest.

INDIRECT LIABILITY *see* CONTINGENT LIABILITY.

INDIRECT LOAN loan sold by a dealer or a retailer of goods, to a third party financial institution that owns the loan contract as a HOLDER IN DUE COURSE and collects principal and interest payments from the borrower. Commercial banks and finance companies buy installment contracts from dealers at a discount from the face value on the notes. *See also* DEALER FINANCING; FLOOR PLANNING.

INDIVIDUAL PROPRIETOR *see* SOLE PROPRIETOR.

INDIVIDUAL DEVELOPMENT ACCOUNT (IDA) savings program, similar to a 401(k) plan, created to help low-income families build financial assets for a specific purpose, such as education advancement, home purchase, or starting a business. Account holders' contributions to an IDA are matched up to a certain amount by a sponsoring organization.

INDIVIDUAL RETIREMENT ACCOUNT (IRA) tax-deferred retirement savings account for individuals or married couples filing jointly. Individuals under age 50 may contribute up to $5,000 annually from personal income, and individuals age 50 or more can make annual contributions of $6,000. IRA contributions are tax deductible regardless of income if neither the taxpayer nor the spouse is enrolled in an employer-sponsored pension or retirement savings plan. Eligibility to claim a fully tax-deductible IRA contribution is reduced for higher-income individuals and individuals participating in an employer-sponsored retirement plan. These limits are reviewed and adjusted annually. In 2011, couples with incomes between $90,000 and $110,000 and individual taxpayers with incomes between $56,000 and $66,000 were eligible to make partially deductible IRA contributions.

Withdrawals from an IRA before age 59½ are generally subject to a 10% penalty tax, although certain types of withdrawals are exempted. Individuals may contribute annually to an IRA account until age 70½. After reaching that age, individuals must begin withdrawing funds according to an IRS schedule based on life expectancy. IRA accounts may be invested in many different types of investments, including stocks, bonds, certificates of deposit, and mutual funds.

See also 401(K) PLAN; INDIVIDUAL RETIREMENT ACCOUNT ROLLOVER; KEOGH PLAN; ROTH IRA; SELF-DIRECTED IRA.

INDIVIDUAL RETIREMENT ACCOUNT ROLLOVER provision in the U.S. tax code allowing the owner of an INDIVIDUAL RETIREMENT ACCOUNT to transfer assets of the account, without penalty, into another IRA account or qualified retirement plan if the funds are reinvested within 60 days. The same rule applies to early distributions of pension fund shares, profit sharing plans, and other tax qualified employee savings plans. This provision allows individuals to shift assets from one form of investment to another, without having to pay the 10% IRS penalty on early withdrawals. Also called "*rollover IRA*."

INDORSEMENT *see* ENDORSEMENT.

INDUSTRIAL BANK state chartered finance company that makes consumer and commercial loans and accepts time deposits and interest-paying NEGOTIABLE ORDER OF WITHDRAWAL accounts. Industrial banks are found mostly in the western United States. The term has its roots in the early-20th-century finance companies that originated loans to industrial workers; back then, most commercial banks did not offer consumer loans. Also called *industrial loan bank* or *industrial loan company*.

INDUSTRIAL DEVELOPMENT BOND municipal bond issued by a state or local government, or by a development agency, to finance private industrial projects generating tax revenues and certain public works projects. These bonds are of two types: development bonds financing the renovation or improvement of public facilities, and industrial revenue bonds, for which a private corporation is responsible for payments to bondholders. Industrial bonds are subject to special IRS rules governing the tax exemption of interest. The tax exemption on many of these bonds, other than bonds financing airports, water treatment plants, and certain other public works related projects, was eliminated by the Tax Reform Act of 1986. Bond ratings on revenue bonds are based on the credit rating of the private corporation backing the lease or rental agreement covering the facilities, because the ultimate source of repayment is the corporation, rather than the bond issuer. *See also* PRIVATE PURPOSE BOND; PUBLIC PURPOSE BOND.

INDUSTRIAL REVENUE BOND *see* INDUSTRIAL DEVELOPMENT BOND.

INET network for exchange of bank card debit and credit transactions among financial institutions affiliated with MASTERCARD WORLDWIDE. MasterCard's card authorization system (INAS) and net settlement system (INET) are now combined in worldwide data communications network known as BankNet. Full name: Interbank Network for Electronic Transfer.

INFLATION economic condition characterized by an increase in prices and wages, and declining purchasing power. Inflation is usually measured by changes in the Consumer Price Index (CPI). The result is diminished purchasing power, and frequently a lower rate of savings as wage earners put more of their disposable assets in consumption, and less in long-term savings. Inflation is a monetary phenomenon. It occurs when there is too much money in circulation relative to the production of actual goods and services. Federal Reserve MONETARY POLICY is the only means of controlling inflation, although FISCAL POLICY can help as well. *See also* DEFLATION; DISINFLATION; HYPERINFLATION.

INFLATION-INDEXED SECURITIES notes or bonds paying a guaranteed RATE OF RETURN above inflation if held to maturity. Inflation-indexed Treasury securities, available since 1997, are offered in the following maturities: five-year and 10-year Treasury notes, and 30-year Treasury bonds. Inflation-indexed Treasuries have two components: a fixed rate of return, paid out as INTEREST, and an adjustable return (the PRINCIPAL) indexed to the rate of change in the consumer price index (CPI). If inflation rises, the interest coupon remains unchanged, but the inflation-adjusted principal (paid at maturity) increases in value. U.S. Treasury inflation-indexed securities are modeled after Real Return Bonds issued by the Government of Canada, and are available from the Treasury Department's Bureau of Public Debt in denominations as low as $1,000. Securities can be purchased electronically through Treasury Direct, the Treasury Department's sales window for small investors, or a financial broker-dealer.

INFORMATION TECHNOLOGY computer based information management systems allowing a financial institution to collect information from many different sources and develop a composite picture about its customers, its market position in different financial centers, and its net exposure in those markets.

INITIAL INTEREST RATE interest rate, often discounted below the fully indexed rate, that is in effect during the period before the first rate change of an adjustable-rate mortgage (ARM).

INITIAL MARGIN *see* MARGIN.

INSIDE DIRECTOR member of a firm's board of directors who is also a member of its management, such as the president or chief executive officer, as opposed to outside directors appointed for their reputation in the community. Directors of banking institutions can be removed by federal banking regulators if they abuse their office, in contrast to directors of nonfinancial companies.

INSIDER INFORMATION legal term for information not available to the general public, but known by inside directors, principals in a firm planning a takeover of another company, and others. Officers, directors, and other corporate insiders owning at least 10% of a company's stock must report trades to the Securities and Exchange Commission.

INSIDER LENDING loans to directors and officers of a bank. Banking laws require that banks make loans to insiders at the same rate and credit terms as loans to other borrowers. The 1991 federal law recapitalizing the Federal Deposit Insurance Corporation imposes new limits on loans to insiders.

INSOLVENCY inability to pay debts as they mature, or as obligations become due and payable. A person may still have an excess of assets over liabilities, but be insolvent if unable to convert assets into cash to meet financial obligations.

A financial institution, such as a bank, generally is considered to be insolvent if its ratio of capital to assets is at, or close to, zero, or if its capital assets, including common stock, are of such poor quality that its continued existence is uncertain. *See also* ACT OF BANKRUPTCY; BANKRUPTCY.

INSTALLMENT CONTRACT written agreement to pay for goods purchased, in payments of principal and interest at regularly scheduled intervals. Also called installment sales paper and installment paper. *See also* CONDITIONAL SALES CONTRACT.

INSTALLMENT CREDIT loan repaid with interest owed, in equal periodic payments of principal and interest. Installment loans are fully amortizing loans, repayable over a fixed amortization schedule in monthly installments. These loans can be secured by personal property—for example, an auto loan—but not real estate. If the loan is to a consumer, disclosure of finance charges is required by federal consumer protection laws. *See also* CHATTEL MORTGAGE; CONDITIONAL SALES CONTRACT; CONSUMER CREDIT; PERSONAL LOAN.

INSTALLMENT NOTE promissory note underlying an INSTALLMENT CREDIT agreement, calling for periodic payments of principal and interest to pay off the debt.

INSTITUTIONAL LENDER financial institution or institutional investor that invests its own funds, or funds under management, in corporate equities and debt securities, government securities, residential mortgages, commercial real estate, or mortgage-backed securities. Frequently, these investors buy mortgage loans, either whole loans or pools of loans packaged as securities, and also new securities offerings sold through private placement. In the SECONDARY MORTGAGE MARKET, hedge funds, private equity funds, life insurance companies, commercial banks, and pension funds act as institutional lenders.

INSTRUCTING BANK bank that initiates a transfer of funds as instructed by a customer, as opposed to an advising bank, which notifies the sender that payment has been made. Also called the *ordering party.*

INSTRUMENT legally enforceable agreement between two or more parties, expressing a contractual right or a right to the payment of money. Practically all documents used in credit are instruments, e.g., checks, drafts, notes, bonds. *See also* NEGOTIABLE INSTRUMENT.

INSTRUMENTALITY government agency issuing marketable securities backed by the FULL FAITH AND CREDIT guarantee of the government. The term is normally used in connection with notes, certificates, and bonds issued by U.S. government agencies, such as the Export-Import Bank, the Government National Mortgage Association, or the Small Business Administration, but can refer more generally to any government agency.

INSUFFICIENT FUNDS *see* NOT SUFFICIENT FUNDS.

INSURANCE TRUST IRREVOCABLE TRUST created to receive the proceeds of a life insurance policy, normally established to avoid paying estate taxes. Trust assets are payable to the beneficiary at the death of the insured. A life insurance trust provides additional liquidity to the insured, but has the disadvantage that the person named as beneficiary cannot borrow against the policy, and must survive a gift to the trust by three years.

INSURED ACCOUNT bank account protected from loss of interest or principal by federal deposit insurance, up to $250,000 in ordinary accounts and retirement accounts. Insurance coverage for traditional and Roth IRAs, self-directed KEOGH plans, Simplified Employee Pension (SEP) accounts, public employee "457" plans and employer sponsored 401(k) savings plans was increased in 2006 to $250,000 per account. Accounts in commercial banks, savings banks, savings and loan associations are insured by the Federal Deposit Insurance Corporation's Deposit Insurance Fund. The National Credit Union Share Insurance Fund insures accounts in federal credit unions and most state credit unions. See also UNINSURED DEPOSITOR.

Contrast with *uninsured assets,* which are not protected by federal deposit insurance. Mutual funds and annuities are uninsured investments subject to market risk, but investors with broker-dealer accounts may be protected from a broker's insolvency by the SECURITIES INVESTOR PROTECTION CORPORATION (SIPC).

INSURED FINANCIAL INSTITUTION bank or savings institution that is a member of the Federal Deposit Insurance Corporation's deposit insurance plan, the DEPOSIT INSURANCE FUND. Credit union accounts are protected by the National Credit Union Share Insurance Fund.

INSURED LOAN Residential mortgage loan insured by the FEDERAL HOUSING ADMINISTRATION (FHA) or by a mortgage insurance company. In event of default, the FHA indemnifies the holder of the mortgage for part, or all, of the unpaid principal. FHA-insured loans generally have a high ratio of loan to value, and frequently are pooled for sale to institutional investors as GINNIE MAE (Government National Mortgage Association) PASS-THROUGH CERTIFICATES. Interest rates on FHA insured loans are set slightly below prevailing market rates on conventional mortgage loans. *See also* CREDIT ENHANCEMENT; PRIVATE MORTGAGE INSURANCE.

INTANGIBLE ASSET balance sheet asset having no physical properties, but thought to represent some future economic benefit to its owner. Intangibles, such as GOODWILL, bank card service marks, patents, franchises, and so on, are noncurrent assets amortized over the period held.

INTEGRATED CIRCUIT CARD *see* SMART CARD.

INTER-AMERICAN DEVELOPMENT BANK (IADB) development bank, organized in 1959, to foster economic development in Latin America by arranging project financing with its own funds and loans by private banks. Membership, originally limited to member countries of the Organization of American States, has since been broadened to include the governments of 26 Latin American countries, the United States, Japan, and 14 European countries.

INTERBANK BID RATE *see* LONDON INTERBANK BID RATE.

INTERBANK DEPOSITS deposit held by one bank for another bank, usually a correspondent. Each bank holds a DUE TO ACCOUNT in the name of the other bank. An account on the books of a foreign correspondent is a NOSTRO ACCOUNT to the bank owning the account, and a VOSTRO ACCOUNT as viewed by the foreign correspondent.

INTERBANK MARKET *see* FEDERAL FUNDS; MONEY MARKET.

INTERBANK RATE *see* FEDERAL FUNDS RATE; LONDON INTERBANK OFFERED RATE.

INTERCHANGE exchange of transactions between financial institutions participating in a bank card network, based on a common set of rules. Examples are the Visa and MasterCard bank card systems and regional automated teller machine networks. Card interchange allows a bank's customer to use a bank credit card at any card honoring merchant. *See also* INTERCHANGE RATE.

INTERCHANGE RATE fee paid by one bank to another to cover handling costs and credit risk in a bank card transaction. Interchange fees generally flow toward the bank funding a transaction and assuming some risk in the process. In a credit card transaction, the interchange fee, also known as the *issuer's reimbursement fee,* is paid by the bank purchasing (or accepting) the merchant's sales drafts (the MERCHANT BANK) to the card issuing bank, which then bills the cardholder. The interchange fee (a percentage of the transaction amount or a fixed amount), is derived from an accounting formula that takes into account authorization costs, fraud and credit losses, and the average bank cost of funds, and is periodically revised. In automated teller and electronic debit point-of-sale systems, interchange flows in the opposite direction; when a consumer gets cash at an automated teller machine, the terminal owning bank collects the fee. *See also* SWIPE FEE.

INTERDEALER BROKER specialist brokerage firm acting as an intermediary between broker-dealer firms and dealer banks in the over-the-counter bond market and financial derivatives market. Interdealer brokers execute customer trades and also help broker-dealer firms and banks manage their exposure to credit risk, interest rate risk, and exchange rate risk.

INTERDISTRICT SETTLEMENT ACCOUNT clearing account maintained by the Federal Reserve Board in Washington, D.C., for settlement of transfers of funds among the 12 Federal Reserve Banks. As transactions are made, each Reserve Bank's settlement account is increased (debited) by a due from entry, or reduced (credited) by a due to entry. These accounting entries are settled daily on a net basis, reducing the need to transfer funds between Reserve Banks.

INTEREST money paid for the use of money, expressed as a percentage rate for the period of time in use, generally an annual rate. Bank interest is both an amount paid to attract deposit funds, and a finance charge for money loaned to borrowers. Prior to the federal Truth in Lending Act of 1968, lenders used widely differing methods of calculating loan interest. Since then, interest due on consumer loans must be computed in terms of an ANNUAL PERCENTAGE RATE (APR), utilizing interest rate tables from the Federal Reserve Board or from financial publishers, and the total cost of borrowing disclosed when a loan is made. Federal regulation of credit was intended to make it easier for consumers to shop for credit. Loan interest paid over the term of a loan may in fact be less than the total FINANCE CHARGE cost of borrowing if the lender charges a commitment fee or discount points payable in advance. Interest on loans may also include late payment fees, annual fees, and over-limit charges.

See also ADD-ON INTEREST; COMPOUND INTEREST; DAILY INTEREST; DISCOUNT; EXACT INTEREST; LEGAL RATE OF INTEREST; PRECOMPUTED INTEREST; PRIME RATE; RULE OF THE 78S; SIMPLE INTEREST; USURY.

INTEREST MARGIN *see* NET INTEREST MARGIN.

INTEREST-ONLY LOAN

1. Mortgage in which the borrower pays only interest for a set term. At the end of this term, typically five to ten years in the United States, the loan converts to a fully amortizing loan in which both interest and principal are paid. An interest-only loan reduces loan payments in the early years of a loan, so borrowers who expect their income will grow over the loan term can take out a larger MORTGAGE for purchase of a home.
2. commercial loan or line of credit paying interest at regular intervals until maturity, when the entire balance is due. The borrower makes regular interest payments, and pays down the loan principal during the annual out of debt period, when the borrower is required to be free of debt. *See also* BALLOON MATURITY; BULLET LOAN.

INTEREST-ONLY (IO) STRIP mortgage security consisting of the interest rate portion of a STRIPPED MORTGAGE-BACKED SECURITY. The holder receives interest payments based on the current value of the loan collateral. High prepayments can return less to the holder than the dollar amount invested. *See also* PRINCIPAL-ONLY (PO) STRIP.

INTEREST RATE cost of CREDIT, expressed as a percentage rate, computed from the ratio of INTEREST to PRINCIPAL. Some interest rates are set by supply and demand in the money market, for example, the rate paid by the U.S. Treasury Department when it auctions Treasury bills. Interest rates on bank loans are administered rates, which means they are determined by the lender. The bank PRIME RATE, for example, is determined independently by each bank, even though many banks follow the actions of money center banks in repricing their prime rate. Variable interest rates, such as the rate charged in an Adjustable Rate Mortgage, are determined from an INDEX rate, or COST OF FUNDS INDEX, that by regulation must be outside the control of the lending institution. *See also* ANNUAL PERCENTAGE RATE; BASE RATE; DEPOSIT INTEREST RATE; LEGAL RATE OF INTEREST; USURY.

INTEREST RATE CAP

1. contractual agreement protecting a borrower against a rise in interest rates. In exchange for an upfront fee paid when the funds are advanced, the lender agrees to hold any rate increases to a preset ceiling. For example, a borrower taking out a loan priced at a spread above the LONDON INTERBANK OFFERED RATE (LIBOR) for 90-day Eurodollar deposits pays a cap fee to insure that the loan interest rate does not exceed a preset rate anytime during the life of the loan. The cap seller (the lender) agrees to pay the purchaser (the borrower) the difference between LIBOR and the STRIKE PRICE of the cap when LIBOR rises above that price. Interest rate caps are priced as option contracts, generally using an options pricing formula.

   Most commercial lenders hedge against the interest rate risk created by the cap by buying an offsetting cap from another financial institution, by exchanging a floating rate obligation for a fixed rate obligation in an INTEREST RATE SWAP, or by hedging—selling futures short—in the financial futures market. If interest rates happen to rise, the lender can then sell the futures contract at a higher price. The easiest way to buy protection against interest rate risk is to buy another cap. A bank selling a 15% cap on a $100 million loan could protect itself by taking an identical cap from another lender. Compare to COLLAR.
2. in an ADJUSTABLE RATE MORTGAGE, contractual limits on interest rate adjustments above an INDEX such as ANNUAL CAP and LIFE OF LOAN CAP.

INTEREST RATE FUTURES contract giving the holder the right to buy or sell a financial instrument at a specific price at a given future date. Interest futures began in 1975 when the Chicago Board of Trade began trading futures contracts on Ginnie Mae pass-through certificates. Later commodities exchanges added futures contracts in Treasury bills, notes and bonds, and commercial paper. Financial institutions utilize futures contracts as a hedging device, to minimize interest rate risk in periods of rising or falling rates.

INTEREST RATE MISMATCH *see* GAP; MISMATCH.

INTEREST RATE OPTIONS contract giving the right, but not the obligation, to buy or sell a financial instrument paying a fixed rate of interest at a specified price and future date. Option contracts in standard amounts of financial instruments, at a standard STRIKE PRICE and expiration date, are traded on securities and commodities exchanges, or are arranged in the over-the-counter market by a commercial bank or investment bank. Interest rate options, also called *debt options* or *fixed income options* are traded on the American Stock Exchange and the Chicago Board Options Exchange. Financial instruments traded include U.S. Treasury bills and Treasury bonds. Over-the-counter option contracts, often used when hedging a bond portfolio, are written by commercial banks and investment banks for Treasury notes and bonds, mortgage-backed securities, and money market instruments.

Another type of interest rate option allows option trading in FINANCIAL FUTURES contracts. For instance, the buyer of a call option in Treasury bond futures takes a long position in Treasury bonds of a specific maturity. Futures options in Treasury bonds are traded on the Chicago Board of Trade, whereas options in Eurodollar futures are traded on the International Monetary Market at the Chicago Mercantile Exchange and the London International Financial Futures Exchange.

INTEREST RATE RISK risk that an interest-earning asset, such as a bank loan, will decline in value as interest rates change. Longer maturity, fixed rate loans (for example, 30-year conventional mortgages) are more sensitive to price risk from changes in rates than variable rate loans. Another type of interest risk is REINVESTMENT RISK, or the possibility that maturing loans cannot be replaced by new loans earning the same interest rate.

INTEREST RATE SENSITIVITY *see* INTEREST RATE RISK.

INTEREST RATE SWAP contract in which two counter-parties agree to exchange interest payments of differing character based on an underlying NOTIONAL PRINCIPAL amount that is never exchanged. There are three types of interest swaps: *coupon swaps* or exchange of fixed rate for floating rate instruments in the same currency; BASIS SWAPS or the exchange of floating rate for floating rate instruments in the same currency; and *cross currency interest rate swaps* involving the exchange of fixed rate instruments in one currency for floating rate in another.

Typically, a swap contract exchanges fixed rate obligations for a floating rate instrument in the same currency. In its simplest form, the two parties to an interest rate swap exchange their interest payment obligations (no principal changes hands) on two different kinds of debt instruments, one being a fixed interest rate, the other being a floating rate.

For example, the Student Loan Marketing Association (Sallie Mae) may want to swap rates with a bank—a mutually beneficial transaction, as Sallie Mae, a highly rated institution because of its status as a federal agency, prefers floating rate to match short-term loans in its student loan portfolio. Sallie Mae can sell fixed rate debt at a relatively low cost, whereas the bank prefers to match its long-term fixed rate mortgages with fixed rate funds.

INTEREST RATE SWAP

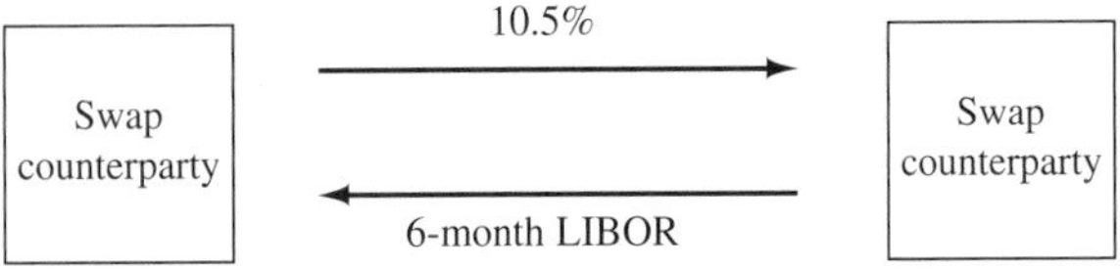

Notional amount: $10 million.
Maturity: 5 years.
Payment frequency: both fixed and floating rate payments are made semiannually.

INTEREST SENSITIVE ASSETS bank assets, principally loans, that are subject to changes in interest rates, either at maturity or when they are repriced according to an INDEX rate. Repricing of these assets is pegged or indexed to the upward or downward fluctuations of a publicly disclosed rate or cost of funds index, such as the six-month Treasury bill, the bank prime rate, and so on. Examples are variable rate consumer loans, variable rate demand loans, and adjustable rate mortgages. *See also* ASSET-LIABILITY MANAGEMENT; DURATION; GAP; INTEREST SENSITIVE LIABILITIES; REPRICING OPPORTUNITIES.

INTEREST SENSITIVE LIABILITIES short-term DEPOSIT instruments paying floating, as opposed to fixed, rates of interest. Since REGULATION Q interest rate ceilings were abolished under the Monetary Control Act of 1980, a significant portion of bank deposits are rate sensitive, including the six-month MONEY MARKET CERTIFICATE, the MONEY MARKET DEPOSIT ACCOUNT, and the SUPER NOW ACCOUNT. Phaseout of deposit interest rate ceilings in 1986 and removal of most penalties for early deposit withdrawals have led to increased volatility in the supply of deposits funding bank loans and new techniques to manage INTEREST RATE RISK. *See also* ASSET-LIABILITY COMMITTEE; ASSET-LIABILITY MANAGEMENT; FUNDS MANAGEMENT; INTEREST SENSITIVE ASSETS.

INTEREST SHORTFALL earned interest unpaid after loan payments have been made. This shortfall occurs most frequently in adjustable-rate mortgages with an interest-rate cap or mortgage loans with a low monthly payment option, resulting in NEGATIVE AMORTIZATION.

INTERIM LOAN *see* CONSTRUCTION LOAN.

INTERIM STATEMENT

1. **Banking.** A customer's checking account statement, dispensed by a self-service banking terminal, listing account debits and credits since

the last regular account statement was mailed, and current collected balance. Also called *mini statement* or *snapshot statement.*

2. **Finance.** A financial statement reporting activity for an accounting period less than an organization's fiscal year, for example, the quarterly 10Q report filed with the SEC.

INTERLOCKING DIRECTORATE commercial bank or savings institution having individuals on its board of directors who also serve on the board of an unaffiliated competitor in the same marketplace. The Financial Institutions Regulatory Act of 1978 prohibits management interlocks by banks in the same Metropolitan Statistical Area (MSA), but exempts smaller banks, and also permits interlocks of up to 49% of a bank's management officers.

INTERMEDIARY

1. financial institution, such as a bank or savings and loan, that acts as a conduit between suppliers of funds (depositors) and users of funds (borrowers). *See also* FINANCIAL INTERMEDIARY.
2. in the SWAP market, a commercial bank or investment bank that makes a market in interest rate and currency swaps to earn fees or trading profits.

INTERMEDIATE TARGETS monetary targets, either monetary growth or interest rates, that the Federal Reserve sets as objectives of its MONETARY POLICY. In recent years, the Fed has shifted its focus from controlling the rise and fall of the Fed Funds rate to emphasis on monetary targets and growth in the nation's money supply. Money supply is one of these targets, although other economic indicators are also closely watched, including total federal funds trading, net borrowed reserves and total reserves, plus total debt in the economy. *See also* OPERATING TARGETS.

INTERMEDIATION process of transferring funds from an ultimate source to the ultimate user. A FINANCIAL INSTITUTION, such as a bank, intermediates credit when it obtains money from a depositor and relends it to a borrowing customer. The opposite is DISINTERMEDIATION, the withdrawal of deposit funds when savers expect to earn a higher yield through direct investment such as stocks or bonds. *See also* FINANCIAL INTERMEDIARY.

INTERNAL CAPITAL GENERATION RATE rate at which a bank generates equity capital, computed by dividing retained earnings (net income less dividends) by the average balance of stockholders equity for a given accounting period.

INTERNAL RATE OF RETURN (IRR) average annual yield earned by investment during the period held. It can be: (1) the effective rate of interest on a loan; (2) the discount rate in DISCOUNTED CASH FLOW analysis; or (3) the rate that adjusts the value of future cash receipts earned by an investment so that interest earned (cash inflow) is equal to the original cost (cash outflow). The IRR is arrived at through trial and error calculation, using a mathematical formula, and in financial instruments is equal to the YIELD TO MATURITY.

INTERNATIONAL BANK FOR RECONSTRUCTION AND DEVELOPMENT (IBRD) international lending organization, popularly known as the World Bank, founded at the Bretton Woods economic conference in 1944 initially to finance the reconstruction of Europe following World War II, and more recently to provide developing countries with long-term, low-interest credit for industrial development when private financing is unavailable. The World Bank works closely with the INTERNATIONAL MONETARY FUND (IMF) and had 187 (in 2011) member countries. The World Bank finances its operations through member subscriptions, sale of its own securities, and net earnings. Most World Bank loans are made at variable interest rates pegged to its current cost of funds. Member countries must also be IMF members. In recent years, the World Bank has redefined its traditional role. The bank has set aside funds for new loans, in response to the world debt crisis, and has added its guarantee to new bank loans made to less developed countries. *See also* MULTILATERAL DEVELOPMENT BANKS; WORLD BANK GROUP.

INTERNATIONAL BANKING ACT OF 1978 federal law, enacted by Congress in 1978, placing U.S. branches and agencies of foreign banks under supervision of U.S. banking regulators. Foreign banks are eligible for federal deposit insurance, are required to maintain noninterest earning reserve account balances and submit to periodic bank examinations, and are subject to the same branching limitations as domestic banks. *See also* EDGE ACT CORPORATION; FOREIGN BRANCHES.

INTERNATIONAL BANKING FACILITY (IBF) separate banking center in a U.S. domestic bank or office of a foreign bank, authorized by the Federal Reserve Board in 1981 to participate in Eurocurrency lending through a separate set of accounts. Essentially, an IBF is an in-house shell branch (a separate book of assets and liabilities) that makes loans to foreign customers, other IBFs, and U.S offices and foreign offices of an IBF parent bank. IBF deposits, limited to non-U.S. residents, other IBFs, and banks owning an IBF, are free from reserve requirements, federal deposit insurance assessments, and some state income taxes. *See also* OFFSHORE BANKING UNIT.

INTERNATIONAL DEPOSITARY RECEIPT (IDR) negotiable bank-issued certificate representing ownership of stock securities by an investor outside the country of origin. An international depositary receipt, or IDR, is the non-U.S. equivalent of an AMERICAN DEPOSITARY RECEIPT. These instruments have been used since the 1970s to facilitate international trading in securities. The securities backing the receipt remain in the custody of the issuing bank or a correspondent.

INTERNATIONAL DEVELOPMENT ASSOCIATION *see* WORLD BANK GROUP.

INTERNATIONAL MONETARY FUND (IMF) international organization, formed at the Bretton Woods economic conference in 1944, to maintain monetary stability in the world community. It has 187 members, including the United States. The IMF works closely with the INTERNATIONAL BANK FOR RECONSTRUCTION AND DEVELOPMENT (the World Bank). The International Monetary Fund's role has changed since the early 1970s when fixed-exchange rates were ended. The IMF currently directs much of its attention toward assisting developing countries manage their debts to foreign creditors.

The IMF makes below-market rate loans in the form of drawings (SPECIAL DRAWING RIGHTS (SDRS) by member countries. In recent years, the IMF has linked its lending activities to stringent internal restraints aimed at bringing inflation rates and the world debt crisis under control by reducing imports and increasing exports of debtor nations. Following the Asian financial crisis of 1997 and its destabilizing impact on developing countries worldwide, the IMF introduced several new credit facilities: a Supplemental Reserve Facility (SSF), established in December 1997 to assist nations with severe balance of payment problems, and a short-term Contingent Credit Lines (CCL) facility in April 1999 to provide countries with strong economic policies a line of defense against economic crises beyond their control.

INTERNATIONAL ORGANIZATION FOR STANDARDIZATION (ISO) organization acting as a central clearinghouse for industry standards drafted by national standard setting organizations. The AMERICAN NATIONAL STANDARDS INSTITUTE is the U.S. representative of ISO.

INTERNATIONAL RESERVES acceptable international means of payments between CENTRAL BANKS, mainly in gold, certain currencies (such as the dollar), and SPECIAL DRAWING RIGHTS at the International Monetary Fund.

INTERNET BANKING financial services accessed via the Internet's World Wide Web. An *Internet bank* exists only on the Internet, the global network of computer networks without any "brick and mortar" branch offices. By eliminating the overhead expenses of conventional banks, Internet banks theoretically can pay consumers higher interest rates on savings than the national average. Banks use the Internet to deliver information about financial services, replace transactions done in branch offices, which eliminates the need to build new branches, and to service customers more efficiently. Internet banking sites offer the prospect of more convenient ways to manage personal finances, and such services as paying bills on-line, finding mortgage or auto loans, applying for credit cards, and locating the nearest ATM or branch office. Some Internet banks also offer 24-hour telephone support, so customers can discuss their needs with bank service representatives directly.

INTERPRETIVE LETTER rules of bank regulatory agencies or other administrative agencies that normally take effect as soon as they are issued. Interpretive letter rulings, although not binding as law, are closely watched in the banking industry for indications of new marketing opportunities or authority given by banking regulators for banks to expand their activities in related financial services, such as brokerage and insurance.

INTERSTATE BANKING banking expansion across state lines through bank holding company acquisitions. Interstate expansion of commercial banking companies began in the mid-1980s when state legislatures enacted laws permitting holding company acquisitions on a reciprocal basis with other states.

Interstate banking has evolved in three distinct phases, starting in the 1980s with REGIONAL INTERSTATE BANKING, where banking companies within a region—the Northeast or Southeast—merged to create larger banks; regional expansion under state laws containing a *national trigger* permitting mergers with banks in any other state after a certain date; and nationwide interstate banking. The Riegle-Neal Interstate Banking and Branching Efficiency Act permitted well-capitalized banks to acquire banks anywhere in the United States after Oct. 1, 1995. *See also* BANK HOLDING COMPANY; BRANCH BANKING; SUPER-REGIONAL BANK.

INTERVENTION action by central bankers to manipulate currency rates in the foreign exchange markets, or maintain an orderly market in currency and securities. Central banks intervene through buying or selling currencies or engaging in currency swaps with other central banks.

Most central banks intervene in the conduct of MONETARY POLICY to one degree or another. The Federal Reserve, acting through the foreign exchange desk of the Federal Reserve Bank of New York, and the U.S. Treasury's EXCHANGE STABILIZATION FUND participate equally in financing exchange market intervention. Exchange market intervention has no effect on bank reserves kept by U.S. banks at Federal Reserve banks. *See also* CURRENCY BAND; EXCHANGE STABILIZATION FUND; SWAP NETWORK.

INTER VIVOS TRUST from the Latin, "between the living," a gift of property from one living person to another, as opposed to a TESTAMENTARY TRUST created by a will. Also called *living trust.*

INTESTATE without a will; a person who dies leaving property but without providing for disposition of his or her estate in a will. A court-appointed representative called an ADMINISTRATOR will be appointed to distribute the deceased's property according to state law.

IN THE MONEY option contract when the market price of the underlying security or instrument is above the strike (exercise) price of a call option (an option to buy) or below the strike price of a put option (an option to sell). *See also* AT THE MONEY; OUT OF THE MONEY.

INTRINSIC VALUE net benefit to the holder of an option contract from exercising the option immediately. It is the difference between the underlying price and the option's exercise price. An option generally sells for at least its intrinsic value.

INVENTORY FINANCING working capital loan to finance the purchase of inventory for resale. As the inventory is sold, the loan is gradually paid off. Inventory financing includes floor planning and warehouse financing. Loans secured by receivables command a higher BORROWING BASE than inventory, because receivables are one step closer to cash and qualify for a higher credit advance. *See also* ASSET-BASED LENDING.

INVERSE FLOATER mortgage-backed bond, usually part of a COLLATERALIZED MORTGAGE OBLIGATION (CMO) bearing an interest rate that declines as an index rate, for example, the LIBOR rate, increases. An inverse floater may have a FLOOR and a CAP. Also called a *reverse floater.*

INVERTED MARKET futures market where the nearer months are selling at premiums to the more distant months.

INVERTED YIELD CURVE unusual money market condition where short-term rates are higher than long-term rates, resulting in a negatively sloping yield curve. The yield curve, under normal market conditions, is positively sloping. Investors holding longer-maturity bonds demand a premium for assuming greater interest rate risks. The yield curve inverts when the Federal Reserve tightens credit. This holds down the supply of lendable funds in the banking system, when demand for short-term business credit is rising. This pushes up short-term interest rates. Long-term rates, on the other hand, are influenced more by inflationary expectations than the Fed's monetary policy. A negatively sloping yield curve is a temporary phenomenon, lasting an average of 15 months or less, and is often viewed as a sign that the economy is weakening or heading into a recession.

INVERTED YIELD CURVE

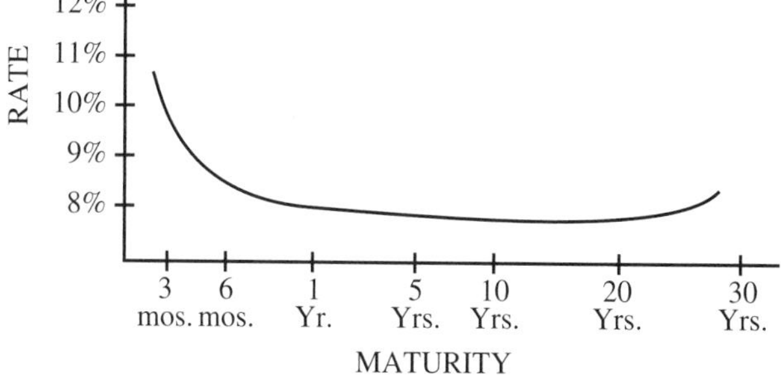

INVESTMENT ADVISOR person or firm supplying buy-sell recommendations and market information to investment clients. Investment advisors are required to register with the Securities and Exchange Commission, and, under the Investment Advisors Act of 1940, disclose any conflicts of interest in recommendations they offer. In general, banks may give limited amounts of investment advice to retail customers, but there are few legal restrictions on investment advice to institutional accounts, such as pension funds, investment management firms and also corporate accounts.

Bank trust departments provide advice and make investments for pension and profit-sharing plans, individual estates, and others. Banks are also active as investment advisors for open-end investment companies—mutual funds—sold to retail and institutional investors, making investment recommendations and managing the securities held in a mutual fund's portfolio.

INVESTMENT ANALYSIS *see* FUNDAMENTAL ANALYSIS; TECHNICAL ANALYSIS.

INVESTMENT BANKING sale and distribution of a new offering of securities, carried out by a financial intermediary (an investment banker), who buys securities from the issuer as PRINCIPAL, and assumes the risk of distributing the securities to investors. The process of purchasing and distributing securities is known as UNDERWRITING. The GLASS-STEAGALL ACT of 1933 prohibited commercial banks from underwriting securities, and required banks to sell their underwriting affiliates, because of abuses by some commercial bankers in selling securities to their own customers.

The Glass-Steagall restrictions were finally removed by the GRAMM-LEACH-BLILEY ACT of 1999, which authorized commercial banks to engage in investment banking activities through affiliated companies, underwriting commercial paper, corporate debt, and equity securities. The act also removed previous restrictions barring banks from underwriting municipal revenue bonds. *See also* SECURITIES SUBSIDIARY; VOLCKER RULE.

INVESTMENT COMPANY company that invests in securities issued by other companies and sells shares to individual investors. Four types of investment companies are authorized by the Securities and Exchange Commission. An OPEN-END FUND (MUTUAL FUND) sells shares to the public and redeems shares' NET ASSET VALUE. A CLOSED-END FUND sells a fixed number of shares and is listed on stock exchanges. *A face amount certificate company* pays a stated amount to investors at maturity dates. A UNIT INVESTMENT TRUST issues redeemable securities representing an interest in specific securities.

Mutual funds are further divided into load funds, which charge the investor a sales commission, ranging from 1¾% to a high of around 8½% of the face value of shares purchased, and no-load funds that do not impose a charge for purchase or redemption of securities. *See also*

BACK-END LOAD; FRONT-END LOAD; INVESTMENT COMPANY ACT; 12B1 MUTUAL FUND.

INVESTMENT COMPANY ACT OF 1940 federal law, enacted by Congress in 1940, requiring companies that market pooled investment funds to the public to register as investment companies with the Securities and Exchange Commission. The act also sets standards for disclosure of financial information, pricing of shares offered to the public and allocation of portfolio investments, and prohibits a regulated investment company from changing its policies without shareholder approval.

INVESTMENT CREDIT federal tax credit resulting from ownership of capital equipment. The tax credit is taken in the year the asset is placed in service. The ITC was repealed by the Tax Reform Act of 1986 for all equipment placed in service after 1985, unless the equipment qualified under special transitional rules. The ITC was originally intended to compensate owners of equipment and equipment lessors for their capital costs. Also called *investment tax credit* or ITC.

INVESTMENT GRADE description of a high-quality corporate or municipal bond, assigned a rating of AAA to BBB by Standard & Poor's and Fitch's Investors Service. (Moody's Investors Service assigns ratings of Aaa and Baa, respectively.) Investment grade securities are those rated Baa or better or BBB or better. These bonds are considered suitable investments for banks, trust departments, and fiduciaries, such as pension funds. U.S. Treasury securities and federal agency securities are also considered investment quality securities for financial institutions. Bonds rated lower than BBB may often carry a higher yield, but are speculative investments. *See also* JUNK BOND.

INVESTMENT LETTER agreement between the buyer and seller in a PRIVATE PLACEMENT of securities, stating that securities are being purchased for investment and will not be offered for resale to the public any time during a specified period, normally two years. These securities, while exempt from SEC registration requirements, may later be sold to the public under SEC Rule 144, provided the securities are held for at least two years and certain other conditions are met. Securities sold under a letter of intent are known as letter stocks or letter bonds. Also called a *letter of intent.*

INVESTMENT SECURITIES marketable securities held by a bank in its portfolio of balance sheet assets. Investment securities, along with bank loans, are the principal source of bank earnings, and generally serve two key functions: as a source of bank LIQUIDITY, or funding to meet loan demand or customers' needs for cash and as an additional source of earnings from the capital gains realized when portfolio securities are sold. Bank investment grade securities are acceptable collateral in meeting PLEDGING REQUIREMENTS for holding federal government deposits, and also deposits of state and local governments.

Bank investment securities are carried at amortized BOOK VALUE, or original purchase cost less amortization or accretion to par value.

Eligible securities that a bank legally can hold as investments include U.S. Treasury securities, federal agency obligations, debt securities of state and local governments, stock in Federal Reserve banks, plus certain other types of investment grade debt (but not corporate securities). The Glass-Steagall Act prohibits national banks and state member banks from investing in equity securities of nonfinancial corporations. As a general rule, banks can own stock in bankers' banks, Edge Act corporations, foreign banks and other companies offering bank-like services, and can hold other investment grade debt so long as securities owned do not exceed 10% of a bank's capital and surplus.

Separated from the investment securities portfolio are TRADING ACCOUNT ASSETS, and other securities a bank is eligible to purchase in securities underwriting for resale to the public or to other financial institutions, and also securities held under repurchase agreements. Assets held in the trading portfolio are marked to market daily. *See also* BARBELL PORTFOLIO; BOND SWAP; LADDERED PORTFOLIO; MARK TO MARKET.

INVOLUNTARY BANKRUPTCY petition by a sufficient number of creditors, claiming a debtor has committed an ACT OF BANKRUPTCY, or is not paying debts on time, asking a bankruptcy court to distribute assets to pay obligations, also called a *creditor's petition*. An involuntary bankruptcy petition can be filed by as few as one creditor; but if the debtor has 12 or more creditors, signatures of at least three creditors are needed. Creditors can file petitions under any chapter of the code: a Chapter 7 LIQUIDATION of the debtor's assets, a REORGANIZATION under Chapter 11, or a Chapter 13 repayment plan. Creditors' petitions are allowed against any business or individual except nonprofit organizations and farmers. Once a petition has been accepted by the court, it is handled as if it were a VOLUNTARY BANKRUPTCY filed by the debtor. *See also* BANKRUPTCY; PRIORITY OF LIEN.

INVOLUNTARY LIEN judgment lien, lien for unpaid taxes or special assessment by a municipality that attaches to a real property without consent of the owner, in contrast with a MORTGAGE lien, which is voluntary.

IRREVOCABLE LETTER OF CREDIT letter of credit, valid for a stated period of time, that may be cancelled or amended only by agreement of all parties to the credit. The issuing bank waives its right to revoke a letter of credit prior to the expiration date, unless the consent of the beneficiary is obtained.

IRREVOCABLE TRUST trust that cannot be revoked by the person creating it, except with approval of the BENEFICIARY, as opposed to a REVOCABLE TRUST, in which the trust instrument can be modified or terminated at will.

ISLAMIC BANKING system of banking consistent with principles of Islamic law and Islamic economics. Islamic law prohibits the collection of interest, commonly called *riba*, although revenue-sharing arrangements are generally permitted. With increased trade between western nations and Islamic nations in the Middle East, Citibank, Deutsche Bank, and other western banks have been opening Islamic banking units since 1996. Because modern Islamic banking is relatively new, rules for financial accounting, bank governance, and lending standards are continually evolving as business practices become more refined. The Institute of Islamic Banking and Insurance, a London organization, says Islamic banks are structured to retain a clearly differentiated status between shareholders' capital and clients' deposits to ensure correct profit sharing according to Islamic law.

ISSUE

1. securities sold by a corporation or government on a particular date or during an offering period, identifiable by maturity date or class of security.
2. to sell or privately place an offering of securities.
3. to approve a credit instrument, for example, a letter of credit, or approve and mail a bank card to a consumer.
4. a person's direct descendants who stand first in line to inherit an estate.

ISSUER

1. corporation, government, or other legal entity having the authority to offer its own bond, note, or stock certificate for sale to investors.
2. financial institution that issues credit or debit cards, for example, Visa or MasterCard credit cards, or automated teller machine debit cards. Card issuers authorize transactions on issued and outstanding cards, and mail monthly activity statements to cardholders.
3. bank that approves a letter of credit on behalf of a particular customer, valid for a stated period.

ITEM banking term for negotiable instruments, such as checks or drafts, representing uncollected funds. In electronic transfers of funds, for example, an AUTOMATED CLEARING HOUSE (ACH) credit or debit transaction, an item is an electronic record of funds moving from one bank to another.

ITEMIZED STATEMENT account activity statement with a line-by-line transaction summary, generally in chronological order, listing account debits, credits, and service charges during an accounting period. If the account is a bank card account, the account statement lists merchant names next to each entry, and terminal locations, for example, automated teller machines, if a debit card is used.

J

JEEP *see* GRADUATED PAYMENT MORTGAGE.

JOINT ACCOUNT

1. bank account owned by two or more persons, who equally share rights and liabilities of the account. Ownership of joint accounts can be set up in either of two ways: (1) a joint tenancy account (commonly used by husband and wife), in which either, acting separately, can make deposits or withdrawals at any time, and when one owner dies, the full account passes to the surviving owner; (2) tenants in common (commonly used by business partners), in which the approval of both owners is needed to make withdrawals. If one owner dies, the other shares the account equally with the deceased owner's estate. *See also* JOINT TENANTS WITH RIGHT OF SURVIVORSHIP; TENANCY BY THE ENTIRETY; TENANCY IN COMMON.
2. investment banking account formed by several underwriters acting as a syndicate. *See also* JOINTLY AND SEVERALLY; SEVERALLY BUT NOT JOINTLY.

JOINT CUSTODY *see* DUAL CONTROL.

JOINT ENDORSEMENT endorsement by two or more persons needed to negotiate a check payable to more than one individual. Many banks require signatures by both owners of a dual account before cashing a U.S. government check, for example, an IRS tax refund.

JOINTLY AND SEVERALLY

1. legal term for the liability of two or more individuals, who each agree to repay an obligation. A creditor holding an unpaid note has the option of suing each person individually or all of them as a group.
2. in UNDERWRITING of municipal bonds, expression for a bond offering in which each member of a syndicate is liable for a portion of any unsold securities, in addition to its own participation. Also called an *undivided account* or Eastern Account. *See also* SEVERALLY BUT NOT JOINTLY.

JOINT NOTE promissory note signed by two or more makers, payable in installments or at maturity. If unpaid, the lender must bring legal action against the borrowers collectively.

JOINT TENANTS WITH RIGHT OF SURVIVORSHIP ownership of bank accounts, real property, or personal property by two or more people, each having full right of usage—the most common form of property ownership by married persons. When a married couple opens a JOINT ACCOUNT, say a checking account, each has unlimited access, and can withdraw funds to the full amount in the account. When one owner dies, the property automatically passes to the co-owner, avoiding probate although estate taxes may be payable. Distinguish from TENANCY BY THE ENTIRETY.

JOINT VENTURE business structure formed by two or more parties for a specific purpose. Joint ventures are similar to partnerships, but are usually limited to one or two projects. In the financial services industry, joint ventures have been widely employed for marketing products or services that one of the parties, acting alone, would have been legally prohibited from doing. Prior to financial modernization legislation enacted in 1999, banks often formed joint ventures with life insurance companies to market annuities and insurance to bank customers.

Federal ANTITRUST LAWS generally treat financial joint ventures as permissible as long as they are pro-competitive, meaning a proposed venture does not interfere with activities of other organizations.

JUDGMENTAL CREDIT ANALYSIS approval or denial of a credit application, based on the lender's evaluation of the credit application, and credit experience with similar applicants, instead of a CREDIT SCORING model that estimates the probability of debt repayment. As defined by Federal Reserve REGULATION B, a judgmental system is any method of credit approval other than an empirically derived, statistically-based scoring model. Even when scoring systems are used, though, lenders may OVERRIDE the model, as when they approve a loan the system rejected.

JUDGMENT LIEN court order placing a lien on a debtor's real property as security for a debt owed to a judgment creditor. The award, which encumbers the property to the extent of the judgment, may be appealed to a higher court. A lien against personal property is an ATTACHMENT.

JUMBO CERTIFICATE OF DEPOSIT high-yield CERTIFICATE OF DEPOSIT with a principal amount of $250,000 or more, paying a rate adjusted weekly to money market rates. Jumbo CDs may be issued in negotiable form, transferable to a new owner before maturity, although many jumbo CDs are not negotiable. The principal amount of CDs over the FDIC insurance limit compensates owners with their higher yield, which makes these CDs appealing investment vehicles to corporations, pension funds and other institutions investors seeking higher money market returns. *See also* BROKERED DEPOSIT; SAFEKEEPING CERTIFICATE; UNINSURED DEPOSITOR.

JUMBO MORTGAGE conventional mortgage exceeding the maximum amount a secondary market buyer such as Fannie Mae or Freddie Mac will purchase from a mortgage banker or mortgage originator, and usually carrying a higher interest rate.

JUNIOR MORTGAGE MORTGAGE that is subordinate to earlier mortgages, for example, a second mortgage if there is an outstanding first mortgage. If the borrower defaults, holders of junior mortgages will be paid after claims by prior lien holders have been satisfied.

JUNIOR SECURITY security with a claim on the assets and earnings of the issuer that is lower in priority, and contingent on payment to the holder of a SENIOR SECURITY. In priority order, claims are generally ranked and paid as follows: mortgage bonds, debentures, preferred stock, and common stock.

JUNK BOND bond issued by companies whose credit ratings are below investment grade, and generally given a bond rating of BB or lower by bond rating agencies. Bond ratings higher than BB are possible, though, through overcollateralization. To attract investors, junk bonds pay a higher interest rate than INVESTMENT GRADE bonds and are regarded as speculative investments, because the bond issuers either are unknown in the market or are well-known companies that are highly leveraged. The bonds pay higher yields because the credit risk is greater than in investment grade issues. Junk bonds are frequently issued by companies to finance a LEVERAGED BUYOUT, a transaction in which investors acquire a company by issuing new debt, using the company's assets as collateral. The takeover debt is retired by selling assets or is paid off from company cash flow. Also called *high-yield bond.*

JURISDICTION legally recognized authority to hear cases and decide issues submitted for review. The term frequently comes up in discussions concerning legally permissible banking activities, as different banking agencies have overlapping authority. For example, the Federal Reserve Board regulates bank holding companies, but many banking companies have opted for state banking charters, as opposed to NATIONAL BANK charters from the Office of the Comptroller of the Currency, to get banking powers not available to national banks. Jurisdictional disputes arising from these differences frequently are settled by a third party—the federal courts.

In international banking, determination of jurisdiction is crucial to resolving issues arising from cross-border loans to foreign borrowers, who may insist that any legal disputes be settled according to the laws of the borrower's country, not the lender. *See also* FUNCTIONAL REGULATION.

K

KEEFE BANK INDEX capitalization-weighted money center and regional banks compiled by Keefe, Keefe, Bruyette & Woods, a New York City investment banking firm specializing in bank stocks. Full name: KBW Bank Sector Index.

KEOGH PLAN salary deferral plan for business owners are similar to other types of retirement savings plans. A Keogh plan's main benefit is the higher contribution limit, allowing business owners to contribute more of their pretax business income to a retirement plan. Employees can generally contribute up to $16,500 a year. An employer can contribute up to $32,000 (for an annual Keogh contribution of $48,500). These contribution limits are revised periodically by the U.S. Internal Revenue Service.

There are two basic types of Keogh plans. The first is a defined contribution plan where funds are deducted from payroll. The second is a defined benefit plan, where plan-funding contributions are determined by an IRS pension funding formula. Many defined-benefit Keogh plans are set up as profit-sharing plans. Regardless of plan type, Keogh plan assets can be invested in stocks, bonds, bank CDs, mutual funds, and other assets. Individual plan participants may also contribute to an INDIVIDUAL RETIREMENT ACCOUNT or a ROTH IRA.

Withdrawals from a Keogh may be made after age 59½, and starting no later than 70½. Early withdrawals are subject to federal income taxes and a tax penalty.

KEY set of instructions governing the encryption and decryption of electronic messages. Each financial institution participating in a wire transfer system or electronic funds transfer network, such as an ATM network, has a unique identification key, called an *issuer's key*.

KEY CURRENCY currency used in international trade settlement, or as a reference currency in setting exchange rates. Key currencies are the U.S. dollar, or, more broadly, any currency issued by one of the GROUP OF SEVEN countries. Central banks hold a portion of their reserves in a key currency.

KEY MAN INSURANCE insurance policy protecting a small business or partnership against business losses from the death or disability of a principal owner. Lenders sometimes require partnerships or closely held corporations to take out such insurance naming the lender as loss payee before extending credit if they believe the loss of a key employee will hinder a firm's ability to repay a bank loan.

KEYNESIAN ECONOMICS economic theory originated by the British economist John Maynard Keynes (1883–1946), and his followers. Keynes maintained that governments should use the power of the budget to maintain economic growth and stability, and overcome the recessionary cycles common in most western economies. Toward this purpose, Keynes argued, in his work *The General Theory of Employment, Interest and Money* (1935), that governments become active managers of the economy, by manipulating taxation and spending policies. According to the Keynesian view, deficit spending stimulates private sector development in periods when the economy is under-performing.

Critics of Keynesian economics, especially the monetarists, say that economic stability is best achieved by controlling credit and growth in the MONEY SUPPLY. Monetarists fault Keynesian economics for relying too much on government spending and taxation policies, which they say over-stimulates the economy, causing high inflation rates and contributing to the boom and bust cycles in the economy that have occurred since the mid-1970s. *See also* FISCAL POLICY; LIQUIDITY PREFERENCE THEORY; MONETARIST; SUPPLY SIDE ECONOMICS.

KEY RATE interest rate that controls, either directly or indirectly, bank lending rates and the cost of credit paid by borrowers. In the United States, the DISCOUNT RATE and the FEDERAL FUNDS (Fed Funds) rate are key rates regulated by the Federal Reserve System's MONETARY POLICY.

KEY RATIO ratio used by financial analysts in evaluation of a bank's statement of financial condition and income. Ratios examined include: the capital to assets ratio; ratio of loan loss reserves to total loans; liquidity ratios; and performance ratios, such as return on assets (ROA), return on equity (ROE), and the earnings per share ratio. Key ratios give a general indication of bank performance and can be compared to prior year figures.

KICKER extra feature in a loan, beyond ordinary payments of interest, demanded by a lender as a condition for extending credit. The effect is to increase the yield over the term of the financing. From a legal viewpoint, kickers have to be disclosed in consumer loans as part of the finance charges, and in some instances may violate state usury laws.

In real estate finance, a kicker is an equity participation in the gross receipts from rental property, or an ownership stake in the property itself. In an *equity kicker*, the lender gets a given interest rate, plus a percentage of the rent over a certain dollar amount. Other forms of kickers are stock warrants exercisable at a future date, and rights to purchase securities.

KINA monetary unit of Papua New Guinea.

KIP monetary unit of Laos.

KITING *see* CHECK KITING.

KORUNA monetary unit of the Czech Republic and Slovakia.

KRONA monetary unit of Iceland and Sweden.

KRONE monetary unit of Denmark and Norway.

KROON monetary unit of Estonia.

KWACHA monetary unit of Malawi and Zambia.

KWANZA, NEW KWANZA monetary unit of Angola.

KUNA monetary unit of Croatia.

KYAT monetary unit of Myanmar.

L

LADDERED PORTFOLIO bond investment portfolio holding equal amounts of each security in each maturity range over, say a ten-year period. In rising rates, assets can be shifted to longer maturities. Money market and foreign exchange traders also utilize portfolio laddering in listing maturities, either day-by-day or month-by-month, of outstanding contracts so they can more easily control the maturity gap or mismatch between different portfolio assets. Contrast with BARBELL PORTFOLIO.

LAGGED RESERVES RESERVE accounting system whereby depository institutions maintain reserve account balances with a Federal Reserve Bank against checking account and other transaction account deposits outstanding two weeks earlier. The Federal Reserve used this method of calculating reserves from the late 1960s through 1984, when it switched to a CONTEMPORANEOUS RESERVES reporting system. In July 1998 the Federal Reserve Board changed the format for reporting reserve balances back to a lagged reserves accounting, meant to improve the accuracy of data reported by financial institutions. Banks reporting reserve balances weekly—a group including all but the smallest banks—calculate their reserve requirements based on account balances as of the prior 30 days.

LAGGING INDICATOR economic indicator that trails or lags behind the business cycle. Factory inventories of finished goods, interest rates, and consumer prices all tend to follow advances and declines in the business cycle, rather than move in advance of the economy, as a LEADING INDICATOR does. The Conference Board, a business research organization, tracks a number of lagging indicators, including the bank prime rate, outstanding consumer loans, and outstanding commercial and industrial loans.

LAND FLIP type of real estate fraud in which undeveloped property is resold from one owner to another, ordinarily at prices well above the fair market value. Financial institutions that make real estate loans to land developers take equity positions through direct investments, or take risk taking losses if real estate securing a loan suffers a decline in value.

LAT monetary unit of Latvia.

LATE CHARGE penalty assessed for delinquent payments on a mortgage or installment loan after a GRACE PERIOD of 10 to 15 days has elapsed. Late fees are calculated as a percentage of the outstanding balance, and, if unpaid, usually are excluded from the loan interest due.

LAUNDERED MONEY *see* MONEY LAUNDERING.

LEAD BANK

1. bank arranging a loan SYNDICATE, in which several banks buy participations. The lead bank collects a management fee for assembling the syndicate and arranging the financing terms. In the Eurobond market, a bank that acts as agent for members of an underwriting syndicate.
2. investment bank managing an underwriting of securities. Also called a *lead manager* or *managing underwriter*.
3. bank holding the primary deposit or lending relationship with an organization, normally a corporation with a multibank servicing agreement for its credit and cash management needs. *See also* CONCENTRATION BANK.

LEADING INDICATORS economic indicator believed to anticipate changes in the business cycle. The Conference Board, a business research organization, tracks the following indicators: the MONEY SUPPLY, changes in business credit employment statistics; new investments; business formations and business failures; corporate profits and stock prices; and business inventories. *See also* LAGGING INDICATOR.

LEADS AND LAGS language in a contract or credit agreement allowing a company to either lead (accelerate) or lag (delay) payment of foreign trade obligations to trading partners or overseas subsidiaries. A decision to pay early or pay late is determined largely from an importer's perception of the monetary strength of the currency it is billed in. If currency devaluation is feared, importers try to accelerate their payments.

LEASE contract giving the right of possession and use of an asset for a specified period in exchange for payments. The party owning the leased property is the *lessor*, the party using it is the *lessee*, and the lease payments are *rentals*. A lease contract may be written for a single piece of equipment, or it may be a master lease governing a continuing arrangement, regardless of the equipment leased. There are several commonly used types of leases.

A tax-oriented lease, sometimes called a TRUE LEASE, gives the lessor the tax benefits of ownership, transferring the use of tax depreciation deductions, and in some cases, investment tax credits, from the lessee to the lessor in exchange for lower rental payments. All others, including FINANCE LEASES, are nontax leases and are treated as conditional sales contracts for tax purposes. On the lessor's books, a lease is treated very much like a loan. Thus, the lessee can deduct only the interest portion of the rentals. *See also*; CAPITALIZED COST; CONSUMER LEASE; OPERATING LEASE; RESIDUAL VALUE; SALE AND LEASEBACK.

LEASEBACK *see* SALE AND LEASEBACK.

LEASEHOLD tenant's right to leased property. The tenant enjoys certain rights of occupancy, but does not hold claim to the property's title.

For example, a tenancy at will, giving occupancy for the term of a lease.

LEDGER BALANCE customer's account balance as it appears on a BANK STATEMENT. The ledger balance differs from the AVAILABLE BALANCE representing total funds as available for use. The sole purpose of ledger balances, or total credits less debts during an accounting period, is to facilitate the reconciliation of book balances.

LEGAL ENTITY partnership, corporation, or other organization having the capacity to negotiate contracts, assume financial obligations, and pay off debts. In contrast with natural persons, legal entities are chartered by the states where they are organized. A corporation is a person in the eyes of the law, and it is responsible for its actions. It can be sued if it fails to live up to an agreement.

LEGAL LENDING LIMIT maximum amount a bank can lend to a single borrower. National banks are limited to 15% of capital and reserves on unsecured loans (25% of capital if fully secured); bank holding companies can lend a bank affiliate up to 10% of the capital and surplus of the affiliate, or up to 20% of the capital of all affiliates owned by the same holding company. Under the FINANCIAL INSTITUTIONS REFORM, RECOVERY AND ENFORCEMENT ACT of 1989, savings and loans are required to follow the same lending limits to a single borrower as national banks.

LEGAL LIST securities approved by a state banking department as acceptable investments for mutual savings banks, pension funds, insurance companies, and other FIDUCIARY institutions. To protect investors and depositors, only high quality debt and equity securities are generally included. As an alternative, some states apply the PRUDENT MAN RULE.

LEGAL OPINION written opinion by an attorney stating that a proposed bond issue complies with applicable securities laws. In a municipal bond offering, the opinion also states that the issuer has a legal right to issue the securities proposed for sale, and also whether the bonds are exempt from state and local taxes. The issuer must obtain this statement before a new issue can be floated. Municipal bond issuers usually print the legal opinion on the back of each certificate.

LEGAL OWNER person who has a legally enforceable claim to an estate or property. This claim may be only a lien, as, for example, a lender's SECURITY INTEREST in collateral pledged by a borrower. Contrast with *equitable owner,* the person recognized by common law as the owner of the property in question.

LEGAL RATE OF INTEREST

1. maximum loan interest rate permitted by state law. An interest rate in excess of the legal rate is considered USURY; the penalties for

charging excessive interest may include stiff fines or forfeiture of interest and/or principal.

2. rate of interest set by state law for legally enforceable claims, such as legal judgments and overdue taxes. This rate is rarely the highest rate allowed by law for any debt.

LEGAL RESERVES portion of demand deposit and time deposit account balances, plus cash in a bank's vault, that can be used to meet RESERVE REQUIREMENTS of the Federal Reserve System. Legal reserves must be kept as vault cash or a deposit in a checking account at a district Federal Reserve Bank.

Legal reserves are a source of bank liquidity, because they can be converted to cash to pay depositors. The Federal Reserve Board regulates credit in the banking system by adjusting reserve requirements. Raising the reserve requirement drains credit, because banks have to keep a higher percentage of deposit at the Fed; lowering the reserve requirement expands credit because banks then have more funds to put out in new loans.

The MONETARY CONTROL ACT of 1980, which extended reserve requirements to state banks allows state chartered banks to use their checking account in a Federal Reserve Bank to meet state reserve requirements, if allowed by state law.

LEGAL TENDER money recognized by law as acceptable payment for debts owed to creditors. In the United States, legal tender (also called *lawful money*) is all forms of circulating paper money, mostly Federal Reserve Notes, and coins. The term means that money offered as payment has the backing of the government and must be accepted by a creditor, unless a contract calls for another method of payment. *See also* FIAT MONEY.

LEK monetary unit of Albania.

LEMPIRA monetary unit of Honduras.

LENDER LIABILITY lender's exposure to financial compensation claims relating directly or indirectly to actions taken by the lender. Lender liability is a complex topic; but lenders may be placing themselves at risk if they assume a controlling interest in a borrower's business.

Under current federal law, bank lenders may be able to defend their actions from claims by borrowers, or third parties, if they can demonstrate their actions were taken solely in their capacity as lender. But, if lenders act as owner, principal, or manager in the management of a business, they may not be able to put up a defensible argument against such claims.

Consider a bank that forecloses on a defaulted borrower and seizes property as collateral. The property is later found to contain hazardous chemicals from an old industrial plant. If the bank can demonstrate its actions were authorized by its loan agreement with the borrower, it may be able to defend itself from legal claims by the borrower or by third parties for any environmental cleanup costs.

In view of lender liability claims in recent years, lenders can no longer rely on traditional views of acceptable conduct in extending credit and collecting repayment once a loan has been made.

LENDER OF LAST RESORT lender who acts as the ultimate source of credit to the banking system. In the United States this role is carried out by the 12 Federal Reserve Banks, which supply credit through the Federal Reserve DISCOUNT WINDOW. Reserve credit is supplied in a variety of forms, including short-term ADJUSTMENT CREDIT to banks needing funds to maintain their reserve requirements, as well as longer-term SEASONAL CREDIT and EXTENDED CREDIT to banks needing funds for a longer period. On occasion, the Fed has loaned money to troubled banks, and even troubled savings institutions, if it believes that failure to do so would undermine public confidence in the banking system. The Federal Reserve is authorized by the MONETARY CONTROL ACT of 1980 to make discount window loans to savings and loan associations and other nonbank financial institutions. Before borrowing from the Fed, though, a savings institution would have to use up all other forms of credit, including credit advances from the Federal Home Loan Banks.

LENDER PARTICIPATION *see* KICKER.

LEONE monetary unit of Sierra Leone.

LESS-DEVELOPED COUNTRY (LDC) country whose state of economic development is characterized by a low national income, a high rate of population growth and unemployment, and dependence on commodity exports. The majority of nations in Asia, Africa, and Latin America, fit this model, which is why they are known collectively as developing countries or third world countries. LDCs generally pay more for the goods they import from more economically advanced nations than they receive in payments. To make up the shortfall or deficit in balance of payments, these nations must resort to bank loans from private banks and from international credit sources, such as the INTERNATIONAL MONETARY FUND.

LETTER OF ADVICE

1. written instructions from one bank to another, directing that a payment be made at a specified future date. For example, a letter instructing a WIRE TRANSFER payment to a third party.
2. written confirmation of a transfer of funds by BANK DRAFT or ELECTRONIC FUNDS TRANSFER to a third party, given normally to both the person receiving the payment and the person initiating the transaction.

LETTER OF CREDIT (L/C) credit instrument issued by a bank guaranteeing payments on behalf of its customer to a BENEFICIARY, normally to a third party but sometimes to the bank's customer, for a stated period of time and when certain conditions are met. A letter of credit substitutes the bank's credit for the credit of another party, for example, an importer or exporter, who is authorized to write drafts up to a specified amount, payable by the issuing bank. Letters of credit are widely used in banking, originating with the commercial letter of credit in trade financing. Importers and exporters wanted assurances that merchandise delivered would be paid for by the buyer, a requirement that was met by obtaining a bank letter of credit. The buyer purchases a letter of credit, which is then forwarded to a correspondent bank in the city where payment is to be made. In trade financing, the bank drafts authorized under the issuing bank's letter of credit are frequently accepted by another bank, creating a BANKER'S ACCEPTANCE, and become credit obligations of the accepting bank.

There are several major varieties of letters of credit, each serving a different purpose. An IRREVOCABLE LETTER OF CREDIT cannot be cancelled before a specific date without agreement by all the parties involved, whereas a revocable letter of credit can be amended at any time by the issuing bank. A CONFIRMED LETTER OF CREDIT carries the endorsement of both the issuing bank and its correspondent, guaranteeing payment of all drafts written against it; an unconfirmed letter of credit, carries no such guarantee that a correspondent will honor drafts presented for payment. A STANDBY LETTER OF CREDIT is a contingent (future) obligation of the issuing bank to make payment to the designated beneficiary if the bank's customer fails to perform as called for under the terms of a contract. Standby letters, for this reason, are considered OFF-BALANCE SHEET ITEMS in computing bank capital-to-asset ratios. *See also* BACK-TO-BACK LETTERS OF CREDIT; CREDIT ENHANCEMENT; DOCUMENTARY COMMERCIAL BILL; OPEN ACCOUNT; RED CLAUSE LETTER OF CREDIT; SIGHT DRAFT; TIME DRAFT, TRAVELER'S LETTER OF CREDIT.

LETTER OF INTENT *see* INVESTMENT LETTER.

LEU monetary unit of Romania.

LEV monetary unit of Bulgaria.

LEVEL PAYMENT AMORTIZATION fixed-term LOAN with periodic payments that remain constant over the term of the loan. A portion of each payment goes to payment of interest, and the balance amortizes, or reduces, the outstanding principal. If the loan has a variable rate, the term may be extended if interest rates rise. Or there may be a BALLOON PAYMENT at maturity. *See also* AMORTIZATION SCHEDULE.

LEVERAGE money borrowed to increase the return on invested capital.

1. **Banking.** The use of funds purchased in the money market or borrowed from depositors to finance interest-bearing assets, principally loans. What banks do, in effect, is invest their depositors' money in loans at rates high enough to cover the lender's cost of funds and operating expenses, and yield a profit margin or SPREAD.

Leverage increases when bank assets grow at a faster rate than equity capital, such as common stock, which acts as a cushion against losses. To keep leverage from getting too high, which might happen if banks grow too rapidly or make too many risky loans, commercial banks and savings institutions have to keep minimum levels of equity capital in relation to total assets. *See also* CAPITAL; CAPITAL RATIOS; LIQUIDITY.

2. **Finance.** The use of debt or senior securities to get a higher return on owner's equity capital. A firm issuing long-term bonds may be able to earn a higher rate of return from the the bond proceeds, which are often invested in capital equipment, than what it pays the bondholders in interest. The result is financial leverage or capital leverage, because any increase in earnings benefits the corporate owners, not the bondholders. Issuing bonds has several advantages, provided the issuer can meet the debt service payments. Bond interest payments are tax deductible, although stock dividends are not, and a bond issue does not dilute the value of shareholders' equity. A bond issuer that is too highly leveraged, though, risks default.

LEVERAGED BUYOUT (LBO) takeover of a company using the acquired firm's assets and cash flow to obtain financing. Typically, these transactions are done by conglomerates selling or spinning off an unwanted subsidiary to the company's managers and outside investors. The buyers of an LBO financing are said to take private the target company. Leveraged buyouts are risky for the buyers if the purchase is highly leveraged. An LBO can be protected from volatile interest rates by an INTEREST RATE SWAP, locking in a fixed interest rate, or an interest rate CAP, which prevents the borrowing cost from rising above a certain level. LBOs also have been financed with high-yield debt, or JUNK BONDS, and have also been done with the interest rate capped at a fixed level and interest costs above the cap added to the principal. For commercial banks, LBOs are attractive because these financings have large up-front fees. They also fill the gap in corporate lending created when large corporations begin using commercial paper and corporate bonds in place of bank loans.

LEVERAGED LEASE long-term lease in which the lessor borrows most of the funds needed to acquire the asset financed from a third party, usually a bank or insurance company. The lessor makes an equity investment equal to, say, 20% of the equipment's original cost, and borrows the remaining 80% by issuing nonrecourse notes to the lenders, and writes a noncancellable lease for the equipment.

The lessor makes an assignment of the lease and lease rental payments to the lender, who is entitled to repossess the asset if the lessee happens to default. A leveraged lease is a true lease for tax purposes, because the lessor, as owner of the asset, is entitled to all of the tax benefits of ownership, including accelerated depreciation write-offs, deduction of INTEREST payments on the bank loan, and the INVESTMENT

CREDIT, if any, for purchase of the asset. Banks write leveraged leases for their own customers through the leasing subsidiary of a bank holding company. *See also* ASSET-BASED LENDING; FINANCE LEASE; OPERATING LEASE; REGULATION Y.

LEVERAGED LOAN loan extended to companies or individuals that already have high levels of debt. Such loans have a higher risk of default and are more costly to the borrower. Leveraged loans are also a financing tool in a LEVERAGED BUYOUT (LBO) of another company.

LIABILITY

1. **General.** A legally enforceable claim on the assets of a company, excluding owner's equity, or the property of an individual, calling for a transfer of assets at a determined future date. Also, any item appearing on the right hand side of a double-entry accounting system or balance sheet.
2. **Banking.** The funds owed by a bank, including time deposits and demand deposits, borrowings from a Federal Reserve Bank or other banks, and Federal Funds in the interbank market. Deposit liabilities, representing claims by a bank's customers on the assets of the bank, are the major source of funds for bank lending. Other liability categories include MANAGED LIABILITIES, or deposits that banks actively solicit from other banks; BROKERED DEPOSITS, which usually are certificates of deposit secured through a broker-dealer; and OFF-BALANCE SHEET ITEMS, which are liabilities that are not direct obligations on the issuing bank, but represent contingent obligations that may become payable in the future.

LIABILITY LEDGER central record of a bank's outstanding loans and discounts to all borrowers, maintained in a bank's loan department. The liability ledger is usually a sub-ledger to a bank's computerized GENERAL LEDGER accounting system. The aggregate total of outstanding loans is the major portion of a bank's EARNING ASSETS.

LIABILITY MANAGEMENT management of bank liabilities, including deposits, to support lending activities and achieve balanced growth in earnings and bank assets without excessive liquidity risk. Liability management involves accepting money from depositors, and securing additional funds from other financial institutions, for use in lending and investing. Other tools of liability management are interest rate hedging against unexpected market moves and managing the difference between asset and liability maturities for controlled speculation on interest rate shifts.

In banking, active management of the liability side of the balance sheet began in the early 1960s when commercial banks began issuing negotiable certificates of deposit, which could be sold to other holders prior to maturity, to solicit funds from other institutions in the money market. *See also* ASSET-LIABILITY MANAGEMENT; FUNDS MANAGEMENT; MANAGED LIABILITIES.

LIAR LOAN slang term for a low-documentation or no-documentation mortgage loan, often a loan extended to a STATED INCOME BORROWER. These were designed for borrowers who had a hard time documenting sources of income, such as with prior tax returns, or who had nontraditional sources of income. Lenders approving these loans relied heavily on credit scores or the mortgaged property's loan-to-value (LTV) ratio to get a loan approved. Many such loans became problem loans in the 2008 financial crisis.

LIBOR *see* LONDON INTERBANK OFFERED RATE.

LICENSEE bank that is granted the right by a licensing authority to distribute financial services in its market area. A license may preclude local financial institutions from offering competing services, or be nonexclusive.

LICENSE TO OPERATE grant of permission to undertake a trade or carry out a business activity, subject to regulation or supervision by the licensing authority. Licenses are granted by state or federal agencies, and also by private concerns, as when a business authorizes another to use its name as a franchise operator. Licenses granted by government authority imply professional competence and ability to meet certain standards set by law or regulation.

LIEN creditor's claim against property to secure repayment of a debt. A lien encumbers the borrower's property pledged as security, up to the amount of the debt, and guarantees the lender's right to collect payment through legal means. For example, a MORTGAGE gives a lender the right to initiate FORECLOSURE proceedings against a borrower in DEFAULT on the mortgage loan. A lien holder has a prior claim compared with creditors whose claims are not secured by the borrower's assets. *See also* INVOLUNTARY LIEN; JUDGMENT LIEN; MECHANIC'S LIEN; SECURITY INTEREST.

LIFE CYCLE FUNDS family of mutual funds, also called *flexible funds,* that blends stock funds and bond and money market funds, tailoring the mix to the investor's age and number of years to retirement. Younger investors have a higher percentage of assets invested in common stock funds, while those nearing retirement age have an increasing percentage in bond funds and money markets. The investor's asset mix is tailored to the investment horizon.

LIFE ESTATE freehold estate giving the person owning it the right to receive income of the estate until death. The beneficiary cannot sell the property and the estate terminates at death.

LIFELINE BANKING limited package of retail banking services offered at a relatively low fixed monthly cost. The concept originated in the early 1980s when consumer advocates began pressuring financial institutions to offer low-cost services to senior citizens and low-income depositors. The term preferred by bankers is *basic bank-*

ing, and these accounts generally are available to all depositors. A basic banking checking account usually includes check writing up to a certain number of checks per month and limited bank teller visits, but unrestricted access to accounts at automated teller machines. The customer pays a flat monthly fee. More frequent teller visits or check writing triggers an additional charge.

LIFE OF LOAN CAP contractual provision in an ADJUSTABLE RATE MORTGAGE limiting the interest rate increase over the amortized life of the loan. For example, a 10% interest rate with a 5% lifetime cap may not increase more than 5% while the loan is outstanding. *See also* ANNUAL CAP; PAYMENT CAP.

LIFT A LEG in financial futures, money market and commodity market trading and foreign exchange, closing out one side of a long-short hedge before liquidating the other side. A trader holding a STRADDLE, is said to *leg out* by selling either side of the transaction.

LIMEAN *see* LONDON INTERBANK MEDIAN AVERAGE RATE.

LIMIT

1. LEGAL LENDING LIMIT on loans to a single borrower. National banks and savings and loan associations cannot make unsecured loans greater than 15% of capital, and secured loans above 25% of capital.
2. bank's own internal credit limit in loans to a single borrower, for example, a guidance line of credit. The guidance line is never disclosed.
3. consumer's CREDIT LIMIT, as in credit cards.
4. in FOREIGN EXCHANGE, a daily trading limit: the maximum amount a dealer is willing to trade or deposit with another bank. Also, a central bank's limit on long or short open positions.
5. COUNTRY LIMIT, amount a bank is willing to lend to a single country.
6. in electronic funds transfers, a BILATERAL CREDIT LIMIT negotiated by two banks to prevent overdrawing a Reserve Account at a Federal Reserve Bank.
7. limit up/limit down: in commodities markets and financial futures, the largest daily price change allowed by a futures exchange on FUTURES CONTRACTS.

LIMITED LIABILITY COMPANY (LLC) type of business organization, recognized as a legal form of business in most states, combining features of a CORPORATION and a PARTNERSHIP. An LLC provides its organizers with liability protection from claims and lawsuits similar to a corporation. It is treated as a partnership for tax purposes; earned income passes through the LLC to its owners, who are taxed as individuals.

LIMITED PARTNERSHIP business in which an individual or party who participates in its affairs as a minority investor receives a share of the profits (or losses) that is limited by agreement. A limited partner can have no role in managing the concern, and has limited liability, as opposed to the unlimited liability of a GENERAL PARTNER. Limited partnerships are typically sold through brokerage firms or private placement (direct sale) with investors.

LIMITED PURPOSE TRUST COMPANY state chartered trust company that performs specific trust functions. Examples are the Depository Trust Company (DTC) in New York, which holds securities certificates in safekeeping so banks and securities firms can participate in book entry settlement of securities trades, and the Participants Trust Company, a depository for mortgage-backed securities.

LIMITED RECOURSE FINANCE

1. financing arrangement where the lender can require the borrower to repay only in special conditions that are spelled out in the LOAN AGREEMENT itself, and otherwise must look to the collateral as a source of repayment. Borrowers may have to pay more for limited recourse financing. *See also* NONRECOURSE LOAN.
2. indirect lending arrangement where a dealer sells installment sales contracts to a bank, which assumes responsibility for collection of the debt as a HOLDER IN DUE COURSE, and the dealer's liability for losses incurred by the bank is limited by contract. The bank's RECOURSE against the dealer expires after a specified period.

LIMITED SERVICE BANK

1. banking facility that is located away from the bank's main office. These offices may accept deposits, but do not make loans or offer trust services.
2. bank that is limited by charter or by regulation to offering only certain services to the public. Limited service banks have narrow product lines, such as credit cards or auto loans, and may offer other services on an irregular basis. *See also* LIMITED PURPOSE TRUST COMPANY; NONBANK BANK.

LIMITED TAX BOND general obligation MUNICIPAL BOND secured by a pledge of tax receipts from a specific revenue source, usually real estate property taxes, a portion of the real estate taxes, or a group of specific taxes. Contrast with an *unlimited tax bond*, which is backed by the general taxing authority of the issue.

LIMIT ORDER order to buy or sell a specified amount of securities at a given price. The order usually specifies a time period but it may have an indefinite expiration, such as a "good til canceled order."

LINE OF CREDIT commitment by a bank to lend funds to a borrower up to a specified amount over a specified future period. Lines of credit are reviewed annually, and do not require fees or compensating balances unless the line is guaranteed by the lender. Bank lines are considered good until further notice and may be withdrawn at the bank's option. When the borrower is officially notified of the credit available, the line is referred to as an *advised* line. When the maximum credit is kept internal by the lender, and not disclosed, it is a *guidance* line. In a commercial line of credit, the borrower may be required to keep 10%

to 20% of the available line in a COMPENSATING BALANCE. *See also* CHECK CREDIT; HOME EQUITY CREDIT; OVERDRAFT; REVOLVING CREDIT.

LINKED SAVINGS ACCOUNT SAVINGS ACCOUNT that has an account number related to a transaction account, usually a checking account or NOW account. It is sometimes called a *package* account. The depositor can keep the bulk of funds in the savings account and transfer money between accounts, and may qualify for lower account service charges or free checking. Balances on both accounts and interest earned are reported monthly in a COMBINED STATEMENT. *See also* AUTOMATIC TRANSFER SERVICE; SWEEP ACCOUNT.

LIQUID ASSET cash or its equivalents—any asset that is readily convertible to cash. For example, Treasury bills, short-term marketable securities, demand deposits, and time deposits nearing maturity. Liquid assets can be sold quickly without significant loss. *See also* NEAR MONEY.

LIQUIDATION

1. conversion of assets into cash or inventory into accounts receivable to meet current obligations and service long-term debt. When an obligation is paid off it is said to be liquidated.
2. termination of a business by selling its assets and distributing the proceeds to meet current liabilities and claims of creditors. Debts are paid in order of priority and remaining assets distributed on a pro rata basis to owner or shareholders. In a VOLUNTARY BANKRUPTCY petition, filed under Chapter 7 of the Bankruptcy Code, the debtor's assets are distributed to meet creditors' claims, in order of priority. A group of creditors can also file an INVOLUNTARY BANKRUPTCY petition, to force the sale and distribution of the debtor's assets.
3. closing out a LONG POSITION or a SHORT POSITION.

LIQUIDATOR *see* RECEIVER.

LIQUIDITY

1. ability of an organization to meet its current financial obligations. In banking, adequate liquidity means being able to meet the needs of depositors wanting to withdraw funds and borrowers wanting to be assured that their credit or cash needs will be met. Liquidity is also measured in terms of debt capacity or borrowing capacity to meet short-term demands for funds. *See also* LIQUIDITY RATIOS.
2. quality of an asset that is readily convertible into cash, with minimal loss in value. Short-term securities, such as Treasury bills that are easily sold to other investors at relatively narrow spreads between bid and asked quotes, and in reasonably large trading volumes, are said to be highly liquid.
3. characteristic of a market where a large amount of securities, futures contracts, and so on, can easily be traded with minimal price distortions occurring. Strong markets are characterized by

stable prices and relatively narrow bid-asked spreads. Thin markets have wide spreads and extreme trading volatility. *See also* DEPTH OF THE MARKET.

LIQUIDITY CRISIS

1. condition in which a business has insufficient cash on hand to repay bank loans, meet other short-term obligations, or pay its employees.
2. situation where a sharp decline in bank lending and sales of commercial paper causes a ripple effect throughout the economy, making it harder for companies to meet their short-term obligations. A liquidity crisis occurred most recently in the 2008 financial crisis.

LIQUIDITY DIVERSIFICATION *see* LADDERED PORTFOLIO.

LIQUIDITY PREFERENCE THEORY in KEYNESIAN ECONOMICS, the desire by investors to hold their money in liquid assets, such as checking accounts, rather than nonliquid assets (stocks, bonds, real estate). This preference is explained by: (1) a transactional motivation, or the desire to keep money available for spending as needed; (2) a precautionary motivation, characterized by the reluctance to keep money tied up in assets not readily convertible to cash; and (3) the speculative motive, a belief that interest rates may be going up in the future. According to the Keynesian theory, INTEREST is the payment to investors to persuade them to give up their liquidity. Longer-term investments, therefore, would command higher rates over shorter-term investments. This premium is known as the liquidity premium. Contrast with EXPECTATIONS THEORY.

LIQUIDITY RATIOS key financial ratios measuring a bank's application of interest-earning deposit liabilities to fund loan growth, expressed as a percentage. There are four primary liquidity ratios: cash and unpledged marketable securities divided by total assets; total deposits divided by borrowed funds; volatile funds divided by liquid assets; and total loans divided by total deposits (most commonly used). A low ratio of loans to deposits indicates excess liquidity, and potentially low profits, compared to other banks. A high loan-to-deposit ratio presents the risk that some loans may have to be sold at a loss to meet depositors' claims.

LIQUIDITY RISK risk that a bank will have to sell assets at a loss to meet cash demands, for example, depositors' demands for funds. Liquidity risk is generally explained as a ratio comparing available liquidity to the demand for funds.

LIRA monetary unit of Turkey.

LIS PENDENS Latin for a pending suit, a legal notice warning all parties that there is a lawsuit that may affect rights in certain property. The notice is published in a newspaper. *See also* LITIGATION.

LITAS monetary unit of Lithuania.

LITIGATION process of filing a lawsuit in the appropriate jurisdiction to settle a legal dispute or controversy. By filing a suit, one litigates the contested matters. Contrast with ARBITRATION.

LIVING TRUST *see* INTER VIVOS TRUST.

LIVING WILL document giving bank supervisory agencies instructions for closing down a large bank or bank-holding company in event of financial crisis. The Dodd-Frank Act overhauling the U.S. financial system requires large, complex, financial companies (banks characterized as TOO BIG TO FAIL financial institutions) to write living wills so financial regulators can more easily unwind counterparty contracts with other banks and bank customers and can liquidate a failing bank's assets.

LOAD FUND mutual fund that charges the investor a sales commission, called a load, as opposed to a NO-LOAD FUND. The sales commission may be due at the time of the sale (a FRONT-END LOAD), or payable at redemption of the securities (a BACK-END LOAD).

LOAN money advanced to a borrower, to be repaid at a later date, usually with interest. Legally, a loan is a contract between a buyer (the borrower) and a seller (the lender), enforceable under the UNIFORM COMMERCIAL CODE in most states. The terms and conditions for repayment of a loan, including the finance charge or interest rate, are specified in a loan agreement. A loan may be payable on demand (a DEMAND LOAN), in equal monthly installments (an INSTALLMENT LOAN), or they may be good until further notice or due at maturity (a TIME LOAN).

There are various methods lenders use to categorize loans, both for internal control and for reporting lending activity to governmental agencies, such as, classification by maturity, industry, security, and type of borrower. Bank loans are normally classified by: (1) COMMERCIAL & INDUSTRIAL LOANS to business organizations; (2) interbank loans, which are mostly FEDERAL FUNDS transactions, from one bank to another; (3) LOAN PARTICIPATIONS, or loans to a single borrower shared by several banks; (4) real estate loans, which may be subdivided into construction loans and long-term MORTGAGE loans; and (5) loans to consumers, such as auto loans and other forms of consumer installment credit. *See also* CONSUMER CREDIT; CREDIT; LOAN PARTICIPATION; PARALLEL LOAN; SECURED LOAN; SYNDICATED LOAN; TERM LOAN; TIME LOAN; UNSECURED LOAN; WORKING CAPITAL LOAN.

LOAN APPLICATION *see* CREDIT APPLICATION.

LOAN CAP *see* PAYMENT CAP.

LOAN COMMITMENT *see* COMMITMENT.

LOAN COMMITTEE management committee that evaluates and approves or declines loan applications exceeding the lending authority of an individual loan officer. This committee first examines LOAN DOC-

UMENTATION and the borrower's financial statements to assure that a pending loan meets the bank's LOAN POLICY standards and regulatory guidelines. Then the lender makes a binding COMMITMENT to fund the loan and disburse the loan proceeds to the borrower. The loan committee also carries out the lender's periodic CREDIT REVIEW of maturing loans, and decides what collection efforts should be taken to restore to health past-due loans and other NONPERFORMING ASSETS.

LOAN COVENANT *see* COVENANT.

LOAN DOCUMENTATION credit-related documents, including the loan contract, FINANCIAL STATEMENTS, business plan, documents of the lender's SECURITY INTEREST, and other papers that are used by the lender in evaluating creditworthiness of a prospective borrower. These documents, detailing the history of a loan, are kept in the borrower's CREDIT FILE, for later review by the loan review committee and by field examiners from the lender's primary supervisory agency.

Proper documentation is important in lending because the quality of documentation in the loan portfolio is directly related to credit quality ratings assigned by bank examiners. For example, a loan with an inadequate loan agreement or poor collateral control is classified by examiners under the heading SPECIAL MENTION. This means the loan is a potentially weak credit, and deficiencies in documentation need to be corrected to assure full repayment according to the original loan agreement.

LOAN FEE lender's fee for making a loan, either at the COMMITMENT time, or as funds are advanced at specific stages, as in construction financing. There are different types of loan fees: an annual fee to maintain a line of credit; a COMMITMENT FEE to hold available the unused portion of a loan or line of credit; and a UTILIZATION FEE for the amount of credit actually drawn down against an approved line. *See also* COMPENSATING BALANCE.

LOAN GRADING loan classification system, or credit scoring system, that assigns ASSET QUALITY ratings to a loan portfolio, based on comparative evaluation of outstanding loans. For example: (1) not reviewed; (2) satisfactory (an acceptable business credit); (3) special mention (missing documentation); (4) substandard (normal repayment in jeopardy); (5) doubtful (full repayment questionable); and (6) loss (complete write-off).

Many lenders use the National Bank Examiner Risk Classification System in assigning risk ratings to commercial loan portfolios, because they are required to use this format in reporting loan quality in the REPORT OF CONDITION filed quarterly with a bank supervisory agency. *See also* ADVERSELY CLASSIFIED ASSETS; NONACCRUAL LOAN; NONPERFORMING ASSET.

LOAN LEDGER *see* LIABILITY LEDGER.

LOAN LIMIT

1. LEGAL LENDING LIMIT on loans to a single borrower—not more than 15% of capital and surplus for national banks (secured loans) and generally 10% to 20% for state chartered banks.
2. authority of a bank lending officer to make a loan without obtaining prior approval from the bank's LOAN COMMITTEE.

LOAN LOSS PROVISION noncash expense item charged to a bank's earnings when adding to the allowance, or LOAN LOSS RESERVES, for possible bad debt. The loan loss provision is reported on a bank's INCOME STATEMENT.

LOAN LOSS RESERVES valuation reserve against a bank's total loans on the balance sheet, representing the amount thought to be adequate to cover estimated losses in the loan portfolio. When a loan is charged off, it is removed from the loan portfolio as an earning asset, and its book value is deducted from the reserve account for loan losses. Lenders also set aside reserves for a nonaccrual loan, in which interest and principal payments are no longer being collected. Recoveries from the liquidation of collateral repossessed from the borrower are credited to the reserve account. The TAX REFORM ACT OF 1986 disallowed the tax deduction of loan loss reserves held by banks with assets over $500 million.

LOAN PARTICIPATION sharing of a loan by a group of banks that join together to make a loan too large for any one bank to handle. Also known as *participation financing,* loan participations are arranged through CORRESPONDENT banking networks in which smaller banks buy a portion of the overall financing package. Large syndications may run into hundreds of millions of dollars, and involve more than one hundred different banks. Syndications are also a convenient way for smaller banks to book loans that would otherwise exceed their LEGAL LENDING LIMITS. By selling most of the financing to an UPSTREAM correspondent, the local bank earns fee income from servicing the loan, and is able to retain other banking relationships, such as checking accounts.

LOAN POLICY loan underwriting guidelines, and the written documentation setting forth these standards, as determined by a bank's senior LOAN COMMITTEE. A bank's loan policy also establishes minimum credit standards in booking new loans, policies and procedures in treatment of past-due and delinquent loans, and more generally, the type of customer a bank wants as a borrower.

LOAN PRODUCTION OFFICE (LPO) banking office that takes loan applications and arranges financing for corporations and small businesses, but does not accept deposits. Loan applications are subject to approval by the lending institution.

LOAN REGISTER journal in which time loans are recorded in chronological order, and consecutively numbered. This is also called a *matu-*

rity tickler. Shortly before the maturity date, the borrower is notified that the loan is about to come due. *See also* NOTE NOTICE.

LOAN REVIEW *see* CREDIT REVIEW.

LOAN SALES sale of loans or loan participations to an investor without the knowledge of the borrower. Loans, if competitively priced, may sell at par or at a slight premium. If originated at rates below current market rates, loan participations are typically sold at a discount from face value. A bank selling participations in 8% fixed rate loans will have to sell them off at a discount if the competitive market rate on similar loans is 10%. *See also* ASSET SALES; SECURITIZATION.

LOAN SHARK lender, other than a regulated financial institution, who makes a business of lending money at rates above legally permitted interest rates. An example is a $5 loan on Monday to be repaid Friday for $6—an annual percentage rate of 1040%, not including interest compounding. Loan-sharking was a pervasive activity through much of the nineteenth century, leading to the formation of cooperative associations, such as mutual savings banks and credit unions, to arrange small loans at reasonable interest rates. State small loan laws generally prohibit loan-sharking, although state laws differ on what is, or is not, an excessive rate of interest.

LOAN STRIP short-term credit advance made under a long-term lending commitment; for example, a 90-day time loan made under a five-year revolving line of credit. Banking regulators treat a participation in a loan strip as a borrowing if the original investor does not want to renew and another cannot be found. In that event, strips are considered deposits and are subject to reserve requirements under Federal Reserve REGULATION D.

LOAN-TO-VALUE RATIO relationship, expressed as a percentage, between the principal amount of a loan and the appraised value of the asset securing the financing. In a residential mortgage loan, this is the percentage value of the property the lender is willing to finance with a mortgage. For example, a $160,000 mortgage on a $200,000 house has a loan-to-value ratio of 80%. Lenders customarily set upper limits on the loans they are willing to make, and may require borrowers taking mortgages approaching the appraisal value of the property—generally any mortgage loan with a loan-to-value ratio above 80%—to take out PRIVATE MORTGAGE INSURANCE as added security.

LOCAL CHECK check deposited in the same Federal Reserve REGIONAL CHECK PROCESSING CENTER as the paying bank, even if payable through a bank located outside the region. For example, credit union SHARE DRAFT payable through a commercial bank. The CHECK ROUTING SYMBOL on the check tells whether the check is paid through a local bank.

LOCK BOX post office box used by organizations to accelerate collection of receivables. Checks are routed to a designated P.O. box number, where they are picked up several times during the day, separated from the envelopes, and submitted to the check collection system for conversion into cash receivables. Many large banks offer lock box processing as a cash management service to corporate customers. A lock box can be retail, designed for remittance processing for consumer accounts, or wholesale, in which payments from other corporations are collected and submitted through DEPOSITORY TRANSFER CHECK or electronic debit payments into a concentration account for investment and disbursement as needed.

LOCKED MARKET said of a market where the bid price equals the asked price. This occurs in very competitive markets, and for only brief periods. The market will unlock, and bid-asked quotes will diverge, after the trades are made.

LOCK-IN PERIOD

1. time period, usually 30 to 60 days, a mortgage lender agrees to hold the mortgage rate and points payable by the borrower to the rate quoted when the application was taken. This is also called *rate lock*. It is not the same as a loan COMMITMENT, although some commitments may contain a lock-in provision. This protects the borrower against rate increases if interest rates rise before the loan closing takes place. Lenders may charge a flat fee or a percentage of the mortgage loan, or add a fraction of a percentage point to the loan's interest rate.
2. period of time in which a mortgagor cannot refinance a mortgage without paying a penalty to the lender.

LOMBARD RATE interest rate set by banks in Germany on short-term loans collateralized by securities. The term officially refers to the lending rate set by the Bundesbank, the German central bank, which usually sets its Lombard rate .05% above its discount rate. Informally it is used by European banks in referring to loans backed by a pledge of securities.

LONDON INTERBANK BID RATE (LIBID) key interest rate at which major banks in the London Interbank Market are willing to borrow funds from each other, as opposed to the lending rate (the LONDON INTERBANK OFFERED RATE) quoted by banks willing to lend surplus Eurodollar deposits. The bid rate is the lower of the two interest rates.

LONDON INTERBANK MEDIAN AVERAGE RATE (LIMEAN) midpoint between the bid rate (LIBID) and the offered rate (LIBOR) in the Eurocurrency market.

LONDON INTERBANK OFFERED RATE (LIBOR) KEY RATE in international bank lending. LIBOR is the rate major banks in London pay to borrow Eurodollars. It is used to determine the interest rate charged to creditworthy borrowers. LIBOR rates, based on daily quotes at 11 A.M. (London time) from five major London banks, are fixed rates quoted for specific maturities. The lending rate in the Euro-markets (LIBOR) and the borrowing rate (LIBID), are quoted for the U.S. dollar and other Eurocurrencies, generally for fixed-term borrowings. Actual rates can vary because different reference banks are used. Syndicated Eurocredits facilities, such as Revolving Underwriting Facilities (RUFs), underwritten by several Eurobanks, are quoted as spreads above LIBOR.

LONG BOND benchmark against which other bonds are compared, for example the 10-year U.S. Treasury note or the 30-year U.S. Treasury bond; also, any widely traded bond with a current maturity (current time to maturity) of 10 years or more.

LONG COUPON

1. bond interest payment for a period longer than the standard six-month interest payment period, normally the first interest coupon. Contrast with SHORT COUPON.
2. bond with an original maturity of ten years or more, for example, the 30-year U.S. Treasury bond.

LONG DATE FORWARD speculative foreign exchange contract involving forward positions longer than one year. Trading is highly risky as there may not be a willing counterparty to take the opposite position.

LONG HEDGE

1. purchase of a FUTURES CONTRACT to lock in the price of a commodity or financial instrument. This is also called a *buy hedge.* In buying a futures contract, an investor agrees to buy the underlying commodity or financial instrument in the cash market. For example, an investor holding a $5 million bond portfolio maturing in two months can lock in the reinvestment rate with a long hedge. *See also* SHORT HEDGE.
2. strategy to lock in current yield, anticipating a drop in rates, with purchase of a futures contract or call option.

LONG POSITION

1. currency, security, or financial instrument owned outright by a dealer, indicating a net asset position. A dealer holding $5 million in U.S. dollars would say, "I am long in dollars." The opposite is a SHORT POSITION, or a net deficit. In financial futures, the term refers to a trader's market position when purchasing a FUTURES CONTRACT without closing out the position by making an offsetting sale; in options, a call option that has not been exercised or allowed to expire.
2. securities held by a broker-dealer, either for a customer or its own trading account.

LONG-TERM

1. loan with an original maturity of more than ten years, for example, a 30-year conventional mortgage loan.
2. obligations, such as bonds, that will not become payable for a year or more.

3. holding period (at least one year) for owning securities that qualifies, under Internal Revenue Service rules, for treatment as a long-term capital gain (or loss). Tax rates on long-term gains are usually lower than tax rates on short-term gains.

LONG-TERM DEBT generally refers to debt maturing in five years or more. For example, the residential mortgage and fixed term home equity loans.

LOSING THE POINTS in foreign exchange trading, market condition that exists when the buying price in the forward market is lower than the SPOT MARKET selling price. If a trader buys at the higher spot rate and sells at the one-month forward rate, he is losing the points. Contrast with EARNING THE POINTS.

LOSS

1. loan written off as uncollectible, and assigned to the loan workout committee if a commercial loan, or to the collection department if the loan is made to a consumer. Also, the formal classification by bank examiners on loans with no tangible value.
2. sale of an asset at less than its acquisition cost or fair market value.
3. reduction in value of a loan considered partially, or fully, uncollectible.
4. in accounting, an operating loss as when costs exceed net proceeds from a transaction, or expenditures are greater than revenues for an accounting period.

LOSS RESERVE *see* LOAN LOSS RESERVES.

LOST CARD bank card reported missing by the cardholder of record, or a card that was never received and is presumed to have been lost in the mail. To get a replacement card, the cardholder will have to sign an affidavit, a legal document.

LOST IN TRANSIT

1. checks, drafts, or other negotiable instruments lost in the clearing process.
2. sales draft lost between a bank card processing center and either the card issuing bank or the merchant processing bank.

L-SHAPED RECOVERY economic recession and recovery with an L-shaped chart pattern—a sharp decline in employment, industrial output, and gross domestic product. Economists refer to Japan since the 1990s as a classic example.

LUMP-SUM DISTRIBUTION single payment to an account beneficiary, for example, the beneficiary of a retirement account, as opposed to scheduled payments at regular time intervals. The holder of an INDIVIDUAL RETIREMENT ACCOUNT, for example, can either reinvest the assets of the account in a rollover account, or the proceeds can be recognized as ordinary income, and taxed at an average rate over a 10-year period.

M

MACHINE READABLE capable of being read by a mechanical device without additional processing. Machine readable characters on preprinted checks—the MAGNETIC INK CHARACTER RECOGNITION (MICR) line—permit high-speed check sorting and remittance processing. Other examples are the bank card MAGNETIC STRIPE, the retail industry Universal Price Code (UPC), and Optical Character Recognition (OCR).

MACROECONOMICS analysis of a nation's economy as a whole, examining aggregate data, such as inflation, industrial production, price levels, and unemployment. Contrast with *microeconomics,* the analysis of business sectors and industry groups.

MAGNETIC INK CHARACTER RECOGNITION (MICR) digital characters on the bottom edge of a paper check containing the issuing bank's ABA TRANSIT NUMBER (bank identifier) and CHECK ROUTING SYMBOL (denoting funds availability). When checks are cleared through the banking system, the dollar amount of the check is added to the machine readable MICR line. Introduction of MICR in the 1950s greatly facilitated check clearing, enabling banks to virtually automate the handling of billions of checks every year. *See also* ENCODING.

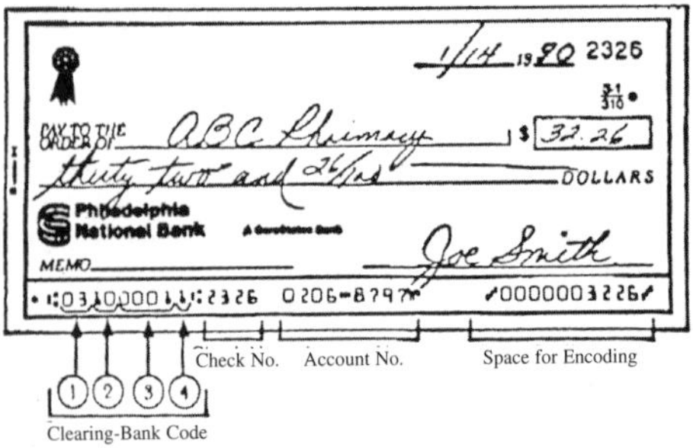

① Federal Reserve District, 2 digits: 01 to 12

② Branch/City Designation & Clearing

③ Bank Number

④ Parity Check Digit (for reading error control)

MAGNETIC STRIPE strip of magnetic tape, affixed to bank credit and debit cards, encoded with cardholder identifying information, such as the PRIMARY ACCOUNT NUMBER and card expiration date, permitting automated handling of transactions. The bank card industry standard for magnetic stripes allows three separate tracks of encoded data:

Track 1: developed by the International Air Transportation Association for automation of airline ticketing;

Track 2: developed by the American Bankers Association for the automation of financial transactions; and

Track 3: developed by the thrift industry for financial terminals operating in an *off-line* mode (not connected to a host processor) for transaction authorization.

MAIL FLOAT clearing delays that slow the PRESENTMENT of out-of-town checks to the paying bank. Mail float is the time lag attributed to checks and CASH LETTERS arriving from distant points.

MAIL TELLER teller responsible for receiving, sorting, and proving deposits arriving by mail. In larger banks, deposits from customers and correspondents may exceed deposits taken at the teller line.

MAINTENANCE FEE periodic charge to maintain an account, such as a credit card annual fee or a monthly checking account service charge. Checking account fees may be waived if the customer keeps a certain minimum balance.

MAINTENANCE MARGIN

1. in futures, money that a customer must keep in a MARGIN account when a position is outstanding. It is usually lower than the initial margin posted. The value of positions are posted to market daily. If position losses exceed the maintenance margin, the dealer issues a margin call requiring the customer to post additional margin.
2. in securities, the margin requirement a brokerage customer must maintain at all times in a brokerage account with a debit balance. Federal Reserve REGULATION T, which regulates broker-dealers, requires an initial $2,000 deposit in a brokerage account and sets the margin requirement (50% since 1974) to cover margin trading on a customer's account.

MAINTENANCE REQUIREMENTS dollar amount that a bank or brokerage customer must keep as MARGIN capital in a trading account. The customer can borrow against the total value of securities in the account, but may be required to post additional margin if the value of the margin falls below a specified level. Maintenance requirements are a selective credit control, and are implemented through Federal Reserve REGULATION T and REGULATION U. In general, margin levels are set at 50% of market value, but can be raised or lowered as needed.

MAJOR INDUSTRY IDENTIFIER first digit in the PRIMARY ACCOUNT NUMBER that is printed on the front of a BANK CARD or TRAVEL & ENTERTAINMENT card. Cards issued by banks and other financial institutions generally have account numbers beginning with the number 4 or 5; those issued by nonbank companies, such as travel & entertainment companies, have account numbers beginning with 3.

MAKER person who writes a CHECK, signs a PROMISSORY NOTE or other negotiable instrument, and assumes primary liability for payment. The maker of a check is also known as the DRAWER.

MALFEASANCE wrongdoing or criminal act, as when a bank loan officer accepts cash gifts from a customer. Contrast with MISFEASANCE, the improper performance of a legally permissible act, and NONFEASANCE, the failure to carry out a contractual obligation.

MANAGED CURRENCY any currency whose EXCHANGE RATE is influenced by central bank INTERVENTION in the exchange markets, as opposed to interaction of supply and demand in the free market. Most major currencies are managed to one degree or another when central banks buy and sell their own currency to maintain market stability and carry out MONETARY POLICY. *See also* CLEAN FLOAT; DIRTY FLOAT; EXCHANGE CONTROLS.

MANAGED LIABILITIES deposits, other than CORE DEPOSITS, that banks actively solicit from other banks, or from brokers, to maintain adequate levels of LIQUIDITY. Managed liabilities are deposits that can be increased or decreased at will, such as large-dollar negotiable time deposits; Eurodollar and other Eurocurrency borrowings; repurchase agreements against Treasury securities and federal agency securities; and Federal Funds purchased, to meet a bank's needs for funds to pay off maturing deposits and fund new loans.

Such borrowings can be increased or decreased as needed to meet temporary funding gaps between maturing assets and liabilities. The negotiable CD, which evolved in the 1960s when Regulation Q imposed interest rate caps on all deposits except those above $100,000, is typically sold in $1 million pieces. These certificates of deposit pay interest at maturity, and usually have an original maturity of one to three months. *See also* BROKERED DEPOSIT; LIABILITY MANAGEMENT.

MANAGING UNDERWRITER commercial bank or investment bank representing an UNDERWRITING GROUP in purchase and distribution of a new securities offering. The managing underwriter arranges the selling group; files the necessary registration papers; acts as AGENT for the selling group, as authorized by the AGREEMENT AMONG UNDERWRITERS; decides the portion of the offering, or ALLOTMENT, to be assigned each member; and acts to stabilize the price of the securities during the offering period. For his or her services, the managing underwriter is paid an extra fee from the syndicate's gross profit. Called LEAD BANK in the Eurobond market and *lead manager* in the United States. *See also* BEST EFFORT; NEGOTIATED UNDERWRITING.

MANAT monetary unit of Azerbaijan.

MANDATORY CONVERTIBLE type of bond with a redemption requirement. Banks issue mandatory convertible bonds, also called equity linked securities, to meet regulatory capital requirements without issuing common stock until some future date. The bonds often pay higher yields than comparable bonds to compensate for the mandatory conversion feature.

MANUFACTURED HOUSING factory-built housing shipped in sections to a building site. Manufactured housing is constructed according to federal standards (the HUD code) for home design and safety from the Department of Housing and Urban Development (HUD). Manufactured homes are popular with low-to-moderate income home buyers because of their low cost. Manufactured housing loans are often sold to investors in the asset-backed securities market.

MARGIN

Banking:

1. NET INTEREST MARGIN (NIM), or the percentage difference between a bank's yield on earning assets (mostly loans) and interest paid to depositors.
2. proportion of the asset pledged as security, for example, inventory or accounts receivable, that a bank will lend against. The difference between the market value and loan value is also called a HAIRCUT. If the collateral declines in value, additional margin will be required.
3. premium a mortgage lender adds to an INDEX rate in determining the loan interest rate in an ADJUSTABLE RATE MORTGAGE. This premium is typically two to three percentage points.

Futures: money or securities put up as a good faith deposit assuring that a future contract will be fulfilled. Also known as a *security deposit*, as in the initial margin and MAINTENANCE MARGIN required when a futures position is open.

Securities: money deposited with a broker that serves as partial payment when purchasing securities. The Federal Reserve Board's REGULATION T sets a MAINTENANCE MARGIN, currently 50%, in purchases or short sales of securities. Margins may be put up in cash or eligible securities. Individual broker-dealers may impose higher margins in trades of OVER-THE-COUNTER securities.

MARGINAL COST OF FUNDS incremental cost or differential cost of each additional dollar borrowed. It is the cost of funding one more loan, assuming that the cost of funds remains unchanged. Under conventional cost accounting theory, the marginal cost of acquiring new funds decreases as scale economies are achieved. Put another way, the marginal cost of funds varies inversely to the capital base of financial intermediaries because the larger banks, which as a rule have larger loan portfolios, can tap into the capital markets and money markets with greater ease than smaller ones. *See also* POOLED COST OF FUNDS.

MARGIN CALL demand by a bank lender, securities broker-dealer, or a futures clearinghouse for additional funds or collateral to offset position losses in a MARGIN account. If a bank loan is secured by marginable securities the lender may call the loan if the customer fails to post additional collateral or pay down the loan. If the margin call is on securities, the customer is asked to post more cash or eligible securities by a certain time the following day, or the collateral can be sold to satisfy the outstanding loan.

MARITAL DEDUCTION portion of an estate that may pass to the surviving spouse exempt from federal estate taxes. There are numerous types of marital deductions: the federal income tax deduction for a nonworking spouse, the deduction under the federal gift tax for lifetime (inter vivos) transfers, and the federal estate tax for testamentary transfers provided by a will.

MARK monetary unit of Germany.

MARKA monetary unit of Bosnia-Herzegovina.

MARKET

1. aggregate of supply and demand that brings together informed buyers and sellers, and sets the public price for products or services. For example, the CREDIT market, the foreign exchange market, the MONEY MARKET, the mortgage market, and the SECONDARY MARKET.
2. public place, such as a stock exchange, or futures exchange, where trading takes place. It implies the presence of market makers who are willing to buy or sell for their own account, or for customers, at quoted prices.
3. to sell anything of value to a willing buyer at a mutually agreeable price.

MARKET CAPITALIZATION an organization's current share price multiplied by the number of shares outstanding. When expressed as a ratio to earnings, the resulting number is the firm's PRICE/EARNINGS RATIO or (P/E) multiple.

MARKET DISCIPLINE public disclosure of a bank's financial condition to depositors and other interested parties. Regular disclosure of a bank's equity capital and its major liabilities are promoted by banking regulatory agencies as an incentive for banks to maintain adequate capital to cushion against potential losses. According to the theory, depositors, creditors and others will want to do business with financial institutions that meet, or surpass, the recommended RISK-BASED CAPITAL standard, a base guideline for banks doing business internationally.

MARKET INDEX CD CERTIFICATE OF DEPOSIT that pays a rate of interest tied to a commodity or a market index. Also known as an *indexed deposit* account or *indexed CD*. These CDs pay stock market-like returns but offer the safety of a CD protected by deposit insurance. Interest is calculated based on the market return of the index. This type of CD carries added protection for depositors; even in a bear market (falling stock prices) no principal can be lost. In a bull market (rising prices), the CD pays 100% of the investment return of the index.

MARKETING business activities relating to delivery of goods and services from sellers to purchasers, and also from businesses to consumers to meet demands of the market. Bank marketing, or selling in the past relied heavily on retail branch networks to distribute financial services, but in recent years banking institutions have employed a variety of marketing approaches, including direct mail, telemarketing mail, telemarketing, and Internet-based marketing. *See also* AFFINITY CARD; INTERNET BANKING; MARKET RESEARCH; PERSONAL BANKER; PLATFORM AUTOMATION; RELATIONSHIP BANKING.

MARKET MAKER person who stands ready to execute buy and sell orders on behalf of customers or his own account, or BOOK. A market maker is someone who assumes trading risk by taking possession of the asset traded, and who executes transactions at publicly quoted prices. A market maker's bid and asked spreads are not so large as to preclude transactions at the prices quoted. In organized exchanges, such as the stock market or futures market, market makers are licensed by a regulating body or by the exchange itself.

MARKET ORDER order to buy or sell securities at the best available price—at the market—the most common way of executing trades.

MARKET RATE OF INTEREST

1. interest rate determined by demand and supply of funds in the money market, such as the Fed Funds rate. Market rates move up or down, depending on demand for funds, economic conditions, and Federal Reserve monetary policy.
2. rate a bank offers to attract deposits, which may match or exceed rates offered by competitors.

MARKET RESEARCH systematic collection and analysis of data relating to sale and distribution of financial products and services. Market research is an early step in the marketing process, and includes an analysis of market demand for a new product, or for existing products, as well as appropriate methods of distributing those products. Techniques in market research include telephone polling and focus group interviews to determine customer attitudes, pricing sensitivity, and willingness to use delivery alternatives. Most large banks have their own market research departments that evaluate not only products, but their BRICKS AND MORTAR branch banking networks through which most banking products are sold.

MARKET RISK probability that an investment will vary in price as market conditions change. Volatile or speculative securities have greater potential for price gains (and profits) or losses than investments that have stable prices.

MARKET SEGMENTATION THEORY theory of interest rates that says short-term and long-term markets act independently of each other and that investors have fixed maturity preferences. This is also called *segmented markets theory.* Supporters maintain that short-term and long-term rates are distinct markets, each with its own buyers and sellers, and are not easily substituted for each other. *See also* EXPECTATIONS THEORY; LIQUIDITY PREFERENCE THEORY.

MARKET TO BOOK VALUE ratio of the market value of a security, such as common stock, to its book value. It is an indication of performance of common stock equity, after accounting for dilution of stock value after a merger and market reaction to unexpected gains or losses and changes in operating income.

MARKET VALUE highest price that a marketable asset will bring in an open and competitive market, assuming that both buyer and seller are informed and acting independently, also called FAIR MARKET VALUE. In theory, this is the highest price a seller is willing to accept and the lowest price a buyer is willing to pay. It may differ from the APPRAISAL VALUE. *See also* MARK TO MARKET.

MARKKA monetary unit of Finland.

MARK TO MARKET daily adjustment of an account or investment to reflect actual MARKET VALUE, as opposed to historic accounting value or BOOK VALUE. Securities and futures are revalued on a daily basis, but bank loans and investment other than securities are evaluated and marked down only when there is a change in the credit relationship. The FINANCIAL ACCOUNTING STANDARDS BOARD Statement 115 (FAS 115) requires banks and other financial institutions to report debt securities and equities eligible for sale at current market value. Only bonds held to maturity may be listed at their original purchase price.

MASTERCARD WORLDWIDE invester-owned nonprofit corporation that licenses financial institutions to issue MasterCard bank cards and market related products and services. Its principal assets are the MasterCard trademarks; a global communications network, BankNet, for authorization and settlement of bank card transactions for member banks; and a nationwide AUTOMATED TELLER MACHINE network, Cirrus System Inc. Member banks issue MasterCard credit cards and MasterMoney debit cards. *See also* VISA.

MASTER MORTGAGE standard mortgage documentation filed by mortgage originators in public land records. The master mortgage simplifies the recording of liens, as mortgages have become increasingly complex in recent years, and also facilitates sales of loans in the secondary mortgage market.

MASTER NOTE *see* REVOLVING CREDIT.

MASTER TRUST custody arrangement whereby a bank or trust company manages pension fund assets for a group of related companies under a single trustee account. A master trust agreement facilitates the administration of defined benefit pension plan assets, including purchase and sale of securities, reporting to corporate plan sponsors, as required by the EMPLOYEE RETIREMENT INCOME SECURITY ACT, and distribution of retirement benefits to individuals covered by the plan. A master trust arrangement facilitates plan accounting when multiple investment managers are used.

MATCHED BOOK portfolio of assets and portfolio of liabilities having equal maturities. The term is used most often in reference to money market instruments and money market liabilities. In contrast, an *unmatched book* is referred to as a short book or long book.

MATCHED MATURITIES in bank ASSET-LIABILITY MANAGEMENT, the funding of loans with deposits of approximately equal durations to minimize interest rate risk. This is the contractual gap approach to funds management, carried out by matching maturities on opposite sides of the balance sheet in a given reporting period. For example, all 90-day loans are matched against liabilities expected to mature or reprice in 90 days. The difference between maturing assets and maturing liabilities is the contractual gap, which will be different for each calendar period. Matched funding gets more difficult as maturities lengthen. A bank could, for example, try to fund its five-year car loans with five-year Certificates of Deposit, but this is often difficult to achieve. A bank cannot prevent its depositors from withdrawing their money before the CD maturity date. Also, a bank may find it advantageous to deliberately MISMATCH maturities when it believes interest rates are about to change. Maturity matching is more common in the Eurocurrency market where Eurodollar deposits, for instance, have fixed maturities, and can be matched easily against fixed term liabilities. Also called *matched funding*.

MATCHED SALE—PURCHASE AGREEMENT action by the Federal Reserve to restrict the supply of funds (reserves) banks have available to lend. The Fed does this by selling securities to dealers and simultaneously agreeing to buy back those securities at a future date. Selling securities drains reserves from the banking system because dealers have to take out bank loans to finance their purchases.

Matched sale—purchase transactions usually have maturities of seven days or less, and are executed by the System Desk at the Federal Reserve Bank of New York, which carries out the monetary policy directives of the FEDERAL OPEN MARKET COMMITTEE. The System Desk accepts dealer bids to buy securities, usually Treasury bills, until sufficient reserves have been absorbed. A matched sale—purchase agreement is the opposite of a REPURCHASE AGREEMENT, which adds reserves.

MATURITY DATE date on which the principal balance of a contract loan, debt instrument or other financial security is due and payable to the holder. Also, the date on which a TIME DRAFT is payable.

MATURITY GAP *see* GAP; GAPPING.

MATURITY TICKLER *see* LOAN REGISTER.

MAY DAY May 1, 1975, the date when fixed brokerage commissions were abolished in the securities industry in the United States. Ending fixed commissions led to DISCOUNT BROKERAGE trading and accelerated the diversification by securities firms into financial services, and increased competition with banks and thrift institutions.

McFADDEN ACT law enacted by Congress in 1927 giving states the power to regulate bank branching, including branching by national banks. The Riegle-Neal Interstate Banking and Branching Efficiency Act of 1994 modified the McFadden Act, allowing banks to open deposit-taking branches across state lines by merging with other banks. *See also* INTERSTATE BANKING; REGIONAL INTERSTATE BANKING.

MECHANIC'S LIEN enforceable claim, permitted by law in most states, securing payment to contractors, subcontractors and suppliers of materials for work performed. The lien, which attaches to real property, plus buildings and improvements situated on the land, remains in effect until the workmen have been paid in full, or in event of liquidation, gives the contractor PRIORITY OF LIEN ahead of other creditors.

MEDALLION SIGNATURE GUARANTEE financial institution's endorsement applied to securities in the process of transfer, certifying the owner's signature is genuine and has legally binding authority. The leading medallion signature gurarantee programs are the Securities Transfer Agents Medallion Program (STAMP), whose members include more than 7,000 U.S. and Canadian banks, savings institutions, and credit unions, and the New York Stock Exchange Medallion Signature Program (MSP), servicing major securities brokerage firms.

MEDIUM OF EXCHANGE any monetary instrument or MONEY accepted as payment for goods and services and settlement of debts, such as checks, bank drafts, or notes. A medium of exchange eliminates the need for direct exchange or BARTER, and is the basis for a modern banking system.

MEMBER, APPRAISAL INSTITUTE (MAI) professional designation by the American Institute of Real Estate Appraisers of the National Association of Realtors, given to real estate appraisers who meet qualifying standards and are certified by the institute.

MEMBER BANK depository financial institution that is a member of the FEDERAL RESERVE SYSTEM. National banks are required to be members of the Federal Reserve; state chartered commercial banks and savings institutions have the option of becoming members. Member banks purchase stock in their district Federal Reserve Bank equal to 6% of their PAID-IN CAPITAL and surplus; keep a portion of their demand deposits and time deposits in LEGAL RESERVES at a Federal Reserve Bank; honor checks drawn on the bank and presented by another bank for collection; and comply with federal banking regulations, and if a state chartered bank, accept supervision and examination by the Federal Reserve System. *See also* NONMEMBER BANK.

MEMO ENTRY debit or credit to a customer's account that is recorded to the bank's transaction journals at a different time than when the transaction actually occurred. Journal entries are entered to the general ledger usually at the end of the day. Many banks that operate electronic banking services, such as automated teller machines, do not record ELECTRONIC FUNDS TRANSFER (EFT) transactions in an on-line fashion, but record them to a memo file, sometimes called a *strip file,* which is used to update customer accounts.

MEMORANDUM OF UNDERSTANDING voluntary agreement by a bank or savings institution, negotiated with a supervisory agency, to refrain from a particular activity deemed by the regulatory agency to be an unsound banking practice. A memorandum of understanding is not necessarily an admission of wrongdoing, but indicates a willingness to take corrective action in the future.

MERCANTILE AGENCY organization that supplies credit information to businesses and to financial institutions in response to a request for a credit history on an individual or business organization. Examples are: credit bureaus affiliated with the Associated Credit Bureaus of America, such as Trans Union LLC; DUN & BRADSTREET, the oldest of the mercantile credit agencies; and credit interchange associations, such as the National Association of Credit Management. Mercantile agencies furnish information on debt repayment and credit history, collected from a wide number of reporting companies.

In addition to Trans Union, the major credit bureaus in the United States are Equifax, Inc., and Experian. *See also* CREDIT BUREAU.

MERCHANT person, firm, or corporation that has a contractual relationship with a card issuing bank to accept bank cards for payment of goods and services.

MERCHANT AGREEMENT written agreement between a retail merchant and a card processing bank. The merchant agreement spells out the merchant's rights and warranties with respect to accepting bank cards, the merchant discount rate, and procedures to follow in handling chargebacks and other disputed transactions.

MERCHANT BANK

1. bank that purchases bank card sales drafts from a retail merchant. The merchant bank converts the merchant's sales drafts to deposits, and collects a processing fee called a *merchant discount.* If the transaction was initiated by a customer at another bank, the merchant bank submits the sales draft information through the bank card INTERCHANGE system, collecting the amount of the draft, less the interchange fee, from the card issuing bank. *See also* MERCHANT DISCOUNT RATE.
2. European or British investment bank that engages in MERCHANT BANKING.

MERCHANT BANKING form of banking where the bank arranges credit financing, but does not hold the loans in its investment portfolio to maturity. A merchant bank invests its own capital in leveraged buyouts, corporate acquisitions, and other structured finance transactions. Merchant banking is a fee-based business, where the bank assumes market risk but no long-term credit risk. A common form of banking in Europe, merchant banking is gaining acceptance in the United States, as more banks originate commercial loans and then sell them to investors rather than hold the loans as portfolio investments. *A banque d'affaire* is a French merchant bank, which has more powers than its British counterpart. The GRAMM-LEACH-BLILEY ACT allows financial holding companies, a type of BANK HOLDING COMPANY created by the act, to engage in merchant banking activities.

MERCHANT DISCOUNT RATE fee charged a merchant for processing bank card sales drafts and crediting the funds to the merchant's account. The merchant discount depends on sales volume; the discount declines as sales volume increases, and is negotiated individually with each merchant. If the merchant discount is 2%, the merchant keeps $98 for every $100 in sales. *See also* INTERCHANGE.

MERCHANT FRAUD scheme to defraud a bank card plan, often a merchant working in collusion with someone else. A common form is white plastic fraud, a scheme in which the merchant submits phony sales drafts to a processing bank and then splits the sales draft income with the person supplying the account numbers that were charged.

MERCHANT NUMBER identification code that identifies card honoring merchants in a bank card plan. Merchants are issued a specially encoded card that is used for end-of-day transaction settlement, in tallying their daily sales volume for reporting to their card processing bank.

MERGER combination of two or more organizations through stock purchase, cash payment, or a combination. Managements in both companies generally consent to mergers in the banking industry, or in the case of a bank acquiring a failed institution, the approval of bank regulatory agencies is necessary. A merger is called an ACQUISITION when one of the parties to the transaction, usually but not always the larger one, takes over a smaller company and consolidates the two organizations into a single entity. *See also* PURCHASE ACQUISITION.

Note that the purchase method of accounting is to be used for all business mergers initiated after June 30, 2001, according to SFAS No. 141. Previously, a business combination could be classified as either a purchase or a pooling of interests. If any of the twelve criteria for pooling was not met, the combination is reportable as a purchase transaction.

MESSAGE AUTHENTICATION CODE (MAC) unique security code, created by an algorithm and used in ELECTRONIC FUNDS TRANSFER (EFT) to ensure that the information has not been tampered with, and that the sender of a message is in fact the originating bank.

MESSENGER bank employee whose job is collection, by direct presentment, of checks, notes, and drafts that are not drawn on clearinghouse banks and thus are not collectible through a clearinghouse. Messengers also collect special items from brokerages and corporations, such as drafts with stocks or bonds attached. Collection by messenger is frequently known as *collections by hand.*

METROPOLITAN STATISTICAL AREA (MSA) federally designated geographical unit consisting of an urbanized area with a central city of at least 50,000 residents and a regional population of 100,000. Federal banking regulations permit FINANCIAL INSTITUTIONS doing business within an MSA to use a single master account in dealing with the Federal Reserve for computing reserve requirements, processing checks, and sending electronic fund transfers. Information about COMMUNITY REINVESTMENT ACT-related lending to local communities, compiled for each MSA, is available from federal banking regulators.

MEZZANINE BRACKET popular name for the underwriters in an underwriting syndicate who subscribe to the second largest portion, following the lead manager, and are listed below the lead manager in TOMBSTONE advertising announcing the transaction in newspapers. Other underwriters, including co-managers, participating in the deal are listed in alphabetical order beneath the major underwriters.

MEZZANINE FINANCING

1. in corporate finance, a LEVERAGED BUYOUT or restructuring financed through subordinated debt, such as preferred stock or convertible debentures. This type of financing is very popular in merger & acquisitions, as the transaction is financed by expanding equity, as opposed to debt. Holders of the securities are also assured of having a greater role in managing the resulting company.
2. second or third level financing of companies financed by venture capital. The mezzanine financing is senior to the venture capital financing, but junior to bank financing, and adds creditworthiness to the firm. It generally is used as an intermediate stage financing, preceding the company's initial public offering (IPO), and is considered less risky than start-up financing.

MICROFILM photographic process that copies checks and other documents for record keeping and storage. Microfilming of bank records is being replaced gradually by document image processing, in which physical documents are converted into computer readable digital images that are stored on optical laser disks for rapid retrieval.

MICROLOAN development loan to a small business arranged by a bank-funded COMMUNITY DEVELOPMENT BANK. Such loans provide startup capital in economically disadvantaged communities, and are often made for amounts as small as $1,000. Microloan programs assisted by the World Bank provide needed funding in developing countries. They are becoming more common in the United States. Also called *microcredit.*

MIDDLE RATE median average of BID and OFFER prices quoted by foreign exchange dealers. For example, say the bid price of a given currency versus the U.S. dollar is $1 = 1.6510 and the offer price is

$1 = 1.6520. Traders will say, "Can we do business in the middle?"—at $1 equal to 1.6515. ($1 = 1.6515.)

MIDGETS popular name for 15-year Government National Mortgage Association (Ginnie Mae) pass-through securities collateralized by pools of biweekly mortgages. As with 30-year Ginnie Mae pass-through securities, midget pools have a minimum principal of $1 million.

MINI-BRANCH specialized branch office that offers a limited number of banking services, less than what is available at a full-service branch. A mini-branch, generally smaller than a conventional branch, may have only an AUTOMATED TELLER MACHINE for taking deposits and dispensing cash, and may refer loan applications to another branch. Also called *convenience branch.*

MINIMUM BALANCE amount required in an account to earn interest, qualify for special services, or waive service charges. Accounts that fall below the minimum balance may be subject to service charges if the average balance is below that threshold, or if the account falls below that balance at any time. To get a free checking account, for instance, a customer may have to keep a certain amount in the account at all times or maintain an equivalent amount in other accounts. Cost accounting systems may give customers an earnings credit for funds kept on deposit. Others, instead, work with a flat charge per check or account. *See also* AVERAGE BALANCE; TARGET BALANCE.

MINIMUM PAYMENT smallest payment a credit cardholder can make toward reducing the outstanding balance owed, while meeting the terms and conditions of the cardholder agreement.

MINI-STATEMENT *see* INTERIM STATEMENT.

MINOR person under legal age, the age when he or she attains full civil rights. The legal age is 18 in most states, but may be 21 in some states.

MINT bureau of the U.S. Treasury that manufactures coins, and holds the U.S. Treasury Department's gold bullion reserves in safekeeping. The Treasury's Assay Office is supervised by the Bureau of the Mint.

MISENCODED payment incorrectly entered encoded in a bank's proof and transit department with an incorrect dollar amount. A misencoded check will have to be processed manually as an exception item. *See also* REJECT ITEMS.

MISFEASANCE performing official duties irresponsibly, or improperly carrying out a lawful act. Contrast with MALFEASANCE, committing an unlawful act in an official capacity; or NONFEASANCE, failing to doing something a person is obliged to do by contract or agreement.

MISMATCH situation in ASSET-LIABILITY MANAGEMENT when interest-earning assets and interest expense liabilities do not balance. The conventional circumstances in banking are that banks and savings institutions borrow short and lend long, for example, funding 30-year mortgages with short-term deposits, expecting that short-term deposits can be rolled over at maturity dates. Also known as a *mismatched book.* Contrast with MATCHED MATURITIES.

MIS-SENT ITEMS checks sent by error to the wrong bank for payment. These are usually returned to the sending bank, delaying payment of these checks.

MISSING PAYMENT loan payment made within the allowed grace period, but, for one reason or another, not posted to the proper account. If not corrected in time, the error may result in the posting of a LATE CHARGE against the account.

MIXED DEPOSIT deposit at a teller window, night depository, or at an automated teller machine, containing both cash and checks. Contrast with SPLIT DEPOSIT.

MOBILE BANKING banking by smartphone or other handheld mobile device with Internet access and e-mail capability.

MODEL mathematical characterization of a process, market condition, or set of variables used to determine how each would behave under different scenarios. Such models are widely used in ASSET-LIABILITY MANAGEMENT, credit scoring, loan pricing, interest rate futures, and financial swaps. *See also* BLACK SCHOLES MODEL; ECONOMETRICS; SIMULATION; WHAT-IF CALCULATION.

MODIFIED PASS-THROUGH CERTIFICATE security that represents an undivided interest in pools of mortgages, backed by federally guaranteed loans of the same maturity and coupon date. Payments of principal and interest are made monthly to certificate holders, and are guaranteed by the Government National Mortgage Association regardless of whether payments are received, as borrowers pay down the loans. There is no holding back of interest payments as with collateralized mortgage obligations and mortgage-backed bonds.

MODIFIED PAYOFF deposit insurance payoff whereby uninsured depositors, persons holding deposits exceeding the FDIC insurance limit ($250,000 per account) receive only a portion of their claim against the assets of a failed bank. The modified payoff was introduced in the early 1980s to cope with bank failures where a sizable portion of the deposits were rate sensitive BROKERED DEPOSITS that paid well above rates offered by competing institutions.

M1, M2, M3 key measures of the U.S. money supply as defined by the Federal Reserve Board. Federal Reserve policy makers and economists closely watch growth in the money supply for signs of future economic growth and potential for inflation.

M1 is the narrowest measure of money supply, representing money that can be readily spent or easily converted to cash. It includes coins and currency in circulation, checking account balances, negotiable order of withdrawal (NOW) accounts, traveler's checks, and credit union share draft accounts.

M2 includes everything in M1 plus savings accounts, certificate of deposit (CD) accounts under $100,000, household money market deposit accounts, and money market funds.

M3, the largest measure of U.S. money supply, includes everything in M2 plus large-value CD accounts, money market fund balances owned by institutions, repurchase agreements, and Eurodollar deposits. The Federal Reserve discontinued publication of M3 in 2006.

MONETARIST economist who believes that control of the MONEY SUPPLY is the key to managing the boom and bust cycles in the economy. Monetarists, most notably Milton Friedman and his followers, maintain that recessions are caused by declines in the rate of expansion in the money supply. The monetarist school of economic thought says that setting annual targets for growth in the money supply is the best means to achieve stable growth in the economy and control inflation. As an economic theory, though, monetarism has its drawbacks. Critics say monetarism ignores other factors, such as government spending and taxation, and bank credit, which are equally important. According to the monetarist view, the VELOCITY OF MONEY is the most important factor influencing economic growth. Velocity is usually defined as the number of times the same dollar is spent in a year; velocity of money is calculated by dividing total sales volume (or Gross Domestic Product output in goods and services) by the money supply in circulation. Finally, there is still no inclusive definition of the money supply itself; consequently, the money supply is observed by the Federal Reserve, but is only one indicator of the effectiveness of monetary policy.

MONETARY ACCORD OF 1951 agreement between the U.S. Treasury Department and the Federal Reserve Board of Governors that enabled the Fed to pursue an active MONETARY POLICY, independent of the Treasury and the federal government. Before 1951, the Fed had to assure low-cost Treasury financing by purchasing Treasury securities at a set price. Afterward, the Federal Reserve Open Market Committee was able to purchase as much, or as little, of Treasury securities offered for sale by the Treasury Department as it wanted, instead of having to buy whatever the Treasury issued at the prevailing rate. Also known as the Treasury-Fed Accord.

MONETARY AGGREGATES *see* MONEY SUPPLY.

MONETARY BASE sum of reserve accounts of financial institutions at Federal Reserve Banks, currency in circulation (currency held by the public and in the vaults of depository institutions). The major source of the adjusted monetary base is FEDERAL RESERVE CREDIT. The monetary base, as the ultimate source of the nation's MONEY SUPPLY, is controllable, at least to some degree, by Federal Reserve MONETARY POLICY. The adjusted monetary base data is compiled weekly by the Federal Reserve Board and the Federal Reserve Bank of St. Louis, and is adjusted seasonally.

MONETARY CONTROL ACT *see* DEPOSITORY INSTITUTIONS DEREGULATION AND MONETARY CONTROL ACT.

MONETARY POLICY actions by the FEDERAL RESERVE SYSTEM to influence the cost and availability of credit, with the goals of promoting economic growth, full employment, price stability, and balanced trade with other countries. Through its monetary policy decisions, the Fed tries to regulate both interest rates and the nation's MONEY SUPPLY. Monetary policy is carried out by the FEDERAL RESERVE BOARD and the FEDERAL OPEN MARKET COMMITTEE, the 12-member committee (including all 7 governors of the Federal Reserve Board), which directs the open market purchase and sale of government securities for the 12 Federal Reserve Banks. The Federal Reserve Board chairman appears before Congressional committees twice a year, in February and July, to report on Federal Reserve monetary policy objectives, as required by the 1978 Humphrey-Hawkins Act. These addresses are watched closely for indications of a change in monetary policy.

The Fed has at its disposal several distinct tools of monetary policy: the purchase or sale of securities through OPEN MARKET OPERATIONS, its power to set financial institution RESERVE REQUIREMENTS, and the DISCOUNT RATE paid by banks and savings institutions when they borrow from one of the district Federal Reserve Banks. Monetary policy can be characterized as being either tight credit or easy credit. When the Fed is worried that the economy is growing too fast or prices are rising too rapidly, it tightens up reserve positions by selling government securities or allowing maturing securities to run off. This process is known as *draining reserves.* If, on the other hand, the Fed becomes concerned that the economy is not growing fast enough, or is headed into a recession, it can inject new reserves into the banking system by buying securities from securities dealers. By buying, instead of selling, securities, the Fed is expanding, rather than contracting the supply of bank reserves, thereby making it easier for banks to meet their reserve requirements and make new loans.

In addition to monetary policy, the Fed also has several selective credit controls regulating the cost of credit. These include the MARGIN requirements on securities purchased through broker-dealers, and the highly effective MORAL SUASION, whereby the Fed tries to persuade bankers to go along with its recommendations through informal pressure. Although monetary policy differs from the federal government's FISCAL POLICY, carried out by its tax and spending policies, both share a common objective: balancing aggregate demand in the economy against aggregate supply, as measured by the gross domestic product, employment, and interest rates, thereby keeping inflation and unemployment under control. *See also* INTERMEDIATE TARGETS; MONETARIST; MONETARY BASE; OPERATIONAL TARGETS.

MONETARY TARGETS *see* OPERATIONAL TARGETS.

MONEY anything commonly accepted as a LEGAL TENDER currency for payment of debts. Money has been defined any number of ways, but it generally serves three distinct purposes, depending on how it is used: (1) as a medium of exchange for payments between consumers, businesses, and government; (2) as a unit of account for measuring purchasing power, or the prices paid for goods and services; and (3) as a store of value for measuring the economic worth of current income deferred for spending in future years.

In the United States, paper currency (FEDERAL RESERVE NOTE), coins, and checking account balances are examples of money. Other forms of money are commodity money (gold and silver bullion and coins, brightly colored shells and so on), and BARTER, the trading of goods and services without monetary exchange. Today, paper currency represents only a fraction of the nation's money supply; about three-fourths of the MONEY SUPPLY is held in the form of bookkeeping debits and credits representing demand deposit (checking) account balances in commercial banks. *See also* CURRENCY IN CIRCULATION; FIAT MONEY; M1, M2, M3; MONETARY BASE; MONEY SUPPLY; NEAR MONEY.

MONEY CENTER BANK bank located in a major financial center that participates in both national and international money markets. Money center banks offer regional banks and community banks access to master trust, foreign exchange, and depository services, as well as check clearings, through CORRESPONDENT banking networks. Money center banks are found mainly in New York, Chicago, and San Francisco, and also in London and other world financial centers.

MONEY LAUNDERING acceptance of large cash deposits from individuals or businesses when the money is suspected of being used for illicit purposes. Under the BANK SECRECY ACT, financial institutions are required to report cash deposits of $10,000 or more, and multiple deposits from the same depositor adding up to $10,000. Such transactions are reported to the Treasury and the U.S. Secret Service.

The Money Laundering Control Act of 1986 further requires that banks and savings institutions have in place a reporting system to monitor cash transactions under $10,000. Under federal regulations, cash transactions under $10,000 are reportable in certain states.

MONEY MARKET market where short-term debt securities are issued and traded. The money market is an informal network of dealers and institutional investors, rather than an organized market like the New York Stock Exchange. A bank selling certificates of deposit, for instance, is engaged in money market activities. Money market securities are generally short-term, typically less than 90 days, and are highly liquid investments issued by firms with good credit ratings. Participants include government securities dealers, banks and other financial institutions, and managers of money market funds. An important part of the global money market is the Euromarket, a largely unregulated market where financial instruments in various currencies are actively traded outside the country of origin. *See also* MONEY MARKET INSTRUMENTS.

MONEY MARKET CERTIFICATE (MMC) nonnegotiable certificate of deposit with a minimum denomination of $2,500 and an original maturity of at least seven days. Prior to January 1983, when the MMC was deregulated, the account was a six-month CD requiring an initial deposit of $10,000 and paying a rate tied to the yield on six-month U.S. Treasury bills. With deregulation, maturities and rates paid depositors are set by management policy in individual financial institutions. *See also* MONEY MARKET DEPOSIT ACCOUNT; NINETY-DAY SAVINGS ACCOUNT; PASSBOOK; STATEMENT SAVINGS ACCOUNT.

MONEY MARKET DEPOSIT ACCOUNT (MMDA) high-yield savings account authorized by the GARN-ST. GERMAIN DEPOSITORY INSTITUTIONS ACT of 1982 to allow depository financial institutions to be fully competitive with money market mutual funds. The MMDA also called a "money market account," pays a market rate of interest with no regulatory limit so long as the account balance stays above $1,000. When the balance drops below $1,000, the MMDA pays the same rate of interest as a NEGOTIABLE ORDER OF WITHDRAWAL (NOW) account.

Banks and savings institutions have the right to require a seven-day NOTICE OF WITHDRAWAL before approving withdrawals or transfers, but most have waived this requirement. Consequently, MMDA accounts are considered liquid assets, paying rates competitive with money market mutual funds, even though individual bank rates will vary. *See also* MONEY MARKET CERTIFICATE; MONEY MARKET FUND; SUPER NOW ACCOUNT.

MONEY MARKET FUND (MMF) mutual fund that invests in short-term debt instruments, such as acceptances, Treasury bills, commercial paper, and negotiable certificates of deposit. Most funds invest in high-quality paper, although some funds have purchased noninvestment grade securities to offer a better yield. Money market funds, managed by investment companies registered with the Securities and Exchange Commission, typically buy paper with maturities of 60 days or less. A fund sells shares to investors, who receive regular interest payments. The amount of interest earned by an investor depends on several factors, including the general level of interest rates, the management fee or commissions charged by the fund's manager, and whether there are redemption fees present. The fee structure in a money market mutual fund and investment characteristics of the portfolio are spelled out in the fund PROSPECTUS. *See also* MONEY MARKET DEPOSIT ACCOUNT.

MONEY MARKET INSTRUMENTS debt instruments issued by private organizations, governments, and government agencies, generally with maturities of one year or less. Such instruments are highly liquid investments, and include Treasury bills, bankers' acceptances, commercial paper and short-term tax-exempt municipal securities, and negotiable bank CDs. Money market instruments are actively traded in the money center financial markets in New York, London, and Tokyo.

Futures contracts on U.S. Treasury bills and certain other money market instruments are traded in the financial futures markets.

MONEY MARKET PREFERRED STOCK class of PREFERRED STOCK with a floating dividend rate. The dividend is reset every 49 days—the minimum time interval that holders own the stock, while claiming the 70% dividend tax exclusion—by investors who tender bids for the stock at a specific dividend rate. Money market preferred issues are meant to insure that preferred stock issues trade at, or close to par value, but have been known to fail if an offering fails to attract enough bids at the dividend rate desired by the issuer. Under the financial regulators' risk-based capital rules, money market preferred stock does not count toward a bank's Tier 1 capital. *See also* ADJUSTABLE RATE PREFERRED STOCK; TRUST PREFERRED SECURITIES.

MONEY MARKET RATES interest paid depositors who invest in money market instruments or federally insured deposits paying market rates of return. Money rates are reported in daily newspapers, and include such key rates as broker call loans, the federal funds rate, rates on bankers' acceptances, Eurodollar time deposits, the 3-month and 6-month Treasury bill rate, and the LONDON INTERBANK OFFERED RATE (LIBOR).

MONEY MULTIPLIER relationship between the MONETARY BASE and the MONEY SUPPLY. The multiplier explains why the money supply grows as excess reserves are added to the banking system. When a bank makes a loan, it creates money, because part of the loan becomes a new deposit.

In practical terms, banks put money in circulation by extending credit. Assume that a bank makes a $100,000 loan and reserves 10% or $10,000 to meet its Reserve Requirement, depositing $90,000 in the borrower's bank. The borrower's bank sets aside a reserve of $9,000, leaving $81,000 available for another loan and another deposit. If carried to its logical extension, the original $100,000 loan would expand into more than $500,000 in deposits and $400,000 in new loans. *See also* FRACTIONAL RESERVES.

MONEY ORDER instrument of exchange issued for a fee, often used by persons who do not have checking accounts to pay bills or send money to someone in a distant city. Money orders are issued by post offices and financial institutions, usually in amounts under $500, and carry both the payee's name and the payer. Those issued by a bank are drawn on the issuing bank or a correspondent.

MONEY SUPPLY total amount of money available for transactions and investment in the economy. The Federal Reserve Board uses various statistical measures to measure the various forms of money that make up the money supply. The monetary aggregates in the money supply are updated weekly by the Federal Reserve Board.

When the Fed is pursuing an expansive MONETARY POLICY, the central bank adds reserves to the banking system and banks are able to make more loans. This stimulates growth in the money supply, because business borrowers keep part of their loans in the form of bank deposits.

Since 1983, when the monetary aggregates were last revised, the components of the money supply have been the following:

M1: currency held by the public, plus travelers' checks, demand deposits, Negotiable Order of Withdrawal (NOW) accounts, Super NOW accounts, Automatic Transfer of Savings (ATS) accounts, and credit union share drafts.

M2: M1 plus savings and small denomination time deposits, Money Market Deposit Accounts, money market mutual fund shares owned by individual investors.

MONEY TRANSFER *see* WIRE TRANSFER.

MONTHLY COMPOUNDING OF INTEREST *see* COMPOUND INTEREST.

MONTHLY STATEMENT ACCOUNT STATEMENT mailed or sent by electronic mail to a customer that lists debits, credits, service charges, and account adjustments during the prior month. A checking account statement includes a list of checks written, deposits, and electronic debits and credits at an ATM, along with cancelled checks. A credit card statement is a descriptive billing statement listing account charges and finance charges that apply to revolving balances if there is an outstanding balance. A consolidated statement summarizes end of month balances in several accounts as of the date the statement was prepared.

MOODY'S INVESTORS SERVICE investment advisory service that publishes financial manuals analyzing corporate securities that are sold to the public. Moody's also rates the investment quality of commercial paper, and bonds and short-term tax-exempt notes issued by states and municipalities.

Moody's Investment Grade ratings assigned to municipal notes range from MIG1 (best quality) to MIG4 (adequate quality); all four are considered investment quality securities for banks. Moody's ratings on corporate bonds and preferred stocks, plus certain common stocks, are graded from Aaa (highest quality) to Caa (lowest quality). Securities rated Baa or better are considered investment quality.

MORAL HAZARD circumstances increasing the probability of loss, for example when a borrower or a party to a transaction gives misleading financial information or has an incentive to take unusual risks.

MORAL OBLIGATION BOND tax-exempt bond issued by a municipality or state financing authority, secured by revenues from the project financed, plus a nonbinding pledge by the state legislature. In the event that project revenues are insufficient to meet debt service payments, the legislature is authorized to step in and appropriate funds in the future to cover principal and interest payments to bondholders. The state's commitment to service the bonds is moral, rather than contractual, as legislatures have no legal obligation to do so if the original OBLIGOR defaults.

MORAL SUASION persuasion by oral or informal pressure, carried out by central bankers and heads of government agencies to convince bankers to do something, or refrain from doing something. Moral suasion, which stops short of legal remedies and formal rule making, can at times be highly effective because of the ANNOUNCEMENT EFFECT Federal Reserve policy has on the markets.

MORATORIUM

1. condition when a borrower declares inability to repay some or all of an outstanding debt, or ceases paying the debt service—interest—on a loan. If declared by a sovereign borrower, it generally leads to rescheduling of the loan with a longer term. *See also* SOVEREIGN RISK.
2. legal moratorium on a proposed activity, for example the one-year moratorium in the Competitive Equality Banking Act of 1987 on securities underwriting by bank holding company affiliates.

MORTGAGE debt instrument giving conditional ownership of an asset, secured by the asset being financed. The borrower gives the lender a mortgage in exchange for the right to use the property and agrees to make regular payments of principal and interest. The mortgage lien is the lender's security interest and is recorded in title documents in public land records. The lien is removed when the debt is paid in full. A mortgage normally involves real estate and is a long-term debt, normally 25 to 30 years, but can be written for much shorter periods.

Originally written exclusively as fixed-rate fully amortizing loans, mortgages have evolved into more flexible contracts. Since the mid-1970s, the financial industry's funding sources have become more volatile and market sensitive. Legislation and regulation have relaxed the prohibitions on alternative types of mortgage financing, such as variable rate and adjustable rate mortgages. Recent innovations in packaging of mortgage loans for resale in the SECONDARY MORTGAGE MARKET to investors have helped to create a national market for mortgage lending and a wide variety of synthetic financial instruments, such as the COLLATERALIZED MORTGAGE OBLIGATION, a multiclass security consisting of several different mortgage-backed bonds that have payment characteristics quite different from the mortgages securing the bonds.

See also ADJUSTABLE RATE MORTGAGE; ALTERNATIVE MORTGAGE INSTRUMENT; BALLOON MORTGAGE; BIWEEKLY MORTGAGE; CHATTEL MORTGAGE; CONVENTIONAL MORTGAGE; DERIVATIVE MORTGAGE-BACKED SECURITIES; GRADUATED PAYMENT MORTGAGE; GROWING EQUITY MORTGAGE; INTEREST-ONLY (IO) SECURITIES; INVERSE FLOATER; LIAR LOAN; MORTGAGE-BACKED BOND; MORTGAGE-BACKED CERTIFICATE; MORTGAGE-BACKED SECURITIES; NEGATIVE AMORTIZATION; PORTABLE MORTGAGE; PRICE LEVEL ADJUSTED MORTGAGE; PRINCIPAL-ONLY (PO) STRIP;

REVERSE MORTGAGE; ROLLOVER MORTGAGE; SHARED APPRECIATION MORTGAGE; ZERO COUPON MORTGAGE.

MORTGAGE-BACKED BOND bond collateralized by a pledge of mortgages and payable from the issuer's general funds. Because the market value of the collateral must exceed the outstanding bond principal, additional collateral may be required if the market value of the underlying mortgages declines. Unlike mortgage pass-through securities, which convey an ownership interest in a pool of mortgages, ownership of a mortgage-backed bond (and usually servicing rights) is retained by the issuer, although mortgage servicing can be sold, at a price, to a third party. Also, for tax purposes, mortgage-backed bonds are treated as issuer debt rather than as a sale of assets. Mortgage-backed bonds also have a more predictable maturity than pass-through securities, thus giving the bondholder a kind of call protection against early redemption. *See also* PAY-THROUGH SECURITY.

MORTGAGE-BACKED CERTIFICATE *See* MODIFIED PASS-THROUGH CERTIFICATE.

MORTGAGE-BACKED SECURITIES investment grade securities backed by a pool of mortgages or trust deeds. Principal and interest payments on the underlying mortgages are used to pay semiannual interest and principal on the securities. Income from the principal and interest payments on the underlying mortgages are used to pay off the bonds.

Most mortgage-backed securities, such as COLLATERALIZED MORTGAGE OBLIGATIONS and REAL ESTATE MORTGAGE INCOME CONDUITS, consist of multiclass obligations that are divided into different classes of bonds to appeal to different investor needs. Because some mortgage pools will pay off faster than others, mortgaged-backed securities are typically issued as a series of several different bonds, each having a different maturity date. *See also* PAY-THROUGH SECURITY.

MORTGAGE BANKER *See* MORTGAGE ORIGINATOR.

MORTGAGE BANKERS ASSOCIATION OF AMERICA *see* TRADE ASSOCIATION.

MORTGAGE BROKER *See* MORTGAGE ORIGINATOR.

MORTGAGE CASH FLOW OBLIGATION multiclass paythrough bond, similar to a COLLATERALIZED MORTGAGE OBLIGATION (CMO). Payments received on a mortgage pool are applied to paying principal and interest on the obligation. Mortgage cash flow obligations differ from CMOs; investors rely on the issuer's contractual obligation to use the cash flow from the mortgage principal and reinvestment income to meet debt service payments on the bonds.

MORTGAGE CONDUIT *see* CONDUIT.

MORTGAGE DISCOUNT amount paid in advance by a mortgagor, computed as a percentage of the loan principal. This is also called

DISCOUNT POINT, points, or *new loan fee*. Points, usually paid at the mortgage closing, increase the lender's yield from the mortgage loan.

MORTGAGEE lender who arranges mortgage financing, collects the loan payments, and takes a SECURITY INTEREST in the property financed.

MORTGAGE INSURANCE contract insuring a mortgage lender against default risk. Mortgage insurance allows a borrower to purchase a home with a down payment as low as 3 to 5% of the purchase price—even less for qualified borrowers—instead of the usual 20% down payment lenders normally require. Insurance premiums are paid by the borrower. The Federal Housing Administration, an agency in the Department of Housing and Urban Development, insures mortgages on one-to-four-family houses and condominiums, and it reimburses the mortgage lender if default occurs. Mortgage insurance purchased from a commercial insurance carrier is known as PRIVATE MORTGAGE INSURANCE.

MORTGAGE INTEREST DEDUCTION *see* TAX DEDUCTIBLE INTEREST.

MORTGAGE MODIFICATION process of adjusting of a mortgage loan's principal, interest, or other terms outside those originally negotiated at loan closing, usually done to avoid loan default or foreclosure. Mortgages are modified by reducing the interest rate, changing to a fixed rate loan interest from a floating rate, lengthening the loan term, reducing the loan principal, forgiving late fees or penalties, or capping monthly payments at a percentage of household income. An example is the Home Affordable Modification Program (HAMP), created by the Financial Stability Act of 2009. The HAMP program was a cooperative effort by banks, mortgage servicers, credit unions, and various federal agencies to create standard guidelines for mortgage modifications. Also called *recasting*.

MORTGAGE NOTE written promise to repay a mortgage loan plus interest. The MORTGAGE gives the lender a security interest in the mortgaged property. The mortgage note is the PROMISSORY NOTE stating the principal amount due, the rate of interest, and the terms for repayment of the funds advanced. The borrower (the MORTGAGOR) signing the note, and any cosigners, are personally liable for repayment of the debt.

MORTGAGE ORIGINATOR Person who works with a borrower to complete a mortgage financing. *Mortgage brokers* have access to a large number of lenders, and they offer the most choices in mortgage loan programs. The broker is paid a fee by the borrower or lender at loan closing and does not service the loan (collect principal and interest payments). *Mortgage bankers* originate loans and sell their loan production to institutional investors in the secondary mortgage market. They may also receive loan principal and interest payments, acting as servicer for the investor owning the mortgage note.

Starting in 2011, residential mortgage originators employed by a federally insured or supervised financial institution must register with the NATIONWIDE MORTGAGE LICENSING SYSTEM AND REGISTRY. Mortgage brokers employed by nonbank mortgage firms must obtain licenses from their state banking department, pass a background check, and take continuing education courses.

The registry, authorized by the Secure and Fair Enforcement for Mortgage Licensing Act of 2008 (SAFE Act) of 2008, was created to curb mortgage fraud and set nationwide professional standards for mortgage originators.

MORTGAGE POOL group of residential mortgage loans classified by original maturity date and type of mortgage (i.e., fixed rate conventional, adjustable rate) for sale to investors in the SECONDARY MORTGAGE MARKET.

MORTGAGE REIT REAL ESTATE INVESTMENT TRUST that supplies funds to the residential housing market by lending capital to real estate developers. Mortgage REITS borrow from banks and institutional investors and relend to developers at a higher interest rate, and frequently take equity participations in the cash flow income from the projects they finance.

MORTGAGE REVENUE BOND tax-exempt bonds issued by state and local governments and by state housing finance agencies to finance the sale or repair of single family homes. These offer below market financing to income-qualified borrowers. Also called *mortgage subsidy bond.*

MORTGAGE SERVICING *see* SERVICING.

MORTGAGE SWAP exchange of mortgage loans for participation certificates or pass-through securities backed by the same mortgages. Mortgage lenders, swap mortgages with FANNIE MAE or FREDDIE MAC, acquiring securities guaranteed by the federal mortgage agencies to improve ASSET QUALITY in loan portfolios, obtain acceptable collateral for REPURCHASE AGREEMENTS and REVERSE REPURCHASE AGREEMENTS, take low-rate assets off the balance sheet, or for other reasons.

MORTGAGOR borrower in a mortgage contract who mortgages the property in exchange for a loan and gives the title to the property to the MORTGAGEE.

MULTIBANK HOLDING COMPANY *see* BANK HOLDING COMPANY.

MULTICURRENCY NOTE FACILITY short-term or medium-term EURONOTE financing denominated in several currencies. The facility allows the borrower to choose the currencies to draw in successive rollover periods, when the loan is refinanced. It is the riskiest credit facility for the borrower, because the lender has the right to set the currency in which the loan will be paid off. The loan will reprice periodically, say every six months, in different currencies, depending on the lender's perception of currency risk in the transaction.

MULTILATERAL DEVELOPMENT BANK international financial institutions organized to provide financial and technical assistance to foster economic development in less developed countries. They are financed by member contributions and borrowings in the world financial markets. In terms of scope they may be global (the World Bank Group), regional (the Latin American Development Bank or Asian Development Bank), or specialized institutions (the Caribbean Development Bank or the East African Development Bank).

MULTILATERAL NETTING *see* NETTING.

MULTINATIONAL CORPORATION corporation owning subsidiary companies operating in several countries. A generally accepted definition is a corporation or enterprise that derives at least 25% of its annual sales from facilities outside its country of origin. Developing countries, including the NEWLY INDUSTRIALIZED COUNTRIES, have also encouraged formation of multinational corporations on their soil. Many multinationals are chartered in tax haven countries for trading and investing on a global basis.

MULTIPLE OPTIONS FUNDING FACILITY (MOFF) medium-term Euronote financing allowing the borrower to choose from several funding options, i.e., a medium-term project financing allowing the option of using different guidelines for pricing, such as prime rate, banker's acceptance rate, and Eurodollar rate. Such options, however, must be listed clearly in the original loan agreement.

MUNICIPAL BOND debt instrument that is an obligation of a state or municipality, and also political subdivisions and agencies of these governments. There are several classifications of municipal bonds, including a GENERAL OBLIGATION BOND and a REVENUE BOND. Special assessment bonds are bonds payable from assessments from benefitted property owners, covering such things as streets and sidewalks. A special tax bond is a bond issued for a special purpose, for which proceeds of a special tax are pledged, but not the taxing authority of the issuer. Water and other utility bonds are payable primarily from utility revenues, but are also supported by taxing authority—so-called double barreled obligations.

Certain classes of municipal bonds issued after August 1986, called PRIVATE PURPOSE BONDS, are fully taxable bonds if, for example, more than 10% of the proceeds from the bond issue are used for private development (as opposed to public improvements, such as highway development), and the debt service is paid by private business organizations. *See also* INDUSTRIAL DEVELOPMENT BOND; PRIVATE PURPOSE BOND; PUBLIC PURPOSE BOND.

MUNICIPAL BOND INSURANCE financial guarantee protecting a municipal bond issue against default risk. Coverage is purchased from a number of private insurance companies, such as AMBAC Assurance Corporation, and MBIA Insurance Corporation. Bonds insured by these firms, which offer to purchase the bonds at par in event default occurs, enjoy an AAA rating, enabling government agencies to issue bonds at a lower cost. Insured bonds ordinarily have a lower yield than uninsured bonds as the cost of insurance typically is passed on to the holder. When a bond defaults, it is paid off immediately so that even if principal is recovered, interest from the date of default to maturity is not earned. *See also* FINANCIAL GUARANTEE.

MUNICIPAL NOTE short-term debt instrument, generally with a maturity of less than one year, issued by state or local government, and repayable from the general fund of the issuer or a defined revenue source. Notes are issued for a variety of purposes: revenue anticipation notes and tax anticipation notes help the issuer overcome a cash flow shortage. *See also* BOND ANTICIPATION NOTE; TAX ANTICIPATION NOTE.

MUNICIPAL REVENUE BOND *see* REVENUE BOND.

MUNICIPAL SECURITIES RULEMAKING BOARD (MSRB) self-regulatory organization established by the 1975 amendments to the SECURITIES ACT OF 1934. The board sets rules for trading of municipal bonds by broker-dealers and bank dealers, and provides an arbitration service. Its rules are approved by the Securities and Exchange Commission and enforced by the National Association of Securities Dealers and bank regulatory agencies. Its 15-member board is comprised of securities firms, bank dealers, and the public, each having equal representation.

MUTUAL ASSOCIATION nonstock financial institutions, such as a SAVINGS AND LOAN ASSOCIATION, that is owned by savers holding claim to funds on deposit, who are known as *members*. Members have no claim to the earnings of the association, but elect directors to its board of trustees. Other forms of mutual associations are credit unions, mutual savings banks, and cooperative banks.

MUTUAL COMPANY nonstock savings bank, insurance company, or savings and loan. The term also has been used in reference to open-end investment companies, which are also known as MUTUAL FUNDS. In a mutual company, profits, after deduction of business expenses, are set aside for the benefit of the depositors of a financial institution, and the policyholders of a mutual insurance company, or are held as surplus reserves to maintain liquidity.

MUTUAL FUND investment company that pools money from its shareholders in stocks, bonds, government securities, and short-term money market instruments. Mutual funds can also invest in other marketable assets, such as futures, options, and collectibles. A mutual fund is also known as an open-end investment company, meaning that there is a continuous offering of new shares and redemption of outstanding shares.

When shares are sold, the fund's capitalization increases; it decreases when shares are redeemed by investors. (Unlike a CLOSED-END FUND, shares are not traded on organized exchanges.) The owners of a mutual fund own proportional shares in the entire pool of securities in which the fund invests, and pay taxes on distributions from the fund. Most mutual fund shares are redeemable at current NET ASSET VALUE, although some have a BACK-END LOAD or redemption charge when shares are liquidated. In any mutual fund, the value of shares owned depends on current market value of the portfolio, which is generally repriced daily. *See also* ANNUITY; MONEY MARKET FUND.

MUTUAL MORTGAGE INSURANCE FUND government sponsored mortgage insurance administered by the FEDERAL HOUSING ADMINISTRATION, which insures mortgage loans on one- to four-family residential housing. The plan is designed to be self-funding, the FHA collects premiums from mortgagors and pays lender claims on losses from mortgage defaults. *See also* PRIVATE MORTGAGE INSURANCE.

MUTUAL SAVINGS BANK (MSB) state chartered nonstock savings institution that accepts deposits from individuals and primarily makes residential mortgage loans. Management is by a board of trustees. These savings institutions offer checking and other transaction account services, and may also originate consumer loans, commercial loans, and commercial mortgages, and invest in limited amounts of corporate bonds and corporate stock. State banking departments are the primary regulators of mutual savings institutions. *See also* FEDERAL SAVINGS BANK.

MUTUAL WILLS separate wills by two people, with similar language, for example, by husband and wife, each naming the other as beneficiary of his or her estate, or naming a common beneficiary.

N

NAIRA monetary unit of Nigeria.

NAKED OPTION option written by a buyer or seller who does not own the underlying asset; either a LONG POSITION by the writer of a call option or a SHORT POSITION by the writer of a put option. Naked options can be written for securities, currencies, commodities, and indexes, and have limited profit potential and unlimited risk, although the holder's risk is limited to the life of the option. Writers of naked options assume a higher level of risk, along with greater profit potential.

NAKED POSITION market position of someone holding an unhedged position. An example is someone holding an outright LONG POSITION or SHORT POSITION in financial futures that is not hedged by an offsetting position, SPREAD transaction, or part of an ARBITRAGE deal; also the holder of a NAKED OPTION. The holder is at risk to changes in market prices.

NATIONAL ASSOCIATION when used in a bank's name, indicates a NATIONAL BANK chartered by the Office of the Comptroller of the Currency.

NATIONAL ASSOCIATION OF FEDERAL CREDIT UNIONS (NAFCU) *see* TRADE ASSOCIATION.

NATIONAL ASSOCIATION OF SECURITIES DEALERS (NASD) nonstock membership organization formed under the Securities Act of 1934 to act as primary regulator of securities sold in the OVER-THE-COUNTER market. A self-regulatory organization, NASD issues the rules of fair practice governing practices by broker-dealer firms in the OTC market. Its members include securities broker-dealers and underwriters other than commercial banks. The NASD governs its members in trading policies and procedures, listing of new issues, and customer relations. It also licenses broker-dealers. Bankers who accept customer orders in discount brokerage operations must pass an NASD qualifying examination, and have a NASD Series 7 brokerage license. The NASD also issues suitability guidelines regulating broker-dealer sales of mutual funds and other investment securities.

NATIONAL AUTOMATED CLEARING HOUSE ASSOCIATION (NACHA) *see* TRADE ASSOCIATION.

NATIONAL BANK commercial bank chartered by the COMPTROLLER OF THE CURRENCY, an agency of the U.S. Treasury Department. A national bank is supervised by the Comptroller and is a MEMBER BANK in the Federal Reserve System.

National banks originally came into existence in the 1860s under the National Bank Acts of 1863 and 1864 when the federal government, lacking a uniform national currency, approved the chartering of banks that would issue their own notes (national bank notes) backed by U.S. government bonds, and imposed a 10% tax on bank notes of state chartered banks. (In response to the new federal tax, state chartered banks persuaded their depositors to begin writing checks instead of taking out their money in cash. This practice led to paying bills by check, and the check payment system as we know it today.) National bank notes have been retired from circulation since 1935.

About 30% of U.S. commercial banks have national charters, but national banks have economic power beyond what the numbers indicate, holding more than two-thirds of the total deposits in federally insured commercial banks. National banks are authorized by the GRAMM-LEACH-BLILEY ACT OF 1999 to engage in any activity determined by the Federal Reserve Board to be financial in nature or related to a financial activity, subject to the approval of the Federal Reserve Board. Insurance underwriting, merchant banking and real estate development are, however, specifically excluded.

NATIONAL BANK SURVEILLANCE SYSTEM (NBSS) computerized monitoring system introduced in 1975 by the Office of the Comptroller of the Currency to monitor changes in condition as reported in call reports of national banks. Its quarterly Bank Performance Report compares each bank with banks of similar size to get an accurate picture of bank financial performance.

NATIONAL CREDIT UNION ADMINISTRATION (NCUA) independent federal agency established by federal law in 1970 to charter and supervise federal credit unions. The NCUA is governed by a three-member board, appointed by the president for six-year terms. Its responsibilities include examinations of federal credit unions; management of the National Share Insurance Fund, which provides deposit insurance for federal credit unions and many state credit unions; and the CENTRAL LIQUIDITY FACILITY, a source of short-term funds for credit unions. The chairman of the NCUA is a member of the policy coordinating body of federal financial regulators, the FEDERAL FINANCIAL INSTITUTIONS EXAMINATION COUNCIL.

NATIONAL CURRENCY any approved currency (monetary unit) issued by a central bank or monetary authority as the official unit of account for valuation of foreign exchange and payment of debts. In the United States, Federal Reserve Notes issued by the Federal Reserve Banks are the official national currency. *See also* LEGAL TENDER.

NATIONAL HOUSING ACT federal act in 1934 creating the FEDERAL HOUSING ADMINISTRATION providing mortgage insurance and below-market financing for home buyers, and the FEDERAL SAVINGS AND LOAN INSURANCE CORPORATION. FHA mortgage insurance protects against default risk in mortgage loans with loan-to-value ratios up to 80%, and mortgages amortized by periodic payments over a 30-year term. FHA-insured mortgage loans are purchased in the secondary market by the GOVERNMENT NATIONAL MORTGAGE ASSOCIATION.

NATIONWIDE MORTGAGE LICENSING SYSTEM AND REGISTRY (NMLSR) database created in 2004 for residential mortgage originators employed by banks, savings associations, credit unions, and bank lenders affiliated with the Farm Credit System. The SAFE Act of 2008 (Secure and Fair Enforcement for Mortgage Licensing Act) requires mortgage originators to pass a background and fingerprint check and to take continuing education courses to maintain their registration. The NMLSR registry is owned and operated by the State Regulatory Registry LLC (SRR), a wholly owned subsidiary of the Conference of State Bank Supervisors. Web site: *http://mortgage.nationwidelicensingsystem.org.*

NATURAL GUARDIAN parent, either the father or mother, recognized by law as the lawful guardian, as opposed to an appointed guardian, who is named by a court or a will to care for a child under legal age.

NEAREST MONTH nearest active trading month of a financial futures market, as opposed to FURTHEST MONTH. Also called *nearby month.*

NEAR MONEY liquid assets, such as time deposits, Treasury bills, and other short-term government securities, that are easily converted to cash on short notice. Near money is, however, excluded from the narrowest definition of the MONEY SUPPLY, because, unlike checking accounts and cash, it does not function as a medium of exchange in everyday purchases of goods and services.

NEGATIVE AMORTIZATION increase in the PRINCIPAL of a loan, when the loan payments are insufficient to pay the interest due. The unpaid interest is added to the outstanding loan balance, so the principal increases, rather than decreases, as payments are made. This situation typically occurs in an ADJUSTABLE RATE MORTGAGE with an ANNUAL CAP limiting any increases in the interest rate, and also in a GRADUATED PAYMENT MORTGAGE (GPM), which has low initial payments so moderate-income borrowers can afford to make the loan payments. Negative amortization can occur on a potential basis (when deferred interest exceeds borrower optional payment caps) or scheduled basis (provided for by loan documents).

NEGATIVE AUTHORIZATION approval of a bank card transaction in which the customer's account number is compared against a list of cancelled accounts numbers. This file is called a *negative file.* The opposite is POSITIVE AUTHORIZATION, in which each request for authorization is checked against the account holder's transaction file.

NEGATIVE CARRY

1. funding gap that occurs when interest earned on a loan is less than lender's COST OF FUNDS. This is also called *negative cost of carry.* Though rare today, such a situation occurred in the early 1980s when mortgage lenders made fixed rate mortgages at rates below rates paid depositors. In many states, lenders were restrained by usury ceilings from charging higher interest rates.

2. situation where the net yield on a dealer's inventory, or a mortgage banker's loan portfolio, is less than the interest rate paid to finance the assets owned. For example, a bond yielding 10% purchased with funds borrowed at 12%. The opposite is POSITIVE CARRY.

NEGATIVE CONVEXITY *see* CONVEXITY.

NEGATIVE GAP repricing or duration mismatch in which interest sensitive liabilities exceed interest sensitive assets. A bank whose interest sensitive liabilities reprice more quickly than interest sensitive assets is said to be liability sensitive.

NEGATIVE PLEDGE clause in a bond INDENTURE whereby the issuing corporation or government agrees not to pledge assets, unless the holders of bonds or debentures are at least equally secured. Also called *covenant of equal coverage.*

NEGATIVE VERIFICATION auditing system whereby a letter regarding balances, loans, or other information is sent to a bank's customer. A reply is called for only if there is a difference between the information reported by the bank and the customer's own records. The information is assumed to be correct, unless the customer disagrees and responds in ten business days.

NEGATIVE YIELD CURVE *see* INVERTED YIELD CURVE.

NEGOTIABLE CERTIFICATE OF DEPOSIT large-denomination CERTIFICATE OF DEPOSIT ($100,000 to $1 million or more) issued by a commercial bank. Negotiable CDs are issued as interest-bearing time deposits, paying the holder a fixed amount of interest at maturity. These negotiable instruments are typically held by wealthy individuals, insurance companies, and financial institutions. Maturities vary from 14 days to 12 months, with the average maturity being about 3 months. Negotiable CDs cannot be cashed before the maturity date. Negotiable CDs also have been issued in discount form, paying the holder the face value at maturity.

NEGOTIABLE INSTRUMENT written order to pay, such as an acceptance, check, bill of exchange, or promissory note, transferable from one person to another, provided certain conditions are met. When a person cashes a check, he negotiates the check by signing his name on the back and presenting it to a bank, thereby becoming the legal owner of funds represented by the writing on the face of the check. He may take the funds as cash or deposit the money into an account. Checks are negotiable by ENDORSEMENT and delivery (also called PRESENTMENT) to the paying bank, which is then obligated to pay the check. If an instrument is payable to the bearer, for example, a bearer stock or bearer bond, negotiation is done by simply presenting the instrument.

Under Article 3 of the UNIFORM COMMERCIAL CODE, an instrument is negotiable if it is: (1) a written instrument signed by the endorser or maker; (2) an unconditional promise to pay a certain amount of money, either on demand or at a future date; and (3) payable to the holder or bearer. A person who becomes a HOLDER IN DUE COURSE of a negotiable instrument by delivery, or by delivery and endorsement, has an unrestricted claim to the instrument, and can sue other people in his or her own name.

See also CHECK; DEMAND DEPOSIT; DISHONOR; DRAFT; NOTICE OF WITHDRAWAL; PROTEST; THIRD PARTY CHECK; WRONGFUL DISHONOR.

NEGOTIABLE ORDER OF WITHDRAWAL (NOW) ACCOUNT interest-bearing transaction account that combines the payable on demand feature of checks and investment feature of savings accounts. A NOW account is functionally an interest paying checking account. The NOW account began in Massachusetts in 1974 when mutual savings banks offered interest bearing transaction accounts (NOW accounts) to compete with commercial banks. These accounts, which paid a rate of interest equivalent to that of passbook savings accounts, were authorized nationwide for all depository institutions by the 1980 Monetary Control Act. *See also* SUPER NOW ACCOUNT.

NEGOTIATED UNDERWRITING sale of securities through exclusive bid by an underwriter, as opposed to COMPETITIVE BID underwriting by several underwriting groups. In negotiated underwriting, the MANAGING UNDERWRITER and the securities issuer agree on the spread, or the difference between the purchase price and the initial public offering price. This form of underwriting is most common in municipal revenue bonds, corporate bonds, and common stock offerings, whereas the alternative, competitive bid underwriting, is preferred—and sometimes required by statute or regulation—in municipal general obligation bonds.

NEST EGG savings account holding funds that are not needed for immediate spending, also known as *rainy day money*. Ordinarily put in time savings account earning a market rate of interest.

NET ASSET VALUE (NAV)

1. in MUTUAL FUNDS, the per share value of assets in a fund, computed by subtracting liabilities from the portfolio value of securities held, plus cash and accrued earnings, and dividing the total by the number of outstanding shares. This is the value all shareholders would receive if all issued shares were redeemed. In a NO-LOAD FUND, this value is the bid price quoted in the mutual fund listings in daily newspapers. In a LOAD FUND, the bid price is figured by adding the sales commission to the NAV. Mutual funds compute net asset value daily, based on closing prices on the previous business day. The asked or offered column in tables in a mutual fund prospectus shows the price after load is added.
2. tangible book net worth of a corporation's securities, usually stated as net value per share. For example, the book value of common stock is the difference between the accounting value of outstanding

stock and all liabilities plus intangibles, such as GOODWILL and DEPRECIATION, divided by the number of shares issued. This value, also called *tangible book value*, also is computed for bonds, preferred stock, and so on, and is unrelated to market value.

NET BALANCE *see* PAYOFF STATEMENT.

NET BORROWED RESERVES statistical measure indicating a shortage of reserves in the banking system. A net borrowed reserves position always is expressed as a negative number, meaning there are more funds borrowed at the Federal Reserve than EXCESS RESERVES available for bank lending. A higher number signals tighter Federal Reserve credit policy and potentially rising interest rates. The opposite is NET FREE RESERVES.

NET CHARGE-OFF gross amount of loans charged off as bad debt, less recoveries collected from earlier charge-offs. Net charge-offs are computed as a percentage of gross loans outstanding recorded, less unearned income and LOAN LOSS RESERVES for charged-off loans. Poor credit quality loans that are not worth keeping on the books are purged from the loan portfolio, usually monthly or quarterly. A minus sign before the net charge off amount means recoveries have exceeded charge-offs for an accounting period.

NET FREE RESERVES statistical measure indicating a surplus of reserves in the banking system, meaning that the Federal Reserve Board is pursuing an easy money policy and that interest rates may ease a bit, or stay about the same. Contrast with NET BORROWED RESERVES.

NET INTEREST COST (NIC) total interest cost of an offering to a bond issuer, including both coupon interest and premium or discount, and usually expressed as the total interest to maturity, using a straight line arithmetic computation that does not factor in the time value of money. The formula for calculating net interest cost is: Total Coupon Interest Payment + Discount (or – Premium) / Bond Maturity in years.

NET INTEREST MARGIN (NIM) percentage difference between the interest income produced by a bank's earning assets (loans and investments) and its major expense—interest paid to its depositors. The net difference between interest earned and interest paid is a key measure of bank profitability.

NET INTEREST YIELD *see* NET INTEREST MARGIN.

NET OPERATING INCOME (NOI) earnings reported by a bank or bank holding company, after deducting normal operating expenses, but before taking gains or losses from sale of securities, other losses and charge-offs, and additions to the reserve account for possible loan losses. Normally, NOI refers to earnings before federal income taxes are paid. Also called *net earnings* or *net income.*

NET PAYOFF *see* PAYOFF STATEMENT.

NET SETTLEMENT in electronic payment systems, settlement of interbank transactions on a net, end-of-day, basis between reserve accounts of banks participating in a clearinghouse. Credit and debit transactions are recorded on the clearinghouse books throughout the business day; final settlement of the net transactions—credits, less debits—occurs when funds due a bank are credited to its reserve account by a Federal Reserve Bank.

NETTING written contract to settle mutual obligations at the net value of the contracts, as opposed to the gross dollar value. Thus, two banks owing each other $10 million and $12 million, respectively, might agree to value their mutual obligation at $2 million (the net difference between $10 million and $12 million) for accounting purposes. There are various forms of netting in banking: *bilateral netting,* an agreement by two parties to settle contracts at net value; *multilateral netting*, a netting arrangement with a third party acting as a central clearinghouse; and *netting by novation,* in which a new agreement replaces an existing contract. *See also* NOVATION.

NETWORK terminals, computers, and processors connected together by telephone lines or cable for the purpose of approving financial transactions. Among the numerous bank-to-bank networks are, AUTOMATED TELLER MACHINE (ATM) networks, which are electronic banking systems comprising numerous ATMs, each connected directly or indirectly to a central computer facility called a SWITCH that routes transactions to the appropriate bank for approval and posting to customer accounts. Other examples of banking networks are AUTOMATED CLEARING HOUSE networks, electronic POINT-OF-SALE systems, the Federal Reserve's FEDERAL WIRE (FED WIRE), and the CLEARING HOUSE INTERBANK PAYMENTS SYSTEM (CHIPS). *See also* FUNDS TRANSFER; SOCIETY FOR WORLDWIDE INTERBANK FINANCIAL TELECOMMUNICATION (SWIFT).

NET WORTH owner's equity in a business, computed as accounting assets, less liabilities. In a depository financial institution, it is generally identical to CAPITAL, and includes capital, surplus and undivided profits in a stockholder-owned institution, and general reserves in a mutual institution. Net worth in a stockholder-owned bank often includes common stock, preferred stock, and certain classes of bonds with a MANDATORY CONVERTIBLE feature; they are convertible into common stock equity according to a fixed schedule.

NET WORTH CERTIFICATE capital assistance certificate authorized by the GARN-ST GERMAIN DEPOSITORY INSTITUTIONS ACT of 1982 to help savings institutions increase their equity capital reserves. These promissory notes would be counted as part of the issuer's net worth.

NET YIELD

1. profit (or loss) from an investment, after deducting out-of-pocket costs and reserves for losses.

2. rate of return on a bond, taking into account the purchase price, the coupon rate, and number of years to maturity. Municipal bonds are quoted on a net yield basis. Also called YIELD TO MATURITY.

NEW BALANCE in credit cards, the balance owed after an unpaid balance is carried over from the previous month and new purchases plus finance charges are added.

NEW ISRAELI SHEKEL monetary unit of Israel.

NEWLY INDUSTRIALIZED COUNTRY (NIC) developing country whose economy is supported to a greater or lesser degree on exports from internally generated industrial production (such as Argentina, Brazil, South Korea, Mexico, and Taiwan) versus agricultural products or commodities.

NEW MONEY

1. deposit of funds into a new account, often representing money transferred from another bank.
2. in a U.S. Treasury refunding, the amount by which the par value of securities offered exceeds that of maturing obligations.

NEW YORK CLEARING HOUSE ASSOCIATION oldest and largest bank clearing house in the United States; organized in 1853. The clearing house reorganized in 2004 as the Clearing House Payments Company. *See also* CLEARING HOUSE INTERBANK PAYMENTS SYSTEM.

NEW YORK DOLLARS funds payable in New York City from interest and other charges, from deposit accounts at a New York bank, as in a correspondent banking relationship. Any check payable at a bank in New York City.

NEW YORK FUTURES EXCHANGE *see* FUTURES EXCHANGES.

NEW YORK INTEREST interest computed by the exact number of days in a month, rather than a 30-day month or other combinations. Contrasting is Boston interest, which is ordinary interest computed on the basis of a 30-day month.

NEW YORK MERCANTILE EXCHANGE *see* FUTURES EXCHANGES.

NEW YORK STOCK EXCHANGE (NYSE) largest and oldest stock exchange in the United States. The New York Stock Exchange, also known as the Big Board, is the most influential stock exchange, listing securities of the largest U.S. corporations, including the 30 firms listed in the Dow Jones Industrial Average. The NYSE is a self-regulatory organization with a 20-member board of governors who regulate the trading activities of its 1300 members. *See also* AMERICAN STOCK EXCHANGE.

NEXT DAY FUNDS funds available for withdrawal or transfer the next business day. This is the earliest date that checks cleared through a local clearinghouse association and most AUTOMATED CLEARING HOUSE payments are available for use. Contrast with SAME DAY FUNDS.

NEXT OF KIN person in the nearest blood relationship to a decedent, who inherits the decedent's property, as provided by state law, if there is no will. State laws vary as to whether surviving spouses are considered next of kin.

NICHE bank that services only a segment of the market in its geographic region, or that offers a limited number of services. Community banks are niche banks in the sense that they offer credit and deposit services to local customers, but they rely on correspondent banks for more sophisticated products, such as foreign exchange and letters of credit.

NIGHT CYCLE second operating shift used by regional AUTOMATED CLEARING HOUSE in processing inter-regional ACH transmissions, ordinarily between 10 P.M. and 1:30 A.M. Night cycle processing, commonly used by corporations to move funds into bank CONCENTRATION ACCOUNTS, gives next day funds availability (same day if after midnight).

NIGHT DEPOSITORY bank vault accessible by key for merchant deposits after banking hours and on weekends. Many banks have night collection boxes for deposit of daily cash, checks, and credit card sales drafts. Some even have an AUTOMATED TELLER MACHINE next to the street level depository giving the merchant an on-the-spot transaction receipt. Deposits are later processed by bank employees and credited to the merchant's account.

NINETY-DAY SAVINGS ACCOUNT passbook savings account with an original maturity of exactly 90 days. The rate paid depositors is sometimes linked to the 90-day Treasury bill. Deposits are subject to a 7-day withdrawal notification, and if left on deposit, are rolled over for another term.

NO ACCOUNT check returned by the paying bank to the originating bank (the drawee bank) because the check writer has no account to pay checks presented for collection.

NO-ACTION LETTER administrative review letter by the Securities and Exchange Commission (SEC). In a no-action letter the agency declines to rule on the legality of a proposed activity, and will not undertake civil or criminal action if the activity takes place as proposed. SEC no-action letters generally are viewed favorably by those requesting comment because it means the agency will not oppose the activity unless the relevant facts change. These letter rulings are specific to each case, and are applicable only to the facts outlined.

NO FUNDS *see* NOT SUFFICIENT FUNDS.

NO-LOAD FUND mutual fund that does not carry a sales commission charge or load. Such funds are typically sold directly by the fund's sponsor and distributor, rather than through broker-dealer networks. Some no-load funds, however, have an annual distribution fee called a 12b-1 fee, that covers advertising and marketing expenses. *See also* 12B-1 MUTUAL FUND.

NOMINAL INTEREST RATE

1. **Banking.** stated rate of interest earned or paid, ignoring compound of interest or other factors. The nominal rate of a SAVINGS ACCOUNT or TIME DEPOSIT is less than the EFFECTIVE ANNUAL YIELD. A mortgage may have a contractual rate of 9%, but an ANNUAL PERCENTAGE RATE (APR) of 9.38% because loan application fees and prepaid DISCOUNT POINTS are included in the computation of the APR.
2. **Investments.** stated rate of interest on an investment or security, without adjusting for inflation or inflationary expectations, as opposed to real interest rates. The real rate of interest is equal to the nominal rate less inflation.

NOMINEE registered owner of a stock or bond if different from the beneficial owner, who acts as holder of record. Typically, this arrangement is done when a broker or trustee holds securities in STREET NAME, or the actual owner may not wish to be identified. Nominee ownership simplifies the registration and transfer of securities held under a corporate name, and often is done by banks, trust companies, custodians, and fiduciaries for institutional or individual clients.

NONACCRUAL LOAN asset, usually a loan, that is not earning the contractual rate of interest in the loan agreement, due to financial difficulties of the borrower. Nonaccrual loans are loans in which interest accruals have been suspended because full collection of principal is in doubt, or interest payments have not been made for a sustained period of time. A reserve for possible loan losses is set aside for these loans, and any payments received from the borrower are applied first to principal, and then to loan interest due. According to the guidelines of banking regulators, a loan with principal and interest unpaid for at least 90 days is considered a nonaccrual loan, unless the lender has adequate collateral. Consumer loans and residential mortgage loans are generally exempted from these guidelines. For bank bookkeeping purposes, a nonaccrual loan is recorded as a CASH BASIS LOAN, that is, a loan in which interest is credited as earned income only when payments are collected from the borrower. *See also* NONPERFORMING ASSET; REAL ESTATE OWNED; RENEGOTIATED LOAN; WORKOUT AGREEMENT.

NONAMORTIZING LOAN *see* INTEREST-ONLY LOAN; NEGATIVE AMORTIZATION.

NONASSUMPTION CLAUSE clause in a mortgage contract prohibiting ASSUMPTION of the mortgage by a third party, at the same rate and payment terms, without the prior approval of the lender. Also known as a DUE ON SALE CLAUSE.

NONBANK BANK type of limited service bank popular in the 1980s. Enactment of the Riegle-Neal Interstate Branching Act of 1994, authorizing nationwide branching and bank acquisitions, eliminated any reason for chartering nonbank banks to gain access to out-of-state markets.

NONBORROWED RESERVES measure of banking system reserves, consisting of TOTAL RESERVES (member bank deposits in Federal Reserve Banks, plus vault cash), less funds borrowed (BORROWED RESERVES) at the Federal Reserve Discount Window. The amount of nonborrowed reserves is computed weekly by the Federal Reserve. *See also* NET FREE RESERVES.

NONCALLABLE bond or preferred stock that cannot be redeemed by the issuer prior to maturity or before a date specified in the bond indenture. Most bonds are noncallable for the first five years, and U.S. Treasury bonds generally cannot be called until they are close to maturity. The bond indenture agreement in most corporate bonds protects holders from loss of income from early redemptions by requiring issuers to pay a premium above par value that is at a maximum at the FIRST CALL DATE and diminishes afterward. In fact, yields on most corporate bonds are quoted from the first date a bond becomes callable. Yield is quoted to the first call date when the trading price is above par and an early call involves loss of principal. *See also* YIELD TO CALL.

NONCASH ITEM check or other negotiable instrument handled as a COLLECTION ITEM, and not credited to the customer's account until payment has been received from the paying bank. For example, checks with special instructions, maturing bankers' acceptances, and foreign checks.

NONCOMPETITIVE BID bid in a U.S. Treasury securities auction that does not require the purchaser to compete with other bidders; also called *noncompetitive tender*. Instead, noncompetitive bids are filled at the weighted average price of competitive bids. Noncompetitive bidding allows smaller investors to take part in Treasury auctions, without having to bid on the same terms as large government securities dealers who make markets in Treasury securities through competitive bids. In Treasury bill auctions, noncompetitive bids range from $10,000, the minimum bid, to as high as $1 million.

NONCONFORMING LOAN SECONDARY MORTGAGE MARKET term referring to residential mortgage loan exceeding the loan size specifications of FANNIE MAE and FREDDIE MAC for purchasing loans in the secondary mortgage market. The conforming loan unit is adjusted annually. Fannie Mae and Freddy Mac are limited by federal law to purchasing loans not exceeding a certain dollar amount.

NONCREDIT SERVICES services performed for corporate customers, or for other banks via a correspondent banking relationship, that do not involve the extension of credit and payment of finance charges.

Such services include check collection, cash management, and trust account services. Noncredit services are a major source of fee income, supplementing interest income earned on outstanding loans.

NONFEASANCE failure to carry out an obligation, such as timely repayment of a loan as called for in a loan agreement. Contrast with MISFEASANCE, the improper performance of a lawful act, and MALFEASANCE, the carrying out of an illegal or improper act.

NONINTEREST EXPENSE salaries, rental of equipment, leases of buildings and equipment, and taxes and other related expenses, including the LOAN LOSS PROVISION for anticipated bad debt. Noninterest expenses are the fixed operating costs in a bank, which may be offset by fee income from loan originations, late charges on loans, annual fees, and credit facility fees, or through noncredit services.

NONINTEREST INCOME net income derived from fee-based banking services, such as corporate cash management, check collection, and consumer annual fees on credit cards, and also monthly service charges on deposit accounts. Also included are many new activities, such as fees from mutual fund commissions, investment advisor fees in merger and acquisition activities, and securities underwriting fees.

NONLEGAL INVESTMENTS securities that do not conform to the statutory requirements—the legal list investments approved by state banking departments—for mutual savings banks and for trust companies. These are generally sub-investment quality securities.

NONMEMBER BANK commercial bank, savings bank, or savings and loan association that is not a member of the Federal Reserve System. Nonmember banks must maintain a portion of their transaction accounts and time deposits at a Federal Reserve Bank to meet RESERVE REQUIREMENTS. They have access to the Federal Reserve DISCOUNT WINDOW and other Fed services on the same terms as Federal Reserve member banks. Contrast with MEMBER BANK.

NONMONETARY TRANSACTION any transaction that does not have a dollar value or result in a transfer of funds, such as a change of name or address, an AUTOMATED CLEARING HOUSE (ACH) notification of change in a customer's bank account information.

NONNOTIFICATION LOAN full recourse loan that is securitized by accounts receivable. The borrower is not notified that the account has been pledged as loan collateral. If the receivables are not paid, the borrower is still liable for repayment of the loan.

NONPAR ITEM check that a paying bank honors at a discount from its par value (face value) when presented by another bank for collection. Nonpar banking, or the practice of discounting drafts and notes drawn on other banks, was commonplace until the Federal Reserve Check Collection System was created in 1916.

NONPERFORMING ASSET loan that is not paying principal and interest according to the original terms of the borrower's loan agreement, plus loans and leases with renegotiated terms and real estate acquired through foreclosure. The total of nonperforming assets usually is expressed as a percentage of the lender's total loan portfolio.

There are various definitions of this term, depending on the loan involved, and the lender's policy. When the principal and interest payments on a loan are past due by 90 days or more, the loan is said to be nonperforming, and the borrower is in a state of DEFAULT. Before a loan gets to that stage, however, a lender usually takes action to protect his security interest, by asking for more collateral or even demanding payment in full. *See also* DELINQUENCY; NONACCRUAL LOAN; WORKOUT AGREEMENT.

NONPERSONAL TIME DEPOSIT time deposits, including money market deposit accounts, held by a depositor other than an individual. The term includes savings accounts owned by corporations, deposits representing the proceeds of a banker's acceptance, deposits owned by Edge Act and Agreement Corporations, and deposits owned by foreign banks. These deposits may be subject to RESERVE REQUIREMENTS under Federal Reserve REGULATION D.

NONPOSSESSORY LIEN *see* LIEN.

NONPURPOSE LOAN bank loan, collateralized by pledge of securities, in which the proceeds are to be used for purposes other than purchase of stocks or bonds. Banks are required by Regulation U to have a borrower execute a purpose statement regardless of the use of the loan, whenever a loan is secured directly or indirectly by securities in a margin account.

NONRECOURSE term referring to the absence of any legal claim against a seller or prior endorser. The seller (or the endorser of a check or other NEGOTIABLE INSTRUMENT) is not liable or otherwise responsible for payment to the holder. The absence of recourse is a key element in determining whether a sale of assets is actually a sale for tax and accounting purposes and a transfer of ownership from seller to buyer.

NONRECOURSE LOAN

1. loan where the lender's source of repayment is the cash flow generated by a project financed by the loan or the collateral securing the loan. The nonrecourse form of financing commonly is used in FACTORING of accounts receivable. The lender fully assumes the credit risk. If the borrower defaults, the lender's only recourse is to foreclose on the collateral backing the loan; the borrower is not liable personally for repayment. In a nonrecourse mortgage loan, for example, the lender must look to the collateral, rather than the borrower, as the ultimate source of repayment.
2. dealer FLOOR PLANNING arrangement in which the liability of the dealer, for example, an auto dealer, is limited to warranties about the gen-

uineness of the paper offered for sale, vehicle title, and so on. The dealer cannot be required to buy back defaulted installment contracts from the lender, as he or she would be required in RECOURSE financing.

3. agricultural loan in which the lender is legally barred from taking action against the borrower if the loan collateral (the farmer's crop), is insufficient to repay the loan. This type of financing is done through the federal government's direct loan program for farmers.

NONRECURRING GAIN (OR LOSS) any profit or expense that is not likely to occur again, as when a bank is liquidating a business or divesting an investment portfolio and writes off a portion of the uncapitalized expenses, or sells its headquarters building and records the resulting capital gain in the quarter in which the transaction occurred. A nonrecurring gain is a one-time event in accounting terms. If an expense item, it is sometimes called an extraordinary charge.

NONREVOLVER

1. bank credit card customer who pays a credit card bill in full every month, within the allowed GRACE PERIOD, thereby avoiding finance charges. Also called a *convenience* cardholder, because the credit card is being used as a convenient substitute for cash or checks.
2. LINE OF CREDIT that can be drawn only once, unlike a revolving line of credit that can be drawn against, and repaid, any number of times while in effect.

NO PROTEST instructions by one bank to another bank not to object to items in case of nonpayment. The sending bank stamps on the face of the item the letters NP. If it cannot be collected, the paying bank returns the item without objection.

NORMAL YIELD CURVE graph showing longer-maturity debt instruments paying out higher yields than short-term debt instruments; also known as a POSITIVE YIELD CURVE.

NOSTRO ACCOUNT *our account* in Latin, meaning an account kept by a bank or company in the currency of the country where the money is held, with the equivalent dollar amount noted in another column. Contrast with VOSTRO ACCOUNT.

NOTARY PUBLIC public officer authorized to administer oaths and witness documents, such as affidavits, property conveyances, and protest notices as when a bank refuses to honor a negotiable instrument. A notary's seal authenticates a document.

NOTE

1. legal evidence of a debt or obligation; A financial instrument consisting of a promise to pay (PROMISSORY NOTE), rather than an order to pay, a bill of exchange, or a certificate of indebtedness, a BOND.
2. dishonored bill of exchange presented by a notary, and if still not paid or accepted, it is *noted.*

NOTE ISSUANCE FACILITY (NIF) revolving credit arrangement in the Euromarket, whereby the borrower issues short-term promissory notes (Euronotes) in its own name, generally with maturities of three to six months. A group of underwriting banks guarantees the availability of funds by agreeing to purchase any unsold notes at each ROLLOVER date, or by writing a standby line of credit. NIFs offer companies the flexibility of short-term financing. The revolving line of credit is often negotiated through a single bank that in turn sells participations to other members of the underwriting syndicate. *See also* REVOLVING UNDERWRITING FACILITY; STANDBY NOTE ISSUANCE FACILITY; TENDER PANEL.

NOTE NOTICE notice of a maturing loan, stating the amount due, the maturity date, and collateral pledged, that a lender mails as a reminder to the borrower several days before the maturity date; also called *notice of maturity*. Typically, the lender may notify the borrower ten days before the loan matures and becomes payable in full.

NOTICE OF DISHONOR declaration signed by a notary public that a check, draft, or bill of exchange has been presented for collection and the drawee bank declines to make payment. *See also* PROTEST.

NOTICE OF WITHDRAWAL written notice of a depositor's intention to withdraw funds from an interest bearing account. Banks may require customers to give notice seven days before withdrawals from time deposit accounts, and also Negotiable Order of Withdrawal (NOW) accounts. Most banks, however, waive the notice requirement in NOW accounts.

NOTICE TO CREDITORS written notice posted in newspapers asking creditors of an estate, or a debtor, to present their claims in court. A notice to creditors is filed in bankruptcy proceedings and in adjudication of estates. In a bankruptcy case, notice to creditors precedes the first meeting of creditors, where creditors who are owed payment are invited to present their claims.

NOTIONAL PRINCIPAL principal balance underlying a SWAP transaction, and the amount used to compute swap payments in an INTEREST RATE SWAP or CURRENCY SWAP. Once the obligation to pay interest is separated from the principal on the underlying security, it becomes a notional amount, and is the fictitious principal generating the cash flows in a swap agreement. The two parties to a swap agreement trade the cash flow yield, not the notional amount. Interest payments accrue as with any ordinary interest-bearing security, even though the investor in fact receives only interest payments.

NOT SUFFICIENT FUNDS (NSF) check that may not be paid or honored because the balance in the payor's account is less than the written amount on the check. Synonymous with INSUFFICIENT FUNDS.

NOVATION

1. substitution of a new contract or obligation for an existing one, and the discharge of the existing obligation. The exchange adjusting or altering existing mutual obligations is by mutual agreement, with either buyer or seller paying the difference in market value to equalize the exchange.
2. substitution of one of the principals to an agreement, either the creditor or debtor. Contrast with ASSIGNMENT.

NOW ACCOUNT *see* NEGOTIABLE ORDER OR WITHDRAWAL (NOW) ACCOUNT.

NUMERICAL TRANSIT SYSTEM *see* ABA TRANSIT NUMBER.

O

OBLIGATION

1. legally enforceable duty to pay a sum of money, or agree to do something (or not do something), according to the terms stated in a CONTRACT. The duty of a borrower to repay a loan, and the legal right of a lender to enforce payment.
2. any form of indebtedness evidenced by a written promise to pay.

OBLIGOR party who has an obligation to pay a debt, including interest due, by a specified date, or when repayment is demanded. The obligor (also known as *obligator*) is the debtor or borrower; the party advancing the funds is the lender, creditor, or *obligee*. In corporate securities, the obligee is the bondholder and the issuing organization is the debtor.

ODD DATE MATURITY DATE in a foreign exchange contract that is neither a spot nor a fixed date. For example, a normal two-month forward contract from April 15 matures on June 15. An odd date would be a June 10 maturity.

ODD DAYS INTEREST interest earned in a mortgage or closed-end installment loan during a time interval that is either longer or shorter than other loan payment periods. This normally occurs when a bank funds a mortgage loan in the middle of a month, or when a dealer sells installment contracts to a bank, and the bank assumes responsibility for collecting the debt. For accounting purposes, the extra days' interest is added to the first loan payment. If the loan is a fixed payment, fully amortizing loan, all remaining loan installments are even amount payments.

OFF-BALANCE SHEET ITEMS obligations that are contingent liabilities of a bank, and thus do not appear on its balance sheet. In general, off-balance sheet items include the following: direct credit substitutes in which a bank substitutes its own credit for a third party, including standby letters of credit; irrevocable letters of credit that guarantee repayment of commercial paper or tax-exempt securities; risk participations in bankers' acceptances; sale and repurchase agreements; and asset sales with recourse against the seller; interest rate swaps; interest rate options and currency options, and so on.

Under the RISK-BASED CAPITAL guidelines approved by banking regulators for bank holding companies and state member banks, banks are required to hold a portion of equity capital in reserve to meet contingent obligations in off-balance sheet items. This is based on a risk-weighted scale that requires holding more capital in reserve for certain assets, up to 100% of the prevailing capital requirement for certain assets, and as little as 0% for liquid, easily marketable assets. Risk weights are determined by multiplying each off-balance sheet item by a conversion factor to yield a credit equivalent amount. Thus, if the required capital-to-asset ratio is 8%, off-balance sheet items given a 100% risk weight would require an 8% capital backing; a 50% risk weighting requires a 4% capital support. Anything qualifying for placement in more than one category is assigned the lowest applicable risk rating.

The risk weights for off-balance sheet items are as follows:

100% risk weight: standby letters of credit, risk participations, asset sales with recourse, risk participations in bankers' acceptances.

50% risk weight: unused portions of loan or lease commitments with original maturities of more than one year; Revolving Underwriting Agreements, Note Issuance Facilities.

20% risk weight: short-term commercial letters of credit, and documentary letters of credit collateralized by the underlying shipments.

OFFER price at which the owner of a security, financial instrument, or other asset is willing to sell. This is also called the *asked price*. This differs from the BID price, or the price a buyer is willing to pay. The BID AND ASKED quotes are the prices a dealer is willing to pay, and the price a dealer wants to charge, respectively. The bid price is always the lower of the two prices. Buyers, who can be individual investors or large institutions, pay the offered price, or the price asked by the seller, frequently after negotiating from the original bid-asked quote.

OFFERING CIRCULAR *see* PROSPECTUS.

OFFERING PRICE price per share at which a new distribution of securities is offered to the public, also known as the *public offering price*. In no-load mutual funds, the offering price is equal to the NET ASSET VALUE of the securities offered for sale.

OFFICE OF THE COMPTROLLER OF THE CURRENCY (OCC) *see* COMPTROLLER OF THE CURRENCY.

OFFICE OF THRIFT SUPERVISION (OTS) federal agency established in 1989 to supervise thrift institutions with federal charters (federal savings banks and federal savings and loan associations). The OTS was abolished in 2011 by the Dodd-Frank Act, its powers transferred to other banking agencies. The Federal Reserve assumed supervision of thrift holding companies. The Comptroller of the Currency took over general supervision and rule making for U.S. thrift institutions. The Federal Deposit Insurance Corporation became supervisor for state chartered thrift institutions.

OFFICER senior administrative official of a bank, appointed by the BOARD OF DIRECTORS, to implement and carry out its operating rules, including the bank's loan policy. The chairman of the board is the highest ranking officer in a bank or bank holding company, reporting directly to the board of directors, whereas the chief executive officer (CEO) is ordinarily the executive with the most responsibility for day-to-day operations. In many smaller banks, it is not unusual for the

CEO to also hold the title of president or even chairman. Under the bank president are other administrative officers: the chief operating officer (COO); the bank CASHIER, who is senior administrative officer (his or her name appears on all official, or cashier's, checks); executive vice presidents; and lesser officers, including senior vice presidents, vice presidents, assistant vice presidents, branch office managers, and calling officers (sometimes called account executives) who market banking services to corporate customers.

OFFICIAL CHECK *see* CASHIER'S CHECK.

OFFICIAL STAFF COMMENTARY Federal Reserve commentary explaining in question and answer fashion the important sections of consumer protection regulation. The Fed has issued staff commentaries covering Regulation E, covering electronic funds transfers, and Regulation Z, covering consumer credit.

OFFICIAL STATEMENT financial disclosure by a state or local government planning a municipal securities offering that states the purpose for the issue and how investors will be repaid. The official statement also discloses pertinent information on the issuer's financial condition. Compare with PROSPECTUS.

OFF-PREMISE BANKING retail banking services provided away from a bank's main offices or its branches, ordinarily through automated teller machines (ATMs) in convenience stores, shopping centers, corporate office parks, and other locations. Off-premise banking networks, such as ATM systems, are costly to set up, but have a lower cost per transaction than conventional branch offices staffed by tellers.

OFFSET either of two accounting entries that cancel each other out.

Banking:

1. SET-OFF CLAUSE: a lender's right to take possession of any bank account balance of a guarantor or delinquent debtor, through GARNISHMENT. This is known as the *right of offset.*
2. number encoded on the MAGNETIC STRIPE of a bank card that, when matched with the cardholder's PERSONAL IDENTIFICATION NUMBER (PIN), verifies the remembered PIN as the correct access code. *See also* PRIMARY ACCOUNT NUMBER.

Futures and options: closing a position by purchase of an equal number of opposite contracts in the same delivery month, or covering a short sale of futures through the purchase of an equal number of contracts in the same delivery month. Either action cancels the obligation to make or take delivery of the underlying commodity or financial instrument.

OFFSHORE BANKING UNIT (OBU) shell branch owned by a nonresident bank in an international financial center that makes loans in the Eurocurrency market, unrestricted by local monetary authorities or governments. An offshore banking unit cannot, however, take domestic deposits. Since the 1970s these financial units have sprung up in major European cities, the Mideast, Asia, and the Caribbean. The major offshore banking centers for U.S. banks are the Bahamas, the Cayman Islands, Hong Kong, Panama, and Singapore, which offer favorable political, regulatory, and tax treatment. Since 1981, U.S. banks have been permitted many of these same advantages through International Banking Facilities, located in major U.S. financial centers. *See also* INTERNATIONAL BANKING FACILITY.

OFF THE SHELF *see* SHELF REGISTRATION.

ONE-BANK HOLDING COMPANY corporation owning at least 25% of the voting stock of a commercial bank. An amendment to the Bank Holding Company Act, enacted by Congress in 1970, extended Federal Reserve supervision of bank holding companies to corporations owning only one bank. Formation of the one-bank holding companies, beginning in the late 1960s, gave rise to the leveraged holding company: commercial banks were no longer dependent largely on depositors' funds to underwrite loans and other investments. Bank holding companies are allowed to issue commercial paper in capital markets.

This ability to finance bank operations through holding company debt gave banks greater flexibility in raising capital to support a wide variety of activities by the subsidiary bank, and by affiliate companies.

The 1970 law also required nonbank commercial corporations to divest their banking subsidiaries. *See also* BANK HOLDING COMPANY; REGULATION Y.

ONE-DAY CERTIFICATE temporary U.S. Treasury Department financing by which the Treasury borrows from the Federal Reserve System when it needs funds. The Treasury issues an interest-bearing certificate called a Special Certificate to the Federal Reserve Bank of New York. No certificates have been issued since June 1979 when federal legislation limited direct Treasury borrowings from the Fed to not more than $5 billion, and required approval by five of the seven governors of the Federal Reserve Board.

ONE-STOP BANKING *see* FULL-SERVICE BANK.

ONE-STOP SHOPPING *see* FINANCIAL SUPERMARKET.

ON-LINE computer system where customer transactions are posted to a bank's central records, and directly to a customer's account, as they are made.

Most electronic banking systems, including AUTOMATED TELLER MACHINE (ATM) networks and electronic POINT-OF-SALE systems, are fully on-line systems, meaning that transactions are approved or rejected as soon as they are entered into the system. *See also* FUNDS TRANSFER; PLATFORM AUTOMATION.

ON OTHERS ITEM *see* TRANSIT ITEM.

ON-US ITEM

1. check payable from funds on deposit at the same bank where it is presented for collection. If there are sufficient funds in the account on which it is drawn (the drawee's account), the check can be cashed or deposited into another account. Also called a *house check.*
2. electronic funds transfer where the paying and receiving accounts are at the same bank.

OPEN ACCOUNT an alternative to LETTER OF CREDIT in international financing, usually extended without formal written contract or promissory note. It is recorded on the records of the seller as unsecured accounts receivable for which payment is expected within a specified period after purchase. Also called *open book account.*

OPEN BOOK Euromarket term for NEGATIVE GAP; also called an unmatched book or short book. If the average duration (maturity) of a bank's liabilities is less than the average duration of its assets, or vice versa, it is said to be running an open book.

OPEN CONTRACT futures market contracts that have not been liquidated by subsequent sale or purchase of the underlying instrument, by taking delivery of the instrument, or by taking an offsetting position in futures. Also called OPEN INTEREST.

OPEN-END CREDIT consumer LINE OF CREDIT that may be added to, up to a preset credit limit, or paid down at any time. The customer has the option of paying off the outstanding balance, without penalty, or making several installment payments. Bank CREDIT CARD and check OVERDRAFT credit lines are two of the most widely used forms of open-end credit. Also called *revolving credit* or *charge account credit.* Contrast with CLOSED-END CREDIT. *See also* CASH ADVANCE.

OPEN-END FUND type of INVESTMENT COMPANY that sells new shares to the public and stands ready to buy back (redeem) its shares at the market price when investors wish to sell. Open-end investment companies are better known to the public as MUTUAL FUNDS, and are so named because these companies are continually creating new shares when they sell securities. Consequently, the NET ASSET VALUE of mutual funds increases or decreases as investors buy shares or redeem them. Funds typically invest in a variety of financial instruments, including common stocks, corporate bonds, tax exempt bonds, and short-term money market instruments. Contrast with CLOSED-END FUND.

OPEN-END INVESTMENT COMPANY *see* MUTUAL FUND.

OPEN-END LEASE lease, usually an automobile or vehicle lease, in which payments do not fully amortize the obligation. The monthly payments ordinarily are lower than closed-end lease financing, but the lease requires a BALLOON PAYMENT at maturity. The size of the balloon is disclosed when the lease is taken out. Contrast with CLOSED-END LEASE.

OPEN-END MORTGAGE clause in a mortgage allowing mortgaged property to be used for additional advances on the same note, up to a preset amount. Subsequent advances are dated back to the recording of the original mortgage deed. Contrast with CLOSED-END MORTGAGE.

OPEN INTEREST financial futures market contracts that have not been offset by opposite transactions, or fulfilled by delivery of the underlying financial instrument. Even though each futures transaction has a buyer and a seller, in computing open interest only one side of the market is counted. Open interest also refers to options contracts that have not been closed out, offset by opposite transactions, or allowed to expire.

OPEN MARKET ACCOUNT Federal Reserve System's portfolio of U.S. government securities, agency securities, and bankers acceptances acquired through OPEN MARKET OPERATIONS. The Open Market Account is maintained by the Federal Reserve Bank of New York, following instructions from the FEDERAL OPEN MARKET COMMITTEE, which meets periodically. Also called *System Open Market Account.*

OPEN MARKET INTERVENTION *see* INTERVENTION.

OPEN MARKET OPERATIONS purchase or sale of government securities by the Open Market desk at the Federal Reserve Bank of New York, as directed by the FEDERAL OPEN MARKET COMMITTEE.

By buying and selling securities, mostly short-term Treasury obligations, i.e., Treasury bills, the Federal Reserve is able to: (1) meet the public demand for cash by adjusting bank reserves upward or downward, as needed, and (2) influence bank interest rates, including rates such as the Federal Funds (Fed Funds) rate that banks charge for short-term sale of EXCESS RESERVES.

When the manager of the Fed's Open Market Desk at the Federal Reserve Bank of New York makes the decision to buy securities, the Fed writes a check on itself to the bank, or other institutional investor holding the securities, and deposits a check in a commercial bank. If the Fed buys $1 billion in Treasury bills, bank reserves are increased by that amount. Selling $1 billion in T-bills has the opposite effect, shrinking the reserves in the banking system, which tends to drive up the cost of credit, and interest rates. When the Fed is worried that the inflation rate is rising, it pursues a tight money policy by selling securities. What results is higher interest rates, because the banks pass the added cost along to the borrowers.

The Fed also adds reserves to the banking system to meet the public's seasonal demand for cash. This demand for cash varies seasonally; it is highest in December, and lowest in late summer.

For these reasons, open market operations are the most flexible monetary tool the Fed has available in implementing its monetary policy objectives. Because commercial banks have about three-fourths of the nation's checking account deposits, the Fed, by managing the level of reserves in the banking system, is able to influence the nation's supply of money (the money supply or money stock), and the cost of credit. Both the Fed Funds rate, which is the market rate banks pay one another for nonborrowed reserves, and the bank prime rate are influenced to a large degree by the Fed's actions in open market operations.

Other tools of monetary policy are the DISCOUNT RATE and RESERVE REQUIREMENTS. *See also* FISCAL POLICY; MATCHED SALE–PURCHASE AGREEMENT; QUANTITATIVE EASING; REVERSE REPURCHASE AGREEMENT; SWAP NETWORK; TERM AUCTION FACILITY; TERM DEPOSIT FACILITY; TERM SECURITIES LENDING FACILITY.

OPEN MARKET RATES interest rates on various MONEY MARKET INSTRUMENTS that have an active secondary market. Open market rates are influenced by a number of factors, including supply and demand, current interest rates, and also trading arbitrage by market participants.

For example, in the FEDERAL FUNDS market, banks with excess reserves sell funds, usually on an overnight basis, to other banks needing cash to meet their RESERVE REQUIREMENTS. The Fed Funds rate is repriced with each transaction, and is highest during periods of TIGHT MONEY when the supply of NONBORROWED RESERVES in the banking system is reduced by Federal Reserve monetary policy.

Other examples of open market rates are the rates banks pay when they buy Eurodollar deposits from a non-U.S. bank or purchase negotiable certificates of deposits and bankers' acceptances from banks willing to sell funds in the money market.

OPERATING LEASE LEASE written for a shorter period than the economic life of the leased asset. These leases ordinarily are written by equipment manufacturers, who are expected to take back the equipment and re-lease it to other users. Both commercial banks and finance companies write operating leases. Operating leases are cancelable leases, meaning the equipment can be returned at any time if it becomes obsolete or no longer is needed. *See also* FINANCE LEASE; LEVERAGED LEASE; RESIDUAL VALUE.

OPERATIONAL TARGETS Federal Reserve MONETARY POLICY objectives, usually expressed in terms of projected changes in monetary aggregates (the MONEY SUPPLY) and credit (NONBORROWED RESERVES). The Federal Reserve Board chairman reports the Fed's intentions, that is, what the Fed expects to achieve through its monetary policy, in twice-annual reports to Congress, as called for by the Full-Employment and Balanced Growth Act of 1978. The growth projections are stated as upper and lower ranges, covering the fourth quarter of one year to the fourth quarter of the following year.

The Fed's ultimate objective in monetary policy is balanced growth in the economy, as measured by changes in the GROSS DOMESTIC PRODUCT, the inflation rate, unemployment, and so on. Since 1979, the

Fed's near-term focus in monetary policy has been management of credit in the banking system, which it attempts to control through OPEN MARKET OPERATIONS.

OPPORTUNITY COST present value of the income that could be earned (or saved) by investing in the most attractive alternative to the one being considered. For example, investing in government bonds instead of originating mortgages. Also called *alternative cost.*

OPTION contract granting the right, and not the obligation, to purchase or sell property, or assets during a specified period at an agreed-upon price, called the STRIKE PRICE. Options are most common in the stock market, but also are used frequently as a hedging device in managing currency positions in foreign exchange, financial futures, commodities, and stock index futures. Option prices are determined by the interaction of the maturity, volatility, and price of the underlying instrument.

There are two basic types of options:

(1) call option—contract sold for a price that gives the holder the right to buy from the option seller a specified amount of securities at a specified price; and

(2) put option—contract sold for a price that gives the holder the right to sell a specified amount of securities at a predetermined price.

The initial cash paid, or PREMIUM, is determined at the beginning of the option contract. Most put and call options are rarely used. They are allowed to expire unexercised, or are sold before the exercise date in trading activity, based on the rise and fall of option premiums. *See also* AT THE MONEY; DELTA; IN THE MONEY; OUT OF THE MONEY; STRADDLE.

OPTION-ADJUSTED SPREAD (OAS) method used in calculating the relative value of a fixed-income security containing an EMBEDDED OPTION, such as a borrower's option to prepay a loan. OAS models, taking into account the effects of prepayments under various interest-rate scenarios, attempt to estimate the future value of a security. The methodology makes it easier to work out a side-by-side comparison of two different bonds, one of which has a call option (or prepayment option) and one that does not. The callable bond often has a higher yield to compensate for the early redemption feature.

Option-adjusted spreads are quoted as a fixed spread, or differential, over a benchmark security. In the United States the benchmark is U.S. Treasury issues in various maturities, since Treasury securities are not considered to have any credit risk. When first introduced, option-adjusted spreads were widely used in pricing mortgage-backed securities, but they have since been applied to other fixed-income securities, including structured notes and callable corporate bonds.

OPTION ARM adjustable-rate mortgage (ARM) that enables the borrower to select from various loan payment options every month. These mortgages are typically structured with a low introductory interest rate and as many as four major types of payment options: a fully amortizing 30-year payment, a fully amortizing 15-year payment, an interest-only payment, and a minimum payment option that adjusts after the first 12 months. Option ARMs are suitable for borrowers who want maximum payment flexibility or who expect to own their property for a short time period. Also called *flexible payment ARM*.

OPTIONS CLEARING CORP. (OCC) corporation, owned by the stock exchanges, providing trade comparison and settlement services for all option trades on U.S. securities exchanges. The corporation's prospectus, given to option traders, describes its rules for ethical conduct and outlines trading risks in exchange traded options. OCC's Intermarket Clearing Corporation also provides a link to the New York Futures Exchange.

ORDER

1. instrument authorizing payment to someone else, such as a CHECK or a DRAFT. Checks are three-party instruments, involving a check writer or MAKER, the financial institution delivering the funds (the payer bank) and the person receiving the payment. A check is different from a NOTE, such as a PROMISSORY NOTE, in that a note is a two-party instrument and merely is a promise to pay, not an order to pay; it is not always negotiable, or transferable to a third party. A check, by definition, is a NEGOTIABLE INSTRUMENT; ownership of a check is transferred by ENDORSEMENT. *See also* DRAWEE; DRAWER; NEGOTIABLE ORDER OF WITHDRAWAL (NOW) ACCOUNT; PAYER; PAYMENT ORDER.
2. trading instructions to a broker or dealer. There are several kinds of orders in futures trading, such as market order, which instructs a floor broker to buy or sell contracts in a specific month. A LIMIT ORDER tells the broker to execute an order only if the market reaches or betters that price. An open order is an order that is good until cancelled or executed. A STOP ORDER tells the broker to buy or sell at the market when a specific price is reached, either above or below the market price when the order was given.

ORDINARY INTEREST interest computed on a 360-day year, using 12 months of 30 days, instead of a 365-day year. Treasury bill yields are quoted on a 360-day year. Corporate bonds, mortgages, and consumer installment loans with PRECOMPUTED INTEREST earn ordinary interest. With larger amounts invested, the difference between ordinary interest and EXACT INTEREST (a 365 day-year) can be substantial. *See also* BASIS.

ORGANIZATION FOR ECONOMIC COOPERATION AND DEVELOPMENT (OECD) official group of 24 nations, including most of the major industrialized countries, that was formed in 1961 to coordinate economic and social policies among its members and promote economic assistance to developing countries. Its members include 18 European countries, Canada, the United States, and Japan. It is based in Paris.

ORIGINAL ISSUE DISCOUNT (OID) amount that the original issue price of a BOND, COLLATERALIZED MORTGAGE OBLIGATION, or other debt instrument is below PAR VALUE or face value. These bonds require special tax treatment from the Internal Revenue Service. The Internal Revenue Service treats the increase in price from the original issue price to par at maturity as interest subject to income tax as ordinary interest. Even though no interest is received, taxes are due on the annual accretion of bond interest. At the extreme, a zero-coupon bond pays no interest at all until maturity.

ORIGINAL MATURITY term to maturity from the issue date of a bond. It differs from the CURRENT MATURITY, which is the time between the present and the maturity date. For example, a 30-year bond issued in 1982 had a current maturity of 13 years in 1999.

ORIGINATION FEE fee charged for originating and processing a mortgage loan application; it is one of the required disclosures at loan closing. The Real Estate Settlement Procedures Act requires that lenders disclose origination and closing costs associated with real estate loans, so consumers can compare fees.

ORIGINATOR

1. bank, mortgage broker, or mortgage banker that initially made the mortgage loan (or loans) backing a pool of mortgages. *See also* MORTGAGE ORIGINATOR.
2. investment bank working on a new securities offering, usually appointed manager of the underwriting SYNDICATE. Also called *originating investment banker.*
3. party initiating instructions for a money transfer or wire payment

OTHER PEOPLE'S MONEY

1. funds borrowed to acquire income-producing property instead of paying all cash.
1. Wall Street slang for funds contributed by private investors or institutions to increase the return on invested capital. *See also* LEVERAGE.

OUT OF THE MONEY term used in options trading when the market value of an underlying security or financial instrument is lower than the *exercise price* of a CALL OPTION (an option to buy) or higher than the strike price of a PUT OPTION (an option to sell). An out-of-the-money option has no benefit or INTRINSIC VALUE, although buyers of these options hope they will move IN THE MONEY by the expiration date. *See also* AT THE MONEY.

OUT-OF-TOWN CHECK *see* FOREIGN ITEMS; TRANSIT LETTER.

OUTRIGHT FORWARD forward market purchase or sale of foreign exchange without a corresponding SPOT MARKET purchase. For example, buying a one-month, two-month, or three-month contract in a given currency.

OUTSTANDING

Banking:

1. checks or drafts that have not been presented to the paying bank for payment, or are still in the process of collection.
2. aggregate amount owed by a bank's credit card holders; this usually is less than total card volume due to early payments.

Finance: uncollected funds, or accounts receivable; also unpaid obligations.

Securities: a corporation's capital stock; stock issued and sold to investors, less stock repurchased by the issuer (treasury stock).

OVER AND SHORT general ledger account where differences in transaction journals are recorded, such as a teller's cash difference. This is also known as a *difference account*. Transaction journals that refuse to balance are one of the daily hazards of banking; the causes usually are bookkeeping or clerical errors, for example, a transposed digit in a teller's transaction log.

OVERCOLLATERALIZATION type of CREDIT ENHANCEMENT by which an issuer of securities pledged collateral in excess of what is needed to adequately cover the repayment of the securities plus a reserve. By pledging collateral with a higher face value than the securities being offered for sale, for example 125% of principal value, an issuer of mortgage-backed bonds can get a more favorable bond rating from a rating agency and also guard against the possibility that the bonds may be called before maturity because of mortgage prepayments.

OVERDRAFT

1. amount by which a check exceeds the AVAILABLE BALANCE in a checking account. Also, the negative account balance that results when a depositor writes checks exceeding the account balance. Bank customers who have an overdraft line of credit, called OVERDRAFT PROTECTION, can write checks for more than the account balance whenever they want, without fear that their checks will be returned or they will have to pay overdraft check fees for bounced checks. Also called "overdraft privilege" a *bounce protection*.
2. DAYLIGHT OVERDRAFT to a bank's RESERVE ACCOUNT at a Federal Reserve Bank created when balances transmitted to other banks or third parties exceed the balance in its reserve account. The resulting funds shortage in the reserve account is a temporary situation ordinarily covered by incoming wire transfers from other banks. *See also* BILATERAL CREDIT LIMIT; OVERDRAFT CAP; UNWINDING.
3. banking system in Great Britain and other European countries where depositors can write checks greater than their average balance, and can even maintain a negative balance, paying interest only on the negative balance. Also called *overdraft banking*.

OVERDRAFT CAP maximum dollar amount a bank agrees to transmit to other financial institutions over private payment networks and the

Federal Reserves FEDERAL WIRE network in a single day. In order to control DAYLIGHT OVERDRAFT exposure, each bank's cap is a multiple of its RISK-BASED CAPITAL. *See also* BILATERAL CREDIT LIMIT.

OVERDRAFT PROTECTION banking service to cover a checking account overdraft. The bank may charge a servicing fee for each check exceeding the available account balance; or, if the account owner has a satisfactory credit rating, pay the overdrafts by drawing down a pre-approved personal line of credit.

OVER-EXTENSION

1. **Banking.** A loan balance or total credit obligation beyond the borrower's ABILITY TO PAY. In situations where the borrower has taken on more credit than he can handle, a debt consolidation loan (combining several obligations in a single loan repayable over a longer term) may be the only alternative to bankruptcy. As a rule of thumb, borrowers who pay more than one-third of their net income to repayment of consumer debt, excluding mortgage debt, may be over-extended in their ability to repay recurring household debt.
2. **Securities.** A trader's purchase of securities above his capital and borrowing power. This situation could lead to losses in a declining market if the trader is unable to meet margin calls.

OVERLAPPING DEBT debt created by a municipality when it issues municipal bonds to fund other development projects by a governmental unit serving the same area. A city may use income from general obligation bonds to service county or school district bonds.

OVERNIGHT MONEY money that is sold in the interbank market by banks with idle funds to those needing temporary funds. The Fed Funds market, where financial institutions sell EXCESS RESERVES from reserve accounts, at Federal Reserve Banks, is the largest source of overnight funds. Fed funds are due back at the selling bank at the start of business the following day. *See also* MATCHED SALE—PURCHASE AGREEMENT; REPURCHASE AGREEMENT.

OVERNIGHT REPURCHASE AGREEMENT *see* REPURCHASE AGREEMENT.

OVER-RIDE

1. decision by a credit analyst or bank lender to approve or decline a credit application, despite the presence of other factors, such as DEROGATORY INFORMATION as released by a credit reporting agency. Over-rides most often occur when a lender grants a loan request, or rejects the application, even though a credit scoring system has determined otherwise. *See also* CREDIT SCORING.
2. set aside of federal legislation by a state legislature during a specified period of time after enactment of federal legislation. *See also* PREEMPTIVE RIGHT.

OVERSEAS PRIVATE INVESTMENT CORPORATION independent federal agency created by the Foreign Assistance Act of 1969 to insure, guarantee, and finance private investments in developing countries. Since 1979 OPIC has operated as a unit of the International Development Cooperation Agency.

OVER-THE-COUNTER (OTC)

1. market for trading securities that are not listed on an organized stock exchange, such as the New York Stock Exchange or a regional stock exchange. U.S. government securities, corporate bonds, mortgage-backed securities, asset-backed securities, and municipal securities also are traded over-the-counter. Trading activity is carried out by broker-dealers who communicate with each other by telephone, and by computer-controlled networks of quotation terminals. In the OTC market, prices are determined by negotiation between buying and selling brokers, rather than auction bidding on the floor of an exchange. Most bank stocks are traded over the counter, although many are listed on major exchanges, as well as regional stock exchanges.
2. market away from regulated exchanges where privately negotiated contracts are traded. Examples are foreign exchange forward contracts, currency swaps, and interest rate swaps. *See also* CURRENCY SWAP; DERIVATIVE; FORWARD EXCHANGE CONTRACT; INTEREST RATE SWAP.

OWNER'S PAPER all forms of mortgages, debt, or second mortgages that are held by the seller rather than a financial institution, for example, a PURCHASE MONEY MORTGAGE. Also called a *seller's mortgage.*

P

P* indicator of the long-term INFLATION rate in the economy. The P* (pronounced P *star*) number tracks the growth of M2, a MONEY SUPPLY measure, as modified by the VELOCITY OF MONEY. If P* exceeds P (expected future prices), the Federal Reserve can be expected to tighten bank credit and interest rates, causing the economy to grow at a slower rate. When P* is less than P, the Federal Reserve can ease its credit policies, allowing bank credit and the money supply to grow at a faster rate.

The P* formula is:

$P^* = M2 \times V^* / Q^*$

where M2 is an official measure of the money supply (checks plus checkable deposits, savings, and time deposit accounts), V* is the velocity of M2, or the number of times that money turns over, and Q* is the estimated value of Gross Domestic Product in the future, assuming the economy grows at 2.5% a year.

PA'ANGA monetary unit of the Tonga Islands.

PACKAGE MORTGAGE mortgage or deed of trust that covers personal property, such as furniture, appliances, and other household items. *See also* CHATTEL MORTGAGE; WRAPAROUND MORTGAGE.

PAID-IN CAPITAL

1. **Banking.** The capital stock of a bank, Federal Reserve Bank, or international development bank subscribed to, and paid by, its stockholders. Paid-in capital is the amount contributed by stockholders to obtain a bank charter and commence business. Federal Reserve MEMBER BANKS are required to purchase shares in their district Federal Reserve Bank equal to 6% of their capital and surplus; only 50% of this amount actually is paid. The remainder, or callable capital, can be called at any time.
2. **Finance.** The difference between par value of a corporation's outstanding shares of stock and current market value. This value is adjusted downward when a corporation repurchases its own stock. Contributions in excess of par value or donations not counted toward capital stock are called *capital surplus.*

PAIR-OFF hedging technique involving trade of a security to offset a previous trade. In mortgage banking, it allows a lender to buy back mortgages or mortgage backed securities committed to a buyer in the SECONDARY MORTGAGE MARKET.

PANIC sudden loss of public confidence in the financial markets, characterized by falling prices and business failures. Financial panics occurred at regular intervals in the nineteenth and early twentieth centuries.

PAPER generic term for short-term debt instruments, such as bankers' acceptances, commercial paper, and documentary drafts. Short-term obligations are a source of credit to businesses needing temporary financing, for example, an importer who needs bank financing to cover the cost of merchandise until his inventory is sold. Short-term paper with maturities under 90 days is eligible for REDISCOUNT at a Federal Reserve Bank; that is, it can be used as collateral for a Federal Reserve credit advance. *See also* DISCOUNT WINDOW; ELIGIBLE PAPER.

PAPER GAIN (OR LOSS) popular name for unrealized capital gain or loss in an investment portfolio or an open position in options or futures. Paper gains are determined by comparing the current market price to the original cost of the investment. They are not realized until securities are sold, a futures position is liquidated, or an option to sell is exercised. Also called *paper profits.*

PAPERLESS ENTRY

1. transfer of funds, initiated by telephone or instruction from a computer terminal rather than a check or draft.
2. electronic deposit of pay or benefit payments from a government agency or private organization into a depositor's account.

See also BOOK ENTRY SECURITY; DIRECT DEPOSIT; ELECTRONIC FUNDS TRANSFER.

PAPERLESS STATEMENT Financial statement detailing activity in a checking, brokerage, or other account; available through a bank or financial institution web site. Also called *online statement.*

PAPER MONEY bank notes designated by the U.S. Treasury as LEGAL TENDER for payment of debts, principally FEDERAL RESERVE NOTES. Paper money is also known as FIAT MONEY, because it is not backed by the issuing government's pledge to exchange paper for an equivalent amount of gold or hard currency.

PAPER PROFITS *see* PAPER GAIN (OR LOSS).

PARALLEL LOAN four-party loan involving parent companies and their subsidiaries in different countries. A parallel loan is an arrangement to borrow in the currency of one country with a promise to pay interest and principal at a later date. The loan is collateralized by a concurrent loan from a multinational parent company to its affiliate in a foreign country. A parallel loan is similar to a BACK-TO-BACK LOAN, or two-party loan, in that it transfers surplus liquidity from one currency to another. The two-party loan is safer from the lender's view because, if the subsidiary defaults, the multinational parent normally is obligated to make good on the loan.

PARIS CLUB *see* GROUP OF TEN.

PARITY

1. in foreign exchange trading, absence of a counterproposal to a bid or offer of another party. The term implies that both traders are dealing at exactly the same prices. Thus, they are at par or at parity.
2. PURCHASING POWER PARITY.

3. in financial swaps, the absence of any price difference between two maturity dates of a swap agreement.

PARTICIPATION *see* LOAN PARTICIPATION; RISK PARTICIPATION.

PARTICIPATION CERTIFICATE (PC) certificate representing an undivided interest in a POOL of conventional mortgage loans. Principal and interest payments pass through to the certificate holders each month. For example, a participation certificate can be a PASS-THROUGH SECURITY that is issued and guaranteed by. *See also* MODIFIED PASS-THROUGH CERTIFICATE; MORTGAGE-BACKED CERTIFICATE.

PARTNERSHIP AGREEMENT *see* ARTICLES OF PARTNERSHIP.

PAR VALUE

1. **Banking.** A check collection system where depository institutions exchange checks at face value, without charging a fee (called an exchange charge) for accepting checks drawn on other banks. Non-par banking was prevalent during the nineteenth and early twentieth centuries. Banks that are member banks in the Federal Reserve System are required by the Fed to honor checks at face value, and in fact, most banks, even nonmember state banks, honor checks at par exchange. The Federal Reserve maintains a list, called the par list, of banks that pay checks at par.
2. **Securities.** The face value of a security or financial instrument. The par value of a common stock is the nominal value assigned by a corporate charter, and has no specific financial relevance after the issue date. The par value of a debt security, for example a bond, is very relevant, as that is the price that will be paid the bondholder at maturity. The bond coupon interest payable semi-annually is a percentage of a bond's par value. Preferred stock dividends normally are stated as a percentage of the assigned par value, but also may be determined by auction bidding at periodic intervals. Par value is unrelated to market value, which is influenced more by market pricing, YIELD on the securities offered for sale, NET ASSET VALUE, and prices of comparable issues in the secondary market. *See also* ACCRETION OF DISCOUNT.

PASSBOOK account at a bank or thrift institution whose ownership is evidenced by entries in a nonnegotiable book that must be presented with each deposit or withdrawal, and for posting of interest. It is usually a SAVINGS ACCOUNT, although a TIME DEPOSIT account may be in passbook form. Contrast with STATEMENT SAVINGS ACCOUNT.

PASSBOOK LOAN *see* SAVINGS ACCOUNT LOAN.

PASSING THE BOOK *see* GLOBALIZATION.

PASSIVE INVESTOR investor who lends money but does not actively contribute to management. For example, a LIMITED PARTNERSHIP in a real estate development project. Passive investors may deduct investment losses only if gains from such investments exceed their losses. Income earned by passive investors may become subject to the federal alternative minimum tax.

PASS-THROUGH ACCOUNT method of maintaining required reserves, whereby financial institutions are able to meet RESERVE REQUIREMENTS by holding deposits in a MEMBER bank that maintains an equivalent deposit at a Federal Reserve Bank. The bank maintaining the pass-through account does not have to be in the same Federal Reserve District as the bank owning the account.

PASS-THROUGH SECURITY security that passes payments from borrowers to investors as loan payments are collected. The issuer remits, or passes through, to the investor monthly payments of principal and interest. Servicing of the underlying loans is usually done by the seller, who is paid a servicing fee.

PAST DUE loan payment not made as of the scheduled payment date, and subject to late charges after an allowable GRACE PERIOD. Continued lateness is noted in the borrower's credit history, and may be reported to a credit bureau or credit reporting agency. Past due loans are reported on a bank's CALL REPORT.

PATACA monetary unit of Macao.

PAYABLE THROUGH DRAFT DRAFT payable through a designated bank, drawing funds from the issuer's own account. The bank, whose name is printed on the face of the draft, verifies neither the signature nor the endorsement, which is the responsibility of the issuer. A credit union SHARE DRAFT, a check-like negotiable instrument, is a payable-through draft, and usually is cleared through a correspondent bank.

PAYCHECK-TO-PAYCHECK description for a person with limited or no savings, with limited access to banking services, and whose income goes mostly to expenses. These individuals often use non bank servicers—check cashing companies and money transfer companies—for their everyday banking needs.

PAYDAY LOAN generic term for short-term cash advance secured by personal check, often at very high interest rates. Also called *check loan* or *payday advance loan*.

PAYDOWN

1. partial reduction of a debt, as when a consumer pays off a part of the outstanding balance on a credit card, mortgage, or installment loan.
2. net reduction of a debt when the amount of new securities issued is less than that of a maturing issue.

PAYEE party named as the beneficiary of a CHECK or NEGOTIABLE INSTRUMENT; the person to whom the written amount on the face of the instrument is paid.

PAYER party responsible for making payment of the amount written on a check, draft, or other negotiable instrument. Also called the maker or writer.

PAYER BANK the bank paying a check, unless the check is payable at another bank and is sent to that bank for payment or collection. Also, a payable through bank, for example, when the writing on a draft (a PAYABLE THROUGH DRAFT) states it's payable through XYZ bank.

PAYING AGENT agent, usually a commercial bank, authorized by a securities issuer to make principal payments and periodic interest payments to bondholders. The bank, or banks, acting as paying agent charges a fee for this service. Occasionally, the treasurer of the issuing organization will be designated as paying agent. *See also* REGISTRAR; TRANSFER AGENT.

PAYMENT CAP clause in an ADJUSTABLE RATE MORTGAGE (ARM) limiting monthly payment adjustments, usually restricting the increase to a percentage of the previous payment. An ARM with a 7½% payment cap and monthly payments of $100 can increase to no more than $107.50 in the first adjustment period, and $115.56 in the second. *See also* ANNUAL CAP; LIFE OF LOAN CAP.

PAYMENT DATE

1. date specified in a bond indenture as the interest payment date or interest and principal payment date for a series of bonds.
2. designated VALUE DATE where funds are transferred by prior arrangement, for example, a payroll or Social Security DIRECT DEPOSIT.

PAYMENT DELAY time delay between the date on which borrowers make their mortgage payments and the date principal and interest payments pass through to investors in mortgage-backed certificates. Because interest is calculated monthly, payment delays result in interest-free delay periods of up to 19 days on Ginnie Mae pass-through securities, 24 days on Fannie Mae participation certificates, and 44 days on Freddie Mac participation certificates, reflecting the actual number of days between payment on the underlying mortgages and payment to the pool investors.

PAYMENT ORDER

1. order directing transfer of funds to a designated account or beneficiary. Payment orders may be sent by mail (or private courier), telex message, or through the SOCIETY FOR WORLDWIDE INTERBANK FINANCIAL TELECOMMUNICATION (SWIFT), a communication network widely used in international banking.
2. check-like instrument directing payment of a specified amount to a third party. Drafts written against a NEGOTIABLE ORDER OF WITHDRAWAL (NOW) account are a common type of payment order.

PAYMENT SHOCK said to occur when the monthly payment rises sharply at the first rate adjustment in an ADJUSTABLE RATE MORTGAGE (ARM), after an introductory period. Consumers can guard against payment shock by taking adjustable rate loans with PAYMENT CAPS limiting the maximum monthly payment, or with interest rate caps that put a ceiling or upper limit on the amount of interest charged.

PAYMENT SYSTEM financial system creating the means for transferring money between suppliers and users of funds, usually by exchanging debits or credits among financial institutions. Checks and drafts commonly are referred to as the paper-based payment system; electronic fund transfers, such as AUTOMATED CLEARING HOUSE debits and credits, and Fed Wire transfers, are referred to as the electronic payment system or paperless system.

PAYOFF STATEMENT document prepared by a lender when a borrower is considering paying off a mortgage or other loan, showing the number of remaining payments, principal balance due, the daily rate of interest, and amount of interest to be rebated if the borrower prepays. Also called *letter of demand.*

PAYROLL CARD bank card that accesses an employee's salary or wages through withdrawals at automated teller machines. Payroll cards are an alternative for people who do not have bank accounts or want to minimize bank service charges.

PAY-THROUGH SECURITY mortgage-backed bond collateralized by a POOL of mortgages. This is also called a *cash flow bond.* The scheduled amortization of the bonds is met by collateral cash flow representing loan payments by mortgage borrowers. Early loan prepayments accelerate bond redemptions. An example of a pay-through bond is a COLLATERALIZED MORTGAGE OBLIGATION.

PAY TO BEARER check, draft, or other NEGOTIABLE INSTRUMENT transferable to the holder by delivery, without endorsement. A BEARER BOND, such as a bond with detachable coupons, is not registered in the name of a particular owner and is payable to whomever receives it in good faith.

PAY TO ORDER NEGOTIABLE INSTRUMENT that is payable by endorsement and delivery. Pay to order instruments are usually written "Pay to the order of XYZ" or "Pay to XYZ or order." Ownership of a check, under the UNIFORM COMMERCIAL CODE, can be transferred only after the person accepting the check endorses it over to someone else.

PEER GROUP classification of commercial banks by asset size and other characteristics. The UNIFORM BANK PERFORMANCE REPORTING SYSTEM classifies banks by 20 different groups. Within each group, banks are compared to other banks of comparable size with respect to profitability (return on assets), and so on. Peer group analysis is used by banks to assess their financial performance vis-à-vis competing banks in their market. Peer groups are determined from bank size, location, and mix of business, and can have as few as five or six banks, in the case of money center banks, or hundreds of community banks.

PEER-TO-PEER-LENDING direct loan from a network of private borrowers, bypassing traditional banks. Borrowers pay interest plus a commission to the sponsoring network. Examples are Prosper Marketplace, Inc. and Lending Clubs Corp. Also called *social lending*.

PEER-TO-PEER PAYMENT money transfer service allowing individuals to send funds directly to another individual or organization by using a computer or smartphone. Examples are PayPal, Google Wallet, or ClearXchange (run by a consortium of banks).

PEG (PEGGING)

1. in FOREIGN EXCHANGE, the process by which a government ties the value of its own currency to the currency of another country, usually the currency of its strongest trading partner, or a basket of currencies. An adjustable peg allows periodic adjustments in exchange rates, to adjust for currency fluctuations; a crawling peg adjusts the pegged currency rate on a more frequent basis, even daily. *See also* FLOATING EXCHANGE RATE; MANAGED CURRENCY.
2. manipulation to maintain the value of a security or commodity, whereby the price is not permitted to fluctuate above or below a certain preset value, known as the PAR VALUE. Pegging or otherwise fixing the prices of securities traded on national exchanges is unlawful under Section 9 of the Securities Exchange Act of 1934. In commodities trading, however, exchanges may legally restrict daily price fluctuations by setting daily trading limits, pegged to the previous day's settlement price or CLOSE.

PENALTY CLAUSE clause in contracts, loan agreements, and other obligations allowing a financial institution to assess penalties for early withdrawal from a savings account, late payments on an installment loan, or breach of contract. Banks have the option of charging a penalty if a depositor fails to give advance NOTICE OF WITHDRAWAL, usually seven days in advance, before withdrawing funds from an interest earning deposit account. *See also* EARLY WITHDRAWAL PENALTY; PREPAYMENT PENALTY.

PENSION FUND fund set up to collect regular contributions from a corporation, government agency, or organization to provide post-retirement income for eligible employees. Employer contributions are set aside in tax-free investments, under authority granted by the Internal Revenue Code. Pension funds are exempt from capital gains taxes and thus any holding period provisions in securities regulations. Pension fund managers are required to follow investment rules, as fiduciaries for pension fund assets held in interest. *See also* DEFINED BENEFIT PLAN; DEFINED CONTRIBUTION PLAN.

PERFECTED LIEN security interest in collateral securing a debt protected from claims by third parties. To properly file a lien and take a security interest, a lender must file the lien with the appropriate legal authority. Perfection of a lien on real estate is accomplished by recording the mortgage deed of trust in public land records of a municipality, such as a town clerk's office.

Perfecting a lien on stocks, bonds, or other assets owned by the borrower (known as PERSONAL PROPERTY, as opposed to REAL PROPERTY, or real estate) occurs when the lender files a FINANCING STATEMENT (UCC-1) listing the type of collateral securing the loan, and its location, in a designated filing place, generally the office of the Secretary of the State or a county recorder's office.

The lender's financing statement gives the lender priority status ahead of creditors filing subsequent liens, and is valid for a five-year period. The filing date is recorded, and the lender's documents are assigned a file number. These documents contain a detailed record of the collateral pledged or taken by the lender, establishing the lender's claim against assets by the borrower in event that the borrower defaults or goes bankrupt. *See also* CONTINUATION STATEMENT; PREFERENCE; PRIORITY OF LIEN.

PERFECT TITLE real estate TITLE free of LIENS, encumbrances, or other defects. Removing prior claims is a legal process known as perfecting a title, allowing sale or assignment to a second party. *See also* CLOUD ON TITLE; QUIET TITLE ACTION; WARRANTY DEED.

PERFORMANCE ANALYSIS *see* RATIO ANALYSIS.

PERFORMANCE BOND

1. bond that calls for specific monetary payment to a beneficiary if the purchaser or maker fails to do something or acts in violation of a contract. It may be a SURETY BOND purchased from an insurance company, or cash held in an ESCROW account by a bank or a third party.
2. STANDBY LETTER OF CREDIT issued by a bank that guarantees the issuing bank will pay a third party BENEFICIARY in the event the bank's customer fails to meet a contractual obligation.

PERIODIC RATE finance charge on consumer credit loan balances, expressed as a percentage. The rate is applied daily, monthly, or at other regular intervals. A credit card account may have a rate of 1.5% on unpaid balances in each BILLING CYCLE. The periodic rate must be disclosed in consumer credit applications or borrowing agreements.

PERIODIC STATEMENT billing summary listing account activity, mailed at regular intervals, usually monthly. A credit card account statement shows new purchases and cash advances during the previous BILLING CYCLE, the MINIMUM PAYMENT and PERIODIC RATE on unpaid balances. *See also* DESCRIPTIVE STATEMENT.

PERMANENT FINANCING long-term mortgage loan, usually covering development costs, construction costs, legal expenses, and other related costs. This loan differs from the CONSTRUCTION MORTGAGE that permanent financing is negotiated after development has been completed and a project is ready for occupancy. It is generally written for periods of ten years or more.

PERMISSIBLE NONBANK ACTIVITIES financial services other than deposit taking and lending, approved by the Federal Reserve Board as permissible activities for bank holding companies and financial holding companies. The list of nonbank activities was significantly broadened by the GRAMM-LEACH-BLILEY ACT OF 1999. In general, financial holding companies may enter into almost any activity considered "financial" in nature, except those activities the act specifically excludes, such as insurance underwriting and real estate development. The Federal Reserve can approve certain nonbanking activities of financial holding companies regarded as *complementary* to banking, on a case-by-case basis, after consultation with the Treasury Department.

The Federal Reserve Board also approves nonbanking activities of bank holding companies on a case-by-case basis, following guidelines in Federal Reserve REGULATION Y, and the Fed's assessment of the expected public benefits, and the likely impact on regulated financial institutions. Examples of approved nonbank activities are operating a consumer finance company, selling mutual funds, equipment leasing, and securities underwriting.

PERSONAL BANKER bank employee who manages a customer's accounts much as a BROKER manages a client's securities portfolio. Each personal banker services specific customers, opens new accounts, takes loan applications, answers questions about other banking services, and in general acts as a personal financial advisor.

See also CROSS-SELL; CUSTOMER SERVICE REPRESENTATIVE; PRIVATE BANKING.

PERSONAL IDENTIFICATION NUMBER (PIN) numeric IDENTIFICATION code used by bank customers when making transactions at a self-service electronic banking terminal, such as an automated teller machine. This is also known as an *access code* or *security number.* A customer's PIN, a numeric code generally four to six digits in length, is his or her signature when making deposits or withdrawing cash at an ATM, or when transferring funds between accounts in a home banking or telephone bill payment service. PINs are cost effective means of customer identification, although banks continue to experiment with other means, such as signature verification and smart cards. From a bank security standpoint, PINs pose several problems. Customers who are prone to forgetting their PINs often write their access code on their bank card. Also, the person who successfully uses a PIN to withdraw money from an account may not be the authorized cardholder. *See also* MAGNETIC STRIPE; PRIMARY ACCOUNT NUMBER.

PERSONAL LINE OF CREDIT *see* LINE OF CREDIT.

PERSONAL LOAN loan granted for personal, family, or household use, as distinguished from a loan financing a business. Such loans are usually unsecured, though in some situations the lender may require a co-signer or guarantor. If unsecured, the loan is made on the basis of the borrower's integrity and ABILITY TO PAY. Generally, these loans are used for debt consolidation, or to pay for vacations, education expenses, or medical bills, and are amortized over a fixed term with regular payments of principal and interest. *See also* INSTALLMENT CREDIT; SAVINGS ACCOUNT LOAN.

PERSONAL PROPERTY tangible and intangible goods, such as furniture, manufacturing equipment, and other assets that are not legally considered as REAL PROPERTY. Personal property is owned by the borrower, and is not fixed or immovable. Personal property can be pledged as loan collateral under a FINANCING STATEMENT filed with a public records office. Also called *personalty.*

PERSONAL TRUST trust created for individuals and their families, typically high net worth individuals. Examples are guardianships and reversionary trusts established during the life of the grantor to reduce tax liabilities or set up an education fund for a minor.

PESO monetary unit of Argentina, Chile, Colombia, Cuba, the Dominican Republic, Mexico, the Philippines, and Uruguay.

PHANTOM INCOME income represented by ownership of a security considered taxable to the holder, even though no cash is received. This may occur when the issuer keeps part of cash flow to cover labor and other out-of-pocket costs, or when investors purchase excess cash flow from mortgage principal and interest payments. REAL ESTATE MORTGAGE INVESTMENT CONDUITS (REMICS), which issue securities from a trust, were designed to overcome this problem.

PIGGYBACK MORTGAGE residential mortgage combining a first lien mortgage financing 80% of the home's value and a second lien mortgage "piggybacked" onto the original mortgage. Both loans are closed at the same time and by the same lender. Taking out a second lien mortgage (normally for 10 to 15% of the house value) enables the borrower to avoid paying private mortgage insurance. The biggest disadvantage is the second lien mortgage often has an interest rate one to two percentage points higher than the first lien mortgage. Also called a *combination mortgage*, *80/10/10 mortgage*, or *80/15/5 mortgage*, depending on the size of the borrower's initial down payment.

PIN PAD numeric key pad a consumer uses to enter a PERSONAL IDENTIFICATION NUMBER (PIN) when paying by DEBIT CARD at a retail merchant or when using an AUTOMATED TELLER MACHINE. In a retail purchase the PIN serves as the customer's signature; in fact, it eliminates the need for a signature in electronic POINT-OF-SALE transactions. A correctly entered PIN approves the sale and the transfer of funds from the customer's account to the retailer's account. An incorrect PIN invalidates the transaction.

PIP dealer's term for the minimum price change in floating foreign exchange rates. For example, a change in a quoted price from 1.7814 to 1.7815 is equal to one pip.

PIPELINE expression for loan applications approved by a lender but not actually closed and delivered to a secondary market buyer, or held in the originator's loan portfolio. A mortgage banker refers to loans for which he or she has a FORWARD COMMITMENT to deliver in 30 days, 60 days, and so on, as loans in the pipeline. In the securities industry, a new issue of securities being readied for a public offering. *See also* CALENDAR; VISIBLE SUPPLY.

PITI short for Principal, Interest, Taxes, and Insurance—the four itemized components of a mortgage payment as listed in a borrower's mortgage statement.

PLACEMENTS *see* PRIVATE PLACEMENT.

PLATFORM AUTOMATION form of banking automation that connects the customer service desk in a bank office with the bank's customer records in the back office. Direct linkage to a CUSTOMER INFORMATION FILE enables branch account officers to book new loan applications directly with the bank's loan processing system, and also permits faster look-up of customer account information to answer questions on rates, new services, and so on. (The term platform originated in the period when banking officers sat at desks on a platform slightly elevated above the main banking floor, but today is used to describe the customer service area in a bank's lobby.) Platform automation in bank branches also can speed the processing time in handling credit applications, because paperwork is reduced. *See also* BACK OFFICE; PERSONAL BANKER; RELATIONSHIP BANKING.

PLANNED AMORTIZATION CLASS (PAC) mortgage-backed bond that protects investors from rising mortgage prepayments. PAC bonds in a COLLATERALIZED MORTGAGE OBLIGATION are paired with faster-paying bonds known as "companion" or "support" bonds, which shield the PAC bonds from accelerating prepayments and early redemption to bondholders.

PLEDGE transfer or assignment of assets to secure payment of an obligation; also called a SECURITY INTEREST. The borrower assigns an interest in the property to the lender, which becomes a LIEN on the collateral. If the borrower offers stocks, bonds, or other securities as collateral, the lender generally takes possession or is assigned ownership of the collateral until the loan is paid. *See also* HYPOTHECATION; MARGIN; PERFECTED LIEN; REGULATION T.

PLEDGED ACCOUNT MORTGAGE (PAM) type of GRADUATED PAYMENT MORTGAGE where principal and interest payments are supplemented by payments from a special savings account. Funds are drawn from the pledged savings account, acting as additional collateral, during the early years of the loan.

PLEDGING REQUIREMENTS administrative, statutory, or contractual requirement that securities be hypothecated (held) as collateral for public fund deposits or serve as a bond or security for specified deposits. Securities backing public deposits are marketable securities, such as U.S. Treasury bills or bonds. Pledged securities generally are kept by the pledging bank in a separate account. They can be placed with an independent trustee, for example, a Federal Reserve Bank, and serve as collateral for deposits by the U.S. government, states, or municipal governments. U.S. Treasury securities generally are counted at face value, commercial paper and bankers' acceptances at 90% of face value, and municipal securities at 80% of value.

PLUS

1. plus sign (+) following a Treasury note or bond price quote, indicating the quote is expressed in sixty-fourths of a percentage point. A quote of 93.16 means 93 and 33⁄64 of par. It appears in published quotations as 93.16 +.
2. indicator showing the closing price of a stock or mutual fund published in a daily newspaper is higher than the previous day's close.

POINT

1. **Banking.** (1) upfront charge equal to one percent of the principal amount of an loan, called a DISCOUNT POINT. This fee, payable at the loan closing, increases the lender's yield on mortgages and other installment loans; for the borrower, it is considered part of the finance charge and is tax deductible in the year the loan is made; and (2) BASIS POINT, or one hundredth of one percentage point.
2. **Foreign Exchange.** In price quotes, the fourth place after the decimal point. For example, if $1 = 1.7855 Euros, an exchange rate of $1 = 1.7854 is one point lower. *See also* PIP.
3. **Futures.** The minimum price fluctuation, or smallest increment of price movement. In interest rate futures this is expressed as 1⁄32nd of a percentage point. A market move of 3 ticks is equal to a change of 3⁄32. Also called a TICK.
4. **Securities.** The trading unit equal to $1 in stock prices or 1% of bond value.

POINT-OF-SALE (POS) retail PAYMENT SYSTEM that substitutes an electronic transfer of funds for cash, checks, or drafts in the purchase of retail goods and services. In a POS system, sales and payment information are collected electronically, including the dollar amount of the sale, the date and place of the transaction, and the consumer's account number. If the transaction is done on a bank credit or debit card, the payment information is passed on to the financial institution or payment processor, and the sales data is forwarded to the retailer's management information system for updating of sales records. *See also* ELECTRONIC BANKING; POINT-OF-SALE TERMINAL; REGULATION E.

POINT-OF-SALE TERMINAL electronic transaction terminal used in an electronic POINT-OF-SALE (POS) system. There are two basic types of POS terminals: electronic cash registers that are used by high volume merchants, such as department stores, and dial-up terminals that automatically dial a special telephone number, often a toll-free number, to obtain authorization. NET SETTLEMENT, when the transfer of funds actually takes place, may occur at the same time as the transaction or soon afterward, or it may occur later in the day.

POINT SCORING *see* CREDIT SCORING.

POLITICAL RISK *see* SOVEREIGN RISK.

POOL group of mortgages, consumer loans, commercial loans, or other credit receivables acting as collateral for an issue of bonds, mortgage backed securities, or ASSET-BACKED SECURITIES. Any group of loans with similar qualities, i.e., term to maturity, interest rate, and so on, can be treated as a unit for purposes of assembling asset-backed or mortgage-backed bonds offered for sale to investors. Rules specifying the types of loans eligible for pooling are established by the issuer, and stated in the bond INDENTURE agreement or the issuer's offering circular. *See also* MORTGAGE POOL.

POOLED COST OF FUNDS cost of funds formula based on division of the balance sheet into different categories, matching specific interest earning assets with interest sensitive liabilities. An example is the pooling of all interest sensitive assets with maturities of one year or less, and matching these loans against all one-year interest sensitive deposits. This costing formula usually is adjusted for LEGAL RESERVES that banks keep as a portion of their total deposits, regulatory capital-to-asset requirements, fee income collected from checking account customers, and float—uncollected checks. *See* MARGINAL COST OF FUNDS.

POOLING AND SERVICING AGREEMENT in asset-backed or mortgage-backed securitizations, the agreement between the loan seller, master servicer, special servicer, and trustee. This document defines the responsibilities of each party and describes how cash will be disbursed, how to correct loan servicing errors, and so on.

POOLING OF INTERESTS *see* MERGER.

PORTABLE MORTGAGE mortgage that allows the borrower to transfer the outstanding balance of an existing mortgage loan at the same rate when selling one house and buying another. The borrower pays a premium over fixed rate mortgages of comparable maturity, in addition to title insurance and appraisal fees. An advantage to the borrower, however, is the absence of closing costs and DISCOUNT POINTS when buying a new home. *See also* ASSUMABLE MORTGAGE.

PORTFOLIO group of loans or assets, classified by type of borrower or asset under management. The largest asset portfolio in a commercial bank normally is the loan portfolio, in which loans are classified by borrower—commercial loan, mortgage loan, and consumer installment loan.

PORTFOLIO LENDER lender, frequently a mortgage originator, who holds loans in portfolio until maturity (or until the loans are paid off by the borrower), and does not sell loans to investors in the secondary market. A portfolio lender derives its net income from the loan spread, or difference between its interest earning assets and deposit liabilities, as opposed to a mortgage banker, whose income primarily is from fees.

POSITION

1. **Banking.** (1) bank's net balance of a foreign currency taking into account all assets and liabilities denominated in that currency; (2) mortgage banker's inventory of mortgages held in portfolio; and (3) lender's status, either secured by collateral or fully unsecured, in relation to other creditors of a single borrower. *See also* CASH POSITION; PRIORITY OF LIEN.
2. **Foreign Exchange.** A dealer's inventory in a particular currency. When interest rates in a particular country go down, dealers sell that country's currency; when rates rise, they add to their net position.
3. **Investments.** An investor's stake in a market, in the form of open (unliquidated) contracts. Investors take a view on the market by GOING LONG (buying) or GOING SHORT (selling) securities. A LONG POSITION also is a dealer's inventory of unsold securities. *See also* SHORT POSITION; SHORT SALE.

POSITIVE AUTHORIZATION retail payment authorization system where all noncash transactions are compared against a bank's customer files for approval. This is a more stringent form of credit approval than a NEGATIVE AUTHORIZATION system, because a positive file may turn down persons who have exceeded the authorized credit limit on a credit card account, but are not delinquent cardholders. *See also* ZERO-FLOOR LIMIT.

POSITIVE CARRY condition where cost of borrowing is less than the yield on the instrument being financed; also referred to as a positive spread. The opposite is NEGATIVE CARRY.

POSITIVE GAP maturity or repricing MISMATCH in a bank's assets and liabilities where there are more assets maturing or repricing in a given period than liabilities. A bank with a positive gap is asset sensitive. The opposite is NEGATIVE GAP.

POSITIVE PAY cash management service—a deterrent to check fraud—by which banks compare a company's record of checks issued with checks presented for payment. Suspicious checks are referred to the check issuer for approval. A less-costly alternative, *reverse positive pay*, calls for the check issuer to self-monitor its checking account and notify the bank when it declines to pay a check.

POSITIVE YIELD CURVE YIELD CURVE in which long-term rates are higher than short-term rates, so-called because yield curve has an upward slope, meaning longer maturities earn a higher rate of interest. It is also known as a *normal yield curve* because investors holding longer maturity securities expect to be compensated for assuming more interest rate risk. If the nominal interest rate on Treasury bonds maturing in, say, ten years, is higher than it is for three-month Treasury bills, the yield curve is said to be positive. Under the LIQUIDITY PREFERENCE THEORY of interest rates, savers who commit their funds for a longer period of time expect to earn more interest than if they put their money out short-term. They give up liquidity, or ease of access to their money, in exchange for a liquidity premium (the higher interest rate), which explains why, under normal economic conditions, longer-term rates are higher than shorter-term rates. The opposite is an INVERTED YIELD CURVE.

POSITIVE YIELD CURVE

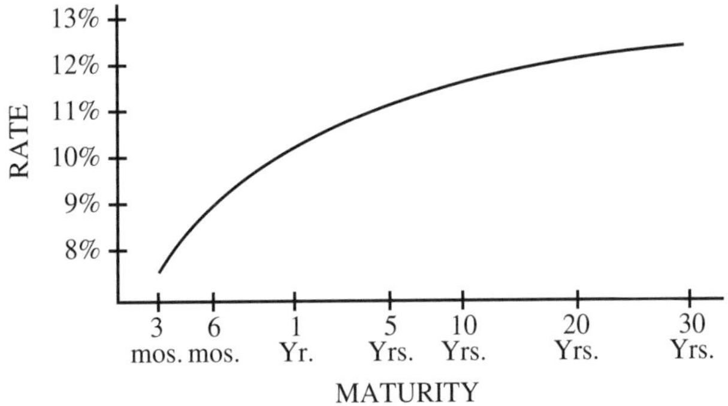

POSTAL FLOAT *see* MAIL FLOAT.

POST-DATED CHECK or negotiable instrument payable on a future date. Checks written with a future date cannot be paid (honored in banking terminology) until that date has passed. Bankers' acceptances and time drafts are always post-dated instruments. Compare to STALE-DATED.

POSTING transferring accounting entries from journals, or records of original entry, to a general ledger. The date transactions actually are credited to an account, such as cleared checks or bank card transactions, is known as the *posting date* or *payment date* or *execution date*.

Some bank credit card issuers charge interest on purchases from the date transactions are posted to the cardholder's account. *See also* MEMO ENTRY.

POUND monetary unit of Egypt, Lebanon, and Syria.

POUND STERLING monetary unit of the United Kingdom, including Great Britain.

POWER OF APPOINTMENT right granted to a person acting as TRUSTEE to appoint others to dispose of or distribute an ESTATE according to the terms of a will or a deed of trust. A general power of appointment authorizes the person receiving the property (called the *donee*) to sell or dispose of it without restriction; a limited power of appointment limits the distribution of the estate to named individuals.

POWER OF ATTORNEY legal document authorizing another person to act as agent. The authority granted may be a full power, or it may be limited to certain acts, and it must be witnessed by a notary public. A person selling property may assign power of attorney if unable to attend the real estate closing.

POWER OF SALE

1. mortgage clause giving the lender the right to sell the property securing the mortgage if the borrower defaults.
2. trust power, either express or implied, giving a TRUSTEE the right to sell assets from a trust.

PREAPPROVED CREDIT credit card or line of credit that is approved in advance and available for use at any time. Federal banking regulation prohibits mailing unsolicited credit cards, but financial institutions are permitted to mail out applications inviting a consumer to apply for credit. Use of the account is presumed to indicate acceptance of applicable credit terms, including interest rates and annual fees. *See also* PRESCREENING.

PREAUTHORIZED PAYMENT automatic transfer of funds from a borrower's deposit account to pay down a loan or obligations owed to third party creditors. A payment schedule is set by written agreement, establishing the payment amount, and the date the funds are to be transferred. Payments to third party creditors are often made by electronic funds transfers. *See also* AUTOMATED CLEARING HOUSE; VALUE DATE.

PRECOMPUTED INTEREST finance charge on consumer installment loans that is computed in advance, and added to the outstanding balance owed by the borrower. The basis of interest calculation is usually the ADD-ON INTEREST method. Contrast with SIMPLE INTEREST.

PREEMPTIVE RIGHT

1. **Banking.** The authority of the Federal Reserve Board to preempt the authority of state legislatures to regulate banking when inter-

vention is deemed necessary to maintain stability in the credit markets. An example is the Monetary Control Act of 1980, which authorized the Fed to set aside state usury ceilings at a time when mortgage rates in some states were at, or close to, the legally permitted limits. In most situations, states are authorized to nullify national preemption if they pass legislation within three years.

2. **Finance.** The right of stockholders to subscribe to new issues of common stock before a public offering is made, protecting against dilution of ownership. Depositors in a savings institution converting from mutual to stock ownership have the same privilege.

PREFERENCE transfer of property within 90 days of a borrower's filing of a bankruptcy petition. A preference may be through a lien or security interest, or transfer of property to a creditor. An unsecured loan paid off within 90 days of bankruptcy also may be declared a preference. Bankruptcy trustees have the power to void preferences that impair the POSITION of general creditors, or that undermine the stability of a business. *See also* SET-OFF CLAUSE; VOIDABLE PREFERENCE.

PREFERRED STOCK stock that pays a fixed dividend and has claim to assets of a corporation ahead of common stockholders in event of liquidation. Preferred stock is sometimes called *preference stock.* Bank depositors have priority of claim over even preferred stockholders. Banks and bank holding companies have issued several classes of preferred stock, including perpetual preferred stock, which has no stated maturity date and is not redeemable by the holder; and limited life preferred stock, or preferred stock with a stated maturity of at least 25 years.

Under the RISK-BASED CAPITAL guidelines adopted by U.S. banking regulatory agencies, nonvoting preferred stock can be counted as part of a bank's core capital or Tier 1 capital. (Tier 1 capital must equal 4% of a bank's total assets. Preferred stock eligible for inclusion as Tier 1 capital can be noncumulative preferred stock, equal to 25% of common stock but not auction rate preferred stock, such as MONEY MARKET PREFERRED STOCK. *See also* ADJUSTABLE RATE PREFERRED STOCK.

PREMIUM

1. **Banking.** A noncash incentive offered customers opening a savings account or taking out a loan.
2. **Finance** difference between the face value of a bond and the ABOVE PAR price. The opposite is DISCOUNT. Bonds purchased at a premium are amortized over their expected life; if purchased at a discount, their book value is said to accrete or grow towards par from the date purchased. *See also* ACCRETION OF DISCOUNT.
3. **Foreign exchange** exchange situation, called *agio*, in which gold or silver coins have a higher exchange value than paper currency of equivalent face value.
4. **Insurance.** An annual, semiannual, or other payment for insurance coverage.
5. **Options.** The price paid by the buyer of an option contract.

PREPACKAGED BANKRUPTCY type of business BANKRUPTCY filing under Chapter 11 of the federal bankruptcy code. Creditors agree in advance of the bankruptcy petition filing to a REORGANIZATION, allowing the debtor company to emerge in a much shorter period from court-supervised bankruptcy protection and resume normal business operations.

PREPAID DEBIT CARD
1. Type of debit card used in some states to disburse government benefits, such as welfare and unemployment benefits, and also used for income tax refunds.
2. debit card linked to a previously deposited cash balance. This card carries major association logos (MasterCard or Visa), can be reloaded with cash deposits or from payroll, and can be used at retail merchants like an ordinary debit card. The card works essentially like a STORED VALUE CARD.

PREPAID INTEREST *see* UNEARNED INTEREST.

PREPAYMENT
1. paying a loan or mortgage before maturity. A prepayment clause in a mortgage gives the borrower the option of retiring the mortgage indebtedness without penalty.
2. making extra payments toward an installment loan, or paying the outstanding balance in full. Early payments may reduce the amount of interest owed. *See also* RULE OF THE 78'S.

PREPAYMENT MODEL financial model predicting prepayment on MORTGAGE loans. Some models commonly used are the CONDITIONAL PREPAYMENT RATE AND CONSTANT PERCENT PREPAYMENT. *See also* AVERAGE LIFE; HALF LIFE; SPEED.

PREPAYMENT PENALTY fee paid to a lender for the privilege of paying off a loan prior to maturity. A prepayment penalty, which may decline in the years after a mortgage was originally booked, compensates the lender for loss of income in future years.

PRESCREENING activity in credit approval in which a lender compiles a list of prospective new accounts from credit bureau records. Prescreening reduces the cost of a new accounts mailing, in that only the accounts considered good credit risks are solicited. These prospects may receive a PREAPPROVED CREDIT offer.

PRESENTMENT demand for payment of a CHECK or other NEGOTIABLE INSTRUMENT. Checks are typically submitted for payment through a bank CLEARING HOUSE association, the Federal Reserve's check collection system, or by direct presentment to the paying bank.

PRESENT VALUE today's value of a payment or a stream of payment amount due and payable at some specified future date. Today's value of a stream of cash flows is worth less than the sum of the cash flows to be received or saved over time. *See also* DISCOUNTED CASH FLOW; INTERNAL RATE OF RETURN.

PREVIOUS BALANCE account balance in open-end credit arrangements at the start of a BILLING CYCLE. The borrower pays interest on the full amount owed, regardless of whether the initial balance is paid down. Compare to AVERAGE DAILY BALANCE.

PRICE/EARNINGS RATIO relationship between the current price of a stock to the earnings over any earnings period. This is also known as the *P/E ratio.* The period in question can be the most recent quarter, a full year, next year's projected earnings, and so on. The P/E is calculated by dividing the current stock price by the earnings per share.

The annualized P/E ratio, also known as the *P/E multiple,* measures corporate earnings power and is used by investors to gauge market demand for stocks. The annualized P/E ratio is calculated by dividing the market value by earnings per share for the most recent 12-month period. Companies with a high P/E have greater earnings potential than low P/E stocks, but also are more volatile and somewhat riskier investments.

PRICE LEVEL ADJUSTED MORTGAGE (PLAM) form of GRADUATED PAYMENT MORTGAGE in which the rate of interest paid remains fixed, but the outstanding balance is adjusted for inflation according to an appropriate price index. Periodically, according to a time schedule approved by both borrower and lender, the outstanding balance owed is revised for appreciation in property values and monthly payments are revised accordingly. *See also* ALTERNATIVE MORTGAGE INSTRUMENT.

PRIMARY ACCOUNT NUMBER (PAN) 14-digit or 16-digit numeric code embossed on the face side of a bank card, and also encoded in the MAGNETIC STRIPE. The primary account number is a composite number containing: the MAJOR INDUSTRY IDENTIFIER of the card issuer; an individual account identifier, which includes part of the account number; and a CHECK DIGIT or code that verifies the authenticity of the embossed account number.

PRIMARY DEALER government securities dealer reporting its daily trading volume and portfolio positions to the Federal Reserve Bank of New York. The New York Fed, which manages the Open Market Account desk for the Federal Reserve System, does business with primary dealers when it sells, or purchases securities in OPEN MARKET OPERATIONS. To be accepted by the Fed as a primary dealer, a dealer must be willing to act as a MARKET MAKER in all Treasury auctions of U.S. Treasury bills, notes, and bonds and to maintain adequate capital reserves, as determined by the Fed. Nonbank primary dealers finance their inventories by engaging in REPURCHASE AGREEMENTS and by pledging securities to obtain COLLATERAL LOANS from large banks.

PRIMARY DEALER CREDIT FACILITY Federal Reserve funding facility making DISCOUNT WINDOW loans to primary dealers in exchange for collateral. First authorized in the 2008 financial crisis, a period of great economic instability, this program allows broker-dealers who do business with the Federal Open Market Committee (FOMC) to borrow directly from the Fed at the current discount rate. Direct borrowing from the Federal Reserve was not permitted previously.

PRIMARY DEPOSITS *see* CORE DEPOSITS.

PRIMARY MARKET

1. market in which a loan is actually made to the borrower, distinguished from the SECONDARY MARKET, where securities backed by loan receivables are sold to investors. A bank or thrift institution that holds its loans on its own books, and does not engage in secondary market sales, is known as a PORTFOLIO LENDER.
2. market where government securities are sold to PRIMARY DEALERS, who then remarket securities to investors in the secondary market.
3. market in which newly issued securities are offered for sale, futures contracts are offered for sale, and options are purchased.

PRIMARY REGULATOR state or federal agency that is a financial institution's principal supervisory agency. It is usually the same agency that issued a bank or thrift institution's operating CHARTER. Banks and other depository financial institutions must file quarterly statements of income and condition, known as call reports, with their primary regulator, and submit books and records to periodic BANK EXAMINATION.

The Comptroller of the Currency regulates national banks; the Federal Reserve Board regulates bank holding companies and state chartered banks that are members of the Federal Reserve System. Federal savings and loan associations and federal savings banks are supervised by the Comptroller of the Currency, and state chartered banks and savings banks by state banking departments. *See also* DUAL BANKING; FUNCTIONAL REGULATION; REPORT OF CONDITION.

PRIMARY RESERVES cash needed to operate a bank, plus the LEGAL RESERVES required to be held in a Federal Reserve Bank or correspondent bank, plus uncollected checks. Primary reserves can be used to cover sudden deposit outflows that might occur in a depositor RUN, or a temporary liquidity crisis. Primary reserves are distinguished from SECONDARY RESERVES, which may be invested in marketable securities, such as Treasury bills and municipal bonds.

PRIME MORTGAGE high-quality mortgage that meets the standards set by Fannie Mae and Freddie Mac and is eligible for purchase or securitization in the secondary mortgage market. Prime mortgage loans have low default risk and are made to borrowers with good credit records and a stable monthly income. Mortgages not classified as prime mortgages are generally called SUBPRIME LOANS.

PRIME RATE reference note that banks use in pricing short maturity commercial loans to their best, or most creditworthy, customers.

Commercial and industrial (C&I) loans are often priced at prime or prime plus a spread. The prime rate is less important today in pricing bank loans to corporate borrowers that have access to the capital markets. Alternatives to the bank prime rate are the lender's own cost of funds, and an index rate, such as the London Interbank Offered Rate (LIBOR). Although the prime rate is the definitive best rate for top-quality borrowers, many banks maintain a two-tier pricing system where major corporations and even middle market firms are able to borrow at an even lower rate.

PRIME UNDERWRITING FACILITY (PUF) form of REVOLVING UNDERWRITING FACILITY in which the lender's yield is pegged to the bank prime rate. Typically, a prime underwriting facility is a short-term note having a maturity of one to three years.

PRINCIPAL

1. face amount of a loan evidencing the amount repayable, exclusive of interest, according to the terms of the NOTE securing the obligation. *See also* HOLDER IN DUE COURSE.
2. original amount of a TIME DEPOSIT or savings account on which interest is paid daily, monthly, or at other intervals. *See also* COMPOUND INTEREST.
3. primary borrower in a loan, as distinguished from the GUARANTOR or co-maker. If the borrower defaults, the guarantor is secondarily liable.
4. person who has controlling interest in a joint venture, corporation, or partnership.
5. person who appoints another to act on his behalf as agent or ATTORNEY IN FACT.
6. property of an estate or investment trust, exclusive of income.

PRINCIPAL EXCHANGE RATE LINKED SECURITY (PERL) bond paying semiannual interest, with a yield tied to foreign exchange rates. A reverse PERL is denominated in one currency, and pays interest in another, for example, a yen-denominated bond, paying interest in dollars. Investor's EFFECTIVE YIELD increases if the dollar appreciates against the yen, decreases if the dollar falls in value.

PRINCIPAL-ONLY (PO) STRIP mortgage security consisting of the principal portion of STRIPPED MORTGAGE-BACKED SECURITIES. PO strips are created by separating the principal payments from the interest payments collected from a pool of mortgage pass-through securities. The principal payments are combined, regardless of whether principal is paid early or at final maturity.

PO strips are priced and traded at a discount from par value, like zero-coupon issues, rising to par at maturity. PO strips can have high yields if prepayments are accelerated (and interest rates decline), but can have returns much lower than expected if interest rates begin rising. At worst, the return to the investor may never reach the purchase price, resulting in a loss. POs are used mostly to hedge interest rate movements, for example, as a protection against prepayment risk, or the risk of portfolio losses from a sudden increase in mortgage prepayments. *See also* INTEREST-ONLY (IO) STRIP.

PRIORITY OF LIEN order in which creditors are paid when the assets of a borrower are liquidated. Creditor priority is established under the *first to file rule* in the UNIFORM COMMERCIAL CODE, and is summarized as follows: creditors holding a SECURITY INTEREST in collateral are paid before unsecured creditors. As a general rule, holders of secured claims are paid in the order their claims were filed, starting with the earliest recorded lien.

In a VOLUNTARY BANKRUPTCY filed under Chapter 7 of the Bankruptcy Code, the debtor's assets are liquidated to meet unpaid obligations. In general, the bankruptcy estate is distributed as follows: (1) administrative costs, including court costs, trustee's fees, attorney's fees incurred by the debtor; (2) wage claims; (3) costs and expenses incurred by creditors; (4) federal, state and local tax claims; (5) debts having priority under federal law, i.e., claims of secured creditors, followed by claims of general creditors (unsecured creditors.) Creditors holding a perfected security interest are paid before other creditors. *See also* PREFERENCE; SET-OFF CLAUSE.

PRIOR LIEN LIEN recorded before other secured claims, and payable ahead of other liens if LIQUIDATION of pledged collateral occurs. A first mortgage has priority over second and third mortgages, known as junior liens. A secured creditor holding a perfected SECURITY INTEREST has priority over liens filed afterward. *See also* PRIORITY OF LIEN.

PRIVACY *see* FINANCIAL PRIVACY.

PRIVATE BANKING

1. banking services, including lending and investment management, for wealthy individuals. Private banking primarily is a wealth management service, and is less dependent on accepting deposits than retail banking. *See also* PERSONAL BANKER; RELATIONSHIP BANKING.
2. nonstock state chartered and state supervised bank that offers banking services to the public. Originally organized as a partnership, private banking was a common form of banking in the United States in the nineteenth century. Among the private banking firms still in existence is the prestigious Brown Brothers Harriman & Co. in New York City.

PRIVATE CONDUIT *see* CONDUIT.

PRIVATE EXPORT FUNDING CORPORATION (PEFCO) trade finance corporation owned by a consortium of U.S. commercial banks and industrial companies that arranges fixed rate medium-term and long-term loans to foreign buyers. Organized in 1970, the corporation works closely with the Export-Import Bank (Eximbank), which guarantees repayment of PEFCO loans. The corporation finances its activities through the sale of debt securities in the capital markets and by credit lines from member banks and the Eximbank.

PRIVATE LABEL CREDIT retail REVOLVING CREDIT plans managed for a retailer, independent dealer, or manufacturer by a bank or commercial finance company. Major department and specialty stores also manage their own private label credit card programs. If managed by a firm other than the retailer, the servicing company issues the cards, funds the credit receivables, and collects the payments from cardholders. Credit criteria are set by agreement between the retailer and the third party servicing firm. By having a private label credit program, a retailer is able to offer his customers extended payment terms, thereby increasing his sales and accounts receivable turnover. Private label credit plans also build customer loyalty, because retailers are able to send marketing promotions to preferred customers. *See also* CO-BRANDED CARD.

PRIVATE LABEL FUND MUTUAL FUND sponsored and managed by an independent broker-dealer, but distributed exclusively through one bank or savings institution.

PRIVATE MORTGAGE INSURANCE (PMI) mortgage insurance provided by a commercial insurer, as opposed to a government agency, when the mortgage loan-to-value ratio is below 80% of the property's appraised value at loan closing. Mortgage insurance, usually added to the borrower's loan payments, is available from three companies: Mortgage Guaranty Insurance Company, Milwaukee; PMI Group, San Francisco; and Radian Group, Philadelphia.

PRIVATE PLACEMENT sale of an entire issue of securities to a small group of investors. This is also known as *direct placement.* Private placements to 35 or fewer investors are exempt from Securities and Exchange Commission registration requirements, under the Securities Act of 1933. Investments with tax shelter provisions do, however, have to be registered, as required by the Deficit Reduction Act of 1984. In a private placement transaction, the buyer or buyers sign an INVESTMENT LETTER stating the securities will not be resold for a specified period of time, normally two years. Buyers of private placements include banks, savings and loans, and large institutional investors, such as insurance companies, mutual funds, and pension funds. SEC rule Rule 144A establishes a safe harbor for resale of privately sold securities to institutional investors, without the need to comply with the registration requirements of the Securities Act of 1934.

PRIVATE PURPOSE BOND bond issued by a state or government agency in which more than 10% of the proceeds are to be used by nongovernmental units, and are repaid from revenues from private trade or business. The Tax Reform Act of 1986 exempted private activity bonds issued in rural areas from federal taxes, but most private activity bonds are fully taxable securities. Other exemptions were granted for state housing and education bonds, bonds financing airports, public transportation facilities and waste treatment or recycling plants. Interest earned on tax-exempt private purpose bonds is also subject to the federal alternative minimum tax. Also called a *private activity bond* or *nonessential bond. See also* INDUSTRIAL DEVELOPMENT BOND; PUBLIC PURPOSE BOND.

PRIVATE SECTOR ADJUSTMENT FACTOR (PSAF) pricing markup that adjusts service fees charged by a Federal Reserve Bank for check clearing and other services. This markup reflects operational costs, taxes paid, and profit margins of private sector firms. The PSAF is based on data collected from major bank holding companies, and is revised annually.

PROBATE validation of a will by a probate court, followed by the appointment of an executor or administrator. A probate court also is known as a court of probate, surrogate's court, ordinary court, or prefect's court. Validation of a will as authentic is the first step in the settlement of an estate. Most states require that a will be signed by at least two witnesses before it can be accepted as a valid document.

PROBLEM BANK bank with a high ratio of nonperforming loans to total capital, also a bank with a CAMELS RATING of 4 or 5 on the 1–5 rating scale of bank performance assigned by a supervisory agency. These ratings are not disclosed publicly. Problem banks are examined on a more frequent basis than banks that are in healthy condition.

PROBLEM LOAN *see* NONACCRUAL LOAN.

PROCEEDS

1. amount given to a borrower after prepaid interest, loan fees, and other costs are deducted.
2. funds received from the sale of assets, or from the issue of securities, after deduction of selling or marketing expenses incurred.
3. sum collected on a CHECK or other negotiable instrument after deduction of exchange or collection charges.

PRODUCTION CREDIT ASSOCIATIONS *see* FARM CREDIT SYSTEM.

PROFITABILITY *see* RETURN ON ASSETS; RETURN ON EQUITY.

PROFIT AND LOSS STATEMENT *see* INCOME STATEMENT.

PRO FORMA STATEMENT hypothetical financial statement showing assets and liabilities, or income and expenses that may be recognized in the future. Pro forma statements also can illustrate projected earnings if a company were to merge with another, or sell off part of its operations. Business firms often are asked to submit pro forma statements when making a loan application. For example, a request for bank financing to purchase and carry inventory ordinarily would include a pro forma statement showing the impact of the amount borrowed on current assets and liabilities in the most recent balance sheet. Banks also use pro forma statements to indicate expected revenues from a bank ACQUISITION or MERGER with another bank, a JOINT VENTURE that involves equity participation with other firms, or anticipated income and cash flow from a new business activity. *See also* BUSINESS PLAN; FINANCING STATEMENT; WHAT-IF CALCULATION.

PROHIBITED BASIS credit practices that are contrary to the nondiscrimination guidelines contained in the EQUAL CREDIT OPPORTUNITY ACT. The act makes it illegal to approve consumer credit applications in a manner that denies creditworthy applicants access to credit on the basis of race, sex, national origin, age, marital status, or dependence on public assistance. Consumers who assert their rights under the Consumer Credit Protection Act also are protected by the statute. *See also* EFFECTS TEST; REGULATION B.

PROMISSORY NOTE written promise to pay, frequently used in installment loans and commercial loans. A promissory note is the legal evidence of a debt. The note may be transferred to a third party as a NEGOTIABLE INSTRUMENT. *See also* ACCOMMODATION PAPER; NOTE; ORDER.

PROOF AND TRANSIT collection and reconcilement of checks, drafts, and notes. The oldest form of proof is teller proof, or the balancing of a teller's cash position at the close of a business day. In check processing, proof and transit have been combined into a single operation involving high-speed check sorting equipment, a READER/SORTER machine that separates checks into different groups, such as checks payable by other banks (on-others checks) and checks payable by the same bank (on-us checks). Proof and transit is a highly automated business, and has made the check a very competitive, low-priced payment mechanism. *See also* PROOF OF DEPOSIT.

PROOF OF DEPOSIT (POD) verification of the dollar amount on a check or draft being deposited. This is done by comparing the handwritten amount on the check to the amount written on the accompanying deposit slip. Proof of deposit is the second step in processing of checks presented for payment, after checks have been separated by a check sorting machine known as a READER-SORTER into on-us and on-others categories, and is the only step in check processing that has not been automated fully. Proof of deposit or proving a check is done manually after checks have been sorted into different categories and the MICR line containing the customer's account number and the bank routing and transit number has been captured by the reader/sorter. *See also* ENCODING.

PROPRIETARY DEBIT CARD DEBIT CARD issued by a retail merchant for use in electronic transfer of funds. Proprietary cards issued by gasoline retailers give the user the same benefits as cash paying customers, for example, a cash discount off the listed price paid by customers paying with credit cards.

PROPRIETARY FUND bank distributed MUTUAL FUND sponsored by an independent investment advisor. The advisor receives investment advice from the bank selling or distributing the fund.

PROSPECTUS informational document stating the intent to issue securities, required by the Securities and Exchange Commission; also called *offering circular.* A prospectus is the legal document stating the purpose of the security issue, describing in detail the primary business of the issuer and the issuer's financial condition, and listing the principal officers. It also describes how shares are offered for sale and dividends paid. A MUTUAL FUND prospectus describes REDEMPTION rights of investors who liquidate their holdings, and also lists management fees, redemption fees, and other charges payable by the investor if the fund being offered is a LOAD FUND. A prospectus is preceded by a preliminary disclosure known as a RED HERRING. The prospectus itself is an offer to sell shares to the public. A prospectus supplement is an additional statement filed with the SEC containing information about the issuer not mentioned previously; supplements are normally issued in conjunction with SHELF REGISTRATION securities and contain further information on the particular issue being sold.

The Securities Act of 1933 requires only that issuers give full disclosure of information pertaining to a proposed offering. The SEC does not approve or disapprove the offering, but it allows the prospectus and the REGISTRATION STATEMENT to clear on the 20th day after the filing date. If the SEC objects to the offering or asks for more information, the 20-day waiting period begins again unless an exception is granted.

PROTEST formal notice that a bank has refused to pay a check or other NEGOTIABLE INSTRUMENT properly and legally presented for payment. Protest is a means of legally proving that presentment was made, but rarely is used. Modern banking systems provide a sufficient AUDIT TRAIL to verify the conditions under which check presentment was made. When a check is dishonored by the drawee bank, it can be presented a second time by a notary public or other public official. If the drawee bank still refuses to pay, an official statement is attached to the instrument, legally certifying that presentment was made and that the instrument was dishonored.

PROVISIONAL CREDIT temporary redeposit of funds in a disputed ELECTRONIC FUNDS TRANSFER while the transaction is investigated. Under the ERROR RESOLUTION procedures in Regulation E, a consumer who claims his bank account was debited erroneously without his or her authorization may challenge the transaction. The consumer's bank has ten business days from the time the complaint is lodged to investigate and if necessary correct the error. If it cannot, the bank must return the funds debited, and it then has up to 45 days in most transactions to investigate the alleged error.

PRUDENT MAN RULE investment standard for trusts and fiduciary investments. The rule, also called the "American rule," originated in an 1830 court case. It states that trustees are free to make investment decisions, applying the same standards—reasonable income and preservation of capital—that a prudent man would use. The rule has been accepted in some states as a guide for trustees. Other states have more formal rules, limiting fiduciaries and bank trust departments to a so-called LEGAL LIST of approved investments.

PUBLIC OFFERING offering and sale of securities by an issuer, after meeting registration requirements of the Securities and Exchange Commission. Offerings usually are carried out by an underwriting syndicate, according to the terms and conditions in an UNDERWRITING AGREEMENT. Also, the secondary distribution of previously issued shares of securities.

PUBLIC PURPOSE BOND bond issued by or on behalf of a state or local governmental unit that is exempt from state or local taxes under the Tax Reform Act of 1986. Qualifying issuers have taxing authority, power of eminent domain, or policing power within its jurisdiction. Such bonds may include GENERAL OBLIGATION BONDS backed by taxing authority, revenue anticipation notes and TAX ANTICIPATION NOTES issued to cover cash flow shortfalls. They are exempt from federal taxes, including the alternative minimum tax but are subject to volume limitations on new issues of tax-exempt securities. Contrast with PRIVATE PURPOSE BOND.

PURCHASE ACQUISITION accounting method that adds the revalued assets and liabilities of an acquired firm to those of the acquirer. The assets and liabilities of the acquired organization are recorded on the books of the acquirer at FAIR MARKET VALUE. The difference between the purchase price and the net fair market value of assets and liabilities acquired or assumed is carried by the acquirer as GOODWILL. The financial figures of the two entities remain combined going forward, but historical costs are restated. This method ordinarily is used when more than 10% of the purchase price is paid with cash, preferred stock, or debt securities.

PURCHASE AND ASSUMPTION method used by the FEDERAL DEPOSIT INSURANCE CORPORATION in closing a failed bank and transferring ownership and control to a healthy institution. Purchase and assumption is used only when it is a less expensive option to a LIQUIDATION, in which the FDIC pays depositor claims and disposes of the failed bank's assets to partially recover its liquidation costs. *See also* MODIFIED PAYOFF.

PURCHASED FUNDS *see* FEDERAL FUNDS; MANAGED LIABILITIES; OVERNIGHT MONEY.

PURCHASE MONEY MORTGAGE mortgage taken by the seller in lieu of full payment in cash, securing the buyer's obligation.

PURCHASE MORTGAGE mortgage taken out to purchase a home. Contrast with a mortgage REFINANCING, in which an existing mortgage is replaced with a new lower-rate loan.

PURCHASE ORDER FINANCING financing method advancing money against a manufacturer's purchase order. Purchase order financing is short term; obligations are typically payable to the financing company within 30 to 60 days of issuance. Compare with FACTORING.

PURCHASING POWER PARITY economic theory linking currency exchange rates to prices paid for goods and services in any two countries. For example, if a basket of goods can be bought with $1,000 in the United States or 150,000 yen in Japan, the parity of the U.S. dollar to the yen is 1-to-150. If either currency has greater purchasing power, the theory goes, it might be better for buyers to convert yen into dollars, for instance, and buy in the United States. The theory applies to tradable goods with low transportation costs. If the price is different in the two countries, people will not buy in the higher price country.

PURPOSE STATEMENT signed affidavit of a borrower stating the intended use for a loan collateralized by margin securities. Federal Reserve REGULATION U requires banks to obtain a purpose statement (Federal Reserve form U-1) when loans are secured by marketable securities. The borrower agrees not to violate any Federal Reserve regulations on sale or purchase of securities.

PUT BOND MUNICIPAL BOND or other bond that has a sell-back provision, or REDEMPTION privilege, allowing holders to sell their holdings back to the issuer at specific intervals up to five years after the original issue date at specific prices determined at the time of issuance. Also known as an *option bond*, put bonds were first offered in 1980 to encourage reluctant investors to buy long-term bonds. Put bonds frequently are supported by CREDIT ENHANCEMENTS.

PUT OPTION contract giving the holder the right, but not the obligation, to sell a security or financial instrument for a specified period of time at a specific price, called the exercise price or STRIKE PRICE. Puts are bought by investors who believe the price of the underlying securities will go down, and they will be able to sell the securities at a higher striking price. The opposite is a CALL OPTION.

PYRAMIDING

1. **Banking.** Using credit with one financial institution to rollover outstanding obligations at other creditors without paying down the principal. Eventually, interest payments become so large the debtor is unable to rollover his debts any longer, and he is often forced to combine obligations in a debt consolidation loan.
2. **Finance.** The use of paper profits to make additional investments, adding to the holder's unliquidated (open) position.
3. **Real Estate.** The acquisition of additional properties by refinancing already owned property, and reinvesting the proceeds.

Q

QUALIFIED ENDORSEMENT endorser's writing on a check limiting his liability in event of nonpayment or nonacceptance of an instrument. It usually is written with the words WITHOUT RECOURSE, or similar words to indicate the endorser is not secondarily liable for payment.

QUALIFIED OPINION opinion by a certified auditor, stating that the auditor is unable to verify completely the accuracy of the financial records of a bank, because of certain omissions in the records or the limited scope of the AUDIT. A qualified opinion does not necessarily mean, however, that there are serious errors or omissions.

QUALIFIED THRIFT LENDER lender that follows guidelines of the 1989 FINANCIAL INSTITUTIONS REFORM, RECOVERY AND ENFORCEMENT ACT for mortgage lenders specializing in home mortgage finance. In exchange for holding 65% of their portfolio in residential mortgages or mortgage-backed securities, such lenders may borrow funds from their district Federal Home Loan Bank. Savings and loans, commercial banks and credit unions can also affiliate with Federal Home Loan Banks as qualified thrift lenders.

QUALIFYING RATIO ratio used by mortgage lenders in determining the maximum amount of mortgage to approve, such as the borrower's total regular monthly debt as a percentage of gross monthly income. The qualifying ratio is the lender's rule of thumb for determining a borrower's ABILITY TO PAY.

QUANTITIATIVE EASING open market purchase of government bonds, mortgage-backed bonds, or other securities by a central bank. Quantitative easing increases the MONEY SUPPLY and EXCESS RESERVES in the banking system. It is a last resort monetary policy tool, usually executed when interest rates are near zero and conventional monetary policy has failed to pull the economy out of recession. The Federal Reserve purchased large amounts of mortgage-backed and government bonds following the 2008 financial crisis in an effort to stimulate the U.S. economy.

QUANTITY THEORY OF MONEY theory correlating the quantity of money and prices in the economy. It attempts to explain how inflation can be controlled by MONETARY POLICY, by control of the money supply. The theory's detractors cite the existence of quasi-money or near money, and also the ability of nonbank FINANCIAL INSTITUTIONS to develop and introduce new forms of credit. Yet, the quantity theory has gained respect in recent years largely through the work of Milton Friedman of the University of Chicago. *See also* MONETARIST.

QUARTERLIES interim financial reports on the condition of a publicly held company, released each quarter of its fiscal year.

QUASI-PUBLIC CORPORATION privately operated corporation that fulfills a public mandate, such as purchasing loans in the SECONDARY MARKET, thereby helping to maintain adequate funding sources for lenders. Quasi-public corporations often have government backing behind their debt obligations, and some issue stock that is publicly traded. The Federal National Mortgage Association (FANNIE MAE) was founded to encourage mortgage lending by purchasing mortgages insured by the Federal Housing Administration or guaranteed by the Department of Veterans Affairs, and also conventional home mortgages.

QUETZAL monetary unit of Guatemala.

QUICK ASSETS current assets of a business, excluding inventories, that could be converted into cash if necessary within a short period, usually one year or less. Also known as *liquid assets.*

QUIET TITLE ACTION legal action brought to eliminate any interest or claim in a property by others. It is the procedure used to remove title defects from a real estate title when a QUITCLAIM DEED cannot be obtained.

QUITCLAIM DEED document in which title, claim, or ownership of property or an estate is relinquished to another, without representing that such title is valid. Usually it contains no covenant or warranty against outstanding claims of previous lien holders.

QUOTATION broker's stated price giving the highest bid to buy or lowest offer to sell. A full quotation displays the price that will be paid (the bid price), and price offered (the offered price). The normal order of listing is bid first, and asked second. The amount of activity is indicated by the spread between bid and asked quotes. Often shortened to "quote."

R

RAISED CHECK check with the written dollar amount fraudulently changed to a higher figure. To protect consumers and financial institutions the dollar amount is written twice: in numeric form after the words "pay to the order of," and in the maker's handwriting on the line below. When the two amounts differ, the paying bank usually accepts the written out amount—for example, "one thousand one hundred dollars"—as the check writer's intention.

RAND monetary unit of South Africa.

RANGE FORWARD FORWARD EXCHANGE CONTRACT combining the purchase of a specific amount of currency with an option contract on currency futures. Range forwards limit downside losses from currency DEPRECIATION to an agreed amount, while giving the holder the option of participating in upside profits.

RAP ACCOUNTING *see* REGULATORY ACCOUNTING PRINCIPLES.

RATE LOCK *see* LOCK-IN PERIOD.

RATE OF EXCHANGE *see* EXCHANGE RATE.

RATE OF RETURN

1. yield obtained on invested capital, also known as the RETURN ON EQUITY (ROE), or RETURN ON ASSETS, (ROA), a measure of operating performance.
2. gross annualized yield on a time deposit or certificate of deposit, the EFFECTIVE ANNUAL YIELD, including compounded interest paid or accrued. This differs from the advertised annual rate or NOMINAL INTEREST RATE.
3. EARNINGS PER SHARE—net income plus after-tax interest charges, divided by the number of outstanding shares. Perhaps the single most useful ratio for assessing a firm's overall operating performance.
4. investor's rate of return, measured by changes in current stock prices and dividends.

See also INTERNAL RATE OF RETURN.

RATE-REDUCTION MORTGAGE mortgage that grants the borrower an option to reduce the loan interest rate at periodic intervals. A rate-reduction mortgage, sometimes called an ADJUSTABLE-RATE MORTGAGE in reverse, may be a good choice when mortgage rates are declining. The mortgage interest rate cannot go up, but it can go lower still. A property appraisal is normally waived at refinancing.

RATE SENSITIVITY *see* INTEREST RATE RISK.

RATING

1. **Banking:** measurement of a bank or thrift institution's CAPITAL ADEQUACY, management and other factors as compared to other

insured financial institutions. There are two broad categories of organizations providing some form of analytical coverage of financial institutions: bank *rating firms* and bank *ranking firms*.

Bank *rating firms* follow a limited number of large banks and thrift institutions, and provide detailed commentary about each financial institution covered, reporting on recent changes in management, the general economic climate and other factors considered significant by rating firm analysts. Different ratings may be released for long-term and short-term obligations of a bank or FINANCIAL HOLDING COMPANY. Some rating firms assign COUNTRY RISK and political risk ratings for banks operating internationally. Bank ratings are available as subscription services.

Among the best known and most widely used *rating firms* are: Dominion Bond Rating Service, Inc. 55 Broadway New York, N.Y. 10016; Fitch Ratings, One State Street Plaza, New York, N.Y. 10004; Moody's Investors Service, 99 Church Street, New York, N.Y. 10007; Standard & Poor's, 25 Broadway, New York, N.Y. 10004.

Bank *ranking firms* generally cover all financial institutions in a category, such as commercial banks, BANK HOLDING COMPANIES, and savings and loans. They assign each institution covered a grade or numerical score using an analytical formula. The assigned rankings are meant to indicate a covered institution's financial strength and ability to protect depositors' funds. Ranking firms compute their evaluations from the same criteria—capital, assets, management, earnings, and liquidity—that bank examiners review during scheduled examinations of insured financial institutions. Bank rankings are also available as subscription services.

Among the best known and most widely used ranking firms are Bauer Financial Inc., P.O. Box 14350, 2655 Lejeune Road, Coral Gables, FL 33134 (*www.bauerfinancial.com*); IDC Financial Publishing, P.O. Box 140, 700 Walnut Ridge Drive, Suite 201, Hartland, WI 53029 (*www.idcfp.com*); Kroll Bond Rating Agency, Inc., 1311 South Main Street, Suite 304, Mt. Airy, MD 21771 (*http://srs/krollbondratings.com*); SNL Financial, One SNL Plaza, P.O. Box 2124, Charlottesville, VA 22902 (*www.snl.com*); Veribanc, P.O. Box 1610, One Social Street, Woonsocket, RI 02895 (*www.veribanc.com*); Weiss Ratings, Inc., 15430 Endeavor Drive, Jupiter, FL 33478 (*www.weissratings.com*).

2. **Credit Rating:** compiled by one of the major CREDIT BUREAUS, recording previous credit history, late payments, charge-offs, and legal judgments reported on an individual.
3. **Bond Rating:** evaluation of a bond issuer's credit risk (probability of default) by a nationally-recognized statistical rating organization (NRSRO) such as Fitch Ratings, Moody's Investors Service, and Standard & Poor's.

RATIO ANALYSIS

1. **Banking:** detailed examination of a bank's financial performance versus similar size banks, as indicated by its return on assets, return on equity, efficiency ratio (non-interest expense divided by revenue), loan CHARGE-OFF ratio, earnings per share, net interest margin, non-interest income, and other criteria. Sources of information include bank annual reports, CALL REPORT data reported to bank regulatory agencies, and FORM 10K and FORM 10Q reports submitted to the Securities and Exchange Commission. *See also* UNIFORM BANK PERFORMANCE REPORT.

   Ratio analysis examines performance and overall profitability of banks and bank holding companies. The four general categories of ratios in assessing performance of banks and bank holding companies include: profitability—RETURN ON ASSETS, RETURN ON EQUITY; capital—CAPITAL RATIO; liquidity—LIQUIDITY RATIO; and asset risk ratio—risk adjusted capital ratio. *See also* CAMELS RATING.
2. **Commercial Lending:** financial ratios used by commercial lenders in analyzing the financial condition of prospective and current borrowers. Trade ratios comparing performance by different firms in specific industries are available from the Risk Mangement Association, the national association of bank credit officers, the U.S. Department of Commerce, and other sources. *See also* BALANCE SHEET RATIOS.

RATIONAL EXPECTATIONS *see* EXPECTATIONS THEORY.

READER/SORTER machine that separates checks received from bank tellers or from other banks, sorting them into different categories. A reader/sorter is a key piece of equipment in preparing CASH LETTERS sent to other banks. It sorts, encodes checks, and distributes checks. *See also* MAGNETIC INK CHARACTER RECOGNITION; PROOF AND TRANSIT; TRANSIT ITEM.

REAFFIRMATION voluntary agreement by a debtor in bankruptcy to pay all or part of a debt, even though the debtor is not legally obligated to do so, and cannot be compelled by his creditors to repay a debt. Under the bankruptcy code, the debtor's attorney files a statement with the court stating that reaffirmation will not harm the debtor financially. Debt reaffirmations are not allowed in Chapter 13 WAGE EARNER PLANS.

REAL monetary unit of Brazil.

REAL ESTATE INVESTMENT TRUST (REIT) investor-owned corporation, trust or association that sells shares to investors and invests in income-producing property. A REIT is exempt from federal corporation taxes, provided that it distributes 95% or more of its income to investors, although shareholder dividends are fully taxable. Assets of a REIT are managed by one or more trustees who control its acquisitions and investments. An equity REIT owns and operates income property, such as shopping centers and apartment buildings; a MORTGAGE REIT lends money to developers, holding a construction mortgage or long-term mortgage as security.

REAL ESTATE MORTGAGE INVESTMENT CONDUIT (REMIC) mortgage securities vehicle authorized by the Tax Reform Act of 1986 that holds commercial and residential mortgages in trust, and issues securities representing an UNDIVIDED INTEREST in these mortgages. A REMIC, which can be a corporation, trust, association, or partnership, assembles mortgages into pools and issues pass-through certificates, multiclass bonds similar to a COLLATERALIZED MORTGAGE OBLIGATION (CMO), or other securities to investors in the secondary mortgage market. Mortgage-backed securities issued through a REMIC can be debt financings of the issuer or a sale of assets. The Tax Reform Act eliminated the double taxation of income earned at the corporate level by an issuer and dividends paid to securities holders, thereby allowing a REMIC to structure a mortgage-backed securities offering as a sale of assets, effectively removing the loans from the originating lender's balance sheet, rather than a debt financing in which the loans remain as balance sheet assets. A REMIC itself is exempt from federal taxes, although income earned by investors is fully taxable. As a tax-exempt entity, a REMIC may invest only in qualified mortgages and permitted investments, including single family or multifamily mortgages, commercial mortgages, second mortgages, mortgage participations, and federal agency pass-through securities.

Federal legislation enacted in 2004 (the American Jobs Creation Act) relaxed some of the restrictions on REMIC issuance, allowing securitization of mortgage-related open-end credit, such as home-equity lines of credit.

A REMIC can issue mortgage securities in a wide variety of forms: securities collateralized by (Ginnie Mae) pass-through certificates, whole loans, single-class participation certificates and multiclass mortgage-backed securities; multiple class pass-through securities with fast-pay or slow-pay features; securities with a SUBORDINATED DEBT tranche that assumes most of the default risk, allowing the issuer to get a better credit rating; and Collateralized Mortgage Obligations with monthly pass-through of bond interest, eliminating reinvestment risk by giving investors CALL PROTECTION against early prepayment.

Among the major issuers of REMICS are FREDDIE MAC and FANNIE MAE, the two leading secondary market buyers of conventional mortgage loans, and also privately operated mortgage conduits owned by mortgage bankers, mortgage insurance companies, and savings institutions. *See also* CONDUIT; GRANTOR TRUST.

REAL ESTATE OWNED real estate acquired by a lender through FORECLOSURE in satisfaction of a debt. A loan secured by foreclosed real estate is counted as a NONPERFORMING ASSET in reporting loan quality in call reports to bank supervisory agencies. Foreclosed real estate is auctioned off through a bidding process. Normally, the lender bids what is owed, and no more. If there are no higher bids, the lender takes the property and it becomes real estate owned. Also called *other real estate owned* (OREO).

REAL ESTATE SETTLEMENT PROCEDURES ACT (RESPA) federal law requiring lenders to give home mortgage borrowers an estimate of total charges prior to the loan closing. Disclosure under RESPA is mandatory in federally guaranteed or insured residential mortgages, and certain types of commercial real estate loans. It requires lenders to make a good faith estimate of closing costs, prohibits borrower kickbacks and sets guidelines for handling mortgage escrow accounts. RESPA is administered by the Department of Housing and Urban Development, and is enforced by the lender's primary banking regulator. *See also* HUD-1 SETTLEMENT STATEMENT.

REAL INTEREST RATE interest rate calculated by subtracting the inflation rate from the stated rate, or NOMINAL INTEREST RATE. The real interest rate, an important tool in comparing effective yields on different investments, can be figured for the current time period, or for future periods by estimating the future inflation rate. Thus, a bond or bank CD earning 11% when the inflation rate is 5% has a (pretax) real interest rate of 6%. As the rate of inflation rises above 5%, the investment begins to lose value because the interest earned falls behind the general increase in prices.

REALIZED PROFIT (OR LOSS) profit or loss when a security actually is sold or otherwise disposed at a price exceeding its purchase price, as distinguished from paper profits.

REAL MONEY money, usually coinage, as distinguished from paper money accepted as LEGAL TENDER; also called HARD CURRENCY. Checks, drafts, and other negotiable instruments would not be considered real money.

REAL PROPERTY land, buildings, and other kinds of fixed or immovable property. This is classified as real, as distinguished from personal property. In some states, it is synonymous with real estate.

REAL RATE OF RETURN rate of return earned by an investment, less the rate of inflation in the country where funds are invested. An investor earning a rate of 8% while the inflation rate is 3%, has a real rate of return of 5%. Rate of return analysis is used in many different economic scenarios, including international capital movements between countries.

REBATE

1. UNEARNED INTEREST returned to the borrower when a loan is paid off early. See also RULE OF THE 78's.
2. pro-rated share of deposit insurance premium returned to a federally insured bank or savings association when the insurance premiums paid exceeds payouts to depositors from an insurance fund.
3. portion of net sales returned to cardholders by a bank card plan, based on card usage. A plan with a 2% rebate nets the cardholder $2 for every $100 in sales.
4. reduction in a credit card merchant's MERCHANT DISCOUNT RATE for credit card transactions above a certain amount.

RECAPITALIZATION any major changes in a corporation's paid in capital, resulting from issuance of new shares of stock, REORGANIZATION in bankruptcy, or exchange of common stock shares for bonds and notes, as in a LEVERAGED BUY-OUT. In banking, it is any restructuring of a troubled bank assisted by a deposit insurance fund, as in a BAILOUT of a failing bank, where the insurance fund pays the acquiring bank the difference between the book value of a troubled bank's assets and the estimated market value. The insurance fund may also take an equity position in the restructured bank.

RECEIPT written record of a transaction or payment of a debt. A deposit receipt is a bank customer's copy of the deposit ticket submitted with a check being deposited. A transaction receipt is a customer's copy of a bank card sales draft or, in an electronic funds transfer, the terminal receipt that is required by REGULATION E. A receipt acknowledging payment of debt is not a promise to pay, and therefore is not a negotiable instrument, but if it is an order to pay, may be transferrable through assignment. *See also* AMERICAN DEPOSITARY RECEIPT; INTERNATIONAL DEPOSITARY RECEIPT.

RECEIVABLES FINANCING form of ASSET-BASED LENDING providing seasonal capital to businesses, collateralized by accounts receivable. Receivables loans, like inventory loans, are sources of short-term funds that are used for a variety of purposes, such as financing a business expansion. Receivables are a better form of collateral than inventory from the lender's viewpoint; they demonstrate that the firm has buyers. Receivables are more liquid than inventory; they are one step closer to cash. A lender's primary risk in receivables financing is that the borrower will divert collections away from repayment of the loan. *See also* BORROWING BASE.

RECEIVER person named by a bankruptcy court to act as agent for a debtor in bankruptcy. The receiver is entrusted with authority to help reorganize the company, or to liquidate it to satisfy obligations to creditors. The receiver is required to maintain the property for the benefit of creditors or others having an equity interest in it, until bankruptcy has been discharged. In a BANK FAILURE the FDIC acts as receiver of the failed bank's assets. *See also* DEBTOR IN POSSESSION.

RECEIVING BANK in the nationwide AUTOMATED CLEARING HOUSE (ACH) system, a bank or other depository institution eligible to receive electronic credit and debit entries from another bank, the ORIGINATOR of an ACH transaction, for posting to a customer's account. Also called *receiving depository financial institution* (RDFI).

RECESSION downturn in a country's economy, measured by a decline in aggregate economic activity. Most economic measures of a recession are at least partly subjective, although a widely held definition says a recession occurs when real gross domestic product declines in two consecutive quarters. Another indicator of a recession is a sudden rise—at least two percentage points—in the unemployment rate. The National Bureau of Economic Research decides when recessions begin and end, based on an analysis of economic indicators. This often means that a recession can be well underway before policymakers in government and business become aware of it and begin taking corrective actions. *See also* FISCAL POLICY; MONETARY POLICY.

RECIPROCAL STATUTES mutually beneficial legislation adopted by two or more states to encourage commerce between them, or for other reasons. For example, state laws approving REGIONAL INTERSTATE BANKING, and also state laws providing comparable treatment of corporation or inheritance taxes. *See also* UNIFORM COMMERCIAL CODE.

RECLAMATION

1. adjustment for errors in processing of a check or other negotiable instrument incorrectly recorded by a clearinghouse association. The net difference is either due, or payable by, a clearing member.
2. securities term for the right of a party to collect money or securities from the party on the other side of the transaction if irregularities in settlement are discovered, for example, if certificates are stolen.

RECORD DATE

1. calendar date used by a bond issuer in determining eligibility to collect future payments of principal and interest. The record date for a holder of a Collaterized Mortgage Obligation is generally one month prior to the payment date.
2. date on which owners of a corporation's stock are declared by the board of directors as eligible to receive dividends payable at a specified future date or vote on corporate issues, as in a RIGHTS OFFERING.

RECORDING (OF LIEN) public acknowledgment of a lien against specific property identified in a mortgage, and recorded in a public land record office. The details of a properly executed legal document, such as a mortgage, deed of trust or extension of a mortgage are noted, and become part of the public record.

RECOURSE ability to compel payment. Under negotiable instruments law, recourse conveys the right to collect from a writer or endorser of a negotiable instrument, such as a check or draft. When an installment sales contract is sold to a bank on a recourse basis, the retailer takes full responsibility for the paper if default occurs. In commercial finance, where a lender purchases a merchant's accounts receivables, the finance company reserves the right to charge back any disputed invoices to the customer and debit the customer's account. In contrast, FACTORING is done on a NONRECOURSE basis; in other words, the factor buying the merchant's credit receivables makes the credit evaluation in advance and assumes all credit risk of nonpayment. *See also* LIMITED RECOURSE FINANCE; NONRECOURSE LOAN; WITH FULL RECOURSE.

RECOVERY

1. collection of payment on an obligation previously written off as a loss. Because the loan already was charged against the reserve account for bad debts, recoveries may be credited against the loan loss reserve or allocated to undivided profits. Recoveries may result from payment by the borrower or liquidation of collateral. *See also* WORKOUT AGREEMENT.
2. improvement in the business cycle, as after a RECESSION.
3. gain in securities prices after a market decline.
4. gain in the value of a currency against other world currencies.

RECURRING PAYMENT regularly scheduled payment of a consumer debt, such as an installment loan, which is payable monthly, a MORTGAGE, which is payable monthly or biweekly, or an insurance premium. Benefits payments to individuals, such as Social Security payments or pension benefits, also are recurring payments. Recurring payments, which change little in dollar amount, are processible through the AUTOMATED CLEARING HOUSE system. A majority of Social Security payments are deposited in this fashion. *See also* DIRECT DEPOSIT; PREAUTHORIZED PAYMENT.

RED CLAUSE LETTER OF CREDIT LETTER OF CREDIT allowing the beneficiary of a documentary credit to receive funds for the purchase of merchandise described in the credit. These funds, known as ADVANCES, are deducted from the face amount of the draft when the beneficiary presents the letter for payment. Most red clause letters are opened in transactions where the beneficiary is acting as agent for the buyer in the exporting country, and purchases merchandise destined for export.

REDEMPTION

1. repayment of a debt security or preferred stock issue by payment of the principal at maturity, or at an earlier date if the issuer calls the security and pays a premium to debt security holders. Also, the liquidation of mutual fund shares by selling shares back to the fund's investment manager at the NET ASSET VALUE price.
2. mortgagor's right, called the EQUITY OF REDEMPTION, to recover foreclosed property by paying principal and interest due, plus the lender's out-of-pocket costs.

3. in bankruptcy, the right of a debtor to reclaim personal property by paying creditors the estimated fair market value of assets secured by a lien.

RED HERRING cautionary statement, printed in red, on the first page of a preliminary prospectus. It states that the document is not an offer to sell, but contains the required public disclosures.

REDISCOUNT process by which a Federal Reserve Bank discounts a NEGOTIABLE INSTRUMENT or commercial finance paper, such as a bill of exchange or acceptance as collateral for advances at the DISCOUNT WINDOW. As a practical matter, however, rediscounting of commercial obligations accepted by a bank, called ELIGIBLE PAPER, has occurred infrequently in the last 30 years.

REDLINING discriminatory practice of discouraging mortgages, improvement loans, and other forms of borrowing by home owners and businesses on the basis of race or ethnic background. Originally, such neighborhoods were outlined in red on a map, hence the name redlining. The practice is forbidden by the COMMUNITY REINVESTMENT ACT and other federal regulations. Lenders also are discouraged from using postal ZIP codes as a credit criterion, because they may inadvertently exclude borrowers whose credit status is protected from discrimination by the Equal Credit Opportunity Act. *See also* REGULATION B.

REFERENCE RATE *see* BASE RATE; FEDERAL FUNDS RATE; LONDON INTER BANK OFFERED RATE; PRIME RATE.

REFINANCE BILL *see* THIRD COUNTRY ACCEPTANCE.

REFINANCE RISK risk that a bank will be unable to refinance maturing deposit liabilities when they come due at maturity, at acceptable prices and terms. When banks go to the market to refinance liabilities, the risk is that they may be unwilling or unable to acquire deposits necessary for making new investments. Refinance risk applies to money market deposits and corporate debt. The risk for the institution is that it may not be able to roll over those liabilities at an affordable rate.

REFINANCING

1. **Banking.** A loan that adds to the principal balance owed, usually for property or home improvements, and alters the payment amount and terms.
2. **Finance.** Issuing new securities at a lower interest rate, or extended maturity. Also called REFUNDING.
3. **Real estate.** To extend existing financing to new properties.
4. **Mortgages.** Revising a mortgage loan and modifying scheduled debt payments, often to reduce finance charges or to modify the loan payments.

REFUNDABLE INTEREST interest refunded to a borrower who pays off a loan before the maturity date; refunding of the UNEARNED INTEREST under the RULE OF THE 78'S.

REFUNDING

1. process of paying off maturing or outstanding debt with proceeds of a new issue, often at a lower interest cost to the issuer. The U.S. Treasury Department uses the refunding process to replace maturing Treasury bills and notes with new issues.
2. redemption of a corporate or municipal bond issue prior to the maturity date. This can be advantageous to the issuer if interest rates fall, but disadvantageous to the bondholders. Bond issues are refundable if there is a provision in the INDENTURE allowing early call or redemption. Some refunding provisions permit early calls with excess funds, but prohibit refunding with the proceeds of a lower interest rate issue.

   A call provision allows the bond issuer to pay part or all of the issue early by paying a specified redemption price to the bondholders. Some long-term industrial revenue bonds, however, are callable except for refunding purposes. *See also* DEFEASANCE.

REGIONAL BANK bank whose primary business is making loans to customers in a regional or metropolitan area and taking deposits within the state where it is chartered. A regional bank has a broader market focus than a COMMUNITY BANK, but smaller than a MONEY CENTER BANK. *See also* SUPER-REGIONAL BANK.

REGIONAL CHECK PROCESSING CENTER (RCPC) check processing center owned by a Federal Reserve Bank, that services depository institutions located in one of the 12 Federal Reserve districts. Fed check collection centers accelerate the nationwide collection of corporate and personal checks, by sorting and delivering checks to paying banks the same day as received. Regional check processing centers also handle collection of checks drawn on the Treasury, postal money orders, and redeemed food stamp coupons, but not cash and securities.

REGIONAL INTERSTATE BANKING banking expansion across state lines, as authorized by state laws permitting bank holding companies to merge with out-of-state banks. Regional interstate agreements, originating in the mid-1980s, were the initial step toward nationwide bank networks and nationwide branching. For example, the six New England states adopted reciprocal interstate banking laws in the mid-1980s, as did states in the Southeast, the Midwest, and Western regions.

Under the Riegle-Neal Interstate Banking and Branch Efficiency Act of 1994, well-capitalized banks were able to merge with banks outside their home state after October 1, 1995, and accept deposits through branches in any state after June 1, 1997.

See also INTERSTATE BANKING; SUPER REGIONAL BANK.

REGISTERED BOND bond whose owner's name is recorded as a book entry on the books of the issuer or its transfer agent. Bonds registered as to principal and interest are fully registered bonds, paying interest by check from the issuer's agent. Bonds registered as to principal are transferable only by endorsement of the holder. Most new corporate bonds and municipal bonds are issued only in fully registered form. The opposite is a BEARER BOND. Both registered bonds and bearer bonds are negotiable instruments.

REGISTERED CHECK check, similar to a MONEY ORDER, purchased at a bank for a fee. Registered checks are used by persons who don't have checking accounts to transfer funds to another, or pay bills. The purchaser writes the payee's name, signs his or her name, and presents the check to a bank teller. The check is payable from funds on deposit. Contrast with CERTIFIED CHECK.

REGISTRAR bank or bank trust department authorized by an issuer of securities to maintain records of the number of stock shares or securities cancelled and reissued. The registrar, by ensuring that only the authorized number of stock shares or securities is outstanding at any time, is protecting the holders' interests while performing a service for the corporation. The registrar normally is a commercial bank other than the stock TRANSFER AGENT. *See also* REGULATION 9.

REGISTRATION STATEMENT document required by the Securities and Exchange Commission for public offerings of securities. The registration statement, required by the Securities Act of 1933, discloses information on the management and financial condition of the issuer, and describes how the proceeds of the offering will be used. The statement also is filed with the appropriate securities exchanges and state securities regulators. Proposed offerings under $500,000 generally are exempt from SEC registration requirements under the 1933 Act. *See also* SHELF REGISTRATION.

REGRESSION ANALYSIS statistical techniques that quantify the relationship between two or more variables. The objective is quantitative prediction or forecasting to find out whether or not the variables being examined can be expected to be closely related to a larger population group. Regression analysis is a frequently used statistical tool in ASSET-LIABILITY MANAGEMENT, CREDIT SCORING, and ECONOMETRICS. Much econometric theory relates to theoretical problems arising from the application of various regression models, based on certain assumptions about economic activity.

Regression analysis allows a bank to set credit criteria for the general public, and build a statistical formula predicting how new accounts will perform in the future, that is, their ability to repay debt, by studying a sample of existing accounts. The banker wants to know the credit characteristics of consumers who are good payers, and those who are poor payers. Consumer credit ideally is suitable for statistical tools such as regression analysis because consumer behavior in handling credit is fairly predictable, based on a study of previous credit experience; even the credit losses are predictable.

REGULATION 9 regulation issued by the Comptroller of the Currency allowing national banks to operate trust departments and act as fiduciaries. Under Regulation 9, a national bank is permitted to act as trustee, administrator, and registrar of stocks and bonds, and engage in related activities, such as management of a COLLECTIVE INVESTMENT FUND, as long as these activities do not violate state legislation. *See also* FIDUCIARY.

REGULATION A Federal Reserve Board regulation governing advances by Federal Reserve Banks to depository institutions at the Federal Reserve DISCOUNT WINDOW. The Fed has two different programs for handling discount window borrowings: ADJUSTMENT CREDIT to meet temporary needs for funds when other sources, including the Federal Home Loan Banks, are not available; and EXTENDED CREDIT, designed to assist financial institutions with longer-term needs for funds. This category includes SEASONAL CREDIT privileges extended to smaller financial institutions that don't have ready access to money market funds. Fed banks may also extend EMERGENCY CREDIT to financial institutions other than depository banks and thrift institutions when failure to obtain credit would affect the economy adversely.

REGULATION B Federal Reserve regulation prohibiting discrimination against consumer credit applicants, and establishing guidelines for collecting and evaluating credit information. Regulation B prohibits creditors from discriminating on the basis of age, sex, race, color, religion, national origin, marital status, or receipt of public assistance. The regulation also requires creditors to give written notification of rejection, a statement of the applicant's rights under the EQUAL CREDIT OPPORTUNITY ACT, and a statement listing reasons for rejection, or the applicant has the right to request the reasons. If an applicant was denied credit because of adverse information in a credit bureau report, the applicant is entitled to receive, at no cost, a copy of the bureau report. Creditors who furnish credit information when reporting information on married borrowers must report information in the name of each spouse. *See also* CREDIT BUREAU; CREDIT SCORING; EFFECTS TEST.

REGULATION C Federal Reserve regulation implementing the Home Mortgage Disclosure Act of 1975, requiring depository institutions to make an annual disclosure of the location of certain residential loans, to determine whether depository institutions are meeting the credit needs of their local communities. Specifically exempted are institutions with assets of $10 million or less. Regulation C requires lenders of mortgages that are insured or guaranteed by a federal agency to disclose the number and total dollar amount of mortgage loans originated or purchased in the recent calendar year, itemized by census tract where the property is located.

REGULATION D Federal Reserve regulation that sets uniform RESERVE REQUIREMENTS for depository financial institutions holding transaction accounts or nonpersonal time deposits. The reserve requirement on transaction accounts (checking, NOW accounts, share draft accounts, and savings accounts with automatic transfer) ranges from 3% to 12% of deposits. Reserves on some time deposits (NONPERSONAL TIME DEPOSITS) may range from zero to a 3% reserve requirement. Time deposits with original maturities of 1½ years are subject to a zero percent reserve requirement. Reserves are maintained in the form of vault cash or a reserve account at a Federal Reserve Bank or at a correspondent bank. Reserves on NONMEMBER BANKS were to be phased in over an eight-year period ending in 1988. See also RESERVE REQUIREMENTS; TOTAL RESERVES.

REGULATION E Federal Reserve regulation that sets rules, liabilities, and procedures for electronic funds transfers (EFT), and establishes consumer protections when using EFT systems. This regulation prescribes rules for solicitation and issuance of EFT debit cards, governs consumer liability for unauthorized transfers, and requires financial institutions to disclose annually the terms and conditions of EFT services. The regulation sets up an error resolution procedure for errors on EFT related accounts. *See also* ERROR RESOLUTION; PROVISIONAL CREDIT.

REGULATION F Federal Reserve regulation requiring banks to adopt internal guidelines limiting their risk in dealings with other financial institutions. Regulation F covers two types of activity: check collection and other banking services that large banks perform for smaller, or CORRESPONDENT, banks; and financial market transactions such as interest rate swaps and repurchase agreements. The regulation requires banks to limit their credit exposure to other banks to a percentage of capital—25% of total capital for most banks. Higher levels are permitted for well capitalized banks.

REGULATION G Federal Reserve regulation implementing provisions of the GRAMM-LEACH-BLILEY ACT requiring reporting and public disclosure of written agreements between insure banks and their affiliates or unaffiliated third parties regarding compliance with the COMMUNITY REINVESTMENT ACT.

REGULATION H Federal Reserve regulation defining membership requirements for state chartered banks that become members of the Federal Reserve System. The regulation sets forth the procedures for state chartered banks to become members of the Federal Reserve System, as well as privileges and requirements for membership. The regulation also requires state chartered banks acting as securities transfer agents to register with the board.

REGULATION I Federal Reserve regulation requiring each MEMBER BANK joining the Federal Reserve System to purchase stock in its Federal Reserve Bank equal to 6% of its capital and surplus. Reserve bank stock, which pays dividends semiannually, is nontransferable and cannot be used as collateral. When a bank increases or decreases its capital base, it must adjust its ownership of Federal Reserve stock accordingly.

REGULATION J Federal Reserve regulation providing the legal framework for collection of checks and other cash items, and net settlement of balances through the Federal Reserve System. It specifies terms and conditions under which reserve banks will receive checks for COLLECTION from depository institutions, and PRESENTMENT to paying banks, and return of unpaid items. The regulation is supplemented by operating circulars issued by Federal Reserve banks.

REGULATION K Federal Reserve regulation governing international banking operations by bank holding companies and foreign banks in the United States. The regulation permits Edge Act corporations to engage in a range of international banking and financial activities. It also permits U.S. banks to own up to 100% of nonfinancial companies located outside the United States. The regulation also imposes reserve requirements on Edge Act corporations, as specified in Regulation D, and limits interstate activities of foreign banks in the United States.

REGULATION L Federal Reserve regulation prohibiting interlocking director arrangements in MEMBER BANKS or bank holding companies. A management official of a state member bank or bank holding company may not act simultaneously as a management official of another depository institution if both are not affiliated, are very large banks, or are located in the same local area. The regulation provides a ten-year grandfather period for certain interlocks, and allows some on an exception basis, such as organizations owned by women or minority groups, and newly chartered organizations, and in situations where implementing the regulation would endanger safety and soundness.

REGULATION M Federal Reserve regulation implementing the consumer leasing provisions of the Truth in Lending Act, and covers leases on personal property for more than four months for family, personal, or household use. It requires leasing companies to disclose in writing the cost of a lease, including security deposit and monthly payments, taxes and other payments, and in the case of an open-end lease, whether a BALLOON PAYMENT may be applied. It also requires written disclosure of the terms of a lease, including insurance, guarantees, responsibility for servicing the property, and whether the lessee has an option to buy the property at lease termination.

REGULATION N Federal Reserve regulation governing transactions among Federal Reserve Banks, and transactions involving the Federal Reserve Banks and foreign banks and governments.

This regulation gives the board responsibility for approving in advance negotiations or agreements by Reserve Banks and foreign banks and governments. A Reserve Bank may, under the direction of the Federal Open Market Committee, undertake negotiations, agreements, or facilitate open market transactions. Reserve banks must report quarterly to the Board of Governors on accounts they maintain with foreign banks.

REGULATION O Federal Reserve regulation limiting the amount of credit member banks may extend to their own executive officers. Regulation O also implements the reporting requirements of the FINANCIAL INSTITUTIONS REGULATORY AND INTEREST RATE CONTROL ACT of 1978 and the GARN-ST GERMAIN DEPOSITORY INSTITUTIONS ACT of 1982. Each federally insured bank is required to include in its quarterly statement of income and condition the total amount of credit extensions to executive officers and principal shareholders, and the number of such individuals who have received loans equaling 5% of the bank's equity capital or $500,000, whichever is less.

REGULATION P Federal Reserve regulation governing consumer privacy. The regulation sets guidelines for disclosure of personal financial information and gives consumers the option to "opt out" of any information sharing between banks and unaffiliated companies if they choose to keep their financial data private.

REGULATION Q Federal Reserve regulation prohibiting payment of interest on corporate checking accounts by Federal Reserve member banks. Regulation Q was repealed, effective July 21, 2011, as authorized by the Dodd-Frank Wall Street Reform and Consumer Protection Act.

REGULATION R Federal Reserve regulation exempting specified banking functions (trust, fiduciary, custody and deposit "sweep" functions) from the registration requirements of the Securities Exchange Act of 1934.

REGULATION S Federal Reserve regulation implementing the section of the Right to Financial Privacy Act of 1978 requiring government authorities to pay reasonable fees to financial institutions for financial records of individuals and small partnerships available to federal agencies, in connection with government loan programs or Internal Revenue Service summons.

REGULATION T Federal Reserve regulation governing credit extensions by securities brokers and dealers, including all members of national securities exchanges. Broker-dealers may not extend credit to their customers unless such loans are secured by margin securities—securities listed and traded on a national securities exchange, mutual funds, over-the-counter stock designated by the SEC as eligible for trading in the national market system. Generally, a broker-dealer may not extend credit on margin securities in excess of the percentage of current market value permitted by the board.

REGULATION U Federal Reserve regulation governing extensions of credit by banks for purchasing and carrying margin securities. Whenever a lender makes a loan secured by margin securities, the bank must have the customer execute a PURPOSE STATEMENT regardless of the use of the loan.

REGULATION V Federal Reserve regulation implementing sections of the Fair Credit Reporting Act and the Fair and Accurate Credit Transactions Act of 2003 (FACT Act) covering consumer privacy and personal financial information. The regulation contains guidelines for sharing of consumer information among financial institutions and affiliated companies, distribution of financial reports to credit bureaus, and prevention of identity theft.

REGULATION W Federal Reserve regulation covering loans by a depository institution to an affiliated company, asset purchases from an affiliated company, and other transactions between a bank and its affiliates. This regulation implements sections 23A and 23B of the Federal Reserve Act.

REGULATION X Federal Reserve regulation extending the provisions of other securities related regulations—Regulation G, T, and U—to foreign persons or organizations who obtain credit outside the United States for the purchase of U.S. Treasury securities.

REGULATION Y Federal Reserve regulation governing banking and nonbanking activities of bank holding companies and the divestiture of impermissible nonbank activities. The regulation spells out the procedures for forming a bank holding company and procedures to be followed by bank holding companies acquiring voting shares in bank or nonbank companies. The regulation also lists those nonbank activities that are deemed closely related to banking and therefore permissible for bank holding companies.

REGULATION Z Federal Reserve regulation implementing the consumer credit protections in the Truth in Lending Act of 1968, The major areas of the regulation require lenders to:

—give borrowers written disclosure on essential credit terms including the cost of credit expressed as a finance charge and an annual percentage rate.

—respond to consumer complaints of billing errors on certain credit accounts within a specified period.

—identify credit transactions on periodic statements of opened credit accounts.

—provide certain rights regarding credit cards.

—inform customers of the RIGHT OF RESCISSION in certain mortgage-related loans within a specified period.

—comply with special requirements when advertising credit.

REGULATION AA Federal Reserve regulation establishing procedures for handling consumer complaints about alleged unfair or deceptive practices by a state member bank. Complaints should be submitted in writing to the Director of the Division and Community Affairs at the Board of Governors in Washington, D.C.

REGULATION BB Federal Reserve regulation implementing the COMMUNITY REINVESTMENT ACT. Banks are required to make available to the public a statement indicating communities served, the type of credit the lender is prepared to extend, and public comments to its CRA statement.

REGULATION CC Federal Reserve regulation implementing the EXPEDITED FUNDS AVAILABILITY ACT of 1987, setting endorsement standards on checks paid by depository financial institutions. The endorsement standard is designed to facilitate the identification of the endorsing bank and prompt return of unpaid checks.

REGULATION DD Federal Reserve regulation implementing the Truth in Savings Act.

REGULATION EE Federal Reserve regulation authorizing banks to settle mutual obligations at net value, rather than gross value, through bi-lateral or multilateral netting contracts. Securities brokers, dealers, and members of clearing organizations may also use contractual netting.

REGULATION FF Federal Reserve regulation creating exceptions to statutory prohibitions against obtaining medical information in determining credit eligibility.

REGULATION GG Federal Reserve regulation requiring U.S. financial institutions participating in designated payment systems to set policies and procedures to prevent payments tied to unlawful Internet gambling.

REGULATION II Federal Reserve regulation setting standards for debit card interchange fees; it also prohibits restrictive network arrangements in debit card processing.

REGULATION LL Federal Reserve regulation governing savings and loan holding companies. It defines the permitted activities of savings and loan holding companies and sets forth employment procedures for savings and loan officers and directors.

REGULATION MM Federal Reserve regulation governing mutual savings associations, mutual association holding companies, and subsidiary companies.

REGULATION QQ Federal Reserve regulation requiring large, systemically important bank holding companies and nonbank financial companies to submit an annual resolution plan (informally called a LIVING WILL document). Bank supervisory agencies would use this document as a guide path if it became necessary to close down a major financial company following a bankruptcy or other significant event.

REGULATORY ACCOUNTING PRINCIPLES (RAP) accounting rules and procedures authorized in the 1980s by the Federal Home Loan Bank Board to assist savings and loan associations with low

NET WORTH (assets less liabilities) in meeting regulatory capital requirements.

Permissive accounting rules, such as RAP accounting allowed many technically insolvent S&Ls to inflate their net worth and stay in business. For example, gains or losses from sales of assets could be amortized over extended periods, contrary to GENERALLY ACCEPTED ACCOUNTING PRINCIPLES (GAAP). In the late 1980s, these undercapitalized S&Ls had to be taken over by the government, contributing to the size of the thrift industry bailout.

RAP accounting was phased out by the FINANCIAL INSTITUTIONS REFORM, RECOVERY AND ENFORCEMENT ACT of 1989, which authorized federal funding to pay depositor claims on the failed S&Ls.

REINSTATEMENT restoring a borrower's credit standing to an acceptable condition. Reinstatement occurs when a borrower has cured a delinquency by making past-due payments plus any applicable penalty fees or late charges. If the account is a bank credit card, the customer's account number is removed from a list of accounts—the WARNING BULLETIN—that limits the consumer's ability to use the card. Reinstatement generally is reported to local or national credit bureaus, so that credit reports can be updated accordingly.

REINTERMEDIATION flow of funds into banks and other depository financial institutions from competing nonbank investments. This occurs when consumers move funds from money market funds and direct investments into bank money market and time deposit accounts, sometimes to take advantage of federal deposit insurance. The opposite is DISINTERMEDIATION.

REINVESTMENT RISK uncertainty about investment opportunity rates that may prevail at some future date. In lending, it is the risk that a bank will be unable to reinvest interest-earning assets at current market rates. An asset with an interest coupon carried at an above market rate may not easily be reinvested at a comparable rate at maturity, or when the borrower repays it early. When interest rates decline, borrowers tend to repay loans early or refinance at lower rates.

REJECTION *see* CREDIT DENIAL.

REJECT ITEMS checks, drafts, or electronic payments that cannot be processed when presented for payment. There are various causes of reject items: an unreadable MICR line on a damaged check; misencoding of the dollar amount or account number; an incorrect routing/transit number; a stale-dated or post-dated check; insufficient funds (NOT SUFFICIENT FUNDS) in an account being debited; or the absence of an account at the receiving institution. Reject items require special handling.

RELATIONSHIP BANKING concept in financial services marketing whereby an account officer or CUSTOMER SERVICE REPRESENTATIVE tries to meet all of a consumer's needs, or to the extent permitted by regulation. Relationship banking is an attempt to advance the sales culture in bank marketing beyond order taking to a more pro-active form of direct selling. Instead of selling financial services one at a time, an account officer attempts to gain an understanding of the consumer's needs and offer services that fulfill those needs. Commercial banks and other financial institutions have attempted to apply the concept of relationship banking through PERSONAL BANKER and PRIVATE BANKING programs. *See also* PLATFORM AUTOMATION.

RELEASE written notification discharging a claim by a creditor. A release of lien discharges secured property from a lien, indicating that the borrower has paid off the loan or substituted other collateral. A release clause in a mortgage or deed of trust stipulates that the property may be released from a mortgage lien if the buyer pays off the mortgage, or certain other conditions are met. A release of mortgage is recorded in public land records. *See also* SATISFACTION OF MORTGAGE.

REMAINDERMAN person who has a FUTURE INTEREST in the estate created by a trust, either as a contingent interest when a life tenant surrenders a claim to the estate, or a vested interest that becomes effective at a specified future date.

REMIC *see* REAL ESTATE MORTGAGE INVESTMENT CONDUIT.

REMITTANCE

1. payment toward satisfaction of a debt, whether in cash or cash equivalents, such as checks, drafts, and other negotiable instruments.
2. payment on an installment loan or open-end credit account, forwarded through the mail to a LOCK BOX, along with a remittance document, a machine readable billing document encoded with the customer's account number, and the amount due, plus any late charges, if the loan payment is delinquent.
3. PROCEEDS from a check submitted to another bank for COLLECTION.

REMITTANCE LETTER *see* TRANSIT LETTER.

REMOTE DEPOSIT check deposit by means of a digital image transmitted from computer scanner or smartphone. The practice has grown in recent years since the federal CHECK 21 law permitted banks to clear checks by sending images instead of actual paper checks. *See also* TRUNCATION.

REMOTE DISBURSEMENT *see* DELAYED DISBURSEMENT.

RENEGOTIATED LOAN loan in which the original payment terms have been altered due to a deterioration in the borrower's financial condition. This usually involves extending the loan maturity or lowering the interest rate to avoid FORECLOSURE on collateral assigned by the borrower, or charging-off the loan as uncollectible. *See also* NONACCRUAL ASSET; TROUBLED DEBT RESTRUCTURING.

RENEGOTIATED RATE MORTGAGE *see* ROLLOVER MORTGAGE.

RENEWAL substitution of a new PROMISSORY NOTE for a maturing one. If the old note is surrendered, it legally is considered a NOVATION. Renewal of a loan is accompanied by cancellation of a maturing note and making of a new one, which is then recorded on the bank's records. Renewal may also mean an extension of the maturity of an existing loan.

REORGANIZATION

1. restructuring of a corporation's financial assets under Chapter 11 of the Bankruptcy Code to return the company to profitability. The debtor corporation, known as the DEBTOR IN POSSESSION if no bankruptcy trustee is named, remains in operation and attempts to work out a plan for repayment of debts under supervision of the Bankruptcy Court. Creditors are prevented from seizing assets of the debtor to satisfy their claims, and must agree to a reorganization plan submitted by the debtor. If no acceptable plan can be worked out, the corporation's assets can then be liquidated, or sold off, to meet its unpaid obligations. Any corporation other than a bank or an insurance company, or a municipal government, may file a bankruptcy petition under Chapter 11. *See also* CRAM DOWN; CREDITORS' COMMITTEE; INVOLUNTARY BANKRUPTCY.
2. combination of two or more related business organizations, resulting in a new corporate structure, but leaving the business units intact. For example, two subsidiary banks of a bank holding company can merge into a single bank. The transaction is similar to a POOLING OF INTERESTS.

REPATRIATION return of financial assets deposited in a foreign bank or foreign branch of a domestic bank to a home country. Repatriation of assets denominated in a foreign currency may be impeded by EXCHANGE CONTROLS limiting the ability of residents of another country to transfer assets.

REPERFORMING LOAN residential mortgage loan that is contractually delinquent but on which the borrower has recently made regular payments. The overdue amounts continue rolling forward. Borrowers whose mortgage loan is classed as reperforming have few refinancing opportunities because of their delinquencies.

REPORTING DAYS *see* RESERVE REQUIREMENTS.

REPORT OF CONDITION bank balance sheet, plus additional schedules detailing major balance sheet and off-balance sheet items, as of a specific date. Banks are required by regulation to file sworn statements of financial condition on the last day of each calendar quarter at the request (call) of a state or federal regulatory agency, hence the name CALL REPORT. The call report also includes the bank report of income and stockholder dividends. A copy of the call report filed by all federally insured banks also is forwarded to the FEDERAL DEPOSIT INSURANCE CORPORATION, which makes these reports available.

Bank call reports are one of the two primary forms of bank supervision by regulatory agencies, the other being on-site visits by bank examiners. Quarterly filing of the Report of Condition allows a regulator to monitor the financial condition of banks with a higher than normal percentage of nonperforming assets, and schedule more frequent examinations if necessary. All three federal banking agencies, the Federal Reserve Board, the Comptroller of the Currency, and the FDIC, have uniform reporting guidelines, compiled by the FEDERAL FINANCIAL INSTITUTIONS EXAMINATION COUNCIL, for filling out call reports. Smaller banks and bank holding companies file less detailed reports than regional banks and money center banks. Full name: Reports of Condition and Income.

REPOSSESSION seizure of collateral securing a loan in default. Repossession occurs most often when other attempts to persuade the borrower to make payments fail to cure the loan delinquency. In most jurisdictions, repossession of collateral in which a lender has a security interest is done by obtaining a deficiency judgment or court order authorizing the lien holder to reclaim the property.

RE-PRESENTED CHECK form of electronic payment used by a company to charge (debit) a consumer's checking account when a check is returned because the account had insufficient funds to pay the check. Previously, checks returned by the depositing bank were processed through the check clearing system; re-presented checks are forwarded through the banking system's AUTOMATED CLEARING HOUSE more quickly and at lower cost.

REPRICING OPPORTUNITIES

1. days when bank loans or deposits are subject to a change in interest rate. Interest rates in variable rate consumer loans and adjustable rate mortgages may reprice at scheduled intervals, for example, semiannually or annually, based on changes in an INDEX rate. Other loan and deposit rates can change more frequently, sometimes even daily. A bank with more one-year deposit liabilities changing rates than one-year assets is said to be liability sensitive; if more one-year assets reprice than liabilities, it is asset-sensitive.
2. maturity date of a certificate of deposit or other time deposit that can be renewed (rolled over) at a different rate.

REPUDIATION intentional refusal to pay an obligation, usually the act of a government or a government agency. Repudiation differs from DEFAULT or MORATORIUM.

REPURCHASE AGREEMENT sale of securities coupled with an agreement to repurchase the securities at a higher price on a later date. A repurchase agreement is similar to a secured loan. Most repurchase agreements (or *repos*, as they are called) are overnight transactions, with the sale taking place one day and repurchase the next. Long-term repos, or *term repos*, can extend for a month or more, usually for a fixed time period. The opposite side of a repurchase agreement is a REVERSE REPURCHASE AGREEMENT, a purchase of securities followed by a sale back to the seller. Securities dealers use repurchase agreements to finance their inventories, selling their inventories to counterparty investors (for instance, a money market mutual fund) that have excess short-term funds they want to invest in higher-yielding securities.

An innovation in repo trading by the Fixed-Income Clearing Corporation, first introduced in 1998, allows dealer firms to freely trade general collateral repos—the most widely traded type of repurchase agreement—throughout the day without intraday trade-for-trade settlement, adding greater efficiency to the repo market. Securities eligible for trading include Fannie Mae and Freddie Mac fixed-rate mortgage backed securities and U.S. Treasury bills, notes, and bonds.

See also MATCHED SALE-PURCHASE AGREEMENT; RETAIL REPURCHASE AGREEMENT.

REQUIRED BALANCE *see* COMPENSATING BALANCE.

RESCHEDULING process of negotiating new loans to replace existing obligations, either by lengthening maturities, deferring of loan principal payments, or reducing interest rates, where the alternative is DEFAULT by the borrower and seizure of collateral by the lender. In commercial lending, rescheduling can take the form of a TROUBLED DEBT RESTRUCTURING, in which the lender offers the borrower a concession, such as a lower rate of interest, that it would not consider ordinarily.

In loans to less developed (LDC) countries, debt rescheduling is often carried out jointly with financial aid agreements, such as multi-year STRUCTURAL ADJUSTMENTS supervised by the International Monetary Fund, which are intended to encourage internal economic reforms and increased private sector participation in the economy of the debtor nation. *See also* BUYBACK; MORTGAGE MODIFICATION; SWAP.

RESCIND *see* RIGHT OF RESCISSION.

RESERVABLE DEPOSITS transaction accounts, savings accounts, and nonpersonal time deposits subject to RESERVE REQUIREMENTS under Federal Reserve Board REGULATION D.

RESERVE funds set aside in anticipation of future payments or obligations.

1. **Accounting.** A valuation reserve from retained earnings to cover anticipated future payments. Also called an ALLOWANCE.
2. **Banking.** There are two basic types of reserves, PRIMARY RESERVES, including cash needed to operate a bank, and cash and deposits at a Federal Reserve Bank to meet the required RESERVE RATIO, and secondary reserves. Required reserves are listed in the balance sheet under the asset category "cash and due from other banks." Secondary reserves are funds that can be kept in liquid investments

such as Treasury securities, and can be sold readily if necessary. There is, however, no category labeled secondary reserves on the balance sheet of a bank. *See also* LOAN LOSS RESERVES.

3. **Mortgage Banking.** A fund established by a bond issuer that may be used by the trustee of a series of mortgage-backed bonds to make principal and interest payments, or to pay administrative expenses. Also known as a debt service fund.
4. **Escrow fund.** A fund that pays property taxes and homeowner's insurance on mortgaged property.

RESERVE ACCOUNT noninterest earning balance that DEPOSITORY financial institutions maintain with a Federal Reserve Bank or with a CORRESPONDENT bank to satisfy the Fed's RESERVE REQUIREMENTS. Aside from their value to the Fed when it implements its MONETARY POLICY objectives, reserve account balances play a central role in the exchange of funds between depository institutions. Large dollar-value payments between financial institutions are processed through the Federal Reserve Communication System, also known as FEDERAL WIRE or Fed Wire, which routinely handles a daily volume exceeding $500 billion. These interbank transfers are made from reserve accounts. Banks with excess balances in a reserve account—balances greater than the required ratio of reserves to transaction account deposits—routinely sell these excess balances, known as FEDERAL FUNDS or Fed Funds, in the short-term MONEY MARKET to get a higher yield on temporarily idle balances. Fed Funds usually are sold on an overnight basis and are due back at the start of business the next day. Banks that have Fed Funds to sell generally are community banks with relatively low loan growth; buyers of Fed Funds typically are large regional or money center banks whose demand for short-term capital often exceeds their deposit liabilities. *See also* BORROWED RESERVES; CONTEMPORANEOUS RESERVES; EXCESS RESERVES; RESERVE RATIO; TOTAL RESERVES.

RESERVE ACCOUNT COMPUTATION *see* REPORTING DAYS.

RESERVE CITY BANK bank located in a city with a Federal Reserve Bank or branch office. These banks generally maintain higher reserve account balances than banks located outside reserve bank cities, which are called COUNTRY BANKS.

RESERVE FOR LOAN LOSS *see* LOAN LOSS RESERVES.

RESERVE RATIO ratio of RESERVE ACCOUNT balances to total deposits subject to RESERVE REQUIREMENTS. With the exception of very small institutions, all banks, thrifts, and credit unions are required to maintain reserve balances equal to 3% of nonpersonal time deposits and Eurocurrency deposits—and 12% on any balances above that. Time deposits with original maturities of 1½ years or more are exempt from reserves. Nonmember depository institutions (state banks and savings institutions) can maintain a pass-through account at a MEMBER BANK acting as a CORRESPONDENT for the reporting bank.

RESERVE REQUIREMENTS portion of their deposits banks and savings institutions are required to maintain as LEGAL RESERVES for the protection of depositors. Reserve requirements also provide one of the monetary adjustment tools the Federal Reserve System employs to regulate the supply of credit in the banking system. By raising or lowering the amount of required reserves, the Federal Reserve can either stimulate or tighten available bank credit, and the ability of banks to lend—known as *fractional reserve banking*. The ratio of required reserves to deposits ranges from 3% to 12% for transaction accounts such as checking accounts and Negotiable Order of Withdrawal (NOW) accounts, and up to 3% for time deposits (certificates of deposit). The reserve requirement may be kept in a separate checking account or with the bank's own cash (VAULT CASH). Commercial banks that are member banks in the Federal Reserve System are required to maintain their reserves in a checking account (RESERVE ACCOUNT) at the nearest Federal Reserve Bank. Other financial institutions have the option of holding reserves at a Federal Reserve Bank or in a checking account (called a PASS-THROUGH ACCOUNT) at a correspondent bank. *See also* BORROWED RESERVES; EXCESS RESERVES; FRACTIONAL RESERVES; NONBORROWED RESERVES; TOTAL RESERVES.

RESET DATE

1. point in time when the contractual interest on a floating rate loan is adjusted—monthly, quarterly, annually, or when specified by terms of the loan.
2. the date when the initial interest rate in an ADJUSTABLE RATE MORTGAGE is adjusted, based on changes in value of a market INDEX.
3. date on which the exercise price (or STRIKE PRICE) of an option is determined or modified.

RESIDENTIAL MORTGAGE mortgage collateralized by a one- to four-family dwelling, and ordinarily owner-occupied. The typical mortgage loan is a CONVENTIONAL MORTGAGE loan by a bank or thrift institution.

RESIDUAL cash balance resulting from the difference between the income stream generated by a POOL of mortgages and the cash flow necessary to fund a series of COLLATERALIZED MORTGAGE OBLIGATION bonds. These excess amounts accrue to the CMO issuer, or to a CMO trustee if a CMO issue has been sold.

RESIDUAL VALUE anticipated value or fair market value of an asset at the expiration of a lease. Fair market value is determined by agreement, or by APPRAISAL. In an OPEN-END LEASE, a consumer lease often used in auto financing, the lessee has the option of buying the car at its assumed residual value. Under Federal Reserve REGULATION Y, bank holding companies are permitted to assume residual values not greater than 25% of an asset's acquisition cost.

RESOLUTION AUTHORITY powers given the Federal Deposit Insurance Corporation (FDIC) by the Dodd-Frank Act of 2010 to step in and manage the orderly closure of a large, failing financial institution. The FDIC has the authority to sell assets, pay creditors, and unwind trading positions with counterparties. The purpose is to avoid a repeat of the Lehman Brothers failure in 2008, which caused a wider panic in the U.S. financial system. *See also* SYSTEMIC RISK; TOO BIG TO FAIL.

RESOLUTION FUNDING CORPORATION government-sponsored corporation established by the FINANCIAL INSTITUTIONS REFORM, RECOVERY AND ENFORCEMENT ACT of 1989 to raise funds for use in liquidating insolvent savings and loan associations. The Resolution Funding Corp., also called Refcorp., was authorized to borrow $30 billion by issuing long-term 30-year zero coupon securities. FIRREA also authorized an additional $20 billion in direct Treasury borrowings, to be used in liquidating insolvent S&Ls.

RESOLUTION TRUST CORPORATION (RTC) government-sponsored corporation established by the FINANCIAL INSTITUTIONS REFORM, RECOVERY AND ENFORCEMENT ACT of 1989 to transfer assets of insolvent savings and loan associations to financially sound institutions. The RTC, managed by a five-member Oversight Board, had responsibility for managing the assets and liabilities of savings institutions that become insolvent between 1989 and August 1992.

The agency's authorization as a receiver of insolvent savings associations expired December 31, 1995, when its liabilities transferred to the FEDERAL DEPOSIT INSURANCE CORPORATION.

RESPONDENT bank that regularly buys check processing and other services from a CORRESPONDENT bank; also known as a downstream bank. Purchased services can include securities clearing and trading, check processing, and foreign exchange trading. A respondent bank, which usually is a community bank, may also maintain its RESERVE ACCOUNT in a PASS-THROUGH ACCOUNT at a correspondent, or sell participations in loans exceeding its legal lending limit, or buy participations in loans originated by other banks.

RESTRICTED ASSET account or other balance with limited right of access or withdrawal. For example, a BLOCKED ACCOUNT.

RESTRICTED CARD LIST *see* WARNING BULLETIN.

RESTRICTED MARKET currency exchange rate heavily controlled by government action, but influenced to some extent by free market interaction. A restricted market is less controlled than a blocked currency market, and much less controlled than a free market (CLEAN FLOAT) exchange rate.

RESTRICTIVE COVENANT *see* COVENANT.

RESTRUCTURED LOAN *see* RENEGOTIATED LOAN.

RETAIL BANKING banking services offered to the general public. Retail banking services are a group of financial services that includes installment loans, residential mortgages, equity credit loans, deposit services, and individual retirement accounts. In contrast with WHOLESALE BANKING or corporate banking, retail banking is a high volume business with many service providers competing for market share. *See also* CONSUMER CREDIT; FINANCIAL SUPERMARKET; INSTALLMENT CREDIT.

RETAIL REPURCHASE AGREEMENT type of REPURCHASE AGREEMENT offered as an alternative to conventional savings deposits. The investor buys an interest in a pool of securities, usually government securities. Retail repos are securities transactions, not insured deposits, and carry some risk. The investor has to look to the selling bank's financial standing as the source of repayment when these contracts mature.

RETAINED EARNINGS undistributed earnings that have not been paid to stockholders or transferred to a surplus account. Retained earnings are part of a bank's net worth, or capital and surplus. In a bank, there is little, if any, distinction between capital and surplus, because all amounts contributed by common stockholders over the nominal value of their equity goes into the surplus account. *See also* PAID-IN CAPITAL.

RETURN ITEMS checks, drafts, or notes returned unpaid to the originating bank because they may result in a loss if honored. They are returned by the drawee bank so that the originator can correct any errors or irregularities and then present the items a second time for collection.

RETURN ON ASSETS (ROA) net income divided by total assets. Return on assets is a KEY RATIO of profitability, indicating how efficiently a financial institution's assets are employed.

RETURN ON EQUITY (ROE) net income divided by total equity; it is a profitability ratio measuring how well equity capital is used.

REVALUATION upward adjustment in the value of a country's currency relative to currencies of other nations resulting in a higher exchange rate in relation to others' currencies. In a revaluation, a country's central bank raises the official exchange rate of its national currency in relation to other currencies. This ordinarily is done by a country with a substantial BALANCE OF PAYMENTS surplus. The opposite is DEVALUATION.

REVENUE ANTICIPATION NOTE (RAN) short-term debt security issued by a municipality to finance operations, repayable from anticipated future revenues, such as sales tax. These notes are usually a general obligation of the issuing government, and interest income is tax-exempt to the holder. *See also* TAX ANTICIPATION NOTE.

REVENUE BOND MUNICIPAL BOND or state bond issue paying principal and interest from the revenues of an income generating project, such as a toll bridge, highway, hospital, or other public facility that is built with the proceeds of the financing. Income generated by the facility goes first toward meeting debt service on the bonds, i.e., paying interest to bondholders and retiring the bonds at maturity. Unlike general obligation bonds, revenue bonds are not backed by the FULL FAITH AND CREDIT, or taxing authority, of the bond issuer. As a rule, revenue bonds are considered tax exempt to bondholders in the issuing state. Commercial banks are authorized to underwrite, and trade in revenue bonds through separate securities subsidiaries, as authorized by the Federal Reserve Board. *See also* SECURITIES SUBSIDIARY.

REVERSE FLOATER *see* INVERSE FLOATER.

REVERSE MORTGAGE MORTGAGE in which the borrower receives periodic payments from the lender, based on the accumulated equity in the underlying property. In a reverse mortgage the ultimate source of repayment is the borrower's house. The most common type of reverse mortgage is the Home Equity Conversion Mortgage (HECM), available through a lender approved by the Federal Housing Administration. HECM loans are insured by the U.S. government. Qualifying borrowers must be age 62 or older, own the property outright or have a small mortgage balance, occupy the property as their principal residence, be current on any federal loans, and participate in a pre-loan counseling session given by an approved counselor.

Starting in October 2010, homeowners have the option of selecting a HECM Saver mortgage, a reverse mortgage with significantly reduced upfront costs. The trade-off in a HECM Saver mortgage is the amount they can borrow is reduced, compared to a standard HECM mortgage.

A second type of reverse mortgage is the life estate transaction in which the home owner sells a house but is granted a life estate and receives immediate cash. A third variation is the SALE AND LEASEBACK transaction.

REVERSE REPURCHASE AGREEMENT transaction involving the purchase of securities by a bank or dealer and resale back to the seller at a future date and specified price. Reverse repos are used several ways in banking: to create short-term investment income or, when used by the Federal Reserve System, a tool of monetary policy. Reverse repos are secured transactions, fully collateralized by government securities, unlike FEDERAL FUNDS (Fed Funds), which are unsecured sales of bank reserves.

In a reverse repo, a bank with surplus deposits can make funds available to another bank by buying an asset, generally a government security. The counterparty agrees to repurchase the asset at the expiration of the agreement at a price calculated to compensate the selling bank for the use of its funds.

Securities dealers use reverse repos to build their inventories for trading; they use the borrowed securities as collateral to obtain more securities. When used by the Federal Reserve's Open Market Trading Desk, a reverse repo is known as a MATCHED-SALE–PURCHASE AGREEMENT. The Fed sells Treasury securities when it wants to drain reserves from the banking system, and agrees to rebuy the same securities at a future date, usually within seven days.

REVERSE SWAP transaction on the secondary swap market. A reverse swap offsets the interest rate or currency exposure on an existing swap. It can be written with the original counterparty or with a new counterparty. Either way, it typically is executed to realize capital gains.

REVOCABLE LETTER OF CREDIT *see* LETTER OF CREDIT.

REVOCABLE TRUST agreement providing transfer of property to heirs that may be altered or revoked any time during the life of the grantor. Estate taxes are paid at the death of the grantor, but the estate does not have to go through probate. Beneficiaries may have the unrestricted use of the property while the trust agreement is in effect. Contrast with IRREVOCABLE TRUST.

REVOLVER cardholder in a credit card plan that pays down principal on outstanding balances, and interest, over several months. The opposite is a NONREVOLVER.

REVOLVING CREDIT

1. LINE OF CREDIT extended to a business; a credit facility that is good for a stated period of time, but does not have a fixed repayment schedule. The borrower may draw down the line at any time, or repay it in full without penalty. The borrower usually pays a COMMITMENT FEE that secures the line of credit when the application is taken by the lender. Contrast with EVERGREEN LOAN.
2. CREDIT CARD, checking account CASH RESERVE, or other consumer credit arrangement that gives consumers the option of borrowing against a pre-approved line of credit. There is no charge when the account is not used. When used, the borrower pays a finance charge on outstanding balances, as stated in the credit agreement or credit contract. A finance charge of 1.5% per month, for example, is equal to an ANNUAL PERCENTAGE RATE of 18%. A monthly rate of 1.65% equals 19.8% APR. In credit card plans, there are several methods of computing finance charges. The most common is the average daily balance method, in which the interest rate is calculated on the daily average of the previous month. Another is the previous balance method. Revolving check credit plans are written like checks, but draw funds from a bank card account. Check credit and checking account cash reserve advances begin accruing interest payable from the date of the transaction (unlike credit cards, where billing on new charges ordinarily is deferred during a GRACE PERIOD of 15 to 25 days) and are payable in the next billing cycle. *See also* REGULATION Z.

REVOLVING UNDERWRITING FACILITY (RUF) medium-term Euronote facility, usually between three and seven years maturity, that guarantees the sale of short-term promissory notes (the Euronotes) issued by the borrower at or below a predetermined interest rate. The revolving credit portion of an RUF is usually done through a single bank, known as the arranger. Typically, the arranger commits itself to a very small share of the total financing (less than 10%) and acts as placement agent for marketing the Euronotes. The Euronotes generally have maturities of one to six months, and are sold through a TENDER PANEL of commercial banks and investment banks. The banks agree to purchase any unsold notes at a given Eurodollar spread over LIBOR. The borrower pays interest only on amounts actually drawn. *See also* EUROCOMMERCIAL PAPER; STANDBY NOTE ISSUANCE FACILITY.

REWARD CARD bank credit card that enables cardholders to earn discounts or rebates based on card usage. Cardholders earn a certain number of "points" for each dollar of purchases charged to a rewards credit card account; accumulated rebates can be applied to pay down bank loans or exchanged for services, merchandise, gift certificates, travel, or cash. Also called *rebate card.*

RIAL monetary unit of Iran, Oman, and Yemen.

RIEL monetary unit of Cambodia.

RIGHT OF FORECLOSURE lender's right to take over mortgaged property, and cancel the mortgagor's interest if the mortgagor fails to meet terms of the mortgage note, such as timely payments of principal and interest.

RIGHT OF REDEMPTION right of a borrower to recover mortgaged property from a judicial sale or foreclosure by paying the lender the outstanding principal and interest due, plus the lender's costs in foreclosure. Also, the right of a debtor in bankruptcy to redeem personal property by paying creditors the fair market value of assets securing their lien.

RIGHT OF RESCISSION option given a borrower in a loan secured by real estate to cancel the loan contract after a three-day cooling-off period. Rescission delays the actual funding commitment for a home equity loan or other real estate secured loan for that three-day period. In open-end equity secured loans, the right of rescission is applied once, at the outset of the loan, under the current interpretation of the TRUTH IN LENDING ACT. *See also* REGULATION Z.

RIGHT OF SURVIVORSHIP right of a surviving married spouse to claim co-owned property, when assets are owned in a joint tenancy relationship.

RIGHTS OFFERING offer by a corporation to sell a new offering of securities, normally common stock to its shareholders, proportionate to their holdings. It is usually an offer to sell newly issued shares or additional shares, at a lower price than the publicly offered price. The offer expires after a certain date if not exercised.

RINGGIT monetary unit of Malaysia.

RISK uncertainty that an asset will earn an expected rate of return, or that a loss may occur. Because banks invest much of their funds in interest sensitive assets, primarily loans, there are several categories of risk, including:

capital risk—risk that a deterioration in asset quality from loan losses will impair a bank's capital, requiring sale of new stock to meet regulatory capital requirements;

credit risk—the possibility that the borrower will be unable to make regular payments of principal and interest, and may default;

delivery risk—the possibility that the buyer or seller of an instrument or foreign exchange may be unable to meet obligations at maturity;

exchange risk—the possibility of a loss on an uncovered position resulting from an appreciation or depreciation of a foreign currency;

INTEREST RATE RISK—risk that an interest earning asset (for example, a bank loan) will decline in value as market interest rates change;

LIQUIDITY RISK—risk that a bank will have insufficient cash or marketable assets to meet needs of depositors and borrowers;

operations risk—the possibility that a data processing failure from fire, other natural disaster, or from other causes (for example, a computer hacker gaining access to bank records) will impede or prevent a bank from maintaining normal service;

political risk—the possibility that political instability in a debtor nation will make it difficult for that country to make regular payments on a loan. Also known as SOVEREIGN RISK; and

settlement risk—the possibility that the failure of a major bank, or its inability to honor payment commitments will have a domino effect on other banks, causing similar failures elsewhere. Also known as SYSTEMIC RISK.

See also BASIS RISK; COUNTRY RISK; REFINANCE RISK; REINVESTMENT RISK.

RISK ASSESSMENT analysis of the various risks faced by a bank depositor or by a financial institution. Among the risks requiring monitoring are credit risk, foreign exchange risk, interest rate risk, and market risk. *See also* RISK MANAGEMENT.

RISK ASSETS

1. **Banking.** Bank assets subject to change in value, due to changes in market conditions or changes in credit quality at various REPRICING OPPORTUNITIES. Examples are maturing bank CDs and bank lines of credit with a FLOATING INTEREST RATE.

2. **Finance.** Equity capital, especially capital in troubled companies that may become subordinated to claims of bondholders.

RISK-BASED CAPITAL measure of a bank's financial strength, taking into account capital reserves for loans, investments, and certain other items off the balance sheet. In general, assets with higher credit risk require more capital in reserve than low-risk assets. The aim of risk-based capital is to: (1) encourage banks to keep a sufficient cushion of equity capital, including common stock, to support balance sheet assets; (2) include off-balance sheet items in the computation of capital adequacy; (3) eliminate disincentives to holding low-risk, liquid assets; and (4) set uniform international guidelines for bank capital adequacy in the GROUP OF 10 countries.

In the United States, the risk-based capital formula raises the mandatory capital from 5.5% of assets to 8%, 4% of which must be in Tier 1 capital (common stock plus noncumulative preferred stock); and 4% in other types of qualifying capital, including loan loss reserves, perpetual preferred stock, hybrid capital instruments, such as MANDATORY CONVERTIBLE debentures, and subordinated debt.

The risk-based guidelines, approved by the Basle Committee on Banking Regulations and Supervisory Practices (the Basle Supervisors' Committee), are a fundamental change in calculation of bank capital from previous measures of calculating capital adequacy. It shifts capital determination from the liability side of the balance sheet to the asset side, using a formula that assigns specific risk weights to different groups of assets. A bank's risk-based capital ratio is computed by dividing its qualifying capital by its weighted risk assets. Assets given a 100% risk rating, such as commercial loans and consumer installment loans, require an institution to maintain total equity capital (TIER 1 and TIER 2 capital) equal to 8% of the asset's book value. So-called riskless assets, having a risk rating of zero (cash, U.S. government securities), require no capital held in reserve.

The risk weights for balance sheet assets are summarized as follows:

—0% risk weight: cash, gold bullion, loans guaranteed by the U.S. government, balances due from Federal Reserve Banks.

—20% risk weight: demand deposits, checks in the process of collection, risk participations in bankers' acceptances and letters of credit, and other short-term claims maturing in one year or less.

—50% risk weight: 1–4 family residential mortgages, whether owner occupied or rented; privately issued mortgage-backed securities and municipal revenue bonds.

—100% risk weight: cross-border loans to non-U.S. borrowers, commercial loans, consumer loans, derivative mortgage-backed securities, industrial development bonds, stripped mortgage-backed securities, joint ventures, and intangibles such as interest rate contracts, currency swaps, and other derivative financial instruments.

See also OFF-BALANCE SHEET ITEMS.

RISK-BASED DEPOSIT INSURANCE deposit insurance system in which banks and savings institutions pay insurance premiums based on financial institution risk. The FDIC switched to variable risk-based premiums in 1994 based on the individual bank's RISK-BASED CAPITAL. Undercapitalized banks pay higher FDIC insurance assessments.

RISK-FREE RATE rate of return on a security whose payoff is highly probable, such as the 3-month Treasury Bill—a direct obligation of the U.S. government. Corporate bonds and asset-backed securities are priced at interest rate spreads above comparable maturity Treasury securities.

RISK MANAGEMENT

1. procedures to manage a bank's exposure to various types of risks associated with banking. This is done through a combination of internal policies, contractual arrangements with insurance companies for BANKER'S BLANKET BOND coverage, DIRECTORS & OFFICERS INSURANCE, and SELF-INSURANCE to reduce the costs from accidental loss.
2. corporate service sold by commercial banks. Risk management is a set of services, rather than a specific product, aimed at controlling financing risk, including credit risk, and interest rate risk, through hedging devices, financial futures, and interest rate caps. The aim is to control corporate funding costs, budget interest rate expense, and limit exposure to interest rate fluctuations.

RISK PARTICIPATION sale by a bank of its participation in a contingent obligation, for example, a bank's participation in a BANKER'S ACCEPTANCE or a STANDBY LETTER OF CREDIT. The originating bank remains liable to the beneficiary for the full amount of the transaction if the obligor fails to pay when payment is demanded. These are treated as off-balance sheet transactions in computing risk-weighted capital, and are not included in a bank's equity capital under the risk-based capital guidelines.

RISK RETENTION portion of a loan retained as a portfolio asset by the originating bank or securitizing company. The Dodd-Frank Act of 2010 requires bank lenders to retain a 5 percent interest in most loans originated, a "skin in the game" incentive to originate high-quality loans.

RIYAL monetary unit of Saudi Arabia and Qatar.

ROLLOVER

1. time savings account or certificate of deposit that is renewed for another term at the prevailing interest rate.
2. profit-sharing plan, 401(k) plan, individual retirement account, or other type of deferred income plan that is reinvested within the permitted 60-day period, according to Internal Revenue Service Rules; assets are transferable without tax penalty from one form of investment to another.
3. EURODOLLAR term loan, which is periodically repriced at an agreed spread over a market index rate, usually LIBOR.

4. **Foreign Exchange.** The sale and purchase of currency for one business day. These transactions take various forms, depending on the trade dates and delivery dates involved. If the trade is made today for delivery tomorrow, the transaction is an overnight rollover, usually involving money market instruments, for example, a repurchase agreement. Other rollover transactions include a SPOT NEXT, a TOMORROW NEXT (TOM NEXT), and SWAP. *See also* SHORT DATE FORWARD.
5. **Banking.** To extend the maturity of, or to renew, a loan or obligation.

ROLLOVER MORTGAGE mortgage in which the finance charge periodically is adjusted. A rollover rate mortgage is a short-term loan that must be renewed periodically, say every three to five years, and the interest rate adjusted to reflect market rates at renewal. The best known example is the Canadian Rollover mortgage, where the loan is renegotiated at a new rate every five years. This is the predominant type of residential mortgage in Canada. Also known as a *renegotiable rate mortgage*. *See also* ALTERNATIVE MORTGAGE INSTRUMENT.

ROTH 401(K) PLAN salary reduction savings plan, similar to a 401(K) PLAN, that allows participants to make after-tax contributions to employer-sponsored accounts. Maximum contributions to a Roth 401(k) are the same as those to a regular 401(k) and can be withdrawn (along with investment earnings) tax-free. Plan participants must begin taking distributions no later than age 70½, as with regular 401(k) plans. Authorized by the tax act of 2001, Roth 401(k) plans are effective January 1, 2006.

ROTH IRA retirement account created by the Taxpayer Relief Act of 1997. Individuals under age 50 may contribute up to $5,000 annually to a Roth IRA, and individuals age 50 or over can make contributions of $6,000 annually. Roth IRA contributions are not tax deductible, unlike funds invested in a traditional IRA. However, the investment earnings in a Roth IRA (the account is named after Senator William V. Roth, who championed an expanded IRA account) are tax free if the funds remain in the account for least five years and the account owner is age 59½ or older. While Roth IRA contributions are not deductible from income taxes, they have advantages over traditional IRA accounts. Roth participants are not required to begin taking distributions at age 70½, nor are they required to take distributions at any time during their life. They can continue making contributions from earned income after reaching age 70½. If the account holder dies before taking distributions, the proceeds go to the beneficiary tax-free. Roth IRA withdrawals for purchase of a first home (up to a $10,000 maximum), to pay college expenses, or to provide disability income if the participant becomes disabled, are exempt from the usual 10% tax penalty on early withdrawals.

Married couples with adjusted gross incomes of $169,000 or less, and single taxpayers earning $107,000 or less, can contribute the maximum amount annually. Contribution amounts are gradually phased out for couples filing jointly with annual incomes of $169,000 to $179,000 ($95,000 to $110,000 for singles). Those with incomes above these limits may not contribute to a Roth IRA account.

ROLLOVER conversions from traditional IRAs to Roth IRAs are permitted for individuals with adjusted gross incomes of $107,000 or less. A Roth IRA rollover is exempt from the usual 10% early distribution penalty, although regular income taxes are due on untaxed earnings. Internal Revenue Service rules permit conversion of a Roth IRA to another type of IRA and reconversion back to a Roth IRA. Because participants often customize Roth IRAs to meet their individual tax and estate planning needs, consultation with a financial professional is recommended.

ROUNDING

1. **Banking.** In consumer credit, the allowed tolerance in computing the ANNUAL PERCENTAGE RATE (APR) finance charge disclosed in loan agreements. Federal Reserve Regulation Z allows rate variations as much as ⅛ of 1% above, or below, the exact interest rate. For example, an annual percentage rate of 10.3333 may be stated as 10.33%, 10.3%, or 10.25%.
2. **Finance.** The practice of shortening publicly disclosed information by adjusting a figure upward or downward to the nearest whole number. The practice simplifies disclosure in annual reports, for example, when zeroes are omitted, and conveys to the casual observer the same information as the fully expressed data.

ROUTING/TRANSIT NUMBER *see* ABA TRANSIT NUMBER; CHECK ROUTING SYMBOL.

RUBBER CHECK slang term for BAD CHECK; a check drawn on an account with insufficient funds, also known as a *bounced check.* A bank may pay the resulting OVERDRAFT if the customer has either a satisfactory credit relationship with the bank or an overdraft line of credit. The customer, however, may still be liable for overdraft charges to cover the bank's costs in processing the check.

RUBLE monetary unit of Russia.

RUFIYAA monetary unit of the Maldives islands.

RULE OF 72 method commonly used to approximate the time required for a sum of money to double at a given rate of interest. The rule of 72 is computed by dividing 72 by the interest rate. For example, a savings account earning 10% will double in less than 7½ years (72 ÷ 10 = 7.2 years).

RULE OF THE 78's mathematical formula used in computing the interest rebated when a borrower pays off a loan before maturity. The Rule of 78's, also known as the Sum of the Digits, is applied mostly to consumer loans in which the finance charges were computed using the ADD-ON INTEREST or DISCOUNTED INTEREST method of interest calculation.

The formula for calculating rebates works as follows: add up the number of months for which payments are scheduled; in a 12-month installment loan, the total is 78. This number, divided by the number of payments to be made, equals the finance charge for that month. In the first month, the borrower has use of the whole amount borrowed, and the finance charge is $^{12}/_{78}$ of the total interest; in the second month, it is $^{11}/_{78}$, and so on. A $3,000 loan, paid in 15 equal installments of $225, has an interest payment of $28.13 in the first month, $26.25 in the second, and only $1.87 in the final month. Thus, under the add-on method, the finance charges in the early months are higher than later on, which means that paying off an installment loan early doesn't necessarily reduce the amount of interest the borrower would have paid. The TRUTH IN LENDING ACT, however, requires that lenders disclose how the finance charge will be computed if the debt is paid in full before maturity, so borrowers can weigh different financing alternatives before signing a loan agreement. *See also* SIMPLE INTEREST.

RUN

1. unexpectedly large series of withdrawals at a bank, resulting from depositor fears of the soundness of the institution. A so-called *silent run* is triggered not by a single event, for example, rumors of a bank failure, but by depositors withdrawing their money to earn a better rate elsewhere.
2. list of securities offered for sale to investors, or bank certificates of deposit sold to other institutions or investors in the SECONDARY MARKET for bank deposit liabilities. Also, a dealer's list of bid and asked quotes.

RUNOFF

1. reduction of a loan portfolio as loans are paid off at scheduled maturity dates, or when borrowers prepay their loans. Loan portfolio runoffs accelerate when interest rates are declining, and borrowers refinance at lower rates.
2. early withdrawal of SAVINGS ACCOUNT or TIME DEPOSIT balances. When depositors take their funds out of depository institutions to put their money in direct investments, such as stocks, bonds, or mutual funds, the outflow of funds from banking institutions is known as DISINTERMEDIATION.

RUPEE monetary unit of India, Mauritius, Nepal, Pakistan, the Seychelles, and Sri Lanka.

RUPIAH monetary unit of Indonesia.

S

SAFE DEPOSIT BOX storage facility maintained in the vault area of a bank that is rented to customers for SAFEKEEPING of personal valuables. Access to a safe deposit box is controlled through dual keys, one kept by the customer and one by the bank, and signature cards. Date of entry is recorded on a signature card. If the safe deposit box is rented by a corporation, a separate corporate resolution must be obtained before access is granted. Safe deposit box contracts usually contain a disclaimer limiting the bank's liability to the bank's failure to provide adequate protection facilities. A bank ordinarily is not responsible for loss of personal valuables, and has no knowledge of the contents of a safe deposit box. *See also* DUAL CONTROL; SIGNATURE CARD.

SAFE HARBOR

1. Securities and Exchange Commission Rule 10b-18, known as the *safe harbor rule,* allowing companies to repurchase their own securities without fear of being charged with securities manipulation.
2. type of tax-oriented lease, called safe harbor leasing, permitted by the Economic Recovery Tax Act of 1981, giving the investor a tax position safe from challenge by the Internal Revenue Service. These tax benefits have since been eliminated by the Tax Equity and Fiscal Responsibility Act of 1982 and the Deficit Reduction Act of 1984.
3. general exemption from liability claims if attempts to comply with a law or regulation can be demonstrated.

SAFEKEEPING

1. agency account managed by a trustee for holding securities, such as stock certificates. A bank, acting as agent, holds in its vaults stock certificates and other securities and returns them at the request of a holder. Safekeeping requires a bank to maintain an itemized record of property in its possession and to issue a receipt for securities held. Distinguish from *custody*, in which a bank buys, sells, and receives securities when instructed. *See also* CUSTODY ACCOUNT.
2. SAFE DEPOSIT BOX where personal valuables are kept.

SAFEKEEPING CERTIFICATE document evidencing ownership of a security or certificate of deposit. The certificate is proof of ownership and also represents the holder's claim against the person holding the instrument. Examples include an AMERICAN DEPOSITARY RECEIPT, representing ownership in registered or unregistered securities that are issued outside the United States and traded on a non-U.S. stock exchange; a certificate issued by a brokerage firm when a BROKERED DEPOSIT, normally a CD paying a market rate of interest, is placed by a broker with a bank or savings institution. *See also* INTERNATIONAL DEPOSITARY RECEIPT.

SAFETY AND SOUNDNESS objective of financial industry regulation. Federal and state supervision of banking is designed to provide a financially stable industry that meets the public's credit and other financial needs, as well as to prevent bank RUNS OR PANICS by providing depositors with assurances that their funds will be protected from loss. Federal deposit insurance, for example, protects depositors' accounts from loss in event of financial institution failure. Supervision is done through periodic site visits and examination of a bank's records, and also through filing of CALL REPORT data with an institution's PRIMARY REGULATOR.

SAFETY NET umbrella protections given bank customers by federal banking regulation. In general, these protections are the following: federal deposit insurance insuring depositor accounts up to $250,000 from the FEDERAL DEPOSIT INSURANCE CORPORATION; access to the Federal Reserve DISCOUNT WINDOW, a source of short-term credit to FINANCIAL INSTITUTIONS; and access to the Federal Reserve payment system for clearing checks and other inter-bank payments. The GRAMM-LEACH-BLILEY ACT OF 1999 did not change the focus of the safety net, but it segregated the non-banking services such as BROKER-DEALER activities, merchant banking, and insurance sales by bank subsidiary companies from insured financial institutions.

SALARY REDUCTION PLAN *see* 401(K) PLAN; 403(B) PLAN.

SALE AND LEASEBACK sale of an asset, usually real estate, and agreement to lease it back from the purchaser on a long-term basis. In commercial finance, this type of financing arrangement strengthens the seller's balance sheet, because a capital asset is sold and converted into cash or a receivable.

It may, however, result in a forfeiting of depreciation and tax benefits. The sale is recorded as a one-time nonrecurring gain.

SALE REPURCHASE AGREEMENT *see* MATCHED SALE—PURCHASE AGREEMENT.

SALES LITERATURE brochures, pamphlets, and other printed booklets containing information on rates, savings accounts, and other banking services, found near the teller counter in a bank or branch office. If the products described are listed securities, sales literature is provided for general disclosure only, and is not an offer to sell. A PROSPECTUS for mutual fund shares, on the other hand, discloses terms and conditions under which securities may be sold to the public, and redeemed, and is available on request in banks offering mutual funds.

SALLIE MAE *see* STUDENT LOAN MARKETING ASSOCIATION.

SAME DAY FUNDS funds that are available for transfer or withdrawal the same day as presented and collected, subject to net settlement of accounts between presenting and remitting banks, or sending and receiving banks. FEDERAL FUNDS transferred from one bank to another over the FED WIRE are same day funds, as are transfers through the CLEARINGHOUSE INTERBANK PAYMENTS SYSTEM in New York.

SAMURAI BOND yen-denominated bond issued in Japan by a foreign borrower. These bonds are unsecured obligations of the issuer and generally have minimum maturities of five years or longer. They are used primarily by corporate borrowers to raise capital in the yen market at reasonable cost. Samurai bonds were first issued in 1970 by the Asian Development Bank. Samurai bonds can be used to hedge interest rate risk. *See also* EUROBOND; YANKEE BOND.

SARBANES-OXLEY ACT federal law enacted in 2002 that introduced major reforms in corporate governance and financial reporting. The act (also called the Corporate Responsibility Act) is regarded as the most sweeping securities legislation since the SECURITIES AND EXCHANGE ACT OF 1934, which established the Securities and Exchange Commission and federal regulation of the securities industry. Among its provisions, Sarbanes-Oxley established an independent five-member watchdog agency, the Public Company Accounting Oversight Board, to oversee audits of public company financial statements; required corporate financial officers to certify accuracy of financial statements; required public companies to certify in annual reports the effectiveness of internal controls on financial reporting; banned corporate loans to executives and directors; and required companies to have procedures for handling whistleblower complaints concerning questionable accounting or auditing practices.

SATISFACTION OF MORTGAGE document releasing a MORTGAGE lien, indicating the borrower has paid the debt in full; also known as a discharge of mortgage or mortgage release. The release of lien is also noted in public land records.

SATISFACTORY loan in which payments are being made on time, loan covenants are met, the collateral is priced right (at fair market value), and the loan is performing "as agreed" in the original loan agreement.

SAVINGS ACCOUNT interest bearing DEPOSIT account without a stated maturity, as opposed to a TIME DEPOSIT. Funds can be deposited or withdrawn at will, and most savings accounts pay interest from day of deposit to day of withdrawal. The account holding financial institution may require up to seven days' notice before approving withdrawals; most, however, have waived this right.

There are two broad types of savings accounts: a MONEY MARKET DEPOSIT ACCOUNT (MMDA), allowing the depositor up to six transfers a month (including three by check, draft, or debit card); and an ordinary savings account, such as a STATEMENT SAVINGS ACCOUNT or PASSBOOK account. In both an MMDA and passbook or statement savings, the depositor can make unlimited number of transfers for loan payments and transfers to another account owned by the same depositor, or make account withdrawals by mail, at a teller window, or at an automated teller machine. A deposit account allowing more than three transfers to third parties, by check, draft, and so on, is a TRANSACTION ACCOUNT in the eyes of bank regulators, and is reportable as part of a bank's deposits subject to RESERVE REQUIREMENTS. MMDA accounts and other savings accounts are exempt from this requirement.

SAVINGS ACCOUNT LOAN COLLATERAL LOAN secured by savings account up to the amount advanced to the borrower. Also called a passbook loan, these are relatively secure and risk-free consumer loans. The lender takes possession of the passbook, or places a hold on the account equal to, or greater than, the amount of the loan, and has right of offset (set-off) against the funds in the account.

SAVINGS AND LOAN ASSOCIATION depository financial institution, federally or state chartered, holding its assets mostly in residential mortgages and collecting its deposits from consumers. Savings and loans date their history to the 19th century, when many were organized as voluntary associations with state charters. The S&L industry as it exists today has its origins in the Home Owners Loan Bank Act of 1932, which created the FEDERAL HOME LOAN BANK SYSTEM, a network of regional banks to lend financial support to state chartered S&Ls. The Federal Home Loan Act of 1933 authorized federal savings and loans, chartered and supervised by the Federal Home Loan Bank Board. Deposits in S&Ls were insured by the Federal Savings and Loan Insurance Fund.

In the 1980s the S&L industry was restructured a second time to provide S&Ls competitive parity with commercial banks. The DEPOSITORY INSTITUTIONS DEREGULATION & MONETARY CONTROL ACT allowed S&Ls entry into some markets previously closed, including commercial lending and non-mortgage consumer loans, and deregulated deposit interest rates. The GARN-ST GERMAIN DEPOSITORY INSTITUTIONS ACT of 1982 accelerated the pace of S&L deregulation, permitted the formation of stock ownership S&Ls, direct investments in real estate, and gave the Federal Home Loan Bank Board wider latitude in helping S&Ls build up their net worth.

Savings and loan associations today offer many of the same consumer and business loans available from commercial banks. *See also* FEDERAL SAVINGS BANK; SAVINGS BANK.

SAVINGS ASSOCIATION INSURANCE FUND (SAIF) *see* DEPOSIT INSURANCE FUND.

SAVINGS BANK depository financial institution that accepts consumer deposits and invests its assets primarily in residential mortgages and high-grade securities. Savings banks are found mostly in the northeastern United States. They can be owned by depositors as MUTUAL SAVINGS BANKS or stock savings banks issuing common stock to the public. Financial deregulation in the 1980s gave savings banks the right to offer checking accounts and credit cards, make commercial loans and consumer loans, discount brokerage, and invest in real estate. Savings banks today offer banking services competitive with many commercial banks. The GARN-ST GERMAIN DEPOSITORY INSTITUTIONS ACT OF 1982 gave state chartered savings banks the option of converting to federal charter and authorized FEDERAL SAVINGS BANKS. *See also* SAVINGS AND LOAN ASSOCIATION.

SAVINGS BANK LIFE INSURANCE (SBLI) life insurance sold in several states savings banks by Savings Bank Life Insurance Co. of Massachusetts. Several types of insurance coverage are available: term life, whole life, limited payment life, and annuities. Insurance is sold over the counter, without sales commissions. The cost of coverage generally is less than comparable insurance from commission paid agents, although there are state imposed limits on the amount of insurance that can be purchased.

SAVINGS BOND U.S. government bond earning variable, market-based interest that is sold to the public through depository financial institutions and Federal Reserve Banks. Savings bonds are issued in denominations from $50 to $10,000 and are available in two forms. Series EE bonds, replacing the Series E bond in 1980, are sold at discount, and pay a rate of interest calculated at 85% of the market average on Treasury securities maturing in five years, or the rate in effect when the bond was purchased, whichever is higher. Series EE Bonds purchased after 1989 are exempt from federal and state taxes if used for education expenses. Savings bonds issued after April 1995 have no guaranteed minimum yield. Savings bond yields are adjusted twice a year, on May 1 and November 1. As of January 1, 2012, U.S. savings bonds are sold only in paperless (book entry) form through the Treasury Department's Treasury Direct sales window.

Series HH Bonds, sold in denominations of $500 to $10,000, are available only from a Federal Reserve Bank or the Commissioner of Public Debt. These bonds can be purchased in exchange for maturing Series E and Series EE Bonds, and U.S. Savings Notes (called Freedom Shares). Series HH Bonds are current income bonds, paying interest semiannually and have a term to maturity of ten years. Interest on Series EE Bonds is reportable annually, but reporting may be deferred until the bonds are cashed or at the maturity date. Series EE bonds issued after May 2005 will pay a fixed rate of interest. Series HH Bonds pay semiannual interest and also permit bondholders to defer federal income tax until the HH Bonds are sold or mature. Savings bond interest is subject to federal tax in the year a bond is redeemed, but is exempt from state and local taxes. *See also* I-BONDS.

SAVINGS CERTIFICATE CERTIFICATE evidencing ownership of a TIME DEPOSIT account paying a fixed rate of interest. A savings certificate is a retail CERTIFICATE OF DEPOSIT that normally is issued in denominations of $500 or more, and has a stated maturity. It is nonnegotiable, or transferable by assignment to another owner. A receipt is issued to the certificate holder, and the instrument is recorded in the issuing bank's ledger accounts. *See also* ALL SAVERS CERTIFICATE; MONEY MARKET CERTIFICATE; SMALL SAVER CERTIFICATE.

SAVINGS CLUB *see* CLUB ACCOUNT.

SCENARIO ANALYSIS in mortgage-backed securities, evaluation that projects expected RATE OF RETURN on a security under different interest rates. The calculation of expected return is based on collection of principal and interest, reinvestment income on cash flows, and price appreciation or depreciation of the remaining principal balance until maturity. Scenario analysis attempts to limit INTEREST RATE RISK.

SCHEDULE

1. list of rates paid on deposit accounts.
2. funds AVAILABILITY SCHEDULE stating when deposited checks become good funds.
3. list disclosing minimum balances and fees charged to an account, for example, the average monthly balance needed to get a free checking account.
4. list of mortgage certificates transferred to a trustee for use as collateral in COLLATERALIZED MORTGAGE OBLIGATION bonds.
5. in factoring, a list detailing accounts being financed, signed by the borrower, that periodically is updated.

SCHEDULED ITEMS *see* ADVERSELY CLASSIFIED ASSETS.

SCHILLING monetary unit of Austria.

SCRIP

1. certificates, coupons, and other documents that have no monetary value, but are assigned a nominal value.
2. paper receipts dispensed by a consumer-activated electronic terminal that substitutes for cash in retail establishments. The terminal prints a coupon and debits the consumer's account for the amount of the sale. The coupon is redeemable for goods or services, and also is the customer's sales receipt.
3. temporary stock certificate or dividend payable in short-term promissory notes to conserve cash.

SEASONAL ADJUSTMENT adjustment for periodic swings in statistical data or changes in supply and demand. The volume of bank debits (checks and check-like drafts, including Negotiable Order of Withdrawal accounts, written by businesses and consumers) is higher in December than the following month's total, due mostly to year-end holiday shopping. Seasonal adjustment would reduce the December number, while raising the January figure. If there is no change in trends, both numbers would be identical.

SEASONAL CREDIT

1. credit arrangement, usually a LINE OF CREDIT, allowing corporate borrowers to finance inventory and receivables, purchase supplies, and pay wages during a manufacturing and sales cycle. The borrower has the option of using the line of credit anytime during a specified period, usually two years. A line of credit may, however, be less enforceable than a revolving line of credit.

   The commitment fees and compensating balances the borrower pays to obtain a line of credit are a less expensive way to borrow than a fixed term loan because the borrower draws only what is needed, and can pay down the outstanding balance at any time.
2. extended credit, supplied by the DISCOUNT WINDOW at a Federal Reserve Bank for periods up to 90 days. Federal Reserve banks make these advances under certain conditions to smaller financial institutions that have a demonstrated seasonal need for funds or have difficulty raising funds from the national money market.

SEASONED LOAN loan that has been on the books for at least a year and has a satisfactory payment record. Mortgage loans that have been on the books for a period longer than a year command a premium over unseasoned loans when sold in the SECONDARY MORTGAGE MARKET.

SEASONED SECURITIES securities that have a track record, that have been on the books at least one year, and that are traded in the secondary market. Seasoned securities are worth more to investors than securities that are less well known to investors.

SEASONING aging of a mortgage, loan, or securities expressed as elapsed time since origination. Mortgage loans that have a satisfactory payment record of at least one year, known as SEASONED LOANS, are more easily sold in the SECONDARY MARKET to investors than loans with payment characteristics that have not been established.

SECONDARY LIABILITIES *see* CONTINGENT LIABILITY.

SECONDARY MARKET the market where existing loans, marketable securities, stocks, bonds, and other assets are sold to investors, either directly or through an intermediary.

1. **Money Market.** The market where marketable short-term debt instruments are offered by dealers for resale to new investors. Trades in negotiable CDs between dealers and their customers are in lots of $1 million or more.
2. **Mortgages.** The nationwide SECONDARY MORTGAGE MARKET for purchase and sale of existing mortgages; the market in which mortgages are originated is the primary market. *See also* SECURITIZATION.

SECONDARY MORTGAGE MARKET national market where residential mortgages are assembled into pools and sold to investors. The secondary market, which originated with the Federal National Mortgage Association (FANNIE MAE) the Federal Home Loan Mortgage Corporation (FREDDIE MAC) and the Government National Mortgage Association (GINNIE MAE), supplies additional liquidity to mortgage lenders. Mortgages are sold through established CONDUITS that assemble pools of loans for resale or through private placement of loans directly with an investor. The secondary mortgage market, although dominated by the federal agencies, also includes private mortgage companies that buy conventional mortgages from mortgage originators, for resale as part of a COLLATERALIZED MORTGAGE OBLIGATION, or through a REAL ESTATE MORTGAGE INVESTMENT CONDUIT.

The single most important contribution of the secondary mortgage market is the creation of a national market for resale of residential mortgages. This assures that mortgage originators, regardless of where they are located, have access to pools of capital managed by pension funds, insurance companies, and other institutional buyers of mortgage-backed bonds. Home buyers are assured an adequate supply of mortgage financing, as the secondary market sales lessen the possibility that a lending institution will become loaned up and cease making new loans. The maturing of the secondary market, beginning in the late 1960s with the organization of the GOVERNMENT NATIONAL MORTGAGE ASSOCIATION, has fostered other developments: standardized mortgage loan documentation; greater diversification in mortgages available from lenders, because most secondary market agencies have purchase programs for fixed rate, adjustable rate, and biweekly mortgages; and the beginnings of a national mortgage market, in which loan originators, some operating multistate or even nationwide networks of mortgage origination offices, are able to make new loans at competitive rates, and quickly sell loans under forward delivery commitments for sale to investors. Nongovernment conduits, or organizations that buy loans from correspondents, became active in the 1980s, for example, Maggie Mae, created by Mortgage Guaranty Insurance Corp., a mortgage insurance company, or HOMAC (Home Mortgage Access Corp.), organized by the National Home Building Association.

See also COMPUTERIZED LOAN ORIGINATION; MORTGAGE-BACKED BOND; MORTGAGE-BACKED SECURITIES; MORTGAGE BANKER; PASS-THROUGH SECURITY; PAY-THROUGH SECURITY.

SECONDARY RESERVES assets invested in short-term marketable securities, usually Treasury bills and short-term government securities. These earn interest and can be used to adjust a bank's reserve position. If loan demand is slow, deposit funds often are invested in short-term securities that are easily converted to cash. Secondary reserves are not listed as a separate balance sheet item. *See also* MANAGED LIABILITIES; RESERVE REQUIREMENTS.

SECOND MORTGAGE mortgage that is subordinate to the lien created by a FIRST MORTGAGE, but senior to subsequent liens. Sometimes called a *second trust,* a second mortgage normally has a repayment term much shorter than a first mortgage, a fixed amortization schedule, and may have a balloon payment. The holder of a second mortgage has rights secondary to the holder of a first mortgage lien in event of foreclosure. In a second mortgage, interest due is computed on the entire principal balance owed, which is advanced to the borrower after the required three-day rescission period. A second mortgage is, in effect, an installment loan secured by the borrower's real estate, and technically, a CLOSED-END CREDIT arrangement with a predetermined repayment table or AMORTIZATION SCHEDULE. Contrast with HOME EQUITY CREDIT.

Second mortgages are used for a variety of borrowing needs, including home improvement, investment in a business, and raising cash. Second mortgages also are commonly used to make a smaller down payment in a first mortgage when a home is purchased. *See also* PIGGYBACK MORTGAGE; RIGHT OF RESCISSION.

SECURED CREDIT *see* SECURED LOAN.

SECURED CREDIT CARD bank credit card that is backed by a savings account. The issuer places a hold on the savings account equal to the cardholder's credit line, and reserves the right to use the deposit account to pay off credit card bills if the cardholder is unable to pay. Secured credit cards normally are issued only to persons whose ability to pay, based on credit history, is uncertain.

SECURED CREDITOR party that holds some form of collateral or claim to assets. A mortgage lender holds a security interest in a borrower's residence. A bank taking a SECURITY INTEREST in a borrower's assets is a secured creditor.

SECURED LOAN LOAN that is collateralized by assignment of rights to property and a SECURITY INTEREST in personal property or real property taken by the lender. A mortgage borrower (the mortgagor) gives the lender a MORTGAGE in the property financed. A business loan can be secured by cash, inventory, receivables, marketable securities, or other acceptable COLLATERAL. In event the borrower fails to repay according to the original credit terms, the lender can take legal action to reclaim, and sell, the collateral. Contrast with UNSECURED LOAN, which is backed only by the borrower's promise to pay—a promissory note. *See also* ASSET-BASED LENDING; FINANCING STATEMENT; SECURITY AGREEMENT; SIDE COLLATERAL.

SECURE ELECTRONIC TRANSACTION (SET) payment protocol backed by MasterCard and Visa and virtually all the major players in the e-commerce industry to facilitate secure transmission of credit card payment information over the Internet and other networks. An open industry standard, SET blocks out credit card details, denying merchants access to a consumer's credit card information. SET enables merchants to verify that buyers are who they claim to be, and it protects buyers by transferring credit information directly to the card issuer for authorization and billing. *See also* TEMPORARY ACCOUNT NUMBER.

SECURITIES ACT OF 1933 act passed by Congress requiring registration of securities offered for sale to the public in interstate commerce or through the mail. The issuer must disclose relevant financial and other information, such as the offering price and the number of shares offered in a REGISTRATION STATEMENT filed with the Securities and Exchange Commission. (The public disclosure of an offering is called a PROSPECTUS.)

SECURITIES AND EXCHANGE ACT OF 1934 act passed by Congress establishing the Securities and Exchange Commission, an independent agency, to enforce federal securities laws. The act extended the registration and disclosure requirements of the Securities Act of 1933 to all companies with securities listed for sale on a national exchange, as well as other companies with assets over $1 million and more than 500 shareholders. These companies must file a registration application with the exchange and the SECURITIES AND EXCHANGE COMMISSION. The act also required disclosure of proxy solicitations, in which an organization attempts to gain the shares of other shareholders.

The act also exempted state chartered banks and national banks from having to register as broker-dealers with the Securities and Exchange Commission. (The GLASS-STEAGALL ACT restricted banks to underwriting *bank-eligible* securities, mainly government bonds, making further regulation unnecessary.) The GRAMM-LEACH-BLILEY ACT OF 1999, authorizing banks to deal in a wide range of securities through subsidiaries, amended this section of the Securities and Exchange Act and put broker-dealer activities of banking companies under the supervision of the Securities and Exchange Commission.

SECURITIES AND EXCHANGE COMMISSION (SEC) independent regulatory agency established in 1934 to oversee the administration of federal securities laws. With limited exceptions, the Commission has authority to regulate issuance and trading of publicly offered securities and require issuers to give investors sufficient information to make informed decisions. The Commission is headed by a bipartisan group of five commissioners, appointed by the President to serve five-year terms.

SECURITIES INVESTOR PROTECTION CORPORATION nonprofit, government sponsored membership corporation chartered in 1970 to protect the customer of insured broker-dealers, up to $500,000 per account. The SIPC has no supervisory powers and does not assist failing firms. The corporation, which is funded by member assessments and portfolio income, also has a line of credit with the U.S. Treasury. Five of its seven governors are appointed by the President;

the remaining two are named by the Board of Governors of the Federal Reserve System and the secretary of the treasury. In addition to SIPC insurance, many broker-dealers also guard against losses through private insurance.

SECURITIES LOAN

1. bank loan collaterized by marketable securities. Such loans are regulated by Federal Reserve REGULATION T if made by broker-dealers, by REGULATION U if made by banks. These regulations set margin limits on credit that may be extended against various kinds of securities.
2. bank's loan to a broker, known as a broker loan or BROKER'S CALL LOAN.

SECURITIES SUBSIDIARY company controlled by a BANK HOLDING COMPANY or FINANCIAL HOLDING COMPANY that underwrites commercial paper, and government and corporate securities for distribution to investors. These companies came into existence in 1987 when the Federal Reserve Board permitted bank-owned securities firms to underwrite and deal in limited amounts of commercial paper and municipal revenue bonds. In 1990, the Fed authorized the firms to deal in corporate stocks and bonds. Bank underwriting of corporate securities was at first limited to 5% of revenues from securities underwriting, a ceiling that was eventually raised to 25% of total revenues in 1996. The GRAMM-LEACH-BLILEY ACT OF 1999 removed these volume limits on corporate underwriting, as long as banking companies involved satisfied bank regulatory capital requirements. The modernization act also imposed limits on bank holding company investments in a securities subsidiary to 45% of consolidated assets or $50 billion, whichever is less.

SECURITIZATION conversion of bank loans and other assets into marketable securities for sale to investors. Securities offered for sale can be purchased by other depository institutions or nonbank investors. More broadly, corporate financing through Floating Rate Notes and Eurocommercial paper, replacing bank loans as a means of borrowing, is a form of securitization.

By securitizing bank loans and credit receivables, U.S. financial institutions are able to remove bank assets from the balance sheet if certain conditions are met—boosting its capital ratios, and make new loans from the proceeds of the securities sold to investors. The process effectively merges the credit markets (for example, the mortgage market in which lenders make new mortgages) and the capital markets, because bank receivables are repackaged as bonds collateralized by pools of mortgages, auto loans, credit card receivables, leases, and other types of credit obligations. As banks look to investors as the ultimate holders of the obligations created by bank lending, banks as an industry are inclined to act more as sellers of assets, rather than portfolio lenders that keep all the loans they originate in their own portfolio. Securitization also redefines the bank definition of ASSET QUALITY, and loan underwriting standards, because lenders will be looking at loan quality more in terms of their marketability in the capital markets than probability of repayment by the borrowers.

For regulatory reporting purposes, a loan that is converted into a security and sold as an asset-backed security qualifies as a sale of assets. The seller retains no risk of loss from the assets transferred and has no obligation to the buyer for borrower defaults or changes in market value of securities sold. Asset transfers where the buyer has RECOURSE against the selling institution are treated as *financings* or a borrowing secured by assets. Securitization of bank assets is further complicated by Securities and Exchange Commission regulations, and accounting guidelines. Tax counsel is advised in structuring new issues for market. *See also* ASSET SALES; ASSET-BACKED SECURITIES.

SECURITY

Banking:

1. Personal assets or property that can be pledged as COLLATERAL; also, a good faith GUARANTY by a co-maker to pay an obligation if the borrower defaults. *See also* SECURITY AGREEMENT.
2. Physical safeguards, internal audits, and written procedures to insure safety of customer assets and account records. Such procedures must comply with minimum standards set by the Federal Deposit Insurance Corporation and the Comptroller of the Currency.

Finance: Certificate evidencing ownership of equity (stock), ownership of a debt obligation payable (bond), and the rights to ownership implied by options and warrants. Securities, when pledged as collateral, may be used to obtain bank financing.

SECURITY AGREEMENT document giving a lender a SECURITY INTEREST in assets or property pledged as COLLATERAL. This agreement, signed by the borrower, describes the collateral and its location in sufficient detail so the lender can identify it, and assigns to the lender the right to sell or dispose of the assigned collateral if the borrower is unable to pay the obligation. The security agreement may contain loan COVENANTS governing the advancement of funds, and a schedule for repayment of principal and interest, or require the borrower to obtain insurance coverage for the assets pledged.

The security agreement may cover nonpossessory liens in intangible property such as accounts receivable, or a possessory lien, in which the lender holds the collateral, for example, stock certificates, until the loan is fully paid. In some loans, the security agreement is also the FINANCING STATEMENT filed with a public records office, if it has the signatures of both borrower and lender.

SECURITY INTEREST lender's claim to assets pledged by a borrower securing payment of an obligation. A lender's interest, also known as a LIEN, is said to attach to the borrower's property, and consists of two limited rights: FORECLOSURE and PRIORITY OF LIEN. A lender who files a FINANCING STATEMENT, which is often the same document as the SECURITY AGREEMENT, with the appropriate state or county official gives legal notice to other creditors that a lien has been filed. This process, known as *perfecting a lien,* commonly is done in commercial lending. It asserts the lien is valid against claims of other creditors and most third parties. *See also* PERFECTED LIEN.

SEED MONEY

Real Estate: The initial capital contributed by a project developer. Also called front end money.

Venture Capital: The initial capital investment in a new company. Venture capitalists generally retain rights or warrants to common stock, when the sponsored company issues stock in an initial public offering. This level of financing precedes intermediate MEZZANINE FINANCING, or second-stage financing. *See also* START-UP FINANCING.

SEGMENTATION

1. division of a pool of mortgages into groups with similar rate and prepayment characteristics, such as a COLLATERALIZED MORTGAGE OBLIGATION, in securitizing bank loans, or converting bank assets into marketable securities for sale on the SECONDARY MARKET. This enhances the value of the securities to investors, as securities offered for sale offer the investor more options than conventional mortgage-backed pass-through certificates. These options include fast-pay or slow-pay mortgage-backed bonds and residual interests in the excess cash flow from mortgage bonds.
2. in market research, process of dividing the population into groups of households for preparation of mailing lists and direct mail advertising. Market segmentation, allows a financial institution to identify the best prospects for new products and services, based on income, life-style, and other characteristics.

SEGREGATION

1. SECURITIES AND EXCHANGE COMMISSION rule that broker-dealers maintain separate customer accounts for purposes of obtaining MARGIN credit from a bank, and may not combine customers' accounts without the customers' approval. *See also* COMMINGLED FUNDS.
2. requirement by the Comptroller of the Currency, the Federal Reserve Board, and the Federal Deposit Insurance Corporation that banks maintain their TRADING ACCOUNT ASSETS, or securities held for trading purposes, separate from loan and investment portfolios.
3. separation of accounts under management by a bank trust department acting in a FIDUCIARY capacity for trust accounts.

SEIGNIORAGE difference between the cost of materials in coins (the ASSAY value), and the face value. The term generally refers to money the U.S. Treasury earns from production of coins, which is credited to the Treasury's surplus account.

SELF-AMORTIZING MORTGAGE residential mortgage in which the loan is fully paid over a scheduled time period, usually fifteen or thirty years, through regular payments of principal and interest. The borrower does not have to make a lump-sum BALLOON PAYMENT at the end of the mortgage. Lenders can provide amortization tables showing exactly how much principal and interest are paid over the full term of the loan.

SELF-DEALING

1. **Banking.** The situation where a lender fails to exercise normal DUE DILIGENCE in approving loans to bank officers or directors, makes loans to insiders at abnormally favorable terms, or illegally accepts kickbacks in exchange for making a loan. *See also* INSIDER LENDING.
2. **Trusts.** The situation where a TRUSTEE sworn to protect the assets of another person or the ESTATE of a decedent consummates a transaction out of self-interest as opposed to his duty as a FIDUCIARY.

SELF-DIRECTED IRA INDIVIDUAL RETIREMENT ACCOUNT that gives the investor the option of switching from one form of investment to another, such as stocks, fixed income securities, and short-term or long-term savings accounts in a bank or savings institution. The account holder also has the option of managing the portfolio, as well as directing funds into various forms of investments.

SELF-INSURANCE protecting against loss by setting aside funds from earnings, as opposed to buying an insurance policy. This form of insurance is often used when self-funding for possible losses is less costly than conventional insurance coverage, or when coverage by an insurance company is unavailable, or available only at great cost. A self-insurance plan, for example, can be set up to cover general liability, workers' compensation, or liability of bank directors and officers, and sometimes is a pooling arrangement sponsored by a trade association. Some companies have funded self-insurance through wholly-owned subsidiaries in offshore financial centers, for example, the Bahamas or the Cayman Islands, or through wholly-owned captive insurance companies.

SELF-LIQUIDATING LOAN short-term WORKING CAPITAL loan that is repaid from the liquidation of inventories. It is used to finance seasonal borrowing needs of a business needing capital to acquire inventory, by a farmer or other business needing bank financing to buy seed, fertilizer, and other supplies. The borrower repays the loan as inventory is converted into cash or a farm crop is sold. Early in the twentieth century, commercial banks made only short-term loans, and self-liquidating loans were a common variety. *See also* EVERGREEN LOAN.

SELF-REGULATORY ORGANIZATION business organization that sets its own rules for fair conduct, licenses or approves firms engaging in market making activities, and supervises the activities of market participants. Examples are the NATIONAL ASSOCIATION OF SECURITIES DEALERS, the MUNICIPAL SECURITIES RULEMAKING BOARD (MSRB), the NEW YORK STOCK EXCHANGE, and the AMERICAN STOCK EXCHANGE.

SELF-SERVICE BANKING system in retail banking whereby consumers perform many routine banking transactions themselves, without going to a bank teller. The supporting theory is that many banking services, such as account withdrawals and deposits, can be automated, generating a stable, and growing, source of CORE DEPOSITS at low acquisition cost. At sufficient transaction volumes, self-service banking lowers the cost of serving the customer and provides greater customer convenience, because consumers are no longer restricted to doing their banking during business hours and have access to their accounts through automated teller machine networks. *See also* AUTOMATED TELLER MACHINE; CUSTOMER ACTIVATED TERMINAL; HOME BANKING; INTERNET BANKING; MOBILE BANKING; 24-HOUR BANKING.

SELL DOWN portion of a syndicated financing offered to interested buyers outside the underwriting group. Sell down financing can be a LOAN PARTICIPATION in a commercial and industrial loan, or in securities underwriting whereby a portion of the offering is distributed through a SELLING GROUP acting as agents for the underwriter. In general, the higher the sell down, the greater the yield for the lead manager or lead underwriter.

SELLER FINANCING *see* PURCHASE MONEY MORTGAGE.

SELLER-SERVICER secondary mortgage market term for a mortgage lender approved by Fannie Mae or Freddie Mac to sell mortgages in the SECONDARY MORTGAGE MARKET, and collect monthly principal and interest payments from mortgagors. The selling institution forwards loan payments, maintains mortgage records, and collects a loan servicing fee.

SELLING GROUP securities dealers who affiliate with an underwriting group on an agency basis to assist in distribution of a new offering of securities. Members collect a commission or concession fee for securities placed. The group ordinarily includes members of the original underwriting group. It may be required in some instances to purchase any unsold portion of the offering.

SELL SHORT *see* SHORT SALE.

SEMIANNUAL INTEREST interest payable twice a year. Bond interest is payable semi-annually.

SENDER NET DEBIT CAP limit imposing a maximum ceiling on the aggregate debit position a financial institution will incur during a business day in wire transfers to other financial institutions. This cap can be applied to the sender's payments made on a particular network or a single cap covering all transfer activities across FED WIRE and private wire networks. *See also* BILATERAL CREDIT LIMIT; DAYLIGHT OVERDRAFT.

SENIOR DEBT debt that has priority of claim ahead of other obligations. A first mortgage holder is payable before a creditor holding a second mortgage in a foreclosure action. A lender holding a perfected SECURITY INTEREST has a claim against the borrower's assets that has priority over subsequent lien holders. Senior debt securities have claim to assets of a corporation before SUBORDINATED DEBT in event of liquidation. *See also* PRIORITY OF LIEN; SENIOR SECURITY.

SENIOR SECURITY security that has a claim against earnings or assets, and must be paid before other holders of other securities. Bonds have priority over preferred stock, and preferred stock has precedence over common stock.

SENIOR STRETCH LOAN loan to a business enterprise that has elements of both asset-based and cash-flow lending. In a typical stretch loan the lender offers funding beyond the lendable value of current and fixed assets if the company demonstrates it can generate sufficient cash from normal business operations to repay the loan. These loans reward companies with strong balance sheets and have a lower financing cost than a straight cash-flow loan.

SEPARATE TRADING OF REGISTERED INTEREST AND PRINCIPAL OF SECURITIES (STRIPS) ZERO-COUPON SECURITY created by separating coupon interest on Treasury bonds from the underlying principal. STRIPS are direct obligations of the U.S. Treasury. Stripping is done by the U.S. Treasury Department at the request of large investors or broker-dealers. The securities are held in escrow and principal and interest portions sold separately. *See also* COUPON STRIPPING; STRIP.

SEQUESTERED ACCOUNT deposit account impounded by court order under due process of law, and from which funds cannot be disbursed without prior approval. These accounts usually are kept under a separate file.

SERIAL BOND bond issued as one of a set of bonds, each having a specific maturity. Serial bonds, commonly issued by state and municipal governments, are bonds that allow the issuer to amortize bond principal over several years, by having bonds mature at periodic intervals, at, say, every six months. Each bond has its own maturity date, set by a schedule in the initial offering. Contrast with TERM BOND.

SERIES

1. group of bonds issued as part of a group of bonds under a single INDENTURE. Bonds offered for sale may be issued in the same year or have a different maturity, accrual schedule, and interest rate, as stated in the prospectus or prospectus supplement. Electric utility bonds and revenue bonds typically are issued in a series over an

extended period of time. A COLLATERALIZED MORTGAGE OBLIGATION (CMO) normally is subdivided into several sets of mortgage-backed bonds, called TRANCHES (from the French, meaning slice), each having its own yield to maturity. The tranches in a CMO series usually are denoted by a different letter or number.

2. options term for call options and put options on the same underlying security, at the same expiration date and exercise price (STRIKE PRICE).

SERVICE CHARGE bank charge to a customer's account, as when an account balance falls below a certain MINIMUM BALANCE, a check is returned for insufficient funds, or for servicing an account. Bank fees are meant to cover the cost of maintaining a depositor's account, or performing a specific service requested by a customer. Banks also impose service fees for late payments on loans and credit card purchases above the cardholder's credit line. Other service charges include the annual charge for renting a safe deposit box and transaction fees for using an automated teller machine.

SERVICE CORPORATION subsidiary of one or more banks or thrift institutions that performs services other than deposit taking for its owners and outside customers. These may be services the owners cannot perform directly, or services a bank is forbidden by regulation from performing directly. These latter include PERMISSIBLE NONBANK ACTIVITIES that bank holding companies may engage in through separate subsidiary companies.

SERVICING

1. **Servicer:** party that collects principal and interest payments when mortgages or other assets are securitized and sold to investors. Among its administrative duties, the servicer forwards payments to investors and transmits periodic activity reports to credit-rating agencies and investors owning asset-backed or mortgage-backed securities. In banking there are several distinct types of servicers: a *primary servicer* performs routine servicing and initiates collection proceedings on past-due loans; a *master servicer* oversees servicing activities when assets from multiple originators are pooled together in a single securitization; a *sub-servicer* collects payments on behalf of a master servicer; a *back-up servicer* stands ready to step in should the primary servicer fail in its duties; a *special servicer* handles collection and foreclosure efforts on delinquent loans and other problem loans.
2. collateral control in ASSET-BASED LENDING, by which a lender (or a factor in FACTORING) monitors its collateral position. Collateral control, also known as *policing*, can be done by the lender or by a third party. It (1) assures an account is in good standing; (2) confirms shipments of goods; (3) protects against diversion of funds; and (4) provides a monthly AGING SCHEDULE of receivables.

SERVICING AGREEMENT contract between a financial institution, as agent, and an institutional buyer, as PRINCIPAL, when a loan is sold in the SECONDARY MARKET. The agreement, in general, covers the duties, fees, and audit requirements expected of the seller, covering (1) the seller's fiduciary role as a trustee to collect and remit borrower payments; (2) the seller's agreement to post a fidelity bond and carry ERRORS AND OMISSIONS INSURANCE; and (3) the buyer's right to conduct periodic audits of the selling institution's books and records.

SET-OFF CLAUSE

1. common law right of a lender to seize deposits owned by a debtor for nonpayment of an obligation. A bank lending $5,000 to a borrower who has $2,500 on deposit at the same bank will set-off $2,500, and file an unsecured claim for the remaining $2,500. An exception is consumer credit transactions, where the right of set-off is prohibited by the TRUTH IN LENDING ACT. A consumer who refuses to pay a credit card bill, claiming the merchandise ordered was defective, is thus protected from collection efforts by the card issuing bank by seizing deposits equal to the debt owed.
2. settlement of mutual debt between a debtor in bankruptcy and a creditor, through offsetting claims. Instead of receiving cash payment, debtors credit the amount owed against the other party's obligations to them. This allows creditors to collect more than they otherwise would have collected under a debt repayment plan approved by a bankruptcy court. Also called *right of setoff.*

SETTLEMENT

1. **Banking.** The accounting process recording the respective debit and credit positions of the two parties involved in a transfer of funds. Funds are available for use and may be drawn at any time afterward. Funds transferred through Fed Wire are available for use at the time the transfer occurs, and are settled by adjusting the RESERVE ACCOUNT balances of the sending and receiving banks. Checks, automated clearinghouse transfers, and other payments between banks are settled on a provisional basis, because the possibility exists that the person initiating the transfer of funds may not have sufficient funds to cover the payment, or the payment cannot be processed for various reasons. *See also* NETTING; NET SETTLEMENT.
2. **Real Estate.** The CONVEYANCE or transfer of property to a purchaser, and recording of the mortgage lien when sale of the property is finalized. Also known as a mortgage *closing.*
3. **Securities.** The delivery of securities by a selling broker, and payment by the buying broker, normally 3 business days (regular way delivery) after the transaction date.

SETTLEMENT DATE

1. **Banking.** The date that funds transferred through the Federal Reserve Fed Wire, or private network are deposited in a customer's account and available for use. Fed Wire and CLEARING HOUSE

INTERBANK PAYMENTS SYSTEM (CHIPS) transfers are settled the same day. Automated clearing house transfers are settled the next day. *See also* FINALITY OF PAYMENT.

2. **Securities.** The date that securities sold actually change hands. Under regular way settlement, transfer of ownership occurs five business days after the transaction. Under seller's option settlement, delivery of securities in completion of a trade can be delayed up to 60 days from the trade execution date.

SETTLEMENT OPTION

1. **Foreign Exchange.** A contract in which the seller has the option to settle a FORWARD CONTRACT at any time within a specified period.
2. **Securities.** A seller's option to deliver securities at any time from three business days after the transaction date (regular way settlement) to as late as 60 days after the transaction date.

SETTLEMENT PRICE in futures, the figure determined by the closing range of prices. Settlement prices are used to determine gains, losses, margin calls, and invoice prices for deliveries. Also, the price of a financial instrument underlying an option contract when then the contract is exercised.

SETTLEMENT RISK *see* RISK.

SEVERALLY BUT NOT JOINTLY arrangement commonly used in corporate UNDERWRITING in which each member of a selling group assumes responsibility for selling a share of the total offering, but is not responsible for actions of the other parties. Each member of the selling group is responsible for a portion of the original contract, but not for any unsold shares. Also called a *divided account* or *Western Account. See also* JOINTLY AND SEVERALLY.

SHADOW BANK financial company that performs banklike functions, such as lending money to corporations, but is technically exempt from bank regulations and supervision. Shadow banks do not accept federally insured deposits but create banklike risks.

SHARE ACCOUNT account offered by a CREDIT UNION, paying earnings to its members as dividends rather than INTEREST. The major forms are regular share accounts, an interest bearing account similar to personal savings accounts at banks and savings institutions; SHARE DRAFT ACCOUNTS, an interest bearing account permitting withdrawals or transfers by writing drafts against the account; money market accounts, often called money market share accounts and share certificate accounts, which are similar to term savings accounts. Credit union shares are subject to RESERVE REQUIREMENTS if they allow more than three telephone transfers or preauthorized transactions a month.

SHARED APPRECIATION MORTGAGE (SAM) residential mortgage combining a fixed rate of interest at below market rates, and lender participation in any equity appreciation in the mortgaged property. A shared appreciation mortgage has a low monthly payment, as compared to a fixed rate CONVENTIONAL MORTGAGE, and typically is a short-term (under five years) loan. This type of mortgage is appealing to mortgagors who anticipate refinancing at a lower rate. *See also* ADJUSTABLE RATE MORTGAGE; ALTERNATIVE MORTGAGE INSTRUMENT.

SHARED NATIONAL CREDIT loan or loan commitment of $20 million or more shared by three or more federally supervised financial institutions. These large loans and loan commitments are examined by the Board of Governors of the Federal Reserve System, the Federal Deposit Insurance Corporation, and the Office of the Comptroller of the Currency for changes in loan underwriting and credit quality. Findings are summarized in a report (Shared National Credits Review), which is issued annually.

SHARED NETWORK electronic banking system, such as an AUTOMATED TELLER MACHINE network, that is open to customers of any financial institution in a geographic region. Sharing rules, to comply with the Justice Department's guidelines on EFT joint ventures, must allow participation by any financial institution wishing to join.

SHARE DRAFT ACCOUNT transaction account similar to a NEGOTIABLE ORDER OF WITHDRAWAL ACCOUNT, or NOW account, that is offered by credit unions. Members of a credit union can gain access to their share balances by writing drafts on the accounts. These check-like drafts are authorized for federally insured credit unions under the Consumer Checking Account Equity Act of 1980.

SHELF REGISTRATION popular name for the Securities and Exchange Commission rule allowing securities issuers to file registration statements and sell the securities in a PUBLIC OFFERING at a later date. The SEC's Rule 415, adopted initially in 1982, allows issuers to register securities they expect to sell within two years of the initial effective date, without having to file additional registration statements with each offering.

This allows issuers to act quickly, possibly getting a better price for its securities offered for sale. Under SEC Rule 415, issuers are expected to file amendments disclosing any changes in financial condition. Delayed offerings originally were used by corporations, but the SEC also has approved their use by limited partnership tax shelters, employee benefit plans, and issuers of mortgage-backed securities.

SHELL BRANCH foreign branch of a U.S. chartered bank that acts as a booking office for financial transactions carried out beyond U.S. borders. Often located in offshore banking centers, in particular the Bahamas and the Cayman Islands, shell branches provide access at low cost to the Eurocurrency markets. An INTERNATIONAL BANKING FACILITY is a domestic shell branch of a U.S. bank. *See also* OFFSHORE BANKING UNIT.

SHERIFF'S SALE public auction of a borrower's assets seized in a FORECLOSURE order obtained from a court, and carried out by a sheriff or other court officer. Assets pledged as loan collateral and secured by attachments, liens, or mortgages may be sold at auction.

SHERMAN ANTITRUST ACT *see* ANTITRUST LAWS.

SHILLING monetary unit of Kenya, Somalia, Tanzania, and Uganda.

SHIPPING preparing and submitting mortgage documents to an investor in fulfillment of a standby commitment or forward commitment to sell mortgages in the SECONDARY MORTGAGE MARKET.

SHORT BOOK *see* UNMATCHED BOOK.

SHORT COUPON

1. bond interest payment for a period less than the standard six months. Normally, only the first interest payment of a new issue has a short coupon, as computed from the ACCRUED INTEREST payable from the issue date until the first coupon payment date.
2. bond with a relatively short remaining term to maturity, usually under two years. *See also* LONG COUPON.

SHORT DATE FORWARD FORWARD EXCHANGE CONTRACT in the foreign exchange markets involving a sale and delivery contract from one week to one month after the trade date. Contrast with SPOT NEXT; TOMORROW NEXT. *See also* ROLLOVER.

SHORT HEDGE

1. transaction that reduces or eliminates risk of a decline in price in a commodity or security. Options are often used for this purpose: for example, buying put options (an option to sell) selling call options (an option to buy) a particular security.
2. sale of futures contracts to limit the downside risk of ownership of a commodity or financial instrument. The futures contract is approximately equal in value to the underlying financial instrument.

SHORT POSITION dealer's net deficit of commodities, securities, financial instruments, and so on. A short position occurs when a dealer over-sells, anticipating falling prices with the expectation of buying back the assets sold at a lower price.

SHORT SALE

1. sale of a security not owned in anticipation of making a profit by purchasing the security later at a lower price, and delivering the security in completion of the short sale. A *regular way* short sale occurs when the seller has no other position in the security; a *short sale against the box* occurs when the seller has an offsetting long position and wants to postpone tax losses until the following year. The box is securities industry jargon for securities owned by the seller, but held in safekeeping by a BROKER-DEALER.

2. in futures, taking a market position by selling a futures contract in a financial instrument not owned by the seller, in anticipation of a price decline.
3. real estate sale where proceeds from the transaction are insufficient to pay off any mortgage loans on the property; often done to avoid foreclosure.

SHORT-TERM FINANCING

1. loan or credit facility with a maturity of one year or less.
2. credit arrangement extended to a mortgage banker, to finance an inventory of loans that are resold to investors. These include short-term lines of credit from a commercial bank, called a *warehouse line*; commercial paper issued by mortgage bankers, known as COLLATERAL TRUST NOTES.

SHORT-TERM GAIN in computing capital gain (or loss), an investment held for a period of less than 12 months if acquired after 1987, as opposed to a LONG-TERM investment owned for a longer holding period. Previously, the holding period for short-term investments was six months.

SHORT-TERM INVESTMENT FUNDS generic name for pooled investment funds that invest in short-term money market instruments or government bonds. Examples are money market mutual funds, collective investment funds managed by bank TRUST DEPARTMENTS, and tax-exempt funds that invest in securities issued by state and local governments. Many of these funds have minimal investment requirements, can be bought or sold at any time, and are highly liquid investments.

SHORT-TERM PAPER

1. notes, drafts, bills of exchange, or promissory notes that have original maturities up to nine months to a year, excluding days of grace or renewal. COMMERCIAL PAPER, for example, is a promissory note with an original maturity of less than 270 days, although in practice most issues of commercial paper are for shorter periods.
2. promissory notes or installment notes payable within a year.

SIDE COLLATERAL pledge of assets or deposits that does not fully collateralize a loan. Personal guarantees, such as a promise not to mortgage or sell property owned by the borrower, also are a form of side collateral and are worth only as much as the character of the borrower. Side collateral rarely is taken in consumer credit arrangements.

SIGHT DRAFT bill of exchange or draft that is payable when presented. It is typically used when the seller of goods wants to retain control of the goods being shipped to an importer or exporter. Money is payable at sight, when the completed documents are presented, or within a specified period called days of grace. *See also* TIME DRAFT.

SIGNATURE CARD card that a customer signs when opening an account at a financial institution. It identifies the account owner. Copies of signature cards are kept in the branch offices. It is also a dual control device, controlling access to safe deposit boxes. A corporate signature card bears the names of the firm's officers authorized to sign checks or transfer funds.

SIGNATURE LOAN unsecured loan backed only by the borrower's signature on a PROMISSORY NOTE. No collateral is taken by the lender. These generally are loans to individuals with good credit standing who are known by the lending officer. Also known as a *good faith loan* or *character loan.*

SIGNATURE ON FILE bank card billing system in which cardholders actually do not sign the sales draft authorizing a charge to their account. Instead, the merchant or merchant processing bank approves the transaction by matching the cardholder's address supplied by the merchant to a home mailing address, according to bank records. Signatures are not actually compared. This form of cardholder IDENTIFICATION is used most often by mail order merchants, and by hotel chains when billing additional charges after a hotel guest has checked out. If the customer disputes a charge, he or she signs an affidavit.

SIGNATURE VERIFICATION examination of a signature on a negotiable instrument to determine whether the handwriting is genuine, and whether the person signing the check is authorized to use the account. Banks have a legal responsibility to examine checks and drafts presented for payment, but as a practical matter, signatures of check makers and endorsers are examined only on an exception basis. *See also* IDENTIFICATION.

SILVER CERTIFICATE U.S. paper currency, issued by the U.S. Treasury Department rather than the Federal Reserve Banks, as circulating money until 1967, when they were replaced by the FEDERAL RESERVE NOTE as the United States official LEGAL TENDER. Until then, silver certificates were redeemable for an equivalent amount of silver.

SIMPLE INTEREST interest computed only on the principal balance, without compounding. Simple interest for a year on $100, borrowed at 8% interest, is $8. If interest is compounded daily, the finance charge is $8.33. Simple interest computation is the basis of variable rate consumer lending, and also is used widely in mortgage lending. When interest payments on loans are calculated on a simple interest basis, the borrower pays finance charges on the principal balance actually used. Interest calculated under the ADD-ON INTEREST method speeds up the rate of interest payment in the early years of a loan. *See also* DISCOUNT INTEREST RATE; COMPOUND INTEREST.

SIMPLIFIED EMPLOYEE PENSION PLAN (SEP) type of retirement account for small businesses (under 25 employees) and self-employed individuals; both the employer and employee make contributions to an INDIVIDUAL RETIREMENT ACCOUNT. Plan participants can set aside 25 percent of earned income, up to a pre-set amount, on a tax-deferred basis. Participants direct their own investments in stocks, bonds, mutual funds, etc., and pay taxes when funds are withdrawn. Special provisions limit tax deferrals for highly compensated individuals.

SIMULATION in ASSET-LIABILITY MANAGEMENT, a technique of using operating account balances to test various pricing models and RUNOFF scenarios and to determine how the asset portfolio (loans) and liability portfolio (deposits) are likely to perform under different interest rate and pricing situations. The purpose is to test earnings performance under different interest rate hypotheses. *See also* FORECASTING; SCENARIO ANALYSIS; STRESS TEST; WHAT-IF CALCULATION.

SINGLE INTEREST INSURANCE insurance policy that protects a lender's SECURITY INTEREST in a vehicle or automobile financed by an installment loan. Also known as vendor single interest insurance, the policy names the lender as loss payee. Such insurance coverage is sometimes required of marginally creditworthy borrowers, and is payable in one installment, or over the life of the loan.

SINKING FUND

1. **In general.** Money accumulated in a custodial account to retire debt instruments according to a predetermined schedule, regardless of pricing changes in the secondary market. Some sinking fund requirements must be satisfied by redemption of a specific amount of the issue during a specified year. In other cases, the requirement can be met through purchases of the issue in the open market.
2. **Mortgage-backed securities.** A provision in an INDENTURE calling for scheduled amortization of mortgage-backed bonds, subject to prepayment activity. For example, a PLANNED AMORTIZATION CLASS tranche in a Collateralized Mortgage Obligation (CMO).

SKIP ACCOUNT delinquent borrower who moves without leaving a forwarding address. Lenders hire professional collectors, known as skip tracers, to locate a skip and try to collect the amount owed or extract a promise to pay.

SKIP PAYMENT PRIVILEGE

1. clause in a consumer loan agreement giving the borrower the option of omitting one or more payments, provided the lender is notified in advance.
2. option in some credit card plans allowing the cardholder to defer payments due in December until the following month, after the end-of-year holiday shopping season has ended.

SLOW LOAN

1. classification of loans that are considered doubtful, with questionable repayment. A bank may set aside cash assets against such loans in its LOAN LOSS RESERVES.

2. working capital loan to a firm with an extended accounts receivable cycle; i.e., a firm that takes a long time to convert assets into cash. For example, an agricultural loan.

SMALL BUSINESS ADMINISTRATION (SBA) independent federal agency chartered in 1953 to provide financial assistance to small businesses. The SBA makes direct loans to borrowers who are unable to obtain conventional financing, participates in loans originated by financial institutions, and also guarantees loans made by banks and other financial institutions. The SBA preferred lender program, allows businesses to get SBA-guaranteed loans by filing loan applications directly with designated financial institutions, significantly reducing the time needed to obtain SBA funding. Typically, the SBA guarantees 85% of a small business loan. The agency also provides disaster assistance to small businesses and financial counseling to minority-owned businesses. The SBA also licenses, regulates, and provides venture capital assistance to a SMALL BUSINESS INVESTMENT COMPANY. The SBA guarantees bank-originated business loans up to $750,000 in loan principal.

SMALL BUSINESS INVESTMENT COMPANY (SBIC) company licensed by the Small Business Administration to provide equity capital and long-term loans, subsidized by the SBA, to small businesses. An SBIC may lend money to, or buy stock or convertible debentures in, firms with less than $5 million in assets, net worth of not more than $2½ million, and after-tax net income not exceeding $250,000. Originally SBICs had special IRS tax treatment, allowing stockholders to write off credit losses against ordinary income. The Small Business Administration matches the capital contribution of investors in an SBIC, which is permitted to make loans equal to four times its initial capital.

SMALL SAVER CERTIFICATE (SSC) fixed-rate TIME DEPOSIT with no minimum balance and a maturity of 18 months, authorized in 1980 so banks and savings institutions could compete with money market funds. In October 1983, interest rate ceilings on time deposits with maturities longer than 31 days were removed, eliminating the need for the SSC.

SMART CARD credit cards and debit cards with embedded microchips found mostly in the European community, although some U.S. banks have issued smart cards to customers traveling internationally. Smart cards are generally more secure than MAGNETIC STRIPE bank cards, an incentive for greater acceptance of chip cards. An emerging card technology, the EMV card (sponsored by Europay, MasterCard, and Visa) may lead to wider acceptance of smart cards worldwide.

SMITHSONIAN AGREEMENT agreement by members of the GROUP OF TEN countries in December 1971 to adopt FLOATING EXCHANGE RATES. The conference, held at the Smithsonian Institution in Washington, D.C., was prompted by the collapse of the fixed exchange rates that had existed since 1944 under the Bretton Woods agreement, and indirectly by the decision of the United States to abandon the gold exchange standard.

SMURF slang term for a person who carries out cash transactions in a MONEY LAUNDERING scheme. A smurf, also known as a *runner*, attempts to deposit cash in small amounts (under $10,000) to disguise the owners of the cash or to conceal the ultimate purpose for which the money will be used.

SNAKE exchange rate system in the Western European countries, adopted in 1972 as a more flexible form of FIXED EXCHANGE RATES. The exchange rate of each country in the EUROPEAN COMMUNITY was allowed to fluctuate up or down within certain upper or lower limits, called a CURRENCY BAND. *See also* EUROPEAN MONETARY SYSTEM.

SNAPSHOT STATEMENT *see* INTERIM STATEMENT.

SOCIETY FOR WORLDWIDE INTERBANK FINANCIAL TELECOMMUNICATION (SWIFT) nonprofit, cooperative organization that facilitates the exchange of payment messages between FINANCIAL INSTITUTIONS around the world. SWIFT was organized in 1973 by a group of European bankers who wanted a more efficient method than telegraph wire (telex) or mail to send payment instructions to correspondent banks. Among its voting members are U.S. money center and regional banks, and major banks in Europe, Latin America, Africa, Asia, and Australia. SWIFT began operations in 1977, providing the framework for an international communication system between financial institutions.

Recent changes in SWIFT rules gave multinational corporations and BROKER-DEALER securities firms direct access (but nonvoting membership) to confirmations of foreign exchange and money market securities trades, and derivative securities transactions. In 2011, the SWIFT network boasted 9,700 member institutions operating in more than 200 countries.

Payments between SWIFT members take place on domestic funds clearing systems. In the United States most international payments are handled by the FED WIRE or the CLEARINGHOUSE INTERBANK PAYMENTS SYSTEM (CHIPS) in New York City. Web site: *www.swift.com*

SOFT CURRENCY *see* WEAK CURRENCY.

SOFT DOLLAR

1. payment for banking services with balances, for example, a COMPENSATING BALANCE, as opposed to paying in fees or explicit bank SERVICE CHARGES.
2. payment of brokerage services through sales commissions instead of direct payment. A broker collecting a full fee often will use part of the revenue to pay for other services delivered to the client, such as a subscription to a financial service, or third party investment advice.

3. in a real estate project, interest and fees paid by an investor that is tax deductible against the current year's income.

SOFT LOAN extended term project financing made at below-market rates, especially in loans to developing countries. Soft loans are made by the special lending facility of a multinational development bank (for example, the Asian Development Fund and the African Development Fund) or the International Development Association, an affiliate of the World Bank. Typically, soft loans have extended grace periods in which only interest or service charges are due, longer (up to 50 years) amortization schedules, and lower interest rates than conventional bank loans. Access to the soft loan window is limited to developing countries with low per capita incomes, and developing countries experiencing balance of payment problems.

SOL, NEW SOL monetary unit of Peru.

SOLE PROPRIETOR unincorporated business owned and controlled by one person, often under a business name (doing business as) other than the owner's. Sole owners are treated as individual accounts, and may open interest bearing checking accounts.

SOLVENCY

1. **Finance.** The ability of a borrower to pay personal obligations or debt service payments as scheduled, or on demand if not subject to a fixed schedule. *See also* ABILITY TO PAY.
2. **Banking.** The excess of a bank's assets over liabilities. *See also* CAPITAL ADEQUACY.

SOLVENCY RATIOS accounting ratios measuring the financial soundness of a business enterprise and its ability to meet short-term obligations as they come due. There are several commonly used solvency ratios:

- The quick ratio (also called the *acid test ratio* or *liquid ratio*), calculated from the following formula:

  cash + accounts receivable / current liabilities

- The current ratio, a comparison of current assets and current liabilities that measures ability to pay current debts:

  current assets / current liabilities

- The current liabilities to net worth ratio, which indicates the amount due to creditors within a year as a percentage of owners' (or stockholder's) capital:

  current liabilities / net worth

SOM monetary unit of Kyrgyzstan and Uzbekistan.

SOVEREIGN RISK risk of default by a foreign central government or agency backed by the FULL FAITH AND CREDIT of the government. A famous banker once said, "Sovereign nations don't go broke." But they can refuse to pay their obligations to creditor banks, making it extremely difficult for a bank to collect full repayment of its loans. *See also* COUNTRY RISK; STRUCTURAL ADJUSTMENT.

SPECIAL DRAWING RIGHTS (SDR) international reserve currency created by the INTERNATIONAL MONETARY FUND and allocated to its member nations. The SDR is made up from a basket of major currencies; the dollar value of SDRs is computed daily. The U.S. dollar equivalent of the SDR is posted daily on the IMF's web site: *www.imf.org*. A nation that has a balance of payments deficit can use SDRs, subject to certain International Monetary Fund (IMF) conditions, to settle debts to another nation or to the IMF.

SPECIAL MENTION potentially weak loans or assets presenting an unwarranted credit risk, but less risky than SUBSTANDARD assets. Bank loans are classified as special mention assets when the lender fails to supervise a loan properly or maintain sufficient documentation, or has deviated from acceptable and prudent lending practices. Assets listed for special mention generally reflect weaknesses in administration, servicing, or collection, as opposed to credit weaknesses. *See also* ADVERSELY CLASSIFIED ASSETS.

SPECIAL PROVISION addition to loss reserves for loans considered doubtful. These loans have doubtful repayment prospects, and are expected to be charged off as a loss.

SPECIAL-PURPOSE VEHICLE (SPV) limited-purpose organization that serves as a passthrough conduit for securities backed by mortgages, credit card and auto loans, leases, and other financial assets. An SPV can be a corporation, trust, partnership, or limited liability company. Most often, the SPV is set up as a trust. The SPV claims the legal rights of ownership of the assets transferred from the loan originator, and it has an arms-length relationship with the originator or sponsoring organization, meaning that assets held by the SPV are immune from creditors' claims should the sponsoring organization file for bankruptcy. Owing to this bankruptcy protection feature, an SPV is sometimes called a *bankruptcy remote entity*. A key question for an SPV sponsor is whether the SPV is reported off the sponsoring organization's balance sheet or is consolidated along with other assets of the sponsor. This accounting issue turns on the question of whether the transfer of receivables from the sponsor to the SPV is treated as a sale or a loan for accounting purposes. The Financial Accounting Standards Board defines a qualifying SPV (in Accounting Statement FAS 140) as an investment vehicle that is "demonstrably distinct" from the sponsor, has limited scope of activities, holds only "passive" receivables, and retains the right to sell noncash receivables if necessary to pay claims by investors holding the securitized assets. Also called *special purpose entity*.

SPECIE money in the form of coins, usually gold or silver, as opposed to PAPER MONEY; also called HARD CURRENCY. Since the gold standard was abolished in the 1930s, gold coins, aside from their higher intrinsic value and demand as collectibles, no longer have any special worth as a standard of value in world trade.

SPECULATION risk taking by buying securities in the hope of realizing a capital gain or profit. Speculators realize they are putting capital at risk and may experience a higher loss than ordinary investors who seek a reasonable return on investment and preservation of capital. In general, investment risk increases as the holding period lengthens. Many investors use the foreign exchange markets and financial futures to hedge, or offset, potential losses from interest rate swings. Traders who buy and sell in these markets for their own account expect to realize gains from short-term price action in the financial markets.

SPECULATIVE SECURITIES

1. securities rated as sub-investment grade paper by an investment advisory service, and thus an unsuitable investment for a bank investment portfolio or trust department. Speculative securities are rated by Standard & Poor's as grade BB or lower, and by Moody's Investors Service as Ba or lower. *See also* JUNK BOND.
2. investment security subject to loss of interest or principal, or both. Banking regulators have discouraged investing in certain types of derivative mortgage-backed securities, unless these are used as a hedging device to limit interest rate risk. These include STRIPPED MORTGAGE-BACKED SECURITIES—such as INTEREST ONLY (IO) STRIPS AND PRINCIPAL ONLY (PO) STRIPS—and also trading in WHEN ISSUED securities, that is, buying a security in the interim between the announcement date and the offering date, in the hope of making a quick profit.

SPEED shorthand reference for prepayment of mortgages underlying mortgage-backed securities. There are various mathematical formulas for calculating loan prepayment that directly influence the calculated YIELD TO MATURITY on mortgage-backed securities: CONSTANT PERCENT PREPAYMENT (CPP), an annualized estimate of mortgage prepayments; constant prepayment rate (CPR), measuring prepayments as a ratio to outstanding mortgages. A prepayment assumption forecasts projected cash flows when a COLLERALIZED MORTGAGE OBLIGATION (CMO) initially is priced and offered to investors. As the CMO portfolio ages, these cash flows in turn determine the expected maturity (DURATION) and AVERAGE LIFE of the issue.

SPIDERS shares in a trust that owns stocks in the same proportion as the Standard & Poor's 500 stock index. Spiders, also known as Standard & Poor's Depositary Receipts, sell for a dollar amount equal to about one-tenth of the Standard & Poor's 500 index level.

SPLIT DEPOSIT deposit where the customer presenting an endorsed check receives part of the amount being deposited in cash. Split deposits are a major source of teller errors and potential fraud in customer statements. Contrast with MIXED DEPOSIT.

SPLIT LEVEL BALANCE

1. in bank credit cards or consumer lines of credit, an outstanding balance above which a lower interest rate can be charged. For example, a credit card may have a finance charge of 15% APR on balances up to $2,000, and a 13% rate on any outstanding balance above $2,000. The split rate is meant to encourage consumers to use credit cards for major purchases.
2. deposit total in a savings account or other interest bearing account that determines the interest rate paid. A split balance can be the minimum balance needed to earn interest, or avoid service charges, for example, a $2,500 average balance requirement in a NEGOTIABLE ORDER OF WITHDRAWAL (NOW) ACCOUNT. Accounts with balances under $2,500 would be treated as ordinary checking accounts, earning no interest. *See also* TARGET BALANCE; TIERED RATE ACCOUNT.

SPOT in FOREIGN EXCHANGE trading, delivery to meet immediate orders for purchase or sale of a currency at current market prices, normally in two business days. The rate quoted is the *spot rate*. For example, a dealer may agree on Tuesday to sell U.S. dollars and buy Japanese yen for current delivery. The contract is completed on Thursday, when funds are exchanged and delivery takes place. The majority of foreign exchange current delivery contracts are settled with two-day delivery. An exception is the Canadian dollar and Mexican peso contracts traded in North American markets, where the delivery date is one business day forward; Tuesday orders are filled on Wednesday. *See also* SPOT MARKET; SPOT NEXT.

SPOT MARKET market for immediate delivery and payment in cash, as opposed to future delivery, of commodities, foreign exchange, or financial instruments. Delivery normally occurs two days after the trade date. In financial futures, the term can also refer to futures contracts deliverable in the current month. Also called CASH MARKET.

SPOT NEXT FOREIGN EXCHANGE term for purchase of currency for delivery on the day after the SPOT date. The delivery price is adjusted for the extra day. A spot one week contract calls for delivery one week after the trade date; a spot fortnight contract calls for two-week delivery. *See also* TOMORROW NEXT.

SPREAD

1. **Banking.** The percentage difference between the interest rate charged on a bank loan and the lender's cost of funds. Contrast with NET INTEREST MARGIN.

2. **Futures.** The simultaneous purchase and sale of futures contracts in the same financial instrument for delivery in different months, or in different but related markets.
3. **Securities.** (1) in underwriting, the difference between the purchase price paid by a dealer acting as principal to an issuer of securities and the price paid by investors when a new offering of securities is sold. Also known as GROSS SPREAD; and (2) the difference between bid and asked prices on stocks or bonds traded OVER-THE-COUNTER.
4. **Finance.** A put and call option on the same security.
5. **Foreign Exchange.** The difference in price between a bid and offer In the spot market it is known as *spot spread.*

SPREADSHEET

1. accounting worksheet organized by rows and columns, providing a two-way system for analyzing related accounts. An organization's income statement and balance sheet are based on data collected in this format. Spreadsheets also are used in security analysis to compare financial ratios and operating performance of similar companies. If used to post original account entries, it is a transaction journal or account ledger. Summary totals from these subsidiary ledgers are later posted to the GENERAL LEDGER. For example, a bank's LIABILITY LEDGER listing commercial loans on the books might list all interest payments received and posted to the ledger, past due interest, noninterest expense, and noninterest income.
2. electronic spreadsheet, often used as a forecasting tool to project the impact of interest rate changes on a deposit or loan portfolio during future time periods, and test various what-if hypotheses or interest rate scenarios in each of those periods. Because of its flexibility, computer simulation based on spreadsheet modeling has become an important part of budgeting, financial planning, and ASSET-LIABILITY MANAGEMENT. *See also* WHAT-IF CALCULATION.

SQUARE POSITION foreign exchange term indicating a dealer's purchase commitments in a given currency are offset by sell commitments. The dealer's inventory is balanced, neither a LONG POSITION nor a SHORT POSITION.

SQUEEZE *see* TIGHT MONEY.

STABILIZATION

1. **Monetary Policy.** The actions of a CENTRAL BANK to limit currency fluctuations in the FOREIGN EXCHANGE markets, by purchasing or selling currency reserves to other central banks. When a central bank intervenes in the open markets and sells reserves of its nation's currency, the value of that currency against other currencies tends to decline or remain about the same. Stabilization funds, for example, the EXCHANGE STABILIZATION FUND maintained by the Federal Reserve Bank of New York, are national government units

involved in foreign exchange operations. *See also* PEG (PEGGING); SWAP NETWORK.

2. **Underwriting.** The actions by a DEALER or issuer of a security to prevent a security from falling below the initially offered price in the period between the registration date and the date these securities have been sold in the public market. Some dealers make an active market in WHEN ISSUED securities.

STALE-DATED check presented to the paying bank six months or more after the original issue date. Banks are not required by the UNIFORM COMMERCIAL CODE to honor stale-dated checks and can return them to the issuing bank unpaid. The maker of a check can discourage late presentment by writing the words "not good after X days" on the back of the check. *See also* POST-DATED.

STANDARD & POOR'S investment advisory service, a subsidiary of McGraw Hill, that supplies debt ratings on ASSET-BACKED SECURITIES, government, corporate and MUNICIPAL BONDS, COMMERCIAL PAPER, common stock, and preferred stock. The company compiles various market indexes—the best known being the Standard & Poor's 500 Index of major industrial firms—and publishes investment guides, including the Standard & Poor's Bond Guide, the BLUE LIST of offered municipal bonds (published through a subsidiary). The company rates commercial loans and loan syndications, and also notes bank loans to sovereign borrowers. Standard & Poor's also maintains the CUSIP NUMBER system used to identify securities issued in certificate form, under a contract with the American Bankers Association.

Standard & Poor's assigns 12 different ratings for corporate bonds and asset-backed securities. It also assigns ratings to CERTIFICATES OF DEPOSIT. Corporate debt securities and municipal bonds are rated from AAA (the highest quality) to D, bonds that are in default of principal, interest, or both.

A bond rating of AAA means the issuer has sufficient income to pay principal and interest over the 5- to 40-year lifetime of the bonds. Commercial paper is rated A1, A2, A3, B, although only the top three grades are relevant because issuers usually will not attempt to market lower grade paper. A grading of NCR (no contract rating) means the issuer has not asked for a rating. A rating of P (for provisional) assigned revenue bonds indicates that repayment is contingent on project completion.

Certificates of Deposit issued by banks and savings institutions are assigned ratings under S&P's Qualified CD Rating Service. These are given ratings ranging from AAA to CCC for long-term CDs (over a year) and A to D for CDs with maturities under a year. (The letter Q following a rating indicates a rating is based on public sources.) *See also* DUN & BRADSTREET; MERCANTILE AGENCY; MOODY'S INVESTORS SERVICE; RATINGS.

STANDARD OF VALUE one of the properties of MONEY, a test of moneyness. A stable national economy depends on an accepted, uniform medium of exchange allowing suppliers and users of funds to set a fair value (price) on money loaned from one party to another, or on goods sold in open, competitive markets. Gold is the ultimate standard, although today most Western currencies no longer are backed by gold, i.e., exchangeable for gold coins or bullion equal to the face value of paper currency. The United States abandoned the gold standard domestically with the Gold Reserve Act of 1934, and internationally in 1971 when it signed the SMITHSONIAN AGREEMENT, which initiated FLOATING EXCHANGE RATES between the major Western countries. *See also* BARTER; BULLION; LEGAL TENDER; MONEY.

STANDARD PREPAYMENT commonly used prepayment model in mortgage-backed securities, based on an assumed monthly rate of prepayment. As an illustration, this model might assume an annual prepayment rate of 0.2% in the first month in the life of the mortgage loans, and 2% in subsequent months until the 30th month.

STANDARD RISK

1. an acceptable loan using normal credit standards; a *satisfactory* credit. This credit classification indicates the asset in question has satisfactory asset quality and borrower liquidity. The borrower has the capacity to repay scheduled debts as called for by a promissory note.
2. risk rating given bank assets requiring 100% of risk-based capital for computing capital adequacy. For example, commercial loans, consumer installment loans, and most off-balance sheet items.

STANDBY COMMITMENT

1. nonbinding commitment by Fannie Mae or Freddie Mac to purchase a specified number of mortgages in the secondary mortgage market. A commitment fee is paid by the mortgage originator.
2. bank lending commitment, convertible to LINE OF CREDIT. *See also* BANK LINE.
3. investment banker's commitment to underwrite a stock or bond offering.

STANDBY LETTER OF CREDIT letter of credit requiring a designated third party (the BENEFICIARY) to step in if the bank's customer is unable to perform. A standby letter of credit is most often used as a CREDIT ENHANCEMENT, with the understanding that, in most cases, it will never be drawn against or funded.

STANDBY NOTE ISSUANCE FACILITY (SNIF) credit facility that arranges project financing through secondary obligations. A standby facility guarantees payment if the original note issuer defaults. It is often used by weak credit borrowers, who pay a commission to the guarantor, who is secondarily liable if the primary issuer defaults. This as an off-balance sheet item in financial reporting. *See also* REVOLVING UNDERWRITING FACILITY.

STANDBY UNDERWRITING form of UNDERWRITING whereby the selling group agrees to purchase any outstanding shares of securities after shareholders have exercised their preemptive rights to purchase new securities (or exchange new securities for old ones) as in a REORGANIZATION OR RECAPITALIZATION. When the underwriter sells securities purchased in an underwriting, he is acting as a DEALER. *See also* ALL OR NONE; BEST EFFORT.

STANDING MORTGAGE interest-only loan with no amortization of principal during the life of the loan. The principal is payable at maturity in a balloon note. Contrast with LEVEL-PAYMENT AMORTIZATION.

STANDSTILL AGREEMENT agreement whereby a lender makes no further collection efforts on an unpaid loan, acting in the belief that FORECLOSURE would jeopardize the ability of a borrower in financial difficulty to repay any portion of the debt. Such agreements are found most frequently in agriculture loans and loans secured by real estate, where both parties agree that a renegotiated loan is better than a defaulted borrower. The lender and borrower negotiate new credit terms that may include a lower interest rate and rescheduling of payment terms. *See also* TROUBLED DEBT RESTRUCTURING; WORKOUT AGREEMENT.

START-UP FINANCING money used to start a business or purchase assets. Banks tend to view entrepreneurial ventures cautiously and rarely make loans to newly organized businesses without taking COLLATERAL, and if the business venture is a corporation, personal guaranties of the starters. If the entrepreneurs obtain VENTURE CAPITAL financing, a bank loan typically serves as a second level of funding; the bank loan becomes a source of WORKING CAPITAL loan to finance conversion of inventory or receivables into cash receipts, whereas the venture capital funding is a source of longer-term EQUITY capital that ultimately becomes the source of profit to the owners if the firm becomes successful. *See also* BUSINESS PLAN; CO-MAKER; CORPORATE RESOLUTION; FINANCING STATEMENT; GUARANTOR; KEY MAN INSURANCE; SECURITY AGREEMENT; SECURITY INTEREST; SEED MONEY.

STATE AND LOCAL BONDS bonds issued by municipal governments, local taxing districts, and state government agencies. These bonds, sometimes referred to collectively as MUNICIPAL BONDS, generally are tax-exempt from federal income taxes on interest earned in the state of origin, although certain classes of bonds issued after August 1986 are subject to federal taxes on interest income. The Tax Reform Act of 1986 placed annual limits on the amount of fully tax-exempt bonds issued by a state or local agency.

Classifications of these bonds include GENERAL OBLIGATION BONDS, REVENUE BONDS, INDUSTRIAL REVENUE BONDS, MORTGAGE REVENUE BONDS. *See also* PRIVATE PURPOSE BOND; PUBLIC PURPOSE BOND; TAXABLE MUNICIPAL BOND.

STATE BANK corporation chartered by a state to engage in commercial banking, and subject to supervision under banking laws in the chartering state. State banks differ from NATIONAL BANKS, which are chartered and supervised by the Comptroller of the Currency. State banks have access to Federal Reserve services, such as check collection, currency and coin delivery, and the FED WIRE, and can become member institutions in the Federal Reserve System.

Regulations in some states give state chartered banks more authority than national banks to engage in selected nonbank activities, such as insurance underwriting and brokerage, securities underwriting, and real estate investments, which accounts for the diversity of banking under the DUAL BANKING system. Supervision of state chartered banks is shared by STATE BANKING DEPARTMENTS and the FEDERAL DEPOSIT INSURANCE CORPORATION, which insures deposits of most regulated financial institutions.

STATE BANKING DEPARTMENT agency that charters and supervises state banks. The chief officer in this department is the designated superintendent of banks or has a similar title. The Conference of State Bank Supervisors is the national association of state bank superintendents.

STATED INCOME BORROWER self-employed individual who has income but does not receive regular wages or salary from an employer. These borrowers are usually asked to provide financial statements and meet financial ability-to-pay tests (e.g., six months' stated income and assets to cover two months of housing expenses). Stated income borrowers typically pay higher mortgage loan rates.

STATED MATURITY latest date on which holders of COLLATERALIZED MORTGAGE OBLIGATION (CMO) bonds will be paid in full, assuming there are no prepayments on mortgages backing the bonds. The date printed on a bond is its stated maturity. A typical CMO issue has several maturity classes (called TRANCHES) that cover a range of maturity assumptions: a fast pay bond with maturities up to five years; an intermediate pay bond maturing in 5 to 10 years; a slow pay bond maturing in 20 to 25 years; and a Z-Bond (or accrual bond) that pays out at the maturity of a 30-year mortgage. *See also* AVERAGE LIFE.

STATEMENT detailed record of a customer's account, listing debits, credits, transfers between related accounts, and service charges during the preceding month. A checking account statement lists checks by the date paid, bank teller deposits, and electronic deposits (for example, a payroll direct deposit); AUTOMATED TELLER MACHINE withdrawals and deposits; preauthorized debits (for example, a loan payment automatically deducted each month); and the beginning and end-of-month account balance. A DESCRIPTIVE STATEMENT lists the payee's name next to each account entry, for example, the merchant name in a bank credit card statement. A COMBINED STATEMENT lists account balances in related accounts, for example, checking and savings accounts that are maintained under a single account number. *See also* BANK STATEMENT; PERIODIC STATEMENT; PAPERLESS STATEMENT; STATEMENT SAVINGS ACCOUNT.

STATEMENT ANALYSIS detailed examination of a borrower's balance sheet and cash flow to determine ability to repay bank debt. A key part of the process is close examination of financial ratios, such as receivables turnover. Unaudited financial statements may require additional verification. *See also* BALANCE SHEET RATIOS; TURNOVER RATIOS.

STATEMENT BALANCE

1. account balance as of the date summary statements are prepared and mailed to customers. Checking account statements list all checks paid before the date the statement is prepared. The ending balance may differ from the actual balance in the account, because checks that have not yet cleared are not included. By comparing the bank statement with checks listed in a checkbook, the customer can verify the accuracy of the account statement.
2. outstanding balance owed on a CREDIT CARD account.
3. closing balance in a deposit account, including interest earned, less service charges.

STATEMENT OF ACCOUNT *see* ACCOUNT STATEMENTS; STATEMENT.

STATEMENT OF CONDITION *see* REPORT OF CONDITION.

STATEMENT SAVINGS ACCOUNT savings account where deposits, withdrawals, and interest credited are recorded as computer entries. The customer receives a periodic statement of account, showing deposits, withdrawals, and interest earned up to the posting date, but does not receive a passbook evidencing ownership of the account.

STATEMENT STUFFER marketing brochure in a customer's ACCOUNT STATEMENT, containing a brief sales message and a short-form application or toll-free telephone number. Statement stuffers are an inexpensive way to market additional products to bank customers or promote special rates on savings accounts.

STATIC GAP the simplest measure of short-term net interest exposure, or difference between assets and liabilities of comparable repricing periods. It generally is calculated for periods under one year, in multiple periods, or time frames of 0 to 30 days, 31 to 90 days, or 91 to 180 days. By itself, interest rate gap is an imprecise measurement, because it fails to consider interim cash flows, loan prepayment, average maturity, and other factors. Contrast with DYNAMIC GAP.

STATUTE OF FRAUDS legislation adopted in most states stipulating that certain contracts must be in writing to legally be enforceable. The purpose is to prevent fraudulent transactions. For example, Article II of the UNIFORM COMMERCIAL CODE stipulates that contracts for sale of goods for $500 or more must indicate terms of the agreement in writing and be signed by the party owing the agreed amount.

STATUTE OF LIMITATIONS state laws specifying the time period within which parties taking judicial action to enforce rights must file the claims. The period varies depending on the type of claim; if based on statute, the claim must be filed within a certain number of years of the action in question; if based on written contract, a longer period is allowed—up to six years in most states for contract claims, and five years for civil liability (TORT) claims. The statutory period for filing claims, however, varies according to state jurisdiction. Claims filed after the statutory period ends are barred.

STEP-UP MORTGAGE *see* TWO-STEP MORTGAGE.

STOCK interest in a corporation, evidencing a claim of ownership. Common stock entitles the owners to receive regular dividends if declared by the board of directors, to vote at annual shareholder meetings, or to authorize other persons to vote on their behalf. Preferred stock usually has no voting rights, pays limited but specified dividends, but has priority claim over common stock to earnings (dividends) and assets (liquidation value) of the corporation. *See also* COUPON; PAR VALUE; STOCK PURCHASE OPTION.

STOCK PURCHASE OPTION employee benefit authorizing purchase of shares of common stock issued by their employer, usually at a price discounted from the book market value. The option may be exercised anytime during a ten-year period. Sometimes called a stock-bonus trust. *See also* EMPLOYEE STOCK OWNERSHIP PLAN.

STOCK SPLIT increase in the number of shares to be offered for sale, done by amending a corporate charter. The amendment approves an increase (a split up) in the number of common shares or a decrease, called a split down or reverse stock split. The transaction does not increase equity capital, as the stated par value of shares owned is reduced proportionately. In a reverse split, the issuer reduces the number of shares outstanding. Compare to RIGHTS OFFERING.

STOP ORDER order to buy or sell at the market when a specified price is reached; also called *stop-out order.* There is, however, no guarantee of execution. In a falling market, for example, a stop order calling for sale at 40 becomes a market order at that price, but the next sale may be at 39 or lower. The security is offered for sale at the market price.

STOP-OUT PRICE lowest price the U.S. Treasury Department accepts in an auction of a new issue of Treasury securities. Securities sold at this price pay the highest yield. When the Treasury auctions securities, it accepts tenders starting at the highest bid price and continues to fill bids at gradually lower prices until the entire amount of securities has been sold. Usually, the Treasury also reports the percentage of stop-out bids accepted in an auction of new securities.

STOP PAYMENT order by the writer of a check that payment should not be honored. Stop payment orders directing the drawee to dishonor a specific check may be given by telephone or in writing. Under the Uniform Commercial Code, stop payment orders that have been confirmed in writing by the check writer or maker are valid for six months.

STOPPED ACCOUNT *see* ACCOUNT HOLD.

STORED-VALUE CARD card used to store money and used to pay cash for goods and services. It can be reloaded with additional value and used many times. Banks have been offering stored value cards as a gateway to servicing the needs of consumers who have income from wages or benefits but lack access to conventional checking or savings accounts. *See also* CASH CARD; CHECK CARD; GIFT CARD; PAYROLL CARD; PREPAID CARD.

STORY PAPER security or investment with unusual features, requiring explanation before it can be sold. This may occur because the security has a limited following with securities analysts, does not have a credit rating, or has other characteristics that must be explained to investors. Contrast with SEASONED SECURITIES.

STRADDLE simultaneous purchase of a call option and a put option with the same exercise date and exercise price. This is an option position designed to profit from an expected increase in the price volatility of the underlying instrument.

STRAIGHT BOND noncallable bond, such as a Treasury bond, Eurobond, or savings bond.

STRAIGHT CREDIT

1. LETTER OF CREDIT requiring presentation on or before the expiration date at the office of the paying bank. Drafts are honored in favor of the beneficiary only.
2. loan that is backed or secured only by the borrower's promise to pay. Also known as a GOOD FAITH loan.

STREET NAME securities term for a registered security held in the name of a bank, brokerage firm, or another third party as NOMINEE, as opposed to a registration in the owner's name. Street name registration eliminates the need to deliver certificates to a selling broker when transferring securities.

STRESS TEST simulation technique to evaluate a bank's survivability if sudden, unanticipated events were to occur. Stress tests help determine the amount of private capital a bank would need to get through a severe economic downturn. The Treasury Department performed stress testing on major U.S. banks in 2009, a period of general economic instability.

STRIKE PRICE dollar price at which the holder of a call option can buy the underlying securities, or the holder of a put option can sell, anytime during the life of the option contract. Also called *striking price* or *exercise price*.

STRIP security created by separating the corpus, or bond principal, from the interest coupons, or interest payments. The stripping is done by a trust fiduciary. Principal payments are grouped together to make large denomination securities, and interest payments grouped with other interest payments of the same date to make other large securities, which are then sold to investors in smaller denominations. Separating the interest coupons effectively creates a ZERO-COUPON SECURITY, a bond that pays no interest until maturity. An investor buying a ten-year $1,000 Treasury Bond, yielding 9%, pays $415 and at maturity receives the full face value of the bond.

In U.S. Treasury securities, there are two general classes of strip securities: so-called generic STRIPS, short for SEPARATE TRADING OF REGISTERED INTEREST AND PRINCIPAL, which are direct obligations of the U.S. Treasury Department, and synthetic strips, which are sold through brokerage houses. U.S. Treasury securities actually are not stripped of coupon interest payments, but are sold at true discount. Some zero-coupons issued by brokerage houses have had such colorful acronyms as CATS (Certificate of Accrual on Treasury Securities, issued by Salomon Brothers), and TIGR (Treasury Income Growth Receipts, issued by Merrill Lynch.) *See also* STRIPPED MORTGAGE-BACKED SECURITIES.

STRIPPED MORTGAGE-BACKED SECURITIES mortgage-backed instrument consisting of two distinct classes: INTEREST-ONLY (IO) STRIPS and PRINCIPAL-ONLY (PO) STRIPS. In its purest form, the mortgage-backed security is converted into an INTEREST-ONLY strip, where the investor receives 100% of the interest cash flow, and a principal-only strip, in which the investor receives 100% of the principal cash flows. Both are highly interest rate sensitive. Investors who expect rising interest rates (and declining mortgage prepayments) tend to buy interest-only strips. Those who anticipate lower rates (rising prepayments) buy principal-only strips, because the principal is repaid faster when rates are declining. *See also* ASSET-BACKED SECURITIES; COLLATERALIZED MORTGAGE OBLIGATION; RESIDUAL; SPECULATIVE SECURITIES.

STRONG CURRENCY currency that lenders are willing to accept as payment, other than their own national currency. Central banks maintain a portion of their reserves in strong currency deposits. In foreign exchange trading, a strong currency trades at a premium in relation to a WEAK CURRENCY. Also known as a *reserve currency.*

STRUCTURAL ADJUSTMENT medium-term credit facility originated by the World Bank in 1979 to assist developing countries in gaining economic self-sufficiency. This form of lending is aimed at reducing a debtor nation's CURRENT ACCOUNT deficit, rather than financing new projects. Under these multiyear agreements, debtor nations postpone repayment of principal to later years when the debt service can be more easily absorbed by a stronger, growing economy. The basis of structural adjustment credit is the borrower's agreement to encourage private development, stimulate exports, and promote economic diversification with the ultimate aim of resuming positive economic growth.

STRUCTURING MONEY LAUNDERING scheme to evade reporting requirements under federal law. This happens when cash in excess of $10,000 is deposited at a bank in several transactions under that amount. Cash deposits of $10,000 or more are reported to federal law enforcement agencies under the Money Laundering Control Act of 1986. The law requires everyone, including lawyers, auto dealers, and so on, to report cash deposits over $10,000. Cash purchases of travelers checks and money orders in amounts as small as $3,000 also are reportable under certain conditions. If structuring is suspected, however, bank tellers still are required to fill out a CURRENCY TRANSACTION REPORT. Such transactions must be reported not only to banking authorities, but also to the U.S. Secret Service and the Internal Revenue Service.

STUDENT LOAN *see* EDUCATION LOAN.

STUDENT LOAN MARKETING ASSOCIATION publicly traded corporation established in 1972 to increase the availability of student loans by purchasing loans in the SECONDARY MARKET. The corporation also known as Sallie Mae, guarantees college education loans under the federal Guaranteed Student Loan Program, and under the Health Education Assistance Program. Sallie Mae purchases a 90% interest in loans guaranteed by the corporation, and finances its secondary market activities by issuing medium-term notes and floating rate notes. Sallie Mae obligations are exempt from state and local taxes, and are backed by the full faith and credit of the U.S. government. Sallie Mae's parent company, USA Education, (formerly SLM Holding Corp.) was to be fully privatized in 2006.

SUBCHAPTER M section of the Internal Revenue Code authorizing favorable tax treatment of regulated investment companies. Companies that choose this form of organization are not required to pay income taxes on realized gains and investment income distributed to shareholders if they: (1) distribute not less than 90% of their net investment income (interest and dividends, less expenses) in any taxable year; (2) derive at least 90% of gross income from dividends, interest, and gains from sale of securities; and (3) comply with other percentage limitations on short-term gains from securities held less than three months. Nonregulated investment companies are taxed on net income and realized gains.

SUBCHAPTER S business concern chartered as a corporation that is taxed as a partnership. An S corporation can use the CASH BASIS of accounting, has 75 or fewer shareholders, and corporate gains (or losses) from operations are taxed to the shareholders as individuals. Also known as a *small business corporation.*

SUBJECT OFFER offer that is not a firm commitment to sell, but is intended for information purposes only, or to solicit a counteroffer from a willing buyer.

SUBJECT TO COLLECTION check drawn on an out-of-town bank and deposited, with IMMEDIATE CREDIT of funds, to a customer in good standing, or one who has sufficient balances to cover the deposit. The deposit is made with the understanding that if the check bounces for any reason, the amount deposited will be charged back to the customer's account. *See also* AVAILABILITY.

SUBJECT TO MORTGAGE assignment or transfer of real estate where the purchaser agrees to take over monthly payments of principal and interest, but does not assume personal liability for the obligation. If the purchaser defaults, the lender must attempt to collect the debt from the original borrower, through FORECLOSURE on the property, or other means. The original mortgage remains intact, and property title is not passed on to the purchaser. Contrast with ASSUMPTION.

SUBJECT TO REDEMPTION *see* CALL PROVISION.

SUBJECT TO VERIFICATION deposit accepted for IMMEDIATE CREDIT, for example, a check drawn on and deposited in the same bank, that may be adjusted later if an error is discovered. For example, if the check amount differs from what the customer wrote on the deposit ticket, or when a bank's customer makes a cash deposit at an AUTOMATED TELLER MACHINE (ATM). Envelope deposits at an ATM must be verified by bank employees to see that the deposit matches the amount claimed by the customer.

SUBORDINATED DEBT debt having a claim against the issuer's assets that is lower ranking, or junior to, other obligations, and is paid after claims to holders of senior securities are satisfied. Credit has differing levels of claim, depending on how a financing is structured; thus, an obligation can be senior to one claim, but subordinate to another. For example, a subordinated debenture is junior to a mortgage-backed bond, but has precedence over dividend payments to stockholders.

A REAL ESTATE MORTGAGE INVESTMENT CONDUIT (REMIC), which invests in a pool of mortgages, typically sells interests in these mortgages through multiclass senior/subordinated securities to improve the marketability of REMIC securities. The subordinated debt class absorbs all the credit risk and default risk of one or more senior debt classes. Subordinated obligations also are used commonly in MEZZANINE FINANCING arranged in corporate leveraged buyouts and restructurings.

SUBORDINATION AGREEMENT

1. agreement signed by a co-maker placing an interest in property owned jointly with a borrower behind the lender's security interest in pledged collateral. Lenders in states recognizing the TENANCY IN COMMON form of property ownership ordinarily require co-makers to sign a promissory note or a subordination agreement if the borrower defaults.
2. instrument acknowledging that a creditor's claim is secondary to claims of other creditors. Thus, under a subordination agreement, a loan by an officer of a corporation to the firm has a secondary claim to assets after a bank loan. The agreement assures that a bank loan will be paid off first.

SUBPRIME LOAN

1. loan to to a borrower with a weak credit history, also called a *B and C loan* or *nonprime loan.* Borrowers with previous charge-offs or delinquencies pay a higher rate of interest than *A-rated* borrowers. Mortgages, home equity loans, and debt consolidation loans are common examples of subprime loans.
2. loan to a business borrower priced at an interest rate below the PRIME RATE, the reference rate for bank commercial loans.

SUBROGATION substitution of one creditor for another in settlement of a claim or obligation, or transfer of ownership, as when a mortgage is sold in the secondary market.

SUBSCRIPTION offer to purchase securities, that may be exercised any time during a specified waiting period, usually one to two months after they are publicly offered.

SUBSIDIARY

1. corporation controlled through partial or complete ownership of its voting stock by another company. Bank owned subsidiary companies are reportable in a bank's REPORT OF CONDITION filed with its primary regulatory agency. A company with 50% or more of its outstanding stock owned, directly or indirectly, by a bank is a majority owned subsidiary. A significant subsidiary of a reporting bank is a company in which the parent bank has a 5% equity capital interest, or a company that contributes at least 5% of the parent bank's gross operating income or 5% of its pretax income (or loss). Banks and other depository financial institutions report income on a consolidated basis, including earnings of subsidiary companies.
2. corporation, owned by a BANK HOLDING COMPANY, offering nonbanking services, such as equipment leasing or securities underwriting, as approved by the Federal Reserve Board under Section 4(c)(8) of the Bank Holding Company Act. A company owned by a bank holding company, rather than a bank itself, generally is referred to as a bank AFFILIATE, to avoid being confused with bank-owned subsidiaries. The GRAMM-LEACH-BLILEY ACT OF 1999

permits national banks to establish or acquire subsidiary companies (called *financial subsidiaries*) that may engage in a broad range of bank-related financial activities, except insurance underwriting, merchant banking, and direct investments in real estate. *See also* SECURITIES SUBSIDIARY.

SUBSTANDARD

1. bank loan or other interest-earning asset that is protected inadequately by current net worth and paying capacity of the borrower, or the collateral pledged. Loans classified as substandard are characterized by the distinct possibility that the lender will sustain some loss if the deficiencies are not corrected. Some loss of interest is anticipated, or may have already occurred, but loss of principal is considered unlikely. *See also* ADVERSELY CLASSIFIED ASSETS; DOUBTFUL LOAN; LOSS.
2. country risk classification for cross-border loans to a debtor nation, in which the country involved has not met external debt payments, accepted an economic adjustment program recommended by the International Monetary Fund, or negotiated a rescheduling of debts with its creditors.

SUBSTITUTE CHECK Paper reproduction of an original check. A substitute check has a digital image of the front and back of the original check and is suitable for automated processing. The CHECK 21 law (Check Clearing for the 21st Century Act), federal legislation enacted in 2003, allows banks to truncate paper checks, process check information electronically, and deliver a substitute check to the depositing bank if that bank requires paper checks. *See also* TRUNCATION.

SUBSTITUTION

1. replacement of one creditor by another, also known as SUBROGATION.
2. replacement of collateral securing a broker's call loan with other collateral of equal value.
3. acquisition of a borrower's tangible property through FORECLOSURE. The lender takes collateral in exchange for the defaulted loan.
4. in the SECONDARY MORTGAGE MARKET, an investor's right to have the selling financial institution replace a nonperforming loan with another.
5. the exchange of a new contract for an existing one, as in a NOVATION.

SUCRE monetary unit of Ecuador.

SUNSET CLAUSE language in a state law stating the law expires at a specified date, unless renewed by act of the state legislature. Legislation in several states raising or abolishing interest rate ceilings on credit card finance charges contains such clauses.

SUPER NOW ACCOUNT transaction account combining features of the NEGOTIATE ORDER OF WITHDRAWAL (NOW account) and the MONEY MARKET DEPOSIT ACCOUNT. Authorized for depository institutions in January 1983, Super NOWs have no interest rate ceilings, but a seven-day withdrawal notice may apply. In addition, they have unlimited deposit and withdrawal capability, but are available only to depositors eligible for NOW accounts, excluding for-profit businesses.

SUPER REGIONAL BANK bank holding company operating subsidiary banks in two or more states. Super regional banks operate multistate banking networks in all major geographic regions of the United States. *See also* BRANCH BANKING; INTERSTATE BANKING.

SUPER-SENIOR TRANCHE high-quality bonds taking priority over more junior debt owed by a debt issuer, a structuring that allows a wider group of investors in a bond offering. These senior-level bonds typically have the highest assigned credit rating and have very low default risk. If the bond issuer defaults, the more junior bonds are liquidated first, starting with the lowest-rated bonds, thus giving holders of the higher-quality senior notes some degree of protection from principal loss.

SUPER SINKER bond TRANCHE in a Collateralized Mortgage Obligation (CMO) or other mortgage-backed security with a shorter average life than other bonds in the same offering. These bonds are retired at a faster than normal rate by early borrower prepayments, reducing the cash flow uncertainty. Super sinker bonds are also a common feature in MORTGAGE REVENUE BONDS. These housing related bonds are attractive to investors who believe that mortgage rates will fall while new housing construction increases. *See also* PLANNED AMORTIZATION CLASS.

SUPERVISORY MERGER consolidation of two or more financial institutions, supervised by a bank regulatory agency, in which a weak institution is acquired by a stronger one. The supervisory agency may arrange assistance to the acquiring bank by purchasing some or all of the bad loans in the troubled institution, or giving the acquirer of a failing bank or savings institution guarantees against losses for a limited period. *See also* BAILOUT.

SUPPLY SIDE ECONOMICS economic theory advocating drastic tax cuts and tax credits to encourage productive investments by corporations and achieve economic targets for growth in national output and employment. Supply side economists argue the importance of lowering *marginal tax rates,* which they say stimulates AGGREGATE SUPPLY encouraging suppliers to produce more, and individuals to earn more, as opposed to stimulating AGGREGATE DEMAND for goods and services by consumers and businesses. In other words, people will work more because they can produce more. Supply siders argue that the economic stimulus of tax cuts and tax credits will offset revenue losses from cuts in marginal tax rates. In the early 1980s, supply side economics was a politically attractive solution to the stagflation (double-digit inflation accompanied by stagnant growth) characteristic of the late 1970s. It is counter to the KEYNESIAN ECONOMICS school; supply siders reject the Keynesian multiplier argument that relates tax cuts to increases in aggregate demand.

SURCHARGE

1. extra charge imposed on those who purchase with a credit card instead of cash. Credit card surcharges are forbidden by the Truth in Lending Act amendments of 1975, which permitted discounts for cash payments.
2. charge assessed by a Federal Reserve bank for access to the nighttime processing cycle of an AUTOMATED CLEARING HOUSE, commonly used by banks to move excess funds from ZERO-BALANCE ACCOUNTS into concentration accounts for corporate customers.
3. DISCOUNT WINDOW surcharge imposed by a FEDERAL RESERVE BANK, on short-term adjustment credit. Used in the early 1980s as a selective credit control to control inflation, the Fed's authority to use surcharges expired in November 1981.
4. transaction fee for withdrawing cash at an automated teller machine. Such fees must be displayed at the ATM site.

SURETY guaranty of debt repayment or fulfillment of contractual obligation. Borrowers unable to obtain credit under their own name often have a third party sign the application. Under a surety agreement, the lender can look to the surety or guarantor for payment if the borrower defaults. A surety who pays a borrower's debt takes an assignment of the creditor's rights through SUBROGATION and can attempt to recover that payment from the borrower.

SURETY BOND agreement by an insurance company to take the place of a defaulted contractor in a development project, and take corrective action, if necessary, to finish the project. The insurance company also may be compelled to pay for damages resulting from default. Surety bonds commonly are required on municipal development projects financed by general obligation bonds or revenue bonds. A surety bond also is required to put a STOP PAYMENT order on an official bank check, such as a CASHIER'S CHECK. Also called an *indemnity bond.*

SURPLUS

1. EQUITY of a corporation, including stock issued at a premium over its par value or stated value, representing the excess of assets over liabilities, including capital stock. The preferred term is *capital surplus*. In banking, there is little difference between equity capital and surplus, because amounts contributed by stockholders over the par value of their stock are counted as part of the capital account in computing bank CAPITAL ADEQUACY.

The Comptroller of the Currency requires national banks to have surplus of 20% over the PAID IN CAPITAL stock before obtaining a charter. Also, national banks must allocate at least 10% of the previous six month's earnings to the surplus account before paying shareholder dividends.

2. net profits of a corporation after payment of dividends. Also called earned surplus, undistributed profits, or RETAINED EARNINGS.

SURPLUS RESERVES

1. **Accounting.** The portion of cash surplus that has not been allocated to a particular account.
2. **Banking.** Reserve account balances above the legal RESERVE REQUIREMENTS; also known as EXCESS RESERVES. Also, unallocated reserves of banks belonging to a clearinghouse association.

SURVEILLANCE

1. computerized monitoring system that alerts banking regulators to sudden changes in a bank's condition. The Comptroller of the Currency has an electronic early warning system, the NATIONAL BANK SURVEILLANCE SYSTEM (NBSS), that watches changes in a national bank's financial condition compared to banks of similar size. The NBSS system helps the Comptroller's office keep track of banks in need of special attention.
2. video cameras and other security systems used to monitor teller line and automated teller machine transactions. Film from monitoring systems can be used to document robberies, unauthorized withdrawals, and other disputed transactions.

SUSPENSION

1. revocation of a bank's charter by a supervisory agency.
2. bank closing ordered by banking or governmental authorities to control a RUN on a bank, or when a bank is declared insolvent.
3. temporary halt in trading of a security, or trading activity on a stock exchange in advance of a news announcement or to correct an imbalance of buy and sell orders.
4. debt repayment MORATORIUM declared by a debtor nation, for example, a temporary halt in interest payments.

SUSTAINABLE GROWTH

1. noninflationary, stable growth in the economy with full employment: an objective of Federal Reserve MONETARY POLICY.
2. income from a firm's operations in future accounting periods that can support debt repayment. It implies a rate of growth expected from retained earnings without external financing, and without altering financial leverage. Lenders usually ask for copies of financial statements before extending or renewing a LINE OF CREDIT.

SWAP

1. **Foreign Exchange.** The simultaneous buying and selling of a currency in approximately equal amounts for different maturity dates.

The swap price is the difference in price between the two maturity dates of the swap.

2. agreement to exchange interest payments in a fixed rate obligation for interest payments in a floating rate obligation (an INTEREST RATE SWAP), or one currency for another (a CURRENCY SWAP), and reverse the exchange at a later date. A cross-currency swap is the exchange of a fixed rate obligation in one currency for a floating rate obligation in another. A swap agreement is based on a NOTIONAL PRINCIPAL amount, or an equivalent amount of principal, that sets the value of the swap at maturity, but is never exchanged. The notional principal sets the value of the interest payments in a swap. Rules governing financial swaps are set by the International Swap Dealers Association, a self-regulatory organization.

   Interest rate and currency swaps are used by bankers and investment managers to minimize borrowing costs, to fund bank loans with liabilities of approximately equal durations, to gain liquidity (in a currency swap) in one currency versus another; to hedge portfolio risk or raise capital in foreign markets, and also to generate trading profits. Swaps most often are used for funding purposes or for creating assets, and have some advantages when compared to bank loans or deposits in ASSET-LIABILITY MANAGEMENT. Unlike loans or deposits, swaps are not disclosed on the balance sheet of the issuing bank, although banks must still reserve a portion of their equity capital to cover their outstanding swap agreements under RISK-BASED CAPITAL guidelines. *See also* ASSET SWAP; BASIS SWAP; CREDIT DEFAULT SWAP; SWAP NETWORK.

3. BOND SWAP: sale of a bond before maturity and purchase of another.
4. MORTGAGE SWAP: exchange of mortgage loans for securities backed by the same mortgages.
5. commodity swap: An exchange of payments in which the value of the exchange is linked to commodity prices. Similar to an INTEREST RATE SWAP.

SWAP EXECUTION FACILITY electronic derivatives marketplace authorized by the Dodd-Frank Act of 2010. Under Dodd-Frank, companies must trade credit default swaps and many other derivative contracts through established exchanges or swap execution facilities. The purpose is to improve accountability in the derivatives market with stronger requirements for audit trails and record keeping.

SWAP NETWORK reciprocal short-term credit agreement between central banks to stabilize currency prices through INTERVENTION in the foreign exchange market.

SWAPTION option contract on an INTEREST RATE SWAP. The contract gives the buyer the option to execute an interest rate swap on a future date, thereby locking in financing costs at a specified fixed rate of interest. The seller of the swaption, usually a commercial bank or investment bank, assumes the risk of interest rate changes, in exchange for payment of a swap premium.

SWAP TRANSFERRING RISK WITH PARTICIPATING ELEMENT (STRIPE) hedging technique combining an INTEREST RATE SWAP and an INTEREST RATE CAP. A percentage of the amount financed, say 50%, is borrowed at a fixed rate; the rest is financed at a floating rate with an agreed-upon cap. If rates fall, the borrower participates in half of the benefits from dips in interest rates on the 50% portion covered by the cap. The borrower also is protected from upward swings in interest rates by the cap on the FLOATING RATE NOTE portion of the debt. The borrower also does not pay a fee on the swap agreement; instead, the lender prices the fixed rate portion of the loan above the rate the borrower would get in a straight interest rate swap. *See also* CAP; COLLAR; FLOOR.

SWEEP ACCOUNT transaction account that offers convertibility of balances above some minimum into a higher-yielding savings or investment instrument, such as a money market mutual fund or overnight repurchase agreement. Balances above the specified amount periodically are transferred. A variation is the repurchase agreement, or sweep repo, in which funds are moved from a depositor's account and invested in government securities. The next banking day, the customer's funds, plus interest, are recredited to the deposit account.

SWEETENER

1. **Banking.** The additional consideration paid by a borrower in periods of high interest rates and TIGHT MONEY, or by a marginally creditworthy borrower. For example, payment of an additional point (one percentage point of the principal amount borrowed) during periods of high loan demand. Also, the pledge of additional securities by a broker to finance securities trading for customers.
2. **Finance.** The addition of a conversion privilege on securities, making them convertible into common stock, and thus more valuable to investors.

SWIFT *see* SOCIETY FOR WORLDWIDE INTERBANK FINANCIAL TELECOMMUNICATION.

SWINGLINE short-term BACKUP LINE of credit that can be called at very short notice, and normally is arranged by a bank for an issuer of COMMERCIAL PAPER. The line provides contingency financing to cover potential shortfalls that may result if the proceeds of a sale are insufficient to retire the debt incurred in issuing the paper, or if the issuer is unable to roll over an issue of maturing paper.

SWING LOAN *see* BRIDGE LOAN.

SWIPE FEE Transaction fee (or INTERCHANGE FEE) a bank collects from retailers each time a consumer uses a debit card at a merchant location; usually a fixed amount for each debit card transaction. *See also* DURBIN AMENDMENT.

SWITCH

1. **Foreign Exchange.** The intended effect of intervention in currency markets by central monetary authorities. Switching policy is intended to reverse the rate at which a nation's currency flows out of, or is absorbed by, domestic markets, and has further impact on a nation's balance of trade.
2. **Futures.** Liquidating an existing position and simultaneously reinstating a position in another futures contract of the same type. Known as *switching.*
3. computer facility in shared ELECTRONIC FUNDS TRANSFER networks that routes transactions between a terminal and a card issuing bank's host computer. A switch in front clears all transactions processed through a network; a switch behind clears only transactions initiated by customers of other financial institutions—on others transactions.
4. **Foreign Trade.** The practice of exporting or importing goods through a third country. This commonly is done when the destination country is short of U.S. dollars and the intermediary country has available dollars and is willing to exchange the destination country's currency. Switch transactions must conform with various laws covering export licenses. *See also* THIRD COUNTRY ACCEPTANCE.
5. **Mutual Funds.** Moving assets from one fund to another, within a family of funds.

SYNDICATED LOAN loan extended by a group of banks to a corporate borrower. The loans—usually made at interest rates tied to a variable rate index such as the London Interbank Offered Rate (LIBOR)—are often sold to investors in the secondary loan market. In recent years, institutional investors such as mutual funds became major buyers of syndicated loans.

Syndicated loans to major corporate borrowers are rated by credit rating firms such as Standard & Poor's, using a rating system similar to that used for corporate bonds. With the creation of a secondary market linking loan-originating banks with investors, multi-bank commercial loans may some day trade as actively as corporate debt securities in the OVER-THE-COUNTER (OTC) dealer market. Contrast with HIGHLY LEVERAGED TRANSACTION, a high-interest rate loan extended to riskier borrowers.

SYNDICATE

1. **Banking.** Project financing common in the Eurobond and Euronote markets, and also in the United States, whereby a group of commercial bankers and investment bankers each agrees to advance a portion of the funding. Typically, the financing is arranged by a single bank at narrow interest rate spreads above the lender's cost of funds. The syndicator acts as investment manager, collecting a loan origination fee or commitment fee from the borrower, and arranging

for the sale of Euronotes to other banks in the group. Typically, the syndicator keeps only a small portion of the total financing, generally less than 10% of the total value of the loan.

The syndicated loan differs from a LOAN PARTICIPATION because the syndicate members are known at the outset to the borrower. Syndication also separates the lead banker from the group of financial institutions that ultimately fund the obligation. *See also* NOTE ISSUANCE FACILITY; REVOLVING UNDERWRITING FACILITY; TENDER PANEL.

2. **Securities.** A group of investment bankers who purchases a new offering of securities from an issuer for resale to the investing public at a fixed price. This is also called the *purchase group* or *underwriting group*. Operating rules of the investment syndicate, led by a MANAGING UNDERWRITER, are spelled out in the AGREEMENT AMONG UNDERWRITERS. The purchase group, which may include commercial bankers, differs from the SELLING GROUP.
3. **Investments.** The purchase of shares in investments promising tax avoidance, or reinvestment of earnings without paying income taxes, usually through LIMITED PARTNERSHIP participations in real estate, oil and gas exploration, and so on, sold through an investment syndicate or a broker-dealer. The Tax Reform Act of 1986 sharply curtailed so-called passive losses in tax shelter investments.

SYNTHETIC SECURITY any combination of financial instruments producing a market instrument with different characteristics than could otherwise be achieved, such as, higher yield, better liquidity, or interest rate protection. These securities mimic conventional financial instruments that may or may not be available to investors. Most such deals are PRIVATE PLACEMENTS involving two investors, and usually are created through INTEREST RATE SWAPS, for example, creating a synthetic FLOATING RATE NOTE by matching a fixed rate bond and an interest rate swap. *See also* ASSET SWAP.

SYSTEMIC RISK possibility that failure of one bank to settle net transactions with other banks will trigger a chain reaction, depriving other banks of funds and preventing them from closing their positions in turn. Carried out to its logical extreme, the possibility exists that institutions that have had no business dealings with the failed bank ultimately will be affected in a general shutdown of normal clearing and settlement activity, a condition known as payment system *gridlock*. High dollar payment networks have special rules designed to prevent system-wide settlement failures from occurring. *See also* FEDERAL WIRE; NET SETTLEMENT; OVERDRAFT CAP.

T

TAIL

1. in U.S. Treasury auctions, the price spread between the average competitive bid on bills, notes, and bonds sold in Treasury auctions and the STOP-OUT PRICE or the largest accepted price.
2. money market term for a financial instrument partially financed by a REPURCHASE AGREEMENT. For example, a dealer buys a 90-day Treasury bill and sells a 30-day repurchase agreement. The maturity difference between the two is the tail.
3. **Finance.** The figures appearing after the decimal point in a bond quotation. For example, in a bid of $95.3712, the tail is .3712.
4. **Estates.** The property inherited by direct descendents, for example, children or grandchildren of a decedent. Called an *estate in tail.*

TAKA monetary unit of Bangladesh.

TAKE A POSITION popular expression for the activities of someone who speculates in the market, with the expectation of making a profit. A position may be long or short at the end of a trading day. A dealer buys securities, foreign exchange, or money market instruments as inventory, with the expectation of selling them later at a profit. If held for other institutions or for customers, the securities are listed as part of the bank's TRADING ACCOUNT ASSETS. Also called *taking a view.*

TAKE DOWN

1. **Banking.** An advance of money to a borrower under a CREDIT agreement or COMMITMENT to lend. A borrower who draws $20,000 against a $70,000 revolving line of credit takes down the line by the amount used.
2. **Municipal Bonds.** The price, discounted from par value, at which members of an underwriting syndicate offer to sell. The difference is the underwriter's profit.
3. **Underwriting.** The portion of an offering of securities each member of an underwriting syndicate agrees to purchase for resale to investors. Also, the price paid by underwriters in a new offering of securities.

TAKE-OUT

1. trading profit from the sale of a block of securities and purchase of another at a lower price. The difference can be reinvested or taken as profit.
2. bid made to the seller of a security to buy out his or her position. *See also* LOCKED MARKET.
3. in lending, replacing a short-term loan with a longer maturity loan, taking out the other lender. *See also* TAKE-OUT COMMITMENT.

TAKE-OUT COMMITMENT agreement between a mortgage banker and a long-term investor under which the latter agrees to purchase a mortgage at a specific future date. The investor, called a TAKE-OUT LENDER, is typically an insurance company or other financial institution. *See also* TAKE-OUT LENDER; TAKE-OUT LOAN.

TAKE-OUT LENDER financial institution that extends a long-term MORTGAGE on real property that replaces the interim financing, or construction loan arranged by a savings and loan, bank, or mortgage banker. The institution extending the long-term loan, or permanent financing, is often an insurance company or institutional investor willing to make a long-term investment in income producing property, realizing a capital gain from the eventual sale of the property, in addition to cash flow from rental payments by property tenants.

TAKE-OUT LOAN permanent financing, usually structured as an amortizing, fixed payment mortgage, on an office development, housing project, or mixed use income producing property. A recent innovation is the ZERO-COUPON MORTGAGE, in which interest is due and payable in one lump installment or BALLOON PAYMENT at maturity.

TAKE THE OFFER expression for buyer's willingness to accept the offered price of a quoting seller. The opposite is HIT THE BID.

TAKING DELIVERY

1. liquidating a futures position and taking (paying for) securities or commodities underlying a futures contract. The buyer takes delivery of the commodity or security and pays for the transaction. Futures traders are more interested in short-term market gains than in the instrument or commodity being traded. *See also* DELIVERY NOTICE.
2. in securities settlement, when a buyer pays for securities purchased, which normally occurs on the *regular way* settlement date, usually three business days after the trade date.

TALA monetary unit of Samoa.

TANDEM LOAN mortgage purchase program under which the Government National Mortgage Association (GNMA) purchases mortgages above fair market value, and resells them through FANNIE MAE. The program provides financial assistance to developers of nonprofit public housing projects. Ginnie Mae pays the difference between the price paid by Fannie Mae and the price at which it buys the mortgages, using its credit rating to guarantee the discount.

TANGIBLE ASSET real property or personal property, such as buildings, machinery, and real property. Tangible assets are distinguished from intangible assets such as trademarks, copyrights, and GOODWILL, and natural resources (timberlands, oil reserves, and coal deposits). Accounting rules are vague on this distinction between tangibles and intangibles. Generally, any asset not expressly defined as an intangible is considered a tangible asset.

TANGIBLE NET WORTH equity capital (common stock) of a bank, less goodwill and other intangibles. It is an indication of the borrowing capacity or strength of a bank or a savings institution. *See also* CAPITAL RATIOS.

TANGIBLE PROPERTY *see* TANGIBLE ASSETS.

TARGET BALANCE desired balance in a deposit account that meets minimum standards for profitability, or the BREAK-EVEN YIELD. There are various formulas for pricing deposit accounts to cover servicing costs. If a checking account is priced separately from other deposit accounts, a bank may insist that the customer keep a minimum balance in the account at all times, say $1,500, to qualify for service charge-free checking. A bank may waive service charges for those customers who have a high-balance savings account, for example, a $10,000 money market certificate, or combination of accounts that are kept on deposit, or a COMPENSATING BALANCE kept by a corporation.

TARGET RATE

1. rate set by a bank's ASSET-LIABILITY COMMITTEE as a desirable objective in repricing maturing deposits or loans. *See also* REPRICING OPPORTUNITIES; RUNOFF.
2. INTERNAL RATE OF RETURN, also known as the hurdle rate in capital budgeting.

TAX ABATEMENT reduction in AD VALOREM real estate taxes granted by a municipality or local taxing authority resulting from an easement, exercise of eminent domain by the taxing authority, natural disaster, or other reasons.

TAXABLE EQUIVALENT YIELD total income, including income earned on tax-exempt securities (municipal bonds). This restates nontaxable income earned in the investment portfolio on a basis that is comparable to taxable income before any taxes actually are paid, excluding PRIVATE PURPOSE BONDS, which no longer are fully tax-exempt.

TAXABLE ESTATE portion of an inheritable estate subject to estate taxes, after deducting allowable expenses incurred in settling the estate, including funeral expenses, taxes owed, and marital and charitable deductions.

TAXABLE MUNICIPAL BOND private activity municipal bond or industrial revenue bond that is subject to federal and state income taxes at the ordinary tax rate. This is also called a nonessential function bond, or PRIVATE PURPOSE BOND. The Tax Reform Act of 1986 repealed the tax exemption for bonds financing convention centers, sports facilities, and other quasi-municipal facilities. Interest income on bonds issued after August 7, 1986 that exceed state caps on issuance of tax-free municipals are fully taxable bonds. Certain investors also are subject to the alternative minimum tax on interest income from private activity bonds. Taxable municipals generally pay higher interest rates than other munis, but are protected from early redemption by call protection features. Such bonds may also be exempt from state and local taxes in the state where they are issued. States that exhaust their allowed limit of tax-exempt bonds frequently issue taxable bonds, generally to finance private development. *See also* PUBLIC PURPOSE BOND.

TAX AND LOAN ACCOUNT *see* TREASURY TAX AND LOAN ACCOUNT.

TAX ANTICIPATION BILL (TAB) U.S. Treasury bill sold on an irregular basis, and scheduled to mature in periods of heavy tax receipts. No tax anticipation bills have been issued since 1974. Instead, the Treasury has raised money on an irregular basis through the sale of CASH MANAGEMENT BILLS, which usually are reopenings or sales of additional amounts of bills. Cash management bills, like tax anticipation bills, are intended to finance the Treasury's funding requirements until tax payments are received.

TAX ANTICIPATION NOTE (TAN) short-term note issued by states and municipalities to finance current operations, with repayment from anticipated tax receipts. These notes are issued at a discount, have maturities of a year or less, and mature either at a specific future date or when property and other taxes are collected. Tax anticipation notes hold first claim on tax receipts when collected. *See also* REVENUE ANTICIPATION NOTE.

TAX-DEDUCTIBLE INTEREST loan interest qualifying as interest deductible from federal income taxes. MORTGAGE interest payments on first and second homes are fully deductible, but mortgage interest on a third home, if for personal use, is treated as nondeductible CONSUMER INTEREST. Interest on a home equity loan—HOME EQUITY CREDIT—is tax deductible if used primarily for home improvements, medical expenses, or education. Interest payments on credit cards, auto loans, and other types of consumer interest is regarded as consumer interest; the tax deduction for such interest ended in 1991.

TAX-DEFERRED ANNUITY *see* ANNUITY.

TAX-DEFERRED SAVINGS savings or investment plan that allows an individual to set aside a portion of current income in a designated savings plan, and defer payment of income taxes on principal amount and earned interest. *See also* 401(K) PLAN; 403(B) PLAN; INDIVIDUAL RETIREMENT ACCOUNT; KEOGH PLAN; ROTH IRA.

TAX-EXEMPT BOND municipal bond that is not taxed by the federal government and is free from state and local taxes in most states if purchased by an in-state resident. Most general obligation municipal bonds are exempt from state and local taxes in the states where they are originated, and certain bonds are triple tax exempt, regardless of where they originate. Five states (Texas, Nevada, Alaska, South Dakota, and Wyoming) do not tax municipal bonds issued by other states. If the yield differential is high enough, a taxable bond issued out of state actually may pay a better return to the investor. *See also* TAXABLE MUNICIPAL BOND.

TAX-FREE ROLLOVER reinvestment of a tax-advantaged savings account, such as an INDIVIDUAL RETIREMENT ACCOUNT, within the statutory 60-day period allowed by the IRS for reinvestment without penalty. Amounts that are not reinvested are subject to a 10% penalty payment.

TAX LIEN INVOLUNTARY LIEN on real estate for nonpayment of income taxes or property taxes. Tax liens have priority over bank liens securing the same property, placing the lender at a less than advantageous position in attempting to collect a debt from a delinquent borrower who also owes back taxes.

TAX LOSS CARRY BACK (CARRY FORWARD) tax benefit allowing an individual or organization to reduce a tax liability by applying net operating losses incurred in the current fiscal year against income reported in earlier years. IRS tax rules permit carrying back losses (the excess of allowable deductions over gross income) over the three prior years, resulting in a tax refund. A tax loss carry forward, on the other hand, is an operating loss charged against income in future years.

In general, banks are subject to the same rules as other corporations in computing a tax loss carry back or carry forward, under the TAX REFORM ACT OF 1986, except for losses attributable to bad debt. Starting in 1987, a bank can apply a net operating loss to taxable income in the previous three years, or forward 15 years. The Tax Reform Act repealed the old ten-and-five rule (ten years back and five years forward).

The Revenue Reconciliation Act of 1993 imposed additional restrictions on tax losses, namely the requirement that short-term losses be applied first to reduce any long-term gains. This effectively reduced the gain available for the more favorable long-term capital gain tax rate.

TAX OPINION legal opinion issued by a bond issuer's tax attorney stating, for computation of federal income tax, the tax benefits available to investors. In municipal bonds, the tax opinion states that the bond conforms to statutes exempting bond interest from federal income taxes.

TAX-ORIENTED LEASE *see* TRUE LEASE.

TAXPAYER IDENTIFICATION NUMBER (TIN) IRS identification number needed before most bank accounts can be opened. For individuals and sole proprietors, the tax number is the individual's Social Security number. A business tax identification number is the employer's identification number, required of corporations, nonprofit organizations, associations, and partnerships. A bank must also withhold 20% of the interest earned on the account in a special escrow account. *See also* BACKUP WITHHOLDING.

TAX PLANNING minimization of tax liability through investing in tax deferred investments, tax-exempt securities, or tax shelters offsetting capital gains from passive investments, such as real estate investment trust. Contrast with tax evasion, the willful nonpayment of taxes legally owed. *See also* FINANCIAL PLANNING.

TAX PREFERENCE ITEMS tax deduction giving the holder special tax benefits, which must be computed in calculating the alternative minimum tax (AMT) liability under federal tax laws. The AMT is due if the amount of tax owed using the AMT calculation is greater. Preference items include, for individuals, capital gains from exercise of stock options, and for corporations, deductions for accelerated depreciation, investment tax credits, and increases in loan loss reserves by banks and savings institutions, and many more.

TAX REFORM ACT OF 1986 act passed by Congress that simplified the tax code and eliminated some deductions. The Tax Act of 1986 was the most significant change in the tax structure of the United States in over 50 years. Important provisions include:

—lowered the top corporate tax rate from 46% to 34%, the individual tax rate from 50% to 28%.

—set a new corporate alternative minimum tax on depreciable expenses such as accelerated depreciation on capital equipment.

—imposed a 5% surcharge, effective in 1988, for some taxpayers.

—limited the special deduction for loan loss reserves in banks above $500 million in assets. Larger banks may claim losses only when loans are written off.

—limited the deduction of interest payments on residential mortgages to principal homes and second homes, granted after August 15, 1986.

—reduced the annual limit on individual contributions to 401(k) employee savings plans from $30,000 a year to $7,000 a year.

—eliminated the 15% investment tax credit previously allowed equipment lessors.

—restricted the use of passive tax shelters to income gains or losses from investment portfolios, instead of a taxpayer's gross income.

—limited foreign tax credits on non-U.S. investments, including financial services income, passive investments, and dividends from foreign corporations in which a U.S. corporation has a minority interest. A transition period for the new tax rules extended through 1994.

—allowed net operating losses to be carried back three years and forward 15 years, except for losses attributable to bad debts. Bad debt losses retained the ten-year carry back through 1993.

—authorized sale of mortgage-backed securities through Real Estate Mortgage Investment Conduits (REMICs).

—eliminated the 100% deduction of the interest attributed to tax-exempt obligations (municipal bonds) acquired after August 7, 1986.

—imposed a 20% corporate alternative minimum tax on nonessential municipal bonds issued after August 7, 1986.

—prohibited use of cash basis accounting by banks after 1986, phased in over a four-year period.

—retained the accelerated cost recovery system for depreciating assets. However, machinery and equipment must be depreciated over a longer period.

—increased the recovery period for residential real estate, for depreciation purposes, from 19 years to 27½ years, and from 19 years to 31½ years for commercial real estate. Both will be depreciated under the straight line basis under the new law.

—limited fully deductible INDIVIDUAL RETIREMENT ACCOUNTS to taxpayers not covered by a qualified pension plan, or individuals whose gross income is less than $40,000 on joint returns (less than $25,000 for taxpayers filing as singles).

—taxed Clifford Trusts to the trust grantor, and required that trusts and estates follow the calendar year for tax purposes.

—limited tax deductions from passive real estate tax shelters.

—eliminated the use of the installment method for sales made under revolving credit plans.

—phased out the deductibility of CONSUMER INTEREST charges over a five-year period, ending in 1991, and ended the deduction for state and local sales taxes.

—limited deduction of only 80% of business related expenses.

TAX SWAP *see* BOND SWAP.

TEASER RATE

1. low initial mortgage rate that lenders charge for an ADJUSTABLE RATE MORTGAGE. The rate is less than the rate charged for standard fixed rate mortgages, and lower than the fully-indexed rate on adjustable rate mortgages. The lower payment makes mortgage financing more available to more potential home owners. The rate typically is reset to the market rate after a period of several months to a year.
2. high initial rate offered depositors who invest in savings accounts paying money market rates. When MONEY MARKET DEPOSIT ACCOUNT (MMDA)S were first introduced in December 1982 (but not yet approved for purposes of accepting deposits), certain banks offered rates as high as 21% through repurchase agreements that were rolled into MMDAs when these high rate accounts became legal.

TECHNICAL ANALYSIS forecasting price movements by analysis of trading volume, supply and demand, short-term and long-term market trends, and other market related factors. An important premise in technical analysis is that certain price-volume factors repeat themselves, and can be illustrated graphically by chart patterns, a process known as charting. Some examples are a *point and figure chart*, showing the upward and downward movement of a security in a given time period;

an *ascending top*, showing continually rising prices and the beginning of a price rally; *a head and shoulders pattern*, depicting the reversal of a trend; and a *double top*, signaling the end of a rally. First used by commodities traders, charting is a frequently used analytical tool in the stock market, foreign exchange, and financial futures. Technical analysis differs from fundamental analysis, which examines financial information, such as company earnings and capital formation, and is concerned foremost with the financial strength and profitability of an issuer of securities.

Technical analysts believe that, by diagramming the movement of a market, they can determine market swings in advance. According to the theory, the best time to sell (take a short position) is the start of a major downtrend; the best time to buy is when prices, and trends, are heading upward. The drawback with this methodology is that chart patterns often are recognized only after the fact, that is, after events have run their course. In most situations, the presumed bargains represented by trading patterns are temporary opportunities and usually disappear once large numbers of people have acted. *See also* EFFICIENT MARKET; FUNDAMENTAL ANALYSIS.

TELEGRAPHIC TRANSFER *see* WIRE TRANSFER.

TELEPHONE BILL PAYMENT banking service allowing customers to pay merchant bills, verify account balances, and transfer funds between accounts.

Telephone bill payment was popularized in the mid-1970s by savings and loan associations that wanted to offer their customers transaction accounts even though, at the time, they legally couldn't offer checking accounts, so the payments were instead taken out of savings accounts. *See also* ELECTRONIC FUNDS TRANSFER; HOME BANKING.

TELEPHONE ORDER

1. verbal instruction to move funds from one bank account to another, or from one bank to another, by check or electronic transfer, such as a payment over the FED WIRE network.
2. mail-order purchase charged to a bank card or travel and entertainment card. No signature is required, and the customer has the same consumer rights and obligations as when making a purchase in person. *See also* SIGNATURE ON FILE.

TELEPHONE TRANSFER transfer of account balances from one account to another, or from payer to recipient made by TELEPHONE ORDER, rather than traditional written authorization or instrument. The accounts being debited can be checking, savings, or, if three or fewer telephone transfers per month, money market deposit accounts. *See also* TELEPHONE BILL PAYMENT.

TELLER bank employee who accepts deposits, cashes checks, and performs other banking services for the public. In most financial institutions, tellers work from behind a counter or enclosure. Large banks assign teller functions by job description: a MAIL TELLER processes incoming bank deposits arriving through the mail; a loan teller keeps a record of payments to customer accounts; and a note teller handles the collection of funds on notes and drafts payable by other banks. *See also* CUSTOMER SERVICE REPRESENTATIVE; HEAD TELLER.

TELLER'S CHECK *see* CASHIER'S CHECK.

TEMPORARY ACCOUNT NUMBER randomly generated account number shielding a credit card or debit card owner's personal information from credit card fraud when conducting online purchases over the Internet. The temporary number, linked to a cardholder's actual account number, is used once and then discarded.

TEMPORARY LOAN short-term WORKING CAPITAL loan to finance a firm's inventory or receivables. These loans have maturities generally under one year, and are evidenced by a PROMISSORY NOTE taken or a WARRANT issued by the borrower. A temporary loan can be unsecured or secured by a lien on the firm's assets. Working assets acquired through temporary financing eventually will be converted into cash through the firm's trade cycle, when it sells inventory for cash or collects its receivables. *See also* COLLATERAL LOAN; TERM LOAN.

TENANCY BY THE ENTIRETY joint ownership of property by husband and wife, recognized in some states. Each has equal rights of possession and enjoyment, and right of survivorship when the other spouse dies. Although similar to joint tenancy, the most common form of property ownership by married couples, tenancy by the entirety treats the estate as a unit, which means that neither spouse can sell assets without the other's consent. Also, creditors cannot force the sale of property to satisfy debts of either spouse. The surviving spouse inherits the entire estate. *See also* COMMUNITY PROPERTY; JOINT TENANTS WITH RIGHT OF SURVIVORSHIP; TENANCY IN COMMON.

TENANCY IN COMMON joint ownership of property by two or more persons, without right of survivorship. This form of property ownership most often is used by partners in a business partnership, and by unrelated persons holding title to real property. Each party has an indivisible share of the property; when they die, their share is inheritable by their heirs, not by the other tenants. Also called *tenants in common*. *See also* COMMUNITY PROPERTY; JOINT TENANTS WITH RIGHT OF SURVIVORSHIP; TENANCY BY THE ENTIRETY.

TENDER

1. BID or request for project financing.
2. notice by the seller of a futures contract of his intention to deliver a commodity or financial instrument.
3. offer of payment owed to a creditor; an offer to settle up an obligation. For example, to tender a check.

4. LEGAL TENDER or cash offered in payment of an obligation.
5. offer to purchase securities at a specified price, called a TENDER OFFER.

TENDER OFFER publicly announced offer to purchase securities at a stated price and for a specified period. It is an invitation to shareholders of a company to sell their shares at the offered price, regardless of whether the issuer approves or disapproves of the offer being tendered. The offering price is often at a premium over the market price, as in a corporate takeover attempt.

TENDER PANEL financing method used in sale of promissory notes (Euronotes) through a REVOLVING UNDERWRITING FACILITY (RUF). A syndicate, consisting of up to 15 to 20 commercial banks and investment banks, is authorized by a borrower (or the borrower's agent) to solicit bids on a BEST EFFORT basis for project financing. The panel acts as a selling agent for the banks arranging a credit facility. The tender panel sale allows placement of Euronotes with a large number of investors seeking medium-term (five to seven years) paper. It also separates the originating bank from the banks actually purchasing the notes, thereby spreading the credit risk among a large number of participants. The originating bank's participation in the offering is small, often as little as 10% of the total financing. *See also* MULTICURRENCY NOTE FACILITY; MULTIPLE OPTIONS FUNDING FACILITY; NOTE ISSUANCE FACILITY; PRIME UNDERWRITING FACILITY; STANDBY NOTE ISSUANCE FACILITY; TRANSFERABLE UNDERWRITING FACILITY.

TENGE monetary unit of Kazakhstan.

TENOR

1. shorthand reference for maturity on a note or financial instrument.
2. designates the time when a draft is payable: on sight (when presented), a given number of days after presentment, or a given number of days after the date of the draft.
3. terms set for payment of a draft, i.e., when delivered (a SIGHT DRAFT) or at a future date (a TIME DRAFT).

TERM

1. maturity of a LOAN or DEPOSIT, expressed in months. Short-term obligations or investments generally are less than a year; long-term instruments may have maturities from 1 year to 30 or 40 years.
2. any condition specifying how a loan is to be repaid, for example, the ANNUAL PERCENTAGE RATE finance charge, monthly payment, number of payments, BALLOON PAYMENT, and so on.

TERM AUCTION FACILITY Federal Reserve MONETARY POLICY tool by which Federal Reserve banks auctions short-term notes to financially stable banks. The auction process, initiated in 2007, allows banks to borrow funds at a rate below the Federal Reserve DISCOUNT RATE, thereby increasing the supply of bank reserves (EXCESS RESERVES) in the banking system and funds available for lending.

TERM BOND bond with a single maturity date, as opposed to a SERIAL BOND. Generally, the issuer makes mandatory payments into a SINKING FUND in the years prior to maturity. Bond issuers meet sinking fund requirements by purchasing the issued security in the open market, redeeming the bonds at market prices, which may be lower than the sinking fund call price. This sinking fund provision spreads the issuer's liability of a GENERAL OBLIGATION BOND over the life of the bond; issuers of REVENUE BONDS match debt service payments with bond revenues.

TERM DEPOSIT FACILITY Federal Reserve MONETARY POLICY tool by which Federal Reserve banks pay interest on funds held at a financial institution's Reserve Bank. Funds deposited in a participating bank's term account are removed from that bank's RESERVE ACCOUNT for the life of the term deposit. The process effectively reduces the overall level of bank reserves available for lending, potentially resulting in higher market interest rates and slowing economic activity.

TERM FEDERAL FUNDS RESERVE ACCOUNT balances purchased for periods longer than a single day, but generally less than 90 days. Banks purchase Fed funds for an extended period when they see their borrowing needs lasting several days, or they believe short-term rates may rise and they want to lock in the current rate. Fed funds purchased for an extended term, like overnight Fed funds, are not subject to RESERVE REQUIREMENTS and sometimes are preferred to other purchased liabilities of comparable maturity. *See also* BROKERED DEPOSIT; MANAGED LIABILITIES; REPURCHASE AGREEMENT.

TERMINAL

1. point of entry in a data communications network, such as AUTOMATED TELLER MACHINES, teller terminals, retail POINT-OF-SALE TERMINALS, and personal computers in home banking. This is sometimes referred to as an *electronic window* in corporate CASH MANAGEMENT. *See also* PLATFORM AUTOMATION; TREASURY WORKSTATION.
2. authorization device that approves transactions charged to bank credit cards, deposit accounts, retail private label accounts, or travel and entertainment cards. Most of these are inexpensive devices that automatically dial a central computer to obtain authorization, hence the name *dial-up terminal. See also* AUTHORIZATION CODE.

TERMINATION STATEMENT statement releasing a lender's claim or SECURITY INTEREST in a borrower's assets when a debt is fully paid, terminating a previously filed FINANCING STATEMENT. The Uniform Commercial Code requires secured lenders to sign a termination statement, generally known as Form UCC-3 to clear the borrower's name of liens listed in public records.

TERM LOAN fixed-term business loan with a maturity of more than one year, providing an organization with working capital to acquire assets or inventory, or to finance plant and equipment generating cash flow. The term loan is the most common form of intermediate-term financing arranged by commercial banks, and there is wide diversity in how it is structured. Maturities range from one year to 15 years, although most term loans are made for one- to five-year periods. Term loans are paid back from profits of the business, according to a fixed amortization schedule. Term loans may be secured or unsecured, and carry a rate based on the lender's cost of funds, the federal funds rate, LIBOR, or the bank PRIME RATE. Loan interest normally is payable monthly, quarterly, semiannually, or annually.

Most business loans contain both affirmative and restrictive COVENANTS that impose certain conditions on the borrower such as acceleration of the maturity if the loan conditions are violated. The lender usually will require the borrower to maintain the business in good order, keep adequate insurance, and file quarterly financial statements with the bank. Larger borrowings often are financed by several banks through a SYNDICATE arrangement. *See also* DEMAND LOAN; SECURED LOAN; SECURITY AGREEMENT; SECURITY INTEREST.

TERM MORTGAGE nonamortizing MORTGAGE, usually with a maturity under five years, that has interest-only payments for a specified period, after which the outstanding principal balance is due and payable in a lump-sum BALLOON PAYMENT. *See also* STANDING MORTGAGE.

TERM REPURCHASE AGREEMENT repurchase agreement with a maturity of more than one day; also known as a *term repo*. Banks and savings institutions that have excess cash often buy government securities instead of certificates of deposit, which have a minimum maturity of seven days. In a repurchase agreement, the bank buys securities from a dealer, or from a nondealer bank, with an agreement to sell back the securities later at a predetermined price. The difference between the purchase price and the resale price represents the payment of interest. Term repos may pay higher yields than overnight repos, because the seller assumes interest rate risk for a longer period than an overnight repo.

TERM SECURITIES LENDING FACILITY Federal Reserve MONETARY POLICY tool by which the Federal Reserve Bank of New York sells Treasury securities to the New York Reserve Bank's primary dealers in exchange for other collateral. The purpose is to add liquidity to the U.S. financial system and help the primary dealers finance their balance sheets.

TESTAMENTARY TRUST TRUST established by the terms of a WILL. After the death of the TESTATOR, it becomes an IRREVOCABLE TRUST. This kind of trust is useful if the testator wishes to set aside funds for the education of children who are minors or have just reached the age of majority. The trust is placed in the hands of a trustee, who may be an individual or a bank trust department.

TESTATOR person who has died leaving a valid will, providing for distribution of assets to heirs. Sometimes called *settler.* Compare with TRUSTOR.

THIN MARKET market characterized by few bids and offers, wide bid-asked spreads, and fluctuating prices. A thin market is said to have a shallow depth and weak demand for trading, and wider price fluctuations than a strong market, where bid-asked spreads are narrow, and prices move upward or downward within a more or less predictable range. Also called *weak market.*

THIRD COUNTRY ACCEPTANCE in international trade, a BANKER'S ACCEPTANCE drawn on a bank in a country other than the country of the importer or exporter, and paid in the national currency of the accepting bank. Third country acceptances, also called *refinance bills,* often are used by exporters to obtain bank financing at competitive rates. Since the mid-1970s, Japanese and South Koreans have financed a large portion of their exports, including exports to European countries, through bankers' acceptances denominated in U.S. dollars, which accounts for much of the growth of these acceptances.

THIRD PARTY CHECK

1. CHECK or DRAFT payable to someone other than the check writer (the MAKER of the instrument) or the person who initially negotiates the check by endorsing the back of the instrument.
2. check transferred by ENDORSEMENT and the words "pay to the order of—." The new holder has the same legal rights as the original endorser, and is free to negotiate the check himself either by endorsing the back of the instrument and depositing it, or by exchanging it for cash at a bank teller. The Uniform Commercial Code allows transfer of a check to a new owner any number of times. In practice, however, multiple endorsed checks are uncommon, and banks may be reluctant to accept them without verifying signatures of endorsers.
3. PAYABLE THROUGH DRAFT. Draft payable through a designated bank, drawing funds from the account of the issuer. Corporations use these instruments to pay bills, and insurance companies use them to pay claims. Credit union share drafts are also payable through draft instruments and are cleared by a correspondent bank.

THIRD PARTY CREDIT credit facilitating the sale of merchandise and services that is arranged by someone other than the seller. Retail merchants accept bank credit cards and travel and entertainment cards as payment for merchandise, which often is less costly than extending credit directly, because the merchant is relieved of the expense of funding the credit receivables and collecting the payments. In return for payment of a MERCHANT DISCOUNT, computed as a percentage of net sales, the merchant can get immediate credit for bank card sales slips deposited with a bank. If the merchant discount rate is 2%, the merchant gets $98 for every $100 in credit sales. As long as the merchant follows the terms of the credit agreement, the merchant also is not liable for credit or fraud losses. *See also* PRIVATE LABEL CREDIT; REVOLVING CREDIT.

THIRD PARTY PAYMENT *see* THIRD PARTY TRANSFER.

THIRD PARTY TRANSFER payment made out to and deposited in the account of someone other than the person who initiates the payment, or who initially receives it. Such payments may be THIRD PARTY CHECKS transferred by endorsement, written or oral instructions directing a bank to pay a consumer's bills, or electronic payments.

THRIFT INSTITUTION depository financial institution whose primary function is promoting personal savings (thrift) and home ownership through mortgage lending. Thrift institutions hold most of their assets in mortgages and collect most of their deposits from consumers. SAVINGS AND LOAN ASSOCIATIONS, SAVINGS BANKS, and CREDIT UNIONS are all considered thrift institutions. Thrift institutions, at one time restricted to mortgage lending, have gained parity with commercial banks and many thrifts offer the same range of nonmortgage credit services—credit cards, auto loans, home equity loans, and business loans—available from commercial banks. *See also* FEDERAL SAVINGS BANK; MUTUAL SAVINGS BANK.

THRIFT INSTITUTIONS ADVISORY COUNCIL advisory body established by the Monetary Control Act of 1980 to advise the Federal Reserve Board of Governors on the needs of savings institutions. This panel is composed of representatives of savings banks, savings and loan associations, and credit unions.

THROWBACK RULE in trusts, an IRS rule requiring that trust assets distributed in any taxable year in excess of the amount allowed that year are, for tax purposes, treated as if the income was earned and distributed in a prior year. In other words, they are thrown back to the previous year, or years.

TICK successive price changes in securities trading; $\frac{1}{32}$ of a percentage point. Treasury bill and bond quotes are given in increments of 32nds. The decimal equivalent of $\frac{1}{32}$ of a $1,000 bond is $31.25, $\frac{2}{32}$ is $62.50, and so on. More generally, the term also applies to price movements in futures contracts of precious metals, stocks, and commodities.

TIERED RATE ACCOUNT savings account that pays a rate of interest scaled according to the amount invested in the account. Typically, the higher the balance in the account, the higher the rate. Savings accounts with longer terms generally pay higher rates than accounts with shorter terms.

TIER 1 bank equity CAPITAL, also called *core capital,* supporting bank lending. Tier 1 capital includes common stock and retained bank earnings. *See also* RISK-BASED CAPITAL.

TIER 2 secondary source of bank CAPITAL financing banking activities. Tier 2 capital includes subordinated debt, convertible securities, and a portion of the LOAN LOSS RESERVES for possible bad loans. *See also* RISK-BASED CAPITAL.

TIGHT MONEY market condition that exists when the Federal Reserve, acting through the FEDERAL OPEN MARKET COMMITTEE, reduces the amount of credit available to the public through the banking system. This is sometimes known as *draining reserves.* During periods of tight credit, borrowers face stricter lending standards at rising interest rates, although interest rates may in fact be quite reasonable considering market demands for credit.

When the System Open Market Desk at the Federal Reserve Bank of New York sells Treasury securities, the supply of bank reserves diminishes and the FEDERAL FUNDS rate that banks charge each other for overnight borrowings tends to rise. Rising interest rates are the result of tight Federal Reserve MONETARY POLICY, and also excessive growth in the economy, creating an inflationary situation of too much demand and not enough goods and services to meet market demands. *See also* EASY MONEY; INTERMEDIATE TARGETS; NONBORROWED RESERVES.

TIME DEPOSIT

1. deposit account paying interest for a fixed term, with the understanding that funds cannot be withdrawn before maturity without giving advance notice. A time deposit is also known as an *investment account* or *time certificate of deposit.* Time deposit accounts, evidenced by either a paper certificate or a statement mailed to the depositor when interest is paid, normally pay a fixed rate of interest, and have maturities of seven days to seven years or longer. The notification of withdrawal requirement ordinarily is waived for consumer deposits, though not for large dollar corporate time deposit accounts. Consumer withdrawals still are subject to an EARLY WITHDRAWAL PENALTY, and partial loss of interest. Time deposit accounts owned by a corporation (NONPERSONAL TIME DEPOSITS) are subject to RESERVE REQUIREMENTS, but at a lower rate than transaction accounts, such as checking accounts. *See also* CERTIFICATE OF DEPOSIT; NINETY-DAY SAVINGS ACCOUNT; PASSBOOK.
2. time deposit open account, an interest bearing deposit account allowing multiple deposits, but limited right of withdrawal before maturity. Some examples are club accounts, such as Christmas Clubs and vacation clubs. The deposit is evidenced by a ledger entry on the books of the depositing financial institution.

TIME DRAFT DRAFT (bill of exchange) payable to a third party on a specified or determinable future date, as opposed to a SIGHT DRAFT. A BANKER'S ACCEPTANCE is a time draft.

TIME LOAN short-term business LOAN that is payable in full at a specified maturity date, e.g., 30, 60, 90, or 120 days. Interest on this type of loan ordinarily is deducted (discounted) in advance when the loan is made. It differs from a DEMAND LOAN in that the lender cannot call or demand repayment of a time loan before the maturity. Time loans are repaid from turnover of assets, for example, the sale of inventory or collection of accounts receivable. *See also*; TERM LOAN.

TIME-SALE FINANCING form of indirect lending (DEALER FINANCING) in which a bank or other third party purchases installment sales contracts at a discount from face value from a dealer, and the borrower makes payments to the lender. This usually is done in conjunction with dealer FLOOR PLANNING.

TIME VALUE OF MONEY *see* COMPOUND INTEREST; PRESENT VALUE.

TITLE legally valid claim to ownership of real property, evidenced by deed, certificate of title, or bill of sale. A lender will extend MORTGAGE financing to a buyer only if the seller holds uncontested ownership of the property in question. Most states treat a mortgage as a lien against the title held by the lender, or MORTGAGEE, but some states recognize a mortgage as a binding obligation of the borrower, or the MORTGAGOR named in the title. *See also* TITLE COMPANY; TITLE DEFECT; TITLE INSURANCE; TITLE SEARCH.

TITLE COMPANY firm that verifies ownership of real property, often done in connection with a conveyance of real property from buyer to seller. The valid owner is determined through a thorough examination of property records in a TITLE SEARCH. The company issues a title certificate, based on its examination.

TITLE DEFECT legal claim, circumstance, or other condition that makes it difficult to identify the true owner of real property or transfer title to another. It is also called a CLOUD ON TITLE or clouded title, as when ownership has not been recorded properly, or when secondary liens have not been removed after the obligations have been paid. *See also* TITLE INSURANCE; TITLE SEARCH.

TITLE INSURANCE insurance against losses resulting from a TITLE DEFECT discovered after property has been conveyed from buyer to seller and a new mortgage taken out by the buyer. This protects the borrower against claims not identified in the title search, or claims not specifically listed as exemptions to the title insurance policy.

TITLE SEARCH process of verifying the actual owner of real property by a careful review of public land records, usually conducted by a professional title abstracter. This investigation also determines whether there are any outstanding liens or encumbrances binding on the property, and results in issuance of an abstract of title by the title company. *See also* CLEAN TITLE; TITLE DEFECT; TITLE INSURANCE.

TOLAR monetary unit of Slovenia.

TOMBSTONE slang term for financial advertising listing acquisitions, new securities offered for sale, listing the underwriting parties in order of their participation—with managing partners listed at the top and participating members below. The name derives from the minimal artwork in financial ads. It lists only the relevant data of the parties to the transaction. Such ads are not an offer to sell, as securities regulations prohibit explicit advertising, other than through a PROSPECTUS.

TOM NEXT *see* TOMORROW NEXT.

TOMORROW NEXT (TOM NEXT) foreign exchange and money market term for trades executed tomorrow for delivery on the next business day. A currency purchased on Tuesday is deliverable on Thursday, or the SPOT delivery day plus one day. The spot market price is adjusted by a premium to account for the extra day. *See also* SPOT NEXT.

TOO BIG TO FAIL notion that a bank or financial company has become so large and its services so connected to the overall economy that government agencies would intervene to prevent its failure and the possibility of catastrophic economic damage, as seen in the events of the 2008 financial crisis—the Lehman Brothers bankruptcy and subsequent near collapse of the short-term credit markets.

TOPPING UP CLAUSE language in a BACK-TO-BACK loan, or a two-currency loan, protecting the lender from currency devaluations. The borrower is required to make additional payments of, say 5% in the depreciating currency if the value of that currency declines by that amount. Such provisions can cause problems if the party on the other side of a back-to-back loan has no use for the additional currency, or is required to report topping up payments as additional income. Dependence on these special payments has been reduced by passing the credit risk to a bank, in exchange for payment of a fee.

TORRENS CERTIFICATE certificate of property ownership issued by government agencies in some states. Originated by Sir Robert Torrens, an Australian land reformer, the Torrens system permits property transfers without the need for title searches. It also simplifies title searches; under the Torrens system, a title discovered after the certificate is issued is no longer valid.

TORT wrongful act, other than a breach of CONTRACT, causing one party to suffer a property loss or bodily injury. Such cases are argued in civil courts, although criminal prosecution also is possible in some cases. A person committing a tort is liable for damages.

TOTAL CAPITAL bank supervisor's measure of a bank's qualifying capital in computing its *risk-based capital* reserves. Total capital is measured as follows: TIER 1 equity capital (common stock and qualifying preferred stock), plus TIER 2 capital (reserves for loan losses, subordinated debt, and preferred stock not counted as Tier 1 capital).

TOTAL LEASE OBLIGATION total of all direct costs of a consumer lease, including monthly rentals, interest, and any contingent payments (BALLOON PAYMENTS) due at the end of the lease, and estimate of fair market value (residual value) of the property at lease termination. Federal Reserve REGULATION M requires disclosure of closing costs in consumer leases. The lessor must also tell the lessee whether the lease contains a purchase option available at the end. An OPEN-END LEASE may require a balloon payment, depending on the value of the leased property, although the Consumer Leasing Act limits such payments to no more than three times the average monthly payment.

TOTAL RESERVES sum of the deposits that depository institutions may count toward their legal RESERVE REQUIREMENTS. Included in the calculation are reserve account balances on deposit with a Federal Reserve Bank during the most recent week, currency and coin in a bank's vault, including cash in transit to or from reserve banks. The Monetary Control Act requires most depository institutions to keep reserve balances either directly or indirectly with a Federal Reserve Bank.

TOTAL RETURN annual return on an investment including interest or dividend payments and price appreciation (capital gains). Total return is usually expressed as a percentage. For corporate bonds, total return is the equivalent of the YIELD TO MATURITY calculation; for stocks, future capital appreciation is projected using the current PRICE EARNINGS RATIO. Mutual funds use a formula worked out by the Securities and Exchange Commission in advertising fund performance.

In mortgage-backed securities and asset-backed securities, total return differs from the yield to maturity calculation because the total return calculation takes into account reinvestment income and borrower prepayments. When interest rates are falling, borrowers tend to prepay their mortgages and refinance their loans at current interest rates, causing investor yields on conventional mortgage-backed securities to drop. *See also* CASH FLOW YIELD.

TOTTEN TRUST informal trust in which assets deposited into an account are controlled by the person creating the trust, the GRANTOR, and held in trust for another, who is named as BENEFICIARY. When the account owner dies, the account is transferred to the beneficiary, but taxed as part of the grantor's estate. If the account is jointly owned, the regulations covering joint accounts apply. When all the owners of the account die, the beneficiary becomes the lawful owner.

TOXIC ASSETS assets of doubtful value that cannot be sold or liquidated without substantial loss. Toxic assets trade at market prices far below their original value when issued. Subprime mortgage-backed securities and collateralized debt obligations were common types in the 2008 financial crisis.

TRADE ACCEPTANCE *see* ACCEPTANCE.

TRADE ASSOCIATION nonprofit mutual benefit organization formed to provide services for its members, promote education and professional standards, and influence governmental agencies through lobbying. There are numerous trade groups representing commercial banks and savings institutions in the United States, operating at the state level and nationwide.

Major trade groups in banking are the following:

—ABA Marketing Network, an affiliate of the American Bankers Association dedicated to financial marketing in commercial banks, Washington, D.C.

—American Bankers Association, national trade association of commercial banks in the United States first organized in 1875. ABA represents the commercial banking industry in dealings with Congress and federal regulatory agencies, and promotes professional development through banking schools, seminars, and its education arm, the American Institute of Banking.

—American Council of State Savings Supervisors, Washington, D.C., representing regulators of state chartered savings and loan associations.

—Bank Insurance & Securities Association, Washington, D.C.; bankers marketing insurance, securities, and investments through financial institutions.

—BAFT-IFSA (Bankers Association for Foreign Trade—International Financial Services Association), New York, representing banks in trade finance, payments, compliance, and asset servicing.

—Community Mortgage Lenders of America, Ferguson, Missouri, representing nonbank mortgage lenders.

—Conference of State Bank Supervisors, Washington, D.C., serving supervisors of state chartered commercial banks and savings banks, and dedicated to maintaining the DUAL BANKING financial system.

—Consumer Bankers Association, Arlington, Virginia, representing commercial banks and savings institutions active in the retail financial services industry.

—Credit Union National Association, Madison, Wisconsin, representing the majority of U.S. credit unions, through state credit union leagues.

—Electronic Funds Transfer Association, Herndon, Virginia, a multi-industry association representing financial institutions, service organizations, and manufacturers dedicated to promotion of electronic payment services.

—Financial Services Roundtable, Washington, D.C., representing executive officers of bank holding companies and commercial banks in cities that have a Federal Reserve Bank.

—Financial Women International, Arlington, Virginia, a group representing women holding executive positions in banking institutions.

—Independent Community Bankers of America, Washington, D.C., representing independently owned commercial banks. About half of the commercial banks in the United States are ICBA members.

—Institute of International Bankers, New York City, representing foreign banks doing business in the United States.

—Mortgage Bankers Association of America, Washington, D.C., residential and commercial mortgage lenders and underwriters.

—National Association of Federal Credit Unions, Arlington, Virginia, representing federal credit unions chartered by the National Credit Union Administration.

—National Bankers Association, Washington, D.C., a trade group representing minority-owned banks.

—National Automated Clearing House Association, Herndon, Virginia, a trade group promoting uniform rules and standards for AUTOMATED CLEARING HOUSE associations.

—Risk Management Association, Philadelphia, Pennsylvania, representing commercial loan and credit officers at banks and savings institutions.

—Securities Industry and Financial Markets Association (SIFMA), New York, New York, and Washington, D.C., representing securities firms, banks, and asset management companies.

—Wholesale Markets Brokers' Association Americas, Washington, D.C., serving swap dealers and swap trading firms.

See also AMERICAN INSTITUTE OF BANKING; BANK ADMINISTRATION INSTITUTE.

TRADE DATE date an order is executed to buy or sell securities, financial instruments, or commodities. It precedes the date funds are transferred to settle the transaction (the SETTLEMENT DATE) by one day in options trading, two days in most foreign exchange trading, and three days in stock market trading. *See also* DELIVERY DATE; RECORD DATE.

TRADE PAPER *see* ACCEPTANCE; SHORT-TERM PAPER.

TRADER party who buys or sells securities, financial instruments, or commodities on behalf of customers, or for his or her own account. A trader may be a broker, dealer, or speculator, and may or may not take overnight positions.

TRADE REFERENCE credit reference furnished by a credit reporting agency listing credit experience of a firm's trade suppliers, including trade terms, highest credit balance, or amount due in the previous year, amounts past due, the terms of sale, and payment history. The report serves as a general credit reference of an organization, and its ability to meet current obligations. *See also* DUN & BRADSTREET; MERCANTILE AGENCY.

TRADE REPORT *see* CREDIT REPORT; MERCANTILE AGENCY.

TRADING ACCOUNT ASSETS separate account managed by banks that buy (underwrite) U.S. government securities and other securities for their own trading account or for resale at a profit to other banks and to the public, rather than for investment in the bank's own investment portfolio. Trading assets are segregated from the investment portfolio. They are recorded separately when acquired until they are disposed of or sold, and are recorded at the price in effect when these securities are purchased or sold. Trading assets held for other banks are marked to market (adjusted to current market value) while held by a bank. *See also* SECURITIES AFFILIATE.

TRADING FLAT *see* FLAT.

TRADING LIMIT maximum number of futures contracts that may trade in a day's trading session, as determined by a trading exchange and the Commodities Futures Trading Commission. Limits generally are based on price, and vary according to markets, and may be adjusted depending on market conditions. *See also* MARGIN.

TRADING RANGE range between high and low prices, or bids and offers, recorded during a stated time period, for example, a daily trading session on a stock exchange, an over-the-counter market, or a foreign exchange market. A trading range also can be from January 1 to the latest date, the last 12 months, and so on.

TRANCHE

1. one of the classes of debt securities issued as part of a single bond or instrument, from the French word *tranche* meaning slice. Securities often are issued in tranches to meet different investor objectives for portfolio diversification. For example, a COLLATERALIZED MORTGAGE OBLIGATION is a mortgaged-backed security issued with several different bond tranches issued under a single bond indenture, ranging from a fast-pay bond to a long-term slow-pay bond (called the ACCRUAL BOND, or the Z-bond). Each is paid off consecutively; as one bond matures, the next is paid down in a stepping stone progression. Each tranche has a different coupon and maturity, and is identifiable by a different CUSIP NUMBER.
2. separate borrowings or funding commitments under a TERM LOAN or other credit facility. A multicurrency loan may be structured with a U.S. dollar tranche, a Euro tranche, and so on. World Bank advances to a sovereign borrower are structured in tranches.
3. single maturity CERTIFICATE OF DEPOSIT sold by a lead bank, which is then divided into smaller denominations for placement with investors.
4. gold tranche: first 25% of a member country's contribution to the International Monetary Fund, normally in gold bullion.
5. reserve tranche: deposit balances subject to RESERVE REQUIREMENTS.

TRANSACTION

1. any event that causes a change in an organization's financial position or net worth, resulting from normal business activity. It is recorded on the general ledger by debit or credit tickets.
2. advance of funds, as in a credit card cash advance, purchase of goods at a retailer, or when a borrower activates a revolving line of credit.
3. activities affecting a deposit account, such as a deposit of funds or a withdrawal, carried out at the request of the account owner.

TRANSACTION ACCOUNT

1. deposit account from which the account holder is permitted to make withdrawals or transfers by writing checks or similar means to make transfers to third parties.
2. demand deposit, NOW account, SUPER NOW ACCOUNT, and other accounts accessible by negotiable instrument, and subject to RESERVE REQUIREMENTS, as defined by the Monetary Control Act of 1980, with a Federal Reserve Bank or CORRESPONDENT.

TRANSFER

1. moving funds from one account to another, as from checking to savings.
2. electronic payment from one bank to another through the AUTOMATED CLEARING HOUSE system.
3. large dollar payment from one bank to another through the FED WIRE or the Clearing House Interbank Payments System in New York.
4. real estate CONVEYANCE from buyer to seller that takes place at a mortgage closing.
5. clause in a LETTER OF CREDIT allowing the BENEFICIARY to make the proceeds of the credit available to a third party (secondary beneficiary). The secondary beneficiary is obligated to present the draft to the advising or paying bank to receive payment.
6. moving stocks, bonds, or other securities from one owner to another, and recording the change of ownership on registration papers.
7. ASSUMPTION of a mortgage by a new borrower.

TRANSFERABLE LETTER OF CREDIT LETTER OF CREDIT giving the BENEFICIARY the option of making part or all of the credit available to third parties (secondary beneficiaries). The credit may be transferred only with approval of the issuing bank.

TRANSFERABLE UNDERWRITING FACILITY (TRUF) Euronote facility allowing the original underwriter, the project manager, to reserve the right to transfer the commitment to an other agent willing to assume financial responsibility. This transfer of authority has to be done with the consent of all the original parties and is both a transfer of responsibility and management.

TRANSFER AGENT company that issues, registers, and redeems securities on behalf of the issuer. The agent, usually a commercial bank, also maintains records of changes in ownership, updates records when securities are sold, and ensures that new offerings of securities are not overissued. If the securities offered for sale are bonds, the agent is known as a REGISTRAR. *See also* AMERICAN DEPOSITARY RECEIPT; BOOK ENTRY SECURITY; CUSTODIAN; DEPOSITORY TRUST COMPANY.

TRANSFER OF MORTGAGE ASSIGNMENT of mortgage by either the borrower (the MORTGAGOR) or the lender (the MORTGAGEE). The person receiving the property may take it SUBJECT TO MORTGAGE, i.e., on the condition that the original borrower maintains the existing mortgage, replaces it with another, or may assume the mortgage at the same rate and terms. In that event, the new owner becomes liable for repayment of the debt. *See also* ASSUMABLE MORTGAGE.

TRANSFER PRICING value placed on transfers within an organization, used as a means of allocating costs to various profit centers. Transfer pricing is used widely in multioffice banks and bank holding companies, serving these important functions: (1) price setting for services performed by business units; (2) evaluating financial performance by business units; and (3) determining the contribution to net income by profit centers in the organization.

An example is determining a bank's internal cost of funds, or the cost assigned bank deposits supplied by retail branch offices to its commercial lending division. The retail branches traditionally are suppliers of funds, and commercial lenders traditionally are users of funds. Transfer pricing schemes also are widely used in pricing bank holding company services supplied to affiliate or correspondent banks, for example, check processing, data processing, and funds supplied by a holding company to a subsidiary bank or a nonbank affiliate company. In lending, transfer pricing can be used as a form of internal credit rationing, by arbitrarily assigning the lowest cost of funds to the least risky loans, encouraging lenders to make loans that are profitable to the bank as well as low-risk. Transfer pricing schemes generally follow one of three cost accounting approaches: (1) market price; (2) cost- based price, generally the marginal cost of funds; or (3) negotiated price, a price determined through negotiation by buyer and seller. Historic cost, on the other hand, normally is used for reference only, and generally is not used in internal pricing.

TRANSFER TAX

1. **Securities.** The tax levied by several states and the federal government on sales or transfers of securities, payable by the seller, determined by the location of the TRANSFER AGENT, not the place where the transaction occurs.
2. **Real Estate.** The taxes paid to a state or local government to cover the costs of recording a property deed in public land records, payable by the seller when the property is sold.
3. **Estates.** The federal or state taxes assessed in settlement of an estate, usually nine months after the date of death. ESTATE taxes are federal taxes on the decedent's property, whereas inheritance taxes are state taxes payable by the heirs named in the decedent's will.

TRANSIT DEPARTMENT department in a bank where checks or drafts issued by out-of-area banks are sorted, bundled together, and sent out (presented) to the DRAWEE bank for payment. Checks from distant banks routinely are honored, and a temporary hold is placed on the deposit until funds are received (SUBJECT TO COLLECTION) from the issuer. Banks send these checks, called TRANSIT ITEMS, to a FEDERAL RESERVE BANK or Federal Reserve REGIONAL CHECK PROCESSING CENTER or to the check issuing bank for collection. *See also* ABA TRANSIT NUMBER; CASH LETTER; CHECK ROUTING SYMBOL; DEFERRED AVAILABILITY; DIRECT SEND; PROOF OF DEPOSIT; REGULATION CC.

TRANSIT ITEM CHECKS or DRAFTS issued by a financial institution other than the bank where it is deposited. These are separated from checks written by a bank's own customers (ON-US ITEMS) and are submitted to the DRAWEE bank by direct PRESENTMENT (direct send), through a local clearinghouse, or a FEDERAL RESERVE BANK or REGIONAL CHECK PROCESSING CENTER. Checks drawn on other banks normally are sorted and submitted for collection before checks drawn by a bank's own customers are posted to accounts. Also called *on others items.*

TRANSIT LETTER documentation accompanying checks or drafts submitted for collection, listing the number of checks (items) being sent and the total dollar amount of the checks. A CASH LETTER accompanies checks presented to other banks for payment; a REMITTANCE letter is used when the sending bank does not have an account at the receiving bank.

TRANSIT NUMBER *see* ABA TRANSIT NUMBER.

TRANSMITTAL LETTER document sent with securities tendered for sale, checks and other negotiable instruments presented for COLLECTION, letters of credit, and so on, explaining the purpose of the transaction and detailing any instructions for special handling.

TRANSPARENCY conditions when key information about a company, security, or market is fully and accurately disclosed and is accessible in a timely manner. When it relates to a company's release of financial information to investors, it is known as *full disclosure*. Transparency is one of the essential prerequisites in any free and efficient market.

TRANSPOSITION ERROR error caused by reversing two or more digits of an amount while posting a transaction. If two adjacent numbers are switched, the resulting error is always divisible by nine. If a teller's closing balance is off by $63, the error probably was caused by switching the numbers 70 and 7, 81 and 18, or 92 and 29.

TRAVEL & ENTERTAINMENT (T&E) CARD charge card used to pay for hotel, airline, and other business related expenses. The first travel card was issued in 1950 by Diners Club, followed by American Express in 1958. Travel cards are 30-day charge accounts, with payment due in full before the next billing cycle; and some T&E card plans, usually corporate cards, give the cardholder a quarterly summary of charges to the card. *See also* GOLD CARD.

TRAVELER'S CHECK SIGHT DRAFT issued through banks acting as sales agents, or sold directly to the public. The purchaser pays for the checks in advance, and signs the drafts twice—once when ordering the drafts and once when cashing them. The drafts are payable by the issuing company, sold in denominations of $10 to $100 and in numerous foreign currencies, and insured against loss or theft. They readily are accepted in lieu of cash by merchants, and may be cashed at bank offices in the United States and most foreign countries. Travelers' checks were first issued by American Express Co., which uses the spelling *traveler's cheque*.

TRAVELER'S LETTER OF CREDIT letter of credit addressed to the issuing bank's correspondents, authorizing them to honor drafts drawn by the bearer up to the authorized credit line. This is also called a *circular letter of credit*. Payments are endorsed by the issuer's correspondents on the reverse side of the letter of credit when they negotiate the drafts. This type of credit often is used to cover travel expenses and usually is prepaid by the customer. *See also* TRAVELER'S CHECK.

TREASURER'S DRAFTS *see* PAYABLE THROUGH DRAFT.

TREASURY BILL short-term U.S. Treasury security issued in minimum denominations of $10,000 and usually having maturities of 13, 26, or 52 weeks. Investors purchase bills at prices lower than face value (at discount). The return to the investor who holds it to maturity is the difference between the price paid and the face value at maturity. Treasury bills are the securities most frequently purchased or sold by the Federal Reserve when it carries out OPEN MARKET OPERATIONS.

The formula for computing the discount price on U.S. Treasury bills, which are issued at a price less than par value or face value, is as follows:

Discount in dollars = Days to Maturity / 360 × Discount Basis

Thus, a six-month Treasury bill selling at a 7% discount has a discount price of $35 per $1,000 of maturity value.

The BOND EQUIVALENT YIELD of a 180-day Treasury bill, which allows comparison with interest-bearing securities, is as follows:

Discount / Purchase Price × 365 / 180 = 7.35%

The Treasury Department also auctions from time to time short-term CASH MANAGEMENT BILLS with maturities up to 50 days that are sold to institutional buyers in lots of $1 million or more. These have replaced Treasury certificates of indebtedness and Tax Anticipation Bills as short-term debt instruments.

TREASURY BOND long-term U.S. Treasury securities usually having initial maturities of ten years or more and issued in denominations of $1,000 or more.

TREASURY CERTIFICATE coupon bearing special certificates of indebtedness with maturities of less than one year. The Treasury Department borrows from the Federal Reserve System from time to time, by issuing these short-term certificates to the Federal Reserve

Bank of New York. The certificates cover overdrafts on the Treasury's account maintained at FEDERAL RESERVE BANKS. Legislation in June 1979 authorized Treasury borrowings from the Fed only in unusual circumstances, and when the borrowings are approved by the Federal Reserve Board of Governors.

TREASURY GENERAL ACCOUNT (TGA) general checking account for the U.S. Treasury Department maintained at the Federal Reserve Bank of New York. All official U.S. government disbursements are made from this account. The account also holds dollars credited to the Treasury in the form of monetized gold. *See also* TREASURY TAX AND LOAN ACCOUNT.

TREASURY NOTE intermediate-term, coupon bearing U.S. Treasury securities having initial maturities of less than ten years and issued in denominations of $1,000 or more, depending on the maturity of the issue. Notes pay interest semiannually, and the principal amount is payable at maturity.

TREASURY SECURITIES generic term for interest bearing obligations of the U.S. government issued by the Treasury to meet government expenditures not covered by tax revenues. Marketable Treasury securities fall into four categories: TREASURY BILLS, with maturities of 91 to 365 days; TREASURY BONDS, with maturities of ten years or longer; and TREASURY NOTES, with maturities between one and ten years.

These currently are issued in book entry form only. Ownership of book entry securities is maintained on the computers of the Federal Reserve Bank of New York. The purchaser receives a statement (a receipt), rather than an engraved certificate.

TREASURY STOCK previously issued shares of stock repurchased and held by the issuer. In banking, treasury stock, whether carried at cost or par value, is deductible from a bank's equity capital, and is reportable under undivided profits in the REPORT OF CONDITION.

TREASURY TAX AND LOAN (TT&L) ACCOUNT checking account balances maintained by the U.S. Treasury Department at depository institutions, primarily commercial banks. Federal withholding taxes are payable through TT&L accounts. A large portion of tax receipts are deposited into these accounts. Some Treasury balances may be kept in interest bearing deposits in local banks. *See also* TREASURY GENERAL ACCOUNT.

TREASURY WORKSTATION cash-management term for computer hardware and software systems that handle corporate treasury functions (such as managing cash, debt, and investment services), access to capital markets, and risk management. Treasury workstations enable corporations to communicate seamlessly over the Internet with their cash management banks, other financial institutions, and their customers or suppliers. Workstations increase the reliability of financial reporting and decision making by reducing, if not eliminating, the repetitive handling of time-sensitive financial data. *See also* ELECTRONIC DATA INTERCHANGE.

TREND ANALYSIS in credit analysis, detailed examination of a company's financial ratios and cash flow for several accounting periods to determine changes in financial position. Trend analysis is a key part of credit underwriting, and is a useful and necessary tool in determining whether a borrower's financial strength is improving or deteriorating. Key ratios examined include debt coverage ratio, turnover ratio (conversion of inventory and receivables to cash), and the QUICK ASSETS ratio or quick ratio (current assets divided by current liabilities). *See also* BALANCE SHEET RATIOS; TURNOVER RATIOS.

TRIGGERING TERM consumer credit term that, when used in credit promotion literature or advertising, must disclose certain pertinent information, as required by the TRUTH IN LENDING ACT. Consumer finance charges, for example, must be disclosed as an ANNUAL PERCENTAGE RATE (APR) to give consumers uniform credit information and compare rates charged by different lenders. Also covered by the rule are annual fees, closing costs, and contingent credit costs, such as balloon payments.

TROUBLED ASSET RELIEF PROGRAM (TARP) government program authorizing the U.S. Treasury Department to purchase up to $700 billion in illiquid mortgage-backed securities or other assets from U.S. financial institutions. TARP, created by the Emergency Economic Stabilization Act of 2008, was an effort to recapitalize banks at the height of the 2008 financial crisis and encourage banks to resume lending.

TROUBLED BANK bank that has an above normal percentage of NONPERFORMING ASSETS when compared to banks of comparable size, and may have a negative net worth (or an excess of liabilities over assets). Troubled banks are listed on the bank regulator's PROBLEM BANK list.

TROUBLED DEBT RESTRUCTURING condition where a lender grants a concession to a borrower in financial difficulty. The Statement of Financial Accounting Standards No. 15 (FASB 15) divides debt restructuring of nonperforming loans, where the loan payments are past due 90 days or more, into two categories: (1) loans where the borrower transfers assets to the lender; and (2) those where credit terms are modified. The latter includes foreclosures, reductions in the interest rate, extension of the maturity date, and forgiveness of principal and/or interest payments. Typically, the lender negotiates a WORKOUT AGREEMENT with the borrower to modify the original credit terms rather than initiate foreclosure proceedings against the delinquent borrower. *See also* ADVERSELY CLASSIFIED ASSETS; CASH BASIS LOAN; LOSS; NONACCRUAL LOAN; SPECIAL MENTION; STAND-STILL AGREEMENT; WRITE OFF.

TROUBLED LOAN NON PERFORMING LOAN, also known as a *sour loan.* There are several warning signals: thin margins, liquidity questions, adverse business and employment conditions, insufficient (under margin) collateral, insufficient income. Payments of interest and/or principal may have been renegotiated or restructured. *See also* ADVERSELY CLASSIFIED ASSETS; SPECIAL MENTION; TROUBLED DEBT RESTRUCTURING.

TRUE INTEREST COST (TIC)

1. ANNUAL PERCENTAGE RATE cost of credit, including finance charges, credit life insurance, discount points, and prepaid interest. The federal TRUTH IN LENDING ACT requires lenders to disclose in consumer credit loan agreements the true cost of credit, using a standard method of computing the borrower's finance charge, plus loan application fees and other costs of borrowing. The true interest cost of a $4,000 installment note at 10% interest payable over 36 months is $645.80. Thus, the total cost of the loan, including interest, is $4,645.80.
2. actual cost of issuing a bond, taking into account the present value (time value) of money. The TIC, commonly used in municipal bond offerings, is the rate of interest, compounded semiannually, required to discount the payments of principal and interest to bondholders to the original purchase price. Compare to NET INTEREST COST.

TRUE LEASE LEASE that meets the Internal Revenue Code and accounting tests allowing the lessor to claim the tax benefits of ownership. The lessor is permitted to depreciate the asset over its lifetime and claim any unused tax credits; the lessee can deduct the lease payments as a capital expense from ordinary income taxes. A lease qualifying for tax treatment ordinarily is a multiyear, LEVERAGED LEASE, for example, a lease of capital equipment to an airline or manufacturer. Also known as a *tax-oriented lease. See also* FINANCE LEASE; OPERATING LEASE.

TRUNCATION

1. banking service in which cancelled checks or drafts are held by the customer's bank, or by another bank in the check collection system, and are not returned to the check writer with the ACCOUNT STATEMENT. The Check Clearing for the 21st Century Act (known informally as the CHECK 21 Law) allows replacement of actual checks with digital check images to improve the overall efficiency of the U.S. check-clearing system. The handling of actual checks is stopped, or truncated, at the depositing financial institution. With the new law, a bank on the West Coast can transmit an electronic check image to the East Coast, where a substitute check is created and presented to the paying bank; the check clearing process is thus shortened from days to hours. A substitute check is the legal equivalent of the original paper check and contains the phrase "This is a LEGAL COPY of your check. You can use it the same way you would use the original check."

2. dropping one or more digits in calculating interest accrued on savings accounts. For example, 1.677754 truncated after the fourth decimal becomes 1.6777. The opposite is ROUNDING.

TRUST

1. fiduciary relationship involving two parties, whereby the second party has responsibility for handling property for the benefit of someone else. The trust business has three broad categories: personal trusts, institutional management trusts created under an INDENTURE, and MASTER TRUST arrangements in which a fiduciary, usually a bank, manages the record keeping for institutional investors. There are four types of personal trusts: a TESTAMENTARY TRUST created by a will; an IRREVOCABLE TRUST in which the person creating the trust (the GRANTOR) transfers property to a trustee but does not have the right to cancel the agreement; a short-term trust, such as a Clifford Trust created to set aside funds for education of the grantor's children; and a revocable living trust that may be terminated by the grantor at any time. *See also* BLIND TRUST; CHARITABLE TRUST; DEED OF TRUST; INTER VIVOS TRUST; TRUST ACCOUNT; TRUST COMPANY; TRUST DEPARTMENT; TRUSTEE; TRUST INDENTURE ACT OF 1939.
2. business combination that attempts to restrain competition in a given market through monopoly control of manufacturing, processing, or distribution of goods and services. *See also* ANTITRUST LAWS.

TRUST ACCOUNT shorthand name for all types of accounts handled by a bank's TRUST DEPARTMENT or by a TRUST COMPANY. *See also* ESTATE; GUARDIAN; TOTTEN TRUST; TRUST; UNIFORM GIFT TO MINORS ACT.

TRUST COMPANY corporation organized for the purpose of accepting and executing trusts, and acting as trustee under wills, as executor or guardian. State chartered trust companies also may offer banking services, such as taking deposits and making loans, depending on their charter. Trust companies also act as fiscal agents for corporations, paying stock dividends and bond interest payments, and as fiscal agents or paying agents for state and local governments. Many trust companies also accept deposits, make loans, and perform other banking services. Federal law permits NATIONAL BANKS to engage in trust activities. State chartered trust companies may become members of the Federal Reserve System and be insured by the Federal Deposit Insurance Corporation. Trust companies are regulated by state law.

TRUST DEPARTMENT department in a bank or savings institution managing TRUST ACCOUNT assets for personal trust, employee benefit trusts, and corporate accounts and providing AGENCY services for trust clients. Smaller trusts are managed commonly as COMMINGLED FUNDS or common account trusts, as it is uneconomical to manage them separately. Bank trust departments also settle estates for individuals and act as TRANSFER AGENTS for corporations. Trust account funds are managed separately and accounted for separately from other assets managed by a bank. *See also* EMPLOYEE RETIREMENT INCOME SECURITY ACT; MASTER TRUST; REGULATION 9; TRUST COMPANY; TRUSTEE.

TRUST DEED *see* DEED OF TRUST.

TRUSTEE

1. person named to administer a trust for a BENEFICIARY according to the terms established by the donor.
2. financial institution, usually a TRUST COMPANY or the TRUST DEPARTMENT in a commercial bank that holds collateral for the benefit of bondholders. The trustee collects principal and interest payments, invests the cash between payment dates, and disburses funds to pay principal and interest on issued and outstanding bonds.
3. U.S. Trustee Official in BANKRUPTCY courts in most states, appointed under the U.S. Justice Department's Trustee Program to administer bankruptcy cases.
4. in asset-backed or mortgage-backed securitizations, the party responsible for making payments to investors, administering the pooling and servicing agreement, and protecting the interests of investors.

TRUST INDENTURE ACT OF 1939 federal law, an amendment to the Securities Act of 1933 that requires issuers of corporate bonds, mortgage-backed bonds, and other debt instruments to disclose terms and conditions under which securities are issued. These disclosures are contained in an INDENTURE agreement, a document specifying the legal obligations of the issuer and any restrictions, such as call provisions applying to the securities. The act requires issuers to name a trust corporation to administer terms of the indenture. The trustee, who must be free of conflict of interest, also makes semiannual disclosures of pertinent information to the securities holders. The act also prohibits impairment of the holders' right to sue individually, and requires the trustee to make available a list of the holders so they can communicate with one another. The act also exempts securities (mostly municipal bonds) that are not subject to securities registration requirements.

TRUSTOR person who establishes a TRUST for the benefit of another, and turns property over to a TRUSTEE for distribution to the BENEFICIARY. Also known as a *donor* or *settlor*.

TRUST PREFERRED SECURITIES securities with characteristics of preferred stock and subordinated debt—hybrid securities in other words. Trust preferred securities are issued mostly by bank holding companies. Trust preferred issues qualify as debt instruments for tax purposes and also meet the bank regulatory definition for TIER 1 capital. Trust preferred stock is bank eligible paper, meaning it can be sold (rediscounted) to investors and other financial institutions.

TRUST RECEIPT

1. written agreement used extensively in LETTER OF CREDIT financing, often extended to a buyer or other importer of goods. The buyer promises to hold the property received in the name of the bank arranging the financing, although the bank retains title to the goods. Trust receipts allow an importer to take possession of the goods for resale before paying the issuing bank.
2. type of SECURITY AGREEMENT now part of Article 9 of the UNIFORM COMMERCIAL CODE that controls credit extensions to sellers of durable goods. The seller, say an automobile dealer, has possession of the cars in the dealer's showroom and pays the lender from a trust account as the cars are sold. The lender may also take a FINANCING STATEMENT from the dealer before making the loan. *See also* FLOOR PLANNING; INDIRECT LOAN.

TRUTH IN LENDING ACT act passed by Congress in 1969 requiring lenders to disclose key terms in extensions of credit. The act, part of the Consumer Credit Protection Act, requires venders to disclose the method of computing finance charges, the conditions under which a finance charge may be imposed, and the finance charge expressed as an ANNUAL PERCENTAGE RATE. These credit terms must be disclosed clearly and conspicuously in consumer credit applications. The act also requires that borrowers who sign credit agreements giving the lender a security interest in the borrower's home have the right to rescind the contract within three business days. This is known as the borrower's RIGHT OF RESCISSION. The Truth in Lending Act, the earliest of the federal consumer protection statutes, has been amended several times, and has been copied in several states by state laws containing similar consumer protections. *See also* ADVERSE ACTION; EFFECTS TEST; EQUAL CREDIT OPPORTUNITY ACT; FAIR CREDIT REPORTING ACT; REGULATION B; REGULATION M; REGULATION Z.

TRUTH IN SAVINGS federal law requiring banks to disclose key terms on interest-paying deposit accounts, including the rate paid and fees charged. The Truth in Savings Act, part of the Federal Deposit Insurance Corporation Improvement Act of 1991, requires financial institutions to make available: the SIMPLE INTEREST rate paid; the ANNUAL PERCENTAGE YIELD or annualized yield; the minimum balance needed to open an account; penalties for early withdrawal of funds, and other conditions that might reduce the yield on the account.

TUGRIK monetary unit of Mongolia.

TURNAROUND purchase and sale of securities, commodities, and financial instruments in a single day, as by a speculator taking profits from short-term market shifts. The trader does not hold the securities in his portfolio overnight. *See also* DAY ORDER.

TURNKEY PROJECT real estate development project in which the builder assumes all risk until a certain point has been reached, usually at completion of the project or where the building is ready for occupancy. Permanent financing by a TAKE-OUT LENDER can be arranged at that point, provided certain conditions are met.

TURNOVER RATIOS financial ratios related to sales or volume, for example, accounts receivable turnover; also known as efficiency ratios, for example, assets turnover, conversion of receivables into cash. These measure efficiency of converting assets into cash. *See also* LIQUIDITY RATIOS.

12B-1 MUTUAL FUND mutual fund that uses part of its assets to cover sales and marketing expenses, named after the 1980 SECURITIES AND EXCHANGE COMMISSION ruling allowing the practice. Instead of charging the customer an up-front commission, or a sales LOAD as high as 8½%, the mutual fund manager assesses an annual charge, usually less than 1% of a mutual fund's net asset value. Originally, fund managers thought they could reduce average expenses by using fund assets to cover management fees and other expenses, thereby lowering costs paid by shareholders as a fund grew in size. The SEC requires disclosure of 12b-1 fees in a mutual fund prospectus, a requirement that caused some fund sponsors to switch from 12b-1 fees to BACK-END LOAD funds with redemption charges when fund shares are sold by an investor. So-called 12b-1 funds have been popular with banks because some mutual fund sponsors have been willing to share these sales fees to help offset a bank's marketing costs.

24-HOUR BANKING self-service banking extending beyond normal banking hours by obtaining cash, making deposits, and transferring money between accounts at AUTOMATED TELLER MACHINES. *See also* INTERNET BANKING; MOBILE BANKING.

TWENTY-PERCENT RULE commercial bank practice of requiring corporate borrowers to maintain average deposit balances equal to 20% of their borrowings under a revolving line of credit or term loan. This is also known as a COMPENSATING BALANCE. Today, fixed balance requirements in bank lending are a thing of the past; in actual practice, compensating balances vary from 10% of borrowings to 25%, or may be waived altogether in lieu of bank service charges. The exact ratio of deposits to borrowings depends on interest rates and local market conditions. Banks require balances, which serve as a liquidity cushion for both borrower and lender, compensate the lender for servicing the loan, and tend to weed out uncreditworthy borrowers.

TWO-NAME PAPER popular name for trade paper—trade acceptances and BANKERS' ACCEPTANCES—carrying two signatures, either as drawer or endorser. In the event the issuer cannot pay a banker's acceptance, the bank accepting the obligation is responsible for payment. Also called *double-name paper.*

TWO-PARTY LOAN *see* BACK-TO-BACK LOAN; PARALLEL LOAN.

TWO-SIDED MARKET market where a dealer is willing to quote both a bid and an asked price, or stands ready to make a market on both sides of a transaction, either as buyer or seller. This kind of market usually is found in the government securities market and the over-the-counter stock market, rather than the municipal bond market, which normally is a one-way market. Municipal securities tend to be less marketable than U.S. Treasury obligations, which actively are traded and have a strong secondary market. Some muni bond dealers, however, quote bid and asked prices on longer maturity term bond issues.

TWO-STEP MORTGAGE type of fixed-rate, 30-year mortgage, that adjusts the borrower's interest rate after an initial five or seven year period. The borrower pays less principal in the early years of the mortgage. After five years have passed (seven years in some loans), the mortgage interest rate is adjusted to either the prevailing fixed-rate mortgage or a variable rate mortgage for the remainder of the mortgage.

U

UCC-1 STATEMENT *see* FINANCING STATEMENT.

ULTRA VIRES ACTS actions beyond the powers of a corporation, as stated in its charter, or the laws of the state where it is incorporated. Broadly defined, an ultra vires act is any act prohibited by a corporation's charter, or an excessive use of powers granted. *See also* ARTICLES OF INCORPORATION.

UNAUTHORIZED INVESTMENT investment that is not approved specifically by a trust instrument establishing a trust, as opposed to NONLEGAL INVESTMENTS by a trust company or a bank's TRUST DEPARTMENT. An investment, if not authorized, may meet state laws regulating investments by fiduciaries, but still violates the intent of the person creating the trust. *See also* LEGAL LIST.

UNAUTHORIZED TRANSFER cash withdrawal or transfer of funds, using a bank DEBIT CARD, from a consumer's deposit account by someone other than the cardholder. REGULATION E limits the consumer's liability to not more than $50, provided the consumer notifies the bank within 60 days of discovering the loss. Otherwise, the consumer's total liability may be as much as $500. In situations where the cardholder made it easy for someone else to withdraw money from a bank account without his approval, say by writing his personal access code or PIN number on the card itself, the consumer may have difficulty persuading his bank to correct the error. Liability in wrongful use of PIN numbers is, however, a legally ambiguous area, and is still open to dispute. *See also* ERROR RESOLUTION; PROVISIONAL CREDIT; UNAUTHORIZED USE.

UNAUTHORIZED USE use of a CREDIT CARD by someone other than the authorized cardholder, for example, after a bank credit card has been lost or stolen and purchases not approved by the cardholder are charged to the account. Federal Reserve REGULATION Z limits the cardholder's liability in such situations to not more than $50, although many banks waive even the $50 fee because attempting to collect such a token amount is usually not worth the effort. The TRUTH IN LENDING ACT limits credit card issuance to consumers who have filled out an application, or have responded to a direct mail invitation to apply for a credit card. *See also* UNAUTHORIZED TRANSFER.

UNBANKED Said of individuals who have no access to banking or financial services (including savings, credit, money transfer, insurance, or pensions) through banks, financial cooperatives and credit unions, or nonfinancial institutions.

UNBUNDLING bank service pricing in which account activity is separated into component categories and account SERVICE CHARGES imposed for each activity. Thus, checking account customers are charged a fee for each check paid and each cash withdrawal from an automated teller machine, as opposed to a monthly account maintenance fee. In unbundling service pricing, a bank may also calculate an EARNINGS CREDIT RATE on balances in deposit accounts, which can then be used to reduce the charges for unbundled services. The purpose in unbundling is to price bank services so each earns a profit, or has a measurable loss, and also to impose service charges fairly on all bank customers. Unbundled pricing also is a potential source of fee income, or noninterest income, which can be used to meet noninterest expenses, such as employee salaries. Contrast with account BUNDLING.

UNCLAIMED BALANCES balances left idle in a bank account, and considered abandoned property. Ownership may revert to the state after a specified period, usually five years, under state ESCHEAT laws. Also called a DORMANT ACCOUNT.

UNCOLLECTED FUNDS

1. checks or drafts that have not been paid by the drawee bank. Also called *uncollected items*. FEDERAL RESERVE FLOAT (FED FLOAT) is the time interval created when Federal Reserve Banks pay these checks before they are in turn paid by the payer bank. Federal Reserve Banks report these clearing checks as cash items in the process of collection in their weekly Statement of Condition.

   Federal Reserve REGULATION CC requires banks to follow a uniform schedule of funds availability, even if funds have not been collected from the paying bank: a local check drawn on a bank in the same Federal Reserve check processing district is to be available for withdrawal funds two business days after a check is deposited; nonlocal checks are to be usable funds in five business days; and the first $100 of any check deposited, the next business day. *See also* CHECK HOLD; DEFERRED AVAILABILITY; IMMEDIATE CREDIT.
2. check that cannot be paid by the drawee bank because the maker's account does not have enough funds to cover the check. Also called NOT SUFFICIENT FUNDS.

UNCOVERED OPTION *see* NAKED OPTION.

UNDERLYING financial instruments that must be delivered in completion of an option or futures contract. The underlying may be fixed rate securities, foreign exchange, or equities of futures contracts (if the security is an option on a futures contract).

UNDERLYING LIEN claim having priority over claims of other creditors, and is repayable before subsequent obligations are fully paid. A first MORTGAGE has priority over second and third mortgages, which are known as junior liens. A lender may ask a borrower to sign a SUBORDINATION AGREEMENT making a bank loan repayable ahead of other obligations, for example, a loan by the individual borrower to a closely-held corporation or partnership in which the borrower is a principal owner.

UNDERLYING MORTGAGE *see* UNDERLYING LIEN.

UNDERWATER LOAN loan that has a market value less than its book value. If sold in the secondary market, the lender would suffer a loss. Loans sink because the borrower is delinquent in payments; the coupon interest rate is below the rate on loans of similar quality and comparable maturities; or the loan collateral is worth less than the loan principal, or is not the principal source of repayment.

UNDERWRITING

Banking:

1. detailed credit analysis preceding the granting of a loan, based on credit information furnished by the borrower, such as employment history, salary, and financial statements; publicly available information, such as the borrower's credit history, which is detailed in a CREDIT REPORT; and the lender's evaluation of the borrower's credit needs and ABILITY TO PAY. *See also* CREDIT SCORING; CORPORATE RESOLUTION; LOAN COMMITTEE; LOAN POLICY.
2. purchase of corporate bonds, commercial paper, U.S. Treasury securities, municipal general obligation bonds by a commercial bank or dealer bank for its own account, or for resale to investors. Bank underwriting of corporate securities is carried out through a separate company called a SECURITIES SUBSIDIARY.

Securities: purchase of securities for resale to the public, either directly or through dealers. Underwriting of a new offering of securities is done by an investment banker, who assumes risk in bringing the issue to market by guaranteeing the issuer will receive a certain price when the offering is sold to investors. Underwriters make their income from the price difference, or UNDERWRITING SPREAD, between the price they pay the issuer and what they collect from investors or from broker-dealers who buy portions of the offering. When a dealer bank purchases Treasury securities in a quarterly Treasury bond auction, it acts as underwriter and distributor. Treasury Securities purchased by a primary dealer are held in a dealer bank's TRADING ACCOUNT ASSETS portfolio, and often resold to other banks, and to private investors. Other forms of underwriting are all or none, BEST EFFORT underwriting, and STANDBY UNDERWRITING. *See also* DUTCH AUCTION; NEGOTIATED UNDERWRITING; PRIVATE PLACEMENT; PUBLIC OFFERING; SECURITIES SUBSIDIARY.

Insurance: agreement by an insurer to accept risk of loss from property damage, accidental death, and so on, in exchange for payment of a premium.

UNDERWRITING AGREEMENT agreement between the managing underwriter, acting as agent for the UNDERWRITING GROUP, and the securities issuer. The agreement sets forth the responsibilities of all parties to the proposed sale and the initial price of securities offered to the public, and specifies whether the underwriter will buy any or all of the unsold securities. The issuer pays the cost of filing registration papers with the SECURITIES AND EXCHANGE COMMISSION, and the securities PROSPECTUS detailing terms of the public offering. Contrast with AGREEMENT AMONG UNDERWRITERS.

UNDERWRITING GROUP association of commercial banks and investment banks that purchases a new offering of securities, generally for immediate resale to investors through a public offering. Also called an underwriting *syndicate*. Members of the underwriting group, acting through an AGREEMENT AMONG UNDERWRITERS, purchase the offering at an agreed price for resale at the public offering price. The group signs a purchase offer, or an UNDERWRITING AGREEMENT with the issuer that defines the terms of the proposed offering, and the amount to be purchased by each member of the group. *See also* NOTE ISSUANCE FACILITY; STANDBY UNDERWRITING; TENDER PANEL.

UNDERWRITING SPREAD dollar difference between the amount paid by the UNDERWRITING GROUP in a new issue of securities and the price at which securities are offered for sale to the public. It is the underwriter's gross profit margin, usually expressed in points per unit of sale (bond or stock). Spreads may vary widely and are influenced by the underwriter's expectation of market demand for the securities offered for sale, interest rates, and so on. *See also* GROSS MARGIN; YIELD SPREAD.

UNDIVIDED INTEREST

1. unrestricted claim of ownership to the assets of a corporation or partnership, as in a joint tenant account or TENANCY IN COMMON account. Each owner has a claim to the whole asset base. *See also* JOINT TENANTS WITH RIGHT OF SURVIVORSHIP.
2. SECONDARY MARKET term for ownership in WHOLE LOANS purchased WITHOUT RECOURSE from a mortgage originator.

UNDIVIDED PROFITS cumulative earnings that have not yet been distributed to shareholders as DIVIDEND payments, or carried over to the SURPLUS account; the term excludes reserves for contingencies and loan losses. It is the equivalent of retained earnings in corporate accounting.

UNEARNED DISCOUNT finance charges received when a loan is made and recognized as income at a later date. Finance charges (called DISCOUNT INTEREST) in discount notes are deducted from the loan proceeds, or the amount actually loaned to the borrower. In accounting terms, an unearned discount is a liability on the books of the lender until the loan matures. Under ACCRUAL BASIS accounting, deferred interest is unrealized income, and is deducted from gross loans carried on a bank's books so it does not overstate earnings.

UNEARNED INTEREST interest income received by a bank, though not actually recognized as accrued, or earned income. Consumer INSTALLMENT LOANS where the finance charges are computed using the

ADD-ON INTEREST method, and DISCOUNT loans, with prepaid finance charges, are loaded in the early months with interest payments that the lender cannot count as income. If the borrower repays the loan early, part of the interest paid must be given back in a REBATE. The early interest payments gradually are amortized over the life of the loan, and credited as interest income.

Also, fees paid by either of the parties to a SWAP agreement, are unearned interest. *See also* RULE OF THE 78'S; UNEARNED DISCOUNT.

UNENCUMBERED free of creditor's liens; property with a clean title, which may be sold or conveyed to another party, and is so noted on the TITLE certificate.

UNIFORM BANK PERFORMANCE REPORT analytical survey prepared by the FEDERAL FINANCIAL INSTITUTIONS EXAMINATION COUNCIL, based on call reports filed quarterly. The report emphasizes trends in profitability, asset quality, liquidity, and asset-liability management (sources and uses of funds). The report uses financial ratios to show the impact of management decisions and changing economic conditions on a bank's balance sheet and earnings, and a bank's ability to cover losses with future earnings, ASSET QUALITY, or condition of the loan portfolio, and the adequacy of LOAN LOSS RESERVES for anticipated bad debt. The data in this report are collected by a survey of financial institutions, and shared with participating banks, though it is not publicly disclosed, unlike call report data. *See also* PEER GROUP; REPORT OF CONDITION.

UNIFORM COMMERCIAL CODE (UCC) set of standardized state laws governing financial contracts. The code was drafted by the National Conference of State Law Commissioners, and was adopted in the 1950s by most states and the District of Columbia. (Louisiana, the only state which has not fully ratified the code, has adopted Article 3 of the UCC, dealing with CHECKS, DRAFTS, and NEGOTIABLE INSTRUMENTS.) The code has nine separate sections, called articles. The most important of these are Article 3, dealing with negotiable instruments; Article 4, dealing with bank DEPOSITS and COLLECTIONS; Article 5, dealing with LETTERS OF CREDIT; Article 7, dealing with WAREHOUSE RECEIPTS and other documents of TITLE; and Article 8 and ARTICLE 9, dealing with SECURED LOANS.

The most recent addition to the UCC, Article 4A, covers corporate-to-corporate electronic payments, such as wire transfers and automated clearinghouse credit transfers, and has been adopted by most states. Article 4A does not address consumer transactions, deferring to the ELECTRONIC FUNDS TRANSFER ACT and Federal Reserve REGULATION E for regulation of consumer payments.

Adoption of the code by state legislatures made it easier for lenders to extend credit secured by PERSONAL PROPERTY, such as a firm's equipment or receivables, as opposed to MORTGAGE loans secured by real estate. The code also cleared up some ambiguities and differences in state laws, and required written contracts for sale or purchase of goods worth $500 or more. *See also* FINANCING STATEMENT; PERFECTED LIEN; SECURITY AGREEMENT; SECURITY INTEREST.

UNIFORM CONSUMER CREDIT CODE law adopted in some states setting standards for consumer credit agreements. The code, applying to consumer credit agreements and installment sales contracts for amounts under $25,000, specifies creditor's remedies when a borrower defaults, and contains borrower protections against unfair or unlawful practices by a creditor.

Several states have in addition adopted their own versions of the federal TRUTH IN LENDING ACT to protect borrowers' rights and equal access to credit.

UNIFORM FIDUCIARIES ACT *see* FIDUCIARY.

UNIFORM GIFT TO MINORS ACT law adopted in most states allowing transfers of property to a minor, supervised by an adult, usually a parent, acting as a CUSTODIAN. Gifts to minors must be irrevocable, and are taxed to the minor, not the DONOR. The custodianship ends when the child reaches legal age.

Interest and dividend income earned by a child exceeding $1,000 is taxable, under the Tax Reform Act of 1986, at the highest tax rate of the parent. This is the so-called kiddie tax, intended to discourage transfers of assets to avoid paying taxes.

UNIFORM PARTNERSHIP ACT law adopted in many states covering the distribution of assets in partnerships. Unless the partners state otherwise, they will share equally in the profits and surplus remaining after liabilities are paid. A *tenancy in partnership* similar to a joint tenant agreement is created, giving each partner the right to use jointly owned property. These rights are not assignable, and partners are not liable for personal obligations of another partner. *See also* ARTICLES OF PARTNERSHIP.

UNIFORM SETTLEMENT STATEMENT *see* HUD-1 SETTLEMENT STATEMENT.

UNINSURED DEPOSITOR depositor who has checking or savings account deposits in a federally insured bank or savings institution exceeding the FDIC insurance deposit insurance limit per depositor ($250,000 in coverage for IRA, Roth IRA, and other self-directed retirement accounts). Depositors holding accounts with principal amounts exceeding the $250,000 limit, for example, a JUMBO CERTIFICATE OF DEPOSIT, risk losing part of their principal and interest earned if the institution holding their account becomes insolvent and its assets are liquidated. The Federal Deposit Insurance Corporation is required by law—the Federal Deposit Insurance Corporation Improvement Act of 1991—to follow the least costly method of handling bank failures, which means that depositors with accounts above the insurance ceiling may suffer a loss.

Despite the limitation, it is still possible for an individual to have more than $250,000 in fully insured deposits—by owning a joint account with someone else, or by holding an account in trust for another and naming that person as beneficiary. Coverage for an INDIVIDUAL RETIREMENT ACCOUNT, ROTH IRA, or KEOGH account is treated separately from ordinary savings or deposit account.

UNITARY THRIFT company that controls a single SAVINGS AND LOAN ASSOCIATION. Unitary thrifts are similar to bank holding companies, but have broader financial powers. As thrift institutions, unitary savings and loan companies must hold at least 65% of assets in residential mortgages or mortgage securities. The GRAMM-LEACH-BLILEY ACT OF 1999 grandfathered existing unitary thrifts, but barred new charters after May 4, 1999.

UNIT BANKING banking system in several states that limits banking operation to one full-service banking office. Restrictive branching laws, most prevalent in the Midwest and the Southwest, encouraged chartering of large numbers of small, independently owned state banks, and large multibank holding companies owning numerous unit banks. Branching laws in most states have been eased, since the 1980s, permitting geographic expansion and branch banking networks across the United States. *See also* BRANCH BANKING; CHAIN BANKING.

UNIT INVESTMENT TRUST *see* INVESTMENT COMPANY.

UNIVERSAL BANKING banking system in several European countries where commercial banks make loans, underwrite corporate debt, and also take equity positions in corporate securities. In Germany, commercial banks accept time deposits, lend money, underwrite corporate stocks, and act as investment advisors to large corporations.

The advantages of this type of banking system have been debated. Universal banking permits better use of customer information and allows banks to sell more services under one roof as a FINANCIAL SUPERMARKET. The main disadvantage is that universal banking permits concentration of economic power in a handful of large banking institutions that hold equity positions in companies that are also borrowers of funds.

UNIVERSAL NUMERICAL SYSTEM *see* ABA TRANSIT NUMBER; CHECK ROUTING SYMBOL.

UNIVERSAL PAYMENT IDENTIFICATION CODE (UPIC) numeric code for processing electronic bank deposits. The code is a unique number that masks the payer's actual account number, a protection against fraudulent checks or drafts. Payments are processed through the U.S. banking system's AUTOMATED CLEARING HOUSE.

UNLAWFUL LOANS loans made for amounts in excess of the LEGAL LENDING LIMIT to a single borrower; loans made at a rate exceeding state USURY laws; insider loans to directors or officers that are made in excess of levels permitted by federal regulation; and loans that are illegal according to banking statutes. *See also* ULTRA VIRES ACTS.

UNLIMITED LIABILITY liability of general partners and sole proprietor owners of a company extending to their entire assets, including personal property. This contrasts with the limited liability of stockholders in a corporation, or the liability of limited partners in a joint venture, whose potential losses are limited to the extent of their investment.

UNLIMITED MORTGAGE *see* OPEN-END MORTGAGE.

UNLISTED SECURITY *see* OVER-THE-COUNTER.

UNMATCHED BOOK

1. asset liability imbalance that occurs when the maturity of a bank's assets differs from its balance sheet liabilities. This is also called a *mismatched maturity.* It refers to the situation where a bank's deposit liabilities have a shorter term than the assets (bank loans) funded by those liabilities. An asset liability gap can be positive or negative, depending on whether the asset maturity is shorter or longer than the liability maturity.

   In the Euromarket, the term is synonymous with *open book* or *short book*, and also applies to unmatched currency exposure, for example, owning more pound sterling liabilities than pound sterling assets. *See also* MISMATCH.
2. foreign exchange FORWARD MARKET or SPOT MARKET purchase that has not been executed, or vice versa.
3. currency trading mismatch, for example, holding more liabilities than assets in British pound sterling.

UNPAID BALANCE outstanding LOAN balance or CASH ADVANCE that is still due and payable. It may be the current balance on a loan, credit card account, or a past due balance, including late charges, if payments are missed. A balance unpaid more than 30 days may be reported as PAST DUE to a CREDIT BUREAU.

UNPERFECTED LIEN security interest in which the holder of lien has not taken all of the necessary steps to assure validity of claim, as required under the Uniform Commercial Code. This can happen when a lender fails to properly record a FINANCING STATEMENT attaching a lien to the borrower's property, fails to discover a previously filed lien in public records, or does not file a CONTINUATION STATEMENT extending an existing financing statement.

The lender risks not being able to collect the full value of its claim if its position as a secured creditor is challenged by another party. Courts generally will recognize the validity of an unperfected claim in litigation involving the lender and its borrower, but an unperfected lien may not stand up to challenge by a third party. Contrast with PERFECTED LIEN.

UNREALIZED PROFIT (OR LOSS) paper profits (or losses) from securities owned. This also called paper gain or loss. Accounting rules state that unrealized losses of marketable securities caused by a market decline must be recognized in the holder's income statement, even though the securities or futures contract have not been sold. In banking, this applies only to TRADING ACCOUNT ASSETS held by a bank for its own trading account or a third party. Paper profits in an investment portfolio or trust account are realized when the securities are sold.

UNSECURED CREDITOR general creditor of a debtor filing a VOLUNTARY BANKRUPTCY petition, who does not hold a SECURITY INTEREST in the debtor's assets or backing by a MORTGAGE. In a Chapter 7 LIQUIDATION, general creditors are paid a pro rata share of the bankruptcy ESTATE after claims of secured creditors are satisfied, which means that most general creditors can receive substantially less than the value of their claim.

UNSECURED DEBT debt offering backed only by the creditworthiness and reputation of the issuer, and not supported by COLLATERAL.

UNSECURED LOAN loan granted on the strength of the borrower's credit history or reputation in the community, earnings potential, and other assets owned, even if unpledged. Assignment of collateral, as in a MORTGAGE, is not required. The borrower signs a PROMISSORY NOTE stating the terms and conditions under which the loan will be repaid. The lender may ask a CO-MAKER or GUARANTOR to sign the note, pledging to repay the loan if the borrower defaults. Also called a *character loan* or *good faith loan. See also* FIVE C'S OF CREDIT; SIDE COLLATERAL.

UNWINDING

1. to close out a market position by executing an offsetting order canceling that position.
2. disengaging from a speculative foreign exchange FORWARD MARKET or LEADS AND LAGS position.
3. in futures, simultaneous liquidation of both short and long positions when the pricing spread between the cash and futures market closes, or returns to normal. If the spread tightens up, the long and short positions would be reversed again. Also known as *spread trading*.
4. removing a bank's WIRE TRANSFER payments to other banks in the event the bank is unable to cover its end-of-day NET SETTLEMENT obligations to other banks.

UPFRONT FEE *see* ORIGINATION FEE.

UPSTREAM

1. CORRESPONDENT bank that buys LOAN PARTICIPATIONS exceeding the legal lending limit of a community bank, also called the DOWNSTREAM bank or respondent bank. Typically, correspondent banks offer other banking services for community banks, such as check collection, foreign exchange, trading, and LETTER OF CREDIT financing.
2. loan or transfer of funds, from a subsidiary to its parent company, a term widely used in banking to denote the internal movements of funds within a bank holding company. Corporate dividends in a multi-

bank holding company are paid out of funds transferred to the holding company by its operating banks.

USABLE FUNDS *see* AVAILABLE BALANCE.

USANCE period of time between the date a bill of exchange is presented and the date it is paid. In a strict sense, the term means the time allowed by custom for bills of exchange involving two countries, which can be anywhere from two weeks to two months or longer. Today, it means the time period for which any bill is drawn, or its TENOR.

USE

1. **Banking.** The ability to draw from a bank line of credit or loan.
2. **Trusts.** An informal agreement giving beneficial ownership of property legally owned by another person; the forerunner of the modern TRUST. Differs from nominal ownership of property put in the care of a TRUSTEE for enjoyment by the BENEFICIARY named in a trust.

U.S. DEPOSITORY FEDERAL RESERVE BANK or commercial bank holding balances in safekeeping for the U.S. Treasury Department or federal agencies. The Treasury Department maintains TREASURY TAX AND LOAN ACCOUNTS in commercial banks for collection of federal taxes and licensing fees. Federal Reserve Banks also buy and hold Treasury securities that are not purchased by government securities dealers at regular Treasury auctions; the reserve banks also buy Treasuries from dealers in carrying out Federal Reserve monetary policy. *See also* TREASURY GENERAL ACCOUNT.

U-SHAPED RECOVERY economic recession and recovery with a U shape in charting—a gradual decline in employment, industrial output, and gross domestic product followed by a gradual rise back to the previous peak. *Compare with* V-SHAPED RECOVERY.

U.S. SAVINGS BOND *see* SAVINGS BOND.

U.S. TREASURY SECURITIES *see* TREASURY SECURITIES.

USURY charging loan interest higher than the rates allowed by law. Interest rates in consumer credit contracts are controlled by state law, and the highest permitted rate is called the *usury rate* or the usury ceiling. Since the early 1980s, many state legislatures relaxed statutory controls on consumer credit because such controls often make it more difficult for consumers to obtain credit. To alleviate this, and to keep banks from moving their credit card operations to states with more liberal statutes, lawmakers revised state statutes to allow interest rates to be set by market competition, rather than specified by laws. Several states have abolished usury ceilings; most states have raised the interest ceilings to encourage more rate competition among financial institutions, and most of these laws have a SUNSET CLAUSE calling for periodic review every three to five years. Some states, including New York, Delaware, and South Dakota have no limits on consumer credit.

New York does, however, have a criminal usury ceiling of 25%, a maximum rate of interest that lenders may charge on consumer credit.

State usury laws generally are enforceable only through civil suits filed by debtors claiming excessive interest charges. Most state laws have stiff penalties for illegal interest, ranging from forfeiture of interest owed on the entire loan balance, or forfeiture of both principal and interest. Commercial credit in most states is exempt from usury statutes; agricultural credit is unregulated, though not exempt from state interest rate controls.

USURY RATE *see* USURY.

UTILIZATION FEE annual fee charged by a lender against the portion of a revolving line of credit or TERM LOAN actually used by the borrower. Contrast with COMMITMENT FEE.

UTILIZATION RATE portion of a revolving line of credit actually advanced to the borrower and on which interest is paid. It is the basis for assessing the annual UTILIZATION FEE the borrower pays to maintain the line of credit.

V

VALUATION *see* APPRAISAL ASSAY; LOAN-TO-VALUE RATIO.

VALUATION RESERVE special account set up to offset changes in one or more accounts. When a bank believes a loan is uncollectible, it sets aside a portion of earnings equal in value to the estimated difference between the loan and the market value of the bad loan in the special account for LOAN LOSS RESERVES. *See also* EARMARKED RESERVES.

VALUE COMPENSATED purchase or sale of foreign currencies between two banks in which both parties agree to fix the values of the currencies exchanged at the SPOT price on the settlement date. This minimizes exchange risk, as the buyer agrees to reimburse the seller for any difference in currency values.

VALUE DATE

Banking:

1. date that a customer can use funds deposited in an account.
2. calendar date on which a transfer of funds through FEDERAL WIRE, AUTOMATED CLEARINGHOUSE, or electronic settlement network becomes available for use by the receiving bank or its customer. Fed Wire transfers are effective immediately, and are available as good funds the same day as transmitted by the sending bank. Automated Clearinghouse transactions generally are available the next day. These dates may be same day, next day, or some specified date in the future. *See also* NET SETTLEMENT.

Foreign Exchange: date on which foreign exchange bought and sold must be delivered, and the delivery price paid in local currency. This is usually two days. In the Eurobond market, it is the seventh calendar date after the transaction date. *See also* DELIVERY DATE; SPOT NEXT; TOMORROW NEXT.

VALUE DATING crediting electronic payments to a customer's account with funds available on a future date. It is used most often in DIRECT DEPOSIT programs, for example, electronic deposit of Social Security benefits into a beneficiary's account, or payroll direct deposit.

VALUE IMPAIRED loan to a foreign borrower that is rated as a NON-PERFORMING ASSET because the borrower is delinquent in interest payments six months or more. The loan is not in compliance with an INTERNATIONAL MONETARY FUND debt restructuring program and there is little immediate prospect for compliance; it has not met debt rescheduling terms for more than a year, or there is little prospect for orderly restoration of debt service in the near future.

VA MORTGAGE *see* VETERANS LOAN.

VANTAGESCORE generic CREDIT SCORING model sponsored by the three major U.S. credit reporting companies—Equifax, Experian, and

TransUnion. VantageScore, introduced in 2006, measures debt payment capability on a numeric scale from 501 to 990. A higher score indicates greater capability to take on and repay consumer debt. VantageScore was designed as an alternative to the credit scoring model developed by Fair Isaac Corporation, the original developer of credit scoring systems. VantageScores are calculated using the same credit variables as Fair Isaac (payment history, credit use, credit balances, credit history, and recent credit inquiries) but also include available credit—the unused portion of a credit line still available for spending.

VARIABLE RATE CERTIFICATE CERTIFICATE OF DEPOSIT carrying a yield set at a spread over a base rate—for example, the current 90-day CD rate—and adjusted quarterly. These were introduced in the United States in 1975. Yields are pegged to an interest rate INDEX, commodity prices, and so on. *See also* MARKET INDEX CD.

VARIABLE RATE LOAN consumer installment loan or commercial loan carrying an interest rate that fluctuates according to changes in an INDEX rate. A variable rate loan is also called *a floating rate loan.* The rate paid by the borrower may rise or fall, depending on changes in MONEY MARKET rates such as the six-month Treasury bill, or the bank PRIME RATE. Most adjustable rate consumer loans are level payment loans, and rates are revised quarterly or semiannually. If the loan rate falls, the installment NOTE is paid early; if rates rise, there is an additional BALLOON PAYMENT. Variable rate consumer loans generally are medium-term loans used in automobile financing, home improvement, home equity lines of credit, or unsecured personal loans.

Variable rate commercial loans are adjusted against changes in a BASE RATE, for example, the banker's acceptance rate or the London Interbank Offered Rate (LIBOR). The base lending rate is typically a money market rate, determined by the buyers and sellers of excess funds in the short-term credit markets. *See also* ADJUSTABLE RATE MORTGAGE.

VARIABLE RATE MORTGAGE *see* ADJUSTABLE RATE MORTGAGE.

VAULT armored storage facility meeting minimum security standards set by the Federal Reserve Board (REGULATION P). It is used for storage or safekeeping of customer valuables in SAFE DEPOSIT BOXES, a bank's portfolio of investment grade securities, such as TREASURY BONDS, and cash balances (VAULT CASH) sufficient to meet daily cash needs.

VAULT CASH cash in a bank's vault that is used for day-to-day business needs, such as cashing checks for customers. On premises cash can be counted as a portion of bank LEGAL RESERVES to meet RESERVE REQUIREMENTS of the Federal Reserve System.

VELOCITY OF MONEY number of times that money balances turn over in the economy. According to the MONETARIST theory of economics, the velocity of money should be the principal objective of Federal Reserve MONETARY POLICY. The velocity of money is computed by dividing the nation's output of goods and services (Gross Domestic Product) by the total MONEY SUPPLY (or circulating currency plus checking account deposits). Velocity of money is also influenced by interest rates. When rates are low, people hold more money in cash; when rates are rising, they put more money in interest paying investments. *See also* MONETARY POLICY; LIQUIDITY PREFERENCE THEORY.

VENDOR EXPRESS marketing name for electronic payments to vendors doing business with the federal government. The U.S. Treasury Department's Financial Management Service (FMS) is the fiscal agent for most federal agencies handling the majority of payments to government contractors. Vendor Express payments are processed through the AUTOMATED CLEARINGHOUSE system.

VENDOR SINGLE INTEREST INSURANCE see SINGLE INTEREST INSURANCE.

VENDOR'S LIEN seller's right to reclaim property sold to a buyer if the purchaser falls behind in payments, for example, a seller's lien on real estate sold through a PURCHASE MONEY MORTGAGE. Seller's liens are a carryover from common law and are relatively uncommon in the United States. *See also* MECHANIC'S LIEN.

VENTURE CAPITAL startup money invested in high-risk companies or small companies specializing in new technologies, often in return for an equity position in the firm. This is also called *risk capital.* Start-up companies generally go through three stages of financing: initial START-UP FINANCING or SEED MONEY to a newly organized company; second-tier financing or MEZZANINE LEVEL financing to firms showing potential for positive growth; and finally, an initial PUBLIC OFFERING by successful companies issuing common stock to the public. Venture capitalists recoup most of their investment in start-up companies by taking common stock WARRANTS, and by taking capital appreciation gains from stock sold at a public offering. Frequently, venture financing is arranged in tandem with a WORKING CAPITAL line of credit from a commercial bank to meet short-term borrowing needs.

VERIFICATION

Banking:

1. employer's confirmation of a borrower's annual income, requested by a lender when screening a CREDIT APPLICATION.
2. auditing procedure whereby the accuracy of bank records is checked by direct contact with customers. Verification, also called CONFIRMATION, can be positive or negative. In negative verification, a bank customer is asked only to notify the bank of bookkeeping errors; in positive verification, the customer is asked to verify an account balance as of a specific date.

3. validation of a PERSONAL IDENTIFICATION NUMBER when a bank card is used at an automated teller machine or point-of-sale terminal.
Accounting: auditor's review of financial statements by comparing journal entries to actual documents, such as cancelled checks, copies of loan documentation, and so on.

VESTED INTEREST right of beneficial interest in real or personal property, which may be deferred for enjoyment in future years. Participants in a company's defined benefit pension plan gain the right to the employer's contributions to the plan after a vesting period normally after ten years of employment. Pension funds must comply with certain Internal Revenue Service rules before they qualify as employee benefit plans eligible for special tax treatment as tax-exempt investment funds.

VETERANS LOAN education loan or MORTGAGE partially guaranteed as to repayment of principal and interest by the Department of Veterans Affairs, providing below-market financing with no down payment to veterans of the U.S. armed services. As an incentive to lenders, the Department of Veterans Affairs (formerly the Veterans Administration) guarantees 80% of 30-year residential mortgage loans against default by the borrower. Lenders may charge interest rates up to a ceiling set by the department. Veterans loans may be paid off at any time without penalty, and are assumable by another borrower at the same rate if the borrower sells a home.

VIRTUAL BANKING *see* INTERNET BANKING; MOBILE BANKING.

VISA investor-owned corporation, based in San Mateo, California, that licenses Visa service marks to financial institutions issuing Visa CREDIT and DEBIT cards, and provides net settlement services for its members through its BASE I authorization and BASE II transaction settlement networks. Formerly National BankAmericard Inc. (until 1977), Visa manages a global electronic communications network, called VisaNet, connecting financial institutions, merchant authorization terminals, and automated teller machines around the world. In recent years, Visa has expanded its operations from bank cards to electronic banking, acting as a payment processor for point-of-sale debit card and automated clearing house (ACH) transactions for financial institutions in several states. Visa member financial institutions issue Visa credit cards and Visa Check Card debit cards. *See also* MASTERCARD WORLDWIDE.

VISIBLE SUPPLY calendar of new issues of securities coming to market in the next 30 days, used as a measure of available investments in gauging market acceptance of new issues. Originally, a commodities market term, the term has been adapted to municipal bonds and other types of debt securities offered to investors. Municipal bond issues offered for sale in the dealer market are advertised in the BLUE LIST. Also called *thirty-day visible supply.*

VOIDABLE PREFERENCE transfer of assets by a debtor filing a VOLUNTARY BANKRUPTCY petition in favor of one creditor at the expense of other creditors. If the transfer was made in the 90 days prior to filing the petition, or was made in anticipation of a bankruptcy filing, the bankruptcy trustee may set aside the preference.

VOLCKER RULE section of the Dodd-Frank Act of 2010 that limits trading in securities (proprietary trading) by commercial banks and Wall Street investment banks. The Volcker Rule, named after former Federal Reserve Chairman Paul Volcker, aims to minimize conflicts of interest between banks and their customers.

VOLUME

Futures. The number of transactions in a futures contract (one side only) during a specified period of time. A market with a high number of contracts is good for trading.

Banking.

1. aggregate purchases and cash advances on a credit card program during an accounting period. Outstanding credit receivables usually are less because some cardholders will pay off their credit card bill every month.
2. dollar amount of loans booked by a lender during a calendar or reporting period.

Securities. The aggregate number of shares traded on an exchange during a given day.

VOLUNTARY TERMINATION cancellation of a swap contract by mutual agreement of the counterparties, usually involving a lump-sum payment from one party to the other.

VOLUNTARY TRUST type of living trust (an INTER VIVOS TRUST) in which the person setting up the trust (the settlor) retains legal title of the gift transferred to the beneficiary, even though the beneficiary has actual title and possession. Contrast with GIFT INTER VIVOS.

VOLUNTARY BANKRUPTCY legal proceeding whereby a debtor voluntarily files a petition for relief from creditors in a federal bankruptcy court. The debtor's property is placed in the hands of a court appointed trustee, who distributes assets to pay debts owed to creditors. A business intending to remain in operation can act as its own trustee (called a DEBTOR IN POSSESSION) if no bankruptcy trustee is named. When a petition is filed, an automatic stay prohibits creditors from making further collection efforts until a debt has been discharged, a repayment plan is accepted by creditors, or a petition is dismissed by the bankruptcy court. Individuals and businesses other than railroads, municipalities, banks, and savings institutions can file petitions under any of the three main chapters in the bankruptcy code: a Chapter 7 LIQUIDATION, in which the debtor's assets are sold to pay creditors; a Chapter 11 REORGANIZATION, normally filed by a business; or a Chapter 13 WAGE EARNER PLAN filed by persons with regular income who agree to make partial payments toward their obligations. Contrast with INVOLUNTARY BANKRUPTCY. *See also* BANKRUPTCY; CREDITORS' COMMITTEE; REAFFIRMATION; REDEMPTION.

VOLUNTARY CONVEYANCE *see* FORECLOSURE.

VOSTRO ACCOUNT account used by a bank to describe a demand deposit account maintained by a bank in a foreign country. It is the NOSTRO ACCOUNT of the other bank, and is used primarily to arrange FOREIGN EXCHANGE transfers between the respective banks.

VOTING TRUST CERTIFICATE receipt issued to shareholders of a company placing voting rights in the hands of a few individuals, who are known as *voting trustees.* Shareholders owning common stock exchange their shares for voting trust certificates giving them the same rights of ownership and equity as before, but give up the right to vote their shares during the period of time the voting trust remains in effect. A voting trust is a limited life trust, normally expiring after five years, but can be extended indefinitely by mutual agreement of shareholders and the trustees.

VOUCHER

1. document authorizing disbursement of cash to cover a liability.
2. legally acceptable evidence of debt repayment, such as, cancelled checks, remittance documents, and so on. *See also* ACQUITTANCE.

VOUCHER CHECK CHECK with a detachable form indicating the reason for payment. The endorsing party deposits the check and retains the attached stub as a record of payment. In trade credit, the amount appearing on the payment stub is the posting medium for crediting the seller's accounts receivable ledger, and the buyer's accounts payable ledger.

V-SHAPED RECOVERY economic recession and recovery with a V-shaped charting pattern—a sharp decline in employment, industrial output, and gross domestic product followed by a rapid rise to previous levels.

W

WAGE ASSIGNMENT clause in a loan agreement allowing the lender to attach a borrower's wages if the borrower defaults, without notifying the borrower.

WAGE EARNER PLAN popular name for a debt repayment plan under Chapter 13 of the Bankruptcy Code. The debtor voluntarily agrees to repay over a three- to five-year period a portion of obligations due creditors in exchange for a promise by creditors to refrain from further collection efforts. Court supervised repayment plans help debtors earning a regular income restore their credit ratings without liquidating their personal or financial assets. *See also* LIQUIDATION.

WAGE GARNISHMENT *see* GARNISHMENT.

WAITING PERIOD popular name for the SECURITIES AND EXCHANGE COMMISSION rule mandating a 20-day cooling-off period dating from the filing of the REGISTRATION STATEMENT and a preliminary PROSPECTUS. The regulatory intent is to encourage disclosure to potential investors, but not actual selling. The SEC allows the offering to clear the registration process by not objecting to anything disclosed in the registration papers. Any objection by the SEC automatically would restart the 20-day period, unless the agency has accelerated the process.

WAIVER a voluntary relinquishment of a right to property owned, claim against another's property, or to any legally enforceable right. In banking, the term has numerous meanings, such as an agreement not to charge a credit card annual fee during the first year after a new card is issued, or an agreement to forgo overdraft charges on bad checks.

WAIVER OF DEMAND *see* WAIVER OF NOTICE.

WAIVER OF EXEMPTION clause in a loan agreement whereby the borrower waives a right to exempt personal or real property from attachment or seizure in the event of default. This credit practice was prohibited by banking regulatory agencies in 1985.

WAIVER OF NOTICE

1. agreement by the endorser of a CHECK, DRAFT, or NOTE to accept legal responsibility, without being notified formally, in the event the original maker defaults. Also called *waiver of demand.*
2. waiver of a bank's customary right to be notified formally when it presents ELIGIBLE PAPER (drafts, acceptances) for REDISCOUNT at the Federal Reserve DISCOUNT WINDOW. Endorsement by the bank is legally considered a waiver of demand, notice, and protest by the Federal Reserve, should the original signer default on the notes.

WALL STREET popular name for the financial district in New York City where the New York Stock Exchange, the American Stock

Exchange, leading securities firms, and several major banks and insurance firms are located. In a more generic sense the term is broader in scope, referring to the investment banking and securities brokerage industry regardless of where the firms involved actually are located.

WARD an incompetent person or a child whose affairs are put in the hands of a GUARDIAN appointed by a court, who acts as a FIDUCIARY. The child's guardian administers the child's estate on behalf of the child until the child reaches the age of adulthood.

WAREHOUSE

1. bonded storage facility where commodities, finished goods, or works in process are under a WAREHOUSE RECEIPT. Also called a *field warehouse.*
2. swap maker's book listing inventory of swaps to be held or traded, either for other financial institutions or to profit from position taking. A FINANCIAL INSTITUTION that manages a swap book is known as a MARKET MAKER.

WAREHOUSE FINANCING *see* ASSET-BASED LENDING; INVENTORY LENDING.

WAREHOUSE RECEIPT document giving proof of ownership of goods held in inventory, for example, unfinished goods temporarily stored in a field warehouse by a manufacturer. The receipt is a TITLE document for its holder and may be negotiable or nonnegotiable. A *negotiable* warehouse receipt is deliverable to the bearer or to another party named; a *nonnegotiable* receipt specifies to whom the stored goods are deliverable. Most warehouse receipts are issued in negotiable form, making them eligible as collateral for WORKING CAPITAL loans from a bank. *See also* ASSET-BASED LENDING; INVENTORY FINANCING; UNIFORM COMMERCIAL CODE.

WAREHOUSING

1. holding of mortgages by a mortgage banker on a short-term basis until the loans are sold to an investor. The mortgage originator finances the inventory of unsold loans with a short-term line of credit, using the mortgages as loan collateral. This is used by mortgage bankers to raise working capital funds until mortgages held in inventory are sold to a permanent investor.
2. temporary storage of transactions by an AUTOMATED CLEARINGHOUSE (ACH) or a financial institution, as for corporate customers. ACH associations may hold transactions for financial institutions up to 31 days prior to the VALUE DATE when funds actually are moved.
3. pledging a MORTGAGE as collateral for short-term loans, usually called a hypothecated mortgage.
4. interest carryover in an ADJUSTABLE RATE MORTGAGE subject to a periodic rate cap. When a rise in borrowing costs exceeds the interest rate cap, lenders may defer interest payable to future time periods if allowed by the mortgage contract.

WARM CARD bank card with restricted usage. Withdrawals or deposits may be permitted, but not both. An example can be a deposit-only card, allowing merchants to deposit their daily cash receipts at a night depository and get a transaction receipt from an AUTOMATED TELLER MACHINE.

WARNING BULLETIN listing of over-limit or past-due credit card accounts and stolen cards, compiled by Visa and MasterCard. Merchants are instructed to obtain authorization before accepting the cards listed. Also called *cancellation bulletin, hot card list,* or *restricted card list. See also* ZERO-FLOOR LIMIT.

WARRANT

1. short-term interest bearing note issued by a state or local government to pay debts, repayable from a defined income source. Some examples are notes issued in anticipation of future tax revenues (a TAX ANTICIPATION NOTE) or future cash receipts (a REVENUE ANTICIPATION NOTE).
2. certificate giving the bearer the right to buy securities, gold, or other commodities at a stated price for a stated period or at any time in the future. The offered price usually is above the market price, in contrast to a rights offer of newly issued securities at below market prices. These instruments are offered to the public in negotiable form, and are traded freely on the stock exchanges. They differ from STOCK PURCHASE OPTIONS, which normally are offered only to the issuer's employees. Also called a *subscription warrant.*
3. CURRENCY WARRANT. The yield and price of the instruments covered are fixed at the time of the original sale.

WARRANTY statement, either written or implied, that assertions made in completion of a contract are true. In mortgage banking, a lender may assert that loans offered for sale to a secondary market CONDUIT meet the buyer's specifications for pooling with other loans and are not in arrears. Under a warranty agreement, the buyer has recourse against the seller. A SELLER-SERVICER of loans sold in the secondary mortgage market agrees to buy back an agreed-upon portion of losses from borrower defaults.

WARRANTY DEED deed conveying the seller's interest in real property to the buyer. The seller, also known as the GRANTOR, certifies that the title on property being conveyed is free and clear of defects, liens, and encumbrances. If a third party claim is not exempted specifically, the buyer (the grantee) may sue the seller for any resulting losses.

WASH SALE

1. sale and repurchase of securities within a short period of time to give the appearance of trading activity, sometimes done by stock manipulators to give the impression of trading activity and to raise stock prices. Sales between two people to boost prices, and induce investors to buy, are prohibited by stock exchange rules.

2. disallowed tax loss resulting from sale of a security at a loss in a 30-day period, followed by a repurchase of the same or a substantially identical security, or purchase of a call option, in the next 30 days. Internal Revenue Service rules disallow tax losses involving sale and purchase of the same or substantially identical securities within a 61-day period. To be dissimilar, securities must have different interest rates, voting power or earnings power, or, in the case of bonds, different maturities. Only traders are exempted from the IRS rule that losses from wash trading have to be recognized when the trades took place.

WASTING TRUST TRUST account that allows the TRUSTEE to use part of the trust PRINCIPAL to make payments to a BENEFICIARY if the interest income is insufficient. The term also applies to trusts that invest largely in depreciating assets such as oil and gas reserves.

WATCH LIST

1. list of banks regarded by bank examiners as having earnings problems or IMPAIRED CAPITAL. These generally are banks given a rating higher than 3 on the CAMELS RATING scale used by federal banking regulators to identify banks needing closer supervision. (A CAMELS rating is a composite score, based on six criteria: Capital, Assets, Management, Earnings, Liquidity, and Sensitivity to market risk). A CAMELS rating of 4 or 5 indicates financial weaknesses in the balance sheet, such as a higher ratio of nonperforming loans to total assets than banks of similar size. If uncorrected, these problems could impair a bank's future viability. A bank placed on the watch list is considered a PROBLEM BANK, and is examined more frequently by bank supervisory agencies than other banks. (In contrast, a bank given a CAMELS rating of 1 is a bank with strong earnings and few nonperforming assets.) In any event, a CAMELS rating is never disclosed publicly.
2. list of banks issuing CERTIFICATES OF DEPOSIT to the secondary market that have potentially weak balance sheets, compiled by credit rating agencies, such as Standard & Poor's.
3. list of countries whose ability to meet debt service payments on external debt is followed closely by federal banking agencies for changes in financial condition. The list, a rating of COUNTRY RISK associated with loans to developing countries, is compiled by the Interagency Country Exposure Review Committee, whose members are drawn from the Federal Reserve Board, the Comptroller of the Currency, and the Federal Deposit Insurance Corporation.
4. any list of loans or credit exposures compiled by a bank for internal monitoring. This could be a maturity tickler of time loans maturing in the next 30 days and commercial loans with a perfected SECURITY INTEREST due to expire in the next six months, unless renewed.

WEAK CURRENCY currency said to be a less desirable form of payment than other currencies. Weak currency countries have frequent currency devaluations against currencies of major trading partners, balance of payment deficits, or political instability. These currencies generally trade at a discount in relation to currencies of economically developed countries. Foreign exchange dealers generally do not make markets in weak currencies, except for currency speculation. A dealer who expects a weak currency to decline in value may sell that currency short, making a profit from the difference in exchange rates.

Acceptability of one currency versus another is dependent, of course, on local market conditions. Contrast with STRONG CURRENCY.

WEAK MARKET *see* THIN MARKET.

WEDNESDAY SCRAMBLE last-minute buying or selling of FEDERAL FUNDS on the day that banks report their deposit account balances subject to RESERVE REQUIREMENTS. Banks temporarily short of reserves make up the shortfall by buying overnight funds—Fed Funds—from a bank with EXCESS RESERVES. Federal Funds purchased ordinarily are returned to the selling bank at the opening of business the following day.

WEIGHTED AVERAGE COUPON (WAC) weighted average of the underlying COUPON interest rates of mortgage loans or other loans backing ASSET-BACKED SECURITIES or MORTGAGE-BACKED SECURITIES, as of the issue date, using the balance of each mortgage as the weighting factor. This calculation is used only when the underlying loans have variable interest rates. WAC is computed by multiplying the coupon rate of each mortgage or mortgage-backed security by its remaining balance, adding the products, and dividing the result by the remaining balance.

WEIGHTED AVERAGE LIFE *see* AVERAGE LIFE.

WEIGHTED AVERAGE MATURITY (WAM) weighted AVERAGE LIFE of the remaining terms to maturity of the underlying loans of a mortgage certificate at the issue date, using the balance of each loan as the weighting factor. Weighted average maturity is computed by multiplying the maturity of each mortgage in a given pool by its remaining balance, adding the products, and dividing the result by the remaining balance.

WEIGHTED AVERAGE REMAINING TERM (WART) remaining maturity of MORTGAGE-BACKED SECURITIES or ASSET-BACKED SECURITIES at any given point in their life, measured in months. It is affected by prepayments and must be adjusted monthly. The weighting factor is each loan in the pool.

WHAT-IF CALCULATION forecasting computation that allows testing of different hypotheses for repricing assets and acquiring funds. These hypothetical calculations usually are executed with a spreadsheet program using a microcomputer. In asset-liability management, a what-if calculation can estimate the difference between maturing assets and liabilities for different time periods in the future. These models also can forecast changes in pro forma financial statements under different interest rate scenarios, and are an analytical tool used in credit analysis. *See also* STRESS TEST.

WHEN ISSUED securities term for *when and if issued*, referring most often to conditional trading in bonds or other securities in the interval between the announcement date and the actual date of issue. Securities dealers trade offerings of new securities, stock splits, and government securities, among others, in the period before the effective listing date. Although the U.S. Treasury Department tries to discourage trading in Treasury securities on a when issued basis, government securities dealers frequently can arrange preauction bond swaps (yield swaps) for the issue to be offered for sale.

WHOLE LOANS loan sold in its entirety, without any participation kept by the seller. The investor assumes all contractual rights and responsibilities, and may pay the seller a SERVICING fee for collecting principal and interest payments. The purchase price usually is discounted when the mortgage COUPON is below current market rates.

WHOLE POOLS mortgage PARTICIPATION CERTIFICATE representing an UNDIVIDED INTEREST in an entire pool of MORTGAGE loans, rather than a pro rata share, or fractional interest, in the loans packaged for sale to an investor.

WHOLESALE BANKING banking services offered to corporations with sound financial statements, and institutional customers, such as pension funds and government agencies. Services include lending, cash management, commercial mortgages, working capital loans, leasing, trust services, and so on. Most banks divide wholesale banking into several different businesses: the Fortune 500 and Fortune 1000 market, composed of the 500 and 1,000 largest U.S. corporations, respectively; the Middle Market; and the small business market.

Commercial banks, responding to increased market competition from alternative financing sources, such as commercial paper and junk bonds, have begun to place more emphasis on fee-based corporate services, including foreign exchange and securities trading, advisory services in corporate mergers, and acquisitions, merchant banking, and corporate cash management, and securities underwriting. *See also* COMMERCIAL AND INDUSTRIAL (C&I) LOAN; COMMERCIAL MORTGAGE; INVESTMENT ADVISOR; LEVERAGED BUYOUT; NONCREDIT SERVICES; SECURITIES SUBSIDIARY; SECURITIZATION.

WIDOW'S ALLOWANCE allowance of personal property made by a court or by statute to give a widow sufficient funds from an ESTATE for household expenses during the period immediately following her husband's death.

WIDOW'S EXEMPTION allowed deduction from state inheritance taxes, claimed by a widow for her share of her deceased husband's estate.

WILDCAT BANKING period in the first half of the 19th century when state chartered banks issued their own banknotes (paper money). Many of these banks were organized more for the purpose of issuing banknotes than for taking deposits or making loans, and many failed. Wildcat banks got their name because many were found in hard-to-reach areas, where the "wildcats" lived.

WILL formal document distributing the assets of an estate after the death of the person signing it—the TESTATOR. A will is usually written, signed by the testator in the presence of two or more witnesses. Most states also allow handwritten or holographic wills if signed in the presence of the testator by two or more witnesses. Preparing a will has several advantages over leaving an estate INTESTATE: the testator can designate how the estate will be distributed and can establish a TESTAMENTARY TRUST for the benefit of children. A will also allows property or real estate owned by the testator to be sold more easily. *See also* INTER VIVOS TRUST; TRUST.

WINDOW

1. market opportunity for new loans or other combination of events that must be acted upon, or lost forever.
2. Federal Reserve DISCOUNT WINDOW, so named because bankers used to apply in person at a Federal Reserve Bank teller window for short-term credit advances.
3. period during the day when AUTOMATED CLEARING HOUSE or WIRE TRANSFER payments may be submitted to a Federal Reserve Bank, clearing house, or other processing organization for settlement between banks. *See also* CUT-OFF TIME.

WINDOW DRESSING special adjustments in financial position to give the appearance of adequate liquidity, often to comply with reporting requirements. It gives the appearance of a healthy balance sheet, whereas actual conditions may state otherwise. An organization might buy U.S. Treasury securities and other cash equivalent securities to build up its cash position.

Window dressing, or sprucing up the balance sheet, takes place just before the statement date, for example, at the end of a fiscal year or quarter, and is intended to add size to the financial institution. Mutual funds sell off securities not preferred by the public, and purchase securities preferred by the public. Fund managers sell junk bonds held for yield, in favor of investment grade securities for appearance.

WIRE FATE ITEM checks, notes, or drafts sent to an out-of-town bank with instructions to notify by wire, usually FEDERAL WIRE, as to whether they were paid or not. Notification tells the sending bank when the check actually was paid, which is especially useful if the check is written for a large amount or if the check is being handled as a NONCASH ITEM.

WIRE TRANSFER order to pay funds electronically by wire or telephone instruction, usually involving a large dollar payment. The Federal Reserve Wire Network (FEDERAL WIRE), and the CLEARING HOUSE INTERBANK PAYMENTS SYSTEM (CHIPS) are wire transfer payment systems. The Federal Reserve Wire Network links Federal Reserve offices, depository institutions, the U.S. Treasury, and other government agencies. It transfers funds, U.S. government securities, and Federal Reserve administrative, supervisory, and monetary policy messages. *See also* AUTOMATED CLEARINGHOUSE; AVAILABILITY; BANK WIRE; ELECTRONIC FUNDS TRANSFER; NET SETTLEMENT; SAME DAY FUNDS; SOCIETY FOR WORLDWIDE INTERBANK FINANCIAL TELECOMMUNICATIONS (SWIFT).

WITHDRAWAL

1. taking funds out of a deposit account by writing a CHECK, DRAFT, or withdrawal slip in the case of a time deposit or savings deposit. Certain time deposits and certificates of deposit require a NOTICE OF WITHDRAWAL before funds are withdrawn in cash or transferred to another account. These may also be subject to an EARLY WITHDRAWAL PENALTY or forfeiture of interest.
2. substituting new collateral securing a COLLATERAL LOAN, allowing the borrower to take back the original collateral pledged.

WITHDRAWAL NOTICE *see* NOTICE OF WITHDRAWAL.

WITHDRAWAL PENALTY *see* EARLY WITHDRAWAL PENALTY.

WITH EXCHANGE writing on a CHECK or DRAFT specifying that any collection costs above the face value are payable by the drawee of the check, or the payer of the draft being presented for payment. Sometimes written "payable with exchange."

WITH FULL RECOURSE clause in an ASSET SALES agreement whereby a bank selling WHOLE LOANS or LOAN PARTICIPATIONS to an investor agrees to fully reimburse the investor for losses resulting from the purchased loans, for example, by taking back any loans that become delinquent in principal and interest payments.

WITHHOLDING *see* BACKUP WITHHOLDING.

WITH INTEREST bonds or securities paying accrued interest to the bearer. When sold, the buyer pays any interest accrued since the last payment date, in addition to the market price.

WITHOUT expression for a market characterized by the absence of either bids or offers, indicating a one-way market. If XYZ at $50 was the bid, and there was no offer, the quote would be $50 without. This is usually a market where rising prices are expected.

WITHOUT RECOURSE

In general: phrase meaning that credit risk, or risk of nonpayment, is assumed by the buyer, rather than the seller, of a promissory note or the holder of a negotiable instrument. In negotiable instruments law, the endorser of a check or draft cannot be held accountable for payment to subsequent holders in the event the MAKER or DRAWER fails to pay if the endorsement contains the words "without recourse." Such an endorsement is a qualified endorsement under Article 3 of the Uniform Commercial Code. *See also* HOLDER IN DUE COURSE.

Banking:

1. financing arrangement or dealer FLOOR PLANNING in which the dealer's liability is limited to warranties about the quality of the installment contracts, which the lender purchases at a discount. Defective installment contracts are not charged back automatically to the dealer. A nonrecourse plan may, however, require the dealer to assist in repossessions and collections of delinquent accounts. *See also* NONRECOURSE LOAN.
2. language in a SECONDARY MARKET sale of loans, certificates of deposit, and so on, in which the seller is under no obligation to reimburse the investor for any losses suffered. Transactions where the buyer can ask for compensation are regarded by bank regulators as *financings* and do not qualify as sales of assets; the loans or deposits involved must remain on the seller's balance sheet.

Finance: financing agreement in ASSET-BASED LENDING, common in FACTORING, whereby the lending institution cannot charge back unpaid invoices caused by the account debtor's financial instability.

WITH RIGHT OF SURVIVORSHIP joint tenant account in which assets of either owner pass to the other tenant when either tenant dies, rather than to the owner's heirs.

WON monetary unit of South Korea and North Korea.

WORKING CAPITAL

1. current assets of an organization, especially cash, accounts receivable, and inventory. Definitions of the term vary. An alternative definition is net working capital, or the excess of current assets over current liabilities. A firm's working capital ratio (current assets divided by current liabilities) is a measure of its liquidity. Also called *liquid capital.*
2. earning assets of an organization, including marketable securities, receivables, and inventory, which can be converted to cash if needed.

WORKING CAPITAL LOAN short-term business loan financing the purchase of income-generating assets, principally inventory. Working capital loans are generally written with lending terms requiring full payment within a specified period, such as 60 days or 90 days from the date the funds are advanced.

WORKING RESERVES *see* FREE RESERVES.

WORKOUT AGREEMENT mutual agreement by borrower and lender to reschedule loan payments, modify payment terms by extending the original maturity, and so on. This normally is done in lieu of FORECLOSURE action, in which the lender attempts to sell at auction any loan collateral pledged by the borrower. Loans in this stage of negotiations already are covered fully by loan loss reserves and have been written off as BAD DEBT. By negotiating new terms with the borrower, the lender expects to collect more from recoveries than from legal remedies, such as foreclosure, liquidation, and bankruptcy. *See also* CREDITORS' COMMITTEE; STAND STILL AGREEMENT; TROUBLED DEBT RESTRUCTURING.

WORLD BANK *see* INTERNATIONAL BANK FOR RECONSTRUCTION AND DEVELOPMENT.

WORLD BANK GROUP collective name for the INTERNATIONAL BANK FOR RECONSTRUCTION AND DEVELOPMENT (the World Bank) and its affiliates: the International Finance Corporation, organized in 1950 to provide long-term project financing to developing countries; and the International Development Association, formed in 1960 to make long-term (up to 50 years) loans at low interest rates. The International Development Association is supported by periodic contributions from World Bank member countries. The World Bank itself raises capital for lending by selling bonds in the capital markets of member countries and from direct contributions of member governments. *See also* SOFT LOAN.

WORN CURRENCY circulating money retired from use as it wears out. The average life of a $1 bill, the most widely circulated FEDERAL RESERVE NOTE, is about 15 to 18 months. Currency no longer fit for use as LEGAL TENDER is removed from circulation and burned by Federal Reserve Banks. Mutilated or partially destroyed currency is redeemable at full face value if more than half the original note is intact.

WRAP ACCOUNT brokerage account placing assets managed by several investment advisors under a single account relationship. In a wrap account, all administrative and management fees, including broker commissions, are rolled into one comprehensive fee, which is paid quarterly. Wrap fees generally vary from 1% up to 3% of the assets managed.

Wrap accounts provide a convenient way for investors to spread their assets over an assortment of mutual funds and have access to top money managers. The broker selects funds matching the investor's ASSET ALLOCATION objective for risk and investment return and receives an ongoing fee to monitor the account. The mix of funds in the investor's portfolio is adjusted, or rebalanced, periodically to stay within original investment objective.

WRAPAROUND MORTGAGE financing arrangement in which an existing mortgage is refinanced, and additional money loaned at an interest rate between the rate charged on the old loan and current market rates. The lender, who agrees to pass through part of the loan payments to the original mortgage lender, combines or wraps the remainder of the old loan with the new loan, and the borrower makes one monthly payment. Wraparound loans generally earn a higher yield for the lender than new mortgage loans because the wraparound lender advances only the difference between the unpaid first mortgage and the combined principal of the two loans, but the wraparound rate is computed on the borrower's total debt. A wraparound mortgage is an alternative to refinancing the entire loan when a borrower needs additional funds.

WRITE DOWN revaluation of securities, loans, or other assets when the market value is lower than the book value at which the asset is carried. Marketable securities carried as TRADING ACCOUNT ASSETS for a bank's trading account or held for other institutions must be adjusted to market value (MARK TO THE MARKET) daily, by either writing down or writing up. Loans and leases are carried to maturity at the original book value, unless a bank is required to write down their value by a banking regulatory agency.

WRITE OFF

1. accounting process whereby a loan determined to be a worthless asset is removed from the books as an earning asset and charged to the LOAN LOSS RESERVES account. Its book value is written down to zero.
2. process of removing a BAD DEBT or uncollectible loan from the balance sheet.

WRITER

1. DRAWER of a check, also called the maker.
2. person who sells an OPTION contract, an agreement to buy (a CALL OPTION), or to sell (a PUT OPTION), a specified amount of securities, currency, or commodities at a specified price at a designated future date.

WRIT OF ATTACHMENT legal document placing a borrower's assets under the control of a court order, for example, when a bank initiates foreclosure action for nonpayment of debt. Basically, this is a property execution that attaches to assets of a corporation, as distinct from a wage GARNISHMENT, which applies to individuals.

WRITTEN NOTICE

1. consumer protection clause in the TRUTH IN LENDING ACT stating that consumers have to be notified in writing of any changes in credit terms. This notice may be included in the periodic billing statement, as for example, a change in the method of computing the interest rate in a credit card account. *See also* REGULATION B; REGULATION Z.

2. notice that banks may legally require from customers before paying DRAFTS from a NEGOTIABLE ORDER OF WITHDRAWAL (NOW) account. *See also* NOTICE OF WITHDRAWAL.

WRONGFUL DISHONOR failure to pay a CHECK or DRAFT properly endorsed and presented for payment. Under the UNIFORM COMMERCIAL CODE, the payer bank has until midnight of the day after it receives a check to pay or DISHONOR it. A bank may return a check with a missing signature or altered date, without penalty. If, however, the DRAWEE (the person presenting the check) suffers financially because of the bank's refusal to HONOR an otherwise payable check, the bank may be liable to its customer for damages. The customer must be able to present proof of financial harm. *See also* PROTEST.

W-SHAPED RECOVERY recession and recovery with a W chart pattern—a sharp decline in employment, industrial output, and gross domestic product followed in succession by recovery in these economic indicators, another sharp decline, and a sharp rise. The middle section of the W may indicate a major bear market in securities' prices or a recovery stifled by another economic crisis.

X

X-MARK SIGNATURE signature made by a person unable to sign his or her own name. To be legally valid, the signature must be witnessed by another person.

X9 financial standards committee of the AMERICAN NATIONAL STANDARDS INSTITUTE, a voluntary association, that sets financial industry payment standards for banks and other depository financial institutions. Its members include banks, retailers, equipment suppliers, and federal agencies. The American Bankers Association acts as secretariat for the X9 committee.

X12 uniform standard for interindustry electronic interchange of business transactions. The X12 committee of the AMERICAN NATIONAL STANDARDS INSTITUTE develops and fosters standards for electronic interchange of trade-related transactions, such as order placement and processing, invoicing, payments, and cash application data. The Data Interchange Standards Association, Inc. in Falls Church, Virginia, is secretariat for the X12 standards committee. *See also* ELECTRONIC DATA INTERCHANGE.

Y

YANKEE BOND dollar denominated bond issued in the United States by foreign banks and corporations. These bonds, the U.S. equivalent of the EUROBOND, pay semiannual interest, unlike Eurobonds, which pay annual interest, and are registered with the Securities and Exchange Commission. They ordinarily are issued when the domestic market is more favorable to investors than the Euromarket, and offer the foreign investor some degree of protection against fluctuating exchange rates. *See also* INTERNATIONAL BANKING FACILITY; YANKEE CERTIFICATE OF DEPOSIT.

YANKEE CERTIFICATE OF DEPOSIT negotiable TIME DEPOSIT issued in the United States by a foreign borrower, usually in denominations of $1 million to $5 million. These certificates pay a fixed or variable rate of interest for a specified maturity, usually under 12 months, and are sold directly or through dealers. They are unsecured obligations of the issuing institution. *See also* YANKEE BOND.

YEN monetary unit of Japan.

YEN BOND any bond denominated in yen, usually issued in the Japanese money market. There are several types of yen bonds. If issued in the Euromarket it is called a Euroyen bond. Yen-denominated bonds issued in Japan to non-Japanese investors are priced by the four major Japanese securities firms, and are known as SAMURAI BONDS. (Contrast with foreign currency Shogun bonds issued in Japan to both Japanese and foreign investors.) A 1984 accord between the U.S. Treasury Department and the Japanese Ministry of Finance was instrumental in opening up the yen market to non-Japanese issuers. *See also* EUROBOND.

YIELD return on a loan or investment, stated as a percentage of price. Yield can be computed by dividing return by purchase price, by current market value, or by any other measure of value. In interest-earning investments, such as bank loans or deposits, yield is interest revenue earned divided by the average balance. In fixed income securities, such as bonds, yields fluctuate as bond prices rise or fall, which means that current yields will differ from redemption yields on the same investments.

1. **Banking.** The return earned by a loan portfolio expressed as a percentage. Yield is computed by multiplying the outstanding balances by the ANNUAL PERCENTAGE RATE paid by the borrowers. PREPAYMENTS and CHARGE-OFFS of bad loans will, however, reduce the portfolio return.
2. **Investments.** The income from a BOND, interest-bearing NOTE, or TIME DEPOSIT, expressed as an annualized percentage rate. The nominal yield is calculated from the amount invested multiplied by

the interest rate paid and the maturity (interest = principal × rate × time). The EFFECTIVE ANNUAL YIELD on a time deposit takes into consideration the effect of interest rate COMPOUNDING on the invested principal balance. CURRENT YIELD on a bond is the current COUPON rate of interest in semiannual interest payments, without taking into account whether the bond price is at a premium or a discount in relation to par value. Net YIELD TO MATURITY is based on the amount payable at maturity, taking into consideration accretion of purchase price discount (or amortization of premium), plus coupon interest payments. *See also* AVERAGE LIFE; BOND EQUIVALENT YIELD; DISCOUNT; TOTAL RETURN; YIELD CURVE.

3. **Securities.** The dividends paid to holders of common or preferred stock as of the dividend paying date, measured as a percentage of current market value. The dividend yield, a ratio comparing the dividend rate to the market price per share of common stock, is computed by the following formula:

   dividend yield = annual dividend per share / market price

   Thus, a stock selling at $30, paying a $2 annual dividend, has a dividend yield of 6.6%.

YIELD BASIS method of quoting the yield on securities that states income earned as a percent, rather than as a dollar amount. MUNICIPAL BONDS issued in different SERIES (as part of a SERIAL BOND) and maturing on different dates, and thus having different prices, are sometimes quoted this way for purposes of comparison, as are railroad equipment trust certificates, and Government National Mortgage Association (Ginnie Mae) securities. *See also* DOLLAR BOND.

YIELD CURVE graph showing the comparative yields of securities in a particular class, such as Treasury securities, according to maturity. By depicting the market yield on the vertical axis and the maturity on the horizontal axis, yield comparisons between short-term instruments and long-term instruments are made more easily. The yield curve for U.S. Treasury securities, comparing securities from 3 months to 30 years in maturity, is the benchmark for comparing yields of other fixed income investments. Corporate bonds, mortgage-backed bonds, and asset-backed bonds are described as having a yield spread, measured in basis points, over Treasury securities.

Under ordinary conditions the yield curve slopes upward to the right, called a normal yield curve or a POSITIVE YIELD CURVE because long-term investments pay higher yields than short-term instruments and borrowers are (supposedly) willing to pay a premium for long-term funds. When the yield curve is positive, no radical changes in rates are expected.

When short-term rates rise above long-term rates, an INVERTED YIELD CURVE or negative yield curve results. Inverted yield curves are characterized by unstable financial conditions, and occur during periods of TIGHT MONEY, when the Federal Reserve drains reserves from the banking system to cool inflationary pressures in the economy.

Under such conditions, lenders resist making long-term loans. A flat yield curve is a sign that investors are undecided about which direction rates are moving. *See also* EXPECTATIONS THEORY; HUMPED YIELD CURVE; LIQUIDITY PREFERENCE THEORY; MARKET SEGMENTATION THEORY; YIELD TO AVERAGE LIFE; YIELD TO CALL; YIELD TO MATURITY.

YIELD EQUIVALENCE restatement of rates paid by tax-exempt state and local bonds to arrive at a YIELD that nearly is identical to the after-tax returns on taxable bonds. This is done for clarity in fiscal year reporting, and takes into account the holder's current tax rate to arrive at a yield quote matching the after-tax return on fully taxable securities.

YIELD SPREAD PREMIUM Payment to a mortgage broker by a lender for originating and processing a mortgage loan with a fractionally higher interest rate (called an above-par loan) in exchange for lower upfront costs. Also called *premium pricing* or *volume-based compensation.*

YIELD TO AVERAGE LIFE annualized percentage return on a bond substituting the AVERAGE LIFE maturity for stated final maturity. This often is used in pricing mortgage-backed securities, such as, COLLATERALIZED MORTGAGE OBLIGATIONS, where PREPAYMENT of the underlying mortgages can influence the investor's return, and bonds with SINKING FUND provisions allowing the issuer to buy back, or redeem, its own bonds. *See also* WEIGHTED AVERAGE MATURITY; WEIGHTED AVERAGE REMAINING TERM.

YIELD TO CALL annualized percentage return on a bond or note redeemed by the issuer at the earliest possible CALL date. When a security can be called by the issuer at the first call date allowed by the bond INDENTURE, the annualized yield to that date is often substituted for the YIELD TO MATURITY in yield quotations. Although some longer-term U.S. Treasury bonds are callable five years prior to final maturity, as indicated by the hyphenated quote in bond tables, in practice few, if any, Treasury securities have been called prior to maturity. The term *yield to first call* is used when a bond issue is trading at a premium over the call price and the investor would lose capital. The yield to first call, taking this loss into account, usually is lower than the yield to final call.

Yield to par is used to describe the yield on securities that are issued at a discount or premium in relation their nominal value, or PAR VALUE and are callable at par. *See also* ADVANCE REFUNDING.

YIELD TO MATURITY annualized percentage return of a bond held until its stated maturity. This is a commonly accepted method of comparing yields on bonds with different coupon interest rates, because it assumes that interest income will be reinvested at the current yield and it takes into account any adjustments for bond premium or discount. For this reason it differs from CURRENT YIELD, which may be higher or lower.

Yield to maturity quotes may also differ from an investor's actual return at maturity because they assume constant reinvestment of interest at the currently quoted yield. This may or may not be accurate if the bonds are sold at prices above, or below, their face value, or PAR VALUE. For easy reference, the yield to maturity of a given bond can be found in the bond tables prepared by financial publishers. Certain types of programmable calculators can also be used to compute yield to maturity. Also called *effective rate of return. See also* BOND EQUIVALENT YIELD; DURATION; YIELD TO AVERAGE LIFE; YIELD TO CALL.

YUAN (RENMINBI YUAN) monetary unit of the People's Republic of China.

Z

ZAIRE monetary unit of Zaire.

Z-BOND *see* ACCRUAL BOND; TRANCHE.

ZERO-BALANCE ACCOUNT checking account used by corporations to accelerate collection of funds from subsidiaries, or control funds disbursed to pay trade creditors. In a zero-balance collection account, collected balances are transferred by DEPOSITORY TRANSFER CHECK or automated clearing house debit from subsidiary accounts into a central CONCENTRATION ACCOUNT, bringing the collecting account to a zero balance at the end of each business day. Zero-balance concentration accounts are generally used by companies wanting centralized control of cash receipts. In a zero-balance disbursing account, corporate funds are transferred from a master account in an amount sufficient to cover checks presented for payment. Zero-balance disbursement accounts are typically used by companies that want centralized cash control but decentralized funds disbursement.

ZERO-COUPON CD CERTIFICATE OF DEPOSIT issued at a discount from the principal amount payable to the holder at maturity, expressed as a discount per $1,000 of principal. Also called a *discount CD.*

ZERO-COUPON CONVERTIBLE BOND

1. single payment bond, sold at an original issue discount, that may be exchanged for COMMON STOCK of the issuer when the securities reach a specific price.
2. single payment MUNICIPAL BOND carrying a conversion feature allowing the holder to switch to a regular interest coupon paying bond after a specific number of years.

ZERO-COUPON MORTGAGE long-term commercial MORTGAGE that defers all payments of principal and interest until maturity. The loan is structured as an accrual note; interest due is rolled into the outstanding principal. At maturity, the borrower must either pay off the note or refinance at current interest rates. The lender arranging financing gets a discounted internal rate of return; the borrower can finance a commercial project with a smaller cash flow, on the expectation that appreciation of the property value over the life of the loan will be sufficient to pay off the loan.

ZERO-COUPON SECURITY debt security, sold at a deep discount from its face value, that pays no interest during its stated life. The holder, in effect, receives interest in one lump sum at maturity. Interest payments are represented by the accretion from the original sale price to redemption at par. This interest deferral is attractive to investors who are not taxed on current income, for example, those investing in tax-deferred savings plans, such as an INDIVIDUAL RETIREMENT

ACCOUNT, Keogh accounts, and so on, or who expect that bond interest when paid will be offset by future expenses, for example, college tuition expenses.

Annual interest earned is treated by the IRS as taxable income, even though there is no cash payment of interest. Thus, the appeal of zero-coupon securities lies in the fact that these securities eliminate REINVESTMENT RISK, or risk of market rates rising or falling, because the interest earned is determined in advance by the interest accruals. Zero-coupon bonds, however, are more volatile in yield than bonds paying coupon interest semiannually.

A number of zero-coupon securities have been issued in recent years. Examples are stripped securities, such as U.S. Treasury STRIPS (Separate Trading of Registered Interest and Principal of Securities), which actually are created by dealers who turn back large blocks of Treasury securities for stripping. The Treasury Department separates the bond CORPUS from interest COUPONS, exchanging the whole-coupon securities for U.S. Treasury STRIPS. Synthetic zero-coupon securities are issued by dealers who separate the principal of Treasury bonds from semiannual interest payments and sell the two pieces separately. A trust receipt is issued to the holder of these discounted securities. Among synthetic strips issued are Certificates of Accrual on Treasury Securities (CATS), Treasury Income Growth Receipts, and ZEBRAs (Zero-coupon Eurosterling Bearer with Registered Accruing Securities) issued in the U.K. Treasury STRIPs are also transferable in BOOK ENTRY SECURITY form, making them slightly more liquid than synthetic strips.

Other variations of the discount, single payment investment are the zero-coupon certificate of deposit, zero-coupon municipal bond, and the ZERO-COUPON MORTGAGE. *See also* ZERO-COUPON CONVERTIBLE BOND.

ZERO-FLOOR LIMIT retail point-of-sale authorization system in which all bank card transactions are approved by checking the transactions against either the outstanding balance due or the WARNING BULLETIN listing over limit or past due accounts. *See also* FLOOR LIMIT; NEGATIVE AUTHORIZATION; POSITIVE AUTHORIZATION.

ZERO GAP condition where a bank's INTEREST SENSITIVE ASSETS and INTEREST SENSITIVE LIABILITIES are balanced perfectly for a given time period. This state of equilibrium occurs when maturities of assets and liabilities subject to repricing are matched evenly. In reality, this rarely happens because the dynamics of a competitive market make it difficult to match maturities of deposits and loans (a process called matched funding), and because banks, as credit intermediaries, have to take some maturity risk when they make loans. Banks can, however, control the INTEREST RATE RISK created by maturity imbalances by engaging in HEDGING tactics such as FINANCIAL FUTURES and interest rate SWAPS.

ZERO-INTEREST LOAN *see* ZERO-COUPON MORTGAGE.

ZERO PROOF manual bookkeeping procedure in which posting entries are subtracted, one by one, from an ending balance. The posting entries balance out when a balance of zero is reached, indicating the account entries have been entered correctly. This method of proof is sometimes used by bank tellers to reconcile posting errors, also known as a *teller's difference.*

ZLOTY monetary unit of Poland.

ZOMBIE BANK bank or financial company with a large amount of nonperforming assets or a negative net worth. Zombie banks, despite their weakened financial condition, may continue operating under government supervision to prevent a wider economic panic. *See also* BAILOUT; TOO BIG TO FAIL.

ABBREVIATIONS AND ACRONYMS

ABA	American Bankers Association
ACH	Automated Clearing House
ACRS	Accelerated Cost Recovery System
ACU	Asian Currency Unit
ADR	American Depositary Receipt
AIB	American Institute of Banking
AID	Agency for International Development
AMEX	American Stock Exchange
AMI	Alternative Mortgage Instrument
ANSI	American National Standards Institute
APR	Annual Percentage Rate
ARM	Adjustable Rate Mortgage
ATM	Automated Teller Machine
ATRR	Allocated Transfer Risk Reserve
ATS	Automatic Transfer Service
AVM	Automated Valuation Model
BAN	Bond Anticipation Note
BIC	Bank Investment Contract
BIF	Bank Insurance Fund
BIN	Bank Identification Number
BIS	Bank for International Settlements
CAB	Controlled Amortization Bond
C&I	Commercial and Industrial
CAMELS	Credit, Assets, Management, Earnings, Liquidity, and Sensitivity
CAPM	Capital Asset Pricing Model
CAT	Customer Activated Terminal
CATS	Certificate of Accrual on Treasury Securities
CBO	Collateralized Bond Obligation
CCD	Cash Concentration & Disbursement
CD	Certificate of Deposit
CDO	Collateralized Debt Obligation
CFTC	Commodities Futures Trading Commission
CHAPS	Clearing House Automated Payments System
CHIPS	Clearing House Interbank Payments System
CIE	Customer Initiated Entry
CIF	Customer Information File
CINS	CUSIP International Numbering System
CLF	Central Liquidity Facility
CLO	Computerized Loan Origination
CLTV	Combined Loan-to-Value Ratio
CMBS	Commercial Mortgage-Backed Securities

CMO	Collateralized Mortgage Obligation
COFI	Cost of Funds Index
CPP	Constant Percent Prepayment
CPR	Conditional Prepayment Rate
CPR	Constant Prepayment Rate
CRA	Community Reinvestment Act
CSBS	Conference of State Bank Supervisors
CSR	Customer Service Representative
CTP	Corporate Trade Payment
CTR	Currency Transaction Report
CTX	Corporate Trade Exchange
CUSIP	Committee on Uniform Securities Identification Procedures
D&B	Dun & Bradstreet
DES	Data Encryption Standard
DIDC	Depository Institutions Deregulation Committee
DIDMCA	Depository Institutions Deregulation & Monetary Control Act
DSCR	Debt Service Coverage Ratio
DTC	Depository Transfer Check
DTC	Depository Trust Company
DVP	Delivery Versus Payment
EBP&P	Electronic Bill Payment & Presentment
ECOA	Equal Credit Opportunity Act
ECU	European Currency Unit
EDI	Electronic Data Interchange
EDIFACT	EDI for Administration, Finance, Commerce and Transportation
EEC	European Economic Community
EFT	Electronic Funds Transfer
EMU	European Monetary Union
ESA	Education Savings Account
ESOP	Employee Stock Ownership Plan
ETA	Electronic Transfer Account
ETC	Export Trading Company
FA	Federal Association
FASB	Financial Accounting Standards Board
FCIA	Foreign Credit Insurance Association
FCM	Futures Commission Merchant
FCS	Farm Credit System
FCU	Federal Credit Union
FDIC	Federal Deposit Insurance Corporation
FDICIA	Federal Deposit Insurance Corporation Improvement Act

FFB	Federal Financing Bank
FHA	Federal Housing Administration
FHFB	Federal Housing Finance Board
FHLMC	Federal Home Loan Mortgage Corporation
FIRA	Financial Institutions Regulatory Act
FIRREA	Financial Institutions Reform, Recovery and Enforcement Act
FHA	Farmers Home Administration
FMS	Financial Management Service
FNMA	Federal National Mortgage Association
FOMC	Federal Open Market Committee
FRB or FED	Federal Reserve Board
FRN	Floating Rate Note
FSB	Federal Savings Bank
FSLIC	Federal Savings and Loan Insurance Corporation
GAAP	Generally Accepted Accounting Principles
GAB	General Agreements to Borrow
GEM	Growing Equity Mortgage
GMC	Guaranteed Mortgage Certificate
GNMA	Government National Mortgage Association
GPM	Graduated Payment Mortgage
GSE	Government Sponsored Enterprise
HELOC	Home Equity Line of Credit
HUD	Housing and Urban Development, Department of
IADB	Inter-American Development Bank
IBAA	Independent Bankers Association of America
IBF	International Banking Facility
IBRD	International Bank for Reconstruction and Development
ICC	Income Capital Certificate
IDR	International Depositary Receipt
IMF	International Monetary Fund
INAS	Interbank National Authorization System
INET	Interbank Network for Electronic Transfer
IO	Interest Only
IOS	International Organization for Standardization
IOSCO	International Organization of Securities Commissions
IRA	Individual Retirement Account
IRR	Internal Rate of Return
IRS	Internal Revenue Service
LBO	Leveraged Buyout
LDC	Less Developed Country
LIBID	London Interbank Bid Rate

LIBOR	London Interbank Offered Rate
LIMEAN	London Interbank Median Average Rate
LIN	Loan Identification Number
LLC	Limited Liability Company
LPO	Loan Production Office
MAC	Message Authentication Code
MAI	Member, Appraisal Institute
M&A	Merger and Acquisition
MICR	Magnetic Ink Character Recognition
MMC	Money Market Certificate
MMDA	Money Market Deposit Account
MMF	Money Market Fund
MOFF	Multiple Options Funding Facility
MSA	Metropolitan Statistical Area
MSR	Mortgage Servicing Rights
MSRB	Municipal Securities Rulemaking Board
NACHA	National Automated Clearing House Association
NAFCU	National Association of Federal Credit Unions
NASD	National Association of Securities Dealers
NASDAQ	National Association of Securities Dealers Automated Quotation
NAV	Net Asset Value
NBSS	National Bank Surveillance System
NCUA	National Credit Union Administration
NG	Not Good
NIC	Net Interest Cost
NIF	Note Issuance Facility
NIM	Net Interest Margin
NOI	Net Operating Income
NOW	Negotiable Order of Withdrawal
NP	Notary Public
NSF	Not Sufficient Funds
NYSE	New York Stock Exchange
OAS	Option Adjusted Spread
OBU	Offshore Banking Unit
OCC	Office of the Comptroller of the Currency
OCC	Options Clearing Corporation
OECD	Organization for Economic Cooperation and Development
OID	Original Issue Discount
OLTP	On-Line Transaction Processing
OPIC	Overseas Private Investment Corporation
OREO	Other Real Estate Owned

OTC	Over-the-Counter
OTS	Office of Thrift Supervision
PAC	Planned Amortization Class
PAM	Pledged Account Mortgage
PAN	Primary Account Number
PC	Participation Certificate
PEFCO	Private Export Funding Corporation
PERL	Principal Exchange Rate Linked Security
PIN	Personal Identification Number
PITI	Principal, Interest, Taxes, and Insurance
PLAM	Price Level Adjusted Mortgage
PMI	Private Mortgage Insurance
PO	Principal Only
POD	Proof of Deposit
POS	Point of Sale
PSAF	Private Sector Adjustment Factor
PUF	Prime Underwriting Facility
RAM	Reverse Annuity Mortgage
RAN	Revenue Anticipation Note
RAP	Regulatory Accounting Principles
RCPC	Regional Check Processing Center
RDFI	Receiving Depository Financial Institution
REIT	Real Estate Investment Trust
REMIC	Real Estate Mortgage Investment Conduit
RESPA	Real Estate Settlement Procedures Act
RFC	Resolution Funding Corporation
ROA	Return on Assets
ROE	Return on Equity
RTC	Resolution Trust Corporation
RTGS	Real-Time Gross Settlement
RUF	Revolving Underwriting Facility
SAIF	Savings Association Insurance Fund
SAM	Shared Appreciation Mortgage
SBA	Small Business Administration
SBLI	Savings Bank Life Insurance
SDR	Special Drawing Rights
SEC	Securities and Exchange Commission
SEP	Simplified Employee Pension Plan
SIPC	Securities Investor Protection Corporation
SNIF	Standby Note Issuance Facility
SSC	Small Saver Certificate
STRIPE	Swap Transferring Risk with Participating Element
STRIPS	Separate Trading of Registered Interest and Principal Securities

SWIFT	Society for Worldwide Interbank Financial Telecommunication
T&E	Travel and Entertainment
TAB	Tax Anticipation Bill
TAN	Tax Anticipation Note
TGA	Treasury General Account
TIC	True Interest Cost
TIGR	Treasury Income Growth Receipts
TIN	Taxpayer Identification Number
TRUF	Transferable Underwriting Facility
TT&L	Treasury Tax and Loan
UCC	Uniform Commercial Code
VA	Department of Veterans Affairs
WAC	Weighted Average Coupon
WAM	Weighted Average Maturity
WART	Weighted Average Remaining Term

WORLD CURRENCIES BY COUNTRY

Afghanistan	Afghani
Albania	Lek
Algeria	Dinar
Andorra	Peseta
Angola	Kwanza, New Kwanza
Antigua	East Caribbean Dollar
Argentina	New Peso
Australia	Australian Dollar
Austria	Euro
Azerbaijan	Manat
Bahamas	Dollar
Bahrain	Dinar
Bangladesh	Taka
Barbados	Dollar
Belgium	Euro
Belize	Dollar
Benin	CFA Franc
Bermuda	Dollar
Bhutan	Ngultrum
Bolivia	Boliviano
Bosnia-Herzegovina	Convertible Marka
Botswana	Pula
Brazil	Real
Brunei	Dollar
Bulgaria	Lev
Burkina Faso	CFA Franc
Burundi	Burundi Franc
Cambodia	New Riel
Canada	Dollar
Cayman Islands	Dollar
Central African Republic	CFA Franc
Chad	CFA Franc
Chile	Peso
China	Renminbi Yuan
Colombia	Peso
Comoros	Franc
Congo	Zaire
Costa Rica	Colon
Croatia	Kuna
Cuba	Peso
Cyprus	Pound
Czech Republic	Koruna
Denmark	Krone
Dominican Republic	Peso
Ecuador	U.S. Dollar

Egypt	Pound
El Salvador	U.S. Dollar
Equatorial Guinea	CFA Franc
Estonia	Kroon
Ethiopia	Birr
Falkland Islands	Pound
Fiji	Dollar
Finland	Euro
France	Euro
Gabon	CFA Franc
Gambia	Dalasi
Germany	Euro
Ghana	New Cedi
Greece	Euro
Grenada	East Caribbean Dollar
Guatemala	Quetzal
Guinea Bissau	CFA Franc
Guinea Rep	Franc
Guyana	Dollar
Haiti	Gourde
Honduras	Lempira
Hong Kong	Dollar
Hungary	Forint
Iceland	Krona
India	Rupee
Indonesia	Rupiah
Iran	Rial
Iraq	Dinar
Ireland	Euro
Israel	New Shekel
Italy	Euro
Ivory Coast	CFA Franc
Jamaica	Dollar
Japan	Yen
Jordan	Dinar
Kazakhstan	Tenge
Kenya	Shilling
Korea, North	Won
Korea, South	Won
Kuwait	Dinar
Kyrgyzstan	Som
Laos	Kip
Latvia	Lat
Lebanon	Pound
Liberia	Dollar
Libya	Dinar
Liechtenstein	Euro

Lithuania	Litas
Luxembourg	Euro
Macedonia, Republic of	Denar
Madagascar	Ariary
Malawi	Kwacha
Malaysia	Ringgit
Maldives	Rufiyaa
Mali Republic	CFA Franc
Malta	Lira
Mauritania	Ouquiya
Mauritius	Rupee
Mexico	Peso
Mongolia	Tugrik
Montserrat	East Carribean Dollar
Morocco	Dirham
Mozambique	Metical
Myanmar	Kyat
Nambia	Namibia Dollar
Nepal	Rupee
Netherlands	Euro
New Zealand	New Zealand Dollar
Nicaragua	Gold Cordoba
Niger Republic	CFA Franc
Nigeria	Naira
Norway	Norwegian Kroner
Oman	Rial
Pakistan	Rupee
Panama	Balboa
Papua New Guinea	Dina
Paraguay	Guarani
Peru	New Sol
Philippines	Peso
Poland	Zloty
Portugal	Euro
Puerto Rico	U.S. Dollar
Qatar	Riyal
Republic of Yemen	Rial
Romania	Leu
Russia	Ruble
Rwanda	Franc
Saint Lucia	East Caribbean Dollar
Saint Christopher	East Caribbean Dollar
Saint Helena	Pound Sterling
Saint Pierre	Franc
Saint Vincent	East Caribbean Dollar
Samoa	Tala
San Marino	Lira

São Tomé and Príncipe	Dobra
Saudi Arabia	Riyal
Senegal	CFA Franc
Serbia	Dinar
Seychelles	Rupee
Sierra Leone	Leone
Singapore	Dollar
Slovakia	Koruna
Slovenia	Tolar
Somalia	Shilling
South Africa	Rand
Spain	Euro
Sri Lanka	Rupee
Sudan Republic	Dinar
Sweden	Krona
Switzerland	Franc
Syria	Pound
Taiwan	New Taiwan Dollar
Tajikistan	Tajikistani Ruble
Tanzania	Shilling
Thailand	Baht
Togo, Republic of	CFA Franc
Tonga Islands	Pa'anga
Trinidad & Tobago	Dollar
Tunisia	Dinar
Turkey	Turkish Lira
Uganda	Shilling
Ukraine	Hryvnia
United Arab Emirates	Dirham
United Kingdom	Pound Sterling
United States	U.S. Dollar
Uruguay	Peso
Uzbekistan	Som
Vatican City	Euro
Venezuela	Bolivar
Vietnam	Dong
Zambia	Kwacha
Zimbabwe	Dollar

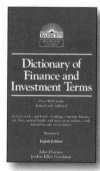

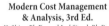